Canadian Film Reader

EDITED BY
Seth Feldman
AND
Joyce Nelson

PETER MARTIN ASSOCIATES LIMITED

In memory of Martin Walsh

Canadian Cataloguing in Publication Data
Canadian film reader
(PMA/Take one film book series ; 5)
Bibliography: p.
Includes index.
ISBN 0-88778-158-6 bd.   ISBN 0-88778-159-4 pa.

1. Moving-pictures — Canada — History — Addresses, essays, lectures.
2. Moving-pictures — Canada — Addresses, essays, lectures.
I. Feldman, Seth, 1948- II. Nelson, Joyce, 1945- III. Series.
PN1993.5.C2C26   791.43'0971   C77-001249-3

© 1977 Seth Feldman and Joyce Nelson
ALL RIGHTS RESERVED
No part of this book may be reproduced or utilized in any form or by any means, electronic or mechanical, including photocopying, electrostatic copying, recording or by any information storage and retrieval systems without permission in writing from the publisher, except for the quotation of passages by a reviewer in print or through the electronic mass media.

Design: Diana McElroy

The PMA/Take One Film Book Series is published by Peter Martin Associates Limited, 280 Bloor Street West, Toronto, Ontario M5S 1W1, in association with *Take One* magazine, Post Office Box 1778, Station B, Montreal, Quebec H3B 3L3; distributed in the U.K. by Tantivy Press, 108 New Bond Street, London W1Y 00X.

General Editors: Peter Lebensold, Joe Medjuck

Contents

Preface	v
Introduction	vii
I "The Possibilities Are Truly Great"	1
Speaking of Movies *Gordon Sparling*	3
American Domination of the Motion Picture Industry: Canada as a Test Case *Garth Jowett*	5
Ernest Shipman and "Back to God's Country" *Peter Morris*	14
Conversations *Gordon Sparling*	22
Conserving the Canadian Image *Sam Kula*	29
II The National Film Board of Canada	35
Grierson's First Years at the NFB *Jack Ellis*	37
Documentary Films: World War II *Ernst Borneman*	48
Before the Guerillières: Women's Films at the NFB During World War II *Barbara Halpern Martineau*	58
The Innocent Eye: An Aspect of the Work of the National Film Board of Canada *Peter Harcourt*	67
An Interview with Terence Macartney-Filgate *Sarah Jennings*	77
On the Candid-Eye Movement *Bruce Elder*	86
Rhythm 'n' Truths: Norman McLaren *Derek Elley*	94
Donald Brittain: Green Stripe and Common Sense *Ronald Blumer and Susan Schouten*	103
Challenge for Change *Patrick Watson*	112
What Challenge? What Change? *Marie Kurchak*	120
Saint-Jérome: The Experience of a Filmmaker as Social Animator *Fernand Dansereau*	128
Memo to Michelle about Decentralizing the Means of Production *John Grierson*	132
III Feature Filmmaking	
The Years of Hope *Peter Harcourt*	139
Pierre Perrault *Louis Marcorelles*	144
Review of "A tout prendre" *Colin Young*	153
The Facts of Life, Toronto Style *Joan Fox*	156
Who's Don Owen? What's He Done, and What's He Doing Now? *Natalie Edwards*	160
A Married Couple: An Interview with Allan King *Alan Rosenthal*	179

Claude Jutra's "Mon Oncle Antoine" *Bruce Elder*   194
Gilles Carle—A Thematic Response or, Scenes From
    Family Life *Piers Handling*   199
Men of Vision: Some Comments on the Work of Don Shebib
    Peter Harcourt   208
Making Films for Your Own People: An Interview with
    Denys Arcand *Judy Wright and Debbie Magidson*   217
Coward, Bully or Clown: The Dream-Life of a Younger
    Brother *Robert Fothergill*   234
Mireille Dansereau: "La Vie rêvée" *Interview by Á.
    Ibrányi-Kiss*   250
What Makes Duddy Run? *Daniel Golden*   258
Grandfather Love Is the Best Kind of Love *Marshall
    Delaney*   262
An Account by a Privileged Hostage of Les Ordres: Brault
    Has Missed His Shot *Pierre Vallières*, translated by John
    Van Burek   264
Filmmaking West Coast Style: Jack Darcus *Á. Ibrányi-Kiss*   268
Fear and Loathing to Order *John Hofsess*   274
Wielandism: A Personal Style in Full Bloom *Marshall
    Delaney*   279

IV Experimental Filmmaking   283

True Patriot Love: The Films of Joyce Wieland *Regina
    Cornwell*   285
The Life & Times of Michael Snow *Interview by Joe
    Medjuck*   290
Michael Snow's "Wavelength" *Bruce Elder*   308
The New Canadian Cinema: Images from the Age of
    Paradox *Gene Youngblood*   323
Review of "The Hart of London" *Seth Feldman*   333
David Rimmer: A Critical Collage *Compiled by Joyce Nelson*   338

V "The Possibilities Are Truly Great" Continued   345

A Place Like Home *Robert Fothergill*   347
Statement from the Council of Canadian Filmmakers
    Sandra Gathercole   364
Introduction *Peter Harcourt*   370
Notes   377
A Selected Bibliography   388
Index   401

Preface

Canadian Film Reader is designed as a source book, providing some of the most lucid commentary available on this area of national culture. Those of us who have worked on the book have envisioned it as a gathering place of ideas, a dialogue, an exploratory tool, a reference work and a preserve for an endangered species of criticism. We also hope that it will serve as both an inspiration and a companion piece to future comprehensive histories of the Canadian cinema, as the first edition of Eleanor Beattie's *Handbook of Canadian Film* did for us.

Credit for the creation and publication of the *Canadian Film Reader* is itself an anthology of names of people concerned with the book's topic. Martin Walsh of the University of Western Ontario had the original idea for an anthology, while Joe Medjuck of Innis College (University of Toronto) and Carol Martin and Peter Martin were personally involved in making that idea a reality. Besides allowing us to include their own material, the following people also recommended worthwhile articles by others: Peter Harcourt (York University), Bruce Elder (Ryerson), Peter Morris (Queen's University), Robert Fothergill and Joe Medjuck. We picked the willing brains of Piers Handling at the Canadian Film Institute, Ken Larose of the National Film Archives, and the library staff at the NFB. Del Mehes and Fran Bates helped in typing the manuscript, and we are very grateful to both *Cinema Canada* and the Canadian Filmmakers' Distribution Centre for providing office space, typing facilities, encouragement and coffee while the project was underway. Alice Smith, graduate student at York University, compiled the bibliography, from which we made selections. We are thankful to the many contributors (editors and authors alike) who expressed their belief in this project by demanding nothing more than printed acknowledgement for the use of their material. Kathy Vanderlinden of Peter Martin Associates guided the work to completion. Finally, we are grateful to the people of Ontario, whose Arts Council money made this book possible.

Introduction

Any anthology attempting to cover as wide a spectrum of cinema history and criticism as we have attempted here will, with any luck at all, generate a productive aura of dissatisfaction. The book has obvious gaps: more material dealing with "Establishment" cinema than with "Independent" cinema; a stress on English-Canadian films rather than Francophone works; maybe even too much "factual" material and not enough critical-theoretical work. We are aware of choices made, sometimes even painfully so when it comes to certain areas left lacking. But perhaps the gaps in this text will encourage others to fill them. We hope there will be responses to the articles included here. We hope there will be new research, new writing, new courses, lectures, conferences and retrospectives on the Canadian films discussed here, as well as those which have gone unmentioned. We know there will be new films. There will also be new books on this subject—at least one near publication now which will serve as the first monograph attempting to encompass the subject of Canadian cinema. We see the *Canadian Film Reader* as a companion piece to these works, especially the new edition of Eleanor Beattie's *Handbook of Canadian Film* which includes current filmographies and relevant information about the industry-at-large. As such, this text is guilty of encouraging the study of films in the context of national cinemas. In order to prevent that concept from being too readily or naively accepted, we feel it necessary to offer the following observations.

While film itself may or may not be an international language, the study of film is undeniably an almost universal pursuit. Not only are there film scholars and critics wherever films are shown, but these scholars and critics seldom limit themselves to the study of a single national cinema. The major film theorists from Munsterberg to Metz have, by and large, taken little account of those similarities between films which might be based on national traits. The historical justification for their attitude can be seen both in the large degree of influence directors from different nations have exerted upon each other and the large body of work made in any given nation which does not in any way reflect that nation's national identity. As a result of these factors, it is possible, for instance, to teach a course in American film in which one would show Hollywood films set outside of the United States whose directors were foreign nationals. By the same token, it would be equally possible to design a European film course or retrospective in which all the material screened was in some way a response to Hollywood.

Thus, to use strict criteria in order to define a national cinema—i.e., those films made in a given nation by its citizens that discuss topics having to do with that nation and its people—is a decision to enter a relatively obscure if not questionable area of film study. Yet these criteria are seen as valid by a small group of scholars. These people have, generally, taken one of three approaches to this pursuit. The first is to write an historical monograph that emphasizes names, dates and capsulized plot summaries at the expense of an overriding theory as to the directions and shape of the national cinema. Rachael Low's massive *History of the British Film* is perhaps the archetype of this encyclopedic approach. Other works in this school range from the officially sponsored *History of Soviet Cinema*[1] to similar official, semi-official, and unofficial works on the cinemas of Hungary, [2] Mexico[3] and Italy.[4]

While works such as these are monuments to historiography, they are in a sense incomplete until some use is made of the material they contain. The second context in which national cinemas have been studied has been that of expanding upon this basic information for the purpose of using cinema as a key to the understanding of the nation in question. In using this approach, scholars have chosen to study films as a reflection of historical and social forces (e.g., Jay Leyda's *Kino* and *Dianying*), expressions of the national psyche (Lotte Eisner's *The Haunted Screen*) or as sociological indicators existing in a sensitive space between industry and culture (Robert Sklar's *Movie-Made America*). In this last instance, the films themselves may be all but disregarded in favour of studying the economics of their production and the social dynamics of the response they illicited from the audience selected for study.

The last and, to date, least explored approach to national cinemas is to use the unique qualities of a single national cinema as a way to come to an understanding of film as a whole. Recent studies of the Formalist and Constructivist aspects of Soviet cinema[5] have worked from this direction, as have Noel Burch's first writings in his proposed study of Japanese film.[6] One might even include Eisenstein's cross-cultural, cross-media studies of Kabuki theatre as an early example of the possiblities of this type of applied anthropology. The advantage of this approach to national cinemas is its potential for expanding our understanding of the definition of film until, perhaps ironically, the medium might be transformed into a true international language. The disadvantage of the approach is that anything it says about a particular culture must be qualified by the understanding that aspects of that culture less relevant to film will have been largely ignored.

How would these three approaches to the study of national cinemas apply in the Canadian context? The first step, in terms of a book length monograph, will probably be in the area of an encyclopedic history of the Canadian film. The umbrella of an historical overview is needed here to cover the fragmented national experience within the medium. It will be impossible to find a common thread among the independent silent productions, the quota quickies, the pre-1939 non-fiction and amateur films, the NFB and postwar English, French and avant-garde work unless all of these individual entities have been studied in some detail. As common sense would indicate, we will have to know exactly what happened to film in this country before we can begin to make sense of it. Slowly, however, the exhaustive research needed for these studies may begin to reveal links between personalities and production units. We may start to dig out common motifs by reading the dozens of plot descriptions of lost and forgotten films.

Armed with detailed historical knowledge, we might then begin to use conclusions reached in studies of other aspects of the Canadian experience in order to add to our understanding of emerging patterns. The histories might provide the bases for more specific inquiries that could, for instance, link artistic, literary and cinematic motifs; trace English-French relations through their respective films and film industries; provide a history of postwar Canadian internationalism through a comparison of commentary in NFB films to public events and/or public opinion polls. These and similar topics are all currently on the verge of accessibility. Properly researched and developed, the data produced could demonstrate how film can be used as a common denominator for scholars in several fields.

In exploring the unique characteristics of Canadian cinema, perhaps we shall find that Canadian films have been able to achieve a kind of link with the topical issues that is unique in the history of world cinema. Or possibly there is something inherent in the Canadian approach to government which has permitted the erection and maintenance of government film agencies that enjoy a creative freedom unheard of elsewhere. Perhaps we shall find that the central fact of Canadian film is that it is inextricably linked to other artistic and literary concerns of the culture. Or maybe Canada has perfected the "genre" of regional films.

On the other hand, maybe we shall find that there are no central motifs, no possible theory of Canadian film, no way that a colonized country divided by regional and linguistic barriers will have produced a "national cinema". If this were the case, we would, of course, be in good company. After all, Sarris tells us that no cinema, save the American, has been able to produce consistently interesting films throughout the bulk of the history of the medium.[7] The great national cinemas of France, Germany, Italy and Japan have all had to endure gaps in creative production. They have all had to endure Hollywood's best efforts to prolong these gaps.

Even if one were to accept Sarris's evaluation of the chances of finding a "national cinema" within a body of disparate works, there are two possibilities that permit us to end the introduction of this book on a sanguine note. The first is that our cinema lies ahead of us. In this regard, it might be useful to cite Dusan Makavejev's description of how his native Yugoslavia began to discover its cinema.[8] The audiences of that nation—a nation which is not only younger than Canada, but, if anything, far more subject to regional divisions and outside cultural influences—began to look for the little things. In their bland local remakes of Hollywood, they found and encouraged, bit by bit, the existence of national traits. One otherwise artless film contained a brief but valid portrait of a Belgrade cop, the first cop who was not simply imitation Hollywood. Audiences responded enthusiastically and the next film contained not only a real Belgrade cop but also a domestic quarrel that rang true. And so on...

The kind of popular construction of national cinema described by Makavejev may well be taking place in Quebec and may occur in the near future in English Canada (where it is possible that one more film or film retrospective will finally convince audiences that not everything produced locally is beneath contempt). Even if it is successful, though, the approach does not give immediate help in understanding the mass of material that all but calls to us from archive shelves. Having seen some of the films preserved by the National Film Archives and the National Film Board, we find it possible to suggest unhesitatingly that these films also have their many moments that ring true, their sequences of extraordinary power, poignancy and delight. These films, too, should be seen by those audiences interested in Canadian film.

And, if all this fails, let us go on to sanguine note number two. That is that we have seen enough in films produced in this country and in the writing about those films to verify the presence of human achievement and, at times, brilliance. If we cannot, when all is said and done, make a national cinema out of what we have seen, if we must admit only to a frustrated unity, then perhaps the following passage from a concluding paragraph of E.M. Forster's *Passage to India* might in some small way be applicable:

> India a nation! What an apotheosis! Last comer to the drab nineteenth century sisterhood! Waddling in at this hour of the world to take her seat! She, whose only peer was the Holy Roman Empire, she shall rank with Guatemala and Belgium perhaps![9]

After all, Canada is an endless mass of contradiction—explorer's heaven. Theorists must take their chances.

Seth Feldman
Joyce Nelson

I

"THE POSSIBILITIES ARE TRULY GREAT"

Speaking of Movies

Gordon Sparling

The notoriety which Hollywood has gained for itself has had a most interesting effect on the civilized world. Hollywood stands, in the eyes of the movie fans, as a symbol of motion pictures and that means a good deal when one realizes that perhaps more people see movies than travel on trains or listen to the radio—not to mention those who go to church. In short, "Movie and the world movies with you; stay away and you stay away alone." A recent experiment by a certain psychologist revealed the fact that Charlie Chaplin is a more familiar name than Coolidge, and Mary Pickford a more widely recognized queen than the wife of King George.

The trouble has been, from all view-points excepting the American, that about 98 per cent of the world's output of motion pictures has come from the United States. This one-sided condition is gradually being remedied as production increases in Germany, England and other countries. Canada, with its much-discussed leanings towards government control, has developed the motion picture industry in an official way. The latest development has been the opening of the Ontario government studio at Trenton. This studio, while small, is well equipped with modern machinery and able to handle all branches of the art from slow motion pictures to animated cartoons. Its situation alone is one of charm. Nestled under a wooded hill and shaded by giant pines, it presents a pleasant spectacle to passers-by on Film Street. On each side and in front are velvety lawns while a short distance to the south is the pictureque Bay of Quinte. Thus in all directions are to be found lovely locations for outdoor scenes. The old town of Trenton itself is ideal with its winding streets and varieties of architecture.

As one enters the front door of the studio the stage is on the right, two storeys high and bristling with banks of Cooper-Hewitts and spotlights. Behind a gallery on the second floor are the dressing rooms where our native Norma Talmadges and Ramon Navarros may don the motley or regale themselves in movie make-up. Under the dressing rooms in a long row are the directors' offices, property room and store room, while beyond are the laboratories. These occupy the whole width of the building and comprise developing, fixing and washing rooms; printing rooms where the continuous click-click of the printers marks the passing of endless ribbons of film; the drying room with its two motor-driven eight foot drums; the title room for making animated and still sub-titles; and last but not least the cutting room in which the test prints are inspected, edited and assembled.

The official opening of the studio, by the Honourable Wm. H. Price, provincial treasurer, which took place on October 8, after an eight month

Reprinted from *Trinity University Review*, vol. 37, no. 1 (October 1924).

probation with regard to efficiency and economy, marked the realization of the dreams of the director, Mr. G. E. Patton, who, in a little over two years, has made motion pictures a factor in education throughout the province. In a single month last spring, 1,500 customers were supplied with films, ranging from technical picturizations of the activities of the European corn borer to scenic travelogues of our province. Mr. Patton is a graduate of OAC and producer of the well-known SOD-BUSTER which toured Ontario shortly after the war. With such a background he will doubtless guide the studio to permanent success.

In the eyes of many people motion pictures are synonomous with society dramas, sex problem stories, trashy amusement. If this were so the days of the industry would be numbered, but a far greater work lies ahead, one which has only been touched, namely that of teaching through the eye. The word teaching, to most people, brings up a vision of dull lecturers pounding away on dull subjects. Herein lies the moving picture's opportunity. If a subject can be shown in an attractive, interesting way it will be impressed on the minds more clearly than an infinite amount of teaching or an endless number of textbooks. The greatest writers have long ago realized that one can teach a lesson without forcing it down the victim's throat. So, wholesome inspiring movies have a place in our educational system which neither church nor state can well afford to ignore. This is the aim of "Province of Ontario Pictures". Dramatic historical incidents, the romance of agriculture and so forth will eventually fill a long-felt need.

There is no reason why Canada cannot eventually become a great motion picture producing country. We have the scenery, we have the ability and, with the necessary progressiveness, we can make full use of our assets. Canada has given to the world great writers, great doctors, great inventors. Perhaps the day may not be far off when she will develop great motion picture directors.

American Domination of the Motion Picture Industry: Canada as a Test Case

Garth Jowett

It was not too long after Thomas Edison's marketing genius saw the development of the motion picture apparatus as a viable economic enterprise, that Canada, and most other industrialized countries, witnessed the unprecedented development of this commercial amusement. The ubiquitous motion picture, in all of its myriad forms—Biograph, Vitascope, etc.—was soon available all across the country, and the larger Canadian cities were as well-equipped as any American cities of comparable size. One theatre, the Ouimetoscope in Montreal, was probably the finest movie theatre in North America in the period before 1910. In this early period, Canada, again like most other countries, depended on an international supply of films, especially from France, Great Britain, but mostly from the United States. Canada also produced some of her own films, but most of these were of the shorter variety, usually of a scene or "newsreel" nature.

With the gradual shift toward longer, multi-reel "feature" films, Canada, like the rest of the world, was dependent upon the few countries which were then equipped to finance and produce such films. In the period just before the First World War, attempts were made to start an indigenous Canadian film industry, and the prospects looked extremely encouraging. However, the war stopped further development on a large scale, and it was several years after the end of the conflict before Canada was once again able to reconsider a domestic movie industry.

The First World War did more to further the growth on an international scale of the American film industry than any other factor, as the conflict paralyzed all but the Italian and American production centres. After the war, the Americans lost little time in establishing distribution centres in Paris despite the protests of French producers, and in Berlin and other European capitals a similar pattern was repeated. By the early 1920s it was estimated that more than half of the films being shown in Europe were American-produced. One knowledgeable film distribution company put the figure at about 90 per cent in 1924.[1] As a further example, in 1925, over 75 per cent of the films shown in France were made in the United States; in Australia, a thriving film market, the figure was 95 per cent. In Germany, the strongest of the European film producing countries, the government had enacted the so-called "*kontingent*" law which required a specific quota of German pictures for each foreign picture exhibited, and even then, American films exceeded the number of German films shown in that country in 1924 and 1925. (However, by 1928 and 1929 a swing toward German films was beginning to take place.) It is also significant that after the initial interest in European films, during the first years of the full-length feature film (1913-1917), American audiences lost their taste for these imports. As an example, German film exports to the United States accounted for less than 2 per cent of the total in 1924.[2]

The British film industry was in an even worse position, as British film producers, caught in the financial squeeze of being unable to make large budget films, could not be sure of the necessary returns on their investments. It seemed as if no one wanted to watch British films during this era, least of all the British themselves. In 1936, the Moyne Committee Report noted that "By 1923 British production had revived to a degree that made it possible for about 10 per cent of the films exhibited in Great Britain to be British made." But this was only a temporary rise in fortunes, for by 1926 the percentage had declined to about 5 per cent. The actual screen time of American films was probably larger because of the various booking agreements then in force.[3] Eventually this situation became so desperate that government intervention was required, which resulted in the imposition of a quota system in 1927.

Even where national film industries were quite healthy, there was often heavy financial investment by American companies, especially in distribution and theatre-owning ventures. The so-called "battle for theatres" which was then raging in the United States spread to Europe, and Famous-Players-Lasky began to acquire first-run movie houses in Britain, France and Germany. The Hollywood studios then lost little time moving into the distribution field; the only thing preventing their transfer of complete vertical integration, which they had achieved in the United States, was the establishment of European production studios. This American intrusion was not always welcomed. As just one of many such examples, Famous-Players caused a tremendous uproar in 1923 when it purchased the historic Vaudeville theatre in Paris and announced its intention to turn the Parisian landmark into a first-run movie house. Famous-Players was not the only company guilty of such indiscretion, and Metro-Goldwyn, through the partnership with Gaumont, also had access to the Gaumont chain of movie houses, including the Paris Gaumont, then the largest movie house in the world. First-National, the largest of the American distributing companies, also moved into the European market, and opened exchanges in France, Belgium and Great Britain.

In all, during the twenties, over 30 per cent of the gross income of the American film industry came from foreign sources. (Some estimates have even placed this higher. Incidentally, the 1974 figure was well over 50 per cent!) The dangerous trend toward quota systems, and the increasing agitation for more control over the proliferation of American films in Europe became the source of a long series of international discussions. In 1926, a representative of the American film industry appeared before a committee of Congress to ask for assistance in warding off the threat of foreign legislative enactments aimed at diminishing American influence in the motion picture industry. Congress duly appropriated $15,000 to finance a section of the Department of Commerce to report information regarding such foreign legislation to American producers.

The venerable Adolph Zukor, then president of Famous-Players, noted that these legislative proposals were merely hysteria, and that "the whole situation has been brought about by interests hostile to the American industry and the movement where it has taken root has materialized in legislation because the lawmakers have not been in full possession of facts and have passed laws of which they have little knowledge".[4]

Whatever Zukor may have felt, the facts were quite obvious; because of the large, dependable domestic market, American films were, on the whole, superior to most European productions, and in the pre-sound era, there was very little difficulty producing films for the European market. In turn, Americans were not prepared to accept European films. A short note taken from the *Film Daily Year Book* for 1922, indicates that 425 foreign films were sent to the United States for sale in that year, but only six were accepted for exhibition![5]

It was not only the economic aspects which concerned the foreign countries, for it had been recognized from the first that the movies were a powerful force for the dissemination of ideas. While social historians have only begun to understand the importance of the motion picture as a major socialization force in the twentieth century, this fact was obvious to anyone concerned with the role of the movies in national life. In 1917, the British government published an extensive report on *The Cinema: Its Present Position and Future Possibilities,* which had been undertaken by the National Council of Public Morals. The report left no doubt about where its compilers stood regarding the importance of the motion picture:

> All other forms of recreation appeal only to a section of the community, but the lure of the pictures is universal; while the cheapness and accessibility of the houses make it possible for the masses to indulge in this enjoyment almost to an unlimited extent. In the course of our inquiry we have been much impressed by the evidence brought before us that moving pictures are having a profound influence upon the mental and moral outlook of millions of our young people—an influence the more subtle in that it is subconsciously exercised—and we leave our labours with the deep conviction that no social problem of the day demands more earnest attention. The cinema, under wise guidance, may be made a powerful influence for good; if neglected, if its abuse is unchecked, its potentialities for evil are manifold.[6]

(It is interesting to note that this was two years after the U.S. Supreme Court had noted in the important *Mutual Film Decision* that motion pictures were "capable of evil".)

Certainly, while the foreign film industries had a legitimate reason for requesting economic protection, it was the threat caused by the dissemination of "foreign ideas" which was uppermost in the minds of many groups and governments concerned with preserving national cultures and identities. So dominant was the Hollywood film in the international market, that the spread of American fads and fashions by the movies became an international cause célèbre. As early as 1921 this cultural invasion was being seriously questioned, and Arthur Weigall, a noted English journalist, pointed out:

> To the remotest towns of England, as to those of America and other countries, these films penetrate, carrying with them this mild but ultimately dangerous poison; and gradually the world, from end to end, is being trained to see life as it is seen by a certain group of cinema producers and writers congregated in a corner of the United States. The world is being Americanised by the photoplay but the trouble is that this Americanisation does not represent the best element of that nation, or even the most popular.[7]

Weigall, in fact, echoed a sentiment popular with many of the reform groups then clamouring for greater control over the motion picture in the United States. Weigall continued to suggest that Hollywood films were a dangerous socializing influence because, "good or bad, they are altering the code of the Englishman; and ... they are lowering our standards and those of the United States, by casually hinting at, or frankly representing as worthy of emulation, an attitude of mind that is not English and not American". Hollywood had long been criticized for its false portrayals of foreigners, and foreign customs, and Weigall went on to make the valid objection that all too often "an Englishman is the recognized buffoon of the American photoplay". He suggested that the solution would be to have a much wider distribution of British films in the United States, for "properly handled, the Cinema could be made to endear the two races to one another by the bonds of mutual admiration and fellow-feeling".[8] (It should be noted that many Americans were, at this time, equally concerned with the portrayal of the image of America by American films on foreign screens.)

Not everyone saw this threat of "cultural imperialism" as a universally dangerous social situation. Since the first days of the motion picture as a major entertainment form, there had been those who optimistically saw the medium as the means for achieving world peace. This feeling reached a peak during the halcyon days of the twenties following the formation of the League of Nations. This world organization was itself very actively involved in trying to oversee the international exchange of motion pictures as an important part of its overall efforts to create a better international climate. Alas, these efforts, mainly through the International Educational Cinematographic Institute of Rome, were as doomed to failure as many other of the League's endeavours.

In 1927, André Maurois, the well-known French intellectual, stated upon a visit to New York: "This is the day of universal culture. The people of the world dress alike more or less, and it is from motion pictures that they get their idea of being alike." He went on to predict that cinema art would become one of the great arts of the future, and compared it to the building of the thirteenth-century cathedrals in its universal appeal to the masses. (This analogy must surely have been lost on the Hollywood moguls!) The American film industry was obviously anxious to encourage any such philosophy which saw in the motion picture a means of providing greater international understanding, as long as it did not entail either governmental control, or the acceptance of foreign films for American movie screens.

Addressing the Better Films Conference in 1927, Carl Milliken, the former governor of Maine, then a popular representative for the Hays Office, announced: "There is an ambitious plan well on the way to fulfillment for circulating around the world in the next few years films of the life, history and customs of each of the different nations of the world so that gradually they will be brought into close contact with each other.[9] Needless to say, nothing else was ever heard of this ambitious project, but Hollywood paid lip-service to the concept of an "international cinema".

Perhaps the most articulate of the spokesmen for "internationalization" of the cinema was William Marston Seabury, an interesting man who had once been the General Counsel to the National Association of the Motion Picture Industry, and who later worked diligently for the League of Nations. Seabury published an important study of the motion picture industry in 1926 (entitled *The Public and the Motion Picture Industry*), in which he suggested that "in reality the motion picture has become and is today the greatest force and instrument in the world for the cultivation and preservation of the world's peace and for the moral, intellectual and cultural development of all people."[10] Seabury called for a "complete commercial renaissance" which would revitalize the industry so that it could fulfill its duties and responsibilities. After a detailed examination of current industry practices he concluded:

> Specifically the remedy in America must include an Act of Congress which will declare the motion picture to be a new public utility and the business of producing, distributing and exhibiting pictures to be charged with the obligation and duty to eliminate the debasing influences, and to articulate friendly relations with the people of other nations and to promote the moral, educational and cultural development of the people.[11]

Through the League of Nations he proposed to set up an official agency to encourage international co-operation which would eventually bring about the renaissance he hoped for. Each country would be induced to recognize the importance of the movies as a means of international understanding, at which point the medium would at last be allowed to realize the latent potential it had been forced to hide because of "commercial exploitation". Seabury expressed the vain hope that:

> With the awakening of each nation to the truth that the business of production and exhibiting pictures had become more than a commercial pursuit, each nation would become conscious of its duties toward the industry within its borders, towards its own people, and towards other nations.[12]

As we know, of course, no such thing happened, and with the entry of Italy into the Ethiopian war, even the Institute in Rome was shut down, and for all intents and purposes attempts at such international co-operation were forgotten until after the Second World War, when once again many of the same optimistic arguments were put forward.

Canada and American Movies

From the outset, Canada because of its geographic situation was considered to be merely one of the many "marketing areas" designated by the American film industry. From an historical point of view, there is surprisingly little source material dealing with the issue of Canadian dissatisfaction with U.S. dominance of the motion picture industry in Canada in the very early period. Such dissatisfaction only comes to the fore in the period after World War I, and reaches a peak just prior to the establishment of the Anti-Combines Investigation in the Motion Picture Industry in 1930-1. There was, however, a considerable minority concern with the cultural influence of American films.

As early as 1911, the great Canadian reformer J.S. Woodsworth had examined the influence of the movies on Canadian life. Discussing the influence of the entertainment medium on immigrants he noted:

> The fact is, that in itself the picture business is neither good nor bad. All depends upon the character of the pictures. Some of these are abominably vile and foster crime and immorality of all kinds. The majority are simply cheap and vulgar or silly. A few provide excellent entertainment and instruction.... There is no reason why the picture show should not become of great educational value. The trouble is that in all such matters attempted reform has rarely been along constructive lines.[13]

It was, however, in the period immediately following the First World War that resentment against the "Americanization" of Canada through the motion picture medium really became a public issue. Much of this resentment was due to Hollywood's misrepresentation of the role of the American armed forces in the great conflict. Canada had suffered great losses, and the nation was in no mood to tolerate American movie claims which showed the Americans winning the war almost singlehandedly. Even when Hollywood lost interest in making such war films, there was always some aspect of movie content which aroused pro-British-Canadian sentiment. As an example, a near-riot ensued in Halifax in January 1933, when an American newsreel suggested that the Island of Bermuda might fitly be handed over to the United States in part payment of British war debts. Paradoxically, Canadians themselves showed no great liking for British films, even though minority pro-British interest clamoured loud and long for better distribution of such films. In 1931, over 95 per cent of the films exhibited in Canada were produced in the United States.

A study done in Nova Scotia in the early thirties among high school students indicated that of the 1,800 interviewed, more than 1,000 showed a preference for American over English films. (A similar study showed even higher preferences in Ontario and the Prairie Provinces.) Those who preferred the American-made product gave as their reasons better acting, more realistic stage settings, and plots which had a "deeper interest".[14] Quite a few of the respondents indicated that they found the British accent difficult to understand, while others noted that "Americans are more like ourselves", and that they preferred the "American type of humour". Also the American stars and settings were more familiar. Interestingly enough the major reason given by those exhibiting a preference for British films was that they were "more clean and decent". The study made a point of noting that a very high proportion of those favouring British films were from Roman Catholic schools.

Much like their American counterparts, Canadian women were active in campaigning for a "better cinema". The concern of most of these groups was with the quality of the theatre, and not in fostering or impairing international friendship. Nevertheless, in relation to morals and British patriotism, the results they reached intimately, though indirectly, connected with their attitude toward the United States. Of all these groups the Imperial Order Daughters of the Empire studied the subject most keenly and persistently. The Nova Scotia chapter of the IODE submitted a declaration to the provincial government which claimed in part:

1) That moving pictures constitute now the most important source from which ideas of United States life are formed, especially by young people....
2) That Canadian feeling is still often irritated by a certain national boastfulness in the American-made pictures....
3) That Nova Scotians often get from the pictures an impression of the United States as indulgent to lax family morals, with a vulgar

> ostentatiousness of wealth, unrefined even in vice [sic], contemptuous of law, and with officials in corrupt connivance with "gangsters".[15]

One IODE official noted that while they were anxious to maintain international goodwill toward the United States, "there is a grave danger to our British citizenship in that our growing Canadian [the child] is imbibing from the press, radio and screen that which tends to loosen the tie of our British connection". Another official was even more vehement in her denunciation of the American influence in Canada through the movies:

> There are certain conventions which must be obeyed in the interests of society as a whole. These are conspicuously absent from American-made moving pictures.... If these features of life are regarded as typically American, whose is the responsibility? and why does not every Canadian cooperate with the I.O.D.E. in demanding British pictures, where these objectionable features do not appear to such an extent?[16]

Canadian Catholics, of course, were vigorous in support of the efforts of the United States Legion of Decency campaign begun in 1933. But then Canadian censorship regulations, as administered through the various provincial governments, have always "protected" Canadians from the worst excesses of the Hollywood product. Ontario passed the Theatres and Cinematographs act in March 1911, which like many similar pieces of law, had no antecedents in previous legislation, but was specifically drafted to control the new phenomenon of the motion picture. Manitoba passed similar legislation on the same day, while Saskatchewan had preempted them by passing its statute the day before. Alberta waited until 1912, as did New Brunswick, British Columbia passed its bill in 1913, Nova Scotia followed in 1915, and Newfoundland in 1916. Surprisingly enough, no specific movie censorship legislation was ever passed in Prince Edward Island. Quebec joined Ontario and Manitoba on that fateful day in March 1911, but it was the only province that had a precedent for film censorship, contained in article 2929 of the consolidation of 1887, which provided that "all public exhibitions of monsters, idiots or other imbecile or deformed persons, tending to endanger public safety or morality, may be prohibited by local councils in the Province". It was to this "sideshow" article that the new motion picture legislation was added. In 1925, Quebec created an entirely new Moving Pictures Act, which also established a board of censorship.

A close examination of the relevant material reveals no great difference in the modus operandi of the Canadian provincial censors from that of the various state and municipal censors in the United States, except for the occasional anti-American incident. This was especially true when it came to dealing with differences between British and American foreign policy. Even British films were banned on occasion, as in 1928 when Herbert Wilcox's DAWN, the story of Nurse Edith Cavell, was banned on the ground that it gave misleading impressions of Miss Cavell and was historically inaccurate. But Canadian internal politics also created some interesting and amusing incidents, as in 1940 when the premier of Ontario, Liberal Mitchell Hepburn, banned the *March of Time* film CANADA AT WAR until after the provincial election because he regarded it as "pure political propaganda" for the Mackenzie King government, which he opposed on personal grounds even though it too was a Liberal government. It is interesting that in the period just before entry into the Second World War most banning of films in Canada concerned political issues, except in Quebec, where almost all of the bannings dealt with moral or religious issues.

Canada finally experienced its great catharsis regarding the domination of the national film industry in 1930-1 when the long and subsequently fruitless Anti-Combines Investigation attempted to outline the extent to which the industry was in the hands of American interests. The evidence was clearly laid out, and one company in particular—Famous Players—was proven to be patently guilty of maintaining virtual control of the motion picture distribution and exhibition facilities in Canada. Sadly, most Canadians didn't seem to care. Why should they? Like their American neighbours, millions of them went to the movies every week, and most were oblivious to the source of their entertainment provided it gave them what they sought—escape, recreation and a few laughs.

It has only been in recent years—in fact since the mid-sixties—that Canadians have become concerned about developing an indigenous film industry. Most Canadian movie-goers still don't care where their films come from, as attendance at most Canadian-made films demonstrates. While for many obvious reasons the situation is different for French language films in Quebec, movies in English Canada are still virtually controlled from Hollywood. The solutions to this problem are not obvious, but tentative steps are now being taken by the Canadian government to create more equitable production and distribution of Canadian-made films.

Ernest Shipman and "Back to God's Country"

Peter Morris

With me, the making of pictures in Canada first appealed as a business, then it became a hobby, now I might fairly say it is a religion. I welcome the opportunity of addressing myself to the Canadian Clubs, believing that I find here perfect understanding from a movement founded for the purpose of quickening a Canadian national consciousness—the spirit which now finds expression not only in a new and distinctive note in Canadian literature, but in a demand for Canadian-made motion pictures, as real and free and wholesome as is Canadian life at its best.

-Ernest Shipman, March 1923.

It is quite difficult in retrospect to decide whether Ernest Shipman was a rogue or a genius. Perhaps like all great entrepreneurs he was a little of both. A typical example of the "Diamond Jim" kind of opportunistic promoters who flourished in North America in the late nineteenth century, he went through two fortunes and five wives during the course of his chequered career—eventually dying at fifty-nine of the *bon viveur's* disease, cirrhosis of the liver. Nell Shipman, the fourth Mrs. Shipman and herself a talented producer, actress and writer, described him affectionately. "Men like Ernie Shipman made the Nineties gay. A vanished breed. He had the bounce of a rubber ball, the buoyancy of a balloon.... He was one of the great cocksmen of his time, not immoral but amoral, not lascivious but lusty. If they named him dishonest he was always within the law's fences contractually and the ten per cent he required of his minion's wages he considered a fair return for his efforts on their behalf." It is possible, of course, to dismiss him as an opportunist who used the lure of Canadian film production during a period of heightened nationalism to extract money from naive investors in cities across Canada. And he did, indeed, have a remarkable talent for separating Canadians from their bankrolls. But this, in any case, is not to tell all of Shipman anymore than it is a description of others like him, from P.T. Barnum up. He did, after all, produce seven feature films in Canada in three years, and in achieving this he stands alone. He realized his films had to be seen outside Canada in the U.S. market if they were to be financial successes. He paid strict and efficient attention to the marketing and promotion of all of them. None (except BLUE WATER) failed on this level as so many previous Canadian films had—and as they were to fail again in the future. His basic theory that films should be produced directly in the locations with which they deal was faithfully put into

This chapter is an extract from Peter Morris's manuscript, *Embattled Shadows, A History of the Canadian Cinema, 1895-1939*. Our thanks to Mr. Morris for his editing of the piece and his permission to print it. Thanks also to McGill-Queen's University Press, who are presently preparing the manuscript for publication.

practice on all seven films. "Telling the Truth in Motion Pictures", Shipman called it. This in itself was something, given the misrepresentations of Canada that were being perpetrated in contemporary Hollywood films. The content of the films was nothing if not Canadian: the life of Bay of Fundy fishermen, the Glengarry lumber industry, Russian immigrants on the prairies, not to forget, of course, the Northwest Mounted Police and north-woods adventure. And more, there was something about his approach to filming that seems rather specially Canadian.

At the time Shipman turned his attentions back to his homeland, Canada was not only in the throes of its post-World War I nationalism, but enjoying an investment boom. There was also a fashion in the movie business for films with Canadian plots. Like all movie fashions it could not last, but for five years or so following the war, films featuring Mounties and trappers, and adventure films in the "high North" were big business. It is against this background that Shipman operated and it was these factors that brought him success.

Shipman never varied his mode of operation. The formula was to find a Canadian story, raise money for its production as a film in the locale in which it was set, excite community participation in the production and promote "in kind" assistance in the form of locations, facilities and personnel. The lead actors and technicians were imported, though they were often, as he was, Canadian-born. He spoke many times of repatriating—permanently—the many Canadians working in movies in Hollywood. He prophesied that new Canadian actors and technicians would not have to leave the country to find work in movies. He promised the construction of permanent production centres, spread across the country regionally based. Canada had almost limitless potential as a major film-producing nation. "There is a market for thirty Canadian features in Canada," he said in April 1922, "but I can make only ten and may make only seven. Centres all over the Dominion will be selected for production. Preference will be given to Canadian authors, Canadian players, and the necessary technical staff will be recruited from Canadians also.... A Canadian picture will not necessarily mean that we are to have snow scenes. In fact, we intend to eliminate the snow scenes and picture Canada during her Summer and Autumn months." A year later his vision had become more grandiose. Comparing the Canadian film industry to a "young giant" which had "no past to live down, no mistakes to apologize for", he noted that he had "carefully estimated that at least one hundred features could be made without duplication of scenery or background". He was an indefatigable defender of Canadian national interests in the film field. His most forceful statement on this was written in September 1921, soon after completing CAMERON OF THE ROYAL MOUNTED, in response to news that the United States would impose a special tariff on the importation of foreign films. He predicted that Canada would respond to this with a "retaliatory tariff" which would "practically prohibit the export of American-made pictures into

Canada and give to Canadian producers a great opportunity and full protection for the making of an increased number of pictures for home consumption". Canadian exhibitors, he wrote, "figure that an increased activity in the making of Canadian pictures would open to them the doors for investment through which they would receive their share of profits from the export of these pictures to all other countries, and at the same time have some voice in the subject matter and the making of these pictures.

"The attitude assumed by the big business interests of the Dominion is that instead of paying so many millions of dollars a year to American producers for entertainment, [the businessmen] will instead receive from foreign markets many millions of dollars, and at the same time demonstrate to the world at large the beauty, resources and virility of the nation."

The films "would be treated from the artistic rather than the commercial standpoint"; free trade relations "would consequently be established between all countries which had not discriminated in their tarrif laws against Canadian-made productions". Canadian films would be exported to Britain, France, Scandinavia, Italy, Spain and Australia, and Canadian exhibitors would purchase from these countries films "in sufficient quantities to fulfill all needs until such time as the Canadian producing units have developed to a point where they can be relied upon for a considerable number of high-grade pictures each year". Meanwhile, markets in the United States would not be closed to the best Canadian films. All that was necessary was to pay "a duty of $30,000 on each $100,000 production"; since BACK TO GOD'S COUNTRY had already earned over $500,000 that was hardly a problem.

Canada also would establish a film school. "A certain educational institution located in one of the Canadian border cities has already suggested the establishment of a school for the teaching of all branches of the motion picture art." Such a school, headed by experienced filmmakers, "would effectually safeguard the student body from all dangers of studio life and lay a practical foundation for the picture industry". (The dislike of "studios" was in line with his oft-expressed belief in "realism with nature backgrounds".)

For a country in the first flush of discovering its existence as a nation following the First World War, Shipman's words were heady stuff. Investors were ready to believe his prophecies. But then, of course, he had an amazing talent for promotion—especially self-promotion. His advertisements were highly imaginative and visually striking—and Shipman's name was itself always prominent. But, more than this, he managed to keep himself consistently in the news section of the movie trade papers. Such stories usually included his name in the headline and more often than not were accompanied by a photograph. Though most of these stories were obviously planted, they are a tribute to his promotional talents. As, on the reverse side, is the fact that no stories ever appeared in the trade papers describing his several failures. For example, not a word appeared in print after the collapse of his Canadian ventures; instead, there are stories about his latest idea—to turn Florida into a rival of Hollywood.

He seems to have been liked—if not exactly trusted—by most of his contemporaries. Rogues like him with an eye always out for the main chance do not survive without a degree of charm to take the sting out of the "con". Certainly women found him lovable—as his sobriquet "The Petticoat Pet of Broadway" suggests.

His son, Barry Shipman (who himself became a Hollywood scriptwriter), recalls that he "was not a businessman". Ernest's penchant was in promoting schemes that remained just on the right side of the law. From these Ernest took his cut, as he did from the theatrical stock companies he managed in his early career—hence the name "Ten Per-Cent Ernie" which stuck with him throughout his life. The monopolistic drive of twentieth-century capitalists was beyond him. He had none of the hunger for power and control that motivated the Adolph Zukors of the film industry. Though he liked money, he lost it almost as quickly as he made it. His methods and peculiar sense of independence were out-of-date in an industry already falling prey to the thrust for massive centralization that characterized so much of American industrial development. And it was the new tycoons of that industry—the Adolph Zukors, the William Foxes, the Marcus Loews and the Joseph Schenks—who were eventually to force him out into the cold.

Ernest G. Shipman was born in Hull, Quebec, December 16, 1871. He was the eldest of four brothers, three of whom—Ernest, Frederick and Joseph—had careers in show-business. His father, Montague, was a descendent of the Shipman family that founded Almonte, a small town near Ottawa. He was educated at the Ryerson School in Toronto and became interested at an early age in promotion and publicity. His early career was as a promoter of travelling theatre companies, but after 1911 and his marriage to Nell Shipman he increasingly interested himself in motion pictures. Initially he worked as promoter, distributor and publicist, but tried several times to involve himself directly in production.

In 1918 he got his first big chance. Nell Shipman had been a great success in two films based on stories by James Oliver Curwood, GOD'S COUNTRY AND THE WOMAN, and BAREE, SON OF KAZAN. What was now proposed was that Shipman and Curwood sign a contract under which Curwood agreed to give exclusive film rights to his stories to Nell Shipman for two years while she agreed to star exclusively in films based on his stories. Ernest Shipman was a co-signatory to this agreement, dated November 1, 1918. Ernest could not have made a better deal. James Oliver Curwood was an extremely popular and very prolific author, writing two novels and ten screenplays a year and producing a short story every two weeks. His novels were always bestsellers and his name associated with a film was a certain selling point. Most of his stories were outdoor adventures and, though he was an American, many of them were set in northern Canada where he usually spent three months a year. They were, in fact, considerably responsible for the popular portrait of Canada as a land of endless ice and snow.

The first story selected for production was "Wapi the Walrus", a story then being published in *Good Housekeeping Magazine*. It had the usual elements of a Curwood plot: a melodramatic triangle of heroine, hero and villain, a setting in the "wilds of North Canada", a dog as co-hero, plus "bears, moose and elk, living amid their natural surroundings in the snow vastness of the North" and the omnipresent Northwest Mounted Police.

Ernest Shipman still faced the problem of raising money to produce the film. For this he went to Calgary. Why is not clear. Likely, it was at the invitation of William R. Marshall, manager of the Imperial Film Company of Canada. Marshall, a long-time theatrical manager and film journalist (working in New York where he may have known Ernest) had recently installed "a complete motion picture plant" in Calgary and produced a film, HELLO, DAD!, for the Calgary Rotary Club. In December 1918, Marshall was predicting that "at some not far distant date it would not be surprising to find one of the largest dramatic studios on the continent located here". Only weeks later, on January 22, 1919, Ernest Shipman was in Calgary to address the Board of Trade. Not surprisingly, he drew his listeners' attention to the "enormous profits" and the apparent potential of Alberta as a film location, but he emphasized that if Calgary were made the production centre for the Shipman-Curwood films, "it would be necessary for a considerable portion of the capital to be raised locally". The twin lures of immediate profits and the development of their favourite city as a rival to Hollywood could not be resisted by Calgary investors. On February 7, 1919, Canadian Photoplays Ltd. was incorporated in Alberta with a capitalization of $250,000. Their prospectus stated they did not intend to compete with Hollywood "in the production of studio-made pictures, but in the great pictures of outdoor life with their intense dramatic interest". For which, of course, they claimed "no country in the world can surpass Canada". Among the principal shareholders were W.R. Marshall of the Imperial Film Company, H.P. Carver, apparently a friend of Curwood's and later to be associated with him in financing Curwood-Carver Productions, and A.E. Cross, later to be president of another Calgary film company, British Canadian Pictures. Ernest Shipman assigned to Canadian Photoplays the benefits of the Shipman-Curwood contract for up to two years in order to produce not less than two films, neither of which was to exceed $65,000 in cost. He was also hired by the company as business manager with responsibility for "publicity, advertising and selling". Net profits from all films were to be divided equally between Canadian Photoplays and Ernest Shipman. The first production was to be WAPI, THE WALRUS, soon to be retitled BACK TO GOD'S COUNTRY for no other reason than to capitalize on Nell Shipman's success in GOD'S COUNTRY AND THE WOMAN.

Cast and crew began to arrive in late February. David M. Hartford, a Hollywood director of action films, was to direct. Joe Walker and Del Clawson were photographers, Bert Van Tuyle was production manager, and Bill Colvin was involved as Shipman's personal associate and general factotum. The cast included Wellington Playter, Ronald Byram, Charles Arling and Ralph Laidlaw. Nell Shipman herself arrived March 1 and announced she intended to make Calgary her permanent home.

Curwood had already arrived and was not at all happy with the screenplay Nell had written from his story. Ernest, aware that much of the company's financial backing was being subscribed on the strength of Curwood's name, pleaded with Nell to placate the irate author. This she did with some reluctance, having no liking for the *macho*-big-game-hunter image Curwood projected. Nell had enlarged the role of the heroine and downplayed that of the dog, Wapi, the centre of Curwood's story. In her screenplay the story revolved around Dolores, who is finally rescued from the villain by Wapi, a dog considered vicious but which she had earlier befriended. Nell accepted Curwood's changes, planning to re-write again once he had left. Everything was smoothed over and by mid-March the company left for Lesser Slave Lake in the Peace River country where the winter scenes were to be filmed.

Their experiences on location were far from comfortable. Working in temperatures that touched sixty below zero and living in cabins abandoned by fishermen for the winter, they faced unprecedented problems. Cameras had to be left outside at all times to avoid static caused by temperature changes. Ronald Byram, playing the lead opposite Nell, contracted a severe cold which developed into pneumonia; he was taken to a hospital in Edmonton and later died. He was replaced by Wheeler Oakman. The script called for a whaling ship frozen in the ice. Studio carpenters refused to work on the second day when they realized the temperature was forty-seven below. They returned south, taking their tools. Bert Van Tuyle, the production manager, had to build the ship himself with the help of a local Indian. Not surprisingly, he suffered severe frost-bite which left him with a limp for the rest of his life.

Shooting was finished by the end of March and the company returned to Calgary, en route to California where the rest of the film was to be shot. While in Calgary, Nell learned that her father had died suddenly.

Production was completed in May and the film was released by First National in September 1919 to almost universal acclaim. Contemporary reviews were glowing, with praise lavished on the film's sense of atmosphere and on Nell Shipman for her ability to appear at ease with the numerous wild animals who, as she intended, became almost her co-stars. One of the most striking scenes had Nell Shipman diving nude into a pool while being observed by the lecherous villain. It had been intended that Nell play the scene in a discreet pink leotard. But the leotard wrinkled visibly when wet, so Nell determined to play the scene in the nude. Nell was not the first actress to play a nude scene; Annette Kellerman had preceded her by some three years in A DAUGHTER OF THE GODS, successor to NEPTUNE'S DAUGHTER. But it is some measure of the times that the scene created as little furor as it did—certainly less than that aroused in the thirties by Hedy Lamarr's brief nude scene in ECSTASY.

BACK TO GOD'S COUNTRY was seen across North America, in Britain, Japan, Europe and Australia. It was an enormous financial success, grossing more than a half-million dollars in its first year of release and netting the Calgary backers a 300 per cent return on their investment.

The plot itself tells the story of Dolores LeBeau, who lives in the Canadian woods with her father and who has a sympathetic rapport with the wild animals of the forest. She falls in love with Peter, a Canadian government official and writer, and marries him after escaping from the villain, Rydal (disguised as a Mountie), who tries to rape her and then kills her father. Later, Dolores and Peter travel to the Arctic on a whaling schooner whose captain turns out to be Rydal, still intent on "possessing" her. She manages to foil him until the ship becomes frozen in, then she escapes on a dog-sled with her husband. Rydal and his partner pursue her, but the dog Wapi, ill-treated by Rydal's partner and befriended by Dolores, assists her by attacking and crippling the dogs of Rydal's sled. Rydal dies in an ice-hole while Dolores and Peter return to "God's Country" and her animal friends.

Nell Shipman had been proven right in emphasizing the "incidents" of the narrative and her own role, for what the critics and the public acclaimed were the magnificent snow scenes, the woodland scenes, the wild-life studies—"always interesting and occasionally irresistibly funny"—and dramatic scenes such as "Dolores' magnificent dive and swim through the rapids".

Nell Shipman makes a striking heroine. Though her Junoesque appearance is at odds with the coyness of some scenes, her real talents are evident in the scenes in which she has to do something, whether it is struggling with Rydal, rescuing her father, or merely bathing. Even the scenes with her and the animals have a natural quality that could only have come from an essential sympathy.

Promotion of the film was in the hands of Ernest Shipman. Having raised the money for the film, he had left director and cast to produce it, only reappearing when his talents for publicity were needed. The promotional campaign for the film was as extensive as one might expect for a film costing ten times that of BACK TO GOD'S COUNTRY. Exhibitors (still largely independent or part of small chains) must have been not a little intrigued by the advertising illustrations which showed a nude girl threatened by a menacing bear and an even more menacing villain. "Don't Book BACK TO GOD'S COUNTRY—Unless You Want to Prove the Nude is Not Rude" was the slogan Shipman used to tantalize prospective customers. This, combined with various tricks used to entice movie-goers into the theatre, helped ensure the film's success.

Shipman's role throughout was identical to the one he played on later productions: an entrepreneur rather than an artistic contributor. As long as he felt he had brought together the right talents in terms of the author and cast needed to sell the film, he stayed strictly away from production decisions. Given the situation of Canadian films at the time, this entrepreneurial role was arguably more creative than any narrowly artistic one. Shipman's talents could ensure not only that a film was made but that it was marketed—a noticeable lack in Canada before his arrival. On the strength of his success in Calgary, he was to travel across Canada for the next four years, attempting to repeat the experience though never again matching the returns of that first production.

Canadian Photoplays never produced their second promised film, though as late as April 1920 it was being discussed. The reason why is unclear. By that date they had received $170,000 on their investment and were "receiving cheques monthly". There was still nearly a year to go on the company's two-year exclusive contract with Curwood and Nell Shipman. It is possible Curwood was upset by Nell Shipman's tampering with his story and broke his contract. In any case, in February 1920 he announced formation of his own company, Curwood Productions, to produce film versions of his novels. David Hartford (director of BACK TO GOD'S COUNTRY) would direct; Ernest Shipman would be in charge of sales and publicity. Two films were produced: NOMADS OF THE NORTH (1920) and THE GOLDEN SNARE (1921), neither of them Canadian but both of which were exploited by Ernest Shipman. Nell Shipman appeared in neither. Ernest and Nell had separated soon after BACK TO GOD'S COUNTRY was completed and were divorced in 1920. This, too, may have had an influence on the break-up of the Curwood-Shipman partnership. In turn, it meant Canadian Photoplays had no scripts lined up. It may also be, very simply, that the backers of Canadian Photoplays were delighted with the 300 per cent return on their investment and content to retire from active production with their money secure. Whatever the reason, Canadian Photoplays, the company that produced Canada's most financially successful film, went into voluntary liquidation.

Conversations
Gordon Sparling

While working on CARRY ON SERGEANT! at the studio in Trenton, Ontario, I made several good friends among the technical staff from New York, notably Sam Corso, the art director. He urged me to come to New York for experience in "the Big Time". However, I accepted an invitation from Frank Badgley to become his assistant at the Canadian Government Motion Picture Bureau in Ottawa. After a rather unproductive eleven months there, handicapped by—as Badgley put it—"only enough money to pay salaries but not enough to make good pictures", I headed for New York.

Sam Corso smoothed the way for me to get on the payroll of Paramount's big studios at Astoria across the Fifty-ninth Street bridge from Manhattan. The next two-and-a-half years were invaluable, working in various departments and studying many top-notchers such as Lubitsch, Cukor, Mamoulian (I was an extra in one of his first features), Chevalier, Colbert, Wanger, and so on, as well as real pros in all phases of production.

The only sour note occurred when I fell for an old con game. We had been shooting on a Sunday and were paid overtime rates in cash. The union shop steward came around collecting for memberships in an Assistant Directors' Union which was being organized. The fee was exactly my day's pay. Later he couldn't recall the transaction—and the union never got off the ground.

One day I received a letter from Clarke Ashworth, vice-president of Campbell-Ewald (now MacLaren Advertising) in Toronto, saying that General Motors had decided to make an inspirational trailer for theatrical release across Canada. The Depression was severe by 1931 and the trailer they had in mind would show Canadians that with their great resources, a lot of hard work and positive thinking, prosperity was just around the corner. He wanted me, a Canadian, to make the picture. I was very much attracted to the idea and left New York immediately for Montreal where the film was to be produced at the bustling Associated Screen News Ltd. I should explain that this firm had been established ten years earlier solely as a news-gathering agency for the major international newsreels—Pathé, Paramount, Universal, Gaumont, News-of-the-Day, etc.; it also produced travelogues and scenics for its largest shareholder, the Canadian Pacific Railway. Many of those early CPR pictures were titled by Terry Ramsaye, who later wrote the classic film history, *A Million and One Nights*.

By 1924 ASN had persuaded many of the American feature producers to forward their negatives to its lab for making the number of prints required for Canadian distribution. The Americans soon found that the

Revised and adapted by Gordon Sparling from *Motion*, no. 2 (January-February 1973).

wild Indians up here were not shooting their precious negatives full of holes and that they were able to save a great deal of money they had formerly been paying in import duty. Incidentally, another large beneficiary was Kodak which set up a plant at Weston, Ontario, to make the raw stock.

One of the pleasures of making the trailer FORWARD WITH CANADA was putting it all together with the lively and amazingly hard-working staff (some of whose marching feet appeared on the main title which was shot by Roy Tash—and used again in the same place on RHAPSODY IN TWO LANGUAGES) and also teaming with a newcomer to movie-making, the well-known journalist B.K. Sandwell, later the illustrious editor of *Saturday Night* magazine.

When the job was finished, B.E. Norrish asked me to stay and set up a production department, quite separate from their newsreel operations. The experience at Paramount had been a tremendous liberal education in up-to-the-minute production techniques at a time when the industry was adjusting to the changeover from silent to sound pictures.

I quickly agreed, on condition that I could make a series of all-Canadian theatrical short subjects. Observation and bitter recent experience made me leery of feature production in Canada. Features required large sums of money. They could not hope to recoup their investment from the home market but must depend on foreign distribution for the bulk of their revenue. (The opposite was true for American producers who counted on their local market to recoup production costs while foreign markets would provide the "cream".) As the American grip tightened more and more on distribution and theatres (even in Canada), available outlets dwindled to seedy "state rights" operators.

All too often in our fledgling Canadian industry it was (to quote a magazine article I wrote forty-three years ago!) a case of "let's make a movie" and then, with scant preparation, insufficient money and a colossal amount of inexperience, a picture was made and forgotten.

> Success in Canadian movie-making will depend, as it does in any other industry, on sound business principles. When a producing group comes into being which will place experienced people in jobs that demand experience; which is willing and able to pay for "production values"; which will study its market before its production; and, above all, which will remember that while it is nice to speak of "the movie game" it is really the movie business; we will surely find that motion pictures can be made here just as successfully as anywhere else in the world.

Those principles are, I believe, still true today. One giant helping hand is the new CFDC. The other (and even more vital one) has yet to come. It must be some just form of access to exhibition profits at home and abroad.

At the beginning of the thirties, the only hope I could see of getting a wedge into the theatrical market was by producing shorts which were thought of as "fillers" and no threat to the movie-making establishment.

Mr. Norrish agreed, but added his own condition that we also make commercial non-theatrical films. This stipulation worked out well because the revenue from the commercials enabled us to buy the latest equipment and eventually to build a fine sound studio—the first in Canada.

But we soon found that it was hard to sell our kind of picture (carefully-scripted, novelty presentation, production value, entertainment and glamour, integral use of music, etc.) when it was under the "Screen News" banner. Don't get me wrong. My attitude was not a disparagement of the newsreels. Theirs was an exciting, demanding, fascinating branch of the filmmaker's art. But there is a basic difference between the two techniques. A good newsreel man strives to put together a good motion picture by utilizing to the best of his capability the material with which he has to work. The production man, on the other hand, organizes and controls his raw materials to produce the motion picture he envisions. The difference is in *taking* pictures and *making* pictures.

Norrish was naturally unwilling to change the name of his very successful company, but he finally did allow the production department to operate under the name Associated Screen Studios. Our product was An Associated Screen Picture.

When we started our theatre shorts we announced an ambitious program of two series: "Canadian Cameos" and "Sport Chats". But after a few releases all were combined into the "Canadian Cameo Series". It took many years to develop wide public acceptance for these one-reelers. Our publicity likened them to the dessert in a well-balanced dinner. Our slogan was "A little gem carved in high relief". We appealed to Canadians to see these home-grown tidbits with the phrase, "It is not a matter of patriotism; it is a matter of national pride."

The "Canadian Cameos", with very modest budgets, gave us the opportunity to experiment with many production techniques, such as in MUSIC FROM THE STARS, a glamour studio musical featuring Horace Lapp and his orchestra with singers Madeleine Pedlar and William Morton; RHAPSODY IN TWO LANGUAGES, feeling our way in the complex Rhapsodic Technique with Canada's first specially-written score composed and conducted by Howard Fogg; ACADIAN SPRING SONG, a romantic, dramatized treatment of a scenic without words, only music and sound effects; THE THOUSAND DAYS, a flowering of our Rhapsodic Technique blending, through visuals, sounds, juxtaposition and music, a two-reel "special" on Canada's "inactive" period of the war. The American government bought 200 prints of that one to acquaint Americans with their northern ally—and gave us a tremendous boost in publicizing Canadian filmmaking.

There were, of course, many and various highlights to compensate for the inevitable frustrations and apathy encountered in promoting our series. An early break happened by chance. Mr. Norrish was a great friend of J.C. Campbell, director of publicity for the National Parks. Several of their silent non-theatrical films were lying around without much circulation. But they had some terrific nature and wild animal footage which needed tighter editing and continuity. A friendly deal was made whereby in exchange for processing Parks Branch negatives we could make blue prints and combine any of them to make subjects for theatrical release as we saw fit. The only stipulation was that Campbell had to approve our sound versions. Out of that arrangement came GREY OWL'S LITTLE BROTHER, of which more prints are said to have been made than *any* other Canadian film, either feature or short.

Another was SHE CLIMBS TO CONQUER which we released in 1932. It was made up from several reels of wonderful stuff shot by Bill Oliver. The leading lady was a photogenic and very expert mountain climber, Gloria Englehart. She and Oliver and a couple of guides climbed the 11,000-foot Mount Victoria in the Canadian Rockies, lugging up all the heavy 35mm equipment required in those days. It was a spectacular beginning for the series—but one Canadian theatre chain refused to run it because Chateau Lake Louise, where the opening scenes had been shot, was mentioned in the narration and that was sinister, undercover advertising! The narration was written by B.K. Sandwell and spoken by Corey Thomson.

We felt that a lovely novelty short could be made based on the spectacular ice carnival presented each winter by the Toronto Skating Club in Maple Leaf Gardens. I think it is safe to say that Shipstad and Johnson got the idea for their professional ice shows from these exciting amateur carnivals which were then a unique Canadian phenomenon. But in those days motion picture negative was very slow—even shooting hockey games under a blaze of white light was an underspeeded presentation of shadows. We heard of a new film which could be "hypersensitized" just before use. I brought up from New York as hand baggage just enough of this film to shoot a one-reeler. An hour before leaving our hotel in Toronto the cameraman ran his shower with steaming hot water until the atmosphere was a soggy pea-soup fog. Then in total darkness he slowly rewound the raw stock, which miraculously became almost twice as fast as normal. Dr. Mills, an amateur genius of stage lighting, and the professional electrician at the Gardens were most co-operative in furthering our experiment. They arranged for increased intensity of lighting on the big numbers and even took the coloured gelatines off for some vital shots. Close-ups of the skaters were shot on another night at the club's own rink on Dupont Street, where camera angles could be arranged without showing any background.

Audiences liked CARNIVAL ON SKATES, so we made another skating Cameo a couple of years later. We shot a lot of spectacular footage in Toronto but were trying to dream up some novel framework for presenting it. Margot Blaisdell was our staff scenarist at the time. She was a real genius—not much common sense, but all kinds of brains. (Her grandfather had invented the Blaisdell paper pencils.) She reworked the Cinderella story which, instead of having a Royal Ball, introduced the Skating Carnival. Montreal actors played the Fairy Godmother and Prince Charming, but the amateur skating star of the real Carnival, Doris Gillespie—who had never done any acting—came down to the studio and created a beautiful Cinderella. Trick photography helped the Fairy Godmother change Cinderella's rags to the glittering costume which Doris had worn for her number in the carnival, and again at midnight when she must run from Prince Charming. For that scene we used a split screen, shot with precisely-cut masks in the camera's aperture plate. As the girl runs past a lamp post in her gorgeous costume, she is in rags again on the other side of it. CRYSTAL BALLET went around the world under the Twentieth-Century Fox banner. We retained the Canadian rights for our Cameo series but for most of the films we were able to obtain wider deals.

Just before the war we went into colour. The Dufay process had recently been introduced in England. Technicolor was beyond our reach. You had to rent their great hulking cameras which ran three 35mm negatives simultaneously and hire their own cameramen—all for $500 per day. Dufaycolour, on the other hand, was a single negative which ran in any regular camera without adaptation. The stock was coated with microscopic dots which acted as filters. If you sat very close to the screen all you saw was a dancing "snowstorm" of these brilliantly coloured specks. But at a reasonable distance the effect was a lovely, soft, realistic colour which many viewers liked better than the garish Technicolor of the time. (Dufaycolour went out of business after the war when those chemical miracles Kodachrome and Agfacolor came on the market.)

The Dufay people sent us 2,000 feet of raw stock free to try out. Ross Beesley and I headed for the Laurentians and shot a skiing quickie, practically editing in the camera in order to get a one-reeler out of it. Peggy Johannsen, daughter of the famous "Jackrabbit" Johannsen, was our photogenic and expert leading lady. The stock was rushed back to England for processing and when the prints were returned everyone was elated. We had cracked the world of colour.

Now we wanted to use Dufaycolour on something special. Just before the war, in June 1939, the King and Queen came to Canada and we thought that the pageantry of their visit to the nation's capital would be a terrific subject for a Cameo. But the Canadian government was controlling all shooting through a pool system to reduce the number of cameramen flocking in from two continents at any given position. Colour was ruled out because the different processes could not be pooled.

All our cameramen had been borrowed by the government except two—the elderly Alfred Jacquemin and the very young Bob Martin. They were very steamed up at being left out, and longed for a chance of revenge. I asked Frank Badgley, who was in charge of all motion picture arrangements, if he would actually forbid us to shoot, or could we scrounge what we could. "You can scrounge all you can," he replied. "But without official status, you won't get much." "So sez you," the three of us muttered, and away we went. Since all the company's good equipment had been taken by the others, Jacquemin had to tape an antiquated telephoto lens to his camera, which by some miracle held steady when he needed it. Bob Martin flirted with the girls in the hairdressing salon of the Chateau Laurier, and managed to get a fine overhead shot of the Royal procession from their window.

Our Roy Tash, who was shooting for the pool in a very preferred position just to the right of the steps into the Parliament buildings, beckoned me over from the crowd, explaining to the Mountie, "I need my assistant." When I rushed across with the hand-held Eyemo which Martin had ready, Tash quickly set the correct aperture just as their Majesties reached the top of the steps, and I became a temporary cameraman. There were only five feet left on the roll! But through pure luck I got the most beautiful close-up of the Queen anyone could ask for.

Mr. Norrish gave the O.K. to take the negative to England so that processed, recorded prints could be returned to Canada before the Royal Tour was over. The captain of the *Empress of Britain* (there was no commercial transatlantic flying yet) was so impressed with his role that he personally carried the film cans to his wheelhouse for protection. The Dufay people were on hand when the ship docked and their lab worked all that day and night. Next morning they screened the complete rushes which were edited during the day. That night an English orchestra leader discussed the music and took the key footages. All night an expatriate scriptwriter, Caesar de Lom, who had at one time worked at Associated Screen, hammered out the narration. Next day we recorded voice and music simultaneously at Merton Park Studios; that night Dufay turned out six release prints of the one-reel "Canadian Cameo" ROYAL BANNERS OVER OTTAWA which were placed (again with the captain on the bridge!) on the *Empress of Britain* on her return trip to Canada. Twenty prints were also banged out for theatres in England—all this within eleven days of the event. I cabled Norrish that the prints were on their way and that I was taking a week's sleep and holiday in England. Incidentally, that short made more money than any other in the series, and enough to pay for the production of all the other Cameos that year.

Soon after the war, we experimented with another new process—Ansco Color (Dufaycolour had by that time discontinued its motion picture activities, superseded by the "chemical miracles" of multi-layer colour stock.) Several postwar "Canadian Cameos" were made in Ansco Color, the chief one being DESIGN FOR SWIMMING. This featured a lovely ornamental swimming group called the Mermaid Swimming Club of Toronto. A mining magnate's pool on his beautiful estate near Oakville was lent for our "set". We built a chamber which could be lowered into the deep end of the pool. The top, above the water-line, was open and the front was plate glass an inch thick. The chamber was held down by a ton of lead ingots on the floor. The girls wore specially designed bathing suits in several colour groupings and their patterned swimming was orchestrated to Tschaikovsky's "Swan Lake Ballet". DESIGN FOR SWIMMING was a delightful little short which, after its Canadian run, was bought by MGM for the balance of the world—but unfortunately Ansco had in the meantime changed from its original reversal method to the negative-positive process. MGM couldn't get reversal prints, so our nice deal fell through!

One of my favourite Cameos was a skiing comedy, SITZMARKS THE SPOT, featuring the Canadian comedian John Pratt. He had made a tremendous hit in the wartime Navy Show with his song, "You'll Get Used to It", so we built a story around him singing a skiing version of it. Before SITZMARKS THE SPOT even had its normal premiere as a "Canadian Cameo", Warner Bros. insisted on having world rights, and offered such a good price that Mr. Norrish snapped at it—over my dead body. Our own series was losing a dandy subject. They only changed the main and end title to read "A Warner Bros. Vitaphone Picture". (The original test print and the only print in existence carrying the "Canadian Cameo" titles is in the archives of La Cinémathèque québécois in Montreal.)

All together there were eighty-five "Canadian Cameos". The first was released in 1932 and the last in 1955—THE BELOVED FISH shot in Ansco Color by Jack Hynes and enhanced by a score composed and conducted by Lucio Agostini. But by then ASN was in its troubled days and the "Canadian Cameo" series was cancelled. The new owners of the company were chiefly interested in its real-estate value and couldn't care less about production. As a sort of last gesture of defiance I obtained their permission to ship this last unreleased reel to the new Stratford International Film Festival in July 1957. It was accepted. This boost was unavailing; the machinery for distribution had been irrevocably disbanded.

Seventeen years later (May 1970) when most of these stirring events had been forgotten, I walked into the local picture house to see the feature, BATTLE OF BRITAIN. And there on the same bill was THE BELOVED FISH—in a mysterious black-and-white print! It seemed a sort of surprise epitaph for the long-deceased "Canadian Cameo" series. R.I.P.

Conserving the Canadian Image

Sam Kula

The film experience in Canada is at least as old, if admittedly not as illustrious, as it is in the United States. No later than July 1896, the Holland Brothers were exhibiting to an astonished audience in Ottawa the wonders of the animated moving picture machine, Edison's Vitascope; and by the end of 1897 itinerant cameramen working for Lumière, Edison, and the Biograph Company were filming Niagara Falls. In 1898 the Edison Studio produced the world's first sponsored film for the Massey-Harris Company, which was the hit of the Canadian National Exhibition in Toronto that summer. Two years later the ubiquitous Charles Urban was contracting with the Canadian Pacific Railway to film a series of travelogues along the railway's right of way to lure British immigrants out west. The cameramen, including the legendary Joe Rosenthal, were under strict instructions to avoid snow scenes!

The early years were also auspicious for a native Canadian feature film industry. By the end of 1913, the year D.W. Griffith defied his employers at the Biography Company to make JUDITH OF BETHULIA in four reels, E.P. Sullivan and W.H. Cavanaugh were producing and directing a *five*-reel version of Longfellow's poem, "*Evangeline*", for the Canadian Bioscope Company. Shot in the Annapolis Valley of Nova Scotia, EVANGELINE was released in February 1914, but despite good trade reviews neither the film nor its makers seemed to have made much impact on the public, and a second effort by the Canadian Bioscope Company failed to secure a general release. The same fate probably befell Arthur Larente's MADELEINE DE VERCHERES, reputed to be at least four reels in length. There is evidence to suggest that this epic of the French-Indian wars at the end of the seventeenth century was photographed on the outskirts of Montreal sometime in 1912, which could conceivably make it the first feature-length film shot in North America. Hard facts on both the production and exhibition of MADELEINE DE VERCHERES are, however, difficult to ascertain, and neither claimant to the title of first Canadian feature film has yet been recovered from the attic or basement in which it may be waiting to be discovered.

Very few of the estimated seventy feature films produced in Canada (with and without foreign participation) before 1939 are now known to have survived; the total at present is thirteen. There may not be any unknown masterpieces among the missing (the few survivors do not tend to raise that expectation), but they would document the continuing struggle to establish a Canadian presence in the medium, despite government indifference, foreign competition, and American domination of distribution and exhibition.

Government indifference extended, of course, to conservation of the

Reprinted from *The Journal of the University Film Association*, vol. 27, no. 3 (1975).

films that were produced. The universal acceptance of motion pictures was a social and cultural phenomenon without parallel in recorded history, and the almost total neglect of the medium by the custodians of cultural artifacts was a phenomenon almost as marked. Their performance in Canada, unfortunately, met or exceeded the usual international standard.

The evidential value of motion pictures was being preached as early as 1900 (Boleslas Matuszewski, who had been appointed Royal Court Cinematographer to Czar Nicholas II in 1896, issued a manifesto in Paris in 1900 arguing for the preservation of film records in an international chain of film archives to embrace all the world!), but the converts were few in number and weak in resources. It was not until 1935 that the National Film Archives in London and the Museum of Modern Art Film Library in New York began to conserve films in the public interest, and these first efforts were echoed in Canada by the formation of the National Film Society (later the Canadian Film Institute) in Ottawa. By then it was estimated that roughly half the productions of the international film art had been lost through neglect of the original, inherently unstable, nitrate stock, and World War II did little to improve the prospects for recovery. Film archives were hardly a high priority in the immediate postwar period. Even the need for them had to be established and defended. Film history, after all, was something adults did to relive their adolescent fantasies.

Despite the fact that millions of Canadians (and more than 100 million Americans) were going to the movies each and every week, a statistic that dwarfed attendance for all the other arts, the centrality of film in contemporary culture—as art, as entertainment, as a medium of mass communication, and as an agent for social change—was consistently ignored. The academic gate-keepers in the social sciences still largely refused to recognize that film was one of the most pervasive cultural products of the twentieth century. If they rightly suspected as simplistic Kracauer's concept of film as reflecting the collective subconscious of a nation, there still was no serious refutation of Panofsky's contention, made forty years ago, that film directly affects the opinions, the taste, the language, the dress, the behaviour and even the physical appearance of millions of people.

Voices were raised, however; individual condemnations of the wanton waste of historical and cultural resources were posted; and if the pleas and protestations largely fell on deaf ears in government, private, non-profit organizations moved to conserve and document at least the acknowledged masterworks of the day. In Canada the Canadian Film Institute in Ottawa established the Canadian Film Archives in 1964, with the divisional responsibility of conserving and documenting the Canadian film, while in that same year, the Connaissance du cinema in Montreal became La Cinémathèque canadienne (now La Cinémathèque québécoise) with the special responsibility of conserving and documenting French language film.

Conditions varied from country to country; but the common experience was that conserving the national film heritage was a very expensive business. What is essential is not only substantial funding, but reliable, long-term funding. The image of an archive living from hand to mouth, never knowing if the laboratory bills will be met, or even if the doors will be open on Monday morning, is hardly conducive to persuading reluctant depositors that their films will be permanently safeguarded. To add to their difficulties, the privately supported archives, operating in a wasteland as far as resources for film study were concerned, felt obligated to offer a full range of services involving exhibition and distribution which further strained their inadequate budgets.

Despite these handicaps both the Canadian Film Archives and La Cinémathèque québécoise safeguarded thousands of films and collected and organized stills, posters and manuscript material that were disappearing as rapidly as the films themselves. A measure of the problems they faced, however, is that neither of the organizations had the resources to build or lease nitrate storage facilities. They had to rely on the good offices of the National Film Board, which as a crown corporation, was the only federal agency seriously involved with film. Unfortunately the board's mandate did not include conservation, aside from board productions. And even for board productions funds were never allocated for adequate nitrate storage. Nevertheless the board continued to act as an unofficial depository and the private organizations stored their nitrate films along with the board's nitrate (which included the productions of its predecessor agency the Canadian Government Motion Picture Bureau, 1917-1941, as well as the news footage of Associated Screen News and the Canadian Army Film Unit) in a warehouse at Beaconsfield, outside Montreal.

The stage was set for tragedy and in July 1967 (the nation's hundredth birthday), the warehouse was totally destroyed by fire taking with it roughly half the films that had survived in Canada. The loss is incalculable with regard to master material, but fortunately film is replicable and prints of a substantial proportion of the titles have been traced to other depositories in Canada, the United States and throughout the world.

Given the total neglect of the medium by federal departments (the Public Archives of Canada, like the Library of Congress in its turn, had decided that conservation of nitrate films was too hazardous, too technologically complicated, and perhaps too unrewarding), the disaster of 1967 may be said to have galvanized the government into action. Two years later, on the recommendation of the secretary of state, the Public Archives initiated a nitrate film recovery program, borrowing William Galloway from the National Film Board (where he had specialized in film research and preserving historically significant film when his financial comptroller's back was turned) to direct the project. The results were spectacular. In four years a nitrate storage facility was secured (on the Rockcliffe Air Force base on the outskirts of Ottawa) and almost filled to capacity with twelve million feet of film pulled in from government departments, industry sources, and individual depositors scattered from St. John's, Newfoundland (one of the last havens of the itinerant exhibitor with a stock of seemingly timeless prints) to Victoria, British Columbia (the unlikely centre for "quota quickie" production in the thirties).

An even more important accomplishment of the project was that it established the viability of a film archives operation within the administrative structure of the Public Archives, basing its acquisition programs with regard to government departments and agencies on the legislative authority of the Dominion archivist over all government records. This aspect of the program was particularly important in Canada because of the central role played by the National Film Board and the Canadian Broadcasting Corporation in film production, and the critical role played by the Canadian Film Development Corporation and the Canada Council in stimulating film production in the private sector. The project demonstrated the immediate and the potential value of consolidating in one institution the product of the federal government's involvement in film, both as research tool and as production resource.

In May 1972, the Cabinet authorized the Secretary of State Department to investigate the feasibility of establishing a national film archive for the acquisition and conservation of film resources in the national interest (with film defined as carriers of continuous images of every kind, nature or description) and with authority to document and to make available film resources for scholarly and cultural purposes. The result, after some two years of deliberation and consultation with archival and educational organizations, all components of the film and television industry, and government agencies in and out of film, was the establishment of the National Film Archives as a division of the Public Archives of Canada.

To many observers in the universities, regional film study centres, and the industry, the establishment of a national film archive within a government department raised questions of autonomy, both in terms of organization and in relations with the film and television community. Galloway's pilot project demonstrated that operational relationships with the industry could be established that would meet their needs and yet not threaten the integrity of the archives. The experience since 1972 has been that the divisional structure within the historical branch of the Public Archives allows complete freedom (within the ever-present budgetary limitation) to acquire, conserve, catalogue and service the collections. The rules and regulations of the National Film Archives are peculiar to that division, and they represent the attempt of a media-orientated staff (drawn from film study organizations, the industry or industry-related organizations) to be responsible and responsive to the community they serve. Elements of bureaucracy do, of course, intrude, but as far as it is practicable the public face of the National Film Archives reflects a total involvement with film.

At present, the five-year plan for the National Film Archives calls for the "elimination" of the nitrate problem through the transfer of roughly three million feet of nitrate stock now in the archives to safety film, and the acquisition and transfer of approximately one million feet more which is in private hands; the implementation of bilateral agreements now in force or in negotiation so that a copy of every feature film and every historically or culturally significant film or television program produced in Canada will be deposited within a year of production; the consolidation of existing production resources made publicly accessible through a single catalogue and totally available for reference on the premises of the archives—the use of three-quarter-inch videotape cassettes will sharply reduce the money and the time required to achieve this objective; the creation of a core collection representative of international film production, both "classics" and contemporary productions —membership in FIAF (The International Federation of Film Archives) will be an important factor in achieving this objective with the best possible prints; and the development of a study centre incorporating books, periodicals, stills, posters and basic documentation on all aspects of film and television production.

On the last two components in the master plan the arrangement worked out with the Canadian Film Institute not only rationalized the film conservation effort in Canada and eliminated the possibility of competitive programs, it also enabled the National Film Archives to begin serving the film and television community almost as soon as it opened its doors in adequate quarters (March 1975). Under an agreement signed in October 1974, the institute undertook to deposit the total resources of its division, the Canadian Film Archives, comprising a collection of more than 5,000 films, a library of 7,000 books and 800 periodical titles, a stills and poster collection, and a collection of basic documentation which includes more than 80,000 files and a main title index of roughly 125,000 cards. Under this arrangement, the institute, supported by the Canada Council, will concentrate its efforts on distribution (the availability of important foreign films and Canadian productions is still an obstacle to the expansion of film study at the university level) and exhibition—through the National Film Theatre in Ottawa and a network of regional theatres. The National Film Archives will support these programs as well as the institute's publications program, rather than develop competitive services. The same attitude will colour the NFA's relationships with regional film study organizations and provincial archives. The effort will be to work with them (with a Film Archives Advisory Committee as the main organ of consultation) in order to expand their services and to stimulate the flow of federal funding.

Beyond the rhetoric lies the rare opportunity to create a public institution in film and television that will take its place along with the art galleries and museums established with federal support in order to safeguard the nation's cultural heritage; to build a national collection that will be exhaustive for Canadian feature films (and for the work of leading filmmakers), comprehensive for all Canadian production in film and television, and authoritative for foreign films that have influenced the art and history of the medium. The urgent need has been, and is today, to locate and acquire films that have survived in Canada and to repatriate films that have been lost in Canada from foreign libraries and archives. An allied need, and in some ways more pressing if we are not to be condemned to repeat our recent history, is a national program to select, acquire and conserve current productions of enduring value. The mandate of the National Film Archives is broad enough to encompass both these goals. The question, as always, is whether the budget will be broad enough to accomplish them before more film joins the legion of the lost.

II.

THE NATIONAL FILM BOARD OF CANADA

Grierson's First Years at the NFB
Jack Ellis

At the outbreak of World War II Canada was something of a sleeping giant. In certain ways it was also a geographical and cultural anomaly which no orderly-minded nation-planner would have perpetrated. Larger in area than the United States, its sparse population stretched across a 200-mile-wide strip along its southern border, it represented physically a virtual extension of the United States up into the uninhabitable Arctic. Its prodigious breadth of forest and prairie, blocked at the western end by a fierce mountain range, took considerable conquering before the Atlantic was finally linked to the Pacific with steel rails. By 1939, as a result of railroad building, it was able to make fully available its enormous natural resources—lumber, wheat, minerals and ores—to a world plunging into war. And with the air age, Canada's former remoteness would accommodate a mainline global air route, and the newly-established Trans-Canada Air Lines, a government monopoly, would reduce some of the unwieldiness of its own size.

In addition to the formidable task of taming a wilderness, Canadians had always faced a struggle for national identity. At first it was the matter of establishing independence from Britain, greatly aided by the Balfour Declaration, which emerged from the Imperial Conference of 1926. It had declared the Dominions "autonomous communities within the British Empire, equal in status, in no way subordinate one to another in any aspect of their domestic or external affairs, though united by a common allegiance to the Crown, and freely associated as members of the British Commonwealth of Nations".[1] More recently the gravitational pull of its powerful neighbour to the south was smothering Canada's distinctiveness. Economically and culturally, as well as geographically, Canada was something of an extension of the United States. Citizens of the United States had even appropriated the name "American". What did it mean to be a Canadian anyway? What were Canada's arts and traditions; what was its special character? The national image was further blurred by the many ethnic divisions within its population. Almost four of its twelve million people were French-speaking and there were many immigrant minorities. Quebec seemed to have as close an affinity with France as with North America; parts of British Columbia were England transplanted; and much of the rest of the vast land was a somewhat drab and pale reflection of Iowa or Montana.

Politically, too, Canada represented a fusion of Britain and the United States, with vestiges of old French civil practice persisting among the Habitants. There were three major political parties: The Conservative, the Liberal, and, since 1932, the Co-operative Commonwealth Federation (the CCF, later called the National Democratic Party, was socialist).

Reprinted from *Cinema Journal*, Fall 1970.

The Liberals had come into power in 1935 with Mackenzie King as prime minister. The National Film Board and Grierson's appointment as commissioner both came about ultimately because of King's favourable impression of Grierson's brightness and dedication to public service.[2] The prime minister, Grierson said, gave him "his personal backing and almost a blank cheque in support".[3]

In 1938, when Grierson first met him, King was sixty-five years old to Grierson's forty. He had successfully led the Liberal Party for more than twenty years; fourteen of those years it had been in power. In spite of differences in age, citizenship, and station, the similarities between King's and Grierson's backgrounds are remarkable. Both had been born of Scottish ancestry in rural locales—King in western Ontario; Grierson in Sterlingshire, Scotland. King's famous maternal grandfather, William Lyon Mackenzie, had come to Canada from Scotland in his early twenties; his paternal grandfather, John King, was a native of Aberdeenshire. Both Grierson and King had a heritage of radical political activity on their mother's side (William Lyon Mackenzie led the Canadian Rebellion of 1837 and had to flee for a period to New York State for refuge) and liberal conservatism on their father's. King, like Grierson, had a brother to whom he was very close; both men's brothers were doctors in military service—Macdougall King in World War I, Anthony Grierson in World War II.

Both were exceptionally industrious students in the social sciences (King at the University of Toronto; Grierson at Glasgow University); both engaged in journalism early in their careers (King as a reporter in Toronto; Grierson writing prolifically on art and then film for numerous newspapers and periodicals). Both attended the graduate school of the University of Chicago (King 1896-7; Grierson 1924-7) and were much interested in the newly arrived foreign populations and their problems. (King lived at Hull House, in the Halsted Street area which Grierson knew well and frequently recollected.) Both careers were, in fact, founded on ideas worked out in the States.

Even the Post Office Department of Canada figures in King's career, as the British General Post Office Film Unit did in Grierson's: after his return from Chicago, King wrote an exposé of Canadian working conditions which implicated the Post Office. King then took a post-graduate course in political economy at Harvard and, like Grierson in reverse, won a travelling fellowship to Europe in 1899 to inquire into the social and labour problems of Great Britain, France, Germany, and Italy. He lived for a while in London. Grierson received a Rockefeller research fellowship in social science which permitted him to study the mass media in relation to public opinion in the United States. King also had a later connection with the Rockefeller Foundation, as its director of industrial research. Arnold Toynbee's *Industrial Revolution* had been to King what Bertrand Russell's *Social Reconstruction* was to Grierson: a major influence. (Arnold Toynbee was an uncle of the now more famous

Arnold J. Toynbee.) King was offered a position as instructor at Harvard, as Grierson had been at the University of Durham, but chose instead to enter the civil service in Canada as Grierson would follow a civil service career.

In 1900, as a very young man only five years out of the University of Toronto, King became attached to a new and experimental branch of government. As deputy minister of labour, he was slightly outside the bounds of established government activity and built up his own department and staffed it, much like Grierson at the Empire Marketing Board Film Unit at the beginning of the British documentary movement. Both, incidentally, had barely decipherable handwriting, which plagued their subordinates. As Grierson had done in Britain and would do even more extensively in Canada, King travelled continuously, from one side of the Dominion to the other. He became leader of the Liberal Party at the age of forty-five; Grierson became film commissioner at forty-one. The words one of King's biographers applied to him anent his assumption of political leadership would do equally well for Grierson in his new post: "... he brought with him a dogged determination to succeed, the ability to think coolly and methodically, and a passion for study and research which was to confound many an opponent in the future".[4]

There were differences, too, of course, equally strong, which would lead to some tension. King was a deeply religious man, with shades of mysticism, while Grierson was an agnostic. King viewed the war as being not so much against he Axis powers as against "the Spirit of Darkness, the Spirit of Evil, the very anti-Christ himself".[5] Grierson offset this view with a resolute geopolitics based on early study.[6] King was temperate to the point of abstention while Grierson was a drinker of considerable practice and capacity. When new restrictions on the sale of liquor were imposed in 1942, King urged the nation to temperance in "a regular sermon" and himself abstained from all alcoholic beverages throughout the war.[7]

King's attitudes about his own and others' sexual activity were severely Puritan—he was a bachelor and apparently celibate;* Grierson's were very free. Not only did King not smoke but he disliked the odour, and his associates made a habit of knocking out pipes and snuffing out cigars and cigarettes whenever he entered the room.[8] Grierson was a chain-smoker with an incredible daily consumption. Nonetheless, King's observation about what he sought among his appointees clearly accounted for the value he placed on Grierson:

> Integrity, of course, is essential. But what I most look for is a sign that a man is anxious to do something for his fellow men, that he is interested in public service or in the job of doing a job. If he has not this zeal or enthusiasm the future is not encouraging. You have to be careful, too, that a man's enthusiasm is not for personal advancement.... the first question must be "does he want to work for his fellow men?"[9]

---

*Recent evidence however suggests he engaged privately in activities he publicly condemned. [Ed.]

In relation to the development of documentary, Forsyth Hardy found it worth noting that "at a time when Britain and the British Commonwealth needed the dramatic psychological leadership film could help provide, it was not the Britain of Chamberlain but the Canada of Mackenzie King that had the vision to offer documentary the opportunity of expansion".[10]

The National Film Board of Canada, which had been "pulled off the sky", to use Grierson's phrase,[11] began in one and then two rooms in the west block of the Parliament buildings in Ottawa. Besides Grierson there were English colleague Stuart Legg and two secretaries—Janet Scellen, who would remain Grierson's personal secretarial assistant throughout his years in Canada, and Jean McIntyre. Legg was serving as liaison to the Motion Picture Bureau, housed in a former sawmill on John Street, with Captain F.C. Badgley as director. In existence since 1916, the bureau was a pioneer government unit rather heavily inclined toward travel films. In November of 1939, Ross McLean was hired as assistant to the new commissioner and occupied the outer room with the two secretaries while Grierson and Legg inhabited the inner one. In December, veterans of British documentary joined the NFB: Raymond Spottiswoode, who had recently been in Hollywood, and Evelyn Spice, a Canadian.

In those first few months, at the invitation of the film board, the March of Time began production for a February 1940 international release depicting Canada's economic contribution to the war effort as well as the part to be played by its fighting forces. In it Grierson himself made a "brief but electrifying appearance in the act of censoring a screen battleship",[12] presumably for security reasons. Already in the theatres was a Canadian epilogue to the British film on methods of air raid defense entitled THE WARNING. The epilogue was an interview in which Norman Rogers, minister of national defense, stated Canadian war aims and means of fulfilling them. Two films by Legg on the special problems of youth in a world at war were about to be released non-theatrically. Badgley's film of THE ROYAL TOUR was enjoying success in theatres across the country. And Grierson was discussing plans with the commercial producers—Associated Screen News of Montreal, Audio Pictures of Toronto, and others in the west. The first films of the board's new scheme of national projection were scheduled to appear in March.[13]

With production under way, and after a trip to New Zealand and Australia, Grierson resumed the hiring of a staff that would assume huge proportions. By December 1940, a little over a year after the board had become operative, there were still fewer than twelve full-time employees with a number of others, such as scriptwriters, working on a special assignment basis; the Motion Picture Bureau maintained its separate staff of from thirty to thirty-five. By October 1941, largely as a result of the merger of the bureau with the board, there were fifty-five NFB personnel. Then the phenomenal expansion began: by December of 1942 there were 293 employees and the number continued to increase. Near the end of Grierson's administration, in April 1945, there were 739.[14]

Grierson looked for the same kind of educated young people he had found in Britain. "So far as my own operation is concerned," he wrote, "the surest way to apprenticeship in documentary is a good degree in political science or economics."[15] The interview method and capacity for spotting talent remained much the same as it had been at the EMB and GPO units. James Beveridge, one of the earliest of the young Canadian hirelings, stressed Grierson's "fantastic ability to size people up—to judge their worth—quickly and accurately. A remarkably acute intuitive psychologist," Beveridge concluded.[16] Interviews with job applicants usually consisted of discussion on what books they'd read or what they thought about paintings. If they said all they really wanted to do was to make movies they weren't hired.[17] To the young and inexperienced who passed the scrutiny Grierson might say: "You want to be a director? You've got lots of imagination. Report for work Monday."[18] Another applicant, however, Nicholas Read, an American in search of training who joined the board at the beginning, recalled his first meeting with Grierson as a very down-to-earth affair. "He fixed me with those sea-blue eyes under his bushy eyebrows," said Read, "and his first question went right to the point... 'How many films have you made?' He then went on with a whole list of embarrassing inquiries, such as, 'You can operate a camera? You know how to operate a hot splicer?'" When Read and many others failed to measure up fully to Grierson's standards they were ushered off to the sawmill, where Legg was busy training and organizing young hopefuls to become filmmakers.[19] Grierson was right about 85 per cent of the time in his choice of people, one observer estimated.[20]

Though very conscious of waste, Grierson was resolute in getting a staff that could do the job. If he never overspent, he did have trouble matching salary, travel and other expenditures to government categories.[21] This was a particularly pressing problem because, starting almost from scratch, he had to form a unit that could expand into an industry. Given the size and urgency of wartime requirements he needed to have his own producer-teacher function supplemented by other experienced filmmakers, as he had done in Britain, in fact, with Flaherty and Cavalcanti. There was, consistently, a tremendous turnover of personnel at the board, which Grierson justified as the positive value of change.

From England there was, first of all, Stuart Legg, who would be a pillar of strength throughout Grierson's tenure. Much of Legg's wartime experience at the NFB could be described by a Grierson remark at one early point: "Legg is looking after his own films and fifty or sixty more on the stocks while I am away."[22] Legg was especially skillful as an editor and script writer, and the people who worked closely with him greatly profited from and were very fond of him. Others, however, found his intellectualism formidable. A cool type, he was said to be unable to establish relationships with others.[23]

If Legg was "cynical" and "sardonic", as some alleged, Raymond Spottiswoode was "prickly". A trained technician and director, he was assigned to work with a commercial firm, Audio Pictures of Toronto, on a film board production entitled WINGS OF YOUTH, about the Commonwealth air training plan. Spottiswoode became supervisor of technical services for the board. Grierson had also invited over Stanley Hawes, who arrived in Ottawa in February 1940. Hawes was a veteran of about ten years experience in British documentary. In 1941, after the board had taken over the bureau, he became senior producer of non-theatrical productions while Legg was senior producer of theatrical productions. Hawes was a film craftsman, interested especially in labour and sociological matters. Once described as "a stocky, stubborn Midlander",[24] he was referred to by Grierson as a "clerk", a "greengrocer", and respected for his lower-class English doggedness.[25]

J.D. Davidson, the cameraman who joined the Empire Marketing Board Film Unit in 1930, arrived in Canada in mid-November of 1940 to serve as director-editor. Norman McLaren was in New York City, having left the General Post Office Film Unit in 1939, when Grierson phoned him just before Christmas of that year. Working for Caravel, a producer of sponsored films, McLaren was torn between his desire to join the NFB and his dislike of unpleasantness with Caravel, for he was mid-picture. (Grierson once called McLaren "one of the film world's gentlest people".) When he hedged, Grierson simply passed word to the Canadian ambassador. Within a week McLaren was hard at work in Ottawa.[26] In 1942 he set up the board's animation unit and—using his technique of drawing directly on film, which was at once cheap, practical and extremely painstaking—produced brief trailers such as MAIL EARLY, FIVE FOR FOUR, V FOR VICTORY, HEN HOP, and DOLLAR DANCE to promote early mailing for Christmas, war savings, and anti-inflation curbs.[27] Another of the old boys, J.P.R. Golightly, was seconded from the British Army at Grierson's request to become London representative of the NFB; and Basil Wright, in some ways principal disciple, made two extended trips to Canada during the war and was English editor of the board's "World in Action" and "Canada Carries On" series.

From the United States Grierson drew another contingent. Irving Jacoby was the first to arrive, from New York, early in 1940. He had had considerable experience in making Hollywood shorts and industrial films and had spent a year in England. Working under Legg and in collaboration with the novelist Morley Callaghan, Jacoby "snow-shoed all over Canada" to make HOT ICE, on the national sport of ice hockey. He followed that with HIGH OVER THE BORDERS (1941), a beautifully-made film on the facts and mysteries of bird migration in the Western Hemisphere,[28] the cost of which Grierson, in a feat of persuasiveness, managed to charge to the Royal Canadian Air Force.[29] After Pearl

Harbor Jacoby returned to the States to join the Office of War Information. Roger Barlow, the fine documentary cameraman (e.g., THE CITY), arrived in 1940 to work on half a dozen films. The first, WOMEN IN THE WAR, was directed by Stanley Hawes. After that he became associate director and cameraman with Spottiswoode on the aforementioned WINGS OF YOUTH, the sixth in the "Canada Carries On" monthly series. Among other American filmmakers who worked at the board were Nicholas Read (now of Potomac Films in Washington, D.C.), Gordon Weisenborn (abducted by Grierson from the University of Chicago at the age of nineteen), Leo Seltzer, Leroy Robbins, John Lenauer, Milton Shiffman (an editor), Harold Rawson, Harry Alpert (an excellent cameraman), Fred Lasey, and Harry Randall (later film officer for the Heart Association in New York). Robert Flaherty did some shooting, and the Negro novelist Richard Wright also worked for the board for some time. The Americans, of course, carried Grierson's influence back into the States as well as helping to build a Canadian film movement.

The Hollanders Joris Ivens and John Ferno, who had been working in the United States, began their wartime filmmaking in Canada. ACTION STATIONS!, about the struggle of the Canadian Merchant Marines against German submarines, was Ivens' first film at the board, and Ferno edited HIGH OVER THE BORDERS. From Occupied France came Boris Kaufman (Jean Vigo's, and later Elia Kazan's, great cameraman). His was the principal teaching influence on the board's camera work. Alexander Alexeieff, extraordinary animator of the pin-board technique (e.g., NIGHT ON BALD MOUNTAIN), also arrived from France to work at the board.

Canadians who had gained filmmaking experience elsewhere were invited back to assist the new national effort. Evelyn Spice, Grierson's long-time associate in England, already mentioned, was one of these. Julian Roffman was another. Roffman came to Ottawa in September 1941. Something of a child prodigy in New York (e.g., AND SO THEY LIVE, 1940), he made at the board the admirable 13 PLATOON, about a young lieutenant and his understanding of and relationships with his men. Along with the British films of the time, it was an early use of synchronous sound recording with non-actors. In setting up the production Grierson told the generals, "This small young man is a great filmmaker. Let him do whatever he wants." Roffman regarded Grierson as his "film father". There are two pictures on his office wall, one of his own father and one of Grierson. The latter gave him the feeling he could do anything, and he reveled in the free and creative atmosphere at the board.[30]

Ross McLean, whom Grierson had hired on as an assistant, had had no previous filmmaking experience. He produced and directed some films during the board's early days, but his talents were chiefly administrative. Grierson was said to have remarked that he was "all right as a scribbler, a clerk, but not much imagination".[31] McLean was extremely knowledgeable and well-connected in the Liberal Party. It was he, in part, who made it possible for Grierson to operate as effectively as he did.[32] McLean became assistant film commissioner in September 1941. With Grierson travelling and in conference much of the time it was McLean who made many of the daily decisions that kept the organization functioning properly. While away on one of his trips, with McLean in general charge at Ottawa, Grierson wrote of him: "McLean represents as well as anyone what Canada is about nowadays and keeps it marching into a dream of the Canadian future which in these parts excites almost everyone under forty. I support him in this, with a special affection for the French Canadian viewpoint."[33]

Donald Fraser, the first of the young Canadian apprentices who would gather around the core of British veterans, was hired late in 1939. He had met Grierson in England in 1938 and, during the year prior to commencing his film board career, had been executive secretary of the National Film Society, a group that worked with audiences along adult-education lines. At the NFB Fraser first became a cameraman. James Beveridge was another of the early recruits who later became senior members of the production staff. In the beginning he worked as a director and cutter on non-theatrical films. F. Radford "Budge" Crawley had had some amateur experience before working for the board and he and his wife became professional 16mm producers and colour specialists, soon with their own firm which continued to undertake much work for the board. Tom Daly, whose name is attached to a disproportionately high number of the finest of the NFB films, graduated from the University of Toronto in English language and literature in June 1940. In September he was interviewed by Grierson, home ill and sitting up in bed in an old gray sweater while people flowed in and out of his bedroom. Since there was as yet no stock footage library, Daly was assigned to start one, with out-takes lying about the rooms at the Motion Picture Bureau. He became Legg's assistant, researching in the stock footage and also editing.[34] Michael Spencer also met Grierson in 1940 and was hired to work with Crawley, already on his second film for the board, as cameraman and editor. He would later move into distribution at the NFB.[35]

Guy Glover joined the board through his friendship with Norman McLaren. Trained as a biologist, he then went into the theatre; his first film work was at the board, under Legg and Spottiswoode. When Grierson was impressed by an animated film he had worked on, MARCHING THE COLOURS, he was placed in a supervisory position. Glover conceded that he found the English intolerable at times and that he fought with Grierson to give the Canadians more responsibility. Instead of disciplining the rebel, Grierson promoted him: Glover headed the French unit during the second half of the war.

With the expansion of personnel and production, the Motion Picture Bureau had to use its meagre equipment at John Street to the best advantage of everyone. The day shifts would bustle around the cutting rooms and laboratories, concerned with their own projects, to be followed at night by other workers intent on different productions altogether. The difficulties of the board and the bureau were similar to those of trying to pour a quart of milk into a pint bottle. Raymond Spottiswoode recalled:

> Back in 1941, a four-reel review of the second year of the war was produced in little over a week by the entire staff splitting up the cutting processes among them—editing, music, effects, negative, and so on—and putting themselves on 24-hour shifts to do it. A year before that, our chief engineer would often find himself awakened in the middle of the night to come down to the Board and fix a broken printer working on a late shift. Arriving, he would go out into the back yard, clip off a piece of barbed wire fence, file a cotter pin out of it, and set the printer going again.[36]

Problems of equipment, time and manpower were overcome in part by assigning productions to the few outside firms such as Associated Screen News of Montreal, where Gordon Sparling made the highly popular PEOPLES OF CANADA for the board in 1940, and the newly-formed Crawley Films.[37] But Grierson was beginning to see that the real impediment to the board's development was the administrative anomaly by which it set policy but did not itself produce. Inevitably there had grown up friction between the enterprising, ambitious new people of the board and the members of the original bureau who wanted to retain the status quo, and who resented the way films were now being made. Standing in Grierson's path most prominently was the bureau's director, Captain Frank Badgley.

Grierson had tried to maintain an amiable relationship with Badgley and was reluctant to take the step he now felt necessary. Badgley had been an "intimate, if only an alcoholic one",[38] who claimed to have loaned equipment for Grierson's first film, DRIFTERS, of 1929, and was under an exaggerated impression that he had been responsible for Grierson's being invited to Canada in the first place[39] —assistance which, if rendered, he had clearly come to regret. Apparently he was disappointed that he had not been appointed film commissioner and he did not like Grierson's kind of film.[40] By October 1940 Badgley had become a "mule and a nuisance"[41] and Grierson had decided he would have to take action.

The action was dramatic, to say the least. At the December meeting of the board, Grierson tendered his resignation. He stated his ground as the unmet need for: (1) more money and flexibility in hiring filmmakers to remove them further from the strict civil service categories, and (2) full supervision by the film commissioner of the Motion Picture Bureau. He was resigning, he said, so that he could speak on these two matters crucial to the future of creative government filmmaking without it being charged that he was simply trying to increase his personal power in government. A year before this contretemps, Grierson had written of W.D. Euler, chairman of the film board and minister of trade and commerce, that he had "served with many distinguished British Ministers in the development of the film as an instrument of National Information but (had) known none who more handsomely took the big view".[42] Now, in an exchange of letters with Euler immediately after the December board meeting, Grierson reaffirmed his intention of resigning —pointing out that he had taken the job for only a short time and that there was good reason for a Canadian to be film commissioner—and re-emphasized that the two central problems mentioned would face the new incumbent. Euler replied that Grierson was trying to get out altogether from under regular control by the Treasury, "contrary to the established principles of democratic government". Grierson, furious, went "to see a lot of very high officials indeed".[43] During this crisis the French were most loyal in their support of him, Grierson said; with his "special affection for the French Canadian viewpoint" he had seen to it that more French films were produced than had previously been the case.

At first, Grierson's intention was to depart around the end of January. Badgley was to be given back the film work, at least his own. In February the resignation still stood but no replacement was available or qualified, and the Griersons planned to be in Ottawa another six months, wrote Margaret, "but nothing definite has been decided".[44] In March the resignation still hadn't been accepted. There had been a prompt and continuous press response urging that he be retained and, it was reported, "In view of the Prime Minister's announcements of his special interest in the retention of Mr. Grierson in Canada for further development of the National Film Board, it is indicated that he will stay on for at least some months."[45] During those same months Grierson held his ground, and the government eventually capitulated under mounting pressure.

On June 11, 1941, by Order in Council P.C. 4215, the board absorbed the bureau and the film commissioner established himself in the John Street premises in July. Badgley's checks were mailed to his home; he was paid for a year after he stopped work.[46] It was thus that the NFB became responsible not only for planning and advising on all government films but also for making them or having them made by outside producers. On June 11, also, the powers and duties of the minister of trade and commerce as defined by the National Film Act were transferred to the minister of national war services, Maj. Gen. L.R. La Fleche. Two months later the stills division of the Motion Picture Bureau was transferred by another Order in Council from the Department of Trade and Commerce to the NFB.[47] The way was now clear for total co-ordinated effort.

Collectively and anonymously (there were no personal credits on the

NFB wartime output) the production personnel set out to make hundreds of films. The first year had closed in October 1940 with some forty pictures either in distribution, in production, or in script preparation; by the fiscal year of 1943-4 the annual rate of release had increased to 200. Films were to become weapons of war, helping to weld together home-front efforts and also telling the story of Canada's contribution to her partners in the world struggle. But under the pressure of wartime urgencies Grierson never lost sight of the ongoing requirements of peacetime. His social conscience and vision led him to accentuate the positive and to avoid the negative propaganda of hate made so easily accessible by war. In his conception, the board was using films as they had never been used before, "in a planned and scientific way to provide what might be described as a supplementary system of national education".[48] "All our Canadian war films were also peace films," Grierson wrote, "there was nothing we founded that was not founded to stay on for peacetime purpose."[49]

All his life he preached that "a country is only as vital as its processes of self-education are vital".[50] The National Film Board of Canada remains as legacy, as testament to that belief.

Documentary Films: World War II

Ernst Borneman

In 1938, the Canadian government invited John Grierson to come to Canada and suggest legislation by means of which all the government's film activities might be centralized and co-ordinated. As a result of his recommendations, the National Film Act was passed on May 2, 1939, creating a National Film Board with authority to devise, from all the government departments' separate requirements, a unified policy, an integrated production schedule and a plan for distribution to meet the needs of the respective departments. In 1941, the board absorbed the functions of the Government Motion Picture Bureau, and in 1943, it took over the graphics division of the Wartime Information Board. The film board thus became the first organization to apply the documentary idea not only to motion pictures, but, under a centrally effective policy, to film strips, still photographs, displays, posters, wall hangers, cartoons and government publications as well. It rose within five years from four to 785 members and represents today (1945) the largest single unit engaged in the documentary field the world over.

The Native Documentary

But, from the beginning, documentary was a movement that served not only government but all other masters of good will and public purpose, and it was not surprising therefore to find the forward-looking heads of private enterprise in Canada among the first supporters of the native Canadian documentary group.

In Flaherty's wake there came the younger Canadian school of documentary cameramen—Bill Oliver of Calgary, Leslie P. Thatcher of Toronto, F.R. Crawley of Ottawa, Father Lafleur of the Oblates and the Reverend Maurice Proulx of Ste. Anne de la Pocatière. All of these men showed a singularly fine appreciation of the values and subtleties of the Canadian landscape but, except for Crawley in his later years, none of them were much concerned with the social pattern that gave life and meaning to the man within the landscape.

Oliver's GREY OWL AND THE BEAVER series was full of superb animal and wild life studies; Thatcher's ANOTHER DAY, which won a New York prize as the best 16mm movie of the year 1934, was a romantic kind of city rhapsody, while his FISHERS OF GRANDE ANSE pieced out, with slow deliberation, a sequence of beautiful compositions along the St. Lawrence Fishing Banks; Crawley's L'ISLE D'ORLEANS in 1939, his STUDY OF SPRING FLOWERS during the same year, his two BIRDS OF CANADA films in 1939 and 1941 and his PORTAGE in 1942 marked him from the beginning as the most subtle and sensitive of the native Canadian school, but it was

Edited from a manuscript dated October 20, 1945.

only in his HISTORY OF POWER IN CANADA that he seemed to become aware of the dramatic pattern in the social and industrial evolution of the nation, and it was in the series of films in which he co-operated with the NFB that he reached his maturity.

These films fell into two groups—studies of regions or communities tracing the relation of an individual or group to the landscape or township, and studies of artists in relation to their regional background. To the first group belonged OTTAWA ON THE RIVER which showed the relation of Canada's capital to the lumber industry of the region; and his masterpiece, THE FOUR SEASONS, the story of a single year in the valley of the Gatineau, in which he tried to present the images and symbols of rural Canada in the sensual flow of his own home valley. There is a phrase in the first reel of the picture which reveals Crawley's own deep attachment to the landscape: "The child is rare who has not travelled upstream from his home to where the forest begins. Here, *in the timeless fairyland of childhood*, he knows as friends the creatures of his Canadian woods."

Much of the same feeling for the native image emerged from Crawley's co-operation with Graham McInnes in the NFB's "Canadian Artists" series—CANADIAN LANDSCAPE, WEST WIND, and PAINTERS OF QUEBEC. Here was the visual bond between the artist and his community, the direct plastic relation between the pattern of the region and the pattern of the canvas. Curiously, tentatively, the camera examined the landscape, selected a frame and came to rest on it, then switched dramatically to the same image on the canvas, examined a detail, enlarged it hugely to the size of the theatre screen, and moved away again to observe it in relation to its model. But always it was the artist, and the artist in relation to the community, whether in closest union with it as in CANADIAN LANDSCAPE and PAINTERS OF QUEBEC, or in wilful isolation from it as in WEST WIND, who served as measure of his work, and always, in the long run, it was the relation of the artist to his native audience which was thus considered as the measuring stick of his art.

But the regional school of documentary was by no means the only native Canadian school. In the missions and monasteries of Quebec there had arisen a functional school of cinema which had long put the camera to the purposes of the church. Father Lafleur's missionary films of Indian tribal patterns and Maurice Proulx's series of forest settlement and northern mission films are therefore not to be ranked with the travelogues or scenic films of the Government Motion Picture Bureau. They are closer, in pattern and purpose, to the films of the prairie group that gathered around Evelyn Spice and Lawrence Cherry, which in turn are closely allied with the aims of the NFB in its insistence upon a cinema of public purpose. BY THEIR OWN STRENGTH and NEW HORIZONS, both of them directed by Evelyn Spice and photographed by Lawrence Cherry for the Saskatchewan Wheat Pool, were powerful films of protest against anomalies in the economy of wheat farming and played a considerable role in the battle for the establishment of co-operative marketing in the prairies. Spice and Cherry finally joined the NFB and established the food and agriculture unit for the board, but before doing so they completed LANDMARKS OF THE PRAIRIES, which ranks with J.B. Scott's HERITAGE and their own later SOIL FOR TOMORROW, among Canada's most vigorous and purposeful critiques of farming methods in the prairies.

The Documentary of Social Purposes: Legg's First Canadian Films

In March 1939, two months before the passing of the National Film Act and seven months prior to Grierson's appointment as government film commissioner, Stuart Legg came to Canada at the behest of the government to make two films for the Dominion-Provincial Youth Training Plan. It was with these films that the Canadian documentary movement first reached a mature level of social purpose appropriate to an industrial nation. Legg did what none of the Canadians had dared to do: he walked right into the slums of the coal town of Glace Bay and came out with a story that went to the core of all the hushed-up hopes and fears of unemployed youth.

Immediately, and to no one's surprise, there came the reactions from the guardians of the polished surface who considered it poor propaganda for Canada to show its "darker aspects". The obvious answer—and it came from Grierson—was that while it was perfectly natural for Canadians to think well of their country and desire that others do likewise, it was disrespectful of other countries to believe they would approve of a patently denatured account which viewed the pattern of national achievement out of its human context. And, as Grierson pointed out at the time, where the commonness of man is forgotten, the common man himself is disfranchised. It therefore devolved upon documentary, with all its powers of juxtaposition, to take the scraps of reality, the rough with the fine, and bring them to order and significance and therefore to beauty.

And there were those in Canada like Donald F. Buchanan, the founder of the National Film Society of Canada, who immediately came to Legg's and Grierson's assistance and said loudly and for all to hear that such a youngster as Legg's Charlie Gordon of Glace Bay was "much more a typical Canadian than were most of the characters generally depicted in our recognized literature, certainly more so than the peasants of MARIA CHAPDELAINE or the complex middle-class sons of JALNA".

There were wonderful things in these two films, THE CASE OF CHARLIE GORDON and YOUTH IS TOMORROW, such as the chimney stacks blowing smoke rings after Charlie got his job, or the tough youth-training officer signalling to Charlie from behind his back that everything is O.K. or the youth-training officer's businesslike question, "What would you like to be?" and Charlie's unhesitating answer, "A detective," and the officer's reaction, first awkward then glib: "Well, there's not much detecting to do around here. What else are you interested in?" and Charlie's immediately pat second choice: "Aviation," and the officer's sudden realization of the source of Charlie's dream world: "Ah, the movies...."

Much of the technique of CHARLIE GORDON which derived initially from the "human story" method of the British documentary group, was applied four years later by Dallas Jones in A MAN AND HIS JOB, while Legg himself began to dissociate himself more and more definitely from the "drama-on-your-doorstep" mentality and began to develop the "Canada Carries On" and "World in Action" technique of editorial internationalism which was to become one of Canada's major contributions to documentary.

The National Film Board

By the time CHARLIE GORDON was completed, Legg had been appointed director of production for the old Government Motion Picture Bureau, while Grierson, in a different building, was beginning to construct the National Film Board with an ingenious interpretation of the status of his personnel. The creative staff was hired on a temporary basis, neither subject to civil service regulations, nor secured in their positions by these regulations. Compulsion was not applied, but deliberately withheld. This reversal of government policy was devised by the film commissioner to "specify responsibility and to encourage initiative" and it had a great deal to do with the shape the documentary movement finally took in Canada.

Among the first apprentices were young Canadians such as Jim Beveridge, Donald Fraser and Tom Daly; young Americans such as Nick Read, and young Englishmen such as Mike Spencer. In October 1940, Stanley Hawes came from England, and in 1941 Raymond Spottiswoode came from Hollywood to complete the nucleus of the more or less old-time documentarians. Canadian newspapermen such as Morley Callaghan and Jim Wright came in as writers on a per-picture basis, and the nucleus of a French-Canadian group was laid with Phileas Coté and Vincent Paquette. But soon the international character of the staff, which had been noticeable in the appointment of the first apprentices, began to assert itself with increasing vigour. Graham McInnes came from Australia, Ernst Borneman from Germany, Ferno and Ivens from Holland. Canadian Icelanders such as Margaret Anne Bjoernson and Gudrun Bjerring came in, and the French Unit was dramatically extended; from the United States, from Great Britain and from Latin-America came others.

"Canada Carries On" and "World in Action"

In April 1940, ATLANTIC PATROL, the first issue in the "Canada Carries On" series, was released. It aimed, as all later issues did, at showing Canada in her social, economic and military relation to a world engaged in a global struggle, and it said in a firm voice that Canada was only important as it was related in this manner to other nations around the globe. The fact that Legg had picked on the theme of naval communications for the first item in the series was of more than incidental importance. The fact that Canada had a brave little Navy which was doing more than its share of Atlantic convoy duty was proud enough to make the Canadian heart beat quicker, but it was of greater urgency to articulate and bring home the fact that Canada was linked by ineluctable lines of transport and communication to every part of the world. It was of the greatest importance at that very hour because the danger of isolation and parochialism was always present in a young and thinly settled nation separated on all sides by water barriers from the actual battlefront. So Legg returned again and again to those themes of transport and communication which would help to extend the perspective of the nation and relate the interests of the people to the new dynamic world forces of the fateful years. In HEROES OF THE ATLANTIC and FREIGHTERS UNDER FIRE he returned to the theme of naval lines of communication; in WINGS OF YOUTH, WINGS OF A CONTINENT, FERRY PILOT, and GLOBAL AIR ROUTES, he and his team of editors explored the new world of international air routes, while VOICE OF ACTION did the same job in terms of radio communications.

Two films in the series, HIGH OVER THE BORDERS and WAR BIRDS, went so far as to use the migration and flight of birds as symbols of a world without frontiers, while other films in the series showed how groups of Canadians overseas fitted in to the total pattern of the war: LETTER FROM ALDERSHOT and LETTER FROM OVERSEAS placed the troops in a British setting, while GUARDS OF THE NORTH followed them up to Iceland. Another group of films in the series reversed this process and showed various regions of Canada in their outward-facing relation to the war: WARCLOUDS IN THE PACIFIC and GATEWAY TO ASIA applied this pattern to Canada's west coast region, while QUEBEC, PATH OF CONQUEST applied it to French-Canada, and LOOK TO THE NORTH dealt with Canada's sub-arctic.

While the British filmmakers were concerned with the local tactics of defensive warfare, Legg in the "Canada Carries On" and "World in Action" series went to the very limits of his authority in stressing the urgency of an aggressive total strategy. The difference in approach between the British and Canadian documentary units in this respect was neatly posed by Grierson: while Anstey in England was making a film on how to put out an incendiary bomb, Legg in Canada was cutting captured German footage into an analysis of the larger strategic plans required to defeat the very strategies Germany had tried to exhibit in such films as FEUERTAUFE and SIEG IN WESTEN. Thus, in THIS IS BLITZ, FORWARD COMMANDOS, THE ROAD TO TOKYO, PINCERS ON AXIS EUROPE, INVASION OF EUROPE, ZERO HOUR, BATTLE OF EUROPE, BREAK-THROUGH and ROAD TO THE REICH, Legg and his team presented the strategic-history of total war on the screens of Canada, and the very understatement of the Canadian part in total battle served to bring home the message of humility and global exfoliation with greater insistence than any pat-on-the-back production could ever have done. In all these films, Legg was less concerned with individual bravery or even military teamwork than with the integration of all national forces and with the release of co-operative and corporate energies on the largest possible scale.

What held true in terms of broad military strategy was equally true in terms of the social and economic sphere. Legg's next step therefore was a series of films which noted the common denominators of the world's social and economic structure and presented them on the screen in a plastic pattern of international cross-relations. BATTLE OF BRAINS showed the international ramifications of scientific research, STRATEGY OF METALS applied the pattern to some of the raw materials of warfare and BATTLE FOR OIL to the fuels of war, FOOD, WEAPON OF CONQUEST and FOOD, SECRET OF THE PEACE compared the international essentials of man's nourishment in war and peace, while BATTLE OF THE HARVESTS and THOUGHT FOR FOOD focussed on Canada's own economy. On the social level, WOMEN ARE WARRIORS compared and examined the role played by women in the democratic and totalitarian countries, TOMORROW'S WORLD investigated the whole social and moral pattern of the postwar world, LABOUR FRONT posed the most acute questions of local and international labour relations, while THE WAR FOR MEN'S MINDS investigated the whole complex of education and propaganda at the highest level of social and political action. This approach finally culminated in the dramatic presentation of the world's functional international bodies (eg., UNRRA, the Food and Agriculture Organization, the International Fund and Bank, and the United Nations Organization) in such films as IN THE WAKE OF THE ARMIES, UNRRA and NOW—THE PEACE.

From the beginning of the series Legg had considered it fully within the scope of his work to examine countries other than Canada on a social, economic and political basis so that Canadians might draw their own conclusions. Thus CHURCHILL'S ISLAND and the later JOHN BULL'S OWN ISLAND investigated the changing face of Britain; INSIDE FIGHTING RUSSIA and RUSSIA'S FOREIGN POLICY presented Canada's northern neighbour; FIGHTING NORWAY, THE FIGHTING DUTCH, INSIDE FIGHTING CHINA and INSIDE FRANCE examined Canada's allies overseas; ATLANTIC CROSSROADS (Newfoundland) and FIVE MEN OF AUSTRALIA looked at the members of the Commonwealth; THE GATES OF ITALY, THE MASK OF NIPPON, FORTRESS JAPAN, and GEOPOLITIX, HITLER'S PLAN FOR CONQUEST compared the effectiveness of Canada's enemies, while BALKAN POWDER KEG and WHEN ASIA SPEAKS were perhaps the two most searching political investigations of large regional cross-sections ever presented on the screens of the world.

Technique of CCO and WIA

The gathering of footage as well as the editing and the commentary of these globe-spanning films posed entirely novel difficulties, yet there was very little discussion of technical or aesthetic problems. The style developed out of the job. Since it was a question of encouraging a pattern of thought and feeling about the individual Canadian's relationship to international events, the visuals as well as the commentary had to relate local strategies to world ones. If the commentary had a touch of the ex cathedra manner, it was because the people's bewilderment had needed that antidote since Munich. If the maps looked upside-down it was because it seemed time that people saw things in relativity. If the manner was hard and objective, it was because the Wehrmacht seemed a good deal harder at the time than it seems to us now, and because it was time that the people of the western hemisphere faced the answer with all the objectivity they could muster. If the tempo of cutting and delivery seemed swifter than anything seen before in documentary, it was because much had to be accomplished quickly if the public mind was to be tuned in time to what, amid the swiftly unfolding scenes of 1940, was required of it. A sense of urgency had to be created to gear people's minds to the hardness and directness required for decision and action. And since events moved speedily and opportunities seemed to be passing just as speedily, the tempo of production as well as the pace of continuity had to change accordingly.

Yet none of these tasks could have been accomplished with quiet efficiency if the technical and aesthetic groundwork had not been laid by units as widely different in purpose as the French avant-garde and the early Soviet schools. Legg's juxtaposition of contrasting images (country versus country, social system versus social system, waste versus conservation of resources, etc.), or his comparison of widely separate images of social progress or of parallel military and economic developments in different countries, was clearly unthinkable without Kuleshov's and Pudovkin's experiments in montage, and his constant effort to link images by visual continuity and by carrying over movement from one shot to the next, clearly stemmed from the first experiments of the French avant-garde in obtaining such visual flow for entirely different purposes and with an entirely different aesthetic in mind.

Since it was entirely impossible to send shooting crews to distant spots of the globe for coverage of half a dozen shots, all such material had to be selected from newsreel and stock library sources, and for this purpose the film board trained two highly specialized gatherers-of-material whose sense of the aesthetic, like Chesterton's, was largely a matter of a sense of smell. But the finely developed nose for news and sources also and inevitably had to develop a sense for the symbolic in the topical, and for the most highly condensed meaning within the shortest possible footage. The logic of the argument ran somewhat like this: Remember, you have only one or two reels at your disposal, and within that space you must be able to tell as much as a feature director in nine. That means you'll have to get more than three times as much into every one of your shots, and the ideal shot therefore is the one which has a kind of three-level action—something happening in the foreground and something in the background in addition to your main action. Since you have no time to cut from longshot to mid-shot to close-up, you'll have to telescope all three of them into each single shot, and since you can't waste your time on inessentials, however pretty, you'll have to strike the most chary balance between the immanent and the transcendental values.

All this was new and vigorous and exciting in its discipline, but the most interesting aspect of it all was the integration of visual and sound. Since visual, music and effects tracks were running side by side in a highly complex three-part counterpoint, and since the visual by itself constantly skipped from place to place all over the globe, it became doubly important for the commentary to draw the two other tracks and the visual together into a single continuity, and this had to be done in such a manner as to make its points through the spectator's subconscious as well as through his conscious.

Aside from active verbs and pseudo-quotations ("The experts say that . . . ") the most important innovation here was the use of metaphors and similes created by the juxtaposition of an incidental aspect of the visual and an incidental aspect of the commentary in such a way that they became meaningfully, though to the spectator imperceptibly, welded together—as in the following examples:

INSIDE FRANCE (Reel 1)
Pix: LS White chalk cliff coastal wall.
Comm: "Behind the familiar facades there has long stood a France speaking with two divided voices."

BATTLE IS THEIR BIRTHRIGHT (End of Reel 2)
Pix: Airman looks down and sees destroyed cities, shots of devastation, ending with pan to statues of dancing children in ruined Russian square.
Comm: "Masters already of the gigantic forces of the physical world, they who are young today, gazing upon the ruins of a bitter human past, well know that the future of mankind itself is in their hands; that beyond the devastation another task is waiting—that of creating in their own image, the bright image of youth itself, another and a greater world."

BALKAN POWDER KEG (Reel 1)
Pix: Peasant lying down in field and covering self in cloak.
Comm: [Hungary's aristocrats] "still wrapping themselves and their people in a cloak of injured pride."

NOW—THE PEACE (Opening Reel 1)
Pix: Aerials—clouds parting over San Francisco.
Comm: "Once again... the nations face the solemn challenge history has thrust upon them: to build—amid the parting clouds of war—a peace which shall be real and indivisible."

At times, this method went no further than the use in the commentary of single words suggested by the visual:

"Down to the very shores of the Arctic Ocean" (shot from descending plane).
"Rising in the hills" (camera tilts up)
"The snouts of U-Boats" (low CU of bows)

But at other times, the similes and metaphors became so complex that they obtained a double, triple, and at times, quadruple value:

NOW—THE PEACE (End of Reel 2)
Pix: Marching massed troops dissolve to VHS San Francisco and bridge (Horizon shot).
Comm: "... that when—this time—the men come marching back, it may be to a world on the march itself to new horizons of adventure."

JOHN BULL'S OWN ISLAND (Reel 1 or 2)
Pix: Bank of England—Montague Norman—grilled vaults. Sinister gent opening combination on lock, door swings open. Huntsmen running to hounds.
Comm: "Through the Bank of England [passed] the destinies of men and markets half a world away. No wonder that for those who held a share in England's trade the door was opened to a green and pleasant land."

JOHN BULL'S OWN ISLAND (Reel 1)
Pix: Surf against breakwaters; aerial shots of dark skies followed by shot of parting clouds and long shot of bright English landscape.
Comm: "Against the walls of Britain, the tempests of the second war with Germany have raged for nigh six years. And now—across the Island Kingdom's darkened skies—the clouds are parting at long last, as though to promote brighter times ahead."

These examples were mainly meant to impart their meaning through the spectator's subconscious. Other examples, however, made use of conscious irony, and still others of contrast rather than of similarity in word and visual.

Here are two examples of ironic simile, the first one particularly remarkable because of its use of direct quotation:

GATES OF ITALY (Reel 2)
Pix: Sequence of Mussolini trotting around turning the soil, heaving a pick, laying a brick, scattering seeds, kissing babies, being cheered, and ending with baby clinic.
Comm: "Already I control the forces of Politics and those of Economics. Soon I shall even control the great forces acting in Nature."

BALKAN POWDER KEG (Reel 1)
Pix: Ox scratching ass with horn.
Comm: "Hungary, the country whose rulers have gazed irritably backward at the past...."

At other times, cutting or sound effects rather than visuals were drawn into commentary in the same manner:

FORTRESS JAPAN (Reel 1)
Pix: Asiatic workers carrying sacks and bales. Tempo increases till they are actually trotting.
Comm: "But today the Japanese are driving their slave labour to the limit of endurance. Every mine and mill and man, they say, must give the utmost in the shortest time. And time, they know, is swiftly running out across the Empire of the Rising Sun."

MASK OF NIPPON
Pix: Sync sound sequence, in which singing and playing get out of sync.
Comm: "They [the Japanese people] heard the strains of 'Deutschland Uber Alles'; but, perhaps significant of 'mystic ferments' yet to come, band and people got out of time."

And here, finally, is one of the most dramatic uses of contrast rather than simile:

WAR FOR MEN'S MINDS:
Pix: Chinese refugees and woman crawling on hands and knees.
Comm: "With such proof of their own towering strength, the people of the earth march forward into their new age—march in the certainty that the gates of hell cannot prevail against them.

Small wonder, then, that the "Canada Carries On" and "World in Action" films broke not only into Canadian but also into American and other theatres outside Canada. In a recent Canadian quiz, the question was posed: "Are Canadian-made films shown in more theatres in Canada or in the United States?" And, of course, every Canadian logically answered: "In Canada." But, in fact, the answer was: "In over 6,500 theatres in the United States; in about 800 in Canada." But in spite of the fact that the film board's weekly Canadian theatrical audience finally rose to 3,500,000, or to nearly a third of the total population, the Canadian documentary makers never forgot the proverbial seating capacity outside the theatres, and it was in this non-theatrical sector that the film board made its main dent.

Editors' note: We have ended Borneman's piece at this point, but it should be noted that he goes on to discuss other categories of film board work during this period, including rural, industrial, union, regional, consumer, educational, and French unit films.

Before the Guerillières
Women's Films at the NFB During World War II
Barbara Halpern Martineau

The women say, unhappy one, men have expelled you from the world of symbols and yet they have given you names, they have called you slave, you unhappy slave. Masters, they have exercised their rights as masters. They write, of their authority to accord names, that it goes back so far that the origin of language itself may be considered an act of authority emanating from those who dominate. Thus they say that they have said this is such or such a thing, they have attached a particular word to an object or fact and thereby consider themselves to have appropriated it. The women say, so doing the men have bawled, shouted with all their might to reduce you to silence. The women say, the language you speak poisons your glottis tongue palate lips. They say, the language you speak is made up of signs that rightly speaking designate what men have appropriated. Whatever they have not laid hands on, whatever they have not pounced on like many-eyed birds of prey, does not appear in the language you speak. This is apparent precisely in the intervals that your masters have not been able to fill with their words of proprietors and possessors, this can be found in the gaps, in all that which is not a continuation of their discourse, in the zero, the O, the perfect circle that you invent to imprison them and overthrow them.

—Monique Wittig, *The Guerillières*, 1969.

Transcript of a speech delivered at the Conference on Canadian Film in Its Historical Context, November 13, 1976, Ottawa, Ontario.

One should not connect the voices with the image film. They are doubtless escapees from another material than that of film. And doubtless they could have come into a quite different film from this one. Provided it were vacant, poor, made with holes.

—Marguerite Duras, preface to
La Femme du Gange, Paris, 1973.

Dobson said his work was like breaking a code. He wasn't only interested in the ordinary Chinese words, but perhaps more so in what the Chinese call empty words. "They are like squeaks and noises that come in between other words and their function has never been analyzed, but in fact they are the whole grammatical apparatus of the language."

—Toronto *Star*, February 18, 1976
(article on A.C.H. Dobson, compiler
of Chinese language dictionary).

To speak of women in the dominant film culture is to speak of absence, gaps, discontinuities, of appropriation and distortion. Women in recent years have looked extensively at the images of women in feature films, particularly those coming from Hollywood. General observations are that these images are distorted, inflated, and most recently, absent. It is noted that except for the extraordinary phenomenon of so-called "women's films" made in Hollywood in the forties, especially by Warner Brothers, women have been portrayed as adjuncts to men, seen through men's eyes, representing men's obsessions, symbols of otherness in a male-dominated world. This is held by feminist critics to be a reflection of the filmmaking situation in a world of power which is in fact male-dominated. Although women have made considerable contributions to cinema throughout its history their work has been obscured and underrated, their voices and visions suppressed.

The rediscovery of women's contributions to film history is an exciting aspect of the work of cultural reconstruction undertaken by the women's movement. It is a massive undertaking fed by the research of women organizing film festivals, conferences, and study groups. We have seen the resurrection of such pioneers as Alice Guy, who made the first edited fiction film (LA FEE AUX CHOUX, 1896), Esther Shub, who invented the art of compilation film (THE FALL OF THE ROMANOV DYNASTY, 1927), Lotte Reiniger, a living genius who made a brilliant feature-length animated film twelve years before Disney (THE ADVENTURES OF PRINCE AHMED, 1926).

One of the recurrent questions concerning this virtual rewriting of film history is whether there is any observable consistency to films made by women, whether there is in fact a distinct women's film culture. I have repeatedly argued that this is something of a red herring, a question which is at best premature. Women working in film have been too scattered, their films too little-known to each other, for the long deep interchange which is the basis of any distinct culture to take place. The interchange has just begun to happen, the culture is in the process of development. And where significant numbers of women are working in situations which encourage interchange, certainly it can be said that their films show this, that new concepts of films made by women-conscious women are in fact being developed. Rather than trying to fit all films made by women into an *a priori* slot, we will do better to evolve working value judgments based on present needs, and to reevaluate those qualities of women's films which are often attacked or ignored because they don't conform to the expectations of conventional phallic criticism. As for women's films of the past, the pressing need is for rediscovery and description.

Traditionally, partly because of the place women have held in the cutting room, partly because of the economics of film, the largest output of films by women has been in documentary and experimental genres. Women have been making features since features began, but in very small numbers—this situation has just barely started to change. Only this year was it possible to organize a festival program of recent films directed by women which was substantially composed of features. Given the increasing interest in documentary techniques used in feature filmmaking today, and the documentary background of many new feature directors, it is not surprising that we find new women's features strongly influenced by documentary developments. This is true both in terms of filmic approach and subject matter—the first impact of the new women's movement on filmmaking was seen in a spate of low-budget documentaries which literally created a new aesthetic for thinking about women on celluloid. The importance of women's documentary films in the sixties and early seventies has yet to be widely recognized.

In English-speaking Canada documentary film is the backbone of the industry, and the place of most beginnings for filmmakers. This is where almost all of the women who have made a professional place for themselves are to be found. As for feature films, since Nell Shipman left Victoria, B.C. in 1905 to seek acting and then production work in the United States, there has been a long silence, broken sporadically by Sylvia Spring's effort (MADELEINE IS, 1970) and the splendid isolation of Joyce Wieland's career, newly manifested in THE FAR SHORE. Only in Quebec, and only recently, have women made a slightly more substantial mark on feature filmmaking: Mireille Dansereau, Anne-Claire Poirier, and Brigitte Sauriol have produced respectable feature films in the past few years, and now Denyse Benoit is completing a new feature, LA CRUE.

The history of women in documentary film work in Canada begins with the formation of the National Film Board by John Grierson in 1939. Until then, with the single exiled exception of Nell Shipman, there was virtually no involvement of Canadian women in any kind of filmmaking. In production credits compiled by the CFI there are three women listed for the years 1913-1940, as scriptwriters. (It should be noted that Canadian women have played a strong role from the first in the development of a national literature—no one could keep them from pens and paper.)

John Grierson was no Canadian but a pragmatic Scot, concerned with gathering talent wherever he found it to produce his kind of films in this obscure corner of the British Marketing Empire. If he found talented women, he used them, and as it was wartime there was a distinct shortage of talented men available for training in film. Grierson brought some trained documentarians with him from the GPO unit in London —among them were two Canadians who had gone to London to learn how to make documentary films: Laurence Cherry and Evelyn Spice, who became Evelyn Spice Cherry. The Cherrys were co-heads of the NFB agricultural film unit, and they produced and directed wartime films stressing the need for greater productivity and thrift in the use of food. They had a small child at the time, and were very conscious of the need for organized day care to release women for work in the war effort. It is a great paradox that the most phallic, aggressive, absurd extension of patriarchy known to humanity—I mean war—resulted in opening economic and social possibilities to women which in turn led to women realizing, as never before, the extent of their oppression and the extent of the changes needed if they were to begin to develop their great potential. (The paradox dates back at least to Euripides; it was to bear modern fruit in the American Civil War, in World War I and the concurrent waves of the Russian revolution.) Evelyn Cherry today, at seventy, is still head of Cherry Productions in Regina, still active in producing films to provide information to Canadians, still emphatic about the pressing need for widely available good day care, and clearly aware of the fact that day care during the war was made available solely because of war needs and neglected after the war in the widespread push to bring women back to the kitchen and out of the salaried work force.

In addition to Evelyn Spice Cherry, there were significant number of women employed by Grierson who assumed key positions in the wartime film board. Gudrun Bjerring Parker directed educational films, sometimes with all-women crews, using Judith Crawley on camera and Sally MacDonald on sound; she became head of the educational unit. Margaret Perry began in 1942 as a traveling projectionist in New Brunswick, joined the Ottawa Film Board, worked as negative cutter, editor, and then camera operator for Gudrun Parker and Beth Zinkan. She eventually became film producer for the province of Nova Scotia. Laura Boulton, an American from Arizona, directed a series of films on the peoples of Canada, one of which, ESKIMO ARTS AND CRAFTS, is interesting for its presentation of a culture in which both sexes were considered equally important and productive. Marge McKay, affectionately known as

Grierson's prime minister, was virtually *the* film board administrator —her unpublished manuscript, a history of the NFB, is still the best source for knowledge of how the NFB functioned in its early years. Margaret Ann Adamson (now Lady Elton) and Daphne Lilly (now Daphne Anstey) chose footage for compilation films and made substantial contributions to the "Canada Carries On" and "World in Action" series. Evelyn Lambart worked with Norman McLaren in the experimental unit and Alma Duncan was in charge of graphics. Beth Bertram was the head of personnel. (In his introduction to the book *Grierson on Documentary*, Forsyth Hardy attempts to be witty by remarking that "when suitably provoked, Grierson will maintain that 'the National Film Board was a matriarchy ''.)

Because of the extremely flexible organization of the NFB under Grierson (anyone could do anything as long as the end product was acceptable to the master), and because of Grierson's policy that NFB films carry no production credits since they were collectively produced (the Ottawa Film Board was in fact a functioning collective headed by a dictator), it is difficult, almost impossible, to delineate precisely the work done by women on films made in the war years. By talking to people from that epoch still working at the NFB and checking production files on film titles they mentioned, I was able to compile a list of some fifteen films indisputably directed by women during the war years. More to the point is the evidence given by women of that period who came to Montreal in May 1975 for a four-day workshop,[1] who participated in seminar discussion and whom I interviewed for a film history of women at the NFB. It is clear from their testimony and the corroboration of their male colleagues that they indeed played vital, central roles in the astonishing output of documentary films by the NFB during the war. It is also indisputably clear that this extensive participation of women at key levels in NFB production and administration diminished rapidly after the war ended and Grierson left the board, and that the next twenty years of film board production were heavily male-dominated, with almost no participation by women except at menial levels.

I found it very significant that the list of films directed by women (on which research and scripts were invariably done by women) included so few war films, although they were all connected in some way with the war effort and fed into Grierson's scheme to unify Canada as a patriotic country by fostering national self-awareness. Women who took the initiative required to direct films chose to concentrate on agriculture, education, anthropology, regional interests, arts and crafts, children's films. Those who worked in supportive positions—editing, choosing stock footage, cutting negatives, doing research for films directed by men—were centrally involved in the production of war films. The women who worked under Grierson made no collective attempt to analyze the significance of NFB films for women or the special contribution women could make to filmic vision. Films directed by men showed men in active roles; women, if present, in supportive roles. Women who worked on these films did not criticize that orientation. Neither, in their own situations, did it occur to them to complain that they were paid far less than their male colleagues. Nor did they complain after the war when their positions were regraded, when they were expected to give up their careers if they conflicted with their husband's work, or when women leaving significant positions at the board were invariably replaced by men.

There was one woman at the NFB who did object (she remarked recently that women under Grierson "were so grateful to be working in interesting jobs that they didn't realize they were slaves".) She was the one woman actively involved in the production of war films at a decision-making level—Jane Marsh, director of WOMEN ARE WARRIORS, INSIDE FIGHTING CANADA, and AIR CADETS for the "Canada Carries On" series, who became *de facto* producer of that series after Stuart Legg. She was by no means addicted to making war films and is best remembered for her successful treatment of the life of rural Québécois, ALEXIS TREMBLAY, HABITANT. Jane Marsh's original title for WOMEN ARE WARRIORS was WORK FOR WOMEN; in her research for that film she compiled statistics on the socio-economic position of women in fourteen countries. She began her report (1941) with a list of quotations as evidence of misogyny dating back to ancient Egypt:

> A general consensus of opinion of women as expressed by men during the last six thousand years leads one to believe that although quite indispensable they are also dangerous because incomprehensible and unpredictable, and they should therefore be kept apart as much as possible, either by being
> 1) Put up on a pedestal and hypnotized into thinking they are frail, incompetent and dependent; or
> 2) Subjugated for the expediency of
>   a. Lust
>   b. Cheap labour
>
> and that all of them have two duties which should occupy the whole of their lives, thoughts and ambitions, i.e.,
> 1) To make men comfortable
> 2) To bear children
>
> and that on no account should they be allowed to use their faculties for anything else as this would bring about disorder by upsetting the status quo.

She remarks that:

> In 1792 Mary Wollstonecraft began the revolution which has been hampered up to the present day by the three complexes which affect women, namely:
> 1) Inferiority (I'm only a woman, it doesn't matter about me)

2) Chivalry (I'm a weak, frail, dependent flower, please protect me)
3) Slump complex (hell, what does it matter and who cares?)

Under the heading "Uses and Occupations" she says:

Women are generally used in wars as
1) Whores
2) Nurses
3) Spies
4) Factory workers in all defense industries
5) Home defense including communications and agriculture
6) Welfare and morale, looking after war orphans, wounded, etc., this includes feeding, etc.
In this war they are also being used as
1) Guerrillas
2) Auxiliary to armed forces (as in WWI), ferrying planes, ground mechanics, AA guns, etc.
3) Fire fighters
4) Reporters

They are used for everything except actual combat and physical labour demanding great strength. But in China and in Russia as well in the Spanish War they have taken part in actual combat and there is actually no type of manual labour that they haven't performed.

Jane Marsh and Grierson battled over the "Canada Carries On" series, when a producer was needed and she was the obvious choice. Grierson didn't want a woman as producer of that series. He offered her anything else, but she stuck to her guns. He took another approach. As she tells it, the series had just found its rhythm in two-reelers, when Grierson decided that instead they would produce twice the number of one-reelers. Jane Marsh argued that the quality of the films would be destroyed, and resigned in protest. To her chagrin Grierson accepted her resignation. Years later, meeting her in New York, he told her she had been right, but he would never give in to a woman.

Given the nature of the research report for WOMEN ARE WARRIORS, I wonder why the finished film bears such different emphasis. It remains an astonishing document, markedly different in tone from other films on the same subject. A film called WOMEN AT WAR, for instance, gives the impression that the ladies have temporarily exchanged their aprons for overalls out of necessity, but that they're all looking forward to a return to "normality" after the war. WOMEN AT WAR shows women primarily as volunteer workers, and an ultra-feminine narrator remarks that "the women's guilds no longer make pinchushions and pillowcases, now they make shirts for hospitals". The concluding line of WOMEN AT WAR is: "Women may not be heroines, but they are brave soldiers."

Another film, WINGS ON HER SHOULDERS, from the "World in Action" series, emphasizes men's feelings about women in the war effort. Men are needed to fly bombers, so women are brought into the air force to perform ground duties. There is considerable attention paid to the uniforms and hairdos of the women, and their dormitory life. We are told that women don't fly planes, although both WOMEN ARE WARRIORS and WOMEN AT WAR show women pilots. And there is an extraordinary sequence in WINGS ON HER SHOULDERS examining the effect on male egos of the work of airwomen on the ground. It seems to be a warning when the male commentator notes that many airwomen have no intention, after the war, "of returning to a life of privacy and ease". The film ends with a tribute to "women who wear wings on their shoulders, that men may fly".

WOMEN ARE WARRIORS is, like WOMEN AT WAR and WINGS ON HER SHOULDERS, a compilation film—it is entirely composed of clips from stock footage, newsreels, other documentaries. It is unique among these women's war films for linking the participation of women in the war effort to their national/political contexts, examining the work of women in three widely different Allied countries: England, the USSR, and Canada. It starts gently, showing women doing the sort of maternal, volunteer work they might traditionally be expected to do, and it moves steadily towards a celebration of women's abilities to do anything at all: heavy factory work, skilled mechanics, active participation in the front lines. Skillful cutting and explicit commentary shows how previous domestic work by women has prepared them to adapt to factory work—a shot of a women at a sewing machine is inserted in a factory sequence, and it's pointed out that for some skilled work women's hands are defter than men's. Unlike WOMEN AT WAR and WINGS ON HER SHOULDERS, WOMEN ARE WARRIORS makes it clear that these women were not leisurely idlers before the war—they were domestic workers, secretaries, doing whatever work was available for women.

But just as the implications of Jane Marsh's original title, WORK FOR WOMEN, were suppressed in favour of WOMEN ARE WARRIORS, so the implications of the film's structure and commentary are suppressed by the use of a male narrator—the same patriotic, reassuring voice heard in so many films showing men at war. Presumably the rationale was that a male voice gave "seriousness" and "authenticity" to the visual presentation. In WOMEN AT WAR a feminine voice trivializes even the powerful material shown, and in WINGS ON HER SHOULDERS a male voice presents a male vision. It was apparently inconceivable that a "serious" look at "serious" women's work could be presented by a dignified woman. (Note that work is "serious" if it contributes to a male-dominated effort, such as war.)

Although the visuals have strong subversive implications, and although some of this is suggested in the script (though with nothing of the force of the research report), the male narrator defuses the film's explosive potential. With no credits to individuals (the CFI pamphlet *NFB: The War Years* attributes the film to Stanley Hawes) the film appears to have been made by men. It becomes a patronizing look at the contributions women can make, when needed, to the patriarchy.

Media manipulation of the women's movement today is a contemporary example of the force which transformed a film conceived by a woman for the enlightenment of women into another plug for the great war effort. WOMEN ARE WARRIORS was withdrawn from distribution after the war, along with other controversial films such as WAR FOR MEN'S MINDS and MASKS OF NIPPON, and it is not normally available for public screening.

Jane Marsh's point was that "individual women have been and done everything that individual men have done at some time or other if only to prove that they could". The operative word for our purposes is "individual". The case of Jane Marsh illustrates the often-proved point that women working alone and out of context can do very little to change the dominant power structure, or the dominant codes which uphold it. Film is a collective medium controlled by capitalist interests which are fundamentally patriarchal. While celebrating the illusion of individual worth and freedom, most films in fact suppress any genuinely individual vision, particularly if it comes from a woman—they perpetuate the codes of the status quo. Changing this requires simultaneous work on two fronts: 1) to understand and render accessible the working of various code systems (and by render accessible I mean speaking in language which itself struggles against dominant codes of mystification, i.e., the jargon of semiologists and other academics); and   2) to understand the practical structures of production which ensure that anarchistic voices are muffled even while token representation is given to women and minority groups.

> In order to change the face of the world, it is first necessary to be firmly anchored in it; but the women who are firmly rooted in society are those who are in subjection to it.... it is not the inferiority of women that has caused their historical insignificance, that has doomed them to inferiority.... To tell the truth, one is not born a genius, one becomes a genius; and the feminine situation has up to the present rendered this becoming practically impossible.
>
> The antifeminists obtain from the study of history two contradictory arguments: 1) women have never created anything great; and   2) the situation of women has never prevented the flowering of great feminine personalities. There is bad faith in these two statements: the successes of a privileged few do not counter or excuse the systematic lowering of the collective level; and that

these successes are rare and limited proves precisely that circumstances are unfavourable for them.

—Simone de Beauvoir, *The Second Sex*

Is it not possible that if we knew the truth about war the glory of war would be scotched and crushed where it lies curled up in the rotten cabbage leaves of our prostituted fact-purveyors; and if we knew the truth about art instead of shuffling and shambling through the smeared and dejected pages of those who must live by prostituting culture, the enjoyment and practice of art would become so desirable that by comparison the pursuit of war would be a tedious game for elderly dilettantes in search of a mildly sanitary amusement—the tossing of bombs instead of balls over frontiers instead of nets? In short, if newspapers were to tell the truth about politics and the truth about art we should not believe in war and we should believe in art.

—Virginia Woolf, *Three Guineas*

The Innocent Eye

An Aspect of the Work of the National Film Board of Canada

Peter Harcourt

We could begin with THE LIVING MACHINE (1961). Ostensibly a film about cybernetics—about the complexities of electronic technology and its place in the modern world—it is finally about something else as well, something not so easily defined. Shot in two parts of approximately half an hour each, the film describes some of the work being done at the Bell Telephone Laboratories in New Jersey and at the Massachusetts Institute of Technology. While conveying its information and displaying a fascination with the luminous intricacies of machinery—a fascination that dates back at least to Eisenstein, to the moving pistons in the final section of POTEMKIN or to the over-lit montage of the cream-separator sequence in THE GENERAL LINE—it also includes some playful and

Reprinted from *Sight & Sound,* vol. 34, no. 1 (Winter 1964-65).

humane elements: an actual frog swallowing an actual fly, quite comically magnified to fill the entire screen, which follows a demonstration of an electronic replica of a frog's eye that buzzes hungrily at all fly-shaped objects; and in Part I, a game of checkers staged between an IBM computer, programmed for half an hour before the game begins, and Mr. Arthur Gladstone, checker champion of New York.

Mr. Gladstone's warm New York face and voice add a touching element to the first part of this film. Mr. Gladstone, who has spent his life in mastering the complexities of the checker-board, now finds that he can win this particular game only by avoiding all the standard moves. For a while he is worried; but he finally comes to admire the machine for its tenacity in persevering with the game to the very end. "I usually shake hands with my opponent," he smiles, as he reaches out for the hand of the programmer. For Mr. Gladstone, as for us, the game has been a disquieting experience, its implications inimical (we might feel) to our self-respect. Part I ends with the question: "If man is to remain master of his new machine, what is man that a machine is not?" It is in the course of Part II's attempt to investigate this question that the film becomes something more than a film about electronic brains. In the pursuit of this problem, THE LIVING MACHINE looks into a void.

As Part I is framed by the game of checkers, so Part II is framed by Allen Sheppard's flight into space. But the film is really built around an interview with Dr. Warren McCulloch, an eminent mathematician at M.I.T. By reporting his words alone, it is difficult here to convey the effect that Dr. McCulloch has upon us when we can see him on the screen, as it is difficult to explain the central position he occupies in this film. There is a chilling sense of greatness about him: chilling because so little concerned with the sentimentalities, the elusive irrationalities, that for most of us seem so much a part of the human fabric of life; great because so learned in his own particular field and so unself-conscious in his speech and dress, so careless of what anyone else might think about what he says and is.

For Dr. McCulloch, all the mysteries of life have an explanation and that explanation is mathematical. Having been early seduced away from his destined theological career by the fascination of mathematics—"because as anyone acquainted with theology will know, the ideas in the mind of God are mathematics and logic"—Dr. McCulloch explains that there have been only two things in his life that he has wanted to know. As he puts it, "What is a number that a man may know it and a man that he may know a number?" He has had to content himself with an answer to only the first part of this double quest.

Yet Dr. McCulloch believes that machines may inherit the earth, may eventually take over and carry on from man. He is detached and thoughtful as he considers this. We see him at his summer home in New England, first swimming naked with his grandchildren in an artificial lake that he has dammed up himself, then sitting on the grass as he talks to us.

There are the sounds of a dog and children in the background, plus the buzz of bees and the occasional protest of a crow. In this setting, the interviewer/filmmaker is troubled by the easy way Dr. McCulloch discusses the eventual extinction of man and the possible reign of the machine.

"But with man gone, wouldn't the machines be purposeless?" the troubled Canadian voice asks.

"No, I think they would be purpose*ful*," he replies, emphasizing the final syllable, "as man's life is purpose*ful*."

"Would there be nothing gone, nothing missing?"

Here, a pause as he looks around him, as if thinking about this aspect of the problem for the first time, trying to be exact in reply:

"You mean in the sense that the dinosaurs are missing?"

"No, something important, something... "

"Aren't they important, I mean weren't the dinosaurs important?"

Here, a cut-away to the children playing close by, and again we might be conscious of the hum of summer life around. The interviewer is even more troubled and tries to explain that he is talking about human emotions, about the way that Dr. McCulloch must feel about his grandchildren. The doctor remains unperturbed: he sees no reason why machines could not be designed that would be able to feel.

"I'm certain that if I do it, there's a mechanism that can do it," he explains. The camera continues to run, as if by its very presence it might probe more successfully than the now exhausted questions have been able to. Again there is a cut-away to the children and still the summer sounds. Dr. McCulloch smiles at them amusedly, and we might hear him murmur the caution, "Don't shake the table!" as the camera continues to run.

This is a moment of great embarrassment in the cinema, as if the filmmakers were no longer in control and no longer knew what to do. As by his eyes Dr. McCulloch seems so much more sure of himself than we could possibly be, instinctively we want to look away. And it is largely because of this moment that many people who have seen the film consider it unsatisfactory, even people who work at the National Film Board. Yet for me, it is a moment of greatness in the cinema, of an honesty of presentation where man has been faced with an ultimate—the relativity of the values of his own existence—and, confronted by the explanations, can find nothing more to say. The camera still runs on as Dr. McCulloch stops smiling at his children and looks up at the camera and then into the eyes of the interviewer, and again smiles as if to say, "What do you want me to do, what more can I say? I am not embarrassed faced by your machine." He looks out at the filmmakers and at us.

Quick cut to Margaret Mead explaining Dr. McCulloch's views as a new kind of anthropomorphism, the invention of a new kind of god. She is most exuberant and pleasing to watch. After Dr. McCulloch, she seems more normal, closer to us in her ways of thought, and is therefore more manageable, more comforting to listen to. Yet, more intelligent?

More far-seeing? The film lets us decide this for ourselves, but the troubled note remains.

In fact, like so many of the films that I shall be concerned with here—such as CITY OF GOLD (1957), UNIVERSE (1960) and LONELY BOY (1961)—THE LIVING MACHINE is studded with questions, questions genuinely the result of a desire to understand. Part I begins with "What kind of machine is it that in half an hour can learn to play checkers with a champion?", while Part II carries on into more metaphysical regions, asking questions about the basic tenets of existence to which there are no cosy replies. With Allen Sheppard in his Mercury capsule we hear: "What is this creature who chooses to attempt a journey through an alien world where only the machinery around him, if it works, will keep him alive?" And when we return to Sheppard at the end of Part II, after we have been taken on a tour through the history of man's billion years —shoes squeaking, footsteps echoing, down the corridor of a natural history museum at night, a torchlight picking out the replicas of the preserves of the evolution of man—again we hear the commentary, reverential, questioning: "Behind man a billion years. A billion years to grow flesh and blood and brain and to begin to understand and shape our world.... What incredible machines will man have made in another billion years? What sights will our adventurers then be seeing with their own eyes? What is this creature of flesh and blood, feeling hope and fear?"

Sheppard in the capsule in outer space, photographed in a ghostly light by the camera in the capsule with him; a medley of buzzes on the sound-track along with his own reporting voice, buzzes perhaps recalling the bees that we have just heard, but mostly the electronic buzz of the frog's artificial eye that we heard towards the opening of the film. Thus, there is an unobtrusive aural symmetry as the film ends with these questions, diffused throughout with a sense of awe: "What is this creature of flesh and blood, feeling hope and fear?"

THE LIVING MACHINE is the work of one section of one unit operating within the quite vast structure of the National Film Board. It is the work of the old Unit B. Originally, when the unit system was devised some fifteen years ago (c. 1950), there were four separate units, each with a shooting schedule of about twenty films a year; while by last year (1963), when it was decided to replace the unit system with a new kind of structure within the film board, there were seven units which produced on an average a total of fifty short films a year.

In principle, each unit was in charge of a certain area of interest; one unit concentrating on French productions; one on theatrical shorts, news-magazines, and the like; another dealing largely with sponsored work for the various government departments. Even at the outset, Unit B seemed to have the widest range of activities, including as it did the animation department, while producing some films on art, some classroom films, and some science films, as well as the "candid" documentaries which I shall be concerned with here.

At its best, the unit method of filmmaking was good because it was organic, allowing a transference of understanding from one member of the unit to another, helping to make for a group maturity. "Craftsmen who care about the whole want to be involved in the whole," the executive producer of Unit B, Tom Daly, explained to me when I visited Montreal in 1963. But, of course, there were also disadvantages: some people felt confined within a particular unit, expected to produce the same kind of film over and over again. So a new system has been evolved, a system that also more sharply divides the English sections from the French. But it was very much the growth of television in the early fifties that helped Unit B to develop its own particular style, a style seen at its most probing in THE LIVING MACHINE and at its most brilliant in LONELY BOY, the film on Paul Anka.

"Television was the excuse and also the opportunity," as Tom Daly described it. The television screen was enormously hungry, while at the same time standards were not too high. This made possible a number of fresh principles. First of all, television encouraged them to shoot on 16mm, which for the same amount of money allowed them to think in terms of maximum footage and editing time, with a minimum of scripting and artificial lighting. On most of the television films there was virtually no script at all. The script and commentary were devised in the process of editing; while Wolf Koenig, who along with Roman Kroitor directed the film, estimated that the shooting ration for LONELY BOY was about $1/20$—that is, one foot of film used for every twenty shot. Also, the general lightness and flexibility of the 16mm equipment made for a greater flexibility and versatility of effects, something best seen in the Freedomland sequence at the end of the Anka film. With Wolf Koenig on camera and Marcel Carrière on sound, they managed to capture all of what we see from only four performances, two performances on two consecutive nights. Until this was explained to me, I had assumed a multiple camera technique had been at work throughout the film, but this was not so. In fact, between them, Wolf Koenig and Roman Kroitor shot all the externals necessary for both LONELY BOY and THE LIVING MACHINE within a period of from five to six weeks, sharing the directorial credit for the Anka film, Kroitor taking it for THE LIVING MACHINE. In fact all the Unit B films were really co-operative efforts, as Tom Daly put it, "the credits being apportioned at the end of the filming according to where they felt the centre of gravity lay".

As its executive producer, Tom Daly is the hub around which all thirty-five members of Unit B turned. Add to his name those of Koenig and Kroitor and then of Colin Low and you have within the unit the four men who have contributed most creatively and consistently to its individual style. Of course there are many others who have helped to make up the team. In the films that I am concerned with, I should perhaps mention Guy Côté, who worked as editor on both THE LIVING MACHINE and LONELY BOY; Eldon Rathburn, who has contributed such effective musical scores to so many NFB films, but especially to UNIVERSE and Colin Low's CITY OF GOLD; and most importantly (it seems to me) the voice of Stanley Jackson, himself a director of some of the unit's more specifically educational films—the quite admirable SHYNESS (1953), for example—who speaks the commentary on the majority of the films with just the right degree of respect and awe, as in THE LIVING MACHINE, or the right tinge of irony in LONELY BOY or I WAS A 90-POUND WEAKLING.

Yet these films are so thoroughly the product of a group that the names do not matter. Although as one grows closer to the films and comes to know them better, one can detect the personal contributions of the individual men, while we commonly talk of a Franju film, a Chris Marker film, or even if we know them of a Robert Vas film, we tend to refer to an NFB film as if less personally conceived. One might think as well of the Canadian Stratford players, universally praised for the vitality of their team-work while, in the old days, boasting no stars.

There is something very Canadian in all this, something which my own Canadianness prompts me to attempt to define. There is in all these films a quality of suspended judgment, of something left open at the end, of something undecided. And if one thinks of the films of Franju, Marker or Vas, of their insistently personal quality, there is also something academic about the way the Canadian films have been conceived. There is something rather detached from the immediate pressures of existence, something rather apart.

The sharpest foil would be Humphrey Jennings and his films about the war. Jennings was a man who to a large extent had the personal quality of his films thrust upon him by the conditions of his time. He also experienced, both in his films and in his life, an immediacy of contact with his fellow men and a certainty of identity in relation to the world in which he lived. Like the poems of Wilfred Owen, Edward Thomas, and others of the First World War, the films of Humphrey Jennings sprang immediately out of his experience of the Blitz and spoke and still speak directly to all Londoners who endured it. Similarly, if on a smaller scale, in all the images of threat, demolition, and insecurity that pervade Robert Vas's early films, there is the felt presence of the Hungarian uprising that has so disrupted his life.

In contrast, the Canadian films have none of this personal urgency about them, none of the autobiographical emotional charge that we tend (I think confusedly) to equate with seriousness or sincerity in art. Yet the films of Koenig and Kroitor are the result of their Canadian experience and they are true to that. Conditions in North America, and particularly Canada, can allow a man to spend an easy, comfortable life without great physical hardship; and if he is a serious person, offer him the facilities to contemplate the Great Problems of our Age. "What is a number that a man may know it and a man that he may know a number?" is not a question that would have been in the minds of many Londoners during the Blitz or in the minds of many Hungarians in 1956. It is essentially a question for a leisured, unharassed, middle-class culture, as are the questions that the Canadians themselves ask in both THE LIVING MACHINE and UNIVERSE. It is the presence of these questions, veering constantly towards some ultimate, that give the films their abstract and slightly rhetorical air, as they give them that quality which might strike Europeans as a boyish sense of wonder.

"If you were to hover in space beyond the moon, speeding up in imagination its movement, you would see a majestic procession in the sky...." Or later on in UNIVERSE, as the camera appears to be whizzing out into the night at an enormous pace, we hear the commentator's reverential voice again saying: "If we could move with the freedom of a god so that a million years pass in a second, and if we went far enough—past the nearest suns—beyond the star clouds and nebulae, in time they would end and, as if moving out from behind a curtain, we would come to an endless sea of night." At this point in the film, we seem to shoot out into this black sea, with dim puffs of light shimmering in the distance. "In that sea are ... the galaxies." There is about this entire film a sense of awe at the immensity of its chosen subject which distinguishes it sharply, I should think, from Professor Hoyle's astronomical writings, where man is made to seem in charge of it all, conducting his investigations with confidence.

Chiefly the work of Roman Kroitor and Colin Low, UNIVERSE takes pains to establish a human frame for the vastness of its subject, starting off with the setting sun on the horizon, followed by its reflection multiplied in a number of office windows, then by its almost horizontal rays refracted across busy city streets. We then move into the David Dunlap Observatory near Toronto to see the astronomer at work —watching, photographing through the night; after our filmed celestial journey through a heaven composed of telescopic photographs and animation techniques, we return to the watchful man alone leaving his post at the observatory, this time in the light of the almost horizontal rays of the rising sun, while a church bell is heard in the distance, plus the bark of a dog and the twitter of birds—a gradual modulation back to our terrestrial life as we habitually experience it.

Wolf Koenig and Roman Kroitor seem to work in perfect unison as a team, "Roman more the shaper, the thinker; Wolf the director, the shooter", as Tom Daly explained it. To speculate from my own knowledge of their films and my first meeting with them one summer afternoon, it seems that this sense of wonder, this questioning probing about the nature of our existence, might very well come from Roman Kroitor, as well as from Colin Low; while the sharp, often ruthless observation of the idiocies of modern life, the witty juxtaposition of this absurdity to that, might more frequently be the contribution of Wolf Koenig. It is perhaps indicative that Wolf began as an animator, making his own contribution to the facetious little film designed by Unit B as long ago as 1953, the ROMANCE OF TRANSPORTATION IN CANADA; during the same year, Roman was directing what I think was his first film for the NFB, a sensitive if slightly over-indulgent observation of an aged Polish immigrant in Winnipeg, PAUL TOMKOWICZ, STREET RAILWAY SWITCHMAN—Wolf early on being concerned to startle and amuse, Roman patiently observing, anxious to understand.[1]

Speculating like this about their individual contributions, I find that Colin Low's work seems a little apart, quieter perhaps, certainly more nostalgic. He has been in charge of three films which are all re-creations of recent Canadian history and are undisguisedly autobiographical in feeling: CORRAL (1954), CITY OF GOLD (1957), and DAYS OF WHISKY GAP (1961). Although he too began as an animator, in CORRAL, though externally dealing with the breaking in of a horse on a ranch in southwest Alberta, Low is really concerned here with something else, something more inward. Beautifully shot by the ubiquitous Wolf Koenig and with an effective musical score for two guitars by Eldon Rathburn, the film seems to be a re-creation less of an actual event than of an atmosphere that has vanished. As there is to a degree in all of his films, there is here the feeling of a quietly private world, of something reflective, plus the sense of something lost. There is the atmosphere of events more deeply felt than thoroughly understood—again something that I find characteristically Canadian.

CITY OF GOLD is personal in a rather different way: here Pierre Berton narrates his boyhood memories of his early life in Dawson City, the centre of the Klondike Gold Rush in 1897. The substance of the film is a montage of still photographs depicting the excitements and hazards of that time: photographs of the girls of Paradise Alley in their Paris-imported costumes, girls who struggled northwards to be the comforts of the gold-ambitious men; an incredible photograph of a line of human beings, strung up along a 45-degree slope of sheer ice in the Chilkoot Pass in an "endless human chain". But as with UNIVERSE, it begins and ends with actuality photography, with shots which link us more closely to our own living world; and miraculously, between stills and location cinematography, there is the continuity of low-angled northern light. Derelict houses, once resplendent, are shot through stalks of waving grass; and as with the early morning sounds that punctuate the close of UNIVERSE, this slight movement serves to emphasize the stillness of the rest.

Throughout this film, too, there is a sense of wonder, this time at the limitless endeavour of man. Concerning some of the people who ventured north, Pierre Berton explains: "... after the long months on the passes and lakes and rivers, they found themselves seized by a curious mixture of feelings, not the least of which was a strange elation ... many of them never bothered to look for gold at all. It was as if somehow they had already found what they were seeking." This time co-directed by Wolf Koenig and Colin Low, with the story line supervised by Roman Kroitor, another most evocative score by Eldon Rathburn, and produced and edited by their chief, Tom Daly, CITY OF GOLD, while superficially about a gold rush, becomes an emblem of the incomprehensible motivation of man.

The National Film Board is a large organization that, since its establishment by John Grierson in 1939, has produced a great many films of real quality. In this article I have been concerned with only a handful of the products of one section of one of the units and have made no attempt to be comprehensive in my selection. The films talked about are simply those that I know best and most admire. The work of Norman McLaren has gone unmentioned, as has Arthur Lipsett's VERY NICE, VERY NICE. And even within Unit B, I have said nothing about I WAS A 90-POUND WEAKLING, an investigation into the obesity scare and health club craze of the present time. Tom Daly explained how the boys were unhappy about this film until they discovered Swami Vishnu-Devananda, who teaches yoga in Montreal. In his unself-conscious dedication to his art and creed and by the charm with which he interviews the interviewers, Swami Vishnu-Devananda gives to even this generally light-hearted and satirical film its own note of seriousness and a reference outwards to other matters.

Nor have I more than mentioned the particular feat of LONELY BOY, the best known example of Unit B's dexterity, though also the most easily misunderstood. In its minute observation of characteristic behaviour, LONELY BOY is indeed the candid documentary that Wolf and Roman wanted it to be. But at the same time, in its editorial juxtapositions, its skillful counterpointing of pictures with sound, in the odd little cut-aways that so fill this film, it acquires within its general documentary intention an almost surrealist intensity. As we hear Paul Anka explaining the necessity of his compositions, we see him silently gesturing as if in song at the Copacabana in New York, an editorial device that momentarily makes his explanations and his gestures seem unrelated and so ridiculous. As we hear him trying out a new song, "In the wee small hours of the morning... ", the filmmakers mix over the voice of his manager, Irvin Feld, explaining how he has many times discussed Paul's obligations to his talent "till the wee hours of the morning". Not only is there the coincidence of phraseology, but also the implication that Feld's management dominates Paul's musical gifts. "And this is the way I groomed him," as he earlier says. Finally, again in the Copacabana, as with self-conscious suavity Paul lights a cigarette for the owner of the club, we catch a glimpse of a chorus girl slipping furtively away, giving an odd quality of ominousness to the scene, as does the flash-bulb camera that repeatedly refuses to work in the earlier dressing-room sequence. Although all small touches, perhaps scarcely noticeable, these effects create a kind of cumulative anxiety, as if things were not all that glorious within this monied, pop-cultured world that we have been observing; as if Anka were trapped within the image of himself created by his manager for his fans, as he seems trapped in the car at the end of the film—fatigued, a bit unsteady, shut away from the world outside.

Something also scarcely noticeable in this article is the fact that the National Film Board is also L'Office national du film. But it would require another article to do justice to the work of the French-speaking units, and, indeed, another writer—someone closer to their specifically French-Canadian concerns. For with the exception of LA LUTTE (1961)—an immensely, wittily perceptive film about wrestling co-directed by four of the best-known names in the French-Canadian section: Michel Brault, Marcel Carrière, Claude Fournier and Claude Jutra—the French-speaking films seem less concerned with subjects that open out upon some world-wide interest like astronomy or pop art than they are to depict minutely some little-known aspect of French-Canadian life. "This is how we live," films such as LES RAQUETTEURS or LES BUCHERONS DE LA MANOUANE seem to be saying, "this is what all the trouble is about, for this is what we want to be allowed to develop, this is what we wish to preserve!" Films such as A SAINT HENRI, LE 5 SEPTEMBRE (1961) or the highly-praised POUR LA SUITE DU MONDE (1962), while certainly moving social documents, most lovingly observed, lack any reference outwards to the larger world beyond Quebec.

Finally, it would be wrong to end this piece without so much as mentioning the board's recent ventures into feature-film production. There have been, of course, some educational, historical re-creations such as the John Cabot film; and there has recently been a feature film actually made independently but which utilized a number of NFB men: Claude Jutra's A TOUT PRENDRE. But DRYLANDERS exists as the first NFB fictional feature film, and it has been followed by NOBODY WAVED GOODBYE, and most recently by Gilles Groulx's LE CHAT DANS LE SAC.

Although LE CHAT DANS LE SAC managed to carry off the prize in Montreal as the best Canadian feature of the year, most interesting in the context of this article is NOBODY WAVED GOODBYE. Produced by Tom Daly and Roman Kroitor and directed by Donald Owen, whose short on Toronto's Bruce Kidd, RUNNER, was shown at the seventh London Film Festival, NOBODY WAVED GOODBYE seems like a logical extension of the work of the old Unit B. It is a remarkable accomplishment and may well suggest the way that NFB productions will grow in the future. Very much in the zooming, tracking style of Unit B's television documentaries, shot on 16mm, the film registers the nuances of a teenage rebellion against the complacent affluence that the young couple see around them in Toronto. Although it is a fiction film with invented plot and characters, the actuality techniques are so persuasively handled that everything looks as if it had been caught *sur le vif*. In spite of some narrative weaknesses in the final third of the film, the dialogue and gestures are so realistically, so spontaneously evoked and are so convincingly, so familiarly Canadian, that it seems that NOBODY WAVED GOODBYE succeeds in doing what Sidney Furie tried to do all alone some eight years ago with A DANGEROUS AGE, and even, in its improvisational techniques, what John Cassavetes only partially brought off in SHADOWS.

No mean achievement, and an extraordinary flowering of a government-sponsored film unit, originally set up (as the original Film Act stated) "to interpret Canada to Canadians and to the rest of the world and to make films in the national interest". The National Film Board has moved a long way from any utilitarian interpretation of that clause.

An Interview with Terence Macartney-Filgate

Sarah Jennings

Sarah Jennings: What was your first film experience with the NFB?
Terence Macartney-Filgate: I started at the board as a scriptwriter, on sponsored films, in military training films in 1954, and learned my craft there by writing very dull scripts and, at the same time, working in the cutting rooms, going out on location as an assistant director, doing all the tremendous lot of joe-jobs that one had to do in those days. At the time I joined the board, very few people were taken in and therefore one had to do everything.

SJ: Had you done anything in film before then?

TMF: No, I always wanted to go into film. I had a varied career, I'd spent four-and-a-half years in the services during the war, and gone to the university after the war, taken a degree in economics, in politics, at Oxford and then had worked in various business occupations rather unsuccessfully and miserably. It was quite fortuitous, as I had been trying to get into the board for quite a long time and I arrived at the right day at the right time when they wanted somebody to write those sort of scripts. I had a certain amount of technical knowledge about the RCAF at that time, so that's how I started. I worked from '54 to '57 on

Reprinted from *Terence Macartney-Filgate: The Candid Eye,* edited by Charlotte Gobeil (Ottawa: Canadian Film Institute, October 1966).

sponsored films; I also wrote and directed some; others I directed, some I edited. I wrote commentaries for travel films, agricultural films, etc.

SJ: What about the Candid Eye films? What frustrations and/or stimulants caused you and the others to develop them?

TMF: At this time the board was involved in two main films, one was a television series which changed its name each year (one year they were called "On The Spot", another year they were called "The Spectre"), but essentially they were acted-out documentaries. They were written scripts with dialogues, sort of poor man's feature films. Quite often they were done in the studios. This did not interest me personally, and in '56 some "Free Cinema" films made in England were screened at the board, notably MOMMA DON'T ALLOW, which was shot in a jazz club and this was a revelation, not in its style or technique, which was nothing new, but perhaps the approach to the subject. It was shot in situ, it was lit, they had put in some lighting. There was some direction, but it was an attempt to take people in situ, as they were rather than forming them to a story—in the sense that Flaherty would take people and write a story or create a story around them and then fit these people into the story which might or might not be part of their existence. I suppose the best example would be the Aran Islanders going after a whale or a shark when they've never hunted whales or sharks in their lives. But this was an approach to reality. There were some other films of that time, including one—of course I always have to be careful about my dates—it was called THURSDAY'S CHILD by Lindsay Anderson, with deaf and dumb children, a beautiful film. And at that time I had become friendly with Wolf Koenig and Roman Kroitor who had worked for B unit, not in sponsored films. They had quite a different, freer film background than my own and we talked and kicked around various projects quite irrelevant to anything that subsequently came out. At one time the board had expressed the wish to make a film in economics and we kicked around the idea of doing a crazy science fiction film on a planet which was a sort of... you could make anything go on a planet to suit any economic fact. It could have been a weird sort of TENTH VICTIM style world. Anyway, nothing came out of that, and then we talked on and on and on and I think it was Roman who got the money for the first one which was THE DAYS BEFORE CHRISTMAS, and I went out with a cameraman, Michel Brault, to shoot, and Wolf Koenig—I can't remember if Wolf shot, but he may have directed some of the sequences. And the thing was very confused. We didn't quite know what we were doing, but we went into Montreal—it's a fascinating city—and tried to catch the spirit of what goes on in a big city just before Christmas. But without putting in the clichés or, if we dealt with the clichés—like the choirs or people in stores—we tried to deal with them like they actually were.

SJ: Did you work out a treatment, a scenario, or have any specific idea of what you wanted?

TMF: No, this was a pilot film, the money was there, and this was the first great experimentation with—well, if you want to call it direct camera or observation film or cinéma vérité. This was Christmas 1957, and I shot sync in a taxi. There's a scene in there with a cab driver talking which is, as far as I know, the first time that sync was ever shot for real in a car. The French very shortly afterwards were shooting sync sequences. This film took a long time to cut. Roman Kroitor cut it because there was a mass of footage, many good things, and it was how you structure, how you put things together—he was particularly strong in structuring films. The film looked good, the material looked good.

 The board's approach to television was becoming somewhat stale. They were perhaps looking for a new approach. They gave us some money and we sat around trying to think of a title. The title was "Candid Eye" because that seemed to describe it. It wasn't "Candid Camera", but the way we looked at things we thought it was candid because it wasn't editorialized. I then did the next one, BLOOD AND FIRE, which was on the Salvation Army and shot in three weeks. I remember Wolf Koenig shot some of it, and Georges Dufaux, and it was the first film I ever shot anything on. I shot some of the tavern sequences, the interiors. It was the first time I'd ever taken a camera in my hands, a movie camera, and used it.

SJ   It seems there were a lot of minds working on an idea....

TMF: Well, this was a sort of symbiotic relationship during the "Candid Eye" series which ran '57 and '58. This was during my time. I think it ran one more year here after I left the board. People had interchangeable jobs. I don't need to go over the particular films, but for instance in one film I might direct and Wolf might shoot for me, and in another film—I remember a thing called A COUNTRY HARVEST or COUNTRY THRESHING, I shot a great chunk of it and I shot a great chunk of the Glenn Gould film. We interchanged our jobs.

SJ: Do you think that shooting yourself also gave you a certain view of a subject? I mean, do you think that if you had been directing a cameraman you could have got the kind of results that you got by shooting it yourself, and because you were all working so closely together you understood each other much more?

TMF: Well, I will split this in two portions. One, when we were working on this series, we all knew each other's camera styles and we could put two or three cameras on situations, sometimes as many as five. And by selecting the people who were shooting we knew that it would intercut, that the styles would come up the same. So if I ever shoot with a person like Brault, Dufaux, other people who have come later at the board, Labrecque, I know their style will fit in with mine. It will all cut together. And to answer your other question, to shoot yourself, you can only rarely get what you want, but this is not always technically feasible—to shoot and direct—and therefore if you use a cameraman you must use one who in a sense sees the same things you see at the same time in the same way, without you having to tell him. It's an instinctive thing. I myself felt that what we were after was the attitude of Cartier-Bresson who presses his button one second, one micro-second before the event happens, before the fat lady laughs, or the man's tears roll down his face. It is no good pressing it afterwards. It's a question of a style of filmmaking, of looking for things like a hunter. You have to be reasonably certain that there is a tiger in the jungle and that you are going to get that tiger. The editors who were working on this series were brilliant people. There was a man called Phil Greaves, an American negro, who is now working as producer-director in the States, a wonderful editor. There was a man called John Spotton who was an ex-cameraman. Roman Kroitor himself was a brilliant editor. Jim Beveridge cut a couple of shows, and a lot were extremely good at it. I always felt that if you could find somebody better than yourself, let them do it.

SJ: You have said that you felt a divide between yourself and the others. What did you mean by that?

TMF: Well, we went on quite happily then, but there had been a tendency within the film board, within this group or section of people known as Unit B, to philosophize about films. As I have said, there are many routes to heaven; but I have a feeling they thought that there was only one route and that they knew that path. Therefore, for them to do anything specifically, Wolf and Roman and Daly, there had to be a philosophical reasoning before they did it. I am not a particularly philosophical person, therefore I work instinctively. I never know why I choose the subject for a film. I have no philosophical reason. Anyway, they wanted to philosophize and look on films as statements on man and the universe, God or nature, and these things bore me, frankly. I used to state that rather loudly, perhaps not always in very kind terms, and a certain tension started to grow up in the last years. I was an impossible person to work with, I know. Of course, if I feel other people think I am impossible, I always make sure they are correct. And it came up to the end.

The last film I did there was THE BACK-BREAKING LEAF, which nobody was keen on me doing. I wanted a cameraman to do it; I had never shot a complete film by myself. I was offered a cameraman I didn't think could get that sort of material, so I stuck my neck out and said I would do it. I had, at that time, one young assistant, Gilles Gascon, who is now a cameraman-director/ director-cameraman at the board, and Gilles and I went down to the tobacco fields and slaved away there. It was before the days of portable, really portable equipment, so it was much harder to get any sound, and I had a producer phoning me up saying the rushes were awful and weren't saying anything, which was sort of disturbing me somewhat, disturbing me greatly, and I wasn't in a good mood when I came back. Anyway, things went from bad to worse and I asked to leave the board. I took a leave of absence, I didn't resign or anything, for a year. I thought I should go out into the wide world of film and see what it was about.

I went to New York primarily because it seemed to offer more filming, work—I don't think necessarily opportunities—just to shuffle meals inside myself. They continued the Candid Eye, ending with a beautiful film on Paul Anka, LONELY BOY. I think it was the last one.

You see, there was the physical thing of—perhaps the challenge. For a long time I had been walking around the board saying that it was too cloistered and that people should be encouraged to leave and work in the outside world. I wished at that time there had been some way to be able to leave the board and come to the CBC. But the board makes you rather security-minded and therefore people are afraid to lose their pension schemes and health schemes and God knows what, paying off their wives and mortgages and children, lawnmowers and country cottages. At any rate, I said that one should leave, so eventually I thought I ought to take my own advice. I applied for a year's leave of absence. I went to New York because New York seemed a challenge. Nobody from the board had ever gone there. Well, some people may have gone down for one or two weeks but had come flying down to mother's wing again; and it just seemed a place to go. So I went to New York and I worked on PRIMARY, the *Time* film. I shot about a third of it; it was the Kennedy film. Actually, PRIMARY was shot by Leacock himself and Maysles—Al Maysles. They were trying to prove things that we'd already done at the board. They had been done two years before. And they were also trying to do things the hard way by proving you could cut films without Movieolas, just using table wheels—which struck me as perhaps slightly archaic, and so I left.

After PRIMARY was shot, I left. I don't think my name is on the credits. I think it is on the French version. I did go back to Time-Life, and I worked on some other film, an education film in the South, and I did a film on the X-15, on the pilot who was flying the X-15 then [PILOT X-15], and again I left afterwards, after completing my assignment. I hear that George Stevens Jr., who runs the USIA, called me an iconoclast. I think it was said to somebody that if I didn't have troubles or wasn't in troubles, then I could be certain to create them. I don't know if this is true or not.

SJ: But you yourself said that you do your best work in a situation of conflict.

TMF: In conflict, yes I think so. So many people misunderstand my benign nature and think conflict is a personal thing. But somehow I have to come up kicking and scratching and causing screaming and crying, and I talk far too much.

SJ: But you're not cynical in your general view of it.

TMF: No, I speak cynically, I enjoy that tremendously. I'm ironic, I suppose, and irony is not a thing that is dear to people's hearts here. Anyway, I make my own bad luck or my own evils, ills or failures. I think that if I had conducted my filmic life with more caution and perhaps better perspective, I would be in a better position than I am now. Perhaps I would have done more good films. My main feeling is it is my own fault that I haven't been able, in a sense, to put myself in a position of getting enough films that I would like to do. But then, if somebody says "What films would you like to do now?", I never know. It has to come by an osmotic process out of working in an environment with other people that I respect. I don't have to like them, but I have to think that what they are doing I like.

SJ: What are you aiming at when you are making films?

TMF: I haven't the faintest idea. It's one of my great weaknesses. I've arrived at a late stage in life without knowing really where I am going, why I'm going.

My subjects interest me, they interest me filmically; they may not be a burning passion—like the Salvation Army, you know, it's not a hobby of mine, the Salvation Army, or the shrine, or tobacco. I don't smoke, I'd given up smoking when I made the tobacco film. Actually I loathe rural areas and farms [but] the people interested me. I'm a city dweller by nature.

People are the reason I make films, because I don't like to make films particularly about things or work on idea films. Sometimes you get a film where there's an idea—it may be industrial or a corporation in the stage of evolution, justice, truth, peace—I'm not interested in those things in any way.

TMF: I want perhaps two things in film: to show people things they haven't seen before—the Salvation Army [BLOOD AND FIRE] is a good example of that—and also, when they see it they say, "My God, that's real; that's the way things are. That man is real, it's not a put-on, he's not being directed," though I do direct people a lot. This is a part of some form of reality. I'm very indistinct; I'm the worst person to talk to about reality. I'm a nebulous person.

SJ: When [Allan King] describes this point of view he tries to avoid making an intellectual interpretation of the world. He doesn't want to say how he interprets the world, but can you try to describe how you interpret the world?

TMF: No, I couldn't give you an answer. When I make a film, I look at a problem—the film-problem. If there was a film I wanted to do, I would see elements that just seem to be the things that one ought to film. It would be partly conditioned by physical circumstances—they would just seem to be the things that ought to go with this sort of film. It would not be an intellectual approach. I would think of balance in the film, sort of balancing it out. When I say balance I mean an artistic balance and dramatic balance of sequences. One needs strong sequences or connectives, but I would have no intellectual approach. To take the example of the Indian—what an Indian represents in the white man's world, or the adaptation—this does not interest me at all. I would just take it and look at the subject for real, and somehow when I'm dealing with people on film I seem to get the things out of them or have them talk about themselves quite freely. On interview material I suppose I'm a psychiatric interviewer. I don't push my own personality. I would much rather interview somebody than be interviewed, and I usually get people to say what they want to say, follow their own bent, and I guide them gently.

I am extremely weak in film structure unless I'm pushed to it—I'm not really interested. I'm a strange filmmaker, I'm not really interested in a film after I've shot it. I like spewing out films; I like thinking about the subject, I like going at it, I like getting it, I like getting great blocks of raw material and excavating it, but I lose interest after that. This is a great weakness. Funnily, I don't mind cutting other people's material, which I've had to do in some of the sponsored films. I seem to have a block on that, even though I worked as an editor for some time. Therefore when the hard business comes to sitting down and discussing the structure, my mind just goes blank and I daydream quite often. I'm not considered to be contributing my fair share. On the other hand, I think I have a good story sense. In some way I find stories or see stories that other people wouldn't understand. I did a film on the shrine—the St. Joseph's Oratory in Montreal—which nobody would touch, because I was interested in it. I like the French and everybody thought I was mad to do what they called two religious films because I had never been considered excessively religious, and I did the Salvation Army and the Oratory. But somehow something came out of those stories and people saw something in them, but I could never philosophize as to why I was doing them.

SJ: Are you influenced by any political views?

TMF: No, I have political views but they would never influence anything I did in film—or any social views. That is something I think any artist has to keep apart, as Cyril Connolly wrote in *Enemies of Promise*, how people's artistic integrity goes down the drain. He was writing during the Spanish Civil War, and I agree that people who get hung up politically can often go off the tracks, or get hung up socially.

SJ: How do you feel your work has evolved since you started the Candid Eye technique? How has it made you evolve?

TMF: Physically, mechanically, I've become a very fast cameraman and, therefore, I like to shoot things myself. I'm not so energetic as I used to feel. If I have to work through problems of lighting it makes me rather impatient sometimes, as the technicians are not as fast as I know I am myself. How has it made me evolve? I don't know if I've evolved at all.

SJ: Have your ideas evolved? Have you tried things that you wouldn't have dreamed of trying before?

TMF: No, all I think I've really done in the last few years involves technique.

SJ: In what way?

TMF: I've evolved a cinematic technique which gives me far more competence in how to go about something. But this is a technical thing. How to live dangerously with camera flairs or back-lit lights, colour in auspicious places. But this is really a technical business. Intellectually in film—I don't think I've evolved at all. I think I'm probably where I was or where I am. I don't have any feeling that I've evolved.

SJ: You say that you are in an "artistic crisis". What do you mean?

TMF: Yes, I feel that I've explored all the possibilities in documentary. I might make good or bad films, but this is largely a matter of finding good or bad subject matter. I don't think that these films would be any better in an artistic sense than anything that I've done before, and therefore I feel that I have worked this end of the—I don't want to use a McLuhan word—of the "medium", this end of this art form, or information form, as far as I can go. Therefore, I feel very much in a cul de sac. I don't know where I'm going. I've never known at any time in my life where I was going and I seem to be particularly aware of it now.

Sometimes I felt I was making many false starts, but just now I don't know in which direction I ought to turn, apart from just waiting for fate—I've often done that.

SJ: Do you think then that documentaries have reached their ultimate? That nothing further can be done in them?

TMF: No, I don't. There's a tremendous field. I think their place is in television. I think actually that the amount in television is relatively small and is largely straight TV reportage, but in straight reportage there is a very low grade of film . . . documentary has to explore emotional content. Sometimes I think documentaries that are not specifically concerned with a specific person produce an emotional content. Take NIGHTMAIL;

you never identify with any of the particular people. But I think you must think of documentaries in the context of television. It's synonymous, that's the outlet for it, and on television essentially people work, characters work, the screen is small and the way you observe it—the audio end of it—is strong, the visual end is weak, and therefore it tends to work on people. An emotional feeling can come through and does come through, if the thing is good.

SJ: What are some of your films that you like?

TMF: The two films I've done that I like best—one was the tobacco film, THE BACK-BREAKING LEAF, and the other was a film most people don't like; it's about the Salvation Army [BLOOD AND FIRE]. I don't know why I like those better than the others. They have quite different subjects, they were done in quite different conditions, but they please me more perhaps because in those films I felt that whatever my talent, I was managing to show something or get something out of the people, or to see a facet of their lives, personalities. That's all I have to say about films I like.

SJ: What do you think is the special quality in your films?

TMF: I don't know what's in my films. I often wonder if I have any real talent or if I latch onto the right circumstances. To some people, my films have always had a large element of somebody else's skills and talent in them, in growing degrees, in varying ways. I don't pretend to be the lonely filmmaker who does everything. I think that I don't even want to go out with a camera, make a film, sit and cut it, write it and do the whole thing. I think I would get bored doing that. I suppose I'm a driven personality, people would say nowadays. I don't seem to be able to settle down. I'm constantly ill-at-ease. I'm always unsure of myself.

Whenever I start a film, as soon as I take on a project, I wish I hadn't taken it. If I could only get out of it and win the Irish sweepstakes and go away. I don't want to come to the starting line. That's what I feel at the very first, whatever film I do, good-bad-or-indifferent, I don't want to do it. But, having committed myself to do it, I have to put myself in the position of committing myself and, of course, I'm hungry, I do it. I'm always committing myself to things I don't want to do. But even if I feel that it's a good subject, I suffer, then I start to shoot, and I like that, if things go well. The stuff starts to come in and other people start to like it and I've respect for other people's opinion and I'm always testing those opinions. But when it's over, I feel immensely depressed because I realize that it all should be done in another way, completely different, and that I've done all the things wrong, and I should have gotten more of this or that.... Sometimes I think I'm merely a hewer of raw material, that I have an ability to just go out and pan for gold and get enough and then it's up to the refinery and the people who make the ingots to shape it and sell it, wrap it, which are all the creative processes that I'm not in.

On the Candid-Eye Movement

Bruce Elder

It is a commonplace of the history of documentary film that at the end of the fifties there developed in the United States, France and Canada (including Quebec) a school of cinema known as cinéma-vérité. The fact that these allied movements did develop in so many different countries at one particular historical moment no doubt indicates a substantial change in the geological rockbed of cinema—a change which even today continues to affect the course of development of the cinema, turning it towards a greater realism. That all these movements, moreover, attempted to incorporate aspects of the real into the work of art and so share with certain other movements in art ("musique concrète", "objet-trouvé", "choisisme", etc.) certain common aspirations clearly must be accounted for, and the willful obscuring or neglect of these similarities could only be accomplished at the expense of understanding why the cinema took this particular course at this particular historical moment.

All of these movements shared certain features in their reaction against the aesthetic of the preceding cinema. The aesthetics which subtended the silent cinema were, for the most part, material-formalist in character; the major innovations of the heroic period of the silent cinema—the fracture of space and time, the use of rigorously formal compositions involving closed forms, the structuration of montage devices on a linguistic model, and the use of an increasingly formal narrative with the concomitant increasing alienation of the cinematic diegeses from the reality—can all be considered in these terms. All of this meant, of course, that the aesthetic value of these works depended upon the rupture between the cinematic object and reality.

During the fifties, allied with those movements in modern art mentioned above, there developed several scattered movements in cinema, the aesthetic of which rested not upon the formal categories opened up by the transcendence of reality, but rather upon the tensions which could be developed in the dialectic between artifice and nature and, more particularly, between fiction and reality.[1] The strategies which characterize the works of these schools—the photographic respect for the integrity of space and time in the use of the long take, the use of more open and less formal compositional devices, the use of non-actors and real locations—were all calculated to integrate the real into the architectonic defined by the dramatic form.[2]

Though this much can readily be admitted, the degree of attention given the similarities among the movements taking place in different countries has resulted in some extremely misleading notions. It is, of course, a commonplace to distinguish between American- and French-style cinéma-vérité, usually on the basis of the rejection of interviews in the former (but not in the latter), and the supposedly lesser degree of intervention on the part of the filmmaker in the pro-filmic event, though it seems to me the full measure of the difference between these two schools has not been fully appreciated. As for the Canadian brand of cinéma-vérité, it seems to be considered of secondary consequence and derivative of either the American or the French version. According to the usual accounts, the fact that Canada developed the style so close in time to the American and French developments reflects the degree of intimacy between Canadian cinematic culture and that of the United States and France.

The trouble with these accounts is not only that they are historically inaccurate, inasmuch as the developments in Canada actually anticipate those in the United States upon which they supposedly draw,[3] but also that the styles of cinéma-vérité developed in these countries differ radically from each other.

The work of Drew Associates, like that of the other allied schools to which we have alluded, usually exploited the tensions inherent in the dramatic form.[4] It is from this use of the dramatic form, in fact, that many of the characteristics which distinguish American cinéma-vérité from Canadian Candid-Eye cinema derive.

It has often been commented upon that the Drew films were journalistic in character inasmuch as they depended for their interest on the supposed noteworthiness of the event documented. In fact, the characteristics of the event necessary to sustain the structure on which the vast majority of the Drew films are built can be more precisely specified than this. As Mamber has pointed out,[5] typically these films are based on a contest-type situation. The fact that such a situation is constituted by a struggle between opposing forces—a struggle which by its very nature is decisive inasmuch as it is assured that one of the forces will achieve victory at the expense of another—guarantees that by conducting a simple track on the event, following contours of its external physical development and recording its key incidents, one will arrive at a work structured on the crisis-climax-resolution pattern which constitutes the basis of the dramatic form. The selection of these contest-type situations is therefore largely pragmatic; one can be sure that following such a situation over a specific period of time and recording only its external appearance will result in a workable structure which possesses a measure of dramatic intrigue.[6]

Further evidence of the dramatic quality of American-type cinéma-vérité can be found in the nature of its concern with character. The centrality of this concern is seen in the fact that the typical problematic underlying the films can be stated in the form "Will A (the protagonist) succeed in some real contest-type situation?" (e.g., will Hubert Humphrey win the Wisconsin primary? Will Eddie Sacks win in the Indianapolis 500? Will Jane Fonda's initial Broadway appearance be successful? Will Susan Starr win her piano competition?). Typically the introductions to the works in this corpus serve to elicit audience sympathy for the protagonist by showing him engaged in a contest-type situation in which he is strongly motivated to win, since something of very appreciable consequence is shown to be at stake. Thus the conflict situation is calculated to put a stress on the character. The resolution of the film, typically the aftermath of a thwarting of the protagonist's will (consider PRIMARY, EDDIE SACKS, SUSAN STARR, JANE FONDA, in all of which the protagonist fails to achieve his goal), portrays the stripping away of his illusions (defined by his ambitious goals) and the emergence of his real character.[7]

Although the sorts of tensions which characterize the dramatic form are imported into the American-type cinéma-vérité film, they are, nonetheless, profoundly altered in character; for whereas in an orthodox dramatic work, the actions of the characters are determined by a body of conceptual material which demands that in order for a certain idea to be expressed a certain piece of behaviour must occur, in a cinéma-vérité film, the parallel dialectic is transformed into one existing between a person's appearance and his real nature, between his mask and his reality. Thus, in these works, the principle of structuration has shifted from a body of conceptual material to reality.[8]

In the traditional fictional cinema, the factors affecting the articulation of the diegesis are many. If a verisimilitude of reality is desired, as it usually is in conventional cinema, its requirements will be one controlling determinant of the work; competing with this, however, will be other determining factors—those resulting from the nature of the body of conceptual material which constitutes the principle determinant of the structuration of the work and particularly the internal logic of this body of material; those resulting from the aesthetic demands of developing tension, etc. All these factors act to deflect the diegesis away from perfect verisimilitude.

In cinéma-vérité films, however, this kind of competition among determing principles is eliminated as the structure of the real event itself substitutes for the logic of the body of conceptual material as the principle of structuration of the work, at the same time guaranteeing the existence of dramatic tensions.

The issue here, then, is not simply one of creating an accurate facsimile of the real. There is a deeper ontological issue involved. The diegesis of the traditional cinema is clearly an artifice, a construct; it is only for this reason that strictly aesthetic categories can be applied when considering its articulation. The representation of the world presented in a cinéma-vérité film is not a parallel construct to the real world articulated in accordance with certain aesthetic demands; it is a trace of the real world informed by the same structural principles as the real itself.

This of course profoundly affects the nature of the filmmaker's enterprise. His task is no longer creation but rather revelation. The process of making such a work is not the forging of an imaginative construct through an act of will but rather one of allowing the forms of nature to manifest themselves through an act of attentive submission on the part of the filmmaker; the goal of art is no longer seen as that of producing beauty but rather truth—or perhaps more precisely, truth in beauty.

Having elucidated the formal structures of American-type cinéma-vérité films, we are now in a position to grasp the full measure of the difference between the English-Canadian and American versions of "direct cinema", for the history of the Candid-Eye movement can in part be written as a history of the rejection of the dramatic forms. One of the most obvious examples of this rejection occurs in THE BACK-BREAKING LEAF. The film begins by establishing a contrast between the well-to-do townspeople who own the prosperous tobacco fields and the itinerant labourers who work the fields in late summer. For a few minutes at the beginning of the film it appears that this contrast will develop dramatically into a conflict between the two groups. So strong is this suggestion that in one remarkable scene we are shown the townspeople practicing archery at their recreation centre. The camera holds for a long time on a tautly drawn bow whose very tension seems to emblemize the tensions between the two groups, while the activity of archery itself is suggestive of the hostilities between them.

The dramatic conflict which this seems to foreshadow indeed appears to be developing as we are shown the labourers in an employment office rallying against exploitative labour practices and unfair wages. This, we sense, is a decisive moment; a show-down between labour and employer is arising which will develop into a crisis-type situation.

Our expectations are thwarted, however, as a remarkable thing occurs: the conflict situation is abruptly abandoned as the film proceeds to document the manner in which tobacco is picked and dried. Indeed, the film concludes as a text on the hazardousness of the enterprise of tobacco-growing.[9]

The contrast between Koenig and Kroitor's LONELY BOY and Leacock and Pennebaker's JANE, both portraits done in 1962 of young performers at early stages in their careers, is equally illustrative of the point we are considering. Whereas the American film is based on the crisis-type situation of the opening appearance of an actress in her first major role and develops fully the dramatic potential inherent in such a situation, the Canadian film eschews any situations involving conflict, and so lacks any sense of drama whatsoever. It restricts itself to documenting the ordinary day-to-day activities of the young pop star and the factors behind his success.[10]

The reasons for the rigorous stance against the use of dramatic form on the part of the Candid-Eye filmmakers are several. Some of them are related to "end-of-ideology" ideology which was current when this style was forged; others have to do with those colonial attitudes so often found expressed in Canadian arts. But the key reason lies in the particular character of the journalism which provided the basis for the Canadian version of "direct cinema". Both the American and the Canadian versions of "direct cinema" were, as we have seen, essentially journalistic in character; the character of the journalism to which each group was committed, however, differed radically. The American-style of cinéma-vérité was, of course, developed under the auspices of Time-Life and the films themselves retained certain features of the Luce-type of journalism which those magazines practiced. Mamber, in his book *Cinéma-Vérité in America*, has demonstrated conclusively the important influence exerted by Robert Drew in the development of cinéma-vérite in the United States, documenting the important role played by Drew's concept of the "key picture"—an image of the moment in which the full drama of a situation emerges—in the formation of the American-type of cinéma-vérité. The photojournalism to which the Candid-Eye filmmakers held allegiance, on the other hand, reflects the influence of Henri Cartier-Bresson.[11]

Cartier-Bresson's approach breaks sharply with the traditions of photojournalism, including the Luce type, which prevailed at the time he began working as a photographer. Whereas earlier photojournalists were concerned with the extraordinary event (consider, for example, the subjects of Drew's "key pictures": catastrophes, the photo finish, etc.), Henri Cartier-Bresson captured in his photographs the ordinary and the unexceptional.[12]

One aspect of Cartier-Bresson's work, then, and an aspect which the Candid-Eye doubtless found important, is that it represents a forward step of the demotic tradition in photography. Photography was first called into being when acceleration in the rate of change prompted the recognition of the radical limitations of human vision; it enabled man to capture and freeze a moment within this realm of flux, preserving it for scrutiny in a way that eyesight never could.[13]

Thus, photography was forged to capture the everyday, the ordinary, that which was subject to change. Accordingly, there developed in the early days of photography a genre dealing with the street, for the locus of the acceleration in the rate of change was the city, and the central symbol of the city is the street. Soon, however, an "artistic" approach to photography was developed. In the attempt to elevate photography to the realm of art, a pictorialist style was developed which was based upon strategies in the use of texture, atmosphere, composition and framing which attempted to purge the image of its literalness and worldliness and to raise the subject matter of the photograph to the realm of the transcendental.

By the thirties, a sharp challenge to the pictorialist ambitions of art photography was being posed in the work of Walker Evans, Alfred

Steiglitz and Paul Strand. These photographers rejected the use of painterly devices and those strategies designed to elevate the subject matter of the photograph to the transcendental, and took a more literal approach to the photographic image.[14]

This conflict between the pictorialist and literalist approaches to photography rehearsed the conflict between premodernist and modernist concerns[15] in the arts inasmuch as it exemplified a struggle for a modern way of seeing which included the factual, the literal, as a part[16]—a struggle for the right of the real, the everyday, the fleeting and the momentary to occupy a legitimate position in a work of art.

Initially, however, this right was not asserted without reservation, for in the work of these photographers the real found its place only by virtue of a kind of formal appropriation in which the real was transformed to conform to certain formal aesthetic canons. The dialectic between real object and its formal transformation constitutes the major source of tension in an overwhelmingly large proportion of the works of this school.

Once the right of the real to take its place in an art object had been established, on those terms, the struggle became one to allow the real to enter the art-work more on its own terms. The first stage in this struggle was conducted primarily in the field of photojournalism. Certain photojournalists began to develop a style of documentation which precluded the necessity of the real to conform to certain formal canons, thus gaining a victory in the overthrow of those conventions exemplified in the work of Steiglitz, Strand and Evans. Their victory, however, was again qualified in that they took as their subject matter scenes from the underbelly of society. In this way they transformed the document into an image of the exotic, the strange, at times even the bizarre.[17]

Thus, although adherence to formal conventions was markedly reduced in the work of these photojournalists, new conventions arose which derived from the choice of the exotic as subject matter.[18] Full victory in the struggle for the right of the real to enter the work of art had still not been gained for it was only by conformity to certain criteria of the dramatic that the real was allowed to occupy that place.

In the photojournalism of Cartier-Bresson these tendencies towards dramatization were to a considerable degree repudiated. Cartier-Bresson's work does not treat that special class of events (e.g., the catastrophic, the photo-finish), which lent a dramatic quality to the photojournalism which preceded him. His photographs are instead drawn from the everyday. This turn away from the dramatic towards the ordinary is, however, accompanied by a renewed formal interest, for "the decisive moment" approach to photography practiced by Cartier-Bresson consists in selecting from the everyday occurrence precisely that moment in which the pictorial elements in the scene interrelate to form a rigorously composed design.[19] Thus, his works depend upon the tension arising from the dialectical relationship existing between the ordinariness of the occurrences selected for representation and the precision of the formal framework in which these occurences are represented.

In an important sense, therefore, the "decisive moment" approach in photography still rested on the sense of privilege attaching to certain selected fragments of reality by virtue of their conformity to certain formal canons. It is important to note, however, that this conformity obtains in the photographs of Cartier-Bresson in a somewhat different manner than it did in photographs of Steiglitz, Strand, Evans and Weston. In the work of this group the conformity was photographically imposed—it was obtained by using such techniques as the manipulation of depth of focus, of framing, of the control of tones in printing. Cartier-Bresson refuses to impose such a formal framework on the event;[20] rather he discovers it in the event as it runs its natural course.[21]

The Candid-Eye filmmakers in Unit B of the National Film Board followed Cartier-Bresson's lead in rejecting as object matter those special events so valued by the "direct cinema" filmmakers of the American school, and in repudiating the use of dramatic frameworks within which to represent these events. They chose, for the most part, everyday events—tobacco harvesting, the daily round of police activity, days before Christmas, the very ordinary side of the making of a popular music star—and, as did Cartier-Bresson, allowed the formal structure of the work to evolve organically out of the events themselves. Moreover, like Cartier-Bresson, the Candid-Eye filmmakers leaned towards formal rigour rather than dramatic importance in the selection of their images. It is for this reason, I believe, that the Candid-Eye films always have a more polished surface than those of their American counterparts. This refusal to impose forms in the matter being represented and the concomitant desire to allow the forms to evolve organically stem from a particular conception of the photographic image—one which holds that the particular virtue of the photographic essay lies in the character of presenting a detached and objective model of representation.[22]

In keeping with this conception of the virtues of the photographic process, the structures which the Candid-Eye group developed were observational in character; i.e., they are imitative of the acts of an observer witnessing the unfolding of a spectacle. This general character, however, was further specified by two additional conditions: first, in order to remain within the realm of the non-dramatic, the events that were chosen as object matter had to be limited to everyday events; second, in order to remain fully consistent with that quality of photography just described, the structures had to imply a radically detached, non-involved spectator who is neither physically engaged in effecting the course of action of the pro-filmic event nor intellectually active in imposing a preconceived grid on the events. Generally, the most effective sort of structure which evolved to meet these conditions was one whose progression is homologous with the process by which an outsider develops familiarity with an event, character or situation.[23]

The ideological implications of this sort of structure are revealing. The extreme sense of detachment which this suggests and which in the Candid-Eye films often passes over into a kind of self-abandonment in the face of reality implies a form of consciousness which is alienated from the world and whose sole activity is limited to passive observation —a consciousness then which plays no role in the structuring either of reality or of our perception of it. The continual rehearsal of the process of becoming familiar with the everyday things around one suggests the extreme alienation of this consciousness as it tries to come to terms with a world beyond itself. Behind this lies a view of reality which, because it is thought to be beyond the individual's control, appears as mystified and needing continually to be demystified. It is hardly surprising, for it is in keeping with the colonized outlook which all of this embodies, that the structures employed in the Candid-Eye films should suggest that the attempt of the overcoming of this alienation occurs only at a the level of cognition.

In all of this, one is reminded of Frantz Fanon's analysis of the stages of development of colonial art.[24] According to Fanon, the development of national art occurs in three stages: the phase of assimilation of the colonizer's art; a phase of the affirmation of past, native culture but articulated from an external point of view—the view of the colonizer; and finally a fighting phase in which the artist becomes an awakener of the people. The consistently national/object matter of the Candid-Eye films situate them within the second phase of Fanon's historical schema.

The benchmarks of this second phase, described by Fanon, precisely characterize the Candid-Eye work. Fanon states that this phase is characterised by an ironic sort of humour. This sense of irony arises from the dialectic inherent in the position of the artist in this period of development: on the one hand he is committed to a national culture, while on the other he views the national culture from a detached, external and hence often amused point of view. The Candid-Eye films frequently exemplify this kind of detached, ironic humour. LONELY BOY again is a case in point; the object matter is Canadian but the vantage point taken is a detached one from which the singer is ironically viewed as a kind of amusing, manufactured commodity whose appeal is that of an adolescent curiosity-piece. How far this is from the point of view taken by Leacock and Pennebaker on Jane Fonda's attempt to achieve stardom, which is seen as the stuff of real human drama.

Another contrast between the two films, explainable on Fanon's model, concerns the difference in the degree of rigour of the structures of the two works. The American work employs a very tight structure, as all the incidents of the film relate directly to that one single contest-type situation which provides the central focal point for the entire work. The Canadian film, by comparison, is extremely diffuse and episodic, presenting us with a number of incidents which purport to give us an in-depth portrayal of the man behind the star and of those forces which operate in shaping his stardom.

The effect of this lack of a central focussing event is that the incidents in the film tend to break up into a kind of shower of discrete particulars. Fanon's model would explain this in terms of the artist's grasp of historical realities at this stage in the evolution of national culture. The artist's detachment prevents him from understanding the inner workings of reality or the logic beneath the unfolding of events. As a result, he can see reality as a series of accidental occurrences, that is, only as a kind of assemblage of separate particulars. For this reason, that structure employed in the films of Drew Associates which depends upon a grasp of the homology between the dramatic form and the structure of conflicts which characterize the inner working of reality is not available to the colonized artist of this phase. His work is restricted to presenting merely the surfaces of reality. Thus, what was claimed to be the result of a meritous, willful detachment shows itself, on deeper study, to be a meretricious, alienated lack of understanding. This sort of realism surely deserves the appellation it has sometimes been given—"naive realism".

Rhythm 'n' Truths: Norman McLaren

Derek Elley

It is difficult at any one point to separate the names of Norman McLaren and the National Film Board of Canada. Yet paradoxically neither has impinged on the other's international reputation: the NFB has certainly provided the working conditions for McLaren to experiment, but in its turn the board has produced a vast output of films which, except for those from certain East European schools, bear the most instantly recognizable stamp of any film centre in the world.

In retrospect it seems more than a happy coincidence of fate that Norman McLaren grew up in the area from which John Grierson had sprung sixteen years earlier. He was born in 1914 in Stirling, Scotland, and showed no special interest in cinema as an art form until well into his teens. "As a kid I went to the movies about once a week, but that was routine, just entertainment. Later I went five days a week, because my best pal at school was the son of the owner of the three cinemas in town. We got in free. But they didn't mean a thing, movies, until I was about twenty years old. It was thanks to the Scottish Film Society Movement that, as an art student [at the Glasgow School of Art from 1932 to 1936], I

Reprinted from *Films & Filming*, June 1974.

saw things like the Russian silent classics and, incidentally, quite a number of unusual shorts. I became very excited about cinema as an art and felt that that was what I wanted to do. This tied in with some feelings I'd had before becoming an art student. When I was at high school we had a very good radio at home—radio was fairly new then—which reached all sorts of European stations; for the first time in my life I was flooded by music I'd never heard before. I would lie back, close my eyes, and listen to this music, and I couldn't help myself visualizing moving images—jumping, leaping, wobbling, squirming. The images kept moving, grouping and regrouping. This was before I had any inkling that I was interested in cinema, and I wondered how it could be done. So I sent to the local library and got two books that told about the history of colour organs, going back a few centuries about people who had experimented. I thought, 'This is it,' and went back and created a very simple sort of light machine at home. That was when I was in my mid-teens."

The preoccupations upon which McLaren was later to capitalize were already sprouting at that time: music, colour and movement. The next step was almost inevitable. "When I was twenty and saw the films, I realized this was the way to do it. I remember the excitement with which I awaited a short by Oscar Fischinger [BRAHM'S HUNGARIAN DANCE, 1931]; it was the first abstract film I ever saw—and there was my world and my dream on the screen! After seeing that, Stewart McAllistair and myself got together and started painting on film; we figured we didn't have a camera, so how could we do those things like Fishinger?" The answer for McLaren was clear; he went to a projectionist at a local cinema and scrounged a worn-out 35mm print, which they then proceeded to scrub clean until left with a reel of clear celluloid. "We started to paint meticulously about ten frames, which took us ages, and then we thought, why not slap the paint all over the films, in lengths rather than in frames. So we made not so much a film, just footage. It doesn't exist now because we screened it so much it just wore out."

Unlike many animators, McLaren has always been just as interested in extending his techniques as in deepening his subject matter. Painting directly onto celluloid—a process first used by the Australian Len Lye in the GPO short COLOUR BOX (1935)—is just one of many methods used by McLaren to realize his differing views of movement and rhythm. Famous works such as LOVE ON THE WING, HEN-HOP, BLINKITY-BLANK, FIDDLE-DE-DEE and BEGONE DULL CARE show directly drawn images of amazing profusion and inventiveness working in harmony with a musical soundtrack; the Oscar-winning NEIGHBOURS and A CHAIRY TALE use the technique of "pixillation"—moving actual people and objects at a frame-a-time to create an extraordinary sense of unreality; LE MERLE, ALOUETTE and NOW IS THE TIME (the latter also exploring 3-D) show his use of paper cut-outs; ALLEGRO, RUMBA, and DOTS his attempts to create artificial sounds by drawing on an optical soundtrack; PAS DE DEUX and BALLET ADAGIO his beautiful use of overlaid images (chronophotography) and slow motion. In short, McLaren's work is as much *about* the diverse forms of animation as it is an artistic use *of* them. Even when using humans he has a tendency to abstract and enlarge certain qualities without giving his audience the complete person—in NEIGHBOURS he makes his stars move like puppets, in A CHAIRY TALE like comical strutting Chaplins (both the chair and the live actor), and in PAS DE DEUX like the very personifications of grace and fluidity. Finding the correct materials to achieve his aims has always been a problem, especially in the matter of inks.

"In the early days we tried watercolour, but it chipped and flaked off. I remember trying shoe polish, which stained but was very messy. We tried oil point, which was very transparent but took weeks to dry. We found something, though, that worked fairly well; I don't remember what it was. And finally I found an ink made in America called Craftint Dyes—they're very good transparent dyes, but went off the market about twelve years ago."

After McLaren's first untitled effort with Stewart McAllistair, things began to move, albeit slowly. "Very luckily, at the School of Art a film production club was formed by several of the younger members of the staff. One of them had a very simple 16mm camera and the school itself had lights and a lot of space and facilities for building sets, etc. The club had about twenty members and met once a week, and we would spend several hours discussing ideas. They were all too ambitious, though; I thought they were crazy, but being one of the younger people I couldn't say a thing. Little by little over the months, members started not coming until the club was whittled down to about half-a-dozen. Then I thought, here's my chance, I'll submit a proposal for a film. It was just a paragraph."

That paragraph, with the help of McAllistair and Rory MacLean (who owned the camera), became SEVEN TILL FIVE, showing a day in the life of the Glasgow School of Art. This was submitted to the Amateur Film Festival, of which Victor Saville was judge that year (1933), and he awarded it the top prize. Cherishing its first silver cup, the film production club decided to give the filmmakers a small sum to continue their work, the result being, in McLaren's case, CAMERA MAKES WHOOPEE, a fifteen-minute exploration of stop-frame animation and trick effects. "At the same time we made a little abstract film in colour, called COLOUR COCKTAIL, to music from some ten-inch 78s. We used a turntable with several objects on it rotating at various speeds, lit in different ways and shot very out-of-focus."

The following year saw the turning-point in McLaren's Life—his all-important first contact with John Grierson, who was to be his personal cinematic magus. "Grierson came to be the judge at the Amateur Film Festival, and I submitted these two pictures thinking he would be terribly impressed by the techniques in CAMERA MAKES WHOOPEE. The other I was shamefaced about, because I knew he was interested in the social film and here was a little abstract, fanciful effort. The first one, however, he took and blasted it to hell! He mentioned it was brilliant technically, but it was a mess: it had no sense of shape, form or phrasing—nothing. He then went and gave the other little one first prize. I was dumbfounded." Grierson, as ever, had acted contrary to expectations, but more importantly, he invited McLaren to join the GPO Film Unit in the south and gain proper professional experience. In the year before taking up this offer, McLaren made a series of advertising films for a local butcher who had earlier lent him a Cine Kodak Special camera—his first taste of commissioned work. It was then, also, that he first recorded his pacifist feelings, in a fifteen-minute silent short called HELL UNLIMITED, using animation, live footage and puppets.

"A few months after I arrived at the GPO Grierson asked me if I would like to go to Spain as a cameraman for Ivor Montagu, for just less than a month, to shoot footage which Montagu would cut and screen immediately in clubs to gain funds for the Red Cross." The film was DEFENCE OF MADRID, concerning the Spanish Civil War. The GPO Unit was at that time full of people who have since become recognized as masters in their own fields, but McLaren had little artistic contact with them. "I occasionally travelled in the train with Britten from London to Blackheath (where the studios were) but it was only idle conversation. Auden I never met. And funnily, I only met Len Lye once, at a special gathering; he made his films at his own studio; not at Blackheath.

"For the first six months I worked as an assistant to Evelyn Spice in the cutting-rooms, then Cavalcanti became my producer and I was asked to make a live-action documentary on the London Telephone Directory books. So I rushed off to the British Museum to study up the history of the first telephone directory, and later wrote it all up into a script with little pictures. Cavalcanti looked at this, tore it up, and said, 'That's not going to work at all. Never write down everything precisely in advance.' I'd never written down things in Glasgow as an amateur, but somehow I'd felt that being a professional I must do this. He pointed out to me how, given a situation in a room with three or four people that you're going to cover, if you plan it all shot-for-shot on paper ahead of time, your thinking is likely to be much less imaginative than if you plan what's going to happen (and rehearse it) but not the viewpoints you're going to take. You'll find it much richer than your imagination could devise beforehand. This struck me as obvious when he said it. So Cavalcanti taught me always to beware of typed planning and leave latitude wherever possible; I'd already grown up in that way of thinking, anyway, but he had a very strong influence on me."

Finally, Cavalcanti suggested that McLaren go to the factory where they printed the directories and follow the process through from start to finish. The result was BOOK BARGAIN, his first short for the GPO Unit. In his two years there (1937-9) McLaren made three other works, the last two of which employed animation techniques. Of these, LOVE ON THE

WING is his most famous, a five-and-a-half minute colour demonstration of hand-drawn figures, publicizing the new air mail service of the time. To the music of Jacques Ibert's "Divertissement", a hen shapes and re-shapes her outline in a dazzling succession of patterns and lightning allusions. Does he now feel, looking back, that the film is rather too hectic for full appreciation? "No, in fact, I've been seeing the film a number of times during the last few weeks because we've been putting a fresh soundtrack on it (the same music). But I am surprised that things go so fast. And I know why: in that way of drawing, the image, though simple, was fairly complex for me at that time, and the natural thing for it to do was to move very fast. If it had been easier I would probably have made it considerably slower."

In 1939 McLaren made a twenty-minute short for the London Film Centre about cooking gas—THE OBEDIENT FLAME—but he was finding the atmosphere in Europe progressively uncongenial. A man of declared pacifist sympathies (most forcefully stated in his film NEIGHBOURS), he did not find attractive the prospect of spending the new few years producing war propaganda material. His leanings had also been away from straight documentary. "The war was coming, and I visualized myself doing hard-sell war propaganda films. I hated the thought of it so much that I wanted to escape, and I thought of America. I reckoned it might have opportunities; it was just a guess. In my early teens I'd been pacifist, then in my mid-teens I'd caught up with politics and joined the Communist Party in Scotland when I was sixteen. I still had an underlying streak of pacifism, though, which could conflict with my Marxist activities, and I later saw things in Spain that shattered me so much that my pacifist streak was reinforced. That was certainly a consideration in going to America."

McLaren moved to New York late in 1939, and after directing a New Year's greetings film for NBC started to experiment with hand-drawn soundtracks. This was occasioned as much by lack of expensive sound equipment as by anything else, but during the two years there (up to 1941) he certainly developed his uncanny talent for relating image to music and vice versa. Again it was Grierson who assumed the role of magus in McLaren's career: in 1941 came the contact that changed the entire course of his life. "He phoned me in New York one day and said, 'Can you come to Canada?' I knew that he was head of some new organization there and I said, 'Well, I'll have to think about it, because I'm tied up here in the middle of a film which I've just scripted and am about to shoot. It's a very long film and I don't know if the company will be able to find anyone suitable in my place.' Well, two weeks later he turned up in New York and talked to me directly. I said, 'I've got two things to ask you: when I come to Canada, what will I be doing? Hard-sell war propaganda?' He said, 'No. You just hang around.' Well! I said, 'The second one is: you'll have to arrange for me getting divorced from this company because I'm so tied up that they'd take a dim view of me leaving at this point.' He said, 'Leave that to me.' So I left him and he did it through diplomatic channels, me still being a British subject. That's how I came to Canada."

The rest is animation history, and apart from two sabbaticals abroad for UNESCO—to China in 1949 and India in 1953—McLaren has quietly worked for the National Film Board ever since. Much has been said and written, by both McLaren himself and other writers, on the various techniques employed in his films. As he is the first to admit, he has always had a struggle to balance his technical fascination with true content, and it is only in recent years that he thinks he has been truly successful. The common element in all his films is an attempt to impart rhythm and movement to inanimate and animate objects—not as obvious an ambition for an animator as might at first seem. Thousands of practitioners make drawings and objects move before our eyes, but only a handful are concerned with extracting the musical rhythm of movement from their subjects. It is here that McLaren excels, with an intuitive musical sense which clearly derives from those high school days in Stirling spent listening to the radio. The great majority of his works are directly expressed to a music soundtrack; does he agree that this was just as important a factor in his films as the concrete image? "Absolutely. In fact, in some cases probably more important than the image; that must be so for more than half of my films." And what music moves him? "That's changed with the times, but it's always been a very wide variety. I've always, until fairly recently, steered clear of any classical music, and always rationalized it by saying, 'Well, it's perfect in itself. It's been completed to be listened to as music, with nothing added, while any dance music has been made for the accompaniment of something, whether visual or tactile or mobile. Light music of any kind, background music for conversation—it's all justifiable, I would never be desecrating the music.' But then I started using classical music on one or two of my films recently—SPHERES, for example—and I realized that ballets had been composed to it for a long time, so why not me! Personally, I like music for small groups, like in France during the twenties and thirties, also military march music, folk music, folk songs, country fiddler music, and, of course, jazz. I've always had a passion for Argentinian folk and tango music, and for the past year I've been playing an awful lot of ragtime."

McLaren's images can vary from the recognizable (hens, birds) to the decorative (motifs, dots) to the abstract (washes of colour, moving patterns). FIDDLE-DE-DEE (1947) is a famous example of the latter, a three-and-a-half minute hand-painted visualization of a fiddler's rendition of "Listen to a Mocking Bird". The work is entirely abstract, and seeks to evoke a mood rather than precise images; it can be seen now as a lead-up to his masterpiece in this style—BEGONE DULL CARE (1949), a seven-and-a-half minute work co-directed with his assistant of this period, Evelyn Lambart. The same intentions had been painfully worked out in Walt Disney's FANTASIA nine years earlier—notably in the opening abstract sequence to the Bach/Stokowski "Toccata and Fugue" and the interlude with the "Soundtrack". McLaren's work is far superior, however, although it demands fine musical sensitivities in its audience. "It's the movement in the music, not particularly the instrumentation or colouration or harmony. The movement is the common denominator between the picture and the sound. Mind you, I'm very sensitive to things like dynamics; in a pianissimo passage I will reduce the contrast within the colour or the tones to a minimum, or else keep the movement very small; and vice versa with fortissimo. The thing to do is to go by instinct.

"We made BEGONE DULL CARE in shots, as it were, the shots being defined by the length of the musical phrase. We'd do maybe five or six versions, after which we'd run them on the moviola and choose the best. Some were painted as the moviola was moving, and we'd dance the brush full of paint to the rhythm of the music in the picture-gate. All the middle-section with the little white dots on black [a superb, shadowy evocation of the adagio of Oscar Peterson's score, comparable in effect to Bela Bartok's 'Night-Pieces']—that was done with a knife on black emulsion running through the moviola, going tick-tick-tick in step with the music, but running about half-speed."

At the opposite end of the scale, however, McLaren has also shown his interest in the mechanics of music with such works as CANON (1964), a ten-minute colour demonstration of the form of counterpoint in which the same melodic strand is overlaid at successive intervals without substantial alteration of its original form. Canon differs from fugue in that the former is a far more severe exercise in musical harmony, and lacks the fragmentary, self-generating power of a fugue. McLaren and Grant Munro's visual demonstration of its technique posed exceptional problems. "As a kid I studied musical theory and the violin for three years, and improvised a lot on the piano, but never had a proper formal training. I had to illustrate a big book on six musical forms (like the fugues, the sonata, the minuet, the canon) and I was asked if I would consider now doing a film. So I had learned about these classical forms enough to go ahead. I started with the canon and planned to make more, but CANON was so much trouble that I dropped the idea. We shot the picture before the music, and decided to use a man walking across and make him do every canonic device possible. Some were very difficult, like reversing in time and turning upside down, but we did it and then called the composer in. We'd done it all to a strict beat (the little man always walked to a tick on the moviola), but we should have brought the composer in much earlier to be sketching music as we planned it. He found that, although what we'd done was correct, musically it didn't make good sense often to have a reverse of a phrase which should have been four phrases to make it read clearly. It's all theoretically there, but ineptly expressed."

McLaren's own harsh judgment of CANON should not obscure the fact that it is a highly entertaining picture quite apart from its didactic element. Canon is a complex musical form, and if for some audiences the film itself becomes over-complex, it never fails to conjure up a sense of awe. The same can be said for many of McLaren's films, from LOVE ON THE WIND to RHYTHMETIC (1956), and most definitely for his two major exercises in picturing human rhythmical patterns to musical soundtracks—the legendary PAS DE DEUX (1967) and the even finer BALLET ADAGIO (1971). BALLET ADAGIO is a ten-minute film, in colour, showing the husband and wife due of David and Anna Marie Holmes executing a series of arabesques, lifts and jet—as to Albinoni's "Adagio for Organ and Strings" (a piece made famous by Orson Welles's THE TRIAL. Filmed in slow motion, with the dancers wearing a minimum of concealing clothing, it is a work of exquisite beauty, a hymn of flesh, muscle and grace which is both deeply erotic and sublimely moving. Almost perversely, its genesis was rushed, and its intentions far removed from its effect.

"The film sprang up by accident. Someone else at the board was making a film on the two dancers and I met them socially one evening. I asked them if there were many teaching films in ballet, and they said there were very few, most being for beginners. They knew of none which showed things like pas de deux or adagio work. It immediately struck me as an idea for a film to shoot them in slow motion doing some such very difficult thing to reveal it for ballet students. At the same time the slowness would lend beauty and grace to the film for the general audience. I mentioned that to them and they liked the idea, so we decided either to have something specially choreographed or choose a piece from their repertory. I decided the speed then and there—four times slower than normal—which meant that it had to be about two-and-a-half minutes long, no more. There wasn't time to have anything specially choreographed, so they arrived months later to do this with about five different adagios, which we looked at right away. The choices of camera angles and so on were dictated by the fact that they could only stay for three days. We had two cameras; one was fixed all the time, and the other without a zoom. It was all done in such a hurry—the fastest film I've ever made. Shot in three days and edited in about ten days!"

Such information speaks volumes for McLaren's intuitive skills, and is not at all apparent in the exquisite final product. "Normally a work takes about a year; PAS DE DEUX took more, because of the technical difficulties. I myself work alone on a film most of the time, though not always. On NEIGHBOURS I had Grant Munro acting in it and editing with me; on CANON, too, he did the same thing. But I don't have any unit or production assistant—although if I need anybody I can go ask for them." One major problem about slow-motion films like BALLET ADAGIO and PAS DE DEUX is linking the final soundtracks to the dancers' retarded movements. "In BALLET ADAGIO they danced to the original music that they're accustomed to—Rachmaninoff's 'Spring Waters'. I had to discard it (I didn't like the music, anyway) but I found it was pretty easy to get suitable music if the tempo and mood are right. The other things don't matter very much."

PAS DE DEUX, the more famous work of the two, employed the optical process of chronophotography, duplicating a certain movement up to eleven times in the printer with time lapses between each inception. The effect is similar to "ghosting" on television, and makes one think the blurred effect of movement has been progressively frozen en route. Running for thirteen-and-a-half minutes, in harsh black-and-white contrasts, it shows Margaret Mercier and Vincent Warren dancing to the pastoral pan-pipes of Dobre Constantin and the United Folk Orchestra of Romania. The beginning, with Mercier on her own, is dawn-like in atmosphere, and as the film progresses McLaren's techniques proliferate, the dancers' poses both mirrored and anticipated by the optical printer. "In PAS DE DEUX they danced in silence, which the dancers like because some of the ballets they do in the company for public performance are in silence. It was Maurice Blackburn [a long-time musical associate of McLaren's] who came up with the final music; he had this record at home. I had searched around and found a number of fairly suitable things, but he said, 'I think I've got the perfect record.' It was three minutes long and the film fourteen, but he said, 'Leave it to me, I'll expand it'—which he did by adding a harp. The orchestra holds a chord all the way through, except for a momentary switch to another chord, so he recorded a harp in various registers, in variations of this chord, made loops of different lengths, and fed them all into the mix system. It worked."

McLaren's trip to India in 1953 exposed him to the music of that country, and in A CHAIRY TALE (1957) he animated a live actor (Claude Jutra) and a chair in a battle for independence and domination to the music of Ravi Shankar, Chatur Lal and Modu Mullick. "From Indian music I became interested in the structure of the classical form, and found myself relying on it in the picture part of my films. It isn't a simple ABA structure; it just starts very thinly and builds and builds, becoming faster and faster. Films like MOSAIC, LINES VERTICAL and SYNCHROMY all have that shape—like Ravel's 'Bolero'. Even a work like NEIGHBOURS has pretty much that shape."

Since BALLET ADAGIO McLaren has worked as adviser on a non-commercial film for the board about the uses of the French animator Alexandre Alexeieff's pin-screen. He is currently (1974) working on a two-part, mainly didactic picture called FRAME BY FRAME, which will explain the various techniques of animation and the uses to which the art can be put. A likeable, but essentially solitary man, Norman McLaren admits to only four influences from his brother animators, Oscar Fischinger, Alexeieff, Emile Cohl and Len Lye. "I must say that no other animators have had much impact on me outside of them. I like their stuff—for instance, George Dunning's work moves me greatly—but they could never influence me." His own definition of his craft is also disarmingly straightforward: "I define animation as the art of controlling the difference between one frame and the next. You always have to make a decision how much you're going to change."

Donald Brittain: Green Stripe and Common Sense

Ronald Blumer and Susan Schouten

Documentary filmmakers in general do not tend to be household names, but even among the inner circle of those familiar with this genre, the name Donald Brittain is surprisingly unknown. While there are magazine articles and book chapters appearing on Richard Leacock, the Maysles, Allan King, Fred Wiseman and other such documentary luminaries, nothing has been written on Donald Brittain. What's strange is that here is a man who has not only made more films than most of the others (for example, in 1966 he worked on seven major films), but during his career has managed to pick up an astonishing number of awards. The list reads like a film festival atlas; Grand Prize at Leipzig, major awards at Melbourne, San Francisco, New York, Venice and the American Film Festival; twice nominated for an Academy Award, and three times winner of the Mulholland Awards as the best Canadian director. Many of the classics of the National Film Board in the last ten years, the films we tend to remember, are the work of this one man. In addition to his own films, he is frequently called in as a "film doctor", often uncredited, to salvage a film that others have made a mess of. Not surprisingly, though his public image is virtually non-existent, he is known and respected by those in the business.

"I had heard a lot about Don before coming to the board," says Les Rose, a rookie in the growing league of Brittain apprentices who inhabit the damp basement editing rooms of the NFB several floors below the bureaucrats. "Before I met him, I imagined him as some immense impressive character. He was the master at whose feet all of us could sit and learn. And then this guy walked into the room with scotch stains all over his jacket, his shirt hanging out, his hair ruffled and his glasses crookedly falling off his nose and I said to myself, 'My god, is this supposed to be the giant of documentary films?'"

Reprinted from *Cinema Canada*, no. 15 (August-September 1974).

Brittain has spent all but five years of his career making movies for the National Film Board. A large number of his films have been on television and although not many people know his name, most Canadians have seen and remember at least one of his films.

One of the most remarkable of these, MEMORANDUM, was made in 1966. Described by one reviewer as a film that yells innuendos and screams its quietness, the film is an account of a reunion of Jewish survivors of the Nazi death camps, twenty years later. Bosley Crowther, who rarely ever mentions documentaries, gave it a glowing review in the New York *Times* and it won Brittain five prizes, an Academy Award nomination and "The Lion of St. Mark", grand prize at the Venice Film Festival. Equally honoured was the film FIELDS OF SACRIFICE commissioned three years earlier by the Department of Veteran Affairs on the rather unpromising subject of "showing Canadians, young and old, how well the graves of our war dead in Europe are being maintained". Brittain took this subject, one which everyone at the board had been trying to avoid, and in the words of NFB executive producer Tom Daly, "turned it into a film that everyone wished they had made".

It is his epics that are best remembered but most Don Brittain films are just about people. His portrait of Leonard Cohen, which won an award at the American Film Festival in 1966, captured the poet's wit and love of life with an impressively deft lightness. In another film he puts us into the swimming pool of a considerably heavier subject, Lord Thomson of Fleet, a real life Mr. Magoo "who owns more newspapers than any other man in the world". Called NEVER A BACKWARD STEP it is again a profoundly telling portrait and again captured the prizes. But Brittain's most exceptional film must be BETHUNE. "Six hundred million Chinese know his name" and in 1964 Brittain introduced him to his fellow Canadians and got himself a job offer from Otto Preminger.

After a brief romance with multi-screen filmmaking here and in Japan and a stab at feature film production, "making a bunch of deals by the pool in Beverly Hills, all of which fell through", Brittain has returned as a freelancer to the National Film Board. Like some prodigious chess master, denied his game for the last couple of years, he has returned to documentary with a vengeance; ten productions last year (1975), five more coming up.

Cigarette dangling unlit from his mouth, Brittain himself comes on as a character from a 1930s movie—the unkempt sardonic newspaperman with an off-handed sense of humour, a good taste for whisky (Usher's Green Stripe, "a real bargain at $9.80 a bottle") and a passion for baseball. At work, he battles with his material often late into the night, but his sense of drama and fun surrounds him with young and enthusiastic apprentices who look up to him as "The Veteran" and consider him their best friend.

Brittain is a very unusual filmmaker in many ways. He started his career twenty years ago and made his name on films that most other filmmakers would not want to touch, sponsored documentaries by government agencies such as the Department of Labour and the Dominion Fire Commissioner. He was able to turn mediocre subjects into great films because of a basic originality; he has an ability to set things on their head and see old material from a fresh perspective. He seems to have the knack of approaching each new film with a total openness and he is not impeded, as are so many others, by a preconceived idelogy. The result is a sort of courage vis-a-vis the subject and he is not afraid to show what is happening, warts and all.

One unique aspect of Brittain's professional character is a strong desire to work with other people on a project, double teaming or sometimes even triple teaming a film. He loves the excitement and energy of people working together. Although he long ago hung up "old number 6" at Ottawa's Glebe Collegiate, the cutting room has just become another locker room complete with camaraderie and towel-snapping repartee. It is in this informal but "serious business" atmosphere that Brittain conducts his one-man film school. For the less experienced filmmaker, he is the ideal collaborator. He asks you what *you* want to do and how can *we* do it.

In terms of technique, Brittain is an unusual filmmaker partly because of his extraordinary use of commentary. For many in the medium film is seen as a visual form of expression and narration is regarded as somewhere between a cop-out and a mortal sin. Brittain sees film as an emotional medium and he is not afraid to use narration, sometimes very strong narration, to orchestrate this emotion. His writing style has that property of which other writers are so jealous, the ability to be profound in monosyllables. His editing style is equally to the point. He seems to be able to pull the right shots and telling moments out of a larger mass of material and structure them to their maximum impact. In the words of one of his editors, "When Brittain gets finished with a film, there is practically blood dripping off the Steenbeck." Many people come to films as equipment freaks; they worry about cameras, lenses, moviolas and timing lights. Others are in film because they are interested in social causes and political ideology. Somehow, "people" are often at the very bottom of the list even though they are the raw material of most documentaries. Brittain hardly knows one end of a camera from another and he is not a crusader, but he genuinely likes people, their strength and heroism, but also their frailities and eccentricities. Marrin Canell, presently researching a film with Brittain, tells about his love of details. "He sent me out to see someone lately and he wanted to know if the guy's teeth were loose or if he drank. When he deals with people, he wants to know their stature, their physical being and if you can get into their mental and moral state, even better." Essentially, it is this love of human detail—the gossip—that distinguishes Brittain as a filmmaker and makes every film he touches consummately interesting.

"I'm not particularly interested in making films for converted people on subjects which they adore. I love making films for a mass audience. To hit most people and hold their interest is not that easy to do and most people consider documentary dreary by definition. It has to do with being honest with the subject, but it also has to do with making all the curves. The moment the audience can predict what is going to happen next, you're dead. You've got to fool them, but you've got to fool them in the right way.

"I think film, essentially, is not intellectual but a totally emotional thing. Even the most straightforward documentary is all emotion if it's to be good. That's what makes it work. The pacing, the trying to find something that the audience doesn't expect but which is inevitable the moment you turn the corner. It's done with subtle things, it's the tone of someone's voice combined with a certain visual set up against something that went before. All these things make a moment work in a film and you can't just put a formula in a computer, you have to sit there in the editing room, month after month and figure it out.

"I learned filmmaking from watching other National Film Board films. I was impressed with Stanley Jackson's commentaries and the work of Unit B. Kroitor, Koenig and Daly, these were men I really respected. A film like LONELY BOY knocked me out when I first saw it, it showed me what could be done with film. But these guys, they worked! I think they used to sleep in the hallways at night. Maybe I started to feel guilty because in the early sixties I seemed to be spending most of my time playing football during working hours with the guys in distribution. You see a film like LONELY BOY and you say to yourself, 'Shit, I wouldn't mind making something half decent.'

"When I came to the film board in 1954, I was hired as a writer, but I started out as a location manager to learn the trade. Now at this time, I had hardly been out of Ottawa. As foreign correspondent for the Ottawa *Journal* (or the New York *Times* of the North, as the management liked to call it) you were lucky if you made it as far as Smiths Falls or Pembroke. I had never been on a commercial airline before and suddenly I found myself supposedly in charge of organizing things, furiously driving to Sydney to meet a plane that would be taking us to some outport of Newfoundland. Allan Wargon was the hot shot director of the film, who came straight from the design department at Eaton's. A very heavy Jew. As we were driving at night, he read to me to keep me awake and he had two books; one was the *Old Testament* and the other was *Eisenstein on Film*. I was driving along and thinking to myself, 'What the fuck have I gotten myself into?'

"When we arrived, I found myself assistant everything—soundman, PR, assistant cameraman, and so on. We sat around in the wilderness for forty-one days waiting for the cloud formations to be just right or some nonsense like that. At nights they had me building trim bins out of wood and at four in the morning they would send me out with this wind-up tape recorder to get the chirp of the Cape Breton cricket. All this for sixty-five dollars a week.

"I came back from location managing and started researching and writing scripts on various subjects. Everyone seemed to hate them and no films ever got made. I kept hearing that they were going to fire me so I kept a low profile. There was this place where you were sent, corridor 'W' in the back of the third floor. The smell of death hung over me when they informed me that my office was being moved upstairs. Seventy-five bucks a week, and I knew my days were numbered.

"Peter Jones, new director of the sponsored film unit, gave me a chance not only to write, but also to direct two films: SETTING FIRES FOR SCIENCE and WINTER BUILDING, IT CAN BE DONE. He told me to get out of town and shoot them and if they were any good then maybe I'd have a job when I came back. I made these two movies and they were pretty bad, but the sponsor liked them, so word went back to the brass and I was saved.

"At this time there was a million feet of war footage sitting in a vault in Ottawa. They kept saying that someone had to put this stuff together but no one would touch it except this guy Stanley Clish. Well he touched it and then they asked me to come and write it and be editorial supervisor. Thirteen films and a year and a half later, I had become a war expert; me, who had never seen a shot fired in anger. The CANADA AT WAR series was a utilitarian job, it had to be done and I got a great deal of credit for doing it.

"BETHUNE was never officially approved by the film board. Throughout the making of the film, they were very lukewarm because of its political implications. We had this one guy Brown, the only Canadian who had been with Bethune in China, and he was dying of cancer so we managed to get permission to film the guy. We got other interviews together and I worked on it on and off for one year. I sweated blood to put that film together and I remember the day it was finished. I walked home and stayed under the covers for twenty-four hours, my nerves were shot and I was completely wiped out. The same thing had happened in the CANADA AT WAR series. I would go to the CBC sound archives and I would listen to war material for ten hours at a stretch. When I came out of there, I didn't know where I was. With BETHUNE, I was so totally involved, that I thought I knew the guy personally.

"Around this time, I was breaking out of scripted filmmaking. I was getting fed up with my needless research that never seemed to get turned into film. Shooting equipment had gotten lighter, easier to use and less lighting was required. Also, by this time, I was getting a track record and could sell a film with just a treatment. Instead of a detailed script, I began to work on a sort of gut instinct of what the film was going to be all about. MEMORANDUM for example, started with two ideas, 'the banality of evil' thing and the fact that some Jews from Canada were going back over there. That was all I had. We just went and shot anything that looked like it would work in any way, shape or form; we started to make connections on the spot. MEMORANDUM took nine months to cut and when we finished we were left with ninety-two edited sequences we never used.

"To make a good documentary, you have to have the time and you have to have the flexibility. A lot of guys go in rigid—'I'm the director, I'm in charge and I'm going to overpower the material.' That's a terrible mistake. When you are out there shooting, you are collecting raw material and that's all. In editing, the fewer your preconceptions toward this raw material, the better. You've got to let the material work on you.

"Editing for me is positioning. A sequence which was dead in one position, becomes fresh in another. The splices are where its happening, and its all in the connections. All of a sudden, you realize that you are getting from one place to another in the right way. In editing I look for intent and emotion and the ability to perceive emotion is what separates a good filmmaker from a traffic director.

"I feel that the film board is a privileged place to work. Most people here don't appreciate it. They should all be sent into the outside world for a year to see what it's like. Ideally they should fire half the staff and start dealing with freelancers, but they can't. They are locked in a box and freelancers are regarded as a threat.

"Film board recruiting has been poor. When I came back from Japan in 1970 I really felt that the creative lifespan of this place was over. The management may have been at fault but that was not the only problem. There are a lot of people around who have brilliant minds but are very mediocre filmmakers. Some of them are wasting their lives here and its tragic that somebody at some point didn't come along and say 'forget it'. Kroitor and I used to sit around at meetings and play this game. Of the seventy-five people around us, how many people would you hire if you were setting up your own company? Maybe a dozen; and the rest just shouldn't be here. I am hard on the film board simply because it's such a fantastic place that it should be getting 100 per cent from everyone here, not its present 30 per cent. I myself am not on staff because I am essentially a very lazy person. If I got into a situation here where I could do nothing, I would do it. Greed is a great spur to creativity.

"Without my hook-up with the National Film Board, I could never have done what I did. Nowhere else could I have gotten the time or the freedom. Aside from those passing moments of suicidal despair I am really very content with what I am doing. I think of myself in a sense as a hired gun, but I must rely on others to give me the right cause."

From the Soundtrack of BETHUNE, 1964:

>An artist enters eagerly into the life of man,
>of all men.
>He becomes all men in himself.
>The function of the artist is to disturb.

His duty is to arouse the sleeper,
to shake the complacent pillars of the world.
He reminds the world of its dark ancestry,
shows the world its present,
and points the way to its new birth.
He makes uneasy the static, the set and the still.

"He considered himself a judge of the bootleg whisky that might be brought to us. He considered that it was not a fit whisky unless it could be drunk like milk. He prided himself that he could remember the taste of both—good whisky and milk."

It was well said that there is a rich man's tuberculosis and a poor man's tuberculosis. The rich man recovers; the poor man dies. This succinctly expresses the close embrace of economics and pathology.

"Madrid. We were heavily bombed today. About twelve noon. Standing in a doorway as these huge machines flew slowly overhead each one heavily loaded with bombs, I glanced up and down the street. A hush fell over the city, it was a hunted animal crouched down in the grass, quiet and apprehensive. There is no escape, so be still. In the silence of the streets the songs of the birds became startling clear in the bright winter air.

If the building you happen to be in is hit, you will be killed or wounded. If it is not hit, you will not be killed or wounded. One place is as good as another.

After the bombs fall, and you can see them falling like great black peats, there is a thunderous roar. From heaps of huddled clothes on the cobble-stones, blood begins to flow. These were once live women and children...."

From Donald Brittain's Commentary for MEMORANDUM, *1966:*

This is one of the more popular sights at the camp.
The gallows where the Poles hanged the camp commandant,
Rudolph Hess, after the war.

His father meant him to be a priest. "I have to pray and go
to church endlessly," he said later, "and do penance for the
slightest misdeed."

They worked for the SS office of Economy and Administration.
Many were family men.
They would go home in the evening
and make love to their wives.

Heinrich Himmler was proud of them. He said once—
"To have stuck it out and remained decent fellows,
This is a page of glory never to be written."

Here they come now: seventeen of them,
Late of the Auschwitz administration.
Some killed with gas and needle and club.
And some with the pointing of a finger.

Mulka, the adjutant, who kept track of things, and then
went into the export trade.

Capesius the druggist, who helped in 8,000 murders,
but said he was always polite.

Doctor Klehr who punctured hearts with a needle
and Bednarek who interrupted torture for prayer
and Wilhelm Boger, who beat men's testicles until they died.

Breitwieser, the camp disinfectant officer,
was accused of dropping the first gas capsule,
but the evidence is conflicting.

Schobert, the Gestapo representative:
"I killed no one personally," he tells the court,
and they let him go.

They rejoin the German crowd.
And who will ever know
who murdered by memorandum,
who did the filing and the typing from nine o'clock to five,
with an hour off for lunch.

And if it could happen in the fairyland of Hansel and Gretel,
and the Pied Piper of Hamelin, could it not happen anywhere?

And could it not happen anywhere,
if it could happen in the cultured land of Bach, Beethoven
and Schiller?

And how could it happen in a land of churches?
There were some martyrs it's true—
but where were the other servants of Christ?

And where were the scholars of Heidelberg?
And how could it all have started in the happy land of Bavaria?
In this, the Hofbrau House of Munich,
Adolph Hitler first laid out his program to the world.
But why should that darken the festive summer night?
A third of them are tourists,
a third were too young,
and the other third is sick and tired of the whole business.

From Brittain's Narration for FIELDS OF SACRIFICE *1963:*

The ruins of Italy speak of them...
The poppies of Flanders stand for them...
They still echo across Vimy ridge
The flatlands of the Dutch can hear them...
They are ghosts on the shores of France
    They haunt the sea of Normandy,
    They have left their scars on the soil of Picardy,
They are remembered by the sand...
They live in the minds of old men who still travel
the roads of the Somme;
    They are the dead
    The Canadian dead of the two wars.
A hundred thousand of them.

The Commonwealth Memorial at Runnymede
On it, along with the others, the names of three thousand
Canadian airmen
who disappeared forever in the sky.

Memories over the gentle green heart of England...
Memories in the searing brown heart of Sicily.
Canadians moved through this cruel and alien land
Once in a burning July.
    The old people remember,
    They had been starving and they were fed
    And they heard stirring sounds of strange music
    And they will tell the children.

An episode to be passed down
Now a part of the Sicilian legend of death
A part of the ancient land of blood.

From Brittain's Narration for Ferguson Jenkins, KING OF THE HILL, *1974:*

    Chewing tobacco is part of the baseball ritual.
    In the old days everyone did it
    Whether they liked it or not.

    Today there are only eighty-six major league managers, players
    and umpires who chew tobacco...
    and most of them mix it with bubble gum to kill the taste.

    The ivy covered walls of Wrigley Field in Chicago have presented
    problems. When Lou Nabokov, the mad Russian, played centre
    field, he
        refused
    to go near the wall for fear he might be allergic to the vine.

As this limited his effectiveness as an outfielder,
the manager tried to alleviate Nabokov's fear by tearing down a portion of the vine and eating it.
Nabokov was unconvinced and continued to ignore long fly balls.

Challenge for Change

Patrick Watson

In a way this story is a continuation of one that began in *artscanada* three months ago under the title "Grass Roots Art". This time the art is film. If sometimes there is more matter and less art that's really no matter. Grass roots film as the National Film Board practices it in the board's three-year-old Challenge for Change program is a way of helping people to move themselves from bad spaces into good spaces—psychic, social or material; whether that is accomplished with cunning matched dissolves and eight-channel soundtrack mixes is secondary to the objectives of this program. Its purpose is not the seduction of the eye and the ear. It is the enlargement of eye, ear and voice, through the film as an instrument for helping people in trouble get out of it.

Get *themselves* out of it. A key qualification. People have long been using film to explore, reveal, guide and provoke in order to accelerate social change. Ask Leni Riefenstahl. About the time that Mao Tse-tung was declaring that "art must serve socialism", John Grierson who started the NFB was declaring that the purpose of documentary film was to reveal social ills so that they might be corrected. Grierson set himself apart from Flaherty, the more pure artist, who simply wanted to use film as a way of knowing.

The Challenge for Change people are on Grierson's side. This doesn't mean they don't give a damn for craft, for technique, for cunning and artistry and handsome pictures and imaginative sound. But if they are the kind of people who are too busy pursuing their main objectives to be distracted by the grade-eight-social-studies-textbook sound of the name of their program, they aren't about to throw away a badly framed shot if it contains vital actions or words.

George Stoney, the executive producer of the program, and Colin Low who with John Kemeny got it rolling in the first place, disagree somewhat about this. For Low the visual elegance of film is expendable when the main purpose is to provide a means of expression for a voiceless community; for Stoney visual power is never expendable, even though it

Reprinted from *artscanada*, April 1970.

may be, in a sense, secondary. If you are using film you are using pictures, and they ought to be good pictures, particularly if they are to be seen by people who are not involved in making the film, Stoney says, unengaged people whom you wish to engage with the film.

But to come back to Grierson, and the purpose of film: the Challenge for Change producers and directors are on Grierson's side in wanting to use film for social improvement. Where they part company with Grierson and indeed with most filmmakers who ever were is that instead of doing it *to* the people they are trying to do it *with* the people.

"Filmmakers are used to playing God," says George Stoney, the executive producer. "Now we're saying to them, 'Let the people tell you what *they* want in a film. Listen to them. The film is going to be *their* film.' And this is tough stuff for the traditional producer or director, who looks on the finished film as *his* signed work, and his reason for existence."

It all began in Newfoundland.

Well it didn't *all* begin in Newfoundland; that's just one of the rhythm-breaking categorical sentences that writers like to use for change of pace. Perhaps the first NFB films to really involve a community in practical decisions about the contents and style of films about their lives were the Fogo Island films that Colin Low showed us during the Expo summer —the first that elaborated clearly the principle of taking equipment and film and technical skill to a people whose problem was at least in part communication with each other and communication with those who governed them, and saying, "Here. Use this."

Now the film board had by then established a long and honorable tradition of taking the camera into a troubled situation to help both those within and without look for the avenues of change.

Films such as WHO WILL TEACH OUR CHILDREN?, GRIEVANCE, STRIKE, have run through countless Canadian projectors helping audiences to find themselves in the puzzle picture and gain some practical insights while doing it.

So it's more accurate to say It all began long ago, than to say It all began in Newfoundland.

However, damn accuracy. The present is now more pertinent than the past, even though the past quite clearly brought it forth. Stick with Newfoundland for the present. Here on Fogo Island in the summer of 1967 a National Film Board crew headed by Colin Low shot twenty hours of film in which the people of this terribly depressed island discussed the hopelessness of their situation, the pressures to get off the island, their sense of despair at the apparent fact that the only life they wanted to live—that of the fisherman and the fishing community—just wouldn't work economically any more. The films were shot with the guidance and the co-operation of the people themselves. The footage was matched with sound for screening in co-operation with their "subjects" (and the quotation marks simply mean that in this approach to film for social change the distinction between filmmaker and subject begins to blur). When the people gathered to see themselves and their neighbours in the movies, they discovered a communion of concern and experience that they had not known about before.

"Our role was to facilitate communication between individuals and between communities and to assist in transferring information from one segment of the community to another."

The entire community was involved in the process. They selected the topics to be discussed and made editorial decisions. No hidden camera techniques were used. People talked to the camera and in a sense came to "use" the camera by suggesting locations and "actors" and topics. As important as anything else, they decided whether the films should be distributed and where: whether they should be seen only in the community that made them, or in other communities on the island, or in St. John's by the Memorial University people (who played a vital role in getting the Fogo experiment started) or by government officials.

Sometimes there was opposition. The clergyman in whose church a screening was held to a hugely appreciative audience, got up afterwards and said he would forbid the films being shown off the island, since their purpose was clearly to hold the Fogo Islanders up to public ridicule.

Not all the twenty-eight Fogo films were problem films. The screenings often began with entertainment films: an old folk-singer, a wedding party, a party with music and dancing. There were warm, unthreatening ways of bringing people together. But the discussion of the problem films that followed revealed divisions in the communities that people simply had not been able to deal with.

The Improvement Committee discovered to its astonishment and dismay that many people thought of them as a strange group that met at the motel and drank beer in secret. Differences emerged between the old fishermen and the young ones. The welfare system, which supported many of the islanders, came under open attack.

The island was being opened up by film. And no one was exploited in the process.

Contrast: THE THINGS I CANNOT CHANGE, a sensitive anguishing film about a poor family, made at the board by Tanya Ballantyne and shown on the CBC a few years ago. When the film was telecast, the family was embarrassed. They had not been warned that it was about to appear. Suddenly the kids were being ridiculed in school, the father accosted on the street and in the local stores, the mother humiliated by whispered and open comments.

How do you handle that? The family had co-operated in making the film. If they had been consulted in advance of telecast they might have objected to embarrassing scenes, such as the father getting into a brawl in the street. Is embarrassment perhaps the human price that has to be paid in order to communicate to an indifferent world?

Challenge for Change says no. George Stoney, examining THE THINGS I CANNOT CHANGE trouble, said this:

"What should have happened—the film should've been screened for the family, in their apartment, privately, with just a few of the crew around. All the response would be sympathetic and understanding. Then, with the family itself doing the inviting and deciding who should come, it could've been screened at the church, at any group where the family had connections and where people would start from a friendly base, and where everybody could see that they were doing something, involved in something important. Gee, they're going to be on TV! All this would be done before the film was actually finished. Then if they wanted changes you could make 'em. And you might even improve your film. I don't think you'd've had to change a single frame; but you would've made it possible for the message to get out without embarrassing or hurting the family if only you'd given them a chance to be involved through the pre-screenings."

While the English half of the board was giving birth to Challenge for Change, the French unit was developing its own Société nouvelle; and the first film that I saw in this series was LA P'TITE BOURGOGNE, a film made with the residents of a community that planners had decided to "renew" without involving the people who lived there.

Through the intervention of the NFB crews, the planners and the residents were brought together, and the development was enabled to take account of the real interests and needs and desires of the residents. But before the residents and the planners could meet, the residents themselves had to get together, and the making of the film was their instrument for doing so.

The most recent production of the French unit that I have seen is called TOUT LE TEMPS, TOUT LE TEMPS, TOUT LE TEMPS, a dramatic feature by the well-known Montreal director Fernand Dansereau. A dramatic feature? How do you carry the participatory idea of filmmaking into the feature mode? Obvious: have the actors invent the scenario. What good is that going to do for people in trouble? Easy: they are the actors.

I was introduced to Dansereau's film somewhat sketchily by someone who hadn't actually seen it. Dialect makes it a difficult film for an English Canadian and maybe even for some French Canadians. I would have foundered without the help of Don Duprey, an NFB distribution officer, who sat in on the screening. He comes from Winnipeg where, as Larry Zolf keeps pointing out, they understand everything.

The film opens with a family reunion in a farm house not far from Montreal, where one of the sons has brought home the girl he intends to marry and another has come burdened with despair about everything in life ranging from his once-again pregnant wife to his unemployability to his actual beer-soaked inability to stay on his feet through the dancing.

As I watched the action unroll and admired the unself-consciousness of the actors I concluded that the crew must have spent a good deal of time with the family to be able to shoot amongst them so unobtrusively. And I began to wonder where the fictional element was; it was all too natural, and absolutely credible. I have been told that this was Dansereau's experiment at doing a fictional film with real people. I couldn't find the fiction. Maybe the fiancée was a fiction. Maybe Polydor's unemployment was a fiction, though that was hard to believe.

At the end, when the credits rolled, it became clear. This family—poor sodden Polydor with his marvellous big-eyed wife; solid, generous Grandfather; Chamber-of-Commerce-people-should-pull-themselves-up-by-the-bootstraps-like-I-did uncle; all the dark-eyed kids—they weren't a family at all! They were members of a community group. In collaboration with the filmmaker and the social animator, they were putting themselves and their neuroses into a family situation, where the dramatization of roles and of tensions produced clarity and communication in a new dimension; but not only for themselves. In this case they approached archetypes, and my guess is that TOUT LE TEMPS will be entertaining (for it is a funny and affectionate film, too) and enlightening Quebeckers for a long time to come.

It is one thing to have people participate in planning and even shooting a film about their lives, quite another to involve them in the editing process. The cutting room is the director's study, his lab, his creative crucible, his sanctuary from all of the world's distractions, the place where the film comes to be. That's where the signature is written on the film; where the pieces are put together, the rhythm polished, the illusions guaranteed, the personal artistry of the filmmaker lovingly enlaced with the rolls of celluloid.

Now the logical extension of everything implied in LA P'TITE BOURGOGNE, in FOGO, in the films of the Indian unit (which I'm coming to), in the principle of using film as an instrument of expression and an instrument of social change for the people who need the change, is that the aforesaid people be involved in the editing too. A really terrible thought for most filmmakers. Editing is the apex of the craft. It is almost a mystery. And yet the NFB participatory theme is invading that cutting room.

In the case of TOUT LE TEMPS the group members, understanding that editing is a highly specialized craft, were content to have it done by the editor and the director, so long as they were consulted along the way, had approval of everything that was done, saw the cutting copy when it was ready for printing and thus in fact ruled the result of the edit, though they did not in fact handle the film itself. Ceding authority over the edit is revolutionary; it requires a curious submission of the director's ego. And the process is already going beyond what I've just described. In at least one project, equipment for screening rushes and for editing have been taken into the community itself so that the participants can keep a running watch on the development of the project.

Willie Dunn said to me one day at the board, "If the NFB has an English unit and a French unit, then it ought to have an Indian unit too and we ought to have our own budgets and decide on our own projects and evaluate them." The NFB has an Indian unit and Willie Dunn is a member of it. I had been looking at his film THE BALLAD OF CROWFOOT. Before he came to the NFB Willie Dunn made his living playing the guitar and singing songs of his own creation. His song about Crowfoot, the legendary prairie chief, has a strong historical anger like that of Buffy Ste. Marie's "My Country 'tis of Thy People You're Dying". It is the soundtrack of the film. The visuals are mostly archival graphics and etchings. Willie has never made a film before. Working in collaboration with skilled NFB technicians he directed (and he really directed it: spend three minutes with Willie Dunn and you know you're with a Director) a powerful document with harsh but brilliant camera movement across the still pictures and an overall effect of challenge. There are some films made about Indians, by white men; few of them are worth anything. The NFB has made a few that were perceptive and honest; most have been crap. John Kemeny, the program's first producer, knew this; that's why he arranged with the Company of Young Canadians for a group of Indian volunteers to start the Indian film unit. Indians should make films about Indians. Now Dunn and his colleagues Noel StarBlanket, Mike Mitchell and others are talking about getting detached from "Challenge for Change" and having complete autonomy, or as much as any other unit in the board. They'll probably get it, though there's some doubt that they are ready for it yet. Only one way to find out. In the meantime, though they haven't made many films yet, they're agitating effectively, and learning the craft, and have played a large role in the making of a near-perfect cinéma-vérité document called YOU ARE ON INDIAN LAND.

YOU ARE ON INDIAN LAND records the closing of the bridge on Cornwall Island last December (1969). The international bridge, and its feeder roads, run through the Saint Regis reservation and were built, says the Indian narrator, without permission from the Indians on the reserve and without even consulting them. When they closed it the mass media managed to communicate to the world that there had been a lot of violence and that Kahn-Tineta Horn had been responsible for the demonstration. Neither point is true. The Indian unit's film simply takes you through the experience of that bitterly cold day, allowing you to see that almost everyone behaved humanely, that the injustice committed against the Indians was ancient in its origins and humiliating in its persistence.

The Indians had called the board for a crew when the blockade got organized, and although it usually takes days to organize a crew at NFB, Stoney got one together in a few hours and down to Cornwall the same night. It was Christmas when they came to sync the rushes and all the white people at the board were, traditionally, into the sauce. The Indians had to do the syncing themselves because the whites were too drunk. After ten screenings on the reservation had united the Mohawks, they arranged screenings for the RCMP, the Cornwall Police, the City administration and representatives from Indian Affairs. Mike Mitchell, of the blockade, said it was the first time these people had ever sat down together with the Saint Regis Indians.

There was some effort made by Ottawa to suppress the film. It is perfectly clear that if Indians across Canada were to see it they would have much more confidence in their own ability to act instead of just sitting around and rotting. The results have not been quick enough to suit the Saint Regis Indians, and while whites in Cornwall are using the film to try to persuade Ottawa to act, it is increasingly difficult to get local Indians to come to the screening. They are too cynical about Ottawa. The answer, however, is not that the film was a failure, but that there should be more like it, both to awaken the white world and officialdom and to help Indians gain confidence in themselves.

Sixteen-millimetre film is an expensive medium. The advent of cheap, portable half-inch videotape gear promoted by enthusiastic salesmen has propelled many groups into the homemade television kick with little idea of what to do with the equipment once they've acquired it. Like kids on Christmas morning with a pair of walkie-talkies. Out into the snow, down to opposite ends of the block, turn on the sets.

"Can you hear me?"

"Yeah, geeze, hear you great. Can you hear me?"

"Sure can. They really work cool, eh?"

"Terrific. I can hear you great."

"Me too. Uhhh...."

"Uhhhh...."

"What'll we say?"

The film board is showing them what to say with tape. VTR for social change makes even more sense than film; it is easier to handle, there is no delay for processing, and the tapes can be re-used. The Challenge for Change gang are heavily into VTR and have made an exciting film of VTR being used in the welfare-ridden community of St. Jacques, to help in the work of a Citizens' Association.

Out into the streets with the portopak camera and recorder. The operators are two young women who live in the area. They know what it's like; and they're not out to exploit anyone. People trust them. Out into the cold streets, stop in front of the welfare office. A guy is coming out.

"Hi. You on welfare?"

"Sure. Just got out of jail."

"How's it going?"

"Not so good."

And he recounts his difficulty in getting a job or keeping a family together or getting decent medical help. And after a while, "Hey, would you like to see yourself on this TV tape we made?"

"Well, yes, I would."

"Okay. Come on over to the parish hall Wednesday night at eight o'clock. We're gonna run it."

So on Wednesday night all the people who have been stopped in the streets by their VTR-wielding neighbours show up to have a good laugh, and stay to join a Citizens' Association. And then a community medical clinic, shown in a film that tells so much about crossing barriers of class and language and ignorance and fear that it made me want to stand up and cheer. These St. Jacques films, quite by the way, are the work of a young American woman, Bonnie Klein, who has become bilingual while working on them. So has her husband: he's a doctor in the clinic; all his patients speak French.

These are very subversive things the film board is up to here. They say to everyone around, Yes you CAN—and we'll help you.

And the really astonishing things is that they are receiving government support; in a time when the NFB is losing many good staff to the current Trudeau austerity drive, the "Challenge" budget is secure. In the Mackenzie River Delta, Northern Affairs officials have bought VTR equipment and are hiring a community development officer to work with native people using this equipment to help them demand their rights. An Indian filmmaker trained at NFB will probably work with him. Are these officials insane?

When UP AGAINST THE SYSTEM was shown to welfare officials in Washington, D.C., they were stunned. "Does the government know you're doing this sort of thing?" they asked. "How long do you think you can get away with it?"

"Quite long," is George Stoney's answer. A tall, soft-spoken Southerner here to work at the board for a two-year stint that has about five months to run, Stoney finds Canadian government officials more mature and secure than the Americans he is used to dealing with, and believes that Canadians understand the idea of government-sponsored subversion. It is an intelligent way to mobilize social revolution without violence.

Hardline revolutionaries will hate it. They say it "co-opts" the revolutionary, defeating him by absorption. Sometimes it seems that the hardliner would prefer to see change delayed if it can't be accomplished by drastic means. Putting the tools of change into people's hands is drastic only in a subtle way. Nobody gets killed. But it does constitute what these filmmaking social activists call "decentralizing the power of propaganda". Another way of saying that is, once the dispossessed and the powerless have access to the means of information they can no longer be misled by Establishment bullshit.

And that is in itself a revolution.

What Challenge? What Change?

Marie Kurchak

The way Sydney Newman, the effervescent seventh director of Canada's National Film Board tells it, the Challenge for Change/Société nouvelle program has brought the NFB back to first principles.

The story goes like this: The first aim of the NFB when it was established in 1939 was to use film to rouse the Canadian people to win the war; its next aim was to win the peace by using educational films to help reintegrate servicemen into civilian life. The pattern of clarifying and mirroring issues of concern to Canadians was set by the NFB's founder and first director, the late John Grierson.

During the fifties and early sixties the films became more beautiful but, according to Newman, "lost the sharp edge of involvement and commitment to people's needs". Production was following its own internal creative logic; and the distribution arm, which once provided feedback on audience needs and reactions, was no longer performing this function.

Enter Challenge for Change in 1967 and its French counterpart, Société nouvelle, in 1969. Experimental in nature (it is slated to end April 1975, according to the original mandate), it was billed as a program designed to "improve communications, create greater understanding, promote new ideas and provoke social change". And, while they were at it, to help eradicate the causes of poverty.

Challenge for Change/Société nouvelle is presently run by an interdepartmental committee comprised of seven federal government departments, who chip in half of the 1.8 million-dollar budget, and the National Film Board, which provides the other half. The idea was that the government departments involved would initiate projects, and perhaps think about film and the film board as more than just the public relations arm of their own departments.

Projects, however, are rarely proposed by the government departments, though the interdepartmental committee must approve each project as it comes up and may withhold funding since it holds the purse. If the committee disagrees on a project it can send it to the Privy Council or the Cabinet for arbitration.

Few projects have been rejected. There is only one recent example: Société nouvelle's proposed series of films about militant groups within Quebec trade unions. The committee turned it down because, they said, the "scenario did not match the research they had done". Militant groups in Quebec are separatist. Spreading their propaganda through film is an obviously political act. One interdepartmental committee-member confessed that the project was indeed turned down for political reasons.

Reprinted from *Take One*, vol. 4, no. 1 (September-October 1972).

Newman: "The committee has a general wisdom... well, let's just say that I'm not aware of any film that has shaken any fundamental institutions." The new war that the film board was battling to win was going to be fought through long-term strategies of cultural and attitudinal change. The camera (both film and videotape) was to be a delicate surgical instrument, not a weapon.

Challenge for Change/Société nouvelle in fact began after the U.S. War on Poverty hit Canadian government hearts, when the Privy Council asked the NFB to do a film that would help people to understand poverty. So young, sensitive filmmaker Tanya Ballantyne made THE THINGS I CANNOT CHANGE, a cinéma vérité film about a poor Montreal family with ten children.

You can't see the picture when you are inside the frame. —Anon.

The films made since have fallen into two categories according to techniques used in production and distribution. One technique is to take a social issue or event or personality and make an animated short such as the award-winning CITIZEN HAROLD (about the perils and joys of citizen participation) or a documentary such as THE THINGS I CANNOT CHANGE. The hope is that the film will close gaps in understanding, provoke discussion by focussing on issues, and cause attitudinal change.

The problem with social documentaries such as THE THINGS I CANNOT CHANGE is that they can be exploitative. The filmmaker may with great sensitivity go about the act of exploring a family's misery, but when the lights are gone the misery remains. It may even be added to: after THE THINGS I CANNOT CHANGE was aired on CBC TV, the family was exposed to the teasing and mocking of its neighbours. This could have been avoided had the family been involved in some pre-screenings with invited neighbours and friends, and if they had had the opportunity to cut out of the film what was embarrassing to them. To its credit, the NFB learned from this experience. Since then, all Challenge for Change films have gone through a test screening process before completion.

But there remains a problem. What the filmmaker has presented is her private vision, packaged in celluloid. The family's isolation is reinforced as the filmmaker impotently withdraws the camera and hopes the message will reach someone "in a position to do something about it". The Challenge for Change answer to this, and one that has made the program known throughout the world, has come to be known as "the Fogo process"; a process in which the filmmaker is as much a community development worker as a filmmaker.

The ethic is not to convince a family or a community that they will be doing society a favour by exposing their most intimate values. Instead the filmmaker uses film as an instrument of inter- or intra-community awareness in order to help people find their strengths as a community, not to reinforce their isolation. The filmmaker must go beyond his "rights" as an artist: he must be concerned with a "process" not just a "product".

The first such experiment involved Challenge for Change filmmaker Colin Low in a joint venture with Memorial University of Newfoundland. Low had insisted on a guarantee—from some neutral institution—for long-term commitment to the region where he hoped to undertake a pilot project in community film: Fogo Island, a fishing community off the north-east coast of Newfoundland.

The 5,000 inhabitants of the rocky island of Fogo live in ten outport communities such as Joe Batt's Arm, Seldom Come By, Tilting and Fogo. Sixty per cent of the people were on welfare. Fishing methods were antiquated and marketing and development organization nonexistent. There was also a severe lack of communication among islanders caused by distance, religious factionalism and just plain hopelessness.

At the same time, the Newfoundland government was about to formulate a policy in the area which could have the effect of relocating many of the people. Fred Earle, a Memorial University community development worker, had been working to organize the islanders and had helped form a development committee. The area was just right for the Challenge for Change experiment in *mediated* intervention.

Filmmaker Low began to develop his influential "process". He shot twenty hours of footage oriented around several personalities and events. He screened the film, unedited, for the participants and asked them to approve screenings to other members of the community. They had the option of cutting out film they might later regret.

Low then made a series of short films (which he called "vertical" films) each about a single personality or event. The films (JIM DECKER BUILDS A LONGLINER; THE SONGS OF CHRIS COBB; FISHERMAN'S MEETING; THE CHILDREN OF FOGO ISLAND; BILLY CRANE MOVES AWAY) were screened for groups all over the island. They worked as catalysts to a discussion of mutual problems, allowing people who may have been reluctant to speak in public to let their films speak for them. They also acted as something external which mediated the hostility that might have erupted in face-to-face confrontation among people with opposing views.

One of the members of the film team remarked that in a "horizontal" documentary intercutting of opinions immediately creates a right/wrong hierarchy which tends to put down some members of the community. The goal of trying to get people to talk to each other is then impeded.

With the permission of the islanders, the films were shown to the official decision-makers whose comments were recorded for the islanders.

The people of the island are said to have found new hope in collective action toward self improvement and new confidence vis-à-vis government. The government altered its plans for relocating people and changed a law stipulating the dimensions of longliners (boats) which didn't conform to the needs of the fishermen. The islanders also started a fishing co-op and marketing board.

Whether the changes would have transpired without the aid of film no one can say. Evaluation has been very difficult. Roger Hart (a Challenge for Change filmmaker who returned to Fogo four years later to make MEMO FROM FOGO) says, "You can hate a film, but it can still have some effect on you, even six months later."

The filmmakers are convinced they helped break some habits of noncommunication and apathy and helped the people define some of their problems. But Hart suggests that at this point they are in trouble. The fisheries co-op and marketing board isn't doing well; the leaders, who were put on a pedestal through the films, didn't in fact have enough skill in the type of leadership needed. The Memorial University Extension Department has had to come to the rescue again by sending in fisheries expert and community organizer Ian Strachan.

As for the reaction of the Newfoundland government, the presence of Memorial University as co-producer and advocate might have had as much influence as the films which may only have provided the convincing emotional arguments.

The technique of using film as a catalyst, mirror, and third party mediator has been used since the Fogo experiment from the Mississippi Delta to Alaska. In some cases half-inch video (VTR) has been used in place of, or in conjunction with, film.

> *People more frequently act their way into a new way of thinking than think their way into a new way of acting.* —Anon.

The problem with a new technique is that it can be seized as a panacea for all kinds of problems, as if the answer lay inside the Arri or the Sony. Perhaps to some extent it does, if the mere presence of the equipment distracts people into doing *something*. Most of us would prefer to believe that the key in any social use of film is a sensitive filmmaker who can get people to open up about the things that concern them. He may use other techniques even before the camera enters the picture. The NFB's Léonard Forest used fiction as a catalyst in Acadian northeastern New Brunswick. He inspired the people of the community to write and act out a feature-length fiction which turned out to be a strong film about politics and manipulation called LA NOCE N'EST PAS FINIE.

Since Challenge for Change uses VTR as well as film, the relative merits of each have been debated. VTR, it is argued, is cheaper, more portable, requires no middle men, is not as intrusive since lighting isn't needed, and playback is immediate. Film, on the other hand, is said to be more effective in encouraging subtle cognitive and attitudinal changes. More planning takes place around it because it has a greater mystique. The processing time also gives people a chance to reflect on their words. And when it comes to target audiences, it is easier for a bureaucrat or decision-maker to watch a well cut film than a shaky little videotape. (The portapack VTR equipment used is primitive as a technique. It is essentially a toy which was never intended by its manufacturers to be put to such uses. It is estimated that 1,000 of them are being used for various purposes in Quebec alone.)

VTR, however, is much more widely used than film as an organizational device. People gain confidence by watching themselves do the kind of things they thought only people in power could do. The Parallel Institute of Montreal has used videotape to help a group of poor people confront welfare authorities. The first thing the instrument does is deflect energy: the authority is likely to say, "Get that camera out of my office" and then listen to the people, rather than saying, "Get those people out of my office." Also, if a larger group of people is being represented by the few in the office, a videotape recording lets the group see what happened inside. If the strategies used weren't very effective, the group also gets a chance to analyze them.

As well as film production and social animation using film, Challenge for Change/Société nouvelle is involved in another area that could broadly be described as "community communications". Although this section has commanded only slight more than 10 per cent of the budget, it has provided seed money, VTR equipment and training to several "community communications" resource groups. Generally what is meant by the term is access—by citizens' groups and people who normally have no means of approach to the established media—to a newer, simpler set of communications tools (such as cable TV, VTR, super-8), the uses of which are just being explored.

Challenge for Change/Société nouvelle became earth mother to many groups whose orientation ranged from cultural (Videographe in Montreal) to militant (the Parallel Institute in Montreal, for whom VTR is a "weapon"). Others included Metro Media of Vancouver, Teled of Halifax, the now-defunct Town Talk of Thunder Bay and Wired World of Kitchener—a group that tried VTR and decided to scrap it in favour of radio only. (Teled also discovered that radio and sometimes print were just as effective for the work they wanted to do, especially as they were less cumbersome.)

At first, assistance from Challenge for Change meant money and equipment to the media-resource-for-the-community groups to enable them to produce programs for the local cable TV outlets. The participants soon discovered, however, that banging out programs every week was short-circuiting energies needed for long-term social change commitments. Not to mention the uneasy feeling they were playing "running dogs" for the cable companies who were under an obligation to the CRTC (Canadian government regulatory agency for broadcasting) to provide just such a community service, in return for a licence.

Perhaps the most successful project in North America in terms of the development of VTR as a medium has been Videographe, a store-front production centre and theatre in Montreal. The project was initiated by Société nouvelle but is now supported by the Quebec government. Anyone who has a project can present it to the Videographe committee. If it is approved, equipment (half-inch portapack, tapes, and sometimes money) is loaned to the tapemaker, who must agree to use original music which he can have recorded in Vdeographe's sound studio. He can also edit the tapes using Videographe's editing facilities. The tape can then be shown in their octagonal theatre, and finally it is transferred to cassette and stored in a library that is accessible to anyone (for play at Videographe) at any time of the day or night.

At the moment, energies of the Challenge for Change community communications section are being concentrated in the activities of seven regional project co-ordinators working on projects for their own areas. At a recent re-organizational meeting, they emphasized their concern for long-range projects rather than social documentaries.

For instance, in a land-use planning project in Surrey (a suburb of Vancouver), co-ordinator Chris Pinney will be using film and VTR to encourage people to participate in community decisions that affect the area in which they live. Pinney looks upon this as "a very conservative notion: getting people to depend on themselves and create their own communities rather than depending on remote governments to make all the decisions".

Another project, led by project co-ordinator Harry Sutherland, involves Tembec, the former Temiskaming plant of the Canadian International Paper Company (an American-owned subsidiary) which folded and was taken over by a consortium of local townspeople, workers in the mill, and the Canadian and Quebec governments. Challenge for Change plans—through the use of VTR—to keep the lines of communication open between the diverse elements (the administration is located in Montreal while the mill itself is far away in Temiskaming, Quebec). For example, a tape made in Montreal of the signing ceremony between the governments and founders of the new mill was shown to the workers, and Challenge for Change also plans a film documenting the progress of what should be an important project for Canadians.

In another Challenge for Change project, sponsored by the Solicitor General's Department of the Canadian government, Jared Finesmith is training prison inmates and staff to use VTR for better understanding and communication. It isn't just a case of inmates making tapes about what concerns them and staff doing the same; training has been carried out in mixed groups and the final VTR crews are made up of both inmates and staff.

The aim of the Solicitor General's Department was to uncover new information on the causes of recidivism. Although nothing new was found, Finesmith succeeded in developing a methodology for the use of videotape in institutions. He also became aware of the importance of involving the community with which the inmate must deal on the outside and plans to do more work in this area. (The prisons involved were Matsqui, Collins Bay and Warkworth.)

Another current experiment, using both film and VTR, is being carried out in some emerging Eskimo communities on the coast of Labrador. The settlements, till now, have been run by the church, welfare offices and supply depots. With the help of a community development worker, the communities are being encouraged to elect councils and seek the legal status necessary to obtain municipal funds from the Newfoundland government. A film dealing with housing, civil rights and education will be used by the Royal Commission on Labrador. Filmmaker Roger Hart transferred all film footage to VTR as it became available and sent it to Labrador for viewing by the people.

> *Everyone can be an artist.*
> *In fact, you have to be an artist to survive.*
> *The problem is, what kind of an artist are you going to be.*
> —Janis Runge, sociologist.

One of the thorniest questions is the one concerning evaluation. The original Challenge for Change/Société nouvelle mandate was so liberal it allowed almost anything to be defined as social change. To reiterate some of the program's accomplishments: it expanded the uses of film and videotape to help people see themselves in new ways; it created films as a focus for discussion about changes that need to be made; and it has helped to put communication production into more hands.

The only outside evaluation that has been done (by James Taylor and Elizabeth van Every-Taylor of the University of Montreal) suggests that "access" is the criterion by which to measure the success of the program's use of videotechnology. In other words, did the program put the "means of production" (not to be confused with Marx's use of the phrase) into more hands? It certainly did. But that criterion seems to ignore the main event: social change. Of course it depends on how social change is defined. One can say, along with the human potential movement, that "self actualizing" is taking place because more people are seeing themselves as creators of information rather than as consumers only. Tim Kennedy, program producer for Challenge for Change, however says, "You can have a lot of people around conversant with the techniques of video but that doesn't mean they are doing anyting important with it." Kennedy argues that long-term subtle attitudinal changes are needed as well as immediate political and economic change, but Challenge for Change Société nouvelle has not defined what it means by social change.

In a sense it can be said that all those people who wanted to get into the mass media to "say something" are now running around using their energies to make tapes while harming nothing, least of all the existing political/economic system. As one Toronto group put it after having made several tapes for the local cable TV station, "We'd rather have two minutes after the national news than ten weeks on cable." They know where the power still lies.

John Grierson, in a memo to Challenge for Change/Société nouvelle[1] just before he died, spoke of his fear of the number of people coming out of college film-production courses, waving super-8 cameras. He said there was great value in the 8mm revolution when it is anchored in necessity (eg., should it be used by the local educators in India). However, he saw in North America an obsession with self-expression which was self-indulgent. He spoke of a confusion between the 8mm revolution and a fascination in the universities with the immature or the 8mm mind.

In its community communications aspect Challenge for Change/Société nouvelle has been concerned with more than self-indulgent media freakery, although there has been some of that in the projects they have supported. The strength of their work lies in making people more critical of the mass media by demystifying it and showing its considerable limits. It has accomplished this in its role as resource organization both materially (by lending equipment, money and training) and spiritually (through its magazine *Access*).

"Spiritually" is not too strong a word to use because there was an almost religious fervour in their opposition to mass media content and style. This citizens' media revolution was the second coming, but there were to be no stars in the east. Stars were out, along with good production values. The result included a great deal of dull, sermon-like tape. "Process" was more important than "product".

This criticism should not obscure the fact that much good work has been done in this area. The encouragement of the use of videotape by citizens has meant the accomplishment of work that could never have been done by the mass media. There are videotape networks in northern Canada that allow Eskimo and Indian communities to share information they could not get out of mass information programs beamed from CBC Toronto via the new Anik satellite. Media resource groups such as Metro Media use tapes to help reinforce community identity and stimulate discussion. In the "Day Care Centre Workers Training Program", the activities of a number of Vancouver day-care centres were taped in order to involve parents in their children's daytime life. In another project, the Yukon Native Brotherhood made a video white paper for the Senate Committee on Poverty.

Many boring tapes may have been made by citizens groups, but this was not the case in the "process" films made by Challenge for Change and Société nouvelle. The professional filmmakers such as Colin Low who did the Fogo series and Léonard Foret who made LA NOCE N'EST PAS FINIE never lost sight of the importance of product in effecting attitudinal change in the viewing audience.

It may have been destructive in the past for Challenge for Change/Société nouvelle to act as its own critic and evaluator. But it is now time that it defined more clearly what it means by social change, and its work should be judged in terms of that definition.

It should also examine in the same light its role in the expanded use of communications tools. Some of the identifying words and phrases used in connection with citizens communication (such as "demystifying", "getting away from mass institutions and alienating influences", "self-reliance and controlling your own destiny") have also been part of the Whole Earth Catalogue or intermediate-technology movement. Comparisons with such movements may create some delusions. Controlling your own destiny means knowing how to survive, to be an artist, to be an entrepreneur.

Perhaps it's time to ask whether the expanded use of communications tools alone can bring that about.

Saint-Jérôme: The Experience of a Filmmaker As Social Animator

Fernand Dansereau

A few years ago, we shot a film that was intended to be a study of a poor neighbourhood in Montreal—SEPTEMBER 5 AT SAINT-HENRI. When the film went into distribution and was televised, it provoked an astonishingly violent negative reaction from the people who had been filmed.

They felt debased by our *outsiders'* observations of them. Worse yet, certain people who played a role in the film felt deeply and personally hurt. One of the families that had been filmed, for example, was overcome with a sort of shame so great they decided to remove their children from the local school.

Because of the severity of these repercussions, a feeling of deep remorse has remained with me, in spite of our undeniable good will.

In December 1966, the National Film Board again proposed a subject of this kind: a study, in a small town in Quebec, of the way individuals and institutions behave in periods of rapid change. Saint-Jérôme, a town of 35,000 inhabitants, thirty miles from Montreal, was to be our centre of operations.

To avoid a repetition of what happened in Saint-Henri, I adopted a special principle: I pledged to all the people I met (except the politicians)

Reprinted from *NFB Newsletter*, Winter 1968-69.

and who could possibly participate in the filming, that they would have the right to censor the material that I would shoot with them. That is, at the stage of final editing each of these people would have the privilege of cutting out of his own interviews anything that he no longer liked. I was abandoning myself to their good will. I told myself that it was placing the same confidence in them that I was asking them to place in me. We did not start shooting until this confidence was sufficiently established. I then found myself embarked on a very special type of filming. Because of this initial pledge, and because of the human relations that were developing between the filmmakers and the residents of the locality, the major part of the shooting was taking the form of interviews. Any efforts at staging, or even creating situations, that I tried at the beginning proved false and frustrating; whereas, when I simply listened to people without trying to change them or trap them, the quality of the things being said and being lived before the camera attained a rare significance for me.

I sometimes worried about this strange film that was slowly taking shape. It looked a bit like television, which didn't make me particularly happy. But then I simply had to continue. My hope was rooted in the fact that I was to keep on filming for nine months in Saint-Jérôme and that I would surely find a way out of my problems.

But the filming finally retained this characteristic. When, a little later, I again attempted to intervene as director, I always had the same feeling of disrespect, of unjustified manipulation on my part. The final footage was composed entirely of interviews and events that had authentically happened quite outside my control.

I found myself in the cutting room with 65,000 feet of film and the job of making something out of it. After a good deal of sweat and anguish it became evident to the editor and myself that only one possibility was open to us: to attempt to bring out, through the editing, a perception that would be our own, that could *not* be presented as an objective documentary about the reality of these people. We would attempt to communicate what we felt about them. The film, finally, is two hours long and has indeed taken a very personal view.

During these months of editing, the thing that impressed me most was how much the people, plus all the research we had done, had taught me about myself. I was forced to clarify my ideas on objective problems —economic, sociological and psychological, of course—but I was also forced, as a total person, to situate myself in the world of today.

We gradually came to feel a strong identification with the people of Saint-Jérôme, in the sense that we shared with them the same confusion before the rapid changes we are living and the same concern for protecting the fundamental human values in ourselves, without refusing progress.

When I had finished the editing, my position as a Québécois was more important to me than my position as a filmmaker.

On the other hand we realized, with hindsight, that our presence in

Saint-Jérôme had had an influence in itself, outside of the film being produced. As an example: we wandered from group to group, asking approximately the same questions, symbolizing the same interrogation. It seemed to me to create new communication between the people, and pushed a number of them to analyze their own situations further.

At different stages of filming we invited our principle participants to screen rushes with us. We continued to do so at different stages of editing. This, of course, taught us a great deal and changed us considerably. But it also changed the people. After seeing themselves in the footage as in a sort of mirror, yet with all the security that surrounds an event that has been lived, is known, and is past, they were free to criticize themselves and to decide to change themselves if they felt the need. I am speaking, of course, not from a filmmaking point of view, but from the point of view of the very being of these persons. In other words, the screenings could, in certain cases, exercise an effect of collective therapy.

I must add right away, however, that we had not planned anything in this direction. It occurred, when it did occur, as a sort of accident.

Finally, our effort in structuring the material for editing, our search for a meaning and a rationality in all this material, may also have played a certain role. Our friends, who were obviously not lacking in structures themselves, found themselves obliged to question their theories and their hypotheses simply because of our approach, and they were obliged to do this in relatively heterogeneous groups. This caused a considerable stirring up of ideas and emotions. This may also explain why the filmmakers at no time received the veto of their close collaborators. The two approaches coincided and grew together and the film was accepted without difficulty.[1]

We have no proof of the influence exercised during the filming. A team of sociologists would have had to accompany us and measure what was happening, if we had wanted to have such proof. But we were not looking for any. Let us say that this has remained a very strong impression with me.

The film is now in distribution. It is long. Most of the time all you can see is people talking. At first we wondered if such a product would have any signification for people other than the citizens of Saint-Jérôme. Experience in distribution seems to indicate that it awakens echoes in all kinds of other Quebec communities. People seem to recognize themselves in it. I am not sure if it would be the same outside of Quebec, but here, the sort of liberation in language and reflection that the film provokes seems to have come at the right moment.

As a matter of fact, we have had to invent new methods of utilization in distribution. Since the film communicates our perception and that of our principal collaborators concerning the reality that we lived, it seemed to be of interest to reconstitute all the footage in a state as close as possible to what it was at the origins, and to offer to viewers a series of satellite films. In this way, it is possible for the viewer to contest our interpretations, and, going back to the beginning, to interpret in his own way, do his own editing. One way this can be done, for instance, is that during the discussion following the screening of the main film, according to the questions that are brought up the animator can refer to one of the satellite films, to complete the first perception of the reality that the main film had offered.

Of course, this type of utilization can rarely be done in commercial theatres, but groups of students, workers or citizens who wish to reflect on their own situation can find within these films a starting point for their work. This is a young, active, impassioned audience, an audience that is *moving* in society, a choice participant, a real public.

Without particularly trying to, we found ourselves making a film-tool. Yet, all added up, the experience was certainly not disagreeable, on the contrary. The filmmaker, in any case, was certainly never bored. The people of Saint-Jérôme brought him, through their actions and sometimes even in words, a particular confirmation: among them, the filmmaker was a useful person, a person who had a particular aptitude for seeing people and objects and transmitting, as a reflection, the image of these beings and these things. The image, of course, is coloured by the personality of the filmmaker, but it is that, really, that seemed appreciated. It is at the same time the confirmation of the aesthetic role and the useful role of my trade that has been offered to me by this experience. And I can feel within me, infinitely stronger and more durable than that from either critics or an anonymous public, the recognition of the people with whom we lived. It is they, finally, who assure me of my function as an artist.

A final, technical note: we worked with light equipment, an Eclair camera, Nagra recorder, virtually no lighting. There were three of us. I was able to observe that the cameraman and the sound man were obliged to have a sort of sixth sense, a talent for divination, to work in these conditions. Sometimes I had the impression, when I saw them brusquely turn towards someone just before something happened, that they really had eyes in the back of their heads.

I think that it is the quality of the relationships that the filmmakers developed with the people that was the essential element. And, in the final analysis, this is the source of beauty in this kind of film. Film is no longer a study in form, but a sudden coinciding of the truth of a moment—an event, a communication—of everything that is cinema and everything that is the reality of people.

Memo to Michelle about Decentralizing the Means of Production

John Grierson

You will remember (*Benedictus benedicat*) Zavattini's idea of arming the Italian villages with cameras, so they could send film letters to each other. This means, in or out of Italy, handing down the means of larger public expression to the people at the grass-roots.

With cameras becoming smaller and lighter and easier to work and cheaper to buy, the decentralization of filmmaking becomes an ever more practical possibility. We see it happening with home movies, with movie-making in research departments, with teaching organizations that make their own films without benefit of clergy.

I have been watching it even more widely manifest itself in the undergraduate circles of the American universities, where the young people have declared an "8mm revolution".

Much is claimed—and rightly—for the technical range of "super-8". But I am sceptical. It troubles me to see people loosely waving a camera around. It is like loosely waving a baby around; for the camera, like the baby, has its rights. I shudder at all catch-as-catch-can film approaches, even when they claim to be catching a falling star. I find it odd that university teachers should spread the doctrine that shooting film any-old-how absolves the student from all need to read and write.

I am told that with the 8mm revolution we have a therapeutic tool of importance: that the youth will not only learn automatically to observe but—o frabjous joy—will also find the magical secret of "play" and "loving contact" with their neighbours.

There is something in this, but there are cheaper and more obvious ways of teaching or inducing observation and collaboration.

There was never a miracle road to observation, whatever passing priests like Mr. McLuhan may say. "Look you, Francois," said de Maupassant to his servant. "To see well and distinguish well, one's eyes must be trained, and to get to that point one must notice everything when one is looking. Never be satisfied with 'almost everything', give one's eyes all the time necessary to see everything that has to be noted, to define things well, to rout out the things one does not see very well; and it is only by long and patient exercise that one arrives at the point of being able to get from one's eyes all that they are capable of. Even the best artists must take great pains to form their eyes so that they will be really good and serviceable."

Reprinted from *Challenge for Change Newsletter*, no. 8 (Spring 1972).

Whatever accounts of observation (and of form) you heed, you will soon have left most of our 8mm revolutionaries far behind. And you needn't depend on classical accounts that are identical in de Maupassant and Plato; there is equally excellent, and again identical, guidance to be got from Paul Klee.

What I hear most about in North America is that the 8mm revolution will provide a magical path to what is all too loosely called *self-expression*. There are philosophical uses of the term which mean a great deal; but the way I hear it, it is more often a refuge from the normal disciplines of work (yes, *and* observation *and* collaboration). There are times again when self-expression means self-indulgence and this often at the expense of others. This matters, very much matters, where self-indulgence means public hurt. Perhaps it doesn't much matter in the midst of North American affluence but the anxiety for self-expression may weaken the political fibre of the next generation. In poorer countries, self-indulgence, involving the selfish use of a valuable means of public instruction and public expression, presents a simple and nauseous example of bad taste.

As you see, I am in a dilemma as I look on the potential of the 8mm revolution and see what, in some quarters, they are doing about it. I am all for easier cameras, lenses et al. I am all for the 8mm revolution, *so long as the 8mm mind doesn't go with it*. I came across a new word the other day: *neaniolatry* meaning, they tell me, "infatuation with the immature". It seems to me that we have got the 8mm revolution all mixed up with this "neaniolatry" at the North American universities.

Having noted this, let us not be put off by it. There are other more vital paths for the 8mm revolution.

The National Film Board of Canada, for one example, is engaged in a more considered effort at decentralizing the production process. They have a continuing program they call Challenge for Change which is concerned with social problems at the local level. What makes it special is that it represents a genuine effort by the NFB to keep in contact with people at the grass-roots. Challenge for Change makes much of cinéma-vérité but has cured itself of one cinéma-vérité deviation which has always been peculiarly attractive to the provincial mind: the secret camera's talent as a Peeping Tom and its ingenuity in catching the embarrassed reaction to the embarrassing question.

Like all harlots, the cinéaste of easy virtue is apt to run into power without responsibility; and it can go to his head.

The basic tendency of the Challenge for Change program is to follow decently in the original cinéma-vérité tradition which the English documentary people associate with HOUSING PROBLEMS (c. 1936). With that film there was talk of "breaking the goldfish bowl" and of making films "not *about* people but *with* them".

But not yet is there a real decentralizing of production. The cinéastes may make their films *with* the people and *in* the villages, but they are soon *off* and away *from* the people and the villages to their normal metropolitan milieu.

The old unsatisfactory note of faraway liberal concern for humanity-in-general creeps in, in spite of these real excursions into the local realities.

What we have is presentation of local concerns without a real re-presentation of local concerns. *Presentation* does not necessarily mean *representation*, much less participatory democracy.

Nevertheless, count the NFB as having contributed uniquely to the decentralization process. You have only to compare its Challenge for Change program with, say, England's BBC-TV (except at Bristol) to realize that it has added, and in intimate terms, to local reporting. Its local portraits are better than any I know and its use of the film to ease and give order to local discussion is important.

Two examples will illustrate the dangers attending the untutored or naive cinéaste in troubled local waters. There was one otherwise excellent film of a long-unemployed man whose tale was sad to tell. Significant of the danger of naiveté was the fact that the director was a woman; and the truth about that unemployed character was what only a man who had been around would have spotted. He was not so much unemployed as unemployable. On a bet, no seaman would have gone to sea with him twice; no docker would have trusted him within fifty yards of a working crane.

The French phrase "*s'écouter parler*" has of course its horrible equivalent in cinema, and not least in cinéma-vérité. The NFB has one ugly example where the local subject gets so starry-eyed and grandiose in his new-found film personality that he destroys himself (or is destroyed) for all further reality.

Yes, naiveté can go with it, however honest the intention of the cinematic stranger from without. Where it matters is when the too too local news is taken all too seriously and out of normal objective context.

The National Film Board has an example of good reportage from a ghost town in the west of Canada: a ghost town left on its uppers after the coal deposit has been worked out. The Challenge for Change program gives the abandoned townspeople, now mostly old people, the chance to discuss and record their complaints. They have no proper water supply, no gas supply, etc., etc. The Challenge for Change program gives the people the opportunity to view themselves, discover their strengths, and bring their ideas to better order. So it does help the townspeople to make their case and (because of the noise and the publicity, no doubt) be heard by politicians. Something indeed gets done.

News-in-depth? Why, in Canada, with its great distances and wild lands between, most mining strikes have their own in-built time patterns. They last so long and no more. I was there when they made the big nickel strike at Moko Lake. They said, with excitement, it would mean not a *fifty*-year city but a *hundred-year city*.

In the wide and difficult land spaces, strike towns are like some island habitations in the wide and difficult sea spaces. The ghost towns are not always nor often worth keeping. The priorities are almost certain to be in a million-and-one distress centres elsewhere.

Many of these points are of course arguable. What is more certain is that the NFB and its Challenge for Change program will have a new and different opportunity of becoming both objective about, and representational of local citizens and local affairs, with the arrival of local TV by cable or otherwise. It is probable that government permits to operate these services will be dependent on the community being represented in the production management by a *community league* or something of the kind. This, as I see it, must mean that municipal authorities, schools, universities, trade unions, industries, chambers of commerce, and other associations, will all have to look to their images and give an account of their stewardship; and, no doubt, all good radicals and true will see to it.

I can't for the life of me see that communities in the future will have the same sort of need for these faraway cinéastes. I start on the ground that a good teacher is, by the fact itself, a good exponent and a ready talent for exposition by film. So for all other professional exponents of cases and causes. The substandard film and the videotape are best seen now as relatively simple tools, to be locally owned and operated within the context of local reporting, local education and democratic representation at the community level. The cost of equipment now puts the 8mm revolution within the reach of most groups and associations—at least in North America. The professional standards need not be lower than the standards associated with local newspapers when they were making their vital contribution to community building in, say, the twenties. These standards were very high indeed, as the memory of William Allen White and the *Emporia Gazette* testifies. Insofar as many associations have their counterparts in other communities, and some have their national fronts, Zavattini may even expect many of his local film letters to have their further circulation.

I leave it to others to say how it will operate in other countries, but I have been looking into decentralization possibilities in India and think I see one possible great development there. In India there is a special imperative for decentralizing the filmmaking process. All the mass media together reach to only a hundred millions of the population, leaving four hundred and fifty millions to word-of-mouth, local educators and the itinerant entertainments of native origin. Obviously the biggest role in economic and social progress of all kinds will be with the local educators; making it necessary to add, in every way possible, to their local powers of persuasion. Here, with the local educators, I associate all developments involving the community welfare. The local activist front is complex.

In India, too, there are many languages to contend with and areas distinctive in ethnic and cultural background. Filmmaking at the district level is, I would think, a logical development, and one to which the various foreign aid programs should soon be giving their attention.

This means, among other peripatetic entertainments, the appearance of peripatetic teachers of filmmaking, moving modestly from district to district, teaching the doctor-teachers and other local educationists how to hold their cameras steady and shoot simply, *as their own native powers of exposition direct them. That would be a real 8mm revolution anchored in necessity.*

I submit this to the attention of any aging documentary types who may be on their way to Benares.

III

FEATURE FILMMAKING

The Years of Hope

Peter Harcourt

I think one returns always to this fact that Canada has given itself a very very big task with a very small population to work on. The result is that you should husband your resources very very preciously. You shouldn't waste them in frittering away the time of television as you do. You've got to look to the building of your imagination, the building of your national intelligence at every level.

—John Grierson[1]

For John Grierson, it was easy. There was no doubt in his mind what had to be done. He knew he was the founder of the documentary movement and he also knew that, for any nation with a sense of itself, film has a vital role to play. Epistemological doubt was not for him. Nor were compromises or half-measures. Grierson belonged to that vanished race of patriarchs who knew exactly what was needed. He also knew how to manipulate governments to achieve the necessary goals.

When he arrived in Canada in 1938, the threat of war provided him with an enormous opportunity. While the federal government had been interested in establishing a documentary unit, the fact of the war made the NFB a national necessity. Its function was obvious: it could help unite the country and mobilize its sentiments towards the inescapable challenge of winning the war. And for once in our lives we couldn't rely upon the Americans to do our work for us. Canada had a real job to do and it set up the film board to help do it.

It is important to stress the energy of these documentary beginnings. They were quite different in character from anything that had happened in the States and more extensive, finally, than anything that Grierson had achieved in England. They were distinctly Canadian and were, by government edict, committed to Canadian themes. While the war provided the impetus to get the film board going, after the war—at the same time as in England the Labour Government was closing down its national film unit—in Canada the film board actually began a period of expansion, searching for the means of carrying on with its charter now that the propaganda needs of the war had been met. Within a very short time, these means were largely supplied by television.

When talking about the film board, one is always talking about a number of different things. Throughout its "heyday"—let us say, from the beginnings of television in 1952 to the achievement of LABYRINTH in 1967—the film board consisted of a number of separate units all concerned with different projects. And while the film board has always been

Reprinted from *Motion*, vol. 5, no. 3 (January 1976).

recognized for the high technical standard of nearly all its films, individual films vary a great deal both in quality and interest, depending upon the subjects treated and the personnel involved. So when I talk about the film board, it should be recognized that I am concerned with only a tiny fragment of its total output—primarily with the productions undertaken by Tom Daly's unit, known at the board in those days as Unit B.

During the fifties and early sixties it was Unit B's task to make films specifically for television, for CBC's "Candid Eye" series. As the executive producer of the unit, Tom Daly had the ability to gather round him a number of people who, at least for a time, worked well together as a group. And while committed primarily to making "candid-eye" documentaries, they managed to extend themselves in other ways as well.

I have elsewhere discussed the artistic achievement of a number of these films, an achievement which (I argue) is inseparable from a philosophical attitude.[2] This attitude has three modes. One concerns the impulse towards investigative reporting, often with a slightly satirical edge. This mode is best represented by the films directed by Terence Macartney-Filgate and later by those of Wolf Koenig. Films like THE BACK-BREAKING LEAF (1959) and BLOOD AND FIRE (1958) showed to television audiences some of the realities of the migrant tobacco workers in southern Ontario or of the down-and-out social rejects who are attracted to Salvation Army hostels; while I WAS A 90-POUND WEAKLING (1960) playfully ridiculed the apparent seriousness of the health-club craze. Yet these films didn't accuse the existing political system. They stood back from their material, observing it sympathetically even when satirically, but drawing no conclusions about the nature of the world they depicted for us. They simply presented us with many facets of how it is to live and work in Canada.

Another mode concerns the impulse towards history, towards the reality of our Canadian past. Here the chief motivating force seemed to be Colin Low. CORRAL (1953) offered us a lyrical observation of the breaking in of a horse, while CITY OF GOLD (1957), one of the most distinguished films to be made from still photographs anywhere in the world, told the story of the great Klondike gold rush of 1897.

CITY OF GOLD is remarkable in many ways. On a technical level it seemed amazing at the time how these old photographs could be brought to life by film; and when Wolf Koenig and Colin Low went up to the Klondike to grab some actuality footage of Dawson City today, they even managed to match the lateral light that characterized the old photographs with the light of their own footage, enabling them to effect smooth transitions between the past and the present. They also employed the services of Eldon Rathburn to compose a music track that beautifully evoked the feeling of that period. Finally, since Pierre Berton had grown up in Dawson and was at that time working on his own book, *Klondike*, they persuaded him to prepare their commentary, thus making the film seem like his story—although it is very much a Unit B film.

It is a Unit B film because of its tone of philosophical enquiry, because it is not simply a presentation of history but an interrogation of that history in terms of what it means to us now. Why did all these men travel north in search of gold? Why did so many of them, once they got there, not even bother to look for gold at all? And on their annual celebration day, a kind of combination of Dominion Day and the 4th of July, what could these people, so far from everywhere, really be celebrating?

In this way, CITY OF GOLD becomes less a documentary than a cinematic poem about the nature of human effort, of human loneliness, and about the meaning of the past. This questioning, at times uncertain tone, provides the third mode within this philosophical attitude that characterized the work of Unit B. While it is present to a degree in nearly all their films, it is most prominent in UNIVERSE (1960), THE LIVING MACHINE (1961), and LONELY BOY (1962). It was also the tone that dominated that cinematic-architectural mind-trip, LABYRINTH, which was prepared for Expo '67 and which effectively brought the work of this unit to an end. Before this happened, however, an interesting "outsider" had joined the board, someone who wanted to shift Unit B into another dimension—the dimension of features.

This outsider was, of course, Don Owen—a poet from Toronto who was as interested in fictive forms of expression as in purely documentary ones; and the feature he eventually produced in 1964 was NOBODY WAVED GOODBYE.

Like the French-language features that were made at about the same time at the board, such as LE CHAT DANS LE SAC (1964) by Gilles Groulx and LA VIE HEUREUSE DE LEOPOLD Z (1965) by Gilles Carle, NOBODY WAVED GOODBYE was achieved by a kind of "cheating". As Gilles Carle has explained it:

> We were quite a group of people working there and doing documentaries. But at this time, policy was changing and we were trying to do feature films. We achieved some feature filmmaking at the National Film Board but with a little cheating—shooting too much, asking for too much film at the lab. And by just working our way around, we ended up with some feature films.

For NOBODY WAVED GOODBYE, Don Owen had to work in much the same way. Sent off to Toronto to make a half-hour film on juvenile delinquency, Owen first of all persuaded the board to let him use actors and then came back with so much footage that they virtually had to let him cut it into a feature. In this way he managed to produce that seminal, English-Canadian film—a film that neither the film board nor Canadian audiences could see much value in until, on a double bill with LONELY BOY, it did well in New York! As Owen has commented:

> Canadians don't really see themselves very well. It's very interesting. When the film was shown in New York, I went with various people to see the film. And seeing the film in New York, it looked so like Toronto. I mean you suddenly heard the way people spoke,

for instance; and you suddenly realized that there's only one place in the world with people like that and that's Toronto. And there's only one place that streets look like that, only in the city, you know. And suddenly it became very recognizable as a special place in the world.

In my view, NOBODY WAVED GOODBYE is more important than most people realize—even today. It records a series of rejections: rejection of school, of the established rules of society, of the values of his parents as Peter sees them, and of the political commitment of a Quebec acquaintance that Peter meets one evening in a coffee-shop. Finally, possibly (for the film is really ambiguous about this), the film records the rejection of the responsibilities of fatherhood. But the quality of the film transcends the negativity of its theme. It achieves greatness (I am prepared to argue) because its style combines the documentary authenticity that characterized the work of Unit B with Don Owen's personal understanding of the feeling of futurelessness experienced by the moneyed kids from the suburbs.

To move from these abbreviated comments about this important film to a comparison with the French-Canadian features produced at the board would really require a separate article; for they too grew up out of their own form of documentary observation. While less cohesive in output than the films of Unit B, the early films of Carle, Groulx, and Jutra were often more experimental in form and more consciously aware of the political realities of the world they were examining.

Particularly interesting from this point-of-view is Gilles Groulx's LE CHAT DANS LE SAC. Made in the same year as NOBODY WAVED GOODBYE, it too records a series of rejections and it too leads its central character into a personal cul-de-sac; but in LE CHAT DANS LE SAC, this cul-de-sac is also seen in political terms. This political reference is largely the creation of its form. Made under the direct influence of Godard's VIVRE SA VIE (an influence which is acknowledged in the film), LE CHAT DANS LE SAC less presents an imitation of real-life situations than it builds up a series of face-to-camera monologues. The film establishes a series of "texts", in fact—texts which we have to "read" as we experience the film in order to make sense of what is going on. In LE CHAT DANS LE SAC, we have to understand not only the personal difficulties experienced by the characters but the political implications of these difficulties as well. In this sense, by way of Godard, the film is more Brechtian in its effect upon us. We have to work at it consciously as we watch it in order to grasp the full implications of the complexities of its form.

Much more could be said about these films, as indeed about other NFB films as well. But the point of these bald statements is simply to suggest that there was a time in the early sixties when there was a lot of talent at the board. From the war years through to the dominance of television, these filmmakers had built up their own way of examining the personal and political realities of the world we live in. When the time came, however, for them to extend themselves into features, the film board couldn't really manage to support this extension. So within six years, most of the real talent left the board.

Except for the films of Norman McLaren, the film board has never known what to do with its most distinguished product, just as we in Canada have been kept from realizing what is distinguished about our own films. We see too few of them in too random an order. Yet a nation is rich in proportion to the pride it takes in its image of itself, an image which can be most persuasively created in our cinemas and on our television screens. Furthermore, I would argue that it can most effectively be created when freed from the pressures of American distribution deals.

The perception of quality is a cultural matter. It is only the international money market that encourages us to think that there are international standards in art. If we are to go on building our imaginations and our national intelligence at every level, as Grierson said we must, then we need a growing group of people who really care about the product on our screens. The Canadian filmmaker's task is hopeless if every gesture he makes is immediately compared with the more established gestures of the Hollywood industry. We must know enough about our own product to recognize its own kind of excellence, its possibly more tentative but genuinely indigenous gestures.

If we care about our own country, it is no longer a question of whether we like Canadian films or don't like them. It is a question of whether we are for them or against them. As far as I am concerned, I am for them.

Pierre Perrault

Louis Marcorelles

Richard Leacock might be called *Homo cinematographicus par excellence*, but Pierre Perrault, who came to the cinema from literature, through the tape recorder and television, is his exact opposite. He brings to filmmaking a strictly critical eye that knows nothing of the established rules, and whereas Leacock makes the cinema burst out from within, from its most fundamental structures (the camera and sound recording, to start with), Perrault feels that these things can be taken for granted. He sees them merely as tools that will give a certain permanence to the extremely interesting work he has been carrying on for ten years in his own country—that is, the province of Quebec—studying its mainly French-speaking people and their paradoxical fate in an English-speaking Canada. Leacock brought the surgeon's knife to reality and sought to reveal man's innermost secrets in the passing moment, whereas Pierre Perrault, instead of writing novels or an epic poem, finds echoes of something greater in what appears to be the banal reality of modest people's everyday lives: this greater quality being the growth of a sense of unity.

When he worked on his first full-length film, POUR LA SUITE DU MONDE (following a series of a dozen half-hour films entitled "Au pays de Neuve France", made by René Bonnière), Pierre Perrault shared the responsibility of direction with his cameraman, Michel Brault. Brault, who was familiar with the techniques of Leacock, Pennebaker and Maysles but also interested in the classical cinema, is ready to do anything anywhere, no matter what the style. For him, the subject orders the technique, not vice versa, as in Leacock's case. "Direct cinema" means more than a light camera and synchronized sound; it demands immediate participation in the event. The performance does not come only from the text, even though this may be constantly improvised; it comes from the very movement of the action itself, with a minimum of interference from the direction team. Ideally the director is his own cameraman, he shares the physical effort of seeking what is real, sticks to the movement of things and of people as it is actually taking place by physical contact, that is, the contact of the camera with reality, and of the director-soundman with the camera. This is not the camera used as a mere gadget, the way Claude Lelouch uses it when he dances around his characters on the station platform at the end of UN HOMME ET UNE FEMME, to express their joy at meeting again through this wild movement. Leacock definitely cuts out symbolism. Here the *"camera-stylo"* which Alexandre Astruc spoke about, but which was then merely a publicity stunt to make people realize that films could be "written" like novels, came into being,

Reprinted from *Living Cinema* (New York: Praeger Inc., 1973).

perhaps for the first time, although now it was not a matter of writing novels in the form of films but quite simply of making films. Not as well as novels, with the extra excitement of the classic 35mm camera, but in another way: a new way of seeing, hearing, feeling, with a refinement of feeling that enriches all our perception, all our understanding of the world.

Pierre Perrault's break with the classical cinema, and with the whole tradition of direct cinema as it already existed in Canada—a tradition inspired by what was happening in New York at about the same time—showed unusual boldness and originality from the outset. Direct cinema in Canada was at first the work of an English team in the National Film Board, the cradle of all Canadian filmmaking. A label was attached to it: "candid eye", which in itself covered everything that was done, because the accent was placed on the eye's candour, the implication being that it concentrated on some primal innocence unspoiled by intervention from outside. Although I have tried hard to find who first used this label I have not been able to do so; it may have been the team of Wolf Koenig-Roman Kroitor, or the Englishman Terence Macartney-Filgate.

In a special brochure of the Canadian Cinémathèque, published in 1967, Wolf Koenig says that the idea of the "candid eye" comes from a British film made by Lindsay Anderson, the creator of "free cinema". This film, THURSDAY'S CHILDREN, made a strong impression on Koenig and his friends in the English-speaking team, an impression even stronger than that made by Flaherty's old films or the English documentaries of the thirties. "All these films," he wrote, "had the colour of reality, the colour we wished to give to what we were doing." Just then television broke through the American market, and the National Film Board of Canada was told to provide the newly-formed television branch of Radio-Canada with films. "We thought this was the chance we had been waiting for: there was an audience, and there was a budget.... This was what we meant to do: catch life as it was, without a script and without frills; take sound on the spot, without careful cutting; make films in a way that would create emotion, laughter or tears, and preferably both at once; show them on television to millions of people and change the world by making them see that life is true, fine and full of meaning." In 1953, Wolf Koenig was given Henri Cartier-Bresson's book of photographs, *Images à la sauvette*, the preface of which, he said, was to become the bible of the whole "candid eye" team....

At the time of DAYS BEFORE CHRISTMAS the French Canadians at the National Film Board began to make their own films; the first of these was LES RAQUETTEURS made by Michel Brault and Gilles Groulx in 1958. It was made in 35mm with synchronized sound, and with cruel irony it shows the odd behaviour of a dressed-up crowd taking part in a curious competition in Montreal. We laugh at these respectable middle-class people with their candid reactions (the "candid eye" is very close), all muffled up in their warm winter clothes, and talking French in their own very special accent. This was the first time French Canadians had been shown directly on the screen. In 1961 Gilles Groulx made a film on his own, GOLDEN GLOVES, about a famous boxing competition. It was the chance to make Ronald Jones, a black boxer, well known. He had made his home, obscurely, in the poorest French district and spoke French at home and English in his boxing world; and he went through the series that led to the Golden Gloves contest which promised riches and success. Groulx was already showing a dual interest that was to make him, with Pierre Perrault, the most personal filmmaker in Quebec; on the one hand he used direct sound knowledgeably, as in the opening of the film where we watch the boxer in training; on the other, he was commenting on a precise social situation—showing how a man here boxed in order to earn a living and how, being poor, he naturally spoke French, the language of the poor, but English in his work, in order to "get on". In 1964 Gilles Groulx made his first full-length film, LE CHAT DANS LE SAC, which today has become a classic of its kind. This film showed quite definitely that direct cinema, its techniques and its aesthetic ideas, in the hands of French teams had acquired a new meaning. It was no longer merely observing life in a humorous way but serving a cause that, in the years that followed, was to become the raison d'être of a whole group of intellectuals and artists, foremost among them the filmmakers in the province of Quebec; to affirm the authenticity, the particularity and the originality of the French ethnic group in a bilingual country that was first dependent on France, then on Britain.

LE CHAT DANS LE SAC carries on the revolution that can be seen in Godard's films as well as in those of the Candid Eye, concentrating on a precise goal—the awareness of being "Québécois". The two young actors are mostly playing themselves, and keep their own christian names. Claude Godbout, an actor in search of identity, is Claude, a journalist in search of himself. Barbara Ulrich, the director's wife, a young English-speaking Jewess, is Barbara, an actress stranded in Montreal, in love with Claude and trying to make her way in the theatre. Claude broods over his own uselessness from morning till night and succumbs to his obsession with politics, so much so that Barbara, who wants to love and work and create, can no longer bear it. Although Barbara belongs to an ethnic minority, she has the confidence that only an English education can give, whereas Claude is completely lost in his efforts to find a national identity. Barbara talks of Brecht, Claude of Jean-Paul Sartre and Franz Fanon. What is admirable about the film is its tone, a sort of monologue in two voices where the characters never cease to be introspective, and which passes from dialogue to monologue to commentaries "off screen", or the other way around. LE CHAT DANS LE SAC is composed like a poem and is what Godard has never been able to produce—a subjectively political film; also Groulx takes advantage of direct cinema to make the characters seem more intensely present and to intensify, too, the audience's participation in what happens to them. In its composition the film still shows signs of the classical cinema but Groulx is a master of both sound and image, sound—words, noises and music—giving its tone to the image. In Groulx's second full-length film, OU ETES-VOUS DONC? (from the title of a pop song in Quebec), actors are placed in a situation that starts from a subject that involves them, and they elaborate the core of the film during the making of it while the director, keeping a strict check on the way work progresses, sees to its general development, which aims to show, once again, what Quebec is becoming.

The wheel has come full circle. French-speaking Canadians have used both the "candid eye" and the "New Wave" methods to their own advantage, and have created an original cinema in which, more intensely perhaps than in any other medium, they have set down the facts about French Canada.

But for a wholly new departure we must turn to Pierre Perrault. At first he had no avowed political aims but was seeking, through the intensity and complexity of his testimony, to go gradually back into history and to try to find the hidden origins of what had survived of France in Canada. This search produced three full-length films: POUR LA SUITE DU MONDE in 1963, LE REGNE DU JOUR in 1967, and LES VOITURES D'EAU in 1968.

The people shown in all these films live in the Ile-aux-Coudres, a small island in the St. Lawrence about fifty miles upstream from Quebec where, until recently—at any rate when POUR LA SUITE DU MONDE was being made—a whole way of life that was quite outside the march of history still continued, at least among the old who lived entirely in the memory of the past when Jacques Cartier stayed on the island on September 6 and 7, 1535, and gave it the name it still bears. At the time he made this film Pierre Perrault had, for more than ten years, been familiar with Baie-Saint-Paul, on the north bank of the St. Lawrence facing the island, and he was married to a local girl; he had known old Alexis Tremblay, the tutelary figure of the first two films, for a long time. A legend, he discovered, had survived about the fishing for porpoise (or more exactly, beluga) which had ended twenty-five years earlier, and in the islanders' memories this fishing had become magnified. Perrault asked them to recall it and made it the subject of his first full-length film, in which Michel Brault's contribution can be seen in the photography. It is often very fine in spite of the very free direction. In LE REGNE DU JOUR Perrault, who this time was solely responsible for the direction, took old Alexis Tremblay, his wife Marie, their son Léopold and their daughter-in-law on a journey to the country of their ancestors—western France, from whence the forebears of the present inhabitants of Quebec emigrated. When they got home, Perrault got the Tremblay family and their friends to talk about the journey and their discoveries. The remarkably good cutting is comparable with that of

Resnais' early films, because Perrault, like Resnais, seems to rediscover old memories that are no longer individual but collective, the subsoil of past centuries. The rites celebrated at the death of a pig, the priest's appearance, are compared in France and in Canada. Suddenly the image Alexis has carved in his imagination of a France that is truly sublime at last comes to life in the person of Robert Martin, a gamekeeper who describes how he was arrested and deported to Buchenwald with a simplicity and a naturalness that take one's breath away. Very fast cutting mixes past, present and future, concentrating on feelings or on the continuity of ideas. To Perrault, each sentence spoken refers back to some wholly concrete experience. Man's imagination does not rise out of nothing, even if it seems to loom up out of an ancient darkness. Is it not burdened with the whole history of man?

In 1969 Perrault's third full-length film appeared. He had made it at the same time as he made LE REGNE DU JOUR, and had worked on it for a long time before showing it publicly. This time we never leave Quebec, and the action all takes place on the Ile-aux-Coudres and the bank of the St. Lawrence. From time immemorial the people on the island have built their own wooden boats, schooners or "water-carriages", as they are called on the island, but these can no longer compete with the large metal ships chartered by the English companies. The islanders find that "progress" comes to them just when they seem to be growing into an awareness that they no longer have the means to fight the other Canada on equal terms — that is, English Canada with its monopoly o of the means of production.

The narrative centres around two parts: one, the building of the last canoe — a sort of small-scale schooner — at the time when the film was made; the other, the departure from the island and the problems encountered in the outside world, particularly a dockers' strike at Trois-Rivières which once again emphasizes the creaky way in which the social machine grinds round. Yet the men who have built these ships are remarkable and have managed to survive terrible historical, economic and physical conditions through the mere strength of their hands. Perrault's technique is honed down to perfection; language remains pre-eminent, yet is closely linked with the living action. Everyone on the island, including the key characters of the first two films, the ancestral Alexis Tremblay, his son Léopold Tremblay, and Grand Louis the story-teller, all show an inexhaustible knowledge of the land and its people. Fast cutting, in which sentences are run together, linked or balanced, emphasizes the critical side of a careful, deeply involved description that centres on a new character, Laurent Tremblay, who owns a schooner but lacks the means to confront the modern world.

Perrault's progress is clear. LES VOITURES D'EAU is in a sense the final part of a trilogy that began with POUR LA SUITE DU MONDE and LE REGNE DU JOUR. Perrault is ready to admit that he has found direct cinema the most powerful method with which to catch life as it really is. But he is not content to catch life raw — he arranges it, edits it in every sense of the word, first of all through his detailed knowledge of the place, the characters and the situation he describes. He does not try to catch reality completely spontaneously or in a sort of primal innocence. The filming takes several months, sometimes a year or two, but it goes ahead at an irregular pace, sometimes even according to the demands of the cutting. The situation described in LES VOITURES D'EAU is crystallized by three events: first, the building of the boat which brings to life not just a craft long practiced on the island but all kinds of memories; second, the strike that keeps Laurent Tremblay and his team immobilized at Trois-Rivières purely by chance; third, the fire in an old unused schooner which shows the growing emotion on Laurent Tremblay's face and arouses other reflections and feelings—this scene was suggested by Bernard Gosselin, the cameraman. Obviously Perrault is in his own way creating a novel and has a deep knowledge of all the elements that form it; but he pushes these elements into real life and the finished product refers to this reality, to the growing awareness of a sense of community, which is ready to be merged with the French-Canadian or Québécois community as a whole.

UN PAYS SANS BON SENS (1970) and L'ACADIE, L'ACADIE (1971), begun almost at the same time in 1968, show the start of a more radical attitude. Produced for the English section of the National Film Board of Canada, UN PAYS SANS BON SENS tries to describe an abstract idea, that of country. The film is divided into three quite distinct parts. The first—"Sketch-book Scenes"—introduces Didier Dufour, a geneticist doctor of science who returns to his village, Baie Saint-Paul, on the mainland facing the Ile-aux-Coudres. The director soon shows us the sort of folklore that falsifies all values. In the second part—"Rejecting the Sketch-book"—a new character, Maurice Chaillot, graduate in literature from the western provinces, describes his experiences as a French Canadian who is ashamed of his origins because he grew up in a situation in which the French language is condemned to disappear and has no future.

Then comes the thesis (or, if you prefer, the hypothesis) on which the film is to be based: a sort of as yet unformed awareness in French Canadians, as Perrault sees them, that their country will henceforth be called Quebec, and that a country does exist in which they belong, in which they are at home. The third part—"Return to the Sketch-book"—gives a logical conclusion to a carefully considered analysis that arises out of what is shown of a particular place and particular characters; and none of it, Perrault insists, is there unnecessarily.

The film's political colour becomes obvious, not merely because René Lévesque appears in it now and then. Opposition is in fact much more deeply rooted in the hearts of individual people. In order to make his point more strongly Perrault not only confronts his two main characters, who through their background are intellectuals, with working-class people but builds up his theme in a threefold way. In the centre is French Canada and Quebec; upstream, if you like, is the example of the Indians, the memory of an almost vanished race which has been unable to adapt itself, yet which occupied the country before the arrival of the French and the English; downstream there is Brittany and the feelings of frustration of a province filled with history and yet unable to find its rightful place in the whole, which is called France.

UN PAYS SANS BON SENS (a paradoxical title that might be translated as "It's a Mad, Mad, Mad, Mad Country") goes far beyond the detail of its own story and becomes a treatise on minorities, not so much because they express an anarchical protest, as because they are rooted in the past, in tradition. Pierre Perrault's film made with Michel Brault, L'ACADIE, L'ACADIE, shows a period of revolt among students at the French-speaking University of Moncton in New Brunswick, previously Acadia, a province from which part of the population was expelled 200 years ago. After the conquest of Canada by the British some of its people went to Louisiana, others returned to Brittany. The whole film takes place against this historical background; on the one hand, there is the memory of a not very distant past still alive in people's minds; on the other, there is Quebec, the neighbouring province, a burning example of a community that still holds the majority but seems condemned to be slowly absorbed.

The film starts from a very small incident. French-speaking students revolt to obtain payment of their fees and to make sure that they will not be handicapped in comparison with the all-powerful and much older neighbouring English-speaking university, the University of New Brunswick. There are three parts: first, a wave of strikes and demonstrations starting in 1968; then the vacation, the return home to the village life of what used to be Acadia; finally the second wave of strikes in 1969, the occupation of the science block, and expulsion by the police. The fight very soon turns on the defence of the students' French-speaking heritage. This awareness comes at a time of transition, when assimilation by the United States and English Canada is taking place increasingly fast yet French Canadians, though they no longer belong to the past, are not yet part of the American future in which all differences are supposed to be flattened out.

In a profound sense this is a political film, but it has no meaning except in relation to its young characters. For the first time Perrault breaks with the world of his elders or, more precisely, with that of the old. His eye becomes sharper, and concentrates on four people: two boys, Michel Blanchard, the younger and Bernard Gauvin, the intellectual, and two girls, Blondine Maurice who wants to believe in the future and Irène Doiron who is haunted by the idea of suicide. In Perrault's now classic manner the analysis is built up on discussions but this time there is a difference because these discussions are linked to an explosive situation, certainly not important compared with other more harshly suppressed revolts, yet fundamental because we can clearly see the nub of the problem, the reason for oppression.

UN PAYS SANS BON SENS and L'ACADIE, L'ACADIE, like all Perrault's work, suffer from having been made in French, which gives them a limited appeal among those who do not speak French. But with the smallest amount of effort and intelligence, it can perfectly well be sub-titled in English or in any other language, so long as the translator really understands the original and its spirit and has a complete mastery of both French and the language into which he is translating. This applies to all direct cinema films. Direct cinema, as it has been defined here, implies a passionate reaction against the cinema of excessive simplification, the kind I have been denouncing: a cinema where visual symbolism reigns triumphant and all is for the best in the best of all possible worlds, pigeon-holed into a few fundamental groups—French, English (and American), Soviet (or Russian), etc. Direct cinema demands really hard work from the audience, and finds its greatest response in its country of origin. It opens up the way, as the whole of Perrault's work has done, to new means of expression made possible by the use of light video tape-recorders, using half-inch, extremely manageable tape on which real montage can now be achieved. Perhaps it is his own truth that Perrault shows us, but in order to do so he goes back to the living sources of a particular society where language was born and the behaviour of people laid down.

In other words, Perrault set off one day to discover his country, as he puts it in an admirable text he wrote in answer to questions from Guy Gauthier which appeared in *Image et Son* in April 1965: "I have got inside people's homes. I have got hold of their past. Nothing is more real than an old man telling of an event he has lived through. Often the facts themselves may not have any value but the telling of them has. I keep quiet. I listen." And suddenly the sense of history shows itself. Perrault is quite unlike Levi-Strauss who, through an interpreter and at a distance, collects the facts brought to light by an inquiry among the Brazilian Indians; he starts from an immediate contact and, if he can, makes two people talk to each other until they forget him. " . . . a living dialogue must be drawn from the very substance of the people, and this is possible only when they are able to stand up against each other, or else against a third party. In other words, yeast is needed. And it means having lived with them for a long time as well." Perrault's aim is "to trigger off a certain action (living, livable, possible, wished, longed for by the actors in spite of the camera) . . . to make events produce themselves before me—and not for me". Perrault starts with the convention of performance in order to multiply it by the whole connected force of the action provoked and the imaginations of the people involved in it. Far from wanting to strip reality, as Leacock does, he exalts it, recreating it in order to transfigure it. An ideal mixture of Leacock's method, which is purely cinematic, and Perrault's, which is more poetic and more literary, in which the "living"—which is more or less spontaneous and more or less organized—and the "lived"—with its historical structure, its sense of becoming—will one day produce an autonomous cinema that has finally broken completely with established methods of expression; but this is still only a dream....

Postscript 1976
Pierre Perrault has now embarked on a new series of films through the Quebec province; the first two, already seen, UN ROYAUME VOUS ATTEND and LE GOUT DE LA FARINE, prove to be still more perfectionist in the classical "Perrault approach" to reality which has no equivalent today anywhere and can be compared only with the work of Robert Bresson in the fiction film. Of course this kind of filmmaking, with words so prominent, raises huge problems in communication outside the native tongue. These films will have to be tackled seriously in the near future, by both film critics and historians.

Review of "A tout prendre"

Colin Young

Within the National Film Board of Canada, increased emphasis is going to the French unit, evidently a reflection of the general resurgence of French feeling in Quebec province, where there is even a certain body of separatist opinion. The present head of the NFB is a French Canadian, Guy Roberge. Members of the French unit come and go between Canada and the continent—Claude Jutra made a short in France (LA BONNE); Michel Brault has worked with Rouch (on CHRONIQUE D'UN ETE) and Ruspoli (REGARDS SUR LA FOLIE), and has just completed an episode for an omnibus feature on adolescence. The Montreal Film Festival is dominated by the French filmmakers and shows much contact with French developments. Leading contenders this year for the top Canadian prize were A TOUT PRENDRE and Brault's POUR LA SUITE DU MONDE. The international jury, chaired by Lindsay Anderson, gave the prize to Jutra's films. (Financed privately and shot on 16mm, it was dubbed two days before the festival showing.)

A TOUT PRENDRE was made without any of the conventional controls: it has the air of freedom and spontaneity missing in any (good) North-American narrative film since SHADOWS. And it is also filled with the inventiveness a man risks when he has a grasp of the medium and is free to explore it.

Thus the film is extremely stylish (in the decorative sense), filled with directorial and editorial flourishes, and it is revolutionary (in its structure and narrative form). We are aware of all this from the unrolling of the credits. We see a young man (Claude—played by Jutra) performing his toilet, dressing, primping in front of a mirror, affecting different guises, and finally shattering his mirror image with a pistol shot. The remainder of the film can be thought of as an embellishment of this opening sequence. We observe Claude as he meets and falls romantically in love with an amazing Negro girl, Johanne. They drift apart, but she announces that she is pregnant and that they are having trouble, perhaps, because he may prefer "the young men". He has a homosexual experiment, Johanne leaves him alone, and then finally he abandons Johanne (after contemplating marriage), dissolving the affair by the simple expedient of sending her some money in the mail—to take care of her pregnancy. He has borrowed the money from a bank, and he feels so good that, to celebrate, he buys himself a new sweater. Stroking himself happily he saunters off. Later Johanne meets a friend. "Any news of Claude?" He replies no. They walk on. The film ends. An image, a series of images, is shattered.

Reprinted from *Film Quarterly,* University of California Press, vol. 17, no. 3 (1963).

There is much more to it than this, of course, but it is all done with so much style, apparent ease, and felicity, that we realize we have finally been given the American [sic] film we have been waiting for since France and Italy startled us with *their* innovations a few years ago. Jonas Mekas has argued repeatedly (*Film Culture, Village Voice*) that the American independent filmmaker must hew his own path and find his own forms independently of his European peers. That sounds all right but the "films" of the New American Cinema have no form and do not seem to be following any useful path. It is thus not surprising that Mekas did not like A TOUT PRENDRE very much, although it is the best American film of many years and certainly the best of its generation.

Why does such a thing happen in Canada, and not the United States? The film board is partly responsible, no doubt—where else in this country is such training available? But the answer lies with the individual filmmakers. Jutra dedicated his film to McLaren and Rouch, and he is close friends with Truffaut. McLaren gives him the courage to jump around in his continuity. Rouch gives him the courage to begin not with a scenario but an event, a feeling, an experience—thus the film's inspiration is in autobiography. But its justification is in its style—and here there is the influence of Truffaut, not considered self-consciously by Jutra, but evident to the viewer.

Our producing filmmakers often see the films of Truffaut, Godard, and Antonioni (Rouch is unknown to them) but few know what to do about what they have seen (any more than do the distributors or exhibitors). Thus we have filmmakers cut off from life *and* art, hesitant to deal with life and when they do, they are either in search of a style (Ben Maddow in AFFAIR OF THE SKIN and Denis Sanders in WAR HUNT), mixing styles (Joseph Strick in THE BALCONY, Strick, Maddow and Myers in THE SAVAGE EYE, Shirley Clarke in THE CONNECTION), leaning stolidly on the past (Frank Perry in DAVID AND LISA, most of Kramer and Frankenheimer) or killing style altogether (Jonas Mekas in GUNS OF THE TREES). Adolfas Mekas at least has some fun with style, in HALLELUJAH THE HILLS, but no one seems capable of finding a style which so accurately fits the subject as Jutra does here (I am excepting the documentary directors —Leacock, Maysles, etc.). Jutra has taken the oldest subject —boy meets girl, boy gets girl in trouble, boy leaves girl—and has found ways of showing the complexity behind the simplest event.

In reconstructing his story from the past he has understood that common-sense usually simplifies the past, not necessarily making it chronological, but leaving out the confusions of the present tense. In A TOUT PRENDRE Jutra deals in confusion and ambiguity—uses them as ingredients of a scene as vital and necessary as the surface event itself. Thus, to take the simplest example: Claude embraces Johanne in his apartment; it should be a moment of concentration, but some small boys are outside the window, shooting cap pistols (there is almost always something going on outside—this is never a closed world); one of them points his gun inside the open window and fires; Claude takes the "shot", staggers limply. The tension of the scene is interrupted and then shifts away from the usual one-track concentration of a conventional scenario ("art" must abstract from "life") to the multivalence of an actual, untidy event.

Thus Jutra dramatizes experience—and in at least three other sequences carries these shiftings of concentration over into fantasy. While walking in the park with Johanne he imagines a sinister stranger stalking them, trying to take Johanne, but in the struggle killing them both. At another time Claude imagines himself attacked and beaten up by two thugs, and yet again, he imagines himself on a fire-escape, fleeing from gangsters, and being shot in the back in the act of shouting out to the world. These incidents are inserted without any technical preparation (dissolves, wipes, or fades)—they are simply cut into the scene and proceed more or less with conventional logic. Rather than existing at the same level of "realism" as the scenes on either side of them (as do the shifting scenes of tragedy and comedy in SHOOT THE PIANIST), they function as escapist fantasy, as illustrations of the emotional fabric of a character, always martyring himself (in imagination) when demands are being made of him (in actuality). It is all very funny.

Jutra now feels that this method unfortunately limits the narrative in A TOUT PRENDRE to the viewpoint of Claude and that the character of Johanne suffers thereby. "Doing it again," he said at the Flaherty Seminar, "I would try to get closer to the character of Johanne." Any autobiographer might feel this weakness in his own work, but an audience need not judge this film as autobiography (although it was the autobiographical element which contributed to the sensation it produced in Montreal—Jutra's father is a well-known doctor, and his mother is represented in the film). A distributor may sell it as "confession", but an audience can see it simply as narrative—certainly the audience at the Flaherty Seminar was overwhelmed by the film as film. The news that it was also autobiography, recreated from memory several years later, added to the quality of the experience that night (Johanne also present), but is scarcely necessary for an understanding of the film.

It *is* relevant for our judgement of Jutra as a director and of Johanne as an actress. The scenes of Claude's first meetings with Johanne are brilliantly romantic and beautiful. It is hard to believe that this is Jutra's first narrative film. It is hard to believe that Johanne has not always been an actress. In a crucial scene Johanne confesses that she has been living a fiction—that she is not the exotic Haitian she has had everyone believe, but was born in the Negro slums of Montreal. Here Jutra reverses his procedure—concentrates on the event itself, allows no element to intrude, prevents our attention from being attracted by anything but the confession itself. In the context of the film as a whole, this scene thus takes on significance that italics lend to prose on a printed page.

It is a rich, suggestive, provocative work—one that I could go back to again and again—and hope to when it becomes available. It is the only thoroughly *contemporary* American (albeit French-Canadian) film of my generation—that is perhaps why it seems so alive. But in a more general way its pleasures and its insights and craft are available to all.

The Facts of Life, Toronto Style

Joan Fox

Whoever would have thought that Don Owen's film, NOBODY WAVED GOODBYE, would acquire the "in" distinction of a review in *Vogue* magazine, that manual and guide of the smart dilettante set, where it is described as "another of those carefully observed, realistic films from Canada... beautifully done in a plain way". It's only a small notice and the reviewer denotes more space to the accompanying film, that accomplished little trouble-maker LONELY BOY, but just the same, such a notice in the heart of American big-magazine taste-making must have been balm to Don Owen after the casual scorn and indifference which his modest film met with in Canada. Here, in the heart of the Canadian film world, Mr. N.A. Taylor, our most eminent exhibitor and distributor dismissed the film as "garbage" and "amateur night in Hicksville". Taken altogether, Canadian response was largely one of "no confidence" until a New York distributor took up the film after the New York Film Festival and spent some money on its promotion. In New York, it was described as "one of the freshest films in years" and the promoter obviously hopes that he has another sleeper success like DAVID AND LISA on his hands. He has something better than that, a more truthful, less contrived film which for that very reason will probably satisfy the public less. Slicker films include answers to the problems they pose.

Don Owen, who wrote and directed NOBODY WAVED GOODBYE, was raised in Toronto and is very much a local product. Owen felt his film as something very personal, and the result is a genuine authenticity of mood which catches the spirit of his subject. He shot the film in Toronto on assignment from the National Film Board to make a television documentary about adolescents. The result is something more than a TV show but slightly less than a full-fleshed feature film.

His hero is an eighteen-year-old boy, ingratiatingly played by Peter Kastner, who is acutely feeling the crisis in identity characteristic of

Reprinted from *Canadian Forum*, July 1965.

adolescents. His home is comfortable and square. His parents are commendable, congenial, honest citizens who completely identify with their materialistic suburban surroundings and fail to understand the source of their son's rebellious beatnik attitudes and irresponsibility.

Owen and Kastner have combined to give a very subtle portrayal of the factors leading a bright well-disposed boy from what is called a "nice" family into the sort of behavior labelled as juvenile delinquency. He has been given neither enough responsibility nor enough challenge as an adolescent. He has that spark of divine discontent which indicates potential, the sort of creative flicker and responsiveness which can turn into criminality if abused by society. He is fed up with school and wants to work because he wants a richer, more demanding life, and he has no cause to give his student life focus, as the French Canadians have. He starts skipping school with his steady girlfriend, and takes a joy ride in one of his father's cars. This leads him right into trouble with both the police and his parents, and so he leaves home to work on his own. He falls into bad company in the person of a parking lot manager whose total philosophy is that of the petty crook. This man is remarkably played by John Vernon with all the suggestion of capable adult masculinity that would be so appealing to the boy.

Finally, caught in a web of complexities that are too much for the youth's comprehension or experience, he desperately decides to flee and steals a car. He takes his girlfriend, who informs him after they begin that she is pregnant. Now the noose is fully tightened around the boy's neck. When she discovers that the money and the car are stolen, the girl opts out and leaves him. The boy goes on, not to return to Toronto to face family and consequences, but away down the highway in the opposite direction—the sure way to turn the incident into the most serious irrevocable kind of trouble for himself.

The girl is more passive and responsible and potentially moral. She is only slightly sullen towards her mother in the expression of her rebellion, and she meets her dilemma with some practicality and common sense. She is played by Julie Biggs as an anonymous interchangeable sort of girl who is at the same time within that small but discernible trickle of Canadian-style heroines. These range from Mary Pickford to Joyce Davidson, the style is World War I—sweet, soft and virginal but realistic and ready to cope without complaint.

Owen shot many scenes using spontaneous dialogue and the result shows surprising identification on the part of the actors (one prominent CBC producer who disliked the film shrugged derisively, "Actors? What are actors?")—particularly from Charmion King as the boy's mother. She is forced into the position of nagging her son to be ambitious on her terms, the only terms society encourages, which are to get to college, work steadily, and never rock the boat. As the boy says, "Why do you have to be such a mother?"

The film grows in mood and credibility as it develops despite an unfortunate opening on a scene of self-conscious teenage discussion of moral values which is as hard to take as it is in life. Owen exhibited a flair for the evocative and lyrical in his film board short on Bruce Kidd called RUNNER and this same touch is in evidence throughout his feature, though it is not the dominant tone. NOBODY WAVED GOODBYE is not a thoroughly satisfying film, but it has virtues that demand attention. It leaves the impression that it has been personally thought out, however naive the result at times, rather than being derivative and imitative. It is more concerned with human values than with being part of a stylistic movement, though it still bears some traces of film board influence in its technique and attitudes. It is neither earnest documentary nor clear-cut drama, but this uncertain style is part of the WASP Toronto thing and in this respect the film is true and reflects its subject matter. It is the first feature film made about English Canada which arrives without effort at a thoroughly native quality, as the French-Canadian films have been doing in Quebec. But unfortunately NOBODY WAVED GOODBYE is isolated and ahead of its time in the context of English Canada. Toronto is not yet a community which thinks of expressing itself in terms of film.

The great lack of sympathy which I have heard expressed for this film hangs largely around the character of the boy. As Peter Kastner plays him, he just simply gets on the nerves of a lot of people who can't imagine themselves with such a son in the family. I think that this merely indicates the incredibly Philistine and smug nature of what is still the major part of English-Canadian society. Why, this kid is so gauche that he asks his sister's fiancé if he's really happy at the prospect of devoting his life to dentistry, and with inordinate bad timing he asks his salesman father for a loan while said father is being groomed in the barber's chair. Apparently nice suburban Torontonians do not do such unthinkable things. Kastner plays the boy with many indications of secret reserves in his personality. For instance, when he is questioned by the probation officer he merely smiles with shy embarrassment and considerable dignity when asked if he has slept with his girlfriend. He chooses to keep this a private matter in what is, I think, a characteristically Canadian manner. All the characters of this film have their untouched internal reserve—their personalities are not all on the surface as in certain American films which deal with "problem" subject matter. Consider this Peter as a rebel without a cause and compare the film with the sensational polemical film of that title which starred the late James Dean. Owen's delinquent is clearly a potential responsible adult and not a psychopath drowning in his own self-pity. This Canadian boy is a reactionary figure in the context of North American popular culture in that he is presented as an individual rather than a type. Again, compare this superficially naive yet complex character with the white-washed stereotypes of such an over-praised small "sincere" American film as ONE POTATO, TWO POTATO which depicts a Negro-white marriage. In order to make this situation palatable the main characters, and particularly the Negro, are sweetly sentimentalized into a state of primitive innocence which would make the heart of David Wark Griffith beat faster. Owen's film is singular in that it has no part of the sticky kind of evasiveness that permeates what pass for liberally-oriented films from America. His adolescent hero's personality is made up of more whole cloth. The assumption is that any kid who wanders around with a guitar slung over his shoulder asking people where they are going in life can be alternately amusing, charming, sweetly shy, offensively aggressive, and in general a bothering pain in the neck.

Another manner in which Owen's film stands apart from the money made on this subject, and I think this is another instance of its indigenous Canadian character, is that the adults are all figures of authority. They are not grotesque caricatures à la Elia Kazan or William Inge stewing in thick brews of Freudian juice and written off as a destructive element in the lives of their offspring. They may not understand their adolescent children but they are allowed to retain their dignity. Peter's parents may bicker incessantly, but they are not engaged in a to-the-death war of sexually biased one-upmanship in which they are prepared to devour one another as well as their children. They are confused human beings rather than case histories.

Owen has also been criticized for not including a great panting sex scene between the adolescents as a prelude to the girl getting in trouble. Such restraint is considered "old hat" and a typical instance of the backwardness of Canadian films. He has chosen to show instead some moments of companionship, tenderness and bickering. By implying the sexual relationship without accentuating it, he has put it into a more reasonable perspective and implied that even for adolescents it is not always the most acutely central portion of their lives. If you reduce most youth problem films to their basic suppositions, you find the easy-think premise that if only adolescents were allowed to express their emotions sexually, calm rationality would prevail in the relations between the generations and presumably youth would stop rebelling. Owen's film stands apart from this class altogether. He never once implies that there are such fatuously easy solutions nor does he stand back and judge this boy or any of these people. These northerners have a sturdy innocence which prevents them from carrying their actions through to the last degree of romanticism. When the girl refuses to go to the bitter end with the boy, one isn't certain why her commitment to the boy ends where it does, but one cannot doubt the reserves that make it possible. She simply has an old-fashioned quantity of eastern North-American self-respect, which includes the capacity to question the roles which circumstances force upon her. Her character has the same quality as the very Canadian style of the film. It is traditional in adhering to the documentary approach but radical in its Chekhovian atmosphere of seeing life and human nature in terms of open rather than closed ends.

Compared to Claude Jutra's A TOUT PRENDRE, or any other French-Canadian film, one is struck by the irresolute nature of this English-Canadian hero's rebellion, not only in the political sense, but also in considering it as a portrait of the artist as a young man. In Quebec it is possible to accept a fully-committed artist like Jutra as hero, or anti-hero if you like, but in Toronto it is hardly acceptable to have as a hero a dilettante beatnik like Peter whose ambition does not exceed strumming away on the folk-song kick. He isn't even sold on knowing himself, his curiosity is directed outwards toward the world. Altogether a good candidate for university who falls into delinquency because of the apathy of the world about him.

Who's Don Owen? What's He Done, and What's He Doing Now?

Natalie Edwards

Personally, I don't give a damn about film as film. I want to communicate with it. As a poet, the only people I reached were my fellow poets. I think it's important not just to make good films, but films that audiences want to see.

Said Don Owen to Howard Junker of the *Montreal Star* in 1964. This relative newcomer to the National Film Board's Unit B was being interviewed by the venerable *Star* because at thirty, with only two small but worthy little black-and-white NFB shorts to his name, he had just shot a full feature-length film called NOBODY WAVED GOODBYE (shoving the NFB's intended first feature, THE DRYLANDERS, in the shade), and was about to make history (Canadian) with it.

Time passes. It's almost a decade since 1964. Those who don't say "Who's Don Owen and what's he done?" may be saying, "What's Don Owen doing now?"

He started out like many a potential filmmaker thinking he was something else—maybe a poet. And he went to the University of Toronto as people do now, taking whatever interested him, skipping the important-paper bit, the degrees. No grants, so he worked summers for Forest Rangers, in a mine, as a fire spotter. He naturally ended up as a CBC stagehand. And he hung around the Greenwich Gallery and worked

Reprinted from *Cinema Canada*, no. 8 (June-July 1973).

at being a poet, just like Irving Layton and Leonard Cohen. And maybe had second thoughts about his poetry. About Leonard Cohen he said in a *Saturday Night* article:

> I could get used to the idea that he was a better poet than I was, but he always seemed to leave the gallery with the most interesting woman there, the one I'd spent all evening trying to get up enough nerve to say hello to.

And he discovered film.

> Living in Toronto when I was a teenager there was very very little film to be seen. Well, that's not accurate. I was not aware of film, that's all. I came from a working-class background and found my way into writing somehow and it took me a while to discover what film was all about. That took place when I started attending meetings of the Toronto Film Society. I saw a few of those masterpieces... and suddenly I began to realize what the fantastic potential of the medium was. And then the TFS had a series on Sundays in which they showed two or three works by one director—and I remember seeing Max Ophul's work, three films I think, something staggering, and the whole kind of possibility of film began to bloom for me. So it wasn't long after that that I took the opportunity of going down to the film board in Montreal to work, and it was there that I began to learn how to put a film together.

In Tom Daly's Unit B of the National Film Board were Colin Low, Roman Kroiter and Wolf Koenig when Don Owen joined it. Daly became a kind of guru for Owen, taught him, encouraged him, let him develop. Daly, himself influenced by Grierson, now heavily influenced Owen, who was ripe for hard work and a direction for his creative energies.

> When I went to the film board... I felt like a man who was desperately escaping from some terrible misery because I was very unhappy in Toronto. I was working as a poet and I had come to realize that my work was pretty poor, and I felt very badly about it and of course I... sort of dried up—all those things having to do with a relatively emotionally mixed-up childhood.

RUNNER (1962)

His first film, RUNNER, was a black-and-white twelve-minute short about Bruce Kidd.

> A film that was in praise of an athlete, but praising him in a rather lofty way... I was interested in the idea of the Pinderian Ode.

Classically constructed, with a commentary written by W.H. Auden at Owen's request, the film was described by the British Film Institute in 1964 as a poem. "It is a film about running or the runner. Matching a very apt quasi-Greek commentary by W.H. Auden, the camera focusses on legs, feet, balancing arms, the body in motion. The style is Spartan, spare and very disciplined; this matches perfectly the control and grace of the runner, and results in a poem to the human body in motion which is wholly successful." Actually, not quite, according to Owen.

> There is a sense in which RUNNER is a kind of perfect film with a very, very serious flaw, and that is the commentary is just too dense to understand.

Owen is grateful to the National Film Board for the training he got with them, and the freedom to work without time or commercial pressures.

> After I'd finished shooting the film the executive producer, Tom Daly, put me in a cutting room by myself and said, cut it. And left me alone for two months.

In this first film Owen's talent of marrying the technique and style of a film to its subject matter, in this case a classical construction to the sense of discipline and single-mindedness of the runner, was already apparent.

Meanwhile, about 1960, the new light-weight, sync-sound, hand-held cameras created cinéma vérité. Godard's BREATHLESS in 1959 was revolutionary; in 1961 Cassavetes made SHADOWS. Owen, at this time, added to his experience by working with the French unit of the NFB as a cameraman on films such as SEPTEMBER 5 AT ST. HENRI (a documentary of a day in a working-class district) and LA LUTTE (on wrestling). He liked the French unit's spirit and use of improvisational techniques.

TORONTO JAZZ (1964)

> TORONTO JAZZ is my first example of working in a candid tradition. It was a film in which I did a lot of experimenting with cinéma vérité, with the idea of shooting things just off the cuff. In a sense I think TORONTO JAZZ is a less successful film, in fact it's considerably less successful—it just never worked.

There are lots of good things in it nevertheless, such as seeing 1964 Toronto again, the streets and trees and buildings (now so changed), the nightclub life, Michael Snow as a little-known artist and musician, Don Francks in one of the ups of his bobbing career. But most of all the film is interesting as part of Owen's work for illustrating the way he again uses a technique that harmonizes with his material. The casual hand-held camera, unscripted dialogue, the scenes whose length is determined only by their interest, the improvisational inventiveness, all are themselves like the jazz they are showing: spontaneous yet controlled. Mind you, it doesn't quite work. Owen, the poet, is not quite a jazzman on film. But by 1972 he had a firm grasp on this technique for his recent film COWBOY AND INDIAN, which has, incidentally, the same subliminal theme: the nature of the creative male, his surroundings, ambiance, the landscape of his creative life.

NOBODY WAVED GOODBYE (1964)

Now, with a twelve-minute and twenty-seven-minute film behind him, Owen was assigned a half-hour documentary about a probation officer and a juvenile delinquent, calculated to be shot in three weeks for about $30,000. And he shot NOBODY WAVED GOODBYE. In five weeks (spread out over a year). For $75,000.

> I proposed it as a kind of half-hour story film, and on the original budget it's a half-hour story film called FIRST OFFENSE. I started shooting and in the first three days we shot almost half our budget of films and I was already into deep trouble because we were doing something that hadn't been done before, certainly at the film board anyway.

John Spotton, who was also Owen's cameraman on RUNNER, just kept shooting....

> ...and I kept on ordering more film. It so happened that all the people were away so that in fact there was nobody at the NFB to say don't send any more film. They kept on sending film and I kept on shooting and the story kept on getting more elaborate and more elaborate, and I added scenes —the great thing about improvising is you're really writing the script while you're shooting—so the thing grew. And when I came back to Montreal four weeks later, I was then something like $10,000 over budget, and I shot 50,000 feet of film instead of 25,000 feet, and I said: I shot a feature.

The NFB didn't fire Owen, and with co-producer Kroiter's backing, Daly's defence, and encouragement from all of Unit B, they let him finish the film. However, the NFB never did quite know how to handle the eighty-minute bastard he gave them, so they slipped their surprise feature almost unheralded into Toronto and Montreal in December 1964. And it died.

> I was really broken by this. I mean it really shook me. It shook my confidence, terribly.

NOBODY WAVED GOODBYE had been shown at the Montreal Film Festival in the summer of 1964, but Gilles Groulx's LE CHAT DANS LE SAC won, and the Canadian Film Awards judges refused to name an over-all 1964 Film of the Year claiming there was just nothing good enough. However, the film won the CIDALC award in Mannheim, Germany, and the Flaherty Award, the British Academy award for best feature length documentary in London, and in September 1964 Judith Crist considered it the highlight of the New York Film Festival.

There was nothing more deadly in 1964 than the word "local". And this was "local" show. Bob Fulford commented in the *Star*: "It seems too bad that the National Film Board is bringing its latest feature into town in such an apologetic way.... It was made here with a local cast and a local director; it's subject is middle-class Toronto suburban society and an adolescent's revolt against the society.... But the film board is bringing it here in something like secrecy. No publicity campaign that you can notice."

Times have changed, and you have to remember 1964 to recall how disheartening the words "Toronto" and "Canadian" were also when Frank Morriss said in the *Globe*: "It is a sad, dreary, ineffectual but sometimes moving little film the New Yorker theatre is showing for Christmas. NOBODY WAVED GOODBYE, a NFB feature movie made in Toronto with a cast of Canadian actors, illustrates the plight of teenagers.... "

In the States, however, the problems the film dealt with were more common, or at least more acknowledged, and as big, broad and superficial films were commonplace, so this lean, honest and original work was a refreshing change. In April 1965 Dan Rugoff distributed it through Cinema V, spending $70,000 (almost its original cost) on promotion, and deliberately keeping its low-budget Canadian art-film origins quiet. And the New York critics loved it.

It was hailed as "an exceptionally fine movie" by the *New Yorker's* Brendan Gill, "commensurate in the purity of its intentions, and even in the artistry of its execution, with *The Catcher in the Rye*" (and oddly enough now shares the fate of Salinger's book by also being offered in high school courses). *The New York Post* found it a film that views "a contemporary reality with shocking cinematic clarity" and is "alternatively fine and uncomfortably simple". Crowther of *The Times* found it "admirably put forth". *The Daily News* liked the "spontaneous effect" of the improvised dialogues. *Time's* reviewer found the poetry in the film: it "conquers its simple ideas and tangled verbiage with cool cinematic assurance, turning a problem play into a poem". And in the *Herald Tribune* Judith Crist declared, "it is a film you should not miss ... it is a 'small' movie—and a universal one" and put it on her Ten Best List for the year.

And so it came back home, and did well, grossing $5,000 a week at the Nortown in Toronto compared to the meagre $3,500 in two weeks it made on its first appearance at the New Yorker.

> NOBODY WAVED GOODBYE was very important to me personally, because it was the first film that I made that really took off, and was very successful.

In terms of style, Owen worked hard on this film to develop the extraordinary marriage of spontaneity and control he desired.

> I was trying to search for the kind of flexibility that you have in candid film, with the formal aspect that RUNNER had... a very controlled kind of improvisation.

To do this he used his own story outline, wrote an analysis of the motivations of each character in each scene, and took the actors aside individually explaining only their own motivation to them.

> ...and telling them two totally different stories of what was going to happen, so they often didn't know when they came together and started to talk that they had two different kinds of information.

Peter's surprised laugh when Julie tells him she's pregnant was authentic. Owen extended his own experiences, using the personalities of his responsive cast, and the result made the film seem very honest.

> The film tries to get at something in North American life, and get at it with a certain honesty. There are mistakes in it. It was made in a rush and it gets talky in places. It needs a little more control —possibly a compromise between improvisation and written dialogue.

And this is the cinematic problem central to Owen's work: how to retain the natural and keep it under control. How to make movies like jazz —spontaneous and responsive, yet artistically formed, defined and limited. Maybe how to live that way. Godard was making films like that: BREATHLESS, UNE FEMME EST UNE FEMME, VIVRE SA VIE. In an interview in *Objectif*, Owen said:

> J'admire beaucoup Godard, et bien que je n'essaie pas de le copier, j'aimerais arriver à avoir la même approche que lui vis-à-vis de la mise en scène.

As the first National Film Board feature to open in New York, NOBODY WAVED GOODBYE made history. The film board continued Owen's training, and Owen concluded:

> Actually the film was under-praised in Canada and over-praised abroad.

THREE SHORTS (1965)

Now if you're somewhat fancifully minded, it's fascinating to note what the film board set this inspired and unruly guy to next. First, he was sent to the top of the girders on a New York construction site where the famous Caughnawaga Mohawks of Quebec work, to film HIGH STEEL, and before he got that cut and finished he was bundled off to zap around two provinces preparing a film on four poets on a university tour, which eventually appeared as LADIES AND GENTLEMEN, MR. LEONARD COHEN, and had to be completed by Don Brittain when Owen was shipped off to Africa to Itu, Nigeria to shoot a documentary on a young CUSO doctor, Alex McMahon and his wife, YOU DON'T BACK DOWN.

HIGH STEEL taught him to handle 35mm colour, and its use in the film is careful and effective. He loved the adventure, and he didn't fall off the girders.

> This was a very scary film to make. But one of the most important aspects of filmmaking for me is the adventure that's always been involved in it. Shooting on the steel meant we had to go up twenty-four stories and we were shooting off very narrow beams... and so we felt at once heroic and foolish at the same time.

Owen wrote, directed and edited it himself, picking up a Canadian Film Award as best editor for it. It was also his first 35mm theatrical short.

> It's a very challenging form because it's a chance to compress a great deal of material into a very short and lyrical form and you don't structure it the way you would a dramatic work.

It was shown on CBC-TV May 1965, and had wide theatrical distribution.

The one-night-stands with the performing poets were hectic — so rushed in fact that it was almost impossible to film. At least for Owen. So instead he got stoned a lot with his friend Leonard Cohen, and shot the Pierre Berton interview, the performance, parties and make-up room sequences, while Don Brittain shot the rest, including some fascinating footage of Cohen musing about himself in a hotel room. LADIES AND GENTLEMEN, MR. LEONARD COHEN is a good film portrait, but Owen considers it mostly Brittain's film.

Filming YOU DON'T BACK DOWN, Owen didn't even get lost in Africa, though the Biafran war was about to start. Driving through a crowd of Ibos in the midst of a political rally, their car was stopped and surrounded.

> Then they started to rock the Volkswagen, back and forth, and there was a moment when I felt — sheer panic — then somebody laughed, and they all laughed, and the tension was broken and they (the crowd) opened up and we drove on. But you could sense that fantastic tension everywhere. It was a great experience.

YOU DON'T BACK DOWN is 28 minutes, shot in 16mm black-and-white.

> In a sense I suppose the big experience for me in this film was making the film, going there, and being like the central character, rather square, and protected, and innocent, and coming up against death and — incredible things.

The work that Owen did on these three shorts, plus an effective CBC "Telescope" on MONIQUE LEYRAC IN CONCERT, greatly increased his technical competence and prepared him for something unique and personal again.

NOTES FOR A FILM ABOUT DONNA AND GAIL (1966)

Using the successful candid style of NOBODY WAVED GOODBYE and 16mm black-and-white, Owen began a probe of the schizophrenic nature of friendship in a pair of working-class girls, Donna and Gail, and, as he experimented with several film styles in order to try to capture the elusive nature of his subject, he logically titled the forty-eight minute result, NOTES FOR A FILM ABOUT DONNA AND GAIL.

This remains his favourite film, despite the fact he is usually very fond of whatever he's just been working on. Unlike NOBODY WAVED GOODBYE, which linked actor Kastner's experiences with Owen's own knowledge of rebellious adolescence—

> I did come to put a lot of my own life into it. People say the boy is very much like me....

DONNA AND GAIL was not so noticeably a personal film and has never been criticized as the later THE ERNIE GAME was, for self-indulgence.

The film is visibly organized in Godardian sections; there's a prologue, and episodes of the two girls meeting, settling their apartment, working, dating, and breaking up, followed by an epilogue. The naturalistic factory sequences are memorable and quite unique in Canadian film, and the performances by Jackie Burroughs as Gail and Michele Chicoine as Donna are downright remarkable.

Although several styles are implemented (direct interview, voice-over interview, story-telling, candid camera) basically Owen still is experimenting with a compromise between the spontaneity of improvisation and the tighter control of scripted dialogue (using Gerald Taafe's "charming script").

> I'm after the real honesty of the situation. And as you work with actresses in the environment of the story, you begin to find ways of doing what is real that even the best writer couldn't, at his desk.

As an undercurrent to the girls' relationship, while the narration (read by Pat Watson) ponders their attraction to each other, and their effects on each other, he also reveals something of his own lonely problems, and of how studying the girls aids him in understanding himself.

In a lecture to a night class on film Owen explained that he was fascinated with the subject because the separate natures of the girls were like parts of himself: the practical, hard and realistic; and the imaginative, immature, responsive, yet separate. He said in *Take One* of the film, that it

168   Feature Filmmaking

> expresses my own particular kind of schizophrenia—my teeter-tottering between two worlds....

Martin Knelman, writing for the *Toronto Star* in 1968, described the film as "intimate, spontaneous, personal, probing... the film is a study, a sketchy and unpretentious effort" whose scope he felt revealed "what we ought to be doing in film in this country right now".

NOTES FOR A FILM ABOUT DONNA AND GAIL won in the medium-length category at the Montreal International Film Festival in 1966, and received a General Information Award, Canadian Film Awards, 1967.

> When I started to make DONNA AND GAIL, I was starting to make a film in which I had to solve all the problems because they were completely new ones in terms of what I wanted to do. I found myself out in areas where I didn't have any examples to fall back on, to do the kind of film that I wanted. And somehow that was the moment for me of really becoming a filmmaker. Nothing I'd done before that really touched that level.

* * *

By this time in Owen's work, after six years and six films with the NFB, several themes are apparent. One concerns the middle-class. He told Dusty Vineberg of the *Montreal Star:*

> The middle-class isn't something I despise. After all, most people want to get married, have children and aspire to that kind of life. But how are we going to survive that kind of life? How do you live a life where you don't destroy your children, which is creative and meaningful, and where there is love, in a society in which all obvious needs are satisfied?

He remains interested in this problem, how you survive and make your life meaningful in an affluent society. After all, he says, if all the social revolutions are successful, what you end up with is well-fed, well-clothed, well-housed people. And once you've achieved that, then what...?

About his African film, YOU DON'T BACK DOWN, he said:

> Nobody caught on but it is really a film about my basic theme. The McMahons are from a very middle-class background. These people are forced to reconsider their values, and that's good.

And NOBODY WAVED GOODBYE was highly praised for its sensitive comprehension of the middle-class. His *au courant* awareness caught the drift of the times accurately.

> NOBODY WAVED GOODBYE was the story of a young man from a middle-class home who had a banjo and ran away from home to sing songs. [It was] just around the time Dylan was about to start singing. I don't think he was on the market. But it certainly wasn't based on Dylan, it was just my intuition about what was going on. And it preceded the whole movement.

And finally, ROSEDALE LADY, the film he should be making now, may once again examine middle-class values.

> There's a sense in which ROSEDALE LADY is a reprise of NOBODY WAVED GOODBYE. NOBODY WAVED GOODBYE is about a young kid breaking out of a well-to-do middle-class home and going out and becoming a thief. And this is the story of a thief breaking his way into an establishment family... and taking up a role in society as a kind of responsible person.

Another theme is the complexity of his own character, the nature of a divided personality. First explored in DONNA AND GAIL, who represented two aspects of his psyche, he prods it further with Ernie of THE ERNIE GAME, who represents the oil-and-water-in-one combination, creating a character so in flux and so evasive of self-understanding that he can only be a loser. This was to be a trilogy, but Owen said:

> The third film I lived through. That's what I've been doing. The idea of the film, "Going to Gail'sville" it was going to be called, was about going to the country to live, something I'm doing right now.

However, there are a lot of uncompleted projects in every filmmaker's life.

> All the things I wanted to do and never did, eh....

But meanwhile Owen became drawn to some highly personal impressions written by Bernard Cole Spencer about mental hospitals and mental illness, that the NFB might use for a documentary on mental health.

> I didn't even know at the time why I was interested in it. It was as though my sensibility was excited by it in an unconscious kind of way.

THE ERNIE GAME (1967)

> ...originally it began as a story of a man who was presumably a schizophrenic and as I started to work on it I became aware first of the appalling ignorance on the subject... the whole nature of insanity is so far away from our understanding. It's like another human existence.

He decided to use the DONNA AND GAIL characters again to help interpret the character of Ernie.

> I wanted to suggest what a schizophrenic was without telling you, and the way I suggested it was to show the relationship between the two girls... two people who are totally opposite in qualities, because that's what schizophrenia is, the inability to resolve one's

impulses going in opposing directions. We all have it. We're all
schizophrenic. To an extent.

A co-production between the NFB and the CBC, THE ERNIE GAME was
intended to be one of a number of such efforts (including Kelly's
WAITING FOR CAROLINE) to be shown on CBC-TV ("Festival") and then
released to movie theatres: a Centennial Project.

> ...an astonishing amount of pressure was put on us, both Ron
> Kelly and myself. I mean we really had a sense that it just had to be
> fantastic. And we had *two* sets of executives to deal with: the CBC
> and the NFB....

The big budget also made people nervous. Shooting was delayed while
Owen replaced an ill director for some adventuresome filming of the
formation of a volcanic island off Iceland, and again when he was
required to shoot a scripted documentary about an adopted boy, A
FURTHER GLIMPSE OF JOEY, for the NFB.

> I was about to shoot THE ERNIE GAME... desperate to get going on
> it, and the film board said to me, before you shoot THE ERNIE GAME
> you have to shoot this film.... [It was] partly to make me get more
> experience working with actors because they were afraid in such a
> big budget film....

Owen prepared a 140-page script, and had a nine-week shooting schedule
and a budget of $265,621. The eighty-six-minute 35mm colour feature
took somewhat longer and went over budget. It was shown on CBC-TV
November 8, 1967.

Time called it a "low budget production ($300,000)" and rated it
"not-to-be-missed". But that December Senator Fournier, a Conservative from New Brunswick, called it and Kelly's WAITING FOR CAROLINE
(which went $190,000 over budget) "indecent, immoral and repulsive"
and hoped the films would "never again be shown in Canada or anywhere else", as he bitterly complained to the Senate about their cost.
The third projected CBC-NFB co-production was not made.

Despite Senator Fournier's help, the film only ran two weeks at
Cinecity in Toronto in October 1968, and a subtitled version didn't open
in Montreal until February 1969. Columbia distributed.

Owen said in *Take One* in 1967:

> THE ERNIE GAME is very modern, very contemporary. The things
> that it deals with are things that are the preoccupation of the
> psychedelic generation—sanity, insanity, consciousness.

The film was beautifully shot in Eastmancolor by Jean-Claude
Labrecque, with Owen carefully guiding the psychological effects of
colour. Background music was by the then little-known Kensington
Market. Leonard Cohen sang a song in a party sequence that suggested a
poetic key to the film: "It's hard to hold the hand of any man, who's

reaching for the sky just to surrender...." In style, Ernie's complex and enigmatic character, and the film's open-ended construction belong to a coolly observant, unromantic novel, and Owen admits to trying to use film personally as if he were writing a book. He experiments with film poetry too, capsulating clues and statements in certain symbolic little scenes such as Ernie kissing and trying to know and love the cold-reflection of himself in a mirror, or the double-edged sequence of Ernie shooting people with an empty camera, watching with delight his momentary influence as they react.

THE ERNIE GAME excited contradictory responses in viewers and critics. At the time Gerald Pratley wrote in the *Toronto Telegram*, "THE ERNIE GAME, viewed in a press preview, is an utter failure.... The character of Ernie Turner in the film, monotonously played by Alexis Kanner, is a totally uninteresting young man.... He walks through the picture, aimless and foolish, and leaves us quite unmoved.... And it is doubtful that he has any appeal for the younger generation which is supposed to be turned on to this kind of outcast, anti-hero."

At the other extreme Mark Slade, a young man writing for the *Montreal Gazette* the same day, gave a four-column praise-laden eulogy to the film: "His dilemma is the dilemma of his age.... he is trapped in a social experiment, which, in a mindless zeal for success, has long since dropped any pretension to human value." Slade's view of Ernie: "As many sided as an insect's eye, this fellow wanders awkwardly into our psychotic space, stays awhile, makes us laugh, makes us cry, then recedes behind the drugged blur of an upstairs window. To live with him much longer would be unbearable; he can hardly live with himself."

People in fact reacted to THE ERNIE GAME as they would have reacted to Ernie. Clyde Gilmour in the *Telegram* found that "the foolish, self-absorbed drifter of the title role, played with undeniable skill by Alexis Kanner of Montreal, is a boring and irritating character", and appears to have small tolerance for "this parasitical fellow, with his condescending smile and his allergy to soap".

Joan Fox, in the *Globe*, noted, "A little warmth in this study would have worked wonders," typifying the irritation felt by many, viewers who wanted to, but just couldn't, take Ernie. Owen's cool, anti-sentimental, anti-romantic direction denied direct empathy with the character.

I was determined to be kind of very cold and outside the character.

Owen's skill at luring the audience into caring and then alienating them the moment they did, kept the character remote, unknowable. It perplexed the audience with the same kind of dual reactions to Ernie that Ernie had himself to society. This induced something like schizophrenic sensations in the audience resulting in uneasiness, irritation, insecurity. It also perfectly illustrates Owen's technique of matching the style of his film to its subject. (McLuhan was then saying, The medium IS the message!)

Bob Fulford observed in the *Star*, 1967: "THE ERNIE GAME exemplifies Owen's method as well as his central theme—it's open-mesh filming, lots of gaps, lots of questions unanswered. It demands participation."

At the Berlin Film Festival in June 1968, critic Elvira Reitze praised the film "... so full of gags and pain", while at home, the wonderful Wendy Michener, whose death was such a sad loss to Canadian film criticism, called it "nothing less than the best English-Canadian fiction film to date and, what's more, a strikingly original, highly personal and engaging film", and after her fourth viewing, added, "All those who can't stand weakness or failure will probably despise both Ernie and the film."

What it's all about were all the things that were wrong with me.

An Etrog for best director was awarded Owen at the 1968 Canadian Film Awards, after THE ERNIE GAME was pronounced best feature.

> [The filmmaker] must expose himself, and that involves the possibility of great pain. When I made THE ERNIE GAME I went through what Ernie went through. By the time I finished I was exhausted.

By this time Owen needed a break and his family life needed mending.

> Working at the film board one tends to neglect one's life. It's [the NFB] inaccessible, so you tend to go out there and stay out there. You are away a lot. By the time I left I had a real patch-up job to do on my life...on my marriage.

Separated from the film board, Owen did a brief stint for the United States Information Agency scripting THE REAL BIG SOCIETY with a group of lower east side kids, then with a Canada Council grant, took off to "study filmmaking abroad" travelling to London, Paris, Rome and Berlin to meet filmmakers and study techniques during actual filming. The family settled in Ibeza (Santa Eulalia), Spain, for ten months of peace and rest.

He sounded confident on his return. He told Melinda McCracken in the *Globe*:

> I'm willing to try anything once. Any drug or experience. It's an obligation you have to your sensibility as an artist. I have to keep changing. I change my appearance about every six months. My hair gets longer or shorter. I get fatter or thinner. Even with a family, I have to keep this insecurity and change in my life. You can do both.

On Judith Crist's recommendation, he was asked by the Albright-Knox

Art Gallery in Buffalo, New York to make a film about their gallery, and given free reign as long as he included the important works.

GALLERY: A VIEW OF TIME (1968)

GALLERY is a classic, inventive and dazzling fourteen-minute colour trip in the Albright-Knox, synthesized with a vivid and unusual soundtrack using electronically magnified footsteps, typewriter sounds, children's voices and twentieth-century noises, generally for harmonic, though occasionally for contrapuntal, effect. McCracken reviewed it in the *Globe* as "a work of art in itself", and it satisfied the gallery well, justifying the opinion of Smith, the gallery director, that "Owen is the best" and of Houston, a member of the board, who felt "he's probably the most promising young film producer in America".

This work proved that Owen has mastered cutting, editing, filmic rhythm, organization, structure, original sound, and the ability to unite all these and say something explicit (about the gallery, its architecture, its uses) and implicit (about modern art, its connections with modern life, its sources) with control and style and with beauty.

He'd already established a reputation as a director who brought tremendous realistic performances out of actors (Peter Kastner and Julie Biggs in NOBODY WAVED GOODBYE, Michele Chicoine and Jackie Burroughs as Donna and Gail, Alexis Kanner as Ernie, and Judith Gault as the later Donna), and now with further proof of his skills as a filmmaker and a shelf of awards behind him, where were the great Canadian films he should be making?

Three CBC "Telescopes" (1971): SNOW IN VENICE, RICHLER OF ST. URBAIN and COUGHTRY IN IBEZA.

> ...it meant going to Europe and shooting three films in three weeks in three totally different locations: one in England, one in Spain and one in Italy. No script... I just shot them right off the cuff.

The two screened on Michael Snow and Mordecai Richler are good film portraits, carefully constructed, cut and balanced, resulting in apparently casual, slightly unorthodox, entertaining programs.

Owen's skill at matching film technique to the characteristics of the film's subject worked particularly well capturing artist-musician-filmmaker Michael Snow, whose extraordinary film WAVELENGTH was the prizewinner at the Venice Biennale. The style of SNOW IN VENICE involved a careful blending of the necessary factual, biographical aspects, a quick look at the Biennale itself (the camera literally rushing around and past things, a scoopy view), some camera trickery with a projected image (raising the question of just what an image is), and a long concluding section just following Snow around as he photographed himself with his Polaroid, while he tried to place a moving blurred portrait of himself in front of a focused background of classic tourist shots of Venice. This section of the "Telescope" expands Snow's statement that "it is central to his art to collaborate with chance" by doing just that as it observes Snow trying to solve the problem he has just set himself, also illustrating his comment that "the artist makes up the rules of the game and then attempts to play it".

> RICHLER OF ST. URBAIN... was just when he was finishing *Horseman*, he was struggling through that tidying-up work. I really got to like him enormously.

The main effort of this "Telescope" portrait was discovering the interest in the character, letting Richler reveal himself, his way of life, his thoughts.

> Another one on Graham Coughtry in Ibeza which never got finished. I still have only the cutting copy of it now. But it's one of my very favourite films. It's very weird, strange—a peculiar film. [Actually] it's finished, but the CBC refused it, so it never got test printed. It's really a very poetic landscape description with some very new things evolving with the camera.

And after that?

> Then I did some commercials. I thought it was great. I learned a tremendous amount about time in film, like how much you can get into a ten-second shot.

COWBOY AND INDIAN (1972)

In 1972 Owen, under a contract from NFB, made COWBOY AND INDIAN for an amount neither he nor the NFB care to mention. "The most expensive," says a critic, "home movie ever made." Maybe the best too.

> I figure it's like a home movie.

Here in COWBOY AND INDIAN Owen pulls together his special ability to view a subject in the subject's manner, to comprehend and communicate the creative person's life, to suggest creativity, to film in an apparently informal, casual, relaxed manner which in reality covers a well-constructed, symmetrical, totally unified skeleton under the loose flesh of the body of the film. The work is truly organic.

This style, begun with TORONTO JAZZ, extended with portraits of Cohen, Snow, Richler, Coughtry, really swings here. As in JAZZ itself the seemingly haphazard, relaxed improvisations within the rhythmical framework, sometimes work really well, sometimes not. The result is a look at the life and times of two artists (here, as in DONNA AND GAIL, he uses the contrast between types to accentuate the individual characteristics of each), Gordon Rayner and Robert Markle, their work, their environments and their way of life, that will stand as one example of how to treat the elusive subject of artists, by avoiding the clichés so often found in informative little films busily proliferating for educational TV, high school film libraries, etc.

"An artist's life is exemplary," says Michael Snow, and indeed it does epitomize what contemporary people are beginning to realize is a desirable way of life. And COWBOY AND INDIAN is every boy's dream come true, it seems to be the perfect life: a world of fun, inventiveness, friends, food and love. In the absolute core of the film Markle's wheezy irresistible laugh seduces the audience into joining him, and when, by the end of the central section, the casual chaotic crowd around the dinner table encourage the filming crew to join them with "Put down the camera!", the invitation is an open one that includes the audience, suggesting: join us, it's great.

Reactions to the film have varied. Some find it incoherent, unfamiliar, they don't understand the language; and some women find it maddeningly chauvinistic, refusing to see the artists as artists, but only as males whose cozy existence is made comfortable by the women quietly in the background.

> [Some] women have very negative reactions to the film because the men are such male chauvinists in a way. You really see it in the film. And in a sense that's what they are. They make that work.

It's a dream world; a perpetual party. And it's hard to make it work.

> I went back to the NFB to make this film, and it's a really funny thing, the film was shot and then, while I was cutting it my whole life just kind of fell to pieces. My wife left, and I had the children, and to cut film, and cook, and it was the beginning of all that experience. Now I find it very easy, but then,... porridge on the film....

Suzanne, who as a dutiful daughter in a large French-Canadian family had accepted a "motherly" role nearly all her life, now left Owen and the children, and travelled to India to follow her guru.

> Why shouldn't she do it? I think it's the only thing to do. I think it's what it's all about, you know.

Which is true, and she does, although somewhat wryly he comments:

> The thing is I feel like I'm one of the martyrs to women's liberation.

Concerning Women's Lib he also says:

> I think the most exciting thing right now is Women's Lib.

ROSEDALE LADY (1973?)

> I don't want to tell you what it is. Briefly, though, it's a film that attempts to examine some of the aspects of the new nationalism in Canada. Essentially, it's a thriller involving the takeover of a Canadian company by a large American conglomerate. This also involves a portrait of a very Toronto family and in a way the American thing is used in a sense to define the Canadian thing. We may not know who we are but we're beginning to know who we're not. Norman Snyder is the writer. We're just completing the third draft of the script, which we hope to start shooting in the fall. The earlier attempt to mount the film on a low budget was a mistake, and we've now decided to do the film in a proper professional way, with stars and technicians experienced in feature filmmaking.

Sounds like an Owen film—contemporary, somewhat controversial, and Canadian, but not in a limiting sense. Owen doesn't feel he'll have any difficulty in acquiring renewed CFDC backing for part of the cost of the revised film. He is, however, on the lookout for a producer.

MEANWHILE

At present Don Owen lives quietly in the country near Green River, Ontario, with two sons, and a cat. Here he writes poetry, shoots film, and meditates.

> There are times when I don't do anything. Don't even think. I just sit, or go for walks and my life is very empty and I love it. I think it's a very hard thing to learn to acquire space in your life. I learned a lot this summer about that.

Is he content?

> I've gradually been more and more pursuing possible ways of dealing with that question—of not so much happiness but, some ultimate solutions for my life, through meditation maybe, or just sitting—really what I do.

To me Owen seems warm and considerate (though I believe him when he says he can be difficult and cold); a quietened man laying in stores of energy for a creative burst somewhere in the near future.

> And this time I feel different in my life. Well, I just want to get working. I've been lying low for a while, but I'd like now to go into a period of intense work.

He hasn't been exactly idle, however.

> I've been teaching myself to be a cameraman. I shot about fourteen little films about two to five minutes long about small towns; each one is a portrait of a different small town, Green River, Locust Hill... they're really documentations for the future of

what it was like here. For the sound track I had people about seventy-five or eighty talking about life in their time; they talk about life in the town, and all you see are the streets and the buildings. Sometimes during a conversation between two people the camera goes back and forth between houses and you have the sense that the houses are speaking. But it's really the life of the houses. I've sold some to the CBC. They're really meant to make one film-an hour-long film all about small towns.

He should be in demand by all the threatened communities to try to help them capture something of what they were before they disappear into condominiums and conformity.

Also I've just finished an hour-long special for CTV on the St. Lawrence River. It's part of a series on the geographical regions of Canada. It was shot and cut very quickly and maybe it shows it, but personally I think it was kind of my-homage to my former wife, Suzanne, who is now in New Zealand. What I know about French Canada I learned from her, and the film contains my love and admiration, with a few misgivings. The film is inspired by a phrase from Gilles Vigneault which would translate as "You think it's a woman, but it's a river." I really enjoyed making this film.

* * *

Summing up for me, Don Owen concludes:

When I look back on my work now I feel a great detachment from most of it. HIGH STEEL and GALLERY seem O.K. because of the careful craftsmanwhip that still stands up. NOTES FOR A FILM ABOUT DONNA AND GAIL has a certain compassion that still seems valid. In THE ERNIE GAME I still like the alternation of "gags and pain". It takes a long time to get off the ego trip aspect of filmmaking and learn what you really have to bring to the craft. I see myself now as being really a catalyst for other people's talents. The knack is to encourage, surprise, challenge the writer, cameraman, actor or editor to give the best they can, so now in making films I'm trying to provide spaces where people can do their own thing.

In a certain sense a film director is the only person on the set who can't do anything. He's totally at the mercy of his collaborators and chance. Most of the really good stuff in filmmaking seems to come out of the blue. It starts to rain—and you keep on shooting—and it looks better than what you had in mind. It's a curious combination of insisting and accepting. So as well as collaborating with a great number of people you are also in a way collaborating with chance.

Finally, I love making films because of the group spirit involved. There's a certain point at which the film takes over and the commitment becomes complete for everybody. You can feel the excitement and unity of people working together—in a sense you kind of disappear into the group. That's why I'd like to make comedies.

Let me explain: We lived in Ibeza a couple of years ago in a small town, a fishing village, where a few other Canadians lived, like Graham Coughtry. At the end of a long winter, there was a very desolate feeling in our group of friends. People were very strung out, for reasons I can't even remember now. Then around the middle of March a Marx Brothers film, in Spanish, showed at the local cinema. I think it was NIGHT AT THE CIRCUS. The audience was about a third expatriate, Canadian, American and British, and the other two-thirds were Spanish farmers. The film completely took us over. Everybody laughed. All the way through. And when the film was over, everybody was beaming. And for days afterward you could see people going around looking changed. It somehow saved us.

I realized that if cinema has anything, like an icon it has a kind of transforming power. If it's really good, and it's got the magic, it can lift you up and help you and that's a very great thing. A privilege. I don't think I'll ever be able to reach that plane, but it's this possibility that keeps me making films. And why I always dream of making a comedy.

*   *   *

Postscript (1977)

Four years have passed. Owen still lives in the country; still meditates, studying the works of the master of crazy wisdom, Chogyam Trungpa; still works with his camera capturing the spirit of the surrounding small towns; still struggles to write and make the films that one day Canadians will appreciate and cherish.

The script of ROSEDALE LADY evolved finally into a new work, PARTNERS, which was released in the late fall of 1976 following a scuffle with the Ontario Censorship Board concerning their desire to cut part of a lyrical love scene. A romantic adventure story featuring the self-discovery of a Canadian girl with a cultivated English-influenced, establishment background and adventurous dissident American lover, the anti-U.S.-imperialism flavour of the tale may have partly caused its cool reception in Toronto, a city constantly media-soaked by the States.

Other works in the intervening time include a three-minute experimental film, FISHING MY FATHER FISHING, in which the camera is used to capture his father in the same manner in which his father fishes, and a four-minute film entitled GROUP PORTRAIT which utilizes a fixed frame in which a cycle of portraits of people replace each other at diminishing time intervals until the faces appear finally to merge into one face. The uncut sound track will be composed of portions of each speaking words from a sentence or two. He describes these works as "like sight gags". "I also make private things," he says, "home movies with my kids, like poems."

The CBC bought his half-hour journalistic film on small towns, NOT FAR FROM HOME, and hired him to direct three shows in the "Collaborators" series. He is now raising money for pre-production of a new script he is writing, a country-western/action romance tentatively titled GREENHOUSE BLUES.

A Married Couple
An Interview with Allan King
Alan Rosenthal

A MARRIED COUPLE (1969) has been variously called a comedy, a psychological study, and a bitter commentary on contemporary life. Allan King, who directed and produced the film, chooses to call it an "actuality drama".

A MARRIED COUPLE, shot in the summer of 1968, covers ten weeks in the life of Billy and Antoinette Edwards. At the time of the filming Billy was forty-two, and his American wife was thirty. Most of the film takes place at the Edwards' home and provides a remarkable insight into the intimate relationship of a rather extroverted, flamboyant, and funny couple. It also provides a grueling look at the tensions of two people who are extremely fond of each other, and yet still capable of tearing each other apart.

Prior to A MARRIED COUPLE one would have said that King's best film was WARRENDALE. Yet by comparison, A MARRIED COUPLE seems to be far more innovative in showing future possibilities in direct cinema. What one sees is neither documentary nor fiction drama, but a curious blend of the two formed by creating fictitious emotional links in the editing of documentary footage.

Allan King was born in British Columbia in 1930. After a short time working in television in Vancouver he pulled off a major film success in 1956 with SKID ROW, his first solo effort. The film predates Lionel Rogosin's ON THE BOWERY but has certain parallels in its examination of the life of the derelicts on Vancouver's skid row. It is a harsh, moody, honest film and marked the first time such subject matter had been treated on Canadian television.

After leaving the protective shelter of television, King went to London, where in 1961 he assembled a highly talented group of filmmakers under the cooperative banner of Allan King Associates. This group included Richard Leiterman, William Brayne, the cameraman on WARRENDALE, and Peter Moseley, the editor of WARRENDALE, THE TRAIN, and the hour-long documentary JOHN HUSTON.

Till 1966 one could say King enjoyed a fairly solid reputation in London based on work for the BBC, work on sponsored films, and RUNNING AWAY BACKWARDS, a description of American jet set living on the island of Ibeza. However, it was left to WARRENDALE to establish King's name in the international class.

WARRENDALE was commissioned in 1966 by the CBC as a portrait of a treatment centre for emotionally disturbed children in northern Toronto. What King produced was not (as misinterpreted by many critics) a

Reprinted from *New Documentary in Action* (Berkeley: University of California Press, 1971), by permission of the Regents of University of California.

rambling discourse on a method of a treatment, but an explosive communication of the nature of the experiences of the children at the centre. In spite of its power and brilliance, it was banned by the CBC and the BBC because of the obscene language used by the children and the violence of a number of the scenes. These "problems" did not stop it being awarded the 1967 Critics' Prize at Cannes.

If one wants to compare King to other cinéma-vérité exponents, two points seem to stand out very clearly. First, I would maintain that films like WARRENDALE and A MARRIED COUPLE show a much deeper and more personal concern on the part of the filmmaker for his subject than is seen or felt in most other vérité films. The second difference lies in the fact that, unlike Al Maysles, Ricky Leacock, or Don Pennebaker, King is no cameraman. His vision has to be translated through the eye of others, and yet there is still a unity to all his films. Possibly his talent lies in conceptualizing, organizing, directing, and a certain flair in guiding the editing.

Yet these things are not enough; there also has to be the ability to draw out the inner truth of the subject. This is one talent King certainly possesses, an ability to capture and present an extremely honest grasp of the subject matter even if it limits his "artistic" scope. Finally there has to be communion, credibility and feeling. And all these qualities King has. Perhaps that's why after seeing WARRENDALE Jean Renoir called King one of the greatest film artists working today.

Q. Can you talk a little about your background?

A. I was born in Vancouver, B.C., in 1930. I went to the University of British Columbia and took honours philosophy. I then drove a taxi for nine months, went to Europe for a year and a half, travelling, hitchhiking—the sort of thing that one did then—and finally got a job in television in Vancouver as a production assistant. I did live television for two years, but in fact after six months switched primarily to film. The first film was SKID ROW, then three or four more in Vancouver. Then I left Vancouver.

Q. What were your jobs in these films—director, producer, worker?

A. Yes, director. We were very lucky out there, because there weren't very many experienced people in the country and television expanded more rapidly than the availability of trained personnel. I was also very heavily involved in film societies in Vancouver when I was a teenager, so one got to see just about everything that was of interest to see. After the Vancouver stint I went abroad and started independent production, first in Spain; I then settled in London and built up an office and production group there. I came back to Canada in 1967, and I've been here ever since.

Q. How does your group work? As a co-operative?

A. More or less. Basically we all function as freelancers except that we work together, are grouped together in one house, and pay a small percentage of our fees to the house. We all have shares in the house, and the house owns the equipment.

Q. How did the concept of A MARRIED COUPLE arise? What was the first sparking point for it?

A. I'm not really sure. I don't think there is ever a single point. I suppose the first point of real action was when I was pretty well to the end of WARRENDALE and wondering what I was going to do next. I knew there was a spot open for an hour and a half film on television at that time, and I thought I would like to do a film about a marriage, about a married couple, recording them over eight to ten weeks, to get some sense, in a way that I don't think has been possible before, of what happens between a couple. One knows about such relationships from one's own experience; one knows from a certain kind of observation of friends which is pretty limited; and one knows from parents, from literature, drama, the arts. But those are all different kinds of knowledge, all useful in their own particular way. I thought it would be fascinating and illuminating to stay with the couple and observe.

Most particularly, I was concerned with a marriage in crisis and wanted to observe the kinds of ways in which a couple misperceive each other and carry into the relationship anxieties, childhood patterns, all the things that make up one's own personality and character. But these inevitably distort the other person and make true intimacy or true connection difficult. As that difficulty gets greater, conflicts and tensions develop in a marriage, so that it becomes less and less rewarding. That is what I wanted to explore. It was something I had been absorbed with since childhood. It had struck me, even when I was a kid in the thirties, that marriage didn't seem to be the kind of rewarding thing in reality that I read about in books or fantasized was going to be mine when I grew up. It puzzled me that people always seemed to get less from marriage than they wanted. My own parents separated when I was a kid, perhaps that gave me a particularly exacerbated view of marriage and made me rather more skeptical or more pessimistic or more aware of, and anxious about, conflicts and difficulties in marriage than say a child whose family had been fairly secure.

Q. As the concept grew, did you have any particular friends or individuals in mind who you thought would be suitable for the film?

A. Not exactly. Billy and Antoinette, whom I ultimately chose, were possibilities, as were many other friends; but first I started talking to a lot of couples I got to through psychiatrists, social workers, and various counselors. Altogether I talked fairly intensively with about ten couples.

I didn't during that early period, talk to Billy and Antoinette. Finally, I decided I would talk to them and see if they were interested.

Q. What was their reaction to the concept of living with a camera?

A. They had been fascinated for a long time with the idea of being in a film. At one stage or another in their lives both of them had dabbled in amateur or semi-professional theater, and many of their friends are in the arts, so it always interested them as a possibility. When they knew I was making a film about a marriage in crisis, or a marriage in conflict, theirs was not in that critical a stage, or at least they didn't acknowledge it. When I finally approached them, Antoinette was ready to be involved in the movie, but Billy was very reluctant. He said, "Our marriage isn't that much of a crisis at the moment, so you would have to make a film simply about an everyday marriage." My own supposition was that the conflicts I sensed to be there, were there, and that they would emerge.

Q. One is very conscious in the film of the style of repartee and wit of the dialogue which goes on about nonessential things. Was this in the back of your mind when you ultimately chose them?

A. I guess it was the major factor—it was the plus that offset the minus that I was concerned about, plus the fact that they can be very funny, and very playful with each other, verbally anyway, and so that was a great advantage. I think a film like this, unrelieved by any lightness, could be very powerful; but it could also run the risk of being overpoweringly depressing and heavy.

Q. Can we go now to preshooting production problems, planning, that sort of stage?

A. I had already chosen the cameraman during the year I was looking for couples and raising money. I had Richard (Leiterman) in mind and Chris to do the sound. I needed Arla Saare to do the editing. I seem to work in a similar sort of pattern every time I set up a film, or once a film starts to go. Once I've had the notion and decide that is what I want to do, I work out a budget. The first thing to see is whether the project is financially possible, and then where I am going to get the money. So I was occupied with that pretty early on, and went through various attempts and routes to finance the film.

First, it was going to be done as a three-country co-production for television. When the Canadian element, the CBC, dropped out, I decided to raise the money privately. A friend of mine thought he could do that and had a go at it, but it didn't work out. So then I went around and simply borrowed money. We set up a company in which the shareholders put in the investment to pay the heart of the cost of the production. They basically put up $75,000 to $85,000, and we sold television rights to follow theatrical distribution in Canada and in England, which made the balance of our production budget. And at that point we were set.

Actually, as the film developed we went way over budget. One of the difficulties is that if you take a year to raise money, your budget is already 10 per cent under right off the bat. We were budgeted at $130,000 to $140,000, and we spent $203,000. This was partly because we went over in time, and partly because we shot a lot more film than I had anticipated.

Having sort of settled the financial questions—raised the money—we finally decided to ask Billy and Antoinette. After they accepted we worked out a fee for them, which was basically union scale and came in the end to about $5,000 for the two of them, plus a small percentage of the profits of the film. Though I have generally no particular commitment to a way of working or an ideology of working, I decided not to intervene in this film, not to direct, not to ask or require anything from Billy and Antoinette, but to allow them to take any initiatives that they might wish to take; this "nonintervention" also covered Richard and my sound man Chris Wangler. We would simply spend as much time as we could physically manage with the couple and record when we felt like it.

We established also that, while we were all friends and knew each other, it wouldn't work if we had dinner with them, or if Antoinette was obliged to make coffee or provide the kind of hospitality that one normally extends to people in one's house. We decided to dispense with all this and to avoid conversation with Bill and Antoinette as much as possible, so that interactions of that kind wouldn't interfere with our ability to observe and record.

Q. In making WARRENDALE you spent three or four weeks with the cameras on location without doing any shooting; did you employ the same method here?

A. In WARRENDALE it was necessary for me to find out something about the children because I didn't know them very well. I didn't know them at all when I started, and they needed a fair amount of time to look at me and get used to me and decide where I was going to fit into their lives. With Billy and Antoinette, that amount of time wasn't necessary; but we did need a bit of time not so much to get them un-camera-conscious or unself-conscious, but for them to work into more intimate feelings, the kind of real expression of strongly felt things. That took a lot of time. What we did do was spend about two weeks with them lighting the house. We could have probably done it much faster but we sort of puttered and fiddled around.

Q. Can you be more explicit on the lighting?

A. As with WARRENDALE we lit the entire house, which was basically the way we did most of our shooting. We had our own power source from the mains. We put a whole new power system in really, so that we could go in first thing in the morning and throw the switch and the whole house would be lit. Actually it took a fair while to work out a lighting pattern that allows you to shoot 360 degrees and shoot so that you are not hitting your own lights or throwing shadows and all those kinds of problems; there is a certain amount of trial and error to that. Also, you can't really anticipate what are the most frequent patterns of movement until you've spent some time with people and get an instinctive sense of where they are going to move and when. That all took about two or three weeks. We also had to adjust the house a bit, and do some decorating. The front room was all walnut paneling, which is very, very dark and just soaked up light. So we put in light paneling instead.

When Billy and Antoinette went on a three-week holiday to Maine and Vermont we followed, taking an extra lighting man. We had him go three days before to rig the two physical locations so that they would be all set, and we would just have to trim, so that again we would have the least possible technical interference with the lights.

Q. Can we get into the actual shooting, and so on?

A. Clearly the ideal would be to spend twenty-four hours a day at the house, but that would have meant two crews and you would split your style. While there were variations, basically our pattern was to spend as much time with them as they were together with each other. Richard and Chris and the camera assistant would go early in the morning, turn on the lights, go upstairs, and be around when Billy and Antoinette woke up. We would stay through breakfast until Billy went to work. Sometimes, though not often, we would stay with Billy or with Antoinette and Bogart, and sometimes we would go with Billy to work and film at work. But the general pattern was to leave them at half-past nine or ten o'clock. Richard, Chris and David would go home and get some sleep and a meal, and then come back about four o'clock to be there at five o'clock when Billy came home. Then they'd stay all through the evening until Billy and Antoinette finally went to sleep, and then back again the next morning. Of course, weekends were very tough. They would start at five o'clock Friday afternoon, and they would get maybe seven or eight hours sleep and time off in the middle of Friday night, Saturday night, and Sunday night—that was very exhausting.

For the first three or four weeks I was around the house a lot. Later, I found it worked best for me to stay away. A director in that sort of situation is a bit irrelevant. You need enough time to observe a lot of things and you drop in; but there is no need, I find for me at any rate, to stand and tell a cameraman "point here, point there, turn on here, turn off there". All you do really is interfere.

Q. Did you discuss with Richard the kind of things you were looking for?

A. I know Richard's style, and he knows my style, because we have worked together for years, so the question of style has been worked out over a long time. We had talked about the problems that anyone has shooting dialogue between two people with one camera, whether to pan back and forth and so on, before we started filming; but it was difficult for Richard to dictate where the camera was going rather than have it dictated by the dialogue. But he very quickly got onto that. What would happen is that we would talk a great deal about the rushes. Either he would see them, or certainly I would always see them. We'd say this or that didn't work, or that seems to be working very well, something seems to be happening here, how do you feel it; and so we would do a great deal of talking on the phone, or before or after work, or wherever it was necessary, so that we could check with each other on what we felt was significant.

In the end I very specifically gave Richard a credit as associate director, because the contribution that he made to the filming was so very, very important. There was no way of doing that kind of a film without an exceptional person shooting, because he had to make the basic choices of when he was going to shoot and when not. We talked a lot about strategy and something about tactics as we were working, but often it was the choice that Richard made; in a very real sense he is the associate director.

Q. How much does the camera interfere? How much do people put on for the camera?

A. It depends on the cameraman. If you get a dumb, insensitive, obtrusive cameraman, the interference is enormous. If you have a sensitive, intelligent, quiet, responsive, unobtrusive and unjudging, impersonally critical cameraman or camera crew, then not only is the camera not inhibitive, but it stimulates the couple to talk, in the same way an analyst or therapist does. You can talk if you want to; you don't have to talk if you don't want to; you do what you want. If you choose to put up smoke screens, or you choose to put on a dialogue, or you try to hide something, this would be evident to anybody with any sort of sensitivity. It isn't possible for people to produce material out of thin air irrelevant to their character. Whatever occurs is relevant to the character, and it gives us that over-all sense we have of the person. So I felt for a long time that we were not concerned with the question, "Is it the real person?" or those kinds of questions. These are really ways in which an audience or some elements of an audience tend to evade the actual feelings they are getting from the film. "Is that really real?"—what the hell does that mean? Either the film means something to you, or it doesn't. On the question again of interference, I think it is well to allow the person to express stuff in perhaps a little more concentrated period of time.

Q. Did you sense that anyone was putting on an act for the camera?

A. There are various places in the film where they do, but there are two kinds of acting. If you ask, "Are they acting for the cameras?" you can say no, and a little while along you would have to say yes. It depends on how much space you have in which to explain. They performed for the camera in the same way they perform for friends. Friends come together, and often they would get into fifteen minutes of bantering back and forth, teasing each other; they'd have a mock row, or they'd set up a whole line of dialogue which they could carry for fifteen or twenty minutes as a way of entertaining themselves and their friends. You can see them do that in the film.

The only thing one has to remember is that we all, at all times and to varying degrees, perform, or perform as if we are different people. At different times we are different persons with different people. I am aware of myself behaving a little differently with a businessman, with a student, with a critic, with my office staff, with my girlfriend, or with my parents. Each of those situations provides a different context and you behave differently. Ideally, when you are totally your own person, you are always the same; you are a consistent character throughout, in all transactions. But that's not the way most people are most of the time.

Q. Did Billy and Antoinette impose any restrictions on you? Obviously you would be getting some very intimate material. Did they see the rushes, or did they only see the final print?

A. Billy wanted the right to veto anything that he thought was unbearably embarrassing. We had a long protracted negotiation about it, and I was profoundly reluctant to allow them to do that—oddly enough not so much because I really felt it would be exercised, but because I thought they would in fact deprive themselves of some of the benefits which would occur from the filming. If they were going to have that right, there would be some area of cheating in the film and some area of withholding. However, Billy felt that he could not be uninhibited, could not be free, unless he had some protection. Oddly enough, Antoinette didn't ask for that until Billy had thought of it; and so she said "if Billy has it, I want it". In fact, the right wasn't exercised. I didn't allow them to see any film except a little bit to show them that there were images on the celluloid, and it was going all right. I didn't allow them to see any film until we had finished shooting, and then they screened all seventy hours.

Q. At that stage did they want to cut anything out?

A. No, they didn't. They didn't have the right of editing or anything like that.

Q. Now, if you can come to the point of selection. The film is mainly Billy, Antoinette, and Bogart; one sees very few friends except for an evening when Antoinette goes out with her girlfriend and on the occasion of the party. Now, friends must have been over at other times. Was this limitation a choice on your part?

A. Yes, the stuff with other people just didn't work out. It wasn't significant. If you want dramatic structure, you want interchanges with other people if they are significant. But there wasn't very much happening with the other friends. For instance, Antoinette was not having an affair with the husband of one of their friends or one of the couples they were friendly with. Had she been, of course, that would have been very pertinent to the film. But just having people over for dinner usually ends up with no more than a scene of people sitting down and having dinner, and it's not very interesting.

Sometimes something explosive will happen at a party, particularly if there is a camera on. People get angry at the lights and so on, or resent other people being the focus of the film. In the first party we filmed, in Toronto, nothing very significant happened. The party in Maine was different. If I were using this technique again and I wanted to involve more people, then I would have to find a particular way in which they were interacting with the other people in the film so that episodes would occur which were emotionally significant.

Q. Let's move on to editing and structure. You shot seventy hours, and you use an hour and a half. Were the choices difficult regarding what to omit?

A. I can't remember—my memory is a bit foggy. I have a bad time once I've cut a sequence out; by and large, I forget it even existed. Yet when you're looking at a rough cut and you argue about what's to come out you say, "I can't take that sequence out; I've got to have that sequence", but once you take it out, you very seldom miss it. However, I can't remember very much; I can't remember sequences, but there must be some which we had in and then took out. It was really much more a question of tightening sections and making them work as sequences and, more than that, making the over-all structure work.

Q. Is the final film in chronological order?

A. No. The opening of the film was shot about two-thirds of the way through; the breakfast scene was shot halfway through. Basically, the main arch of action is at the end of the film when they wake up—after they have had that moment of intimacy when she's sitting on his lap crying, and they wake up the next morning and have a great fight and he throws her out of the house. That whole passage happened the week before we finished filming, and it was what we were waiting for. Not that it had to be a fight; it might have been a very happy episode. But you wait for one significant arch of events that hang together and give you a core. The holiday, and when they're at the lake and so on, and the party around that—they all occurred very early in the filming and are actually unrelated to the rest. All I do is take episodes and put them into a dramatic structure that works for me.

Q. So you are aiming towards a kind of emotional fiction?

A. Yes. It is very often the case that episode (a) is put together with episode (b) to produce a feeling of (c), when in reality they don't have that connection. However, if feeling (c) doesn't have a feeling relationship or isn't true of the characters, then it won't work. What I'm doing is finding conjunctions of events which create for me the feeling I have about that couple and about life, and what I want to express.

One has to be very, very clear. Billy and Antoinette in the film are not Billy and Antoinette Edwards, the couple who exist and live at 323 Rushton Road. They are characters, images on celluloid in a film drama. To say that they are in any other sense true, other than being true to our own experience of the world and people we have known and ourselves, is philosophical nonsense. There is no way ninety minutes in a film of Billy and Antoinette can be the same as the actual real life of Billy and Antoinette.

Q. Did they make any comments on the time rearrangement in the final film?

A. No, because they clearly understood that we would do that. But it was hard at first for Antoinette to handle. For example, there is very little shown where she is very giving or very tender; there is very little shown of how she is with other people, which is often very warm; very little is shown of how she is with her child or the fact that she's a good cook. At other times and in other circumstances, she is all those things. In the middle of a major crisis or conflict, she couldn't be very giving and much of the time was very tense; it was a very tough time. So she comes out in the film—or rather as the character in the film—as someone caught up in those devastating demands of that moment.

A. Can we come back to the dramatic structure and your preparation work with Arla. I am thinking of your problems of reordering the sequences in order to gain maximum dramatic effect, and the things you look for in going through the rushes.

A. First, I think you perceive certain kinds of things, certain things that happened that week and seemed to be something that was a consistent preoccupation, say of Antoinette or Billy. First of all, we went through all the material twice; we went through all the rushes as we were shooting and we went through it all once or twice after that, and then chucked out fifty hours.

Q. What were you looking for when you went through the material?

A. Stuff that connects with other stuff, episodes that connect and illuminate each other. Stuff that contrasts, and stuff that is alive. The trouble with a lot of shooting is that nothing happens, so it's aborted; or you miss half of it because you come in late. You end up with a set of sequences which are alive and are funny, moving, sad and have emotional values. Those are what you start with, and you then try to find an order to those events in which the feelings are amplified, and amplified and amplified, until they've reached a peak. Then you try to resolve them again —rather I suppose in the way you construct a piece of music.

Q. Can you tell me how you work with Arla?

A. Basically, it seems to me that the director and the editor always perceive things a little differently. The director's notion of what's happening is different from the editor's. But as I say, I chucked out about fifty hours, so we had about twenty to work with; if Arla felt she needed something or was stuck, she would go back into that fifty hours. But we then basically screened the twenty hours; we had a list of what those sequences were and a rough idea of what the order of events would be. The twenty hours represented roughly twenty sequences, twenty episodes, and each was roughly an hour long.

We would sit down in the morning and go through an hour. I would say what I liked and what I thought the shape was, and Arla would say what she liked and what she thought the shape was; we would usually very quickly agree on the rough shape of the sequence. Then she would go ahead, pull it out and cut it. The next morning we would come back and screen the rough cut of that sequence, and decide that such and such worked and such and such didn't, or what needed ordering or how we could fix it; and then she would do that, or sometimes she simply set it aside and we would go on to the next one. Arla works extremely quickly, and we would tend to do almost a sequence a day until we had the rough assembly; and then we started polishing.

Q. How long did the assembly take you?

A. The assembly, which was about four or five hours, took about six weeks. Then we were stuck for a month trying to get a shape that would work, and we tried juggling it this way and that way.

Q. Can we tie it down to specifics? What were the alternate shapes you had in mind?

A. It doesn't seem so much like alternatives because you either have the feeling it works or it doesn't work; and if it doesn't work, it's not an alternative, and you keep juggling around until finally it does. But for example, there are two or three major fights in this film. There's the first little fight about the harpsichord. This is a joke fight, but it sort of sets up many of the key strains that emerge later in the film. There's the car fight which is a very bitter fight, but isn't violent and sort of has a semi-resolve to it, and is left with a hooker at the end of it. Then there's the fight where he throws her out of the house. The harpsichord scene isn't a major fight—it's just sort of a way into the film. If you have one big fight at the beginning and one big fight at the end, and the first one is sort of left open and unresolved, all through the middle part you wait for the threads to be picked up. There may be all sorts of little threads in the middle which are significant; but you are really waiting to see what big thing is going to happen next, so it's a matter of how you get those threads to be picked up. There may be all sorts of little threads in the middle which are significant; but you are really waiting to see what big thing is going to happen next, so it's a matter of how you get those threads to develop and amplify each other.

The biggest problem was to put the car fight where it was able to pick up the threads of conflict, so that the earlier clues were expanded and amplified. Another problem was how to make Antoinette's desire for other relationships apparent, rather than merely talked about. She discusses them with her girlfriend, but the discussion is transferred into action when she starts the flirtation with that guy in the red shirt at the party.

Q. You get the development of intensity of their arguments, which serves to increase the tension; but you also have several other sequences, which in a sense could be placed anywhere—the holiday sequence and an explanation of Billy at work. How did you play around with these in the order?

A. It is largely how much relaxation you want from your tension, and so it's merely a matter of gauging the emotional charge or the degree of relaxation that you want before you build to a higher degree. The choices, ultimately, have simply to do with relaxing and heightening tension.

Q. Jack Gold, the English director, has said that when he does a straight documentary, he may have twenty sequences. He then puts those on cards, and in a sense he edits the cards. Do you work at all in this way?

A. I just jot ideas down on paper that feel right—this, then this, then this—and you work out a sequence; and then you think, But if I do that, this isn't going to work here because it's too early, or it's too late, or it doesn't connect with what follows after. Then you try another juggle. And whether you do it on cards or you do it by numbers on a piece of paper, it is the same process.

Q. I asked you before whether Billy and Antoinette had the power of censorship. Now I am wondering if there were times you were using your own taste, saying, "No, I've got this scene, but I don't really think it should be used as a matter of taste." Can you give me some examples there?

A. Well, at that time, Billy had been going to a psychiatrist to help resolve some of the problems he was having. I recorded four sessions with the psychiatrist, and they were absolutely fascinating and indeed hair-raising, as there was some extraordinary material involved. But I decided not to use the material; in some ways it was like a red herring.

When a person is talking to a psychiatrist and talking about something that they feel is quite horrific that they've done, an audience may seize upon that and jump to all sorts of conclusions about the person, conclusions which are misleading or allow them to classify the other person or to depersonalize the other person. So I didn't use these scenes. They were very tempting, and there was a lot of revealing material in them, but I felt they were misleading.

Q. Billy is very funny when he is reading some advertising. Did you catch much of him at work?

A. We spent two, three, four days with him at work, and there were some other funny passages; but you are really looking for that passage that you can get in a minute or thirty seconds which stands for all the things. There were several other episodes, but those were the best ones. There was a long talk with some guy in Saskatchewan. They were planning a Centennial campaign for Saskatchewan, and Saskatchewan wanted to look like Expo, but for only $200,000 or something like that, and the dialogue was very funny.

I was a little unhappy about a couple of sequences that technically didn't work, showing Billy's strength and his forcefulness with other people, because he's rather a different person at work than he is at home. At home, at that point anyway, he was a little more insecure about various kinds of things than he was at work. That extra dimension would have been nice to get included. We did do one other thing. I had a screening with some friends, thirty or forty people, when I had the first sort of rough cut. This was in order to see it with an audience and get a sense of the way other people responded. I did it again with the final cut and then once more, and they were very helpful. It's not so much that people can tell you how to fix a film or what's not working, but you get the sense of an additional perspective, which is very helpful.

Q. Can you remember any of the things said after the rough cut?

A. Yes. There was a lot of imbalance in the reaction to Billy and Antoinette. At one time, people were generally much more responsive to Antoinette, and then there was another point at which they were much more responsive to Billy, and I wanted a balance. It is still the case in the final film that it almost acts as a Rorschach test. People either identify with Billy or with Antoinette, or reject them both, or think they are both marvellous; and you get everything in between that. But you eventually have to decide what is the balance for yourself, and part of that you get from the way the audience is responding. It's also very helpful where jokes are concerned—what's working, and what's very funny to you but is not funny to anybody else; how much pause you need after for the laughter to subside, so that you don't lose lines. We finally blew the film up to 35mm when we had a cut that was one hour and fifty-seven minutes. I knew it was long, but I had gotten too close to the film to decide how much more to cut it, and how much could come out; so we blew it up at that point, and had a number of screenings in New York with other people. Then I cut another twenty minutes, and got it down to ninety-seven minutes.

Q. Was this basically just shortening sequences, or did you take sequences out?

A. Shortening. We didn't take any sequences out; we just tightened up the slack. I took out parts of sequences—after the major fight, after dinner, and after their very funny episode when Bogart picks up a little piece of shit on the floor, which is an extraordinary reliever of the tension of the moment. There was another sequence when they are talking on the bed upstairs; the telephone rings and Antoinette wants to answer it, but Billy doesn't want her to leave the bed and get out of the discussion that they are having, and they have a fight about that. It was a fascinating exchange, but it was just one too many; and I thought, I just cannot take one more fight, so I took it out. In order to tighten up another sequence I cut one bit that I really regret. Billy and Antoinette are in bed the second time in the film. She has been in her bed, and he takes her into his bed. He wants to be intimate with her, and she rejects him; I shortened it a bit and in consequence lost a passage where one really experienced more strongly the anguish and humiliation that Billy felt in being rejected. One still gets a lot out of the sequence, but it is a little diminished.

Q. You said you went way over budget. What were the things that blew up the budget?

A. We were budgeted for seven weeks of shooting, and we shot for ten; we were budgeted for 80,000 feet of film, and I shot virtually 140,000 feet—those were the major things. My own time was double what I said it would be. Editing time wasn't as much as we had anticipated. Our lighting costs were more; we had the trip to Vermont and Maine which wasn't in the budget. Promotion costs were a lot more than I had anticipated; I had budgeted $14,000 to promote the film, and I spent $30,000.

Q. When you finished the film, how did you go about selling it? You said you had a certain number of precommitments on television, but these commitments pay relatively little. How did you begin to get the money back?

A. It wasn't too much of a problem in Canada, except for the amount of time required to do it and the number of speaking engagements and screenings you have to have. I find with a film that it helps a lot if you get out to many locations, wherever the theatre happens to be—St. Catharines or Belleville or Ottawa or Windsor. You go along to see the film, to see the press, and so on; it all helps. The main problem is getting good distribution. This wasn't much of a problem in Canada because we had that settled. But we had a long, long battle with censorship in Ontario, which was very costly and took a lot of time.

Q. What were the problems brought up in censorship?

A. The language, which was virtually unprecedented in Canada. There had never before been so much swearing in a film in Canada—that was really the crux of the problem. The first censor to tackle it had a great deal of difficulty deciding whether it was going to arouse a great public reaction and whether it was within the tolerances of community standards, which is the real basis of most censorship.

Q. How did you eventually win them around? What were the compromises?

A. I made three cuts in Ontario. I haven't had to make any cuts thereafter in any of the other provinces so far, and no cuts in the United States because there just isn't any censorship there any more—or at least no government or state censorship. The key to persuading the censor was that after it became a public controversy, it was clear that more people were going to be upset by the cuts in the film than would be upset by the language in the film. It tends to be a political thing.

Q. You said Canadian distribution was easy; what about American?

A. America was much harder, and we still haven't found an adequate solution to the problem. I have also found greater difficulty with the film in the United States, and I am not quite sure why. I noticed very early on that our screenings in New York had quite a different flavour than in Canada; people seemed to find the film more threatening, personally threatening, personally heavy and painful. I would guess this could be, particularly in New York, because personal relationships there are more strenuous and less secure, and therefore the film seems more painful. In the early American reviews, for example, there was virtually no mention of the fact that the film is very funny in the first half, virtually no mention whatsoever.

The reviews have been of three kinds: from young critics, very responsive and very good reviews; from sort of middle-aged critics or middle-aged married people, an intense involvement in the film, but the reviews tend to say as much about the reviewer as they do about the film (at least that is what we drew from between the lines); with older critics, and this particularly affected us in New York with Judith Crist and a couple of others, a rejection of the film as ugly and the characters distasteful. There was a total inability to take in the film and accept it. In Canada, audiences are a lot more open and easy, especially if there is a very large house, which somehow socializes the experience. In the States, there seems to be a great taste for fantasy at the moment; everybody seems to want an escape, EASY RIDER is enormously popular. It's a good film but I often wonder how much of its appeal is that it romanticizes and fantasizes an experience.

Q. Has the film covered its costs yet?

A. No. It will eventually in Canada and in England. What will happen in the States is still very much up in the air, but I am not terribly optimistic.

Q. This question of using vérité technique and the nonfiction drama, where do you think it is going from here? Do you think you will use the process again?

A. I think I will probably use it on my next film—I am quite sure I will—but more as a way of setting up and recording that kind of feeling exchange; the kind of dynamic that arises out of direct interchange between the characters and the film. But in the next film, I don't think the people will have had actual past relationships with each other. They will be characters that I've deliberately put together in a film, and asked to interact and interrelate.

Claude Jutra's "Mon Oncle Antoine"

Bruce Elder

Most of the critical response to Claude Jutra's recent film, MON ONCLE ANTOINE, has tried to demonstrate that the film belongs within the mainstream of Canadian filmmaking. According to those promulgating this view, the film can be considered as a fictionalized documentary which makes use of a transparent and rather insignificant narrative of an adolescent boy's sexual, moral and social awakening to "document" life in a small village in Quebec. The charm of the film (and most people seem to agree that the film *is* charming) is, in this view, said to lie in the exquisitely sensitive and somewhat ironic portrait of small-town life in French Canada, that is in the documentary aspect of the film an aspect of filmmaking in which Canadian films have traditionally excelled.

This interpretation, it seems to me, has two very serious shortcomings: the first is that it fails to take into account the thematic significance of the time and place in which the film is set; the second and more serious is that this view, since it considers the merit of the film to lie primarily in its documentary aspects and views the narrative only as a means of binding together and extending the significance of the various "tableaux" depicting life in the small village, underestimates the importance

Reprinted from *Descant*, vol. 6 (Spring 1973).

of narrative in the film. The most explicit statement of this view was made by no less a critic than Herman Weinberg who, in *Take One* (vol. 3, no. 3) speaks of MON ONCLE ANTOINE as though its value lay in its documentary aspect and says that he regrets the filmmaker's decision to graft a narrative onto the work. I would argue that when the film is properly considered, its many tableaux are seen to be related in a subtle and complex progression which carries forward a narrative whose significance, far from being of secondary interest in the film, is rather its central focus.

The reason for the failure of most critics to recognize the thematic significance of the choice of locale and historic period for the setting of the film escapes me. Jutra, certainly, is most insistent in calling to our attention the setting of the film. The film virtually opens with the statement that the events depicted in the film are supposed to have occurred "not too long ago". Graffiti scribbled on the washroom walls make even clearer the time in which the events of the film are set, for they refer to Duplessis, premier of Quebec during the forties and fifties.

The location in which the events of the film are set is equally clearly established. Again, right at the opening of the film, Jutra provides the viewer with a title informing him that the events depicted in the film occurred "in the country of Quebec, in the asbestos mining area". And to keep us in mind of this fact, Jutra frequently uses the asbestos mine as a backdrop.

Although the significance of this choice of place and time should be immediately recognizable to anyone with even an elementary knowledge of the history of Quebec, few commentators have remarked upon it. Between 1949 and 1952, strikes at.the asbestos mines were the centre of social ferment which developed into the so-called Quiet Revolution and led to the downfall of a corrupt and reactionary government.

The setting,then,suggests that the work is to have political implications. Directly developing upon this, the first few incidents presented depict the social and industrial conditions of the time. An asbestos miner, Jos Poulin, is shown being harrassed by his English-speaking foreman, worrying about developing asbestosis, and enraged over the inequalities which he sees everywhere around him. Poulin is so disturbed by these conditions that he is forced to leave the wife and family he loves to take work as a lumberjack in the backwoods of Quebec.

In leaving his family to take work in the woods, Jos Poulin follows the course set by that generation of Québécois whose reaction to social and economic oppression took the form of a futile and defeatist back-to-the-land movement. Jutra cleverly conveys the withdrawal and isolationism which characterized the movement by having the Poulin family separated geographically from the rest of the village. This separation of the family is again emphasized when the lonely and distraught Mme Poulin phones Antoine only to find that because of a bad connection she can hardly make herself understood. Jutra underlines the futility of this movement by showing Jos's rage as undirected and ultimately self-defeating. As he sits in the beverage room, Poulin rails against every fact of life—the English, the mine, the winter, the noise, the silence. He is unable to determine the causes of his suffering and take action specifically against those causes.

Once he has established the historical background of the narrative and revealed the oppressive economic and social conditions prevailing at the time, Jutra begins to develop the central narrative line of the film, the story of Benoit's awakening to conditions around him. This narrative development begins with the presentations of two tableaux depicting incidents in Benoit's life. In one Benoit is seen assisting at a funeral, in the other acting as an altar-boy at communion.

Though on first viewing these tableaux may seem to be related only in the most tenuous manner, in fact the interrelationships between them are subtle and complex. Both tableaux show Benoit mocking those in authority. Throughout the mass, Benoit makes sport of the proceedings by pulling faces and carving his initials in the altar-rail. Similarly, when Bernard, after closing the casket, goes in to join the wake, Benoit mocks his hypocritical solemnness by informing him that his tie is crooked. In the opening scenes of the film, then, Benoit is shown to be a youth who refuses to take seriously the hypocritical social conventions of his elders.

In both tableaux, moreover, Benoit is exposed to the difference between what appears to be and what truly is. At the funeral, when the corpse is undressed the apparently complete tuxedo is revealed to be a false front covering only the visible portion of the corpse. Further, as soon as the funeral service is complete, the sham grief of the mourners quickly evaporates to be replaced by their enjoyment of the wake. And at the church, Benoit discovers the apparently exemplary priest secretly imbibing the sacramental wine. In these scenes, then, Benoit experiences the deceptions of the custodians of faith, virtue and power. The remaining tableaux of the film show Benoit's reaction to these revelations. His reaction is one of rebellion against those who hold power—a rebellion which, as the film progresses, becomes increasingly bold.

His daring reaches its height when he and a friend toss snowballs at the boss's horse as the boss rides through the village contemptuously throwing out Christmas gifts for the workers' children.

The reaction of the adults to Benoit's rebellion reveals the difference between the older and younger generations. As Benoit and his friend (after the snowballing incident) stride boldly down the street, the older people look at him with a mixture of admiration for his courage and fear for the possible consequences of his actions. The older generation, it is clear, has been frightened by the boss into passive acceptance of the status quo. It is from Benoit's generation, therefore, that the impetus for social reform must come.

The growing social awareness that leads Benoit to such acts is paralleled by the development of his affection for Carmen. At the beginning of the film, Benoit is shy and awkward with Carmen. He is seen peeking through a keyhole at a woman undressing and bullying her. By the end of the film, the boy's exploitive sexual assertiveness has been replaced by affection for Carmen. Benoit is unwilling, finally, even after all he has been through, to disturb the sleeping Carmen in order to seek her comfort; a short-lived sexual fantasy in which all the horror he has experienced is transmuted into beauty must serve instead.

The second idea announced in the two early scenes, Benoit's recognition of the difference between what seems to be and what truly is, is also of central importance to the film and is developed in the story of the metamorphosis of Benoit's relation to Antoine. In the first half of the film, Antoine is portrayed as a figure of considerable power in the village. This power is cleverly conveyed in one scene by contrasting the townspeople's behaviour when they are some distance from Antoine's store with their behaviour when they are directly in front of it. The workers and schoolchildren are shown spilling out of the factories and schools, the fathers and children meeting and joining in a wild and joyous revelry as they make their way down the street towards Antoine's store. As soon as they arrive in front of the store, the revel ends and all the townspeople line up in row upon orderly row. Antoine is shown gloating over the way in which he controls the pleasures of the ordinary townspeople by concealing the decorated store windows until it strikes his fancy to reveal them. He is even portrayed as presiding over the rituals which attend the elemental transformations of life: as undertaker he presides over the funerals in the village, and as proprietor of the village's only store, he is the sole source of the trappings associated with the marriage celebration.

Antoine, in the first part of the film, is portrayed not only as powerful but also as greedy and exploitive. Thus, he hoards his liquor, not offering to share his bottle of expensive gin even with his wife. And in one scene it is revealed that although Antoine's charge, Carmen, is being cruelly exploited by her father, and that Antoine could end this exploitation by adopting her, he refuses to do so.

The intolerability of these characteristics of Antoine comes to a head during the excursion to the Poulin farm. When starting out, Antoine lords cruelly over Benoit and plays mercilessly on his fears. And when he arrives at the Poulin farmhouse, rather than offering Mme Poulin the comfort which in the absence of her husband she so desperately needs, Antoine proceeds to gorge himself on pork and swill his gin, leaving the corpse of the young man unattended.

Benoit does not go unaffected by his uncle's behaviour. Its impact on Benoit is revealed in a shot from the boy's point of view, showing his perception of Antoine as disgustingly piggish.

Up to this point in the film, Benoit has experienced Antoine only as a strong and powerful, even if callous and exploitive, individual. The events of the next portion of the film, however, reveal that Antoine's strength and power are really only apparent. On the way back to the village from the Poulin farmhouse, Antoine sinks deeper and deeper into drunkenness and Benoit takes over the task of guiding Red Fly home. The coffin falls off the sleigh and Benoit is forced to solicit Antoine's assistance in loading the box back onto the sleigh. Antoine is too drunk to be of any help and breaks into a maudlin, self-pitying sobbing which shows that he is a weak, frightened and impotent man.

Benoit here experiences not only the callousness and cruelty of those who hold power but also their underlying weakness. The radical implications of this insight are clear. To show that those who hold power are evil is to demonstrate the need for, but not the possibility of, social change; only where their weakness is also revealed do we demonstrate that revolutionary action can be successful.

Benoit's awakening perception on that Christmas is paralleled by the story of Jos Poulin's return home. In developing these two stories side by side, Jutra brings out the important contrast between them. Whereas Jos returns home only to experience another defeat, Benoit's new insight could pave the way to his victory. For Jos Poulin, reality is too oppressive to be overcome. Benoit, however, has seen the weakness of those who hold power and the stage is set for him to take revolutionary action. At the end of the film we feel that in that Christmas, the birthday of the Saviour, a force has been born which might redeem the people of Quebec.

One can then read in the narrative of MON ONCLE ANTOINE a meaning of considerable import. Far from being, as the majority of critics have suggested, merely a means of binding the film together or of extending the significance of the document, the narrative is the central focus of the film. The documentary aspects of the work do not absorb but rather are absorbed by the narrative. To conclude from the fact that the film has a realistic texture that the film is a documentary, albeit a fictionalized documentary, is to ignore the intricate *dramatic progression* in the series of tableaux presented to the viewer.

Afterword (1976)

As often happens when such a prospect arises after several years, the republication of this article has forced serious doubts upon me. The article was written several years ago, at a time when I had not undertaken much serious study of the Canadian cinema; in fact, this paper impelled me to do such a study, the results of which are soon to appear in a book I am co-authoring with David Clandfield. The discoveries made and the conclusions arrived at in the course of the research subsequently undertaken would, of course, lead me to recast this paper in a very different form were I to rewrite it today. The most important revision I would make would be to focus on the critical reception of the film in English Canada showing that the interpretation of the film alluded to in the first paragraphs of the essay reflects on the level of cinematic criticism those same qualities of empiricism which characterize the practice of filmmaking in English Canada. On this basis I would attempt to demonstrate that the often alleged rupture in the film's structure (a rupture which is said to occur at the point of Benoit and Antoine's departure for the Poulin's and which is characterized as involving a shift of attention away from the documental aspects of the film towards the dramatic) is simply nonexistent. A study of the ideological and quasi-allegorical determinants of the film would reveal that such criticism of the film is based upon a misreading of the sequences of the first portion of the film. Additionally, I would contrast the critical reception of the film in English Canada, where the film was appreciated for its alleged documental aspects, with its reception in Quebec, where Jutra was frequently criticized for a lack of, or at least a muting of, overt political commitment. The contrast between these two critical responses seems to me to reveal a very profound contrast between the cultures of English Canada and Quebec.

All of this would, of course, mean that the article would have to be entirely rewritten. For several reasons, personal, historical and polemical in nature, I have decided not to undertake a rewriting of this article and to allow it to be republished as it first appeared.

Gilles Carle—a Thematic Response or, Scenes From Family Life

Piers Handling

With the release of LA VIE HEUREUSE DE LEOPOLD Z in 1965, it was obvious that a new talent had arrived on the scene. Ten years later, and with eight features under his belt, we have seen the release of Carle's latest film, LA TETE DE NORMANDE ST-ONGE. Carle's output, while not prolific, has certainly been steady and of a quality that has raised him into the front ranks of Quebec cinema. He is also a filmmaker who has remained remarkably faithful to his roots and while this does not preclude a broadening of his vision, it has allowed him to refine his statements. Within his work it strikes me that there are certain identifiable themes that deserve analysis. While Carle is not a "difficult" filmmaker, he has tended towards visual allegory, and my reaction to LA TETE DE NORMANDE ST-ONGE prompted me to "place" this film in some context. NORMANDE ST-ONGE appears to mark a new step for Carle, but while it moves forward in new directions it is also firmly rooted in the films that preceded it. On reading most of the interviews, reviews and

Reprinted from *Cinema Canada*, no. 26 (March 1976).

critiques, both English and French, on Carle, I have always been left with a vaguely dissatisfied feeling, as if the authors have not fully comprehended what it is that Carle is really trying to do with his films. I offer the following then as a tentative base for further examination, and as Carle's work has been largely inaccessible to English audiences, perhaps it will lead them to a desire to see the films, or to look at them in a new light.

Categories tend to be somewhat facile and pompous, but approaching Carle's work I detected three major trends that are roughly chronological. Although these categories by no means include all of Carle's themes, they are useful in an analysis of his work as a whole.

Urban Absurdity

Carle's first feature, LA VIE HEUREUSE DE LEOPOLD Z, is evidently a germinal work. Produced rather accidentally (it was originally intended to be a short on snow removal), Carle, under the noses of the NFB, expanded it into a feature. It has a charmingly rambling feel to it which coupled with the character of Léopold makes it easy to view the film as one of gentle observation, rather than conscious statement. Episodic in structure and full of comic invention, it follows Léopold, a snowplow driver, on Christmas Eve, the day of a big storm, as he tries to find time to do a series of errands while evading the eyes of his supervisor. But it is also a film replete with instances of a man vaguely uneasy about his place in society—a society that cannot deal with his demands, no matter how unarticulated they are. Throughout we are shown how the mechanical subtly dominates people's lives. The film opens with Léopold trying to start his truck while his wife hangs a telephone receiver out of the upstairs window so he can talk to his irate supervisor who wants to know where the hell he is. He is told when asking for a bank loan that a hole in the computer card means he was once three weeks late on a payment. We see Josita trying to get into the night club she is booked into, only to be told through a loudspeaker above the door that she has to ring a doorbell she can hardly reach. The mileu in which all this takes place is at once disturbing, comical and continually present. On the radio we hear of a bank being robbed by three men disguised as Santa Claus, and in one of the most telling sequences in the film, Josita, in the shower, assumes that the person who rushes in and out of the house is a sex maniac. Of course it is only Léopold, frantically dressing for mass, but Carle undercuts the humour of the scene with Josita's spontaneous reaction, a reaction to which we can only assume she has been conditioned. LEOPOLD Z has an air of unease about it, a sense that things are happening so quickly in the background, in the world around us, that we have little time to absorb it all.

Yet the film also highlights an individual's conflict with aspects of life that threaten to overtake him. Léopold is forced by the restrictions of his job to be conscious of his continual fight against time. He has to find time to pick up the fur coat which is his wife's Christmas present, he has to negotiate a small loan to pay for the coat, and he has to pick up Josita at the train station. When Léopold looks out at the hundreds of cars stuck in the storm during rush hour he mutters, "Why didn't you stay home? Now we have to work like slaves on Christmas Eve." He sees his chances of getting to midnight mass disappear due to the anonymous selfishness of the people who have driven their cars to work. Léopold tells Josita that he once tried to get a job as an excavator when they were building the Metro, but he was turned down—once a snowplowman, always a snowplowman. It is with this statement that Carle makes his most subversive comment, an indictment of a system that pigeonholes people and their aspirations.

In LE VIOL D'UNE JEUNE FILLE DOUCE the tapestry of absurdity is more defined. We begin with a shot of a couple sitting a few feet apart on a park bench, talking to each other through walkie-talkies, a scene which sets the tone for everything that follows. This is in essence a film about a normal girl living in an abnormal society, and in the same way that the *elle* in Godard's DEUX OU TROIS CHOSES QUE JE SAIS D'ELLE refers not only to the woman in the film but also to Paris, the rape in LE VIOL alludes not only to the actual rape that the brothers commit, but also to what is being done to Julie's mind. In the slightly absurd, disquieting society that forms the backdrop to the film, Julie lives as an emotional cipher, her being dominated by what surrounds her. Discovering that she is pregnant, and not knowing who the father is, she flirts with the idea of an abortion but instead decides to take a lover—a Moroccan who is new to Canada and is trying to find his way about.

One of the most disturbing things in the film is the suicide of Susan, Julie's neighbour. As she opens the door one morning to go to work, Julie is confronted with a dead body being carried down the stairs by the police. Turning to tell her lover, and her girlfriend who is also living with her, she cannot wake them. Descending into the street, she occupies the place left by the ambulance that we have just seen drive off with Susan's body. The overriding impression we receive is one of people who cannot or are unwilling to absorb and deal with certain aspects of life.

The three brothers, modern-day gangsters named after angels (Raphael, Gabriel and Joachim) only add to the uneasy feeling of distortion. Their rape of the girl, a hitchhiker they have picked up, is unmotivated, and combined with Julie's lack of reaction as she sits quietly in the car, is extremely disturbing. The subsequent arbitrary discovery of a man they convince themselves to be the father of Julie's unborn child, which culminates with the brothers photographing him for future reference, adds to our feeling of unease. The film is full of such instances—Julie trying to give her new-born baby away, leaving it in the back seat of the car that is driven away, collecting the baby from the police station, typing the autobiography of her Moroccan lover, her girlfriend running off with an Australian only to return days later, and Susan listening to music that obviously exists only in her head. LE VIOL sees Carle stretching himself filmically and artistically, and in this sense of motiveless, incomplete and semi-farcical action, he has found a perfect form for expression.

The impetus of this movement sees its most complete expression in RED, where what formed the backdrop in LE VIOL here intrudes more forcibly and culminates in Red's brutal destruction. RED is a portrait of a half-breed aware both of his white and his Indian heritage. He expresses all the contradictions of our society, and if the tensions within the man are not completely dealt with by Carle, Red's conflict with the society that spawned him is graphically depicted. Red himself is an uneasy amalgam of modern-day playboy, frontiersman and small-time gangster. He is at war with his "family"—a curious mixture of half-brothers, a half-sister and her husband, Frédéric. Red is involved in a car theft ring and the film opens after he has stolen one from Frédéric's car lot. Everywhere that Carle turns his cool eye we have evidence of duplicity, cruelty and unhappiness. The absurdity of much of what happens is again terribly upsetting. Red's mother dies for no apparent reason other than almost willing it, and Red's half-sister Elisabeth is gruesomely killed by an anonymous sniper as she carries groceries into the house. A grotesque stag party given for the impending marriage of one of the half-brothers ends in a whore being viciously stabbed in the leg for failing to arouse the groom-to-be. When Red escapes into the wilds of Quebec, it is only to stumble across a wilderness community of smugglers who live off the surrounding urban society. We are introduced to a couple of its members as they are dismantling a police car, prior to transporting it bit by bit across the lake to their camp. It soon becomes obvious that these people, like Red, are urban dropouts who have been driven into the bush. Unhappy with his new surroundings which offer no solution, Red is drawn back into the metropolis he cannot escape. He decides to confront his pursuers, only to be gunned down in front of Frédéric, who ironically is attending a car show being held in Place Bonaventure.

With RED Carle had reached a transitional phase as a filmmaker. The theme of dissatisfaction with urban life was temporarily laid to rest and, while it has not been banished from his films, no longer preoccupies him in quite the same way.

Rural Escape

RED is a bridge between Carle's first major preoccupation and his second. Society had pushed Red and his girlfriend from the city into the countryside—the Canadian bush. However, for Red, a half-breed, the transposition was not successful. In effect he is more of a white man than an Indian, having adopted most of the external trappings of white society. Furthermore Carle shows that rural Quebec too has been eroded. Unsentimental in his approach, Carle strips away the mythology of the great untouched Canadian outdoors to expose it as a hollow misconception. Bill Sullivan, the leader of the gang of smugglers who inhabit this otherwise deserted part of Quebec, personifies all the contradictions. A Québécois speaking broad joual, he is given an English name, and when we are first introduced to him, he is sitting outside watching his portable television set on a tree stump. Even the bizarre surveyor who pitches his tent on the perimeter of the little camp is an ominous foreshadowing of the intrusion of a society that is never very far away.

But it is with LES MALES and LA VRAIE NATURE DE BERNADETTE that Carle turns to this theme with full force. On the surface LES MALES presents us with what can be interpreted as an idealized retreat into the joys of nature. The two men retire into the bush, presumably to escape the vagaries of a hostile world. This is treated more thoroughly when they trundle off to the local village, desperate for a woman after their months of isolation. Choosing the daughter of the local police chief, they kidnap her and set off a bizarre, manic, almost wild-west chase which lands them in jail. They manage to escape and, lessons learnt—society still does not understand them—they return to their camp, only to find the mirage of Rita Sauvage, the answer to their dreams: the unfettered, uncomplicated woman. Setting up a ménage à trois, their idyllic retreat blooms as Rita dispenses her sexual favours with complete freedom. However, inevitably it seems, masculine jealousies begin to cloud the horizon and when the two men come to blows, Rita vanishes as quickly and as quietly as she came. The men suspend hostilities, reunited by their common aim to find Rita, a search that is never concluded but which finds them finally in Montreal, trying to find her through meditation. Throughout the course of LES MALES we see that disassociation with civilization, or contemporary values, is extremely difficult—if not impossible. Saddled by a cultural baggage that cannot be easily discarded, their new lifestyle is doomed, and when presented with an opportunity to establish a new form of living arrangement, their machismo blinds them to their selfishness. Alone and confused at the film's end, they are almost in a state of suspension as they grope towards some type of self-awareness.

LA VRAIE NATURE DE BERNADETTE was to cover much of the same ground but in a more forceful manner, with many of the tensions held in a finer balance. Bernadette, alone in her apartment one day, impulsively packs up and leaves the city with her child to start a new life in the country. Pursuing a line of development begun with Rita Sauvage, Carle makes Bernadette his most complex character to date. She is an earth mother of immense charm, vitality and energy. In her return to nature Bernadette is determined to discover the joys and simplicity of country living. There she will be able to express her true nature. Ample and generous, she becomes the centre of a community that relies on her energy. She shares herself with anyone who needs her help, yet it is obvious that there is a naiveté about her which while seductively attractive is extremely dangerous. The destruction of Bernadette's dream is ruthless and cruel, but ultimately necessary for her growth, as she begins to comprehend the fact that one cannot escape from reality, or from the imperfections of human nature. While Carle recognizes the inherent attractions of his heroine's move to the country, he is aware of the moralistic, evangelistic impulse that motivates her. She too is saddled with a cultural heritage that views nature as an unspoilt haven. But finally Bernadette is soberly forced to re-evaluate her ideas. Taking up a gun to support Thomas and the farmworkers in their struggle, she has begun to understand his hard-nosed, practical nature, a characteristic that had previously irritated her, as Thomas did not conform to her idea of what a farmer was and should be.

This move towards self-awareness is also to be found in LA MORT D'UN BUCHERON, which immediately succeeded BERNADETTE. Like RED, BERNADETTE is a bridge to another stage in Carle's work, for until that film Carle's world had been predominantly male. Subsequently he was to turn his attention towards the plight of women in Quebec, a theme with which he is still obsessed.

Quebec Women Exploited

Though Carle had not ignored women in his films, until BERNADETTE they tended to play a peripheral role. In LE VIOL D'UNE JEUNE FILLE DOUCE he had dealt with a young, modern girl in a coldly abstract way, but her concerns were overshadowed in his desire to sketch a portrait of her surroundings. In both RED and LES MALES, women are similarly kept in the background or treated superficially. Red's girlfriend is Carle's first example of a woman frustrated and angered by traditional sex roles. Rita Sauvage is more of a catalyst in LES MALES than a fully realized character. She was however the basis for Carle's first complete and complex female character, Bernadette. But it was in LA MORT D'UN BUCHERON and the two features that followed that Carle turned his full focus on women in Quebec society.

LA MORT D'UN BUCHERON is a withering indictment of the exploitation of a young girl who comes to Montreal to find a father who has disappeared. Bewildered and jobless, she looks up an old friend of her mother's, Armand St-Amour, and gets a job with him as a topless singer after innocently auditioning as a folk-singer. Armand is ruthless and cruel, beating her viciously one night when she arrives late for one of her shows. She takes up with a young journalist, François Paradis, who vows to help but ends up exploiting her to further his own career, persuading her to do a sensual, semi-nude dance for a lecherous but influential old man. And finally she drifts from Armand and his bar into commercial advertising and modelling where she is invariably used as a nude mannequin. She is used by men at every turn —used by people who see her as a beautiful and titillating object. Suffocated by this overwhelming masculine influence which ironically extends to the film's very impetus—her search for her father—Maria slowly, painfully moves towards wome kind of liberation. After she finally discovers the fate of her father, her boyfriend pushes her into making love with him. Now that she is freed of her father's shadow, will this male become her new oppressor? In a sequence that is one of the most moving in all Carle's cinema, she pushes him away, and outside in the full light of day reflects in an off-screen narration that finally she is free. Although she is also alone, it is an ending tinged with optimism—unique in Carle's oeuvre.

LES CORPS CELESTES was not to have this ray of hope. It remains Carle's only period piece and deals with a pimp and his covey of prostitutes in a mining town in pre-Second World War Quebec, thus continuing Carle's devotion to the theme of women's exploitation. Ambitious in scope, it is perhaps a trifle imperfect in execution, as if Carle could not balance all of what he wanted to communicate. As he parallels the establishment of a whorehouse with the impending war in Europe, Carle's satire is sometimes incomplete. Desmond's determination to juggle all the conflicting forces of the town—the church, the miners and his harem of girls, one of whom he is attracted to—allows Carle to comment again on a masculine society that is primarily concerned with using its women. Rose-Marie, Desmond's new flame, is subjected to all his jealousies and rages when she does not submit to his desires. Instead she has found a rather innocuous lover of her own with whom she eventually runs off. However, the couple finally returns to the protection of Desmond and his whorehouse when he, and consequently she, cannot survive in the world outside. Her subjugation is complete. After the breath of optimism that ended LA MORT D'UN BUCHERON, Carle executes a total about-face.

The bleak implications of LES CORPS CELESTES were obviously not a vagary in Carle's development, as LA TETE DE NORMANDE ST-ONGE confirms rather emphatically. Normande has certain elements in common with Bernadette. She is the centre of a group of people who depend on her for all kinds of things, and who make a series of demands on her. She will be used and exploited by everyone. While she gives, they take, and Normande, desperate for love herself, is eventually driven mad by their insatiable wishes. She gives money to her sister who doesn't even bother to visit their mother in the hospital, she cares for an elderly neighbour who eventually declares that Normande never did anything for her, and she is used by a sculptor who freezes her beauty in a nude statue while hardly concealing his desire for her. She brings her boyfriend a book as a present, on a subject that means a great deal to him, yet he interacts with her only on a sexual level which leaves Normande unsatisfied. Carol, the magician, at first kind and open, angrily and selfishly denounces her for sleeping with her lout of a boyfriend.

Normande's motives are totally self-effacing—she wants to have her mother with her, a mother who has been consigned to an insane asylum by an intolerant brother. Even here great pain results when her mother shows a preference for her sister, while virtually ignoring Normande. Worn down on all sides, Normande finds it increasingly difficult to deal with reality, and turns to sexual dreams and fantasies where she is always the centre of attention, and where she assumes the dominant role. Finally mad, Normande can register no feeling or emotion. Her madness is a protective device, but the eye that looks out at us stares only into the void.

Conclusion

As has been evident throughout, Carle has remained remarkably faithful to a few major themes. While they cannot explain all the elements that constitute his films, they provide a structure within which to approach his work. But before concluding I would like to touch on a few further points. After seeing LA TETE DE NORMANDE ST-ONGE it struck me that it was less a film about madness and its interchange between mother and daughter, than a film about an attempt to construct and re-establish the family unit. In reflection is this not what all of his films are about? They are all concerned with the family in some way, whether it is the demands it places on Léopold on Christmas Eve, the protective impulse which results in violence, death and rape in LE VIOL D'UNE JEUNE FILLE DOUCE and RED, the ménage in LES MALES, the attempt to establish an extended family based on rural values in BERNADETTE, the search for the father in LA MORT D'UN BUCHERON, the pimp and his family of whores in LES CORPS CELESTES, and the search for the mother in LA TETE DE NORMANDE ST-ONGE. That this goal of setting up some equivalent to the family is never achieved is not a result of artistic failing, of which Carle has so often been accused (i.e., he doesn't know how to end his movies) but it is obviously impossible for him to let this union or resolution take place. And undoubtedly on the evidence of the films his view is becoming bleaker and more despairing.

Furthermore the characters in the films are generally in the process of defining themselves. In RED this results in confrontation and death, but it shows that escape is no answer. The two men in LES MALES ultimately realize what they have destroyed and come to a greater awareness of their divisive impulses. Bernadette is continually in the process of refining her attitudes and ideals until she reaches some kind of understanding, which serves as a basis for action. Maria Chapdelaine explores her father's past in an attempt to purge herself and attain freedom. And finally Normande essentially follows the same path as Maria, but here the self-definition is not allowed to take place—in its place there is its opposite, fragmentation. The first scene in NORMANDE ST-ONGE centres around Normande wondering if she will ever have a child. This obsessive search for the family unit, wherein to some extent the mother becomes Normande's surrogate child, is doomed to failure and nothing is ever allowed to consolidate. Normande's thoughts remain just that —thoughts. At the conclusion of his films Carle's characters more often than not remain alone in a cruel world.

There is one other matter that has intrigued and mystified me: images of fruit and vegetables abound in Carle's films in the strangest contexts. This phenomenon makes its first appearance in LE VIOL, when during the rape Carle cuts back to Julie in the car eating an apple. In the next film Red's half-sister is murdered and she is shown in a pool of blood, surrounded by the fruit she has been carrying into the house. In BERNADETTE there are numerous examples: the film opens on framed paintings of a carrot, a beet, a cucumber and a tomato; Bernadette drives into the country with the back seat of her convertible stuffed with bananas; the three old men play pool on her kitchen table using oranges for balls; and of course there is the image of the farmers dumping all their produce on the highway. And in NORMANDE ST-ONGE, Normande's boyfriend is obsessed with mushrooms. What do these images mean? Contrasted with this is Carle's increasing use of sculptures of one sort or another the papier-maché heads of the lumberjacks in LA MORT D'UN BUCHERON and the nude sculpture that Normande is posing for in LA TETE DE NORMANDE ST-ONGE. For me these props have always had a disturbing edge—they appear where they don't really belong and are perhaps ultimately unexplainable. But on the other hand could they not be images of sterility or growth, images that match the tone and the mood of the films? The sculptures have a frozen, sterile quality, haunting and devoid of emotion. In LA MORT D'UN BUCHERON they anticipate and are reminders of the deaths of the lumberjacks. One could argue that the sculpture in NORMANDE ST-ONGE serves a similar function. But they are also images of the past, of something that is frozen in time, and will not develop or grow any further. The use of fruit and vegetables ironically provides a similar effect, for they usually counterpoint something that is in a state of disruption, or has stopped growing. But I would hesitate to "explain" these images in only one manner as they are open to a multitude of interpretations—the use of fruit in BERNADETTE seems to serve a different role.

What is intriguing is the direction that Carle will now follow. Only RED has as nihilistic an ending as LA TETE DE NORMANDE ST-ONGE, but Carle had the ability to grow beyond that film. The fact that he has left his partnership with Pierre Lamy in Les Productions Carle Lamy and shot a film for the CBC in Toronto points towards a need he must feel for change. On the evidence of the films he has much to give us yet.

Men of Vision
Some Comments on the Work of Don Shebib

Peter Harcourt

There are lots of films that I'd like to make in the States. I'd like to make a film there every couple of years. But basically, I'd really prefer to make films here. If I did leave, it would be like taking a fish out of water. I seem to think that I thrive on the water that I swim in, which is where I am, in Toronto.
—Don Shebib, at the AGO, 1975.

Towards the end of SECOND WIND (1976), there is a tiny moment of some importance. Roger is out on one of his early morning runs, jogging along the Beaches. Apart from his running, things have not been going well for him. His friends have quarrelled with him, his wife has left him and even his career as a stockbroker seems somewhat in jeopardy. During this particular run, he pauses for a minute to walk onto a jetty and look across the lake. It is a quiet moment in the film, a speechless moment, the actual significance of which remains unspecified. There is nothing within the context of this sequence to tell us exactly what Roger may be thinking. His face expresses nothing precisely. Yet, helped by the music, such a moment creates a feeling of inwardness, of self-reflection—as if he is weighing up the values of his life.

I single out this moment for a number of reasons. Partly because, as it doesn't directly advance the narrative, it may have been scarcely noticed by a number of viewers; but largely because it relates to similar moments in nearly all of Shebib's films and to another in this film as well. During the opening sequence of the cocktail party given in Roger's honour—a celebration of his promotion to vice-president of the company he is working for—there is a similar moment of mute attentiveness.

As Roger seems ill-at-ease with the party, indeed with his own success, he goes off alone into the boardroom and looks out of a window down onto the city-scape below. This too is a quiet moment, an introspective moment; but the context of the party encourages more precision in our speculations. Surely there must be something more, Roger's face seems to be saying—something that is more difficult, something that will truly challenge him. Successful though he is, he seems aware of an absence, of something not there. He craves the risks of an actual challenge. He feels not fully stretched in the world as it is.

This feeling of emptiness, of restlessness, often of irrelevance pervades the films of Don Shebib—not only his features but much of his other work as well. And this feeling is often conveyed without the help of words.

Reprinted from *Cinema Canada*, no. 32 (October 1976).

In WE'VE COME A LONG WAY TOGETHER, a film on old people made for OECA in 1974, though stretched by his producers to twice the length that Shebib wanted it to be, there is much the same kind of feeling that we find in his features. For the most part, nowadays, old people are displaced persons. Society gives them no meaningful role to play. They have to be institutionalized, organized, "entertained"—not *that* much unlike Roger in his successful, middle-class life within the institutionalized routine of his middle-class job. The rules are all external. One tries to "have fun" within whatever conditions are offered.

While the people in WE'VE COME A LONG WAY TOGETHER do have fun—dancing to Guy Lombardo's "When I Grow Too Old to Dream..." or playing their small drums and toy trumpets in their own "spasm" band—these scenes of organized activity are counterbalanced with scenes of inescapable loneliness. There is a quiet shot (again, not unlike that early shot of Roger) of an old man by himself looking out of a window; and there are repeated cuts to a shot of an old man walking towards us from a distance—almost like a warning.

These are the moments that give the film its predominant tone, that create the mood we take away with us—whatever apparently cheerful things the people manage to say. Old age leads to isolation and loneliness, to social irrelevance; and this is a fate that moves towards us all.

This feeling of irrelevance is perhaps *the* central mood in all Shebib's features as it is in his most distinguished short, GOOD TIMES, BAD TIMES—a film on war veterans made for the CBC in 1969. GOOD TIMES, BAD TIMES is also about old people, but about old people who once played a most important role—winning our wars. For those of us privileged enough to be aware of European cinema, this film could usefully be compared with Georges Franju's HOTEL DES INVALIDES (1951) or Alain Resnais's NUIT ET BROUILLARD (1955)—films which Shebib may or may not have seen. But whatever the result of such a comparison, GOOD TIMES, BAD TIMES is in its own way a most distinguished film.

Its distinction lies in the balance of its structure, in the interweaving of elements that pull in different ways. These elements, of course, are indigenous to the theme of the film as they are indigenous to war; but Shebib organizes them in a highly original way.

For most people, the experience of war is the ultimate horror. At the same time, for those who survive it, this shared horror creates an extraordinary sense of comradeship, of unquestionable purposefulness. As the voice of a veteran explains in the film: "The comradeship of soldiers is a kind of love," a love that comes about when "you've lived together, slept together, gone on leave together, died together."

GOOD TIMES, BAD TIMES intercuts interviews with veterans with "found" footage of both the world wars. Some of the footage is optically stretched—each frame double-printed to give it the ghostly effect of slow-motion, as if from some nightmare imperfectly remembered. Both through scenes of actual violence and through a sense of violence created in the editing, the found footage conveys the actual horrors of war. Meanwhile there are sequences of the veterans—the survivors —sometimes in a club drinking beer together and singing the old war songs, reminding themselves of the "good times" of intense comradeship, of the days when they really felt useful and united as a group. They tend to forget the "bad times", as one of them explains, because of this sense of dignity bestowed upon them by the war.

Just as the visuals intercut new footage with archival material, so the soundtrack draws upon bits of music (also sometimes "stretched") from Holst's "The Planets", from Samuel Barber's "Adagio for Strings", and from a rock group, The Iron Butterfly. This music contrasts sharply both with the veterans' own singing and with Bing Crosby's rendition of that ironically absurd war song, "Auf Wiedersehen, my dear".

The intricacies of this film could be studied in detail—both the intricacies of the way it has been put together and those of its ultimate meaning. For who, finally, won the war? Certainly not the people who ought it, who experienced the intense emotions of being at the front. Towards the end of the film we see an end-of-war rally in Trafalgar Square in London and hear the legendary sound of Big Ben. Then, over shots of soldiers marching away, as so often in this film, the commentary draws upon lines from an extended poem by Joyce Cary, "Marching Soldiers", which he wrote at the end of the Second World War:

March, march, soldiers, follow away.
We do not belong among these peaceful houses.
Our foreheads are marked with a sign, we have looked at death too long,
Within our eyes his picture sits. March, march, soldiers,
For those who fear that face will put their curse upon us,
Those whom we set free will pay us with hatred,
Because we are guilty of action, of war, of blood.

These lines are accompanied by the plaintive sounds of Barber's "Adagio", creating a rich emotional effect difficult to describe—a fusion of exhilaration plus a sense of loss, a movement into accusation and uselessness.

As the film began with the playing of our (then) national anthem over shots of old coins and little statuettes of soldiers, so it ends with an old veteran singing in his cracked but proud voice, "God Save the Queen." But that is not all. In a way that speaks for this old man personally but which might also sum up the feelings of a good many soldiers, of people who recognize that they have served their purpose, he then says: "Thank you very much. I'm all tired out. Now you can put me to sleep."

All of Shebib's subsequent work can be seen as a development of elements contained within this magnificent short film: the great value he places on male comradeship; his enormous skill as an editor; his feeling for the need for real challenges to give individuals a sense of their dignity; and finally (despite the "jock" sensibility Shebib likes to put forward in his interviews),[1] his sensitivity both to poetry and music. This is a feeling he tries to put to one side, as if as a Canadian it wouldn't be "manly" to let it seem prominent. But it is there in the films nevertheless, both directly and indirectly.

When I first saw GOIN' DOWN THE ROAD when it came out in 1970, I was somewhat perplexed by the role played in the film by the music of Erik Satie. It seemed out of context and therefore pretentious. I now know I was wrong. The context that justifies it is partly provided by Shebib's other films and partly by elements in the film itself.

As most Canadians know by now, GOIN' DOWN THE ROAD tells the story of two lads from the Maritimes who set out for the big city to cash in on the stylish life of the economic centre of this strangely disunited country called Canada. Of course they don't make it. The entire enterprise ends in disaster, leaving them with less at the end than they had at the beginning. But there are moments of hope along the way.

Pete and Joey are pals, real comrades in the way that Shebib believes in; but they are also very different guys. While they are both typical members of the *lumpenproletariat*—unskilled workers with no sense of the political implications of the role society has assigned them—Pete has a more reflective nature. He tries to think about things. Clumsy though his articulations may be (for language, among other things, is the property of the middle-classes), he is doubly aware that life for other people offers something more, something which he wants access to. Sometimes this sense expresses itself simply in crude, "jock" ways, such as when he covets Nicole's resplendant "knockers" as she struts about the Wilson pop factory, tantalizing all the workers but available to none of them. Yet at other times, Pete's awareness expresses itself in more refined ways.

This is where the music of Satie comes in. One night, when the boys are out on the town, doing the Yonge Street strip, they stroll into "Sam's" to pick up some records—country-&-western (obviously), probably from the Maritimes—the kind of music that speaks to the culture they spring from. But Pete notices a well-dressed young woman walking upstairs. He follows her up towards the classical section where she listens, for a moment, to one of Satie's "Gymnopédies". While it is still the scent of sex that is driving him on, there is something in her style and in the style of the music that represents to Pete the world he is excluded from—the world of the cultivated, well-to-do, middle-class. This is the world that allows for contemplation, that provides the leisure in which feelings can be defined. At another point in the film when Pete is having a beer with Joey he is pushed into a kind of articulateness about his feeling of uselessness, his feeling of "alienation", of *Verdinglichung* (as Marx would say).

Pete words all fumble, but his understanding is just. They are talking about salaries, and Pete begins to reckon up the number of cases of ginger ale they have stacked since they began work. "Three hundred and four thousand cases each," Pete finally works out. But there is nothing to show for it. Joey can't understand what he is talking about. He cannot think beyond the weekly pay-package of $80 which is more than they ever got in the Maritimes. But Pete wants something more. "I wanna do something that matters," as he finally puts it, "something that shows for myself, that says I was there. Peter McGraw was there." This is what his work, his life, his whole sensibility has conspired to deny him. And Pete is vaguely aware that this all has to do with a style of life that involves listening to music and reading books.

In another scene, Pete and Joey and their two girls are over at the island, the girls "yakking" on with their hair up in curlers, when Pete notices another middle-class lady absorbed in a book. "Reality" must lie elsewhere, this sequence seems to be saying. Yet Pete can find no way of effectively changing anything.

When everything has failed, after Joey has married his "knocked-up" Bets and they are now both out of work, Pete returns from his job at a bowling alley and puts on the Satie record, as if a reminder of the world they are excluded from. This is the moment of greatest inwardness in the film, once we have come to realize what that Satie means to Pete and to the world of culturally dispossessed people that Shebib has created for us. As the music plays, we cut from tired face to tired face, each one registering something personal but unspecific. Like Roger's look out from the jetty in SECOND WIND, like the faces of the veterans or the inhabitants of the old peoples' home, there is the sense here as so often in Shebib's films that what the characters are feeling lies too deep for words.

Since GOIN' DOWN THE ROAD, Shebib has failed to achieve quite the same degree of critical or commercial success, although I cannot understand why. If on the level of narrative both RIP-OFF (1971) and SECOND WIND seem comparatively slight films, certainly BETWEEN FRIENDS (1973) is not. In any case, whatever individual reviewers might have decided are the "faults" of Shebib's various films, I would argue that they are all important—important both in terms of understanding Shebib's work and in terms of understanding something about the world we live in as Canadians.

If the subject of GOIN' DOWN THE ROAD is (as Robert Fulford put it) "rootlessness, the sense of pointlessness, the sense that no job is worth doing and no relationship worth developing",[2] the same subject can be found in Shebib's next two films. If Pete and Joey's escape to the mythological promises of Upper Canada was a kind of pilgrimage that led nowhere, so the young kids of RIP-OFF also set out on a journey that leads to divisiveness and despair, interfering even with the "comradeship" that had held them together.

The boys are quite well off—like so many North American kids. But there seems nothing *real* that they can do. There isn't anything left to discover. "What a bummer!" as one of them exclaims one day, while they are lying around in an old barn reading about the voyages of Captain Cook; and their efforts to achieve an identity within the high school that encloses them, whether through founding a rock band or trying to make it with the girls, are either ridiculous or humiliating—usually both. Finally the accident of Michael's "inheritance"—a piece of land up north—and their decision to found a commune there gives them an identity—at least for a while. But this too comes to nothing and they return home in defeat.

The penultimate scene involves a confrontation between Michael and his father—perhaps a bit implausible in terms of characterization but right, nevertheless, in terms of the emotional rhythm of the film. This is the first time that Michael actually sees his father as a person and gets some sense of the forces in life that have formed him. Furthermore, in a typically Shebibian way, Michael's response to his father's stories about the hardship of his own youth is more visual than verbal. This means that we, the audience, have to decide what Michael is thinking. Does he partly envy his father for having had so few choices to make in life —rather like the veterans who had to fight in the war? Or does he see a frightening vision of what adult life might be—a lonely routine of unimaginative drudgery, just to earn a living, just to stay alive? What is fine about this film as about other films by Don Shebib is that we have to work at these questions by ourselves.

The film ends on a note of romantic nostalgia. Most of the boys have graduated and, except for Steve (the "Joey" of this film) who accepts an early marriage and a life of common labour, they are going on to university—largely because there is nothing else to do. There is a great feeling of futurelessness, as a long lens and slow-motion photography idealizes the kids throwing about a football, as if to prolong the carefree, if aimless, irresponsibility of their youth. And like so many Canadian films, this sense of futurelessness is consolidated technically by the final freeze-frame. Like Pete and Joey, these kids, while better off, still have no sense of where they are going.

In spite of a fine tribute from Robert Fulford,[3] BETWEEN FRIENDS has not enjoyed either the commercial or critical success of Shebib's first feature. This is truly astonishing because in many ways it is his most complex achievement. In this article I can only point to a few distinguished details; yet they define the sensibility that informs the entire film.

In his public statements, Don Shebib is his own worst publicity agent. He is always complaining that his scripts are weak or that he has had difficulties with his actors. To my mind, the obvious sense of superiority and detached indifference that Michael Parks brought to his role as Toby in BETWEEN FRIENDS, while it may have caused Shebib some annoyance at the time of shooting, contributes forcefully to his effectiveness in the film. Toby (a bit like Pete) is a kind of dreamer. He has had a life and lost it and he now drifts into things—whether into an ill-conceived robbery or into an affair with the wife of his former best friend.

In this way, Toby seems detached from the implications of his own actions. The only signs of true emotion are related to his past—either his prestigious past as super-surfer or his lost relationship with Michael, his young son. He seems to have been closer to the privileged world of "high culture" that Pete seemed to be longing for in GOIN' DOWN THE ROAD; yet he has given it up—for reasons we never fully understand. He is more intelligent and more sensitive than his crude friend, Chino. Yet he doesn't seem to care. And this lack of caring, this sense that there is nothing to live for, as much as Chino's rage brings about the failure and separateness at the end—isolated figures within a snowy landscape, Ellie with her dead father, Toby with his dead friend.

Like many Canadian films, Shebib's are rich in their feeling for landscape, but none more so than BETWEEN FRIENDS. If in SECOND WIND Toronto looks prosperous, beautiful and suburbanly humane; in both GOIN' DOWN THE ROAD and BETWEEN FRIENDS it has a far more hostile atmosphere. Especially in BETWEEN FRIENDS, Toronto appears a city of chilly piers where shady deals are arranged, of grubby little restaurants and impersonal supermarkets where both Chino and Ellie eke out their dreary, minimal-wage existences. And the scenes around Sudbury where the robbery takes place are even more powerful in their wintry bleakness. Slag heaps and lonely chimneys dominate a number of images, making the characters look small and inconsequential by comparison —mere items in an industrial superstructure within which they can play only mechanical roles. Unless they protest: stage a robbery, try to rip the system off. But even then, they fail.

BETWEEN FRIENDS is a film of extraordinary tenderness, of intense compassion for all its characters. With Bonnie Bedelia as Ellie it also offers the only substantially sympathetic female portrait that Shebib has so far given us. Yet as in all Shebib's films her role is to interfere with the strong male companionship that might have existed without her; thus in this way she too contributes to the destructiveness at the end.

In Shelbib's films, women are generally seen as objects, as things men have sex with—whether the decorative housewife with her plants in SECOND WIND or the jaded floozies in BETWEEN FRIENDS that Will, Ellie's father, and Coker make use of for their "love life". But Ellie is something more—more sensitive and demanding. In Shebib's world, of course, this also makes her more dangerous. She is more likely to disrupt the external projects of the men.

Yet the initial love scene between Toby and Ellie is one of exceptional tenderness. The men and their ladies are downstairs drinking and dancing and singing beery songs, when a splinter in Toby's finger gives Ellie an excuse to invite him upstairs to remove it. Obviously she feels apart from this drunken, raunchy fun; and her red maxi-dress, with the refined contours of her body detectable beneath it, lends visual emphasis to this feeling of separateness, to our sense of her sensitivity. Once upstairs, for a while the rowdy singing is drowned out by a bit of opera on the radio—a section of Puccini's "La Bohème". Like the bits of Satie in GOIN' DOWN THE ROAD, this music, and the elegance of Ellie's red dress, sets this scene apart, as if aware of other values. It is placed in parenthesis (so to speak), as indeed it proves to be only a parenthesis in the characters' lives.

Yet Shebib's own sensibility (whether consciously or not) picks up on these elements and introduces them again at later moments in the film—most effectively in the café scene just before the heist. While supposedly working together, Ellie, Will, Toby and Chino are sitting apart from one another in sadness and tension caused partly by Coker's death but mostly by Chino's knowledge of Toby and Ellie's affair. Chino is delivering an angry monologue on the value of friendship—supposedly to the bartender, but actually in his self-pitying way to everyone else in the room. "It's bullshit, that's what it is," he finally cries out. Meanwhile, Ellie is sitting at the rear of the room, plunking out some little classical piece on a piano, the red light at her side casting a red glow on her hair, providing a visual echo of her initial moment of tenderness with Toby. Finally, Toby who throughout the film has seemed directed towards the past, is speaking to his son in California on the telephone. "Do you want to hang up first? Or should I hang up first?" He is trying, as if for the last time, to recreate those playful games of domestic intimacy which he himself has lost.

With repeated screenings, especially when seen in sequence, Don Shebib's films add up to an extraordinary achievement—a mixture of psychological uncertainty and artistic refinement, of boorishness and sensitivity, as, indeed, much of life in Canada is today. But at their centre, there is always the sense of something not there—some kind of challenge, some sense of cohesiveness, something never directly specified that might make life meaningful. This longing is scarcely present in the words his characters exchange: it is more in the way they look at one another or in the way they simply stare off into an empty space—especially the men. What are the qualities in life that hold people together, that might lead us collectively to a sense of identity or a feeling of purposefulness, a feeling of success? This is the question that, cumulatively, Shebib's films seem to ask.

If in SECOND WIND during that extended run with Pete in High Park where Roger is really beginning to discover his pace as a runner, if in this sequence Hagood Hardy's music gives to this moment something like the exhilaration of an American Western (as when the settlers have beaten off the Indians and won their way through to the promised land); so in BETWEEN FRIENDS Coker's funeral is rich in allusions to American culture. But it is an allusion to an absence.

In I don't know how many films by John Ford we have seen a *community* of individuals singing together one of Ford's favourite songs, "We shall gather at the river"—the song helping to unite them as a group. At Coker's funeral, however, all the characters are isolated from one another, separated in extreme long-shot as we hear Will, at the top of his voice and all by himself, singing out that very same song:

> *We shall gather at the river,*
> *That flows past the throne of God.*

This is a moment of great power in the film, simply as it is; but if we pick up on the allusion (probably unintended by Shebib), it becomes more powerful still, with referents not only valid within the film but within our whole culture.

There may be all kinds of "faults" in Don Shebib's films—psychological implausibilities or clumsy bits of dialogue that make too explicit moments that would be stronger left silent. Certainly, in terms of my own response, I feel this is true about Chino's suicidal attack on Toby during the very moment of the robbery in BETWEEN FRIENDS, making too explicit his determination to bring about the destruction of them all. But I don't really care about these faults. There are all kinds of faults in Bergman and Antonioni; but the films are important to us collectively because they add up to something more than any individual moment, be it strong or weak, in any particular film. Cumulatively, they speak to us as a whole.

This much I claim for Don Shebib; and I have only dealt with some of the films and have only begun to scratch the surface of the qualities that are there. Perhaps, as John Hofsess has asserted, Shebib is a Canadian who has outgrown Canada.[4] Perhaps he will have to go elsewhere to develop. Perhaps in SECOND WIND (as a friend of mine playfully suggested), Roger's look out from that jetty really stands for Shebib himself, wondering if there is a place for him in the American industry! But whatever the ultimate answers to these speculations, Shebib's films are less about losers than they are about loners—like a good many Canadian films. And indeed, Canada is a country in which there is very little sense of people working together collectively—especially in Toronto where everybody seems to be working against everybody else.

As I have argued elsewhere,[5] perhaps, in such a culture, it is wrong for us to expect from our cinema the normative values of psychological realism and narrative tidiness—characteristics possibly more germane to cultures that are surer of themselves, where individual roles are more securely defined. If at the present moment conditions of production and exhibition discourage the work of Don Shebib, it doesn't necessarily follow that it is *his* work that has to change. Perhaps *we* have to change the conditions in which he works, conditions which in any case are based on foreign models and controlled by foreign capital.

The films of Don Shebib add up to a statement about life that seems appropriate to us as Canadians. His characters, especially his men, convey a vision of some better kind of life that might be possible elsewhere but *should* be possible here. Whether this is seen in class or cultural terms, this insight is real for us, for many of us, living here in Canada.

It is this search for this vision, however successful it may be in any particular film, that animates the work of Don Shebib as a filmmaker—whoever the writer and whoever the cameraman. And it is this sense of a search that unifies his work and gives it meaning—a meaning relevant to us as Canadians.

Making Films for Your Own People

An Interview with Denys Arcand

Judy Wright and Debbie Magidson

Prior to making LA MAUDITE GALETTE, his first fiction film, Arcand completed a number of shorts while on contract with the film board. The first film, SAMUEL DE CHAMPLAIN, made in 1963, explores Québécois ancestry and the relationship of the white man to the Indian. Excerpts from Champlain's diary serve as the commentary. LA ROUTE DE L'OUEST and VILLE-MARIE were completed in 1964. VILLE-MARIE documents the history of Montreal, its religious and spiritual heritage. VOLLEYBALL, made in 1966, is a poetic study of light and motion. A year later PARCS ATLANTIQUES and MONTREAL UN JOUR D'ETE were finished.

Arcand had by this time become a competent filmmaker. He was no longer interested in assigned projects. In 1970, ON EST AU COTON, a three-hour documentary on the textile industry in Quebec was made as an NFB project. The film is central to Arcand's political growth. ON EST AU COTON remains an underground film, as yet officially unreleased by the film board. Arcand's second feature-length film for the NFB was QUEBEC: DUPLESSIS ET APRES released in 1972. The documentary is a study of the 1970 provincial election campaign in Quebec that shows little has changed since the days of Duplessis.

Reprinted from *This Magazine*, vol. 8, no. 4 (November-December 1974).

Feature Filmmaking

Arcand's first dramatic film was LA MAUDITE GALLETTE made in 1972. The story, set in Montreal, is about a husband and wife team, accompanied by two friends, who decide to rob an old man rumoured to have money stashed away in his house. The heist is aborted by a boarder who lives with the couple. He kills three of the robbers and escapes with the wife (played by Luce Guilbeault). The two of them continue to struggle over the money.

REJEANNE PADOVANI, Arcand's most recent film, tells of the patronage and corruption in the construction industry in Quebec. The film, a hit at Cannes, established Arcand as one of the foremost Québécois directors.

Currently Arcand is completing his third fictional film, GINA, in which Celine Lomez stars as a stripper who goes from town to town. GINA should be released by the end of this year (1974).

The following interview took place in February 1974 at the NFB in Montreal.

Could you tell us something about your growing up years?

Well, I was born in Deschambault, Quebec where I live now. It is a little village between Trois Rivières and Quebec on the north shore of the St. Lawrence. My father was a river pilot. All of my family, my ancestors, did this. It was a sort of free masonry. You couldn't classify me as out of a working-class background nor a bourgeoisie background. It's a middle ground between the two. My father was a well paid technician. When I was about twelve years old my father wanted his family, my two brothers and sister, to have a good education. At the time he thought that he couldn't afford to send us to private scholastic institutions because they were too expensive. So we moved to Montreal, where he bought a house. He thought it would be cheaper to move the family and we could go to classes in Montreal.

In Montreal I went to a Jesuit College. They were very sports oriented and I liked that. It was a very strict education. Now it is the University of Quebec at Montreal. They had a theatre adjacent to the college. It was a professional theatre, Théâtre du Nouveau Monde. I used to work for the professional theatre as a stagehand. It was a little pocket money for me. I grew up in the milieu and loved the theatre. I did an M.A. in history at the university. I figured it was interesting but I didn't know what I was going to do with my life. When I received my degree I went to three places, the CBC, La Presse, and the NFB, thinking that was the sort of work I would like to do. By chance, I presented myself to the NFB the day they had an enormous order from the federal government to prepare films on the history of Canada for Centennial year, 1967. That was in 1962 but they were planning a build-up of historical films. They hired me to do research on the history of Canada. They tried to find a writer and director for the series, based on the research I had done, but nobody at the board was interested. They found the history of Canada boring subject matter. I was then asked to try my hand at writing and directing.

Is that when you made VILLE MARIE, SAMUEL DE CHAMPLAIN *and* VOLLEYBALL?

Yes. That is how I became a director. As soon as I started making films about history, I began to get into trouble, because the way I was seeing history was far different from the way the government thought it should be seen.

What was the difference?

That is complicated. I was taught at the university to take a very gloomy view of French-Canadian history. This is a view that considers conquest the most important thing. That is the basic fact of French-Canadian history, there is nothing else, everything else flows from there—from the fact that it is a conquered people, a colonized people. I adopted this theory. I tried to put this in my films. The NFB thought that these films should be peppy and good for the morale of the people. Mild, smiling propaganda of how happy we all are in Canada. I had some small conflicts in the making of the films, particularly with the commentary. Those with commentary were always refused and I had to rewrite them two or three times. They were not big problems but nagging little things all the time. After three films, the NFB decided to drop the series. By that time I had become part of the staff, and you can't fire somebody in the federal bureaucracy, unless there is bad conduct or something like that. I was a good filmmaker apart from my ideas, so they decided to keep me as a full-time filmmaker. That is when I made VOLLYBALL and a few other shorts.

Were these your ideas or things you were given?

Projects come through the files and you are assigned them. I considered these films like school. An *"exercise de style"* as we say in French, a chance to learn your trade. I always have had a lot of respect for people who are good at what they do. I wanted to be a good filmmaker, technically. Apart from making these historical films, I worked as an assistant director for all of the French filmmakers. I wanted to learn everything, how the lab operates, how the camera works. I became a decent filmmaker while I was making all of these films. Then, I left the NFB in 1967 to try to start an independent company which was called Les Cinéastes Associés with a few other Quebec filmmakers. Gilles Groulx, Michel Brault, Bernard Gosselin and Jean Dansereau were involved. We had a contract to do some insignificant pieces of film for Expo '67 which were rewarding financially but that was the end of it. I did that for a year. At that time there was no CFDC, it was almost impossible to do anything interesting on the private market, as an independent company. I became fed up with the idea that you had to make lots of small films, basically commercials or industrial films to be able to make a living. That is when I decided to go away from all of this and I went back to the country where I was born, Deschambault. I bought a house. I had a lot of money. Expo was good to me. I was rich—not filthy rich, a little rich. I stayed there for a year doing nothing. I played hockey for my village hometown team. I was thinking at the time that I would give cinema a last chance.

Did you want to make a feature?

No. I told myself that I would make only exactly what I wanted to do, or I would do something else. I would become a woodcutter or whatever. I went back to the NFB as a freelancer and presented ON EST AU COTON, as a project. They were fool enough to accept it.

How much of what was later censored was in the original script?

Nothing. The film wasn't based on the original idea at all. The original project was about technocracy. People at the time were always talking about computers and the skills of managers. I wanted to take a crew of seven of the most technically brilliant minds that I could find—an engineer from IT&T, a specialist in mathematics—and confront them with a problem that I thought would be without solution. I would put them to work on this problem. I chose the textile workers problem. After one month of shooting, these people said there was nothing they could do, it was impossible. They said, "It is a problem of the whole society. You want us to work on a plan to change the whole society, that scientifically we can't do because it is not a scientific matter. It is a political matter. You would have to have a revolution, and we can't plan a revolution on our computers. Sorry, we are managers."

What was the problem exactly?

The textile workers' lives. How could you better the lives of these people?

Did you expect this reaction at all?

No. I wanted to have a confrontation just to see what would happen. The NFB at that time was so marvellous. They allowed you to do such things. It was a fantastic intellectual experiment. I must tell you another thing. The problems of the textile workers were so complex that it would have been impossible to stay with the original idea inside my budget, to rent the computer time needed, to try and figure out all the loose ends of this problem. Also, while we were shooting, the textile workers were rushing at the screen with such intensity that we were less interested in the idea of the technocrat. We decided to make an honest film about textile workers.

What kind of research did you do prior to making the film?

We didn't do a lot of research prior to making the film. I just decided to take the textile workers by looking at statistics. By looking through Statistics Canada you could find out, if you knew how to read the statistics, that these people were in a hell of a struggle. I didn't have any personal contact with the people before making the film. The real research was done while we were shooting. Prior to shooting, we had put forth the hypothesis, that people in the workers' situation would revolt. We thought it was impossible to live under those conditions without revolting. Then we started to shoot and tried to find this revolt. We tried to pin-point it. We were never able to do it. We shot for one year, always in total confusion, because we couldn't find what we were looking for. Then we started to do some editing and after two or three months, we saw the light at the end of the tunnel. What we were doing was not a film about revolt, but a film about resignation.

Did you live with the workers?

Sort of. The textile workers all live in small towns, especially in the Eastern Townships. We lived at a hotel, in a little town, in the middle of nowhere for a year.

You were not considered outsiders?

No. First of all, as I told you, I do not come from a very bourgeois background; I don't look bourgeois. I don't speak very brilliant French, and neither do the people who work with me. Sometimes there was hostility. Not from the workers themselves, but from people who were on unemployment, or were soon to be laid off. They would jokingly say to us, "You work for the CBC on a big salary. You are making money off our backs, filming our problems." It was never more than that. It was a little joke.

Did you ever feel hesitant making a film about workers—you telling their story, instead of letting them tell their own?

No, never. I think this is a false problem. It is basically a European attitude, especially prevalent in France and Italy. Correct me if I am wrong. If you are a filmmaker in France and Italy, the social structure, the class structure, is so rigid that it is impossible to find a film director who is not part of the grande bourgeoisie. I know a lot of Italian and French filmmakers who are Communists but who live in pink palazzos and drive expensive sports cars. There, it is true, you would not find a filmmaker who would come from the working class. Whereas I come from the working class and live with working-class people. My brothers-in-law all work at Noranda Copper Mines. I am not different from them and even in strictly monetary terms, I earn about the same as they do.

You don't feel that when you went in to shoot ON EST AU COTON you were being exploitative?

Maybe sometimes. But that is another problem. I think filmmaking is a job. It is a very normal job. I have been at it now for twelve years, and I don't feel that I know all about it. I have a lot of respect for technical competence, as the workers have for their own competence. Now, I couldn't work as a millwright for Noranda because I am not as good as my brother-in-law. He has been at it for ten years. That is his work. I am learning to be quite good as a filmmaker. It would take my brother-in-law ten years to learn what I have learned in that time. You cannot teach somebody by putting an eclair camera in their hands and telling them how to use it. This is a fallacy. They would have to go through the same sort of learning process as I did, and then they would be a cameraman. In ten years time my brother-in-law wouldn't be a millwright, he would be a filmmaker. Then you start the problem all over again. I think it is a false problem here, but has come from Europe where it is a real problem. A film director in Europe is really important. It is very seldom that you see a European film director eating with a crew. The French made a film here last year. There was a director who came here and he was considered very democratic in France because he would invite each day of the week one member of the crew, to have dinner with him. They hired a French-Canadian crew who couldn't believe it. While we are working, I am lucky if I can find a place at the table, if I am late.

Were there any ideas that you originally had before ON EST AU COTON that were shattered for you during the experience of making the film? Or were there any ideas that were strengthened as a result?

No, except the one about resignation that I told you about. I have a sort of anarchist mind and I couldn't stand working in a textile mill. At the most, I could work there for six months and then I would hitchhike to Mexico and stay there for a year. I couldn't lend myself to that kind of day-to-day horror.

So you were shocked that the workers could?

Alienation in that sense is always a mystery to me, especially with the absence of revolt. Alienation means resignation in a way, saying, "It is not so bad."

Before making this film, in your own political thinking had alienation always meant revolt?

Yes. This idea was shattered to pieces.

Could you describe the resignation that you found in the workers?

Well, it is just that they had fought very hard in 1937, 1945, and up to 1960. One of the reasons I chose the textile workers is that they had, at this time, a very militant union. They fought very hard to win these strikes. The fact that the textile workers won, in a certain sense, was their downfall. In the sense that their salaries became better. It became possible for them to live half decently, to buy a Skidoo, a colour television, and so on.

The only revolt we found was in the older workers, the people that were sixty, sixty-five and seventy. They had fought the battles during the economic crisis in the thirties. They were still revolting because they were too old to profit from the "good life". But the middle-aged workers today, although they are not rich and their working conditions are not that good, they say, "Why strike? We have our colour TV's." We discovered through discussion that the attitude among the workers was, "Well things aren't too bad. My basement is finished, the kids play there and it is nice." We always looked for revolt and never found it except in the older workers. That certainly has been a shock for me.

Could you talk about the censoring of ON EST AU COTON?

It is a strange story, because it was the first film that was really censored by the NFB. I had no prior indication. I worked on the assumption that everything would go well.

Because they had accepted it initially?

Yes, I just assumed that it would be the same as ever, that the film would be released. There is an anecdote that might be fun to hear. People in the textile mills asked us, "Why are you always shooting films about poor people? We know poor people. We know our story. We don't have to see it on the screen. Why don't you show us rich people? We never see rich people and that would be interesting for us." We said, "O.K., who would you like to see?" They replied, "The president of Dominion Textiles, we would love to see him." So we decided to include a sequence of the president in ON EST AU COTON.

We phoned the president, Mr. King, and conned him into accepting us for a few days. We disguised ourselves as young executives in grey flannel suits. We were so understanding and full of consideration for Mr. King. He sort of loved us. The other executives at Dominion Textiles found us very interesting people. There is a most interesting story. One of the vice-presidents, who is a very rich man, had a daughter. She had just run away three months before, with a bum or something and was living on Crescent Street. He appealed to us to go and talk to her. As you can see, we had an excellent relationship with the executives.

When I finished ON EST AU COTON, the film board decided to invite Mr. King to see the film because he had a very important part. There was a half-hour strictly on him. He came and had the shock of his life. He just sort of had a heart attack during the film. He went away and at first said he didn't want to be part of the film. Then the film board told me that if I removed the portion on Mr. King, the film would be released. Now I am very sorry that I agreed. I thought at the time they were sincere. I removed the part. Then we had another screening and the NFB said it was O.K. They cut the negative and printed a copy. That is the copy that now circulates underground.

Afterwards, the Canadian Textile Intitute, which is a lobby of all the Canadian textile companies, started pressuring the government and the president of the NFB, Hugo MacPherson. He was afraid. I still don't know if the decision to ban the film was an order from Ottawa or if it was MacPherson's doing. I was never told. The Canadian Textile Institute sent a letter to the NFB and I had a copy of it. I had always had good rapport with them because they were very frank with me, much more so than the film board. The letter said, the film should not go out for two reasons. First, the film promotes class warfare, and second, it creates a bad image of our industry. I agreed with that. When the NFB censored ON EST AU COTON, they couldn't say that. They said the film was inaccurate and biased, which is not true. It is a film that promotes class warfare. They should have said it. The textile people were much more honest.

Did this set a precedent?

Well not exactly. At the time on the French side of the NFB, programming was controlled by a programming committee. Half of the members were from the filmmakers' union. When the programming committee recommended the shooting of a film, the higher authorities like the commissioner would abide by the decision of this committee. Which is not true any more. After ON EST AU COTON, the decisions of the program committee must be approved by the commissioner of the film board. He has the final veto. What is the use of a program committee anyway? The NFB censored another film, Gilles Groulx's 24 HOURS AND AFTER, but it was the only other film. Now, they censor films in the pre-production stage.

In terms of where you get your money, from the government or from a corporation, are there always strings attached?

The problem with cinema in general is that it costs so much. This is a horrible thing. You will always have strings, of one sort or another, because only if you are a millionaire can you afford to make your own films. Filmmaking is not a profitable proposition, by business standards. You can have some money from business but never enough to build up a normal production. If you don't have government money, you won't have any money. You can always think of other systems but that is utopia. The fact is that you need government money, so what can you do about it? I live with this problem every day.

The government gives me a lot of money and I like that. They never ask any questions, and they have been very nice to me. I know they are a part of the federal structure, a part of the whole system. I take their money and do my little films with it. I rip off the system. I deplore the situation but that isn't very helpful, if you are not in a position to change things.

Is film a good medium for political examination?

It is very strange because I never think this way. This is a very theoretical point of view. As I told you, I became a filmmaker by accident and nowadays I am a filmmaker. The only way I know how to express myself is by making films. Now is that the best way, the best medium, or even a good medium? I don't know. I have learned this trade so I practice it. Now, why I make politically oriented films, has nothing to do with filmmaking for me. I am a politically oriented person who is a filmmaker, therefore my end product is politically oriented. If I wasn't a filmmaker, I would be a political newspaperman or a political plumber.

How did you come to make LA MAUDITE GALETTE?

After DUPLESSIS ET APRES I submitted another proposal to the NFB. I wanted to make a film on terrorism on a freelance basis. This was at the time of the Quebec occupation. The project was refused by the boss, Sydney Newman, *not* by the programming committee. Shortly after the events of October, Cinak came to me with the proposition that I make a feature film, LA MAUDITE GALETTE. There wasn't anything else I could do. I was unemployed, so I did it. There is a lot of violence and blood in LA MAUDITE GALETTE but it is really an abortive film on terrorism.

I didn't write the film. It was made in complete depression. It is a film in parenthesis compared to my other films. It was a thriller story set with very poor people who would do anything for money. We decided before production to change the story. We decided that if we shot the film against every law of the thriller, that is, using very long sequences without any cuts, we would break the rhythm horribly. It would be slowly paced, so that the audience would either get out of the theatre, or would start to think about these people and the conditions in which they lived, instead of following the immediate story—who killed who and things like that. It would not be a political film but a social statement. If you get involved in a real thriller, the whole political thing is lost, because the audience wants to know what will happen. If you stop that completely, people have nothing else to do in the theatre but think.

You have worked in both documentary and feature films, which do you prefer?

I couldn't tell you which I prefer. Certainly on the political and intellectual level it's a richer experience to make documentaries, like ON EST AU COTON or DUPLESSIS ET APRES. But it is a lot more fun to make a feature film. A feature is easier to shoot than a documentary. The difficulty in making feature films is of a totally different order. You become enmeshed in aesthetics with the feature film, that is the difficulty. It has to be dramatically correct. It has to be moving. These are problems I never encountered before. When we made ON EST AU COTON and DUPLESSIS ET APRES, we didn't have problems with aesthetics. They were in 16mm black-and-white and everything was shot as it came. The main problem with the documentary is conveying reality. Are we touching the gut of the problem? That is always a philosophical and political problem. For four years we worked on ON EST AU COTON and DUPLESSIS ET APRES. In feature films it is totally different. You are trying to express something through an art medium and you are the artist, something I never considered myself before.

For the audience, which do you think works better in terms of making political statements?

In terms of the audience I don't know. I suppose that, theoretically, a documentary could be a much more solid political statement.

Do you think people go and see documentaries?

Not much. That is the basic problem. The people who go see documentaries are the intellectuals and the students.

It is a matter of accessibility?

Exactly. While we were making ON EST AU COTON, we were having a drink with the main character, and he asked us, "Do you think that you people would be able to make a real movie?" We said, "What do you mean, what are we doing here?" "No," he said, "I mean a *real* movie that I could go to on a Saturday night with my wife." This always stuck in my mind when I was making LA MAUDITE GALETTE and REJEANNE PADOVANI.

Did you make the films for him?

Almost. He was saying, what you are making here with us is something like our union meetings. It is necessary and helpful but dull as hell.

Did he want something more entertaining?

There is something there that is a little deeper than entertainment. If you are making a documentary, you're addressing yourself to the mind, but also to the soul. You express something deeper than just the rational mind. You are asking for an emotional response, which you cannot do to any great extent in a documentary. At the end of ON EST AU COTON we tried to elicit an emotional response by putting military music with images of the workers on the screen. But you cannot go very far with such things in a documentary movie. You have to respect the reality in the documentary, whereas, in the feature film you can do anything you want.

You spoke earlier about the pressure of making a feature film, of having to entertain in a sense because that is part of the role of the feature film. I wonder if that hinders making a political statement?

It is definitely a hindrance. This is a very hard problem. Making a feature film is like writing a novel. You cannot take a political statement and write a novel, nor can you take a political statement and make a feature film. But you can make an excellent documentary with a political statement, because the political statement is bound up with the notion of efficiency. And documentary films are efficient. In feature films and the novel, you are dealing with the human soul. I don't know of any way to reduce the human soul to a rational political statement. It is always broader than that, it is always deeper. In the feature, you have all sorts of things that are unconscious, that you must put in to avoid making a dry film, an exposé. You cannot be efficient with the human soul.

What do you think the strength of REJEANNE PADOVANI is in terms of taking the feature film and injecting political content?

Well, I tried not to *inject* the political content. I just tried to tell a story. A story which I found interesting to depict. I tried to do this as a politically oriented person. It is not the film itself which is primarily a political vehicle. I try to do the best film possible as a politically conscious person. Then again, I try to be in my own life, apart from films, as politically conscious and correct, as a citizen. Now this citizen writes a story to tell the people. This story is not totally conscious. It's not totally political. It is just a story told by somebody who tries to be politically correct. Do I express myself, because it is complicated? We were not trying in REJEANNE PADOVANI to say, let's do a film that will prove this and this. I think had we tried to work like that, it wouldn't have been as good as it is. All of the people who worked on this film are the same people who made ON EST AU COTON and LA MAUDITE GALETTE with me. In REJEANNE PADOVANI we tell a story about people from the mob, who are in the suburbs. We thought it was interesting but we never thought primarily of making a statement.

Do you think that feature film allows people to ignore the political statement because they can say that it isn't reality, it is just a story that you are making up? In fact the political reality becomes fictionalized, so a person in the audience can remove her/himself from it.

We think about this every day.

Is there a solution?

If the actors are good and the situation is realistic, then there can be no escape from the political content.

Is this why the characters in REJEANNE PADOVANI *look like Mayor Drapeau and Premier Bourassa?*

We tried. The fault in REJEANNE PADOVANI is that dramatically it is not good enough. I am not a good dramatist yet. I hope to become one. If it was twice as good dramatically, after the first five minutes, you wouldn't want to leave the theatre. There would be no escape. If you shock the audience while they are seeing a film, even though they say, "It is just a story," something will be imprinted at the subconscious level, and stay there. That is the theory we assume.

Do you think Costa Gavras and Pontecorvo succeed dramatically, so that there is an imprinting. Do their films work politically, or are they like REJEANNE PADOVANI, *not quite there?*

I think the ones you have mentioned are not quite there. I know Costa Gavras personally. STATE OF SEIGE and Z don't work all that well. But the problem is not with the medium itself. Politically he hasn't done his homework. He hasn't read sufficiently. That is the only problem. When I saw Z, I wanted to like it, but it was done too simplistically. The reality in Greece is not like that. It is not as black and white as it was shown in Z. That is why it doesn't work for me. I think STATE OF SEIGE is little better. But it is not yet there. It could also be a personal problem because Costa Gavras is a Greek living in France. He is someone without a country.

Is that a benefit for you, having Quebec as a country?

Sure. At least I can speak of something I know very intimately. The people in REJEANNE PADOVANI, for example, convey that. I think that is why the film works. It was a success in Montreal—80,000 people saw it.

I don't see how you can make a political statement if you don't have a country. It is the only thing that you know. I would love to make a statement about the Palestinians but—I can only make a statement on the theoretical level, because I don't have the gut reaction. I don't know the Palestinians.

Do you think that the passive action of watching films works against using film to involve people in radical action?

Definitely. That is why I don't think filmmaking would ever be a very good political medium. It can be a political medium, but it is certainly far less effective than writing, than making a speech, than having meetings. Maybe even less so than theatre. In the theatre you have people there in the flesh, and they are speaking to you. They can come down from the stage and shake you. When you watch a film you are in a dark room, the seats are usually comfortable, the lights go down, and you are anonymous. That is also the fun of a film; it is like a dream. The difference between films and dreams is thin. Dreams on the screen are the ideal situation because people are unable to resist them.

I find it interesting to work on feature films because you work on the unconscious level with people. Maybe it is there that we should be working politically. It is at least a possibility.

How do you feel about Godard's theory of political filmmaking? That is, in order to make political films, one must not only have a political content, but a truly political form. It is not satisfactory to use the traditional feature film mould. That is not making political films politically.

I think about this every day. I don't know of any filmmaker in the world who has found a decent solution to this problem. Godard has found himself in a cul-de-sac because he is making brilliant political statements but nobody wants to see them. It is the problem of accessibility. Politically, I always agree with Godard. He is brilliant. But on the plane of aesthetics, on the questions of form and content, I do not agree with him. I will have to use an analogy. In Chinese poetry, Mao wrote the most revolutionary poetry, using the most ancient form. It is equivalent to writing revolutionary poetry in the form of Shakespeare's sonnets. The form I think can always bend itself to any kind of statement. You can take the oldest form in any given art and use it politically. I believe that very dearly and that is why I always try to make films which are in appearance, on the first level, very conventional. I think it is a very efficient way to work in terms of accessibility, getting to the audience, and even in terms of pleasure. I like very traditional story-telling. That is just from the point of view of aesthetics. Also, I think it is politically efficient.

It is a fact that nobody other than intellectuals and students go to see Godard.

Exactly. People don't have the keys to open up and understand what his statement is. Whereas, if you give the audience a very traditional format, at least it will be understandable. They understand your story. This one is the wife of this one ... etc. Through this form you can carry a lot of political information.

Your work largely consists of documenting the ills of the system. Is this your way of avoiding the dissension and the division within the leftist framework?

No. I am not a member of a political party and I am not a member of any political ideology. I am just a vague leftist because I haven't found anything on which I could graft my energies. I have not found any political ideology which applies to an industrial country like Quebec.

If I were a Cuban or an Algerian, it would be a totally different story, but I live in Quebec in 1974 and I don't know of any practical political ideology which applies to Quebec. That is why my films do not go further than saying that the capitalist system is rotten. I do not know with what to replace it. I know what I don't like.

Is this why you don't offer any solutions?

Exactly.

This is generally the state of Québécois political filmmaking now. It documents, and shows alienation. It doesn't offer alternatives or solutions.

Filmmakers don't have any solutions and they don't know of anybody who does. At least, they are not convinced by the people who have solutions. That is why the films do not go further than they do. It would be very helpful to have an ideology. It would be very wonderful to have happy endings to our films, that would be the ultimate dream. But it would be totally dishonest to my mind, the ultimate dishonesty. It would be even more dishonest than making crassly commercial films. There is another point. Quebec remains a very mysterious place to most Quebeckers. The basic homework of analysis is still in need. There are a lot of things that can be put on film, which are of interest and contribute to a good analysis of the situation and the society in which we live.

When you made REJEANNE PADOVANI, *did you make it in the form of a feature film because you wanted to get to the people who were not converted?*

It was much more practical than that. The only way that I could make a film last year was to make a feature film. Oddly enough, it is easier for me to make a feature costing $200,000 than to make anything else. Nobody would give me $60,000 to make a black-and-white documentary, but a lot of people would be glad to give me $200,000 to make a feature because it will pay for itself.

Has REJEANNE PADOVANI *paid for itself?*

Well maybe not right now, but it will.

What is the role of culture in political struggle?

I was taught in history class that you can divide an historical process into three parts—economics, politics, and culture. This is the total historical process. So culture is part of politics and politics is part of culture and so on. You can't draw lines like that. Culture reflects the state in which politics is and vice-versa.

Some Quebec filmmakers argue that culture will lead the separating process, because once you have opened the door and allowed culture to express separatist sentiments, the political is almost an afterthought. Do you think it is possible for culture to lead the political struggle?

I don't think culture leads anything. It is not powerful enough. I think basically the economy moves things. I am not a stiff Marxist-Leninist, in the sense that I think the economy itself is the prime, absolute mover of things.... That is where I disagree with Marxists and Marxist interpretations. I think you could say that culture has antennas which monitor the future. It doesn't lead but it can indicate, sometimes fifty years in advance, what will happen fifty years later. Cultural workers who have this "special sensibility" sense things before the whole population becomes convinced. If you read French literature, the French Revolution becomes apparent fifty, sixty, even seventy years before it happened. The same is true for the Russian, Cuban, South American, and Mexican revolutions. Half a century earlier, long-hairs and poets were saying, watch out. However, it is not because the artists were leading the way. They became aware of the objective reality before the mass of the people, that is all.

I think that filmmakers and artists are very sensitive people, but they don't lead the way. Basically, people move by bread and butter issues, they don't move for sensibility. Workers have to make a living. In the textile mills the workers said, "You want us to separate? If we separate we are going to starve." All the companies are English or American owned. There is one textile mill that is Quebec owned. They won't vote for separatism just because they want to preserve the French language or their cultural identity. They couldn't care less about cultural identity. If I were in their position, I would be a federalist too.

How do you feel about co-operative filmmaking as opposed to the alternative, the auteur method? You have worked with an established group on a continuing basis for quite some time.

We are already a co-operative, so that is not a question. I don't consider myself an auteur, neither do the people that I work with. I am the spokesman for the group just for the sake of efficiency. Then again, I think that there is a specific job which is called film director. On the set this is a very practical job. If you are doing a feature film with actors, somebody has to speak to the actors; the actors can't speak to ten people. You can't make a collective film by making all decisions collective. If you are ten people who want to make a film, somebody will have to man the camera, and there is only one eye-piece. It is a matter of normal efficiency.

Now, in a film like ON EST AU COTON or DUPLESSIS ET APRES, it is not necessary to be a director because the cameraman and sound engineer can do it all by themselves while shooting. I was important because I did the editing. You can't have ten people edit a film. For DUPLESSIS ET APRES, we shot 100,000 feet of 16mm and then as the editor, I spoke with the group, after they had seen all the material. I made a rough cut which lasted about eight hours. Then we saw it together; we spoke about it, then reduced it to five hours. We met again and discussed it, then I reduced it to two or three hours. It was pretty collective as a process. You know they had this problem in the cultural revolution in China. They decided to fire the directors in the theatre of the Peking Opera, but it was utter chaos because everything had to be collective. For one lighting problem that you could ordinarily solve in thirty seconds, you had to have a meeting to approach the problem. Realizing the inefficiency of this method, the Chinese started to have directors once again, but on the condition that the director would be the one who would be in charge of expressing the general will of everybody. That is the way I see it. It worked much the same way for REJEANNE PADOVANI, except that I wrote the script.

Who are the people that you work with?

Alain Dostin is the cameraman, Serge Beauchemin is the sound engineer, and my two assistants are France LaChapel, and Jacques Methe. We always work together. We have been friends for ten years. Oh it is fun, it is lovely. We live apart, and we don't see each other too often, apart from films. Once a year we meet together for two months. We live together, sleep together, and see each other twenty-four hours a day. It is fantastic, it is a party. We love to make films.

What is your next project?

It is about a stripper. While we were shooting ON EST AU COTON, we lived in small hotels around Quebec. There was always a big hotel in the centre of town with a stripper, who would go with her suitcase from town to town. Strippers are very, very, defensive. They never say anything about their lives, about where they come from. The only relationship they have with everybody is that everybody wants to take them to bed. We became friendly with one, who was a pool shark. We played pool and hockey together. I will try and make a film on the friendship between a stripper and a group of filmmakers who are making a film about the textile industry.

Have you written the script? Is it with Carle-Lamy?

Yes.

Do you think you can express her sense of exploitation?

I think so. The awful part will be the actual striptease. I don't know what I will do. I don't know how to shoot it. Maybe I won't shoot it at all. How would you do it? It is not very important in my film, it is just her job. The film has nothing to do with her striptease act.

Then why not make her something else?

It is very hard because the people that I know who have led such lives are strippers. In a way she didn't want to become a textile worker and that was her way out. She decided to fight the system but she was not equipped to fight it with anything other than her body.

How do you feel about the role of women in your films?

I have been criticized lately because a few of my actresses are going into liberation, and I have had problems with that. The only thing that I can say is, that I have known women as the ones depicted in my films.

Do you see feminism hooking into a larger social struggle?

Definitely, but I think it has to be done by women. I think women must make their own films to depict their consciousness. I would be a gadfly in the movement. I can only be a sympathetic bystander. It is true that the women in REJEANNE PADOVANI come across only as physical objects, but you must remember that the men appear as total swines. It is not just a question of women. I depict a special segment of society. I am not putting forward the proposition that all women are like this. I know that in this kind of society, women are very often like this and they come across like this on the exterior level. The film doesn't go much deeper than that. It is just an exterior look at such a society. Now in the other films that I do, I hope to go much deeper, but I am sure that I could never go as deep as a woman director.

Why do you think Quebec film tends to be more political than English Canadian film?

Well, it is because generally Quebec society is more political than English Canadian society. Our very survival depends on politics. It always has for two centuries now. People in Quebec are politically motivated. It's a political society. Whereas, in English Canada, politics tends to play a role, but it is far less urgent.

Many English Canadians feel that it is tremendously urgent now because we are about to be sold out.

But it is fairly recent as a movement. Ten years, if that.

And English Canadian filmmakers haven't exactly picked up on it either. Would you label yourself an anarchist politically?

Yes, but not by choice. It is because I have no other alternative right now. If I had been a Chilean, I would have been a Marxist. I feel sometimes that it is helpful to be Québécois, rather than English Canadian, because we have so many problems here that make you feel sympathetic to the Chilean, Greek and Palestinian problems. We feel Quebec's struggle is part of a larger struggle and we have our part to do here, in a very small and modest way. We know it is the only place where we can do something efficient against IT&T. We feel that English Canadians are much more internationally oriented. We feel that sometimes they haven't worked out their own problems enough. English Canadians get very worked up about Vietnam and things like that, but these are basically Vietnamese and American problems. It is not very efficient to walk in front of embassies, which is about all you can do on such issues. It is important to come to grips with your own problems and your own reality. You must make films for your own people, for the situation here. It is the same all over the world, so you start by cleaning your own house first.

Coward, Bully, or Clown:

The Dream-Life of a Younger Brother

Robert Fothergill

Take a dramatic situation—a growing season in a person's life, a challenging encounter, a turning point in a relationship; begin to imagine how things will develop, how the people involved will behave, and what part external circumstances will play. One finds oneself pulled two ways—by what the imagination suggests as conceivable, and by what one's sense of reality insists upon as most likely. The former is subjective, tending to fantasy and dream, shaped by currents in one's own psyche made visible in fictions; the latter is more objective, leaning towards documentation, directed by a critical and perhaps ideological sense of the actual. The one speaks of truth, the other of fact. Out of the tension between them the stuff of the original situation is drawn out into a story which no one else would have developed in quite the same way. Like a Rorschach test, the story tells a lot about one's habitual and half-conscious perception of life.

Reprinted from *Take One*, vol. 4, no. 3 (September 1973).

Then take Canadian filmmakers, imagining for the screen stories located more or less precisely in Canada about recognizably Canadian individuals. If elements of a distinct consciousness (English or French) have indeed been engendered by the emotional and historical experience of being Canadian, then the imaginations of writers and directors will have inherited it to some degree. It will lead them to project themselves into a certain range of experience, and to ignore whole other areas altogether. It will cause them to perceive the unfolding of an action, the revelation of character in behaviour, in recurring patterns. As personal perceptions of reality, screenplays will also, in some measure, express a Canadian mode of seeing and feeling. But even when a film is not a conscientiously developed individual vision, but a manufactured consumer product, or even when the writer/director is an import or an immigrant, still there is a process which can shape the work into a distinctively Canadian reflection of life. For on another level than that of the individual psyche, a screenplay to be located and produced in this country is modified by a more or less conscious sense of what kinds of people and actions will look characteristically, or even credibly, Canadian to an audience. A collective self-image, as exerted on the writer/director's sensibility, sifts out those plot developments and those kinds of behaviour that just don't *feel* like the sort of thing you run across in this part of the world.

So far, this combination of factors has quite noticeably influenced and restricted the representation of life visible in Canadian movies. Think of the many types of film that have made hardly a single appearance among the couple of hundred Canadian features of the past decade. Quebec cinema can show an example here and there, but where among the movies of English Canada will you find, for better or worse: war films, gangster films, passionate love stories, urbane sexual comedies, adventure movies, surrealist fantasies, political intrigue, espionage, costume drama, musicals, or the Bergmanesque? Together with its own conventional cinematic style, each of these movie sub-genres has a cluster of standard roles in which Torontonians and Winnipegers have yet to see themselves reflected. It's not that life in English Canada has never sustained the kinds of experience that such films draw upon. Canadians in their time have been gangsters, pranksters, soldiers and detectives, mystics and sophisticates, adventurers and desperadoes, lovers and *femmes fatales*—haven't they? But their activities, when magnified to the scale of a feature film, continue to seem sufficiently uncharacteristic as to be alien and disconcerting. They conflict with our self-image. Dramatic screenplays exploiting such roles are seldom, if ever, located in a Canadian context.

What, then, is the version of *la condition canadienne* reflected to us by our feature films? It is the depiction, through many different scenarios, of the radical inadequacy of the male protagonist—his moral failure, especially, and most visibly, in his relationships with women. One film after another is like a recurring dream which takes its shape from the dreamer's guilty consciousness of his own essential impotence.

* * *

Time to be specific. Quite recently I asked Winnipeg director John Thompson to tell me something about AND NO BIRDS SING, a film which he made as a student at the University of Manitoba in 1969, and which I hadn't seen at the time. "Well," he said, "it's quite close to being autobiographical for the man who wrote the script. In essence it's about a guy who realizes he's pretty much of a schmuck, and that there really isn't anything he can do about it." Taking such an account in isolation, one might be fleetingly sorry for an author with such a depressing self-estimate, and not especially anxious to see the movie in which it is paraded. But when the capsule summary of a film produced in the cinematic boondocks manages, in less than twenty-five words, to capture the essential theme of literally scores of movies made in English Canada, it becomes a matter of some interest. And as it turned out, the director's summary was pretty adequate. A callow, mediocre university student yearns wretchedly for Virginia, the sophisticated and beautiful "Arts Queen". At a party he makes a clumsy play for her, only to meet with a kind but firm rejection. Later he sees her dancing intimately with the big rich guy whose party it is. Depressed, drunk and apologizing feebly, our anti-hero is taken home by his own long-suffering girlfriend whom he has ignored all evening.

If I have given what may seem to be unnecessary prominence to a medium-length, black-and-white, 16mm student production which very few people will ever see, it is because AND NO BIRDS SING stands in its simple way as a paradigm of the central conception of many of its more ambitious kith and kin. A male imagination has chosen to dramatize and identify with the demoralizing exposure of a male protagonist as shallow and contemptible. The women in whose eyes this exposure takes place are endowed with integrity and generosity; one of them stays by him, her illusions a little faded but her commitment undiminished; the other turns to a more substantial and potent specimen of manhood (albeit a rather unattractive one). And we are not particularly encouraged to respond sympathetically to the protagonist. He comes across as a selfish and unappealing person, trapped in his own limitations. Much of his talk seems hollow and insincere, as though his real feelings are blocked or stunted, and he is relating to other people inauthentically. Moreover, the film doesn't present the humiliation as a wry misadventure of a painful-step-towards-maturity, but more like the pattern of his fate, a nail of his coffin. "... Pretty much of a shmuck ... nothing he can do about it."

The unprepossessing English Canadian male appears on the screen in several guises, which I have labelled Coward, Bully, and Clown. The essential characteristic of the Coward can be summed up in that splendid word, "pusillanimity". He can be quite appealing at times—sensitive, vulnerable, mild—and a woman can find herself drawn to him; but with these qualities comes a deep-down gutlessness that renders him incapable of reciprocating her commitment. In THE ONLY THING YOU KNOW (Clarke Mackey, 1971), he is a pleasant-tempered young schoolteacher who takes up with a quietly serious girl, still in high school. She leaves her oppressive family home and moves in with him, only to discover that his unfailing cheerfulness protects an inability to get in touch with his feelings and encounter her honestly and directly. Dismayed by his retreats and evasions, she turns away from him. In George Kaczender's DON'T LET THE ANGELS FALL (1968) he is considerably older, a Montreal businessman with a neurotic wife and mixed-up teenage children. Hagridden with guilt, he embarks on an affair with the candid, clear-eyed Sharon Acker, whom he meets on some kind of residential training course. She falls frankly in love with him, but when the six weeks are up he succumbs to emotional blackmail and the endemic pusillanimity of his type, and retreats to the dismal safety of his marriage. At the close of the film he is staring miserably at the TV, watching an on-the-street interview in which he himself has been made to look vapid and afraid. On another socio-economic level, Joey, played by Paul Bradley in Don Shebib's GOIN' DOWN THE ROAD (1970), has a good deal of the Coward about him. Bewildered by big-city life, and with a tendency to get maudlin drunk, he finally runs out on the whole mess, leaving a pregnant and newly-evicted wife to fend for herself.

When times are good, Joey and his friend Pete (Doug McGrath) caper about with childish irresponsibility, drinking and frolicking in a fashion that is likeable enough but rather trying to the women who have to put up with it. Pete's repertoire includes a humiliatingly unsuccessful attempt to ingratiate himself with a sexy French lady, Nicole Morin. In their antics, the Canadian male as Coward can be seen shading into another incarnation: the Clown. Like the Coward, but with a greater jauntiness of surface manner, the Clown shies away from the responsibility of a self-determining adult. He is given to "acting up" with irrepressible exuberance, preferably under the indulgent eyes of a woman whose maternal protectiveness is excited by these displays of infantility. As time goes by, however, her expression of good-humoured tolerance gradually turns into a look of weary chagrin. When the Clown abuses her patience once too often, she is likely to turn her capacity for commitment away, in search of a more mature and adequate human being. It is GINGER COFFEY'S luck, in the movie from Brian Moore's novel (1964), that his wife is still prepared to take him back one more time at the end of the film. Shiftless, brash, evasive, dishonest, he has repeatedly sacrificed the welfare of his wife and child to fatuous dreams of instant success in jobs for which he is unqualified and unsuited. With plenty of watery-eyed Irish charm, he manipulates the sympathies of women with his air of rueful, boyish vulnerability. He evades adult responsibility by resorting to the role of the easily-wounded child with the hurt look that no one can be angry with for long. Fred Exley, in A FAN'S NOTES (Eric Till, 1972), presents a similar case. Suffering from a chronic sense of impotence and insignificance, which only a passionate identification with a football hero enables him occasionally to transcend, he divides his time between various manic forms of escapism and helpless dependency, both at the expense of his wife, Patience.

Neither of these latter Clowns is a native-born Canadian. Ginger Coffey recently emigrated from Ireland, while Exley is a New Yorker whose sojourns in Canada probably have something to do with CFDC financing for the film. All the same, something about their roles in the original novels was evidently seen to fit them for inclusion among the dream-figures of the Canadian screen. And certainly this pair of tragic-comic misfits can find congenial company among their fellow protagonists, for example: Ernie of Don Owen's ERNIE GAME (1967), who finally exasperates both of the women who have tried to put up with nutty, child-eternal refusal to face the exigencies of the real world; and Will Cole, the title character of THE ROWDYMAN (Peter Carter, 1972), a Newfie roustabout whose endless skylarking eventually results in the death of his friend, and drives the faithful and pretty Linda Goranson into the arms of a Torontonian. It must be emphasized that unlike, for example, De Broca's KING OF HEARTS, which celebrates lunacy as an inspired and saving condition, the Canadian "Clown" films present their protagonists' aberrancy as a wasting disease.

Will Cole exhibits a quality rare in Canadian films: sexual panache—a gleeful "cockiness", albeit of a rather infantile kind. Far more common, and the central premise of many a would-be comedy, is goofy sexual incompetence. The clown-hero of these scenarios is either too goofy to get it, though he wants it quite badly—in, for example, CHESTER ANGUS RAMSGOOD (Curnick and Wilson, 1971) and FOLLOWING THROUGH (David Beck, 1969); or too goofy even to want it, though several intimidatingly horny women seem to want it at his hands—in, for example, FOXY LADY (Ivan Reitman, 1971). The sad-funny misfortunes of Shebib's quartet of teenage boys in RIP-OFF (1971) all stem, ultimately, from their desire to enhance their sex-appeal, while Harry Barnes, the dumb-cluck cub reporter of WHY ROCK THE BOAT? (Weintraub, 1973), stumbles from one gaucherie to another until at last he wins the girl almost by accident. The point to be made here is that comic films (seldom very funny) tend to be based upon the humiliation and frustration of incompetent characters, rather than upon the exploits of energetic and resourceful ones. THE RAINBOW BOYS (Gerald Potterton, 1973), to cite another case, takes a nutty old ex-Briton, a New Yorker in a Mickey Mouse sweatshirt, and a brawny, bellowing Kate Reid up a mountain in British Columbia, to find some gold which they promptly lose again.

In its third screen manifestation, as Bully, the threatened and insubstantial male ego is shown attempting to assert its dominance through displays of brutal inconsideration and sullen rage. In addition to the hollow nastiness of his general disposition, the Bully specializes in the sexual degradation of his womenfolk. It's the ugliest of the three faces, and the scenarios usually work to punish the characters who display it. A prime example is the protagonist of THE FINISHING TOUCH (1972) in whom real Vancouver director Morrie Ruvinsky has dramatized the human and artistic degeneration of fictitious Vancouver director Mark Van Troyan. Mark is shown kicking his gracious, newly-pregnant wife out of their home, tyrannizing the crew of a film which is obviously getting nowhere under his disintegrating direction, and subjecting his mistress to sexual humiliation in front of the camera. At the end of the film he appears to be heading towards suicide. FACE-OFF, George McCowan's hockey drama (1971), gives us an amitious, selfish jerk of a Maple Leaf rookie, cared for by the truthful, dreamy, liberated, authentic Trudy Young, a much-loved pop singer. She dies in a car crash, and he learns—Alas, too late!—what he has thrown away. Bill Fruet's WEDDING IN WHITE (1972) features Donald Pleasence as a coarse, bullying, piggy-eyed father who discovers that his dimwitted daughter is pregnant, having been raped by her brother's loutish friend, and forces her to marry one of his drinking cronies, a man four times her age. The brother and friend are played with beery, sweat-soaked conviction by Bradley and McGrath, in a repeat of their GOIN' DOWN THE ROAD performances. Another peculiar male, who gets his comeuppance during his ninety minutes on the screen, is the protagonist of EVER AFTER ALL (McLean and Weingartner, 1972). On an expedition to the backwoods with his girlfriend, he smears the blood of a rabbit all over her while they are making love; later his sullen, graceless behaviour culminates in his shooting at a pair of intruders. The intruders tie him up, whimpering, in a cage, and then make love to the girl, with her apparent consent. Considered as a dream or fantasy, EVER AFTER ALL would seem to be the product of a highly paranoid imagination.

If writers for the cinema (outside Quebec) have difficulty imagining a creatively self-realizing male, their conception of women is virtually immaculate. A central quality in Women, to which these films pay tribute, is their greater authenticity. Where men are represented as shallow, insincere, manipulative, women are truthful and direct. They are in touch with their feelings, and they express them, whereas men, it seems, are dishonest with themselves and devious with others. To women is attributed a different and more integrated consciousness which doesn't always calculate before it speaks, which is more open to the world. Stendhal said something to the effect that "in every pair of lovers, there is one who loves and one who consents to be loved". Women, it generally appears, have the power to love and trust and commit themselves without adding up the cost; men have the opportunity to disappoint and betray, and they usually avail themselves of it.

Not surprisingly, this impression of the superior human wholeness of women is reinforced in two films made by women, Sylvia Spring's MADELEINE IS (1971) and Mireille Dansereau's LA VIE REVEE (1971), and in a film exclusively *about* women, AUGUST AND JULY (Murray Markowitz, 1972). Madeleine has been under the subjection of a super-Bully, Torro, a self-proclaimed revolutionary, undisguised ego-tripper and male chauvinist pig, who insists that she go without underwear so that she can "receive" him whenever the spirit moves. By way of escape she has cultivated a fantasy of a friendly Clown who romps with her on a little island. When, however, she meets the living double of her Clown, he turns out to have the ineffectual goofiness typical of the Coward, and Madeleine moves on from him to a state of self-possession indifferent to males. In LA VIE REVEE two young women band together to liberate themselves from the imagery of sexual roles and stereotypes that has enthralled them. Their quest achieves a symbolic culmination when a suave male, for whom one of the girls has trembled from afar, turns out upon closer acquaintance to be impotent. Familiarity breeds a liberating contempt. And finally AUGUST AND JULY, in the form of an "actuality drama", explores the relationship of two women who have turned to each other for the emotional and physical expression of the heterosexual loves which they have left behind.

One might have thought that a recurring male fantasy of impotence and defeat would be accompanied by a half-conscious resentment, generating in turn an imagery of women as somehow to blame for the male condition. Where are the monstrous depictions of smothering Moms and castrating bitches, faithless tramps and frigid demi-vierges? They are almost nowhere to be found. The male psyche is apparently so oppressed that it can seldom project the cause of this oppression beyond itself. There are some exceptions, of course. Fred Exley's functional impotence is exacerbated by his brief engagement to the flawlessly plastic Bunny-Sue, whose mother provides a monstrous foretaste of all-consuming wifeliness. Susan Petrie, in RIP-OFF and other films, establishes herself as the tart with a heart of steel. Far more interesting is the leading "lady" of a little-known Vancouver film, GREAT COUPS OF HISTORY (Jack Darcus, 1969). Mingling actual reminiscences and dramatized scenes, the film looks steadily at an aging woman who has spent her life in the cynical exploitation of men. In between her narratives of how she has always got something for nothing from a sex she despises for its weakness and stupidity, she is shown in action, in make-up and mini-skirt, exerting her wiles on a pudgy Extension lecturer whose classes she's been attending. (O beware of those night-school ladies!) The male is as feeble a specimen as you could wish to see, but the female, for a change, is a hard-bitten predator, startlingly frank and energetic, and hoping to make one of the "great coups of history" with the aid of a Japanese face-lift.

To sum up a little: it is very rare indeed to find an English Canadian film in which a male character of some worth and substance is depicted as growing towards self-realization, achieving or even working towards a worthwhile goal, playing a significant part in any kind of community, or establishing a mature loving relationship with a woman. (I am saving the rare exceptions to this rule for later.) Meanwhile, before we proceed to ask what this dismal tendency of the cinematic imagination may signify, as an expression of national sense of self, we should consider where the films of Quebec fit into this pattern.

In French Canadian cinema the representation of life is far more diverse than in English Canadian films and, as we shall see, has recently begun to include a mode of positive self-realization of a distinct and significant kind. The imagery of male inadequacy is by no means so predominant, yet enough important examples can be found to demonstrate its viability. LE VIOL D'UNE JEUNE FILLE DOUCE (Gilles Carle, 1968) features a pair of taciturn, loutish brothers (played by the ubiquitous Pilon brothers) who, on the way to beating up the putative author of their sister's pregnancy, casually take a hitch-hiker into a field and rape her. The scene is ironically reminiscent of the rape sequence in Bergman's VIRGIN SPRING. In Carle's 1970 film, LES MALES, a poet and woodsman, who have spent two years together in the forest, make an ill-starred attempt to abduct the daughter of the police chief of a nearby township. Returning to their camp they encounter a lovely and generous-spirited girl prepared to share their rustic existence and her own favours. But their growing rivalry and contention drive away this gift from the gods, and they wander into Montreal in a futile search for the vision which their own unworthiness dispelled. LA MORT D'UN BUCHERON (1973) concerns the quest by a girl from Chibougamau for her long lost lumberjack father. Allusively named Maria Chapdelaine, she is attended in her search, around Montreal and into the backwoods, by a ruthlessly exploitative boor of a night-club owner and a young man named François Paradis who claims to love her, but who arranges to sell her favours to a rich old man. LE TEMPS D'UNE CHASSE (Francis Mankiewicz, 1972) takes a Coward, a Bully and a Clown on a weekend hunting trip. The Bully and the Clown—an aggressively handsome ladies' man and a short-winded ne'er-do-well—give $20 to a waitress to take her clothes off, while they goggle appreciatively. Meanwhile, the third hunter, a kindly, hen-pecked man, strikes up a shy friendship with another waitress. Next morning, however, he lacks the courage to opt out of the hunting party and spend the day with her. Reluctantly he is pressured by his friends into another futile trek through the woods, that ends in his being accidentally shot dead by the drunk and desperate Clown.

But take the case of Claude Jutra's autobiographical first feature A TOUT PRENDRE (1963). Here is the story, re-enacted by the actual participants, of a love affair between Jutra and a married mulatto girl living in Montreal. When she becomes pregnant and their relationship descends into crisis, he seeks advice from various sources including a priest, and allows it to reinforce his decision to break off with her, regardless of her obvious suffering. One can reasonably assert that an English Canadian writer/director would have undertaken this autobiographical enterprise in a spirit of self-vilification, rendering the episode as an exposure of his own contemptibility. The woman would have been perceived as candid and courageous, ready to commit herself to a man who is revealed to be evasive and pusillanimous. But in A TOUT PRENDRE Claude Jutra undertakes an honest exploration of what actually happened, seeking neither to vilify nor to idealize. He accepts the reality of past behaviour without capitulating to it as the inescapable pattern for all future relationships. He resists the temptation to imprison himself within a self-limiting, self-defeating version of his experience.

Seven years later, in MON ONCLE ANTOINE (1970), Jutra presents an image of a personal and social condition in which men and women together are rendered in their strengths and frailties, facing the vicissitudes of life and, especially, of death in an asbestos town. The treatment of Clement Perron's script displays a humane and complex awareness of the inter-relatedness of personal limitation and defeat and a demoralizing cultural condition. There is no question that the leading male characters, Antoine and Fernand (the latter played by Jutra himself), come across as distinctly anti-heroic figures; one of the most compelling scenes in the film is that in which Antoine, who is, among other things, the local undertaker, drunkenly confesses to his nephew Benoit the paralyzing horror of death at the core of his miserable existence. Yet the oppressed condition of the male characters is presented neither as contemptible nor as a betrayal of the commitment of idealized women. Moreover, the central consciousness is that of thirteen-year-old Benoit, for whom the events of that memorable Christmas Eve may be the foundation for a maturing independence and realism.

I have been illustrating what seems like a collective debility in the imagination of the English Canadian cinema. What remains to be asked is: what is the relation between this debility and the actual condition, shaped by history and circumstances, of being English Canadian? Does the blight on male characters in our films—our fantasies—genuinely reflect a sense of limitation and inadequacy experienced half-consciously by Canadians in their real lives? If it does not, what has got into our filmmakers that they should be hooked on so demoralized a fiction? If, on the other hand, as I believe, there *is* a consonance between the imagery and reality, is it inescapable? Or can we furnish an account of this constriction of the sense of self that might imply the possibility of liberation—both for the psyche and for its imaginative projections? I do not wish to appear unduly naive; one does not transform one's sense of self overnight, and by a mere effort of will. One cannot abolish one's psychological history or dismiss one's circumstances. But creative changes in the self can, nonetheless, occur, and one can actively collaborate in the process. Insights into the origins of one's psychic debilities are essential as a pre-condition; so too are external circumstances conducive, or at least not hostile, to a reconstituted presentation of self to the world. The process is accompanied *and propelled* by efforts to realize in imagination the self potentially transformed, and by dreams which enact the struggle and its resolution. (Conversely, the compulsive return to a defeatist fantasy militates *against* liberation from the state of being which it manifests.) In the remainder of this essay I proposed to <u>furnish a psychological history for the male ego so unhappily represented on the screen, and to suggest possible modes of liberation and their prefiguration in films.</u>

One way to describe the impediments to satisfactory self-realization by the protagonists of English Canadian films is in terms of the psychological history of a younger brother. Consider the relationship between two brothers. One of them has always been dominant. He grew up faster, was a self-determining adult, making it on his own, while the other was still a juvenile. He has always been the larger and stronger physically, and has tended to be more adventurous and enterprising, achieving great material success and attracting notice everywhere. He has quite naturally grown up with an aggressive self-assurance, assuming leadership automatically and tending to patronize his younger brother—when paying him any attention at all. He operates in the biggest leagues, and with his free-spending, confident manner he has had a lot of success with women. All over the neighbourhood people have pointed him out as the very model of a decent and resourceful prosperity. The fact that he has, for quite a few years now, displayed most of the qualities of an acquisitive bandit has either been politely ignored or genuinely not noticed.

Aware of his more powerful brother as a feature in the landscape, in a way that has never been reciprocated, the younger brother has grown up with a painfully confined sense of his own capacity for self-realization. An abiding sense of himself as inescapably diminished, secondary, immature, has become second nature, has indeed shaped his nature and bred into it a self-thwarting knowledge of personal inadequacy. Back in their family history, in 1776, while his brother was successfully waging the Oedipal struggle with the father, and asserting his autonomy, he refused the combat and stayed dutifully at his father's side. For many years he continued to accept parental supervision of his behaviour and choice of friends, hastening to the scene with willing aid whenever a fight broke out. In the end it was parental indifference rather than filial recalcitrance that reduced the supervision to a formality. And to his helpless chagrin, it was always obvious that the rebellious brother counted for far more than he in the parental regard, precisely by virtue of that rebellion and subsequent success. When it came to competing for the attention of women, he wasn't really surprised to find that, while some of his cousins found him quite attractive and amiable, he could never project the potency, not to mention the sheer prosperity, that brought his brother so many conquest. After all, he had declined the Oedipal battle and had forfeited its psychic spoils.

Seeking to define himself and to chart an independent career, the younger brother finds his options limited. Either he can attempt to follow in his brother's footsteps, to succeed by his standards and in his eyes—in which case he will always come in second, an also-ran, earning belittling recognition for limited achievements. Or he can cast about uneasily for some field of endeavour, some mode of self-realization which his brother has never pursued, and *couldn't achieve if he tried*—for there's little satisfaction in achieving what the other disdained to aim for. One solution would be to move away to another part of the world where he isn't known, and undertake to define himself existentially, free from the conditioning weight of his psychic history. But in Canada's case, this solution has no practical meaning.

The condition of a younger brother is also an affliction of the imagination. It is hard for him to imagine himself, or those who share his condition, successfully acting out the role of an emancipated male. This is not to suggest, however, that the imagination of male America is, by contrast, in splendid shape, delighting itself with a vision of its own poise and potency. Rather, the psychic condition of the American male —undermined, domesticated, "feminized"—constantly gives rise to a literature and a cinema of distress. But the American male experiences and accounts for his condition in different terms, and deals with it in different ways than the Canadian. He doesn't feel the psychic oppression of a more potent ego but, rather, feels trapped and betrayed by an external reality—the conditions of modern, urban, technological life. He blames conditions outside himself, and frequently identifies women as the cause of his malaise. Women have conspired with the technological revolution to subjugate a once noble creature, tameless and swift and proud. Moreover, the American male can always indulge himself with fantasies of aggressively masculine self-realization, ruthlessly mowing down Indians, Germans, Japanese, criminals, policemen and Things From Outer Space. When these diversions pall he can take satisfaction from identifying with the corporate masculinity and big-brotherliness of the American nation in the world.

A faltering Canadian ego has no such comforts. The diminished, younger-brother sense of self tends to find the fault in itself, that it is an underling. You cannot blame large people for the fact that you are smaller than they are. Nor, as we have seen, does the Canadian male project the blame for his condition onto the female. Women are perceived as encouraging him in vain to be a "man", for her sake and his own. As for the compensatory fantasy of heroic self-realization, it is available to him only through a doubly vicarious identification with *American* protagonists, which in turn reinforces the impression that Americans are somehow by nature capable of a vigorous self-assertion, from which Canadians are excluded. His own literature and cinema are busy with anxiety-dreams of failure and defeat. And finally, on the corporate level he may identify with a timid, inoffensive national presence, the United Nations total abstainer, continually allowing itself to be taken advantage of.

If this is an unsatisfactory situation, what alternative modes of liberation are available—to the imagination, at least, if not in reality? One obvious solution would be for Canada to be entirely absorbed into the United States of Greater America. Thus future generations of Ontarians, Maritimers, etc., whatever other natural shocks they might be heir to, would never know the psychic constraints of growing up to younger brotherhood. Instead they would have direct access, for better or worse, to the spectrum of American modes of self-realization and accompanying escape fiction. A second option for the Canadian ego is to identify the stronger brother unequivocally as its oppressor—psychic, economic, political, cultural—and to develop an energetic resistance. (Margaret Atwood speaks of "naming real causes of victimization", and suggests that "successful action against these causes can as yet be taken only in fantasies, or projected into the future". (*Survival*, p. 241.)

In Quebec this process is effectively apparent, the source of oppression being identified in its various aspects as the English, the Church, the Quebec bourgeois establishment, the police, capitalism, American culture, and so on. And in many recent Quebec films the posture of the rebel has furnished a role in which male characters can project themselves as courageously self-determining and worthy of a woman's confidence. Thus, when the young teacher in LES COLOMBES (Lord, 1972), married to a cute, successful pop-singer of working-class origins, discovers her complicity in his rich father's political machinations, he renounces them both. In so doing he wins the respect of his wife's sister, a political activist who had hitherto regarded him as irredeemably bourgeois. In Gilles Carle's LA VRAIE NATURE DE BERNADETTE (1972) most of the men are treacherous and exploitative characters, out to take advantage of the "fool-saint's" naive generosity. The only man of independent worth is the neighbouring farmer, engaged in a battle with representatives of a government department which is trying to pressure him into some sort of collectivization. By the end of the film, he and Bernadette have become allies in an aggressive defiance of the whole corrupt society. Two more films released in 1972—QUELQUES ARPENTS DE NEIGE by Denys Héroux, and LES SMATTES, Jean-Claude Labrecque's first feature—have remarkably similar plots, in which the protagonists become outlaws hunted down by government forces. Héroux's film is a costume drama set in the 1837 uprising; the hero and his beautiful lady-love are victims of the cruel and stupid British soldiery. LES SMATTES, set in the present, shows the Pilon brothers, whose land in the Gaspé has been expropriated for a provincial park, taking to the woods after a shooting accident. In the police hunt which follows, the wife of one of the brothers is shot dead, and the net is tightened on the outlawed pair.

Such films imply, in a manner which is potentially simplistic, that male honour and authenticity derive from being, as the saying goes, part of the solution rather than part of the problem. Not to be on the side of the oppressed is to be numbered among the liberals, the fascists and the cop-outs—in other words, the Cowards, Bullies and Clowns. Significantly enough, the price of rebellion against oppression is frequently depicted as isolation, suffering and death, as the films cultivate fantasies of revolutionary martyrdom rather than revolutionary triumph. A less obviously political work like Clément Perron's TAUREAU (1973) confirms the pattern: the people of Quebec village pool their individual hypocrisies in a vicious persecution of the local pariah family, the town whore, her daughter, and her gentle, slow-witted giant of a son. In the face of the villagers' murderous outrage at his love-affair with the local schoolteacher, "Taureau" hangs himself.

It has to be remembered that most of the Quebec film people are active separatists; to work in film is to participate in the formation and articulation of a dynamically self-aware political culture. Directors in English Canada, on the other hand, are, with some exceptions, "apolitical" bourgeois, aspiring to fame and fortune in the commercial cinema, and ideally in the United States. There are some *cultural* radicals, to be sure, and the beginnings of a women's movement in film, but virtually no socio-political perceptions shared broadly enough to constitute an ideological matrix. This is far from surprising: there simply isn't available in English Canada a developed ideological identity which filmmaking can nourish and be nourished by. Hardly a single film consciously perceives a connection between individual experience and the political condition of being Canadian. (One which does is Don Owen's study of troubled adolescence, NOBODY WAVED GOODBY (1963), in which Peter Kastner conveys to a young Québécois his felt lack of a positive cultural identity to support him through his individual identity crisis.) Occasionally attempts are made to identify with the political counter-culture within the United States. Morley Markson's radical critique of "Amerika", entitled BREATHING TOGETHER (1971), edits together the speeches of a collection of counter-culture-heroes into a revolutionary document with no trace of a Canadian origin. On the other hand, in Robin Spry's PROLOGUE (1969) a young Canadian returns from a fringe participation in the Chicago riots to find that his girlfriend has given up political action as puerile, and is living on a commune with an American draft-evader. What such films fail to provide is an indigenous "resistance movement" through which the individual's need for creative self-assertion can merge with a collective will to self-determination. Of course, it would be easier for a Torontonian, for example, to maintain a conception of himself as colonized, in body and in spirit, if he were not so readily indictable as a colonizer of others—Indians, Eskimos, women and the Québécois.

The cinema, then, has not so far dramatized an ideologically-based resistance to the condition of the younger brother. In the few exceptional instances where an alternative image of maleness has been realized, it has been in personal rather than ideological terms. The integrity of the male ego, and the viable maturity of the relationships between men and women, are not associated with radical alienation but, in some cases at least, with an active commitment to community. They seem to combine, in varying proportions, a traditional-uncorrupted and a radical-liberated conception of the kind of person a man should be, and the kind of relationship between the sexes that gives scope to the integrity of each.

Back in 1962, Don Haldane's modest classic, DRYLANDERS, told the story of a farm family in Saskatchewan, from their arrival and early struggles in the 1900s, through the bumper prosperity of the twenties, and into the devastating years of drought and Depression. Dan Greer, the head of the family, ends his days an utterly defeated man—but he has known many years of deserved success. He has been defeated at last by Nature, and not by any personal insufficiency. The film celebrates an image of tenacious idealism, rooted in a sense of family and community. It is a classic rendering of a particularly Canadian image of heroism—free of hubris and shunning the assertion of individual prowess. More recently, each of the three films which Paul Almond has written and directed has featured a leading male character with strength, substance and integrity. True, the films focus primarily upon the emotional experience of a female character—played in every case by Geneviève Bujold—but within that experience a man plays a positive and constructive part. He is portrayed as sensitive and dependable, capable of responding generously to the haunted intensity that the Bujold character habitually displays. If anything, Almond's work has a tendency towards romantic melodrama, in which the male lead is something of a paragon. This is especially true of ISABEL (1968) in which the handsome young Marc Strange rescues Bujold from imminent rape, and also, it seems, from the clutch of her own obsessions and terrors. In ACT OF THE HEART (1970) she is a God-possessed Montreal Protestant who falls in love with a Catholic priest, in the person of Don Sutherland. A gently self-deprecating, humorous man, unable to match her extremes of mystical intensity, Sutherland's priest nonetheless has the courage to quit the church in order to live with her, thus evincing a capacity for commitment rare among screen males. Finally there is the "visionary allegory" JOURNEY (1972) in which a psychically distressed Bujold finds herself in an agricultural commune uncompromisingly committed to pre-industrial subsistence farming. It is a place out of time, a dream place where she may be liberated from the traumatic effect of her past experience. Embodying something of an archetypal "femaleness"—she comes out of the Saguenay River and bears its name—she encounters Boulder, the leading man of the community. While he clearly embodies a rather traditionally conceived archetype of maleness, he is nonetheless depicted as a mature individual who can aid Saguenay without, as it were, colonizing her. When her stay at the commune seems to have fulfilled its therapeutic purpose, he launches her into the river again to continue her own journey.

Another writer/director capable of freeing himself from the imagery of male worthlessness and the impossibility of authentic relationships is Jack Darcus, whose GREAT COUPS OF HISTORY was referred to earlier. Less loftily allegorical than JOURNEY, his film PROXY HAWKS (1972) is also a great deal more modest in scale and budget. It dramatizes a woman's crisis of revulsion against what she perceives as the oppressive capacity of "maleness", as manifested by her husband, by the perpetrators of My Lai, and in the behaviour of some carrion birds which her husband keeps in captivity. For a time the husband, played by Darcus himself, looks like the typical Bully, authoritarian, surly, intermittently violent. In his wife's eyes, his sexual approach to her become repulsively involved with her images of the ravening birds. But instead of becoming one more vilification of the male, the film goes on to effect a tentative re-establishment and deepening of contact. The man is shown to be capable of acknowledging himself as oppressive, while the woman manages to separate him as a person from the imagery with which he has become associated in her mind. The conclusion contains the possibility of their being able to transcend conditioned roles and stereotypes, and to work out a co-existence for mature human beings.

* * *

The problem, in trying to psychoanalyse the younger brother's dream-life, is that one is caught between advocating the dramatization of a more aggressively "masculine" individualism, and seeking to make a virtue out of impotence. Somewhere in between lies a confident and potent male sense of self which can assert its worth and defend its interests without imposing on others. Women too, in films if not in life, would get a better deal in scenarios where the men are less stunted and immature. If women in Canadian films are usually depicted as long-suffering victims who deserve better than they get—then it's about time they started getting as good as they deserve. One of the tasks of the Canadian imagination is the exploration of roles and relationships which are individually emancipating, collectively responsible, and also culturally possible—that is to say, contained potentially within what we already are. If we do not come to terms with the younger-brother syndrome, recognizing it as mostly crippling and self-defeating (though at some level, perhaps, a source of great maturity), we can only act out its deformities over and over again.

(September 1973, slightly revised)

First postscript (January 1974)

Meanwhile, and by way of a conclusion, let me take brief notice of three films released in the fall of 1973. (I ask the reader to believe that I had not seen them when writing the foregoing article, and that I had no hand in writing their screenplays.) The first, Don Shebib's BETWEEN FRIENDS, shows a strong and candid girl abandoning the flabby, inconsiderate dope she has been living with, for the sake of a visiting American whom he has idolized as hero, mentor, special buddy—in short, as older brother. The pathetically devastated Canadian gets himself shot in a hold-up, and the American, played by Michael Parks, turns out to be emotionally distant and withheld. In PAPERBACK HERO (Peter Pearson) the protagonist, named Rick Dillon, acts out an infantile fantasy of *machismo* by identifying with a legendary American. Known indulgently as "the Marshall" by the people of Delisle, Saskatchewan, Dillon theatrically bullies and swaggers his way around, until one of his women despairs of him, and the other sears him with her infuriated contempt. In a HIGH NOON-style shoot-out which goes awry, Dillon too gets himself shot by the police. It would appear from these movies that the penalty for being an inadequate male is growing more severe.

Finally, there is SLIPSTREAM by David Acomba, in which a Canadian protagonist emancipates himself from a colonized personal condition, and seems to be all the better for it. A rock D.J. broadcasting from a ranch house in the hills for a radio station in Alberta, Mike Mallard rebels against his cynical exploitation by the aggressive, city-slick station owner—played by sometime New Yorker Eli Rill as a very American stereotype. At the same time he refuses to be domesticated by a girl who has moved in on him uninvited, and they separate in mutual anger after she has severed his broadcasting cable with an axe. As his culminating and most radical gesture he sets fire to his ranch-house-cum-studio and watches it burn to the ground, declaring brusquely to a reporter who has come after a story that "it makes sense". SLIPSTREAM is not a major work, for all that it won the 1973 Canadian Film Awards, and the emancipation of an Alberta disc-jockey may not seem to be terribly significant. But the film dramatizes a credible assertion of sovereign identity by a Canadian character who is neither Coward, Bully nor Clown.

Second postscript (November 1976)

I don't want to go on forever mechanically updating this article. If its perspective has any validity, it should serve other viewers as a critical vantage-point in its own right. At this juncture I simply want to make a couple of modifications and a couple of suggestions.

In retrospect I would give less weight to JOURNEY and to SLIPSTREAM. In looking for saving exceptions to the syndrome of the collapsible male, I'm afraid I clutched at straw men. If our films are going to reflect to us protagonists with whom we can identify in their strength, not in their weakness, they must do so first of all in realistic situations, and secondly by way of identifiably Canadian types. The archetypal solemnities of

JOURNEY make it impossible to take seriously or to care about, while Mike Mallard's truculent self-assertion in SLIPSTREAM is vitiated, for me, by the obvious American-ness of the actor. Far more ruinous, in this respect, is the casting of Tony Lobianco in GOLDENROD (Harvey Hart, 1976). Here, in the novel by Herbert Harker, is an honest-to-goodness story of a man who painfully re-achieves a lost self-respect and a lost wife. Lobianco's performance as Jesse Gifford is so blatantly foreign, in accent and manner, that the story loses its Canadian resonance, and ceases to matter for us. The miscasting (for the sake of the U.S. audience) is all the more poignant when we see in a minor role that fine actor Donnelly Rhodes, whose sturdy characterization of Jim King, bloody but unbowed, makes THE HARD PART BEGINS (Lynch, 1974) such an important film.

I certainly do not claim that a good film will inevitably spring from a script which either dramatizes the effective self-assertion of the protagonists, or implicitly links the protagonist's weakness and defeat with a collective Canadian psyche. Thus, for instance, Darcus's third film, WOLF PEN PRINCIPLE (1974), while it eventually conducts its unhappy clown of a leading character to a gesture of liberation, is an awkward, unconvincing, and in places downright silly film. And the attempt in 125 ROOMS OF COMFORT (Loubert, 1975) to make the disintegrated transvestite singer (whose family's hotel is about to be taken over by an ugly American) symbolic of the oppressed condition of Canada, seems to me unsuccessful. The most interesting Canadian cinema will probably be that which bypasses the terms of my formula altogether.

Meanwhile, what is to be said of MONTREAL MAIN, DUDDY KRAVITZ, SECOND WIND, PARTNERS, THE FAR SHORE...?

Mireille Dansereau: "La Vie rêvée"

Interview by Á. Ibrányi-Kiss

CC: Did you feel intimidated at the Awards presentations? You were the only Québécoise filmmaker who made an acceptance speech.

MIREILLE: That's because I am very shy, and I put that as a test. I said to myself, "You have to do that because it is difficult and that means that you have to try." But no, it was because I had something to say, especially since it's a film made by a co-operative. LA VIE REVEE was produced by L'Association coopérative des productions audio-visuelles in Montreal which has been financed by the CFDC. The idea of the co-operative was to try to have people who had never been given the

Reprinted from *Cinema Canada*, no. 5 (December-January 1972-3).

chance to prove themselves in film make their first one. It was almost a condition for making the film. So everybody was doing his first feature. And another way in which we were a cooperative was that everybody invested half their salaries, Danielle Gagne, editor, and I, our complete salaries in the last three months. But as Claude Godbout said, it's more a cooperative way of doing things, not just co-operative. The company he is with, Prisma, helped us a lot by letting us use their editing tables at very low prices. It's the *spirit* which is co-operative.

CC: Who are the filmmakers in the co-op?

MIREILLE: There are forty members. Young filmmakers. All unknown, I guess. All people who wanted to change the way films were produced in Quebec, and who didn't want to work for a big company like Carle-Lamy. Really co-operative filmmaking, in my idea, would be everybody writing the script together, everybody participating in the film; but it was not possible at this point. I think in Quebec we are not ready yet for collective experiences in creation, or in life. Communes are very difficult because we are just starting to know who we are. You can't get that with people who are not secure in themselves. The most difficult thing for me was with my assistant, Patrick Auzepy. He had no ego trip. On the contrary, he was helping. But I was *so afraid* that he would take over, I had to say, "It's my film, not yours." I had to take over the visions. But it was my film in that it's very personal—with the fantasies and all. Nobody could tell me how to do them. So when somebody suggested something, because I wasn't secure enough, I was afraid of being influenced. Before shooting, we thought we might be able to work together in a creative way communally. But it wasn't possible. As long as you make films where, as a director, you are not secure—you can't work collectively. But the ego says yes, we are there and we exist and we create. I do it as a woman. The search of women to create and to exist is the same process as what is happening in Quebec. It is the same pattern for any sort of colonized/colonizer relationship. The same problems exist for women as exist for Quebec in relation to the rest of Canada. It is very difficult for a woman in Quebec.

CC: But in English Canada there seems to be far fewer women involved in film.

MIREILLE: That might be because we look more towards what is happening in France. Editing—for a women—was a very respected position in France. When I went there I met a very great woman editor, but they're always working with men they admire. But I said to myself, I guess unconsciously, that one day I can become a director because of Agnes Varda.

CC: Seeing your film was such an incredible experience for me, because so many of the dreams and fantasies are my dreams and fantasies, too. And that memory sequence of when she was just a little girl—I was so glad to see that in a film! It seems to be a communal memory for myself and so many women.

MIREILLE: I am very glad, because someone in Montreal told me that if I show fantasies that are only mine, I shouldn't make any films. It's true. I don't want to make things only for myself, like I said in the film. Dusan Makavejev told me something marvellous—he said that we see in this film a lot of things that are part of the way people live and that we never see on the screen; and that cinema is a lot about that. I think we should try to put on the screen many things like that—everyday things. That's why I feel very close to what Cassavetes does. My ideal and ambition is to work like that. I haven't found the crew and all that, that he has. He always works with people he knows, and all the people are very involved. I think in a few years I will work like that—with people very involved and who believe in what they are doing. With Cassavetes, it's really life that you see in his pictures. That way of relating to cinema is very appealing to me, even though it's not what you would call spectacular or entertaining.

CC: But your film seems to have gone beyond that, in that his films have a lot of crudity which is depicting the male world. Your film is—

MIREILLE: Yes, but I'm a woman! That's the difference I wanted to show. I am very glad that you see that.

I went to Rimouski in northern Quebec and a few girls told me that they never thought women could get along like that. They felt LA VIE REVEE wasn't honest and true because of that. So I told them that if it exists on the screen, that means they can make it into a reality—and they agreed. It's great. They believe in it now, and for me that is the best thing.

CC: Your film is on such a subtle level—with the nuances of so many feelings and relationships. It's so beautifully subtle. Just as in life—so many important things happen on that level.

MIREILLE: I am sure they didn't pick up on the subtleties and nuances of the dreams. In Montreal the people who liked the film are people who are visual, not linear. Because of the atmospheres. I am a bit disturbed by that—should you *not* make films that are so subtle? The films that work have no subtleties at all. On the contrary, you give everything to the public. It is disturbing because I know that the film hasn't really done well. Yet for me, it is nearly commercial by my idea of films. It is not as experimental as what I would like to do. The world I am in is one of subtleties and atmospheres, and many times I am afraid that it's very European, you know? At least, there are only a few people who can get into that. So in a way I know that I am going more and more towards making films that only a few, an elite, will go into.

LA VIE REVEE played in a very small theatre for six weeks in Montreal, but it didn't pay because the whole system of distribution for cinema is horrible. It made $15,000, I guess, for the man who *owns* the theatre, but all of us who worked on it—nobody got any money. I think if I continue to make very low-budget films I may be able to go on. That is the problem for filmmakers, not knowing if you can go on and make more films. That's why I'm happy about the prize.

CC: Was it at all frightening to make your first feature?

MIREILLE: I wasn't frightened, I felt responsible to the co-operative and the CFDC. The CFDC had just financed a film before mine (a guy's film) which was shot, and all the money was out at the end of the shooting. That was the first co-op production, so it was very bad for all the young filmmakers. The CFDC thought that we could not make features. Michael Spencer told me just yesterday, "You know, it is a big enterprise to make a feature film. I knew it would be difficult." But I told him that I knew if he gave me the money, I would go to the end. That's exactly what we did—we had no money left but we finished it. There was no other way. So there was this feeling that I was almost representing all young filmmakers, and if this film was not financially successful, it could almost be the end for a few years in Montreal for young people, because of that first bad experience. The proof is that now they are starting two features at the co-operative.

They didn't want me to make this first film. The men thought that if I made a film on women, it should be militant. A sociological-Marxist analysis, or something like that. A very political film. But you see, that is a *man's* idea of what is revolutionary about women. They think that we should get together and form a political party and fight, and give intellectual ideas about the problem of women as related to our society and to Quebec. Men thought that what would bring a change in the status of women is a clear analysis of women: sociologically, politically, and financially. They couldn't accept my intuitive, very emotional and personal approach.

CC: I was very surprised at seeing a man's name on the credits, as having written the script with you. I didn't feel his influence at all. How much of it did Patrick Auzepy write?

MIREILLE: That is very hard to say. I had written LA VIE REVEE four or five years ago. All the sequences and the spirit were there. In a way, it's great that you feel that way, because Patrick wanted to let me do my own film and he assisted in really every way. It's very seldom that you see that in a man. He completely tried to understand the film I wanted to make. For two years, I was living with him. At first we were supposed to do it with Paul Almond and people like that. It didn't work, so I was quite discouraged. And he helped me because he felt that if I didn't make this film, I couldn't go on as an individual. From so long ago, this was a very strong thing I had to do. Four years. I believed in this film because of the friendship between the girls and because I was *sure* of the images and dreams, so I stuck with it. I really hope that my next film I can make at the moment that I want to—maybe a few months' difference, but not four years.

CC: The editing of LA VIE REVEE must have been especially difficult because of the slow-motion sequences and the fantasies. But it all blended in so smoothly. It must have been very hard to get that....

MIREILLE: Yes, that's true. At the beginning of the editing I was very unsure and we wound up making many tests. We were always wondering—is it too long or too short by a foot? I always wanted to have it longer, and Danielle kept saying no, no, no. Throughout the whole film, she kept saying, "Shorter!" and I was saying "A bit more"—so it probably came out just right.

CC: And the camerawork was so sensitive and not at all self-conscious.

MIREILLE: I think that is intuitive. I decided every frame and the atmosphere of lighting, because I wanted it to be a very realistic film so people could look at it and really be sure that that's life. Even if there are a lot of dream-sequences—the dreams are true and as real as reality. That was the main quality. I wanted to show two feminine characters being lively and honest, as you would see them in life and not as objects. I purposely didn't want a psychological analysis of two characters. I wanted to have life just bursting out of them!

CC: Was it shot in Super-16?

MIREILLE: That was hard. I had to fight for it. Nobody in Montreal believed in that—I had to come to Toronto. All the labwork was done here. Bob Crone and Film House invested in the film, they even tried a new technique for it.

CC: Did you work very closely with François Gill, the cameraman?

MIREILLE: There was a big conflict between us. In Quebec, the cameraman is the hero. I was making a woman's film and he wanted to be the star. Incredible conflicts. But I think that it is out of conflicts that you get something of value. The conflict with François Gill was the most interesting. He was a man who wanted his ego, but you can see why this is ridiculous; who has the real vision of things? The director. But we still don't have the ability to submit. We think submitting is feminine, and inferior. But in a film, there is one person who wants to impose his vision, which is nearly an aggression. Or not an aggression—a creation. The people around are there to help that person make the best film possible. That is a new realization for me, that submitting is not inferior. There shouldn't have to be a battle between the one who is making and the one who is helping to make. The next day it can be the reverse! But there is always a lot of ego-tripping, and the most difficult is the director—who is doing his own ego trip. (*Laughter*)

CC: Do you find it easier to work with a woman creatively than with a man?

MIREILLE: Danielle and I had no ego trips between us. Insecurity —yes; but not at all the same thing. We were working together, and we were very insecure and not confident, because we were talking about women. I admit that for a good time of my life, and even now, I always admired what men did. So when we were working and thinking about women, we felt that somehow that was not as good as men's work. We didn't feel good about it.

For the past ten years, I have been trying to forget that I'm a woman. I always said to men, "I'm a woman, yes. But I'm quite different from other women. I'm better—I'm almost a man!" That's why I always felt bad about the films I was making. A horrible malaise. Always thinking that people won't like what I'm doing as much as if I were a man doing them.

That is why working at the film board on a project about women is so great, because now I can say that I'm a woman and I'm really glad that I am. And the things I have to say are as important as if I were a man. A lot is changing. When you change as an individual, the things you do change as well. I don't think that I will become aggressive. Men seem to be afraid now. They tell me that I must be a Women's Liberationist because I am questioning marriage and all that. And in their heads, Women's Lib is aggressive. So they see me and I'm not that way—so what kind of Women's Lib am I? I'm a woman trying to find out what I really am, and that's all. The Women's Liberation Movement is very difficult to assume because it is very intellectual, and very badly communicated by the mass media.

The revolution we won as women was in stopping that competition thing, the ego. That is what is so fantastic for me in the group at the film board. We are all women working together. When I started at the film board eight years ago, no one was saying too much about their films because they were afraid that someone would steal their ideas or be influenced by them. It was all very sneaky. With the women's group now, in the Challenge for Change series, it's so great! We read an article, and we bring it in—"Did you see that?" And the other women know I'm making a film about marriage, and if they have a book or something that deals with it, they give it to me or tell me about it. My plans are not to work only with women, or even to make films only about women; but I think this series will bring in a new kind of feeling. Already, at the film board—you look at it, and we are having fun. We laugh a lot, and the atmosphere is this kind of relaxation. The men are really wondering what's happening.

It's strange, you know. For the first time I don't feel ashamed or competitive at all. I feel that the next film I make is going to be much more relaxed. First of all, it's not as big as this one was; in that it isn't dramatic with actresses and all that. But also, I'm very involved.

The way it's done, it's getting very close to the co-operative way of making films. I'm putting myself in the film—so I'm *really* involved. I am making one film in the series. There should be six. I'm very glad that they realized the importance of a series like that. The executive producer, who is a woman, would like it to be nearly permanent. It's for Challenge for Change and it's to go on television. So already, that is a very specific thing. I was called about six months ago to make the film I want to make—just a film by Mireille Dansereau. We did research with women through video for two months, women of all ages and social classes. We did three-hour sessions for three, four days a week. But I was very anguished. I felt that I found things that I knew already. The women were all talking about children, their men, sexual relationships, all fundamental questions that men probably wouldn't talk about so openly. It was marvellous for them. But at the end of two months, I had no thought of making a film about any of that. So I went and really searched.

I felt the responsibility for finding out what was most important about women now—what was most important for women? I researched, and more and more I realized that women centre their whole lives in relationship to marriage. Whether or not to marry at eighteen. At least, for my generation it was that—marriage or career? Marriage meant prison. Career meant freedom, adventure, risk—all of which are very masculine. Career also meant sexual freedom, and that sexuality didn't mean anything. Because men at that time got married and had adventures with women. They looked at their mistresses, at their affairs, as a relationship that was not involving. So we, who wanted to be men, adopted these same patterns. We decided that sexuality was not involving—that we could have all kinds of experiences. Today, I realize that that is a male pattern; that sexual relationships *are* involving—for any individual who is whole and total.

I was really asking myself—what is marriage? Why have I refused it so strongly, so categorically, and so young? That is when the research on fantasies came into it. What I liked most in LA VIE REVEE were the fantasy sequences. What were the most specific fantasies of women related to marriage? Then, I found something really interesting, going back into religion. I saw how the first communion was the first idea of marriage, to Christ. I was starting to work on that, and submitted it to the producer. She said that it was very interesting, but not what we were doing in this series. The film was becoming very meditative and mystical. I still think it is very good, and I am sure that I will go at it again.

But the series is about social change and has to go on television. I went on the idea of what was marriage, and decided to make four portraits.

Four different approaches of women in the same generation—twenty-eight to thirty—what kind of evolution have we done in the past ten years as women, and how we situate ourselves between the generation before ours and the younger generation. Those before us have accepted marriage—with maybe a few mistresses—they have made their own environment; and even when they get divorced, they want to start again. The same pattern always. And the younger generation, those who are eighteen to twenty—ten years away from us—are talking about the end of relationships between two people, and are trying collectives. They are trying to find new patterns. And we, who are between those two generations, are putting into question the institution of marriage, not actually the fundamental relationship of two people. There is no difference between two people living together and two who are married—the patterns are the same. That is what I am showing.

I take four women and I try to really get into their world, and their way of living every day. To show the rhythm of their lives and how they create their everyday lives. I want them to choose, with me, what is most revealing about them and how to illustrate their lives. If they want to dance, or create in music, that is what we are looking at with each of them. I am not only putting my own idea of what these women are, I am helping them realize what they are, and to express themselves. They are going to do the same with me—to provoke me. In a way, I am there and will be asking questions. I'm somebody who is going to see people to know more about why they made choices. But at the same time, it is going to be a feed-back; with them asking me, "Who are you, coming to ask me questions? Do you really love me, or are you just here to make a film?"

I am trying, and I hope that the relationship between the interviewer and the one who is being interviewed is going to be completely changed. These four women are not caught in the usual patterns. One is married and has children, and she was a filmmaker who left everything after twenty-six to have children. Another woman is getting a divorce. She has no children but she has a career. Another is living with a guy and isn't married; and the fourth woman has a child of her own without a father, and a kind of occupation in which she is very involved—but not a career in itself. They are not ordinary women, for they have all questioned the roles of women, and it's interesting to see four women who have questioned and have chosen four different ways of living.

Making the film, and the film itself—neither is more important than the other. I don't like to separate things, I always want to put them all together. Because it is the same thing—the product of the film and the making of it. With LA VIE REVEE, I was so anxious, that most of the time the products was much better than the life I had while making it. People say—it looks so nice, it must have been great to film it. It was not great! It was anguishing and suffering! In our generation, you always have to be cool and have fun and all that ... but everything you do has suffering in it. A woman giving birth to a child—that's the most suffering thing there is. For me, making films is like having children.

But now, I won't be as stressed, I am more secure. You know, I've read about some filmmakers in Quebec and they say, "It was great! Everybody loved each other and tatatatamm!" and I think, how lucky they are.

What Makes Duddy Run?

Daniel Golden

Sirrah ... I am a Jew! and whenever anything Jewish is mentioned I find it necessary to say that I am a Jew. I'm a Jew! A Jew!
—Nathanael West, *The Dream Life of Balso Snell*

It's cretins, little money grubbers like Kravitz that cause anti-Semitism, you know.
—Irwin Schubert in *The Apprenticeship of Duddy Kravitz*

Every ethnic community has its cultural tattletales, artists and writers who go around revealing the family's dirty little secrets to the outside world, the "white men" as Duddy Kravitz learns to call them in THE APPRENTICESHIP OF DUDDY KRAVITZ. Munch and Ibsen painfully expose the icy bankruptcy of spirit and human compassion in their native Norway; George Grosz, Gunter Grass and Fritz Lang dwell on a German psyche obsessed with violence and perverse decadence; Pio Baroja and Luis Bunuel attack their Spanish orthodoxy in all its pious hypocrisy. But when it comes to cultural self-satire and self-hatred Jews are, to borrow a line from the title character of Saul Bellow's *Henderson the Rain King*, "what Gary, Indiana, is to smoke—the world's biggest operation".

Ever since Abraham Cahan explored the ethical price of assimilation in *The Rise of David Levinsky* (1917), Jewish-American writers have assiduously dissected their national character. In doing so, they have created a literature that often documents a movement from isolation to social accommodation. This process of Americanization has not been an entirely satisfactory one, for most Jewish authors have found themselves

Reprinted from *Jump Cut*, no. 5 (January-February 1975).

at odds not only with the dominant external culture, but with Jews themselves. Loss of faith, a strong sense of cultural disaffection, and what another of Bellow's characters aptly calls the "nightmare isolation of the self"—these elements have become both mood and motif for such writers as Mike Gold, Bernard Malamud, Norman Mailer, Clifford Odets, Philip Roth, J.D. Salinger, Budd Schulberg, and many others.

Mordecai Richler is a Canadian Jew whose fiction consistently focuses on the pains and prices of cultural assimilation. His screenplay of THE APPRENTICESHIP OF DUDDY KRAVITZ closely parallels his 1959 novel of the same title, and is an incisive and often unforgiving account of nineteen year-old Duddy Kravitz—hustler, con artist, betrayer. Richler has been accused of anti-Semitism in this film, and at times he envisions Duddy and the Jewish subculture in Montreal as harshly venal, crass, and materialistic. But it is Duddy, played so dynamically by Richard Dreyfuss (AMERICAN GRAFFITI), who complicates and transcends cheap stereotype by revealing compassion, family loyalty, and a curious lonely vulnerability.

In his desperate pursuit of ownership of a large lake and parcel of land in the Laurentian Mountains, Duddy Kravitz descends into duplicity, fraud, and betrayal that leaves him owner of the land for his dream resort, "Kravitzville", but also completely isolated. Repudiated by his loving grandfather, whose adage "a man without land is nobody" feeds his insatiable desire for success, Duddy is also rejected by his mistress and confidante Yvette (Micheline Lanctot) and a young American epileptic, Virgil Roseboro (Randy Quaid of THE LAST DETAIL), who is paralyzed as a direct result of Duddy's ruthless ambition.

Duddy Kravitz seems an anomaly, a Jewish boy without a Jewish mother. Indeed, he shares with some other recent Jewish screen protagonists an unstable and untraditional family background. Duddy's mother is dead, and his father is a cab-driving *tummler*, who pimps on the side for extra cash. In one of the most significant passages in the film, Duddy questions his father, played with fitting bluster and bravado by Jack Warden. When he wistfully asks about his dead mother, "Did she like me?" Max the father gruffly replies, "Sure, why not?" failing to perceive his own son's loneliness. Halfway into the film, this same exchange is repeated, but this time it is Virgil, who is similarly isolated by his epilepsy, who asks Duddy, "Do you like me?" In his relentless pursuit of option monies and new angles, Duddy can only absent-mindedly echo his own father's disheartening response, "Sure, why not?"

In his disrupted and hollow family life, Duddy resembles Neil Klugman, hero in GOODBYE, COLUMBUS, who lives with aunt and uncle in the Bronx after his parents light out for Arizona, and Lennie in THE HEARTBREAK KID, who seems without any ties or family connections. This resemblance points to a common theme carried over from Jewish-American fiction, the loss of "family sense", as Bellow's Tommy

Wilhelm puts it. Family bonds seem to twist or break under the pressure of assimilating, and for many characters, "making it" becomes an incomplete and unhealthy surrogate for a cohesive and reinforcing home life. In THE APPRENTICESHIP OF DUDDY KRAVITZ, there is some redeeming affection and concern for Duddy, especially in the figure of his Talmudically sagacious grandfather, played by Zvee Schooler. But it's not enough to neutralize the emptiness of Duddy's own house and the St. Urbain Street atmosphere of shady deals, arson, and petty chicanery. The ghetto setting is adeptly portrayed, and here one senses the moral ambivalence of the film, something that carries over from the novel. If these hustling Jews are obnoxious and crude, they are also warm and generous. Mr. Farber, the junk dealer, is played by Joe Silver, whose voice rumbles with the phlegm of a thousand cheese danishes. A successful representative of the Street, he is simultaneously an important and compassionate father-surrogate for Duddy and an admitted crook, whose street savvy gets a partner imprisoned for his own criminally negligent homicide. He offers this confession in a steam-bath conversation with Duddy that clearly delineates the groundrules of the young hero's own financial pursuits. And even though his advice is tainted with blatant immorality, and his nouveau riche extravagances so embarrassing (his son's Bar Mitzvah, in chicken liver and carved ice, closely resembles the wedding sequence in GOODBYE, COLUMBUS), Mr. Farber is endearing, perhaps dangerously so. Ted Kotcheff's straightforward direction withholds editorial opinion on this and other questions of moral obligation. Outside the teeming Jewish milieu of catered affairs and convenient fraud, the audience is caught between two equally unattractive extremes—a stolid and vituperatively bigoted French-Canadian peasantry and the genteel bloodlessness of the WASP aristocracy, safely ensconsed above the rabble in their Westmount mansions.

In many respects, Bernie Farber's Bar Mitzvah is the structural and thematic centre of the movie. In its burlesque of the Jewish ceremony of entrance into manhood, it parallels Duddy's own movement from boyish apprenticeship to fully realized mastery of moral and financial wheeling and dealing. Duddy establishes a company to film documentaries of Bar Mitzvahs and weddings, and hires a drunken and blacklisted film director named John Friar (played as a sodden Etonian by Denholm Elliott, who almost walks away with the movie). In Friar's hands, a simple film record of the Bar Mitzvah boy and all his smiling relatives is transformed into a bizarre and hilarious montage of synagogue scenes, diving German Stukas, dancing Zulu warriors, bloody circumcisions, and one especially grotesque scene of a Black sideshow performer chomping on razor blades. It is a marvelous parody of avant-garde technique and pretensions (do the razor blades echo UN CHIEN ANDALOU?), and also a comment on popular tastes and proprieties, since the entire horrified audience at the initial screening is gratefully relieved when the Rabbi proclaims the film "a most edifying experience—a work of art". This film within a film is an indulgence on the part of both Richler and Kotcheff, but it does serve as another indicator of Duddy's insistent and often insensitive pursuit of his dream. Despite the WASP front (the name of his organization is "Dudley Kane Enterprises"), Duddy remains the archetypal *Luftmensch*, in the Yiddish sense of a man who "lives on air", constantly scheming and hustling, with his office in his pocket.

Kotcheff does a yeoman's job of transforming Richler's novel into a screen vehicle. He captures a sense of post-World War II filmmaking in his grainy, high-contrast colour photography. This in turn lends a naturalistic flavour to many of the external shots of St. Urbain Street, especially as the film opens with an over-long sequence of Duddy's high school cadets on parade through narrow littered streets, past an appropriately ethnic melange of urchins, pushcarts, and bagel bakeries. This social backdrop, which includes some obvious documentary-style shots (as when the camera tracks up the squalid inner courtyard and alley of Duddy's apartment building), becomes a significant theme as Duddy ventures beyond the Jewish confines of hustling a roulette game in the resorts or finessing his movie deals.

Dreyfuss portrays Duddy as a pudgy, hyperkinetic hustler, constantly sweating, scratching, and twitching. But despite his nervousness, Duddy (at times) has a charmingly boyish Teddy Bear appearance. This is quite a change from the novel's Duddy, who is an acne-riddled, anorexically skinny chain-smoker. Similarly, the film's Uncle Benjy, played with a slender ascetic reserve by Joseph Wiseman, is in direct contrast to the book's blubbery and pathetic fat man. Uncle Benjy, who has practically adopted Duddy's brother Lennie and financed his medical school career, says to Duddy from his death-bed: "You're a born *pusherke*, a little Jew-boy on the make; people like you make me ashamed." Accurate, perhaps, and this kind of shame wears off on Lennie, who is duped into performing an illegal abortion by his Westmount gentile friends. Only Duddy, street-wise and canny, can rescue his brother from scandal, drag him home from exile in Toronto, and charm the Westmount father whose daughter received the illicit operation.

The film traces Duddy's financial success and ethical destruction; he acquires the last parcel of land by forging a check on the crippled Virgil's account. Duddy's success is a hollow victory, paralleling the fraudulent myth of "The Boy Wonder", a St. Urbain Street alumnus and former friend of Duddy's father, Max. Jerry Dingleman is the boy wonder, a cheap hood who built his fortune on heroin and prostitution, and is fat and crippled in his middle age. Duddy thus also becomes a "somebody", but at the cost of the family love and unity he has so desperately sought, and he pays the price in isolation and degradation.

THE APPRENTICESHIP OF DUDDY KRAVITZ is a troubling film that demonstrates the perversion of the American dream, Canadian-style. If its cinematic technique is undistinguished it is also unobtrusive, and the heavy reliance on location shots and period props helps to establish a sense of place and time. These qualities are essential on-screen, and help to vivify Richler's often scenically sparse and thematically blatant novel. In the film, despite a generally fine level of performance down through the supporting cast, there are flat moments, or times when character becomes easy caricature, and here especially we sense Richler's authorial presence. But THE APPRENTICESHIP OF DUDDY KRAVITZ is ultimately important, for in reflecting Richler's own admitted cultural disaffection, Duddy becomes an ethnic Everyman. Like Sammy Glick, Tommy Wilhelm, and a host of other Jewish protagonists in our recent literature, Duddy is at least in part mythicized from a little Jewish *pusherke* into an eponymous isolate, frantically asserting the success of his self-defeating dream on a desolate and windswept Montreal street corner.

Grandfather Love Is the Best Kind of Love

Marshall Delaney

The relationship between grandfather and grandson is the closest to perfect of all forms of male bonding. I say this as an outsider: I met neither of my grandfathers, nor have I yet become a grandparent. Still, even someone who hasn't experienced it can see the purity of the thing, the flow of love between endlessly hopeful grandfather and endlessly loving grandson—the one, nervously facing death, is eagerly placing his emotional bets on this living hope for the future; the other, nervously facing life, is seizing happily on a plentiful source of available love from the otherwise difficult adult world. No sense of responsibility stands in anyone's way—if anything goes wrong with the child, after all, the grandparent won't be held responsible. There's no sense of manly competition between them, because the difference in age is so great. Equally, there's no Oedipal rivalry, as there is between father and son—even Freud never hinted that we sexually desire our grandmothers. Indeed, such a relationship at its best can produce totally unimpeded love. And it is this love that provides the basis for the charm—let us be obvious about it, the heart-warming charm—of Jan Kadar's and Ted Allan's lovely little film, LIES MY FATHER TOLD ME.

Ted Allan, the Montreal writer, co-author of a Norman Bethune biography (*The Scalpel, The Sword*), originally treated this material as a

Reprinted from *Saturday Night,* November 1975.

short story in 1949. He based it on the largely Jewish world he knew as a child in Montreal in the 1920s, and he peopled it with characters from his own past. He read it on the CBC radio network, where most good Canadian short stories turn up. A few years later he made it into a TV play, and it appeared on CBC television in 1954; it was also, at various times, on TV in Britain and Ireland and on radio in England, Australia, New Zealand, and the United States.

Now, after enormous difficulty, it's a movie. There are a couple of things wrong with the version Kadar and Allan put together in Montreal, and perhaps it's best to get them out of the way early. There's a song by Sol Kaplan under the titles and end-credits, and it's terrible; worse, it's sung in a miserably wispy voice by Kenny Karen. Also, there's a moment in the film when the chicken fat overflows the screen and drenches the audience. That's when the grandfather (Yossi Yadin), in the course of a picnic with his grandson (Jeffrey Lynas), suddenly jumps up and starts singing in Yiddish, accompanied by an off-screen orchestra. At that point the film threatens to turn into a roadshow version of FIDDLER ON THE ROOF; not a happy prospect.

These gaucheries aside, however, LIES MY FATHER TOLD ME is richly enjoyable, indeed one of the best films Canada has produced so far. (And there was Canadian Film Development Corporation money in it, disproving the theory that the CFDC is interested only in violent junk.) Jan Kadar, a Czech director of the greatest distinction—he won the Academy Award in 1965 for THE SHOP ON MAIN STREET—has drawn from the largely Canadian cast some superb performances. Lynas, as the child who loves his junk dealer grandfather and despises his shifty father, beautifully evokes both the shyness and the insufferable cheekiness of a bright six-year-old. Len Birman, as the father who forever prepares get-rich-quick schemes that only make him poorer and more pathetic, demonstrates a talent that's both emphatic and richly nuanced. Marilyn Lightstone, as the boy's adoring mother and the husband's forgiving wife, exudes a glowing warmth that's rare in any film of this period. Barbara Chilcott gives a performance as a mean-minded neighbour that's as authoritative as anything she's ever done. Carole Lazare, as the local whore, charges her character with a sprightliness that's especially refreshing. Ted Allen appears as the neighbourhood Marxist, forever referring difficult questions to the sayings of Lenin. This must have been a peculiar position for him, watching a child playing the boy he once was while himself appearing as the Marxist he later became. He carries it off with great style and charm.

What is most impressive, however, is the care with which Kadar has treated this material. People who gossip about Canadian movies have been telling stories about the years the film was in preparation and its enormous budget problems; but whatever it cost, the result justifies it. The sets are superb, the sense of period close to perfect, the colour always impressive. In certain technical ways (though not, alas, in the soundtrack) this is the best English-Canadian film ever made.

There's no doubt, of course, that it's sentimental. The original story was sentimental (though in different ways) and probably every version since has in some sense played heavily on the emotions of the audience. Kadar doesn't attempt to hide this obvious side of the material: he never plays down the boy's uncritical love of the grandfather, and he makes the grandfather (who was in some earlier versions a rather stern patriarch) into the gentlest sort of immigrant. But at the same time the picture of the father is tough and pitiless. He seems to have grown less likeable as the material has moved through its various versions.

LIES MY FATHER TOLD ME is an account of Europeans and the children of Europeans trying in their different ways—some clumsily, some shrewdly—to adapt to their new surroundings in Canada. The mother does it by turning into a North American tension-managing female, forever making peace between the intransigent males who surround her. The little boy does it by slowly picking up cues from the adults who control him and whom he must eventually manipulate. The father tries to beat North America at its own game by turning into a con man. The grandfather does it best, by remaining himself in spite of all temptations to do otherwise. If the film has a moral, perhaps that's it: the best cultural adaptation is no adaptation. But it doesn't need a moral: the material it presents has a unique richness that makes it emotionally valuable, beyond any cultural lessons that even the most earnest among us can draw from it.

An Account by a Privileged Hostage of Les Ordres: Brault Has Missed His Shot

Pierre Vallières
translated by John Van Burek

LES ORDRES, a film of politics or of fiction? In dealing with events that were real and directly connected with the October Crisis of 1970, was Michel Brault right—indeed, did he have the right—to remain silent about the events that led up to the crisis, be they on the part of the government or on that of the Chenier Cell of the FLQ? Was he justified in

Reprinted from *Cinema Quebec*, vol. 4, no. 2 (December 1974).

ignoring the explosive political debate that surrounded the crisis and which is still going strong, primarily in the form of questions while we wait for more satisfactory answers, and which carry with them a large dose of skepticism vis-à-vis the official explanations, however flimsy, which the political authorities have maintained to this day in the hopes that they can lay the whole thing to rest once and for all? In other words, did he really have the right to forget the fact that the vast majority of people arrested on October 16 were Québécois who were very much politicized and very active.

Even if we do not remain indifferent to the fact of collective powerlessness evoked in Brault's film, we are still unsatisfied. In the past, with regard to THE STATE OF SIEGE, one felt compelled to deplore the absence of any socio-political analysis in a scenario based more on the tradition of the suspense thriller than on any historical reality. With motives quite different from those of Costa Gavras, but with the same consequences, Michel Brault actually contributes to the purging of historical memory, which allows the ruling powers to have yesterday's oppression forgotten so that today's can be organized the more easily.

We all know that one of the greatest weaknesses common to the people of Quebec is their short memory and their fear of following through to the end their analyses of the implications, the causes and the prolongation of political events that condition their lives. In that respect, LES ORDRES calls nothing into question.

On a level of fiction and aesthetics, Brault's film is certainly very beautiful, but at it's première I hardly felt the inclination to cry "masterpiece" that my colleagues did. For the film disappointed me by its obvious wish to silence the essential part of the events from which it draws its raison d'être.

It is not by affirming that LES ORDRES is essentially a film of fiction that I will be convinced that, at least in that respect, it is a major success in our cinema. If it is true that *since* October 1970, the apathy of the Québécois has been better perceived or even affirmed with greater evidence, it is false to pretend that during the crisis, in Montreal, that apathy was not rudely shaken. Moreover, despite the fact that some of the people arrested on 16 October, 1970 and in the days that followed, fell victim to a certain confusion, the majority of "hostages" reacted immediately with a great deal of dignity, pride and courage. It is essential to remember that there were numerous demonstrations in front of the courthouses during the months following the massive arrests: these people were not resigned and comparing, they were enraged (and I'm not only talking about those who were officially connected with the FLQ). Nor must we forget some of the things that were said over the air by ordinary citizens: "the erosion of the public will", as the Hon. Gérard Pelletier would put it, couldn't have been more evident. And finally, we must recall the countless denunciations of the existing system that the crisis provoked, from Montreal to Matane: the mood was not one of domination being accepted as normal, but rather of the desire for radical change. It was not until two years later, at the time of the strike by the Front Commun Intersyndical that the signs of a disquieting return to the general passivity of the Duplessis era reappeared.

Like everyone, Michel Brault is aware of the apolitical attitudes so common in Quebec at the moment, and he certainly does not share in them. But in casting today's political indifference back to the time of the October Crisis, he is not respecting the historical truth and facts upon which he is basing his screenplay. Moreover, by amputating from it the names of James Cross and Pierre Laporte, the politicians, the members of the FLQ and the majority of political victims in the October Crisis, he consciously betrays that truth, of which he is not the owner, but for which he like everyone else is responsible. He betrays it in the name of a Kafkaesque melodrama in which the actors struggle helplessly in utter mystery of their oppression (daily or accidental, it makes no difference).

Due to the capital importance that the October Crisis had, and still has in 1974, on the Québécois' return to a lifeless resignation, a return that all observers have noted, here was the perfect occasion for any cinéaste to put back into question, based on the objective facts and multiple questions that the crisis itself raised, this fatal resignation which if unchecked could constitute in the long run—if not in the short run—the end of a people that has not yet really had the chance to make its place in history, and with it, the end of the "national" cinema which has only barely begun to emerge from the limbo of this endangered race.

Instead of providing the real shock people need these days, LES ORDRES in fact contributes to the eradication from the Québécois' and others' memory, of the machiavellian political power for whom lies, blackmail and the army are instruments inseparable from the necessary maintenance of the people in ignorance and submission.

I can attest personally to the fact that apart from a few exceptions, what Brault shows us is not the way the hostages of October 1970 lived out their imprisonment and its aftermath. The revolt and disgust that was running from one floor to the next at the Parthenais had nothing to do with the sobs of Jean Lapointe, nor with the timid criticisms of Doctor X. Despite the prudence which was very much the rule within those constantly bugged walls, the politicizing of the incarcerated was beyond a doubt. I was able to hold long conversations *out loud* with dozens of these political detainees and I can say in all honesty that the fiction of LES ORDRES does not do justice to the men and women who, in October 1970, payed personally for their "goût du Québec".[1]

I will be answered that indeed the film is fiction and that as such it need not be a flat reflection of historical facts. Quite so. But to that I will answer that any film of fiction which owes its very inspiration to the October Crisis, in turn owes the public a truthful view of that crisis, or else it opens itself to accusations of false representation.

Little matter that Michel Brault's intentions were the best in the world (which I do not doubt for a moment), for me it does not change the fact that his film is politically and morally unacceptable.

If we are right to be so seriously worried about the political indifference that is growing (it is an increase in vacuum) at the heart of the Québécois collectivity, I worry even more at the fact that a cinéaste of Brault's calibre uses this as his standpoint to reduce a major political crisis like the October Crisis to five or six little individual sob stories, and consequently brings along with it a kind of additional justification for the authorities to whom "the people of Quebec are happy with their lot, don't want any trouble, don't want independence, like Papa Trudeau and Little Brother Bourassa", etc... and who fail to understand that the events fully justified the police dragging anyone and everyone out of bed and out of their kitchens.

I do not deny that in 1974 we are absolutely right in taking cognizance of the fact that the people of Quebec have not yet succeeded in rooting fear out of their hearts. But by the same token we should not make believe that in October 1970, at the time of the famous kidnappings, this fear among the population was as manifest as it is today. It was the politicians who, using any means available, worked systematically at reviving it. Alas, they have to a large extent succeeded. The reality of 1974 could justify the impotence expressed by a film like LES ORDRES, but only if used in a screenplay which is founded on that immediate reality, which may be—let us hope so—temporary. But an impotence as hopeless as that presented in Brault's film draws nothing real and nothing lived from the October Crisis to which it refers.

If financing by the CFDC absolutely forced Brault to disguise the essential truths of the Crisis, he would have been better not to have made the film. As it is seen now, in the movie houses of Quebec, LES ORDRES doesn't shake anything or anyone. In fact, it raises fewer questions for its audience than a film like BINGO, which is an openly commercial effort.

René Lévesque was wrong to say that the "how" of the October Crisis was revealed by Brault. No more than the "why", the "how" is not there.

The fiction of LES ORDRES is no more Québécois than it is Libanais or Senegalais. It is closer to the enigmas of Kafka than to the October Crisis in 1970. In other words, if Michel Brault wanted to do a work of the imagination so badly, he was wrong to have dated this fiction October 1970, because he has tried to attach it to the massive arrests of the night of October 16th. Moreover, he has drowned the social and political context of the War Measures Act in a melodrama based on a half-dozen individual dramas, dramas which are momentary, unexplained, and ultimately, anecdotal. He did not know how to choose between fiction and history.

Now it is very difficult to do a film about October 1970 in Quebec without mentioning "the Crisis". In fact, it is probably impossible. Indeed, to attempt such a thing would be an undertaking aimed at mystification. Yet I am the first to admit that "playing with the October Crisis is playing with dynamite". But this is just one more reason for refusing to make believe that the dynamite has gotten soggy by itself, the day when Mr. X and Mrs. Y, in spite of themselves, were handcuffed by the authorities long enough to give them the scare of their lives.

LES ORDRES is a beautiful film in its images and performances, but above all it is a drama totally removed from its causes and its real context. It is a film for the Civil Liberties Union with its overriding interest in mistreated dogs and socially conscious matrons who want someone to feel badly about.

All this is difficult to say to such a respectable and respected compatriot. But why hide it? Michel Brault, cinéaste, took considerable risks in doing a film based on the events of October 1970, not the least of which was that of betraying the historical truth of those events. To try to camouflage the fact that this truth has not been respected, and that this has happened behind the screen of fiction and aestheticism, does not help anyone, neither the Québécois nor the cinema which is supposed to portray them.

Filmmaking West Coast Style: Jack Darcus

Á. Ibrányi-Kiss

Two years ago Jack Darcus was in Toronto with his first two features, GREAT COUPS OF HISTORY and PROXYHAWKS. After making the trek to Mecca (the CBC) and projecting PROXYHAWKS on the film buyer's office door, he was painted a portrait of the Average Canadian Worker who goes home to his TV set and beer and told, "We couldn't do that to the Canadian worker."

This time around, the reaction to WOLF PEN PRINCIPLE was more positive. But as Darcus points out, "I think the reaction is generally more positive because of the CRTC hearings in Ottawa."

At any rate, WOLF PEN PRINCIPLE will be opening in Vancouver shortly and producer Werner Aellen is much more optimistic about its commercial run than he would have had reason to be several years ago.

Jack Darcus is an independent filmmaker from Vancouver. He has three features behind him. All low-budget. All very personal. He has broken every rule in the book, but that has a lot to do with being from the west coast.

Reprinted from *Cinema Canada*, no. 13 (April-May 1974).

Darcus left university in 1963 to pursue painting full-time. He then moved on to stage designing in Ken Livingston's small theatre, the Algonquin, which produced midnight one-act plays; and finally became frustrated by no one taking his desire to direct seriously.

"Larry Kent had made three films by that time out there. The guy was a madman to think he could do what he did, but none of us would be making films in Vancouver if Larry hadn't gotten off his arse and made the first one. He just stood up one day, declared himself a genius, and did it. You can do that in Vancouver. So Larry's approach was very tempting."

At that time Darcus (never having abandoned painting) was doing figurative art—portraits. He met a fantastic lady who eventually became the lead in GREAT COUPS OF HISTORY. "She was an unpaintable portrait. This lady just talked all the time. So I got the idea of doing a film. The Film Society at UBC had a bunch of equipment, they had shot a couple of Kent's films, and wanted to do another film but didn't have the subject matter. By then, Morrie Ruvinsky started a film out there. Morrie was another of those types, he had taken on a tremendously lonely thing. He was the only one doing it. He got his film done and when he finished I had managed to get the Film Society to pay for half my film, sold some paintings, raised around $1,000 and started this film, not knowing what I was getting into."

What he was getting into was making a $6,500 feature film. Impossible? He didn't think so then, and still doesn't.

"It's not unusual in Montreal. When Jean-Pierre Lefebvre made Q-BEC MY LOVE for $24,000 (half cash and half in deferments) nobody screamed and said You can't do that! If you suggest in English Canada that you can make a feature film on a $24,000 budget they say you're crazy, it just can't be done. Well, it's being done in Montreal by other filmmakers as well. There's no point in trying to compete with JESUS CHRIST SUPERSTAR—it costs too much. We need to develop an indigenous cinema here and all we can hope for is to be rough and fresh."

GREAT COUPS was shot in six weeks, two-and-a-half full-time and the rest on weekends. Nobody was paid, everybody was learning on-the-job. "That was the way it was done in Vancouver. Larry did it, Morrie did it. It was the only way of making a film!"

Darcus laughs now thinking of it. Fortunately, he had an experienced cameraman who became his teacher-on-the-set, Terry Hudson. "We just started, and Terry taught me the whole thing. He had shot all of Morrie's films. He said he would teach me the ABC's. We got it shot, and I quickly picked up on what had to be done. Then I was given the basics of editing, taught how to use a hot splicer, and left alone for eight months in a room."

When he came out he had his first feature, and became "Odeon's token filmmaker". It seems the people from Odeon had attended a screening and agreed to run COUPS for a week—longer if it made $2,000 by Sunday night. As soon as the film opened, Vancouver got hit by a newspaper strike, wiping out all publicity. Despite that serious setback, COUPS was only $40 under by Sunday. What's more—it made $3,000 by Wednesday night. Too bad. It was already decided that it would be pulled... so it goes. But Darcus has no bitterness about that: "It was nice. Looking back on it, there are elements of naiveté that are simply amazing. But hell, I wouldn't change much if I had to do it again, and I hope I would do it as well."

In the meantime, Darcus was staying alive by teaching painting, but he was already hooked on cinema. "I liked the process a lot because I like working with people. Painting is a very lonely scene, whereas film—being part of this group of maniacs—was tremendous!"

His second feature, PROXYHAWKS, also came about in a very unorthodox way. One of his art students, hearing about the difficulties he was having raising money for the next film, approached him to say she had $1,000. Darcus was grateful, but refused. However, after three more futile weeks and an initial rejection from the CFDC he called her up asking, "Did you mean it?" PROXYHAWKS was started with $1,000 cash and a lab's willingness to extend credit.

"PROXYHAWKS cost me $16,000. I didn't pay wages but if you add $10,000 to the film so people could have been paid $1,000 each for a couple of months work—it would still have come out cheaply."

The drive to keep making films is obviously very powerful. But does he intend to keep working that way? And to what end?

"There are a lot of directors with a great roster of films behind them but very few who have built a body of work reflecting their point of view. I've expected to do that—to grow and expand and take on form. In North America, that is expected of every other art form—why not film? Filmmakers in Vancouver were always into developing their own subject matter—Peter Bryant, Tom Braidwood, Kirk Tougas, Al Razutis, David Rimmer. Either they're developing truly experimental films like Rimmer, or dramatic subject matter like myself and Peter Bryant. But people like us are considered freaks by the old pros who have been making commercials for twenty years."

A great believer in low-budget films for both artistic and economic reasons, Darcus is nonetheless sympathetic towards the CFDC—even though they've been pushing "commercial" very strongly. "They're a bank. I wouldn't want to trade places with them. All they can talk about on their balance sheet in the yearly report is how much they invested versus how much they got back. When the CFDC was handing out $7,500 grants they were emphasizing that it be spent towards developing features. A great conservative pressure was put on young filmmakers to make a short, show it to a distributor and perhaps get a feature going on that basis. That impetus was conservative because it held them down to making something very glossy—and for $7,000 you can do a feature! If you're working with friends and editing yourself you can do something tremendously experimental and exciting. All this was cut off on those grants. I'm quite sure they're relieved that the Canada Council is taking over film grants. It gets them off that awful hook of having to nurture young ambitious talent while still being a bank.

"I think the Canada Council will be more open to that kind of approach to filmmaking. What is really necessary is for young directors to think in terms of $20,000 and $30,000 films. Canada Council leaves things more open—I can go out and make something brilliant or fall flat on my arse—it's my own thing to do. I can grow that way. I've been hammering at this since I came out here two years ago with COUPS and PROXYHAWKS."

As an example of what was wrong with the old system, Darcus pointed to Sylvia Spring, whose CFDC short for MADELEINE IS was beautiful. But then she was immediately pushed to making a $100,000 feature under heavy pressure and, he feels, she wasn't ready for that. "What they should have done is given her $20,000 to do another film. To buy time. She was done a bit of a disservice. She had far greater potential than she was allowed to grow into."

Wouldn't more low-budget features emphasize the great dichotomy between "art" and "commercial" filmmaking? Darcus doesn't think so. "My ideal is to make a film that all kinds of people will like. I have to feel that I'm growing from subject to subject. That's pure self-indulgence. That's my reason for staying in it. Offer me a year of directing CBC dramas and I'll say no. On the other hand, I realize I'm learning my craft. I have to learn to be entertaining while I do my act. That's where there's a meeting point between commercial directors and myself. Otherwise, we'd break into two camps—the purists on one side versus the vicious capitalists on the other. More analysis has to be done to show that there is a hell of a meeting point between the two."

What compromise wouldn't he make? "I don't wish to produce pure pablum, placebos designed to relieve people of their frustrations, get them back on the job the next day and not enrich their world one bit. You can make a work that's intelligent and also entertaining. That's the apprenticeship I'm serving."

With this approach in mind, Darcus made his third feature for $100,000—WOLF PEN PRINCIPLE. In many ways, it has far more commercial appeal than either of his first two films. For one thing, he was working with Vladimir Valenta, internationally acclaimed actor from CLOSELY WATCHED TRAINS. Months after shooting, that experience still gets Darcus ebulliantly animated.

"Vladimir is incredible. He does things like—for continuity—if he blinks in the middle of a speech, he'll do it the same way for every take. He never misses. An editor's delight—you can cut any place you want! He could always find his light and work with it. He's an old pro film actor, and he was trained as a film actor."

Lawrence Brown, the other lead in WOLF PEN PRINCIPLE, came from the complete opposite pool of talent. He's a high school student from Nanaimo who has acted in only one play before, but his audition floored everyone and he was hired immediately. "Vladimir would take Lawrence aside between takes. He was always showing him things. It was a beautiful teaching process. Lawrence did work for Daryl Duke after that, but what he needs is to go to drama school after graduation and get some bloody craft. He's already on the level of a lot of the other young actors out there, but I hope he does it. He's certainly got the stuff."

WOLF PEN PRINCIPLE deals with a middle-aged theatre manager and a young Indian who both have a fascination for the arctic wolves in the zoo. For very different personal reasons, they conspire to free the wolves, and the film follows their conspiracy and its aftermath. Darcus came by the story while he was working for Stanley Park Zoo treating injured birds of prey (the subject matter, in part, of PROXYHAWKS). He hates zoos. He sees them as concentration camps.

"I used to go down to the zoo and get really angry at seeing the six arctic wolves. In the back of my mind I was searching for a subject, and all of a sudden it just came to me. The fundamental thing about those wolves is that they've become inept. If you let them out, they'd die. They desperately need their cage. If I could, I'd take those wolves and put them in a halfway house in the Yukon and let them adapt back to nature—they have a halfway house for orangutangs in Borneo. Of course the wolves in the zoo were just a nice metaphor for a lot of people. I was getting mad out of self-pity. I was bemoaning their loss of potential, but it was bullshit."

That theme was part of what Darcus was dealing with. His other major concern was with the clash between two cultures—those of the white man and the Indian. "Indian artists are still working according to their traditions but they've lost their connection to what they're doing. When they carve a wolf-mask, it means no more to them than the radio does. It's an object. There's a whole confrontation between cultures that has been lost." Without overly romanticizing the lost culture of the Indian people, Darcus does feel it's a terrible loss.

"The government has invested around $8 million building great shrines for that art out there. And it just sits there mute. I'm glad they're doing it, but nobody has tackled that yet. What is it? Where do the two cultures part ways? In WOLF PEN I hint at it without presuming to be intelligent. I would never pretend to be over on the other side. For me to imagine living in a world where totem poles are an everyday fact of life is almost impossible. All I can do is write in a rather ignorant, white way. Essentially, I'm a comic character and that will probably be my contribution in my next film when I try to tackle this problem."

What sparked off the basic thread of WOLF PEN was meeting an anthropologist who had worked with Indians in northern B.C. for two years and had witnessed an occurrence in which an old woman from the Wolf Clan died and the wolves came around the village and howled all night. As Darcus says, "It's a charming idea and it also doesn't disturb our reality when we walk down the street. We're still connected to our Anglo-Saxon or Northern European-based world. It's that connection which should be shaken a little bit more. As I say, there's a body of subject matter there that is just immense."

Jack Darcus would like to see Vancouver filmmakers start working more on indigenous material. With the growing consciousness on the west coast, this might become possible. "It's like inventing typewriters in Greenland not knowing they exist in the rest of the world and then finding out that everything is computerized—the Canadian film industry has a little bit of that. Where there is some fresh vital energy you also have a very politicized scene, like you have in Montreal. But in English Canada this doesn't exist. If we saw ourselves in relation to Americans as Québécois see themselves in relation to English Canada—we would have all kinds of people standing up and declaring themselves."

As for the Pacific Filmmakers' Co-op, he's been working on getting WOLF PEN on the road, and has had contact only via the telephone. But he's definitely getting involved, "although I think there is a dangerous direction toward founding a service agency that's going to provide equipment and everything else. I'm afraid of toy shops. Unless the emphasis is towards creating scripts, arguing about them, growing a subject matter which is indigenous—it could fall apart. I'm always driving toward opening up people's subject matter—that's the only thing that sustains people in film. That will be my push. There is a lot of possibility in the co-op."

Darcus is presently surviving on a Canada Council grant. As for the future, things look pretty good. "I've got a one-man show touring B.C. and the Yukon now, with paintings and my films. I've got two money scripts I'm almost finished with and a third one I want to make for $7,000 or $8,000. Ten thousand maximum. But I could never sell it to a producer." This film concerns two aging stars of porno films who wind up staying after a shoot is completed and spending a night together. Darcus figures he can keep costs down by shooting on basically one location, an abandoned set, and with only two characters the film should stay simple.

Besides, for the first time in six years, Jack Darcus is out of debt!

Fear and Loathing to Order

John Hofsess

Most countries with busy, profitable film industries produce two distinctly different kinds of movies: there is art or "high culture" for critics, academics and historians of "the cinema"; and there is schlock or "low culture" for "the people"—the ones who actually *pay* to see movies.

A few well-known examples of "low culture" are the CARRY ON movies from Britain (twenty-one of them since 1958) and the Hammer horror films, with those stalwart actors Peter Cushing and Christopher Lee; spaghetti westerns from Italy, erotica from Sweden and Denmark, and the GODZILLA flicks from Japan. Most of these films are low-budget quickies. They entertain many and edify no one.

In Canada as well—though most of the $25 million of government funds invested in feature films since 1967 has gone into high-minded projects that haven't earned a cent—schlock movies have emerged as the most consistently popular kind of film that we produce. Last November, the showbusiness weekly *Variety* published a special issue devoted to Canadian films, and produced the box-office figures for the top ten money-makers in French and English. The French list was led by "skin flicks"—DEUX FEMMES EN OR, L'INVITATION and VALERIE, each of which earned between $1.5-and $2.5 million in "domestic rentals", while the English list was composed almost entirely of the most critically lambasted films that Canadian companies have released—DEATH WEEKEND, BLACK CHRISTMAS, SHIVERS, MY PLEASURE IS MY BUSINESS, RECOMMENDATION FOR MERCY, SHADOW OF THE HAWK, FACE-OFF. The remaining three films—PAPERBACK HERO, LIES MY FATHER TOLD ME and THE APPRENTICESHIP OF DUDDY KRAVITZ—received either mixed reviews, or, as with KRAVITZ, generally favourable ones, but of the total $8.9 million that the top ten English-soundtrack films were reported to have earned in Canada, $5.7 million was earned by schlock items. And of all these films it was SHIVERS—written and directed by thirty-three-year-old Toronto filmmaker David Cronenberg, for $185,000 of government money in 1975—that had the biggest profit-ratio. The film has grossed an estimated $3 million internationally, for SHIVERS has played in thirty-three countries, in fourteen languages. The film had no "stars" to speak of. No KING KONG hype. It succeeded simply by word-of-mouth and widespread public appeal.

Cronenberg has just completed another film in the horror genre —RABID, with Marilyn Chambers (once a famous model for Ivory Snow, but she drifted into porno-flicks), to be released this spring, after what is expected to be a highly successful sales pitch at the 1977 Cannes Film

Reprinted from *The Canadian*, February 26, 1977.

Festival (the British rights were sold, on the basis of "rushes", two weeks into the shooting—nothing unusual for a Hollywood film but highly unusual for a Canadian one). If RABID is also a hit, Cronenberg will have the best track record of any English-Canadian director. "I'll make one claim about myself," Cronenberg says. "I think that my ideas—my obsessions, if you will—have more in common with the tastes and interests of a majority of filmgoers than the standards of any film critic I know. The most valuable thing I've learned from my producers—John Dunning, Andre Link and Ivan Reitman—is that, first and foremost, film is showbusiness. They've found, for example, that it is necessary to make a film that is adaptable to the whims of censors—some excise gory scenes, others snip away at the sex. So we shoot a master version, which we prefer for the most liberal countries, but we also have to know exactly where it will be cut in certain markets so that continuity won't be destroyed. The film is basically the same, like a Cardin suit you buy 'off the rack', but tailored for individual markets."

Cronenberg represents a school of Canadian filmmaking that few people have heard of: he has no heart-rending struggle to describe in his efforts to make the Great Canadian Movie; he doesn't spend his time arguing about the need for tax rebates or quota systems to protect our "fledgling industry"; he just wants to get on with the exciting, and profitable, job of making movies that turn people on—by grossing them out.

Schlock is a Yiddish term for goods that are cheap, trashy, of inferior quality. Compared with *King Lear*, GONE WITH THE WIND is schlock. But the customary use of the term, when applied to cultural "goods" such as movies, is confined to those films that are made on a low budget, have no aspiration except to shock, frighten, titillate or mindlessly entertain, and turn a fast buck in the process. Cronenberg adds a further refinement to the word. "Schlock isn't synonymous with 'bad' movies," he says. "A bad movie is one that *fails* in some obvious way—it is miscast, it is boring, it is dishonest, or whatever. A schlock film, by contrast, may aim low, but it can succeed on its own terms."

To put it another way—schlock films aim straight for the id, which may be why critics with anxious super-egos disapprove of them. They deal with visceral matters, and play upon a wide range of fears and feelings of disgust that people normally have under tight control. There are no "monsters" in Cronenberg's films—all of the horror stems from demonic exaggerations of bodily processes. In SHIVERS, for example, he invents a new venereal disease that spreads like a brushfire through a Montreal high-rise apartment complex. As nature takes its course, each "victim" goes through an incubation period of housing a "parasite" that takes several weeks to reach maturity, and that, finally, having worked its way up through the digestive system, is "born" by making the victim retch, whereupon the parasite assumes an independent life of its own—a bloody, slimey, lumpen-whatzit, capable of all sorts of nasty surprises.

Few horror movies have ever lost money for their producers. Except in rare instances where the budget was excessive and the central idea too frail, as in Roman Polanski's recent film THE TENANT, or the singular case of Tod Browning's FREAKS (which provoked such public outrage when it was released in 1932 that MGM withdrew it from general distribution for thirty years), horror films have had one of the most dependable markets of any movie genre. There are two particular periods, however—the early 1930s and the present—when public interest in horror films has peaked, and made them especially profitable. In recent years THE EXORCIST, THE OMEN, CARRIE and others of diabolical ilk, have been among the top-grossing films, while JAWS set a historic box-office record for films of any kind. Similarly, it was between the years 1930 and '35, in another period of widespread economic instability and growing apprehensiveness about the future, that such "horror classics" (as they are now called, though they were called quite different names in their day) as FRANKENSTEIN with Boris Karloff, DRACULA with Bela Lugosi, DR. JEKYLL AND MR. HYDE, Carl Dreyer's VAMPYR, THE BLACK CAT, the original version of KING KONG and BRIDE OF FRANKENSTEIN, among others, were released and became huge successes throughout the world.

Horror movies, according to Cronenberg, have their roots in such "psychologically revealing fairy tales as *Beauty and the Beast* and *Little Red Riding-Hood*. Whatever seems to be going on at the conscious level is relatively unimportant; the real story is going on underneath. And like dreams, or fairy tales, their impact depends mainly upon their psychological content, which is why, unlike most other kinds of movies, a bigger budget, a more professional cast, more expensive sets and so on do not necessarily make a horror film any better or more successful. Grimm's fairy tales would not work any better if they were written by James Joyce; they would probably work less well, in fact, weighted down with all sorts of irrelevant aesthetic and technical considerations. What matters most in a horror film is simply—do the creators of it have the piercing insight to get under people's skin and make their flesh crawl?

"Personally, I find all films about devil worship and the supernatural to be silly—and therefore not really frightening," he says, "and also, unlike a lot of the horror films made in the 1950s, such as THE THING, THE INCREDIBLE SHRINKING MAN, and so on—terrific films, by the way—there is no fear or hatred of modern science running through my stories. In my own work I never stray far from real possibilities—both SHIVERS and RABID are about contagious physical diseases and everyone in the audience knows that *something* like what they are seeing on the screen could happen to them, and the likelihood of it happening is of much higher probability than the world being visited by Satan's offspring or overrun by giant frogs."

In RABID, Cronenberg gets the plague rolling through a motorcycle accident in the opening minutes of the film. The rider (Frank Moore) isn't badly injured, but his girlfriend (Marilyn Chambers) requires extensive abdominal surgery, including a skin graft, which is depicted with graphic gusto. What happens next—as in SHIVERS, when it turned out that the new strain of VD produced larger and more malignant organisms than usual—is the Cronenberg touch, the absurdist leap in logic. Having read in medical journals about "morphogenetic field theory" he began toying with the possibilities for horrible mishaps. His Dr. Keloid is a brilliant specialist in "neutral field tissue grafting", but even a dedicated doctor who never overcharges the government health-insurance scheme can make fatal errors. He sews up his beautiful patient, with her somewhat impaired digestive system surrounded by "neutralized tissue", hoping that the tissue will "read" the appropriate genetic code and reproduce a new set of internal organs. Well someday maybe, but not today.

Cronenberg's fancy, at this point, sinks deeper into dark dreams. What the tissue "reads", he postulates, is that the patient, who has been kept alive on plasma because of her inability to digest food, needs a steady supply of fresh blood. Instead of recreating the organs required to digest a complex diet, the new tissue develops a proboscis—an elongated feeding organ for sucking blood—that just happens to grow out of the woman's armpit.

"Vampire fangs have been done to death," Cronenberg says cheerfully. "I felt the need for something new. Besides, it's amazing just how many Freudian connotations can be found with this retractable *thing* in an armpit." (I didn't ask him to spell them out.) The thing itself was designed by a special effects makeup artist in Hollywood, Joe Blassco, who made several of them in various sizes. As to how it works—let's just say that few survive the friendly embraces of Marilyn Chambers in this movie, and to make matters worse, like certain insects (MOSQUITO was the original title of the film), she carries a disease fatal to ordinary humans, hence the plague that spreads through Montreal like a new form of the Black Death.

"Horror films—like dreams—are often in 'bad taste'," Cronenberg says, "or so they appear, when judged by a censorious mind. But that in no way denies their validity, even their necessity, for we all need periodic releases from the tyranny of 'good taste'. The trick in making a successful horror film is to give the audience a kick, a shock, a twist it's never had before, but one can't get too far out or the audience will end up being alienated."

Cronenberg would never make a porno film, for example, even though he concedes that the ultimate horror film might have sexually explicit material in it. "But I'll never make that film," he says, "partly because I don't see any point to making films that can only be shown, as far as I know, in about eight or ten U.S. cities, and a few European outlets; but mainly because my imagination doesn't work that way.

"I'm a strong believer in people doing what they *have* to do. I make horror films because I really enjoy them. There are many directors who, if they made films like SHIVERS and RABID, would be slumming, and their condescending and cynical attitude would show up on the screen."

In 1966, a year before his graduation from the University of Toronto with a BA in English literature, Cronenberg began his present career by writing and directing two short films, TRANSFER and FROM THE DRAIN, that were widely shown in Canada along with other underground and student films fashionable at the time. Three years later, he produced his first feature, STEREO (in 35mm, black-and-white) and another feature the following year, CRIMES OF THE FUTURE (in colour). They had running times of about sixty-five minutes each (too short for theatrical distribution, too long for most television slots) and cost, together, around $30,000. Both films were science-fiction stories of an emotionally stoic nature, and while they got good reviews ("An interesting first", Montreal *Gazette*; "Fresh and unconventional", Montreal *Star*; "A very special film, an exceptionally elegant dream", Robert Fulford, *Saturday Night*), they earned in film rentals "slightly less than $1,000".

At that stage of his career, Cronenberg was following a classic syndrome of the Canadian film director of the 1960s—making "personal" films that only a small band of hardy souls wanted to see, and watching his lab bills and production debts mount steadily. At the same time he got married and began raising a family (a daughter, Cassandra, now five). Then, in 1973, he teamed up with producer Ivan Reitman, whose investments ranged from "The Magic Show" with Doug Henning, currently entering its second year on Broadway, to producing films such as CANNIBAL GIRLS. The result of their collaboration was SHIVERS—and even before the film opened anywhere, the producers had sold foreign rights to so many countries that a full return on its production costs was guaranteed. The film also won the Grand Prix at the International Festival of Horror and Fantasy Films, in Sitges, Spain, an annual event for science-fiction and horror movies from around the world.

And now, with RABID, the largest international distributor of schlock films, American International Pictures, has expressed interest in acquiring the U.S. rights, an arrangement that would make all the additional deals to be made in May, at the Cannes Film Festival, "icing on the cake".

"When I was poor and esoteric, I was praised by the critics," Cronenberg says. "Now that I'm making films that are a popular success, I'm panned or cast aside. There's a moral in there somewhere." (At the 1975 Canadian Film Awards, SHIVERS wasn't even permitted to be shown, let alone recognized as an entry.) To Cronenberg, it's all very well to talk about masterpieces and great works of cinematic art but the people who pay for the indulgences and aspirations of the cognoscenti are none other than the much-maligned inventors of schlock, shmaltz, kitsch, smut and trash—cultural blue-collar workers like himself. In matters of culture, to say nothing of engineering, it always pays to remember that it's the broad base of a pyramid that supports the peak.

Wielandism: A Personal Style in Full Bloom

Marshall Delaney

For something like two decades, Joyce Wieland—the Toronto painter, filmmaker, quiltmaker, and lay ecologist—has been creating an individual sensibility and then displaying it, piece by piece, in the various art forms that have suited her purposes. In THE FAR SHORE, her feature film, she articulates that sensibility in detail for the first time. Wieland's spirit has been touched by Pop Art and by the films of what used to be called the New American Underground, but Wielandism—which is how I now think of it—is neither an offshoot of New York painting nor a cul-de-sac of private emotions and impulses. It's a full-blown personal aesthetic, with its own special combination of rules and procedures. Some of its qualities have become evident over the years:

(1) Innocence: Wielandism doggedly refuses to be corrupted, and if necessary it avoids any issue that might force it into compromise or sophistication. Her famous show at the National Gallery in 1971, True Patriot Love, was an expression of innocent nationalism, a nationalism stripped of ambiguities and ironics. The same directness pervades THE FAR SHORE and makes it the most obvious piece of Anglo-Canadian nationalism so far committed to film.

(2) Naive and sentimental charm: From the beginning, Wielandism has equalled sentimentality, and the story line in THE FAR SHORE carries her to new heights of unabashed sentimentality.

(3) Sexuality: In Wielandism, sex is at once romantic and vulgar. In her paintings of fifteen years ago, flowers miraculously turned into penises in a very special artistic trade-off, each object giving to the other some of its most obvious qualities. In THE FAR SHORE the two lovers come together for the first time in a watery northern paradise, but they grunt and groan like animals or porn stars. It's the contradiction that clearly fascinates Wieland and it's the contradiction that she wants to convey in her art.

(4) Melancholy romanticism: A decade ago, Wieland was making little tableau boxes about airplane deaths and paintings about ships sinking. In these objects an air of death was combined with a sickly sweetness, as in a Mediterranean funeral. The same elements occur in the climax of THE FAR SHORE—the two deaths that end the movie are "tragic", so far as the story goes; but, being staged in the northern waters, they are also, in their way, idyllic.

(5) Blantant symbolism: In Wielandism, the subject is distant from

Reprinted from *Saturday Night*, May 1976.

both artist and audience, and at the same time charged with meaning, by its power as a symbol. In her short witty film, RAT LIFE AND DIET IN NORTH AMERICA (1968), the rats "stood for" draft dodgers and ecologists, not in some vague and shifting sense (as with most narrative art) but in the most concrete and open way. In the same sense, everyone in THE FAR SHORE "stands for" something in Wieland's world-view: Anglo-Canadian Rigidity, French-Canadian Sensitivity, Art, Love, he North, etc.

(6) Parody: In Wielandism, parody marches hand in hand with "serious" narrative. Just as her paintings of the 1950s and 1960s were at the same time honest statements and oblique put-ons, so THE FAR SHORE at its climax contains elements of parody—the music score, for instance, sounds during the chase scene like a piano in a silent cinema. In this way Wieland contradicts her own naiveté by introducing parodic elements that are as obvious as the storyline itself.

(7) Ecology and art: In Wielandism there's an equation between art and the natural, unspoiled world. This cropped up in her 1960s films and her National Gallery show, but THE FAR SHORE articulates it clearly for the first time. Tom, the artist, not only lives in but is a part of the Group of Seven wilderness that he paints. Ross, the rich mining engineer from Toronto, is cool to art and anxious to exploit rather than love the northern woods. There's another equation, related to ecology but involving feminist concerns. Wieland seems to see women as a part of nature and men as the spoilers of that nature: those who rape the land also rape the women.

In 1919, a Toronto engineer, Ross (Lawrence Benedict) is doing some work in a small Quebec town. There he meets a pianist, Eulalie (Celine Lomez). He falls in love and asks her to marry him. He proposes by giving a note to a little girl, her niece. Eulalie accepts, also through the niece. The scene is delightful, but it underscores the lack of intimacy between the two of them. Eulalie is escaping something; Ross is possessing something. They marry and he takes her home to Rosedale.

Back in stiff, deadly Toronto, Eulalie is a stranger, and Ross emphasizes her strangeness. "Remember one thing," he tells her, "it may seem to you that you're in with a bunch of foreigners, but really you're the foreigner." She despises his drunken friend Cluny (Sean McCann), and after a while she realizes she doesn't much like Ross, either. And he finds her unsatisfactory: "You're always moping around from room to room, playing that gloomy stuff (it's Debussy) on the piano. It's not healthy.... You think too much."

Ross has a friend, Tom (Frank Moore), based roughly on Tom Thomson. Ross isn't at all convinced of his friend's ability as an artist, and later, when an art dealer rejects Tom, Ross more or less drops him. The dealer, dismissing Tom, says: "He showed me twenty-seven paintings—there wasn't a single cow in any of them." The reference is to the belief, three or four revolutions ago, that only Dutch painters of cows, and Canadians who imitated them, were acceptable to the rich of Toronto. That was the world against which the Group of Seven made its revolution and earned its place as the one enduring myth of modern Canadian culture. Wieland shrewdly attaches that myth—the painters who reacted boldly to our own landscape rather than aping European mannerisms—to her own narrative. At one point Eulalie and Tom are talking:

Eulalie: "Will you paint me?"
Tom: "I can't."
Eulalie: "If I were a tree?"
Tom: "If you were a tree I might have a shot at it."

There speaks a Canadian painter.

Tom also expresses the ecological concerns of Wieland. Ross wants Tom to serve as guide for a silver-prospecting expedition in the woods, but Tom explains that he never does that: he hates silver mining because it makes the land look like the Western Front after the World War. "Ross," he says, "you're rich enough. Leave the land alone." Eulalie naturally sympathizes with this view: she's the sort of woman who hates business but enjoys living off the proceeds of it.

In the end Tom and Eulalie must come together, and death must be the result. The plot proceeds with the force of some ancient myth—or, rather a collection of ancient myths.

At almost any moment during the running time of THE FAR SHORE, the audience must react on at least three levels.

First, there's a response of pleasure and admiration to the film's visual qualities. Wieland and her production designer, Ann Pritchard, have put together a facsimile of Toronto interiors, circa 1919, that's both splendidly evocative and altogether convincing. Richard Leiterman, the cinematographer, has caught Wieland's images on film with exquisite care.

Second, there's our reaction to the heavy freight of symbolic conflict—art versus commerce, Quebec versus Ontario, nature versus exploitation—which makes THE FAR SHORE a public statement as well as a narrative film. Some audiences may find it hard to digest: I found it suggestive and moving.

Finally, there's our reaction to the characters themselves and the actors playing them. Here Wieland's touch is uneven and sometimes forced. Her characters are too often seen as symbols rather than human facts. There are moments when she moves beyond her arguments and mythology and achieves something miraculously tender—as when Tom and Eulalie, falling in love in his cabin, speak to each other by holding a magnifying glass to their faces and moving their lips silently. But often the characters seem too big for the screen—the bumptious Sean McCann character pushes the movie off balance whenever he appears. There are moments, too, when Wieland seems to forget the audience and makes us endure lengthy scenes that task our patience.

Still, THE FAR SHORE has energy, ambition, vision and a marvellously confident sense of itself. A notable accomplishment, and a triumph of Wielandism.

IV

EXPERIMENTAL FILMMAKING

True Patriot Love:

The Films of Joyce Wieland

Regina Cornwell

Joyce Wieland's films elude easy categorization. The body of work as a whole is varied—there are films of a formal nature, and others which are less so. Several are political, concerned with technology, ecology, and her native land, Canada. Her films are informed by her involvement in other, more directly tactile art forms—painting, drawing, construction—and in crafts such as quilting. She makes padded wall hangings, pillowed quilts, and embroidery. There is an evident concern with textures and/or colours and their relationships within the frame and within the shaping of each film as a whole. There is, moreover, a cross-fertilization process at work between film and the other art forms in which she works. For instance, in HAND TINTING, she used fabric dyes to individually colour sections of the film, and the perforations which appear in the segments of tinted leader between shots and scenes were made with her quilting needles. While Wieland's use of titling and subtitling first came from her early work in commercial animation, and appears in four of her personal films to date, she has also incorporated it into her drawing, painting, and quilting. In fact, while making the film LA RAISON AVANT LA PASSION, she did three other related art works, a "Reason Over Passion" etching and a pair of quilts with large stuffed letters, one bearing the inscription in French and the other in English.

Since 1967, Wieland has centred more and more of her artistic energies in film. In considering her work from this period, those short films of a more formal nature—SAILBOAT, 1933, DRIPPING WATER and HAND TINTING—will be examined first. Chronologically, SAILBOAT (1967-8) is the earliest of these. In a series of shots a sailboat is seen moving across the screen from left to right. The title is superimposed on the screen for the duration of the film. Its sound consists of waves mixed with an airplane engine and occasional voices. None of the shots is repeated, but the same boats recur because Wieland carefully anticipated them with her camera by moving down the shore to await their re-entry into the frame. A number of the shots are animated, as when a boat appears to pop back from the right to the centre and off right again. Several other small things occur to disrupt expectancies and make the viewer attend to the images more carefully. As the last two boats begin to fade into the horizon, they seem, at the same time, to be absorbed by the more pronounced film grain in these very light shots. This and other instances in SAILBOAT stress film's dual nature, on the one hand, presenting

Reprinted from *Artforum*, vol. 10, no. 1 (September 1971).

images, while at the same time breaking through the illusions to expose the film material itself. And, as a further example, even while attending to the image, one is forced to note the "presence" of the boats somewhere off-frame, and thus also to note the frame itself, delimiting the image. And the flat letters of the title contrast sharply with the illusory images over which they are superimposed.

While the superimposed title in SAILBOAT literalizes itself through the images, the title 1933 (1967-8) does nothing of the kind. Wieland commented that one day after shooting she returned home with about thirty feet of film remaining in her camera and proceeded to empty it by filming the street scene below. She explains in notes: "When editing then what I considered the real footage, I kept coming across the small piece of film of the street. Finally I junked the 'real' film for the accidental footage of the street. It was a beautiful piece of blue street.... So I made the right number of prints of it plus fogged ends." The street scene with the white streaked end is loop-printed ten times, and 1933 appears systematically on the street scene for only the first, fourth, seventh, and tenth loops. Wieland says of her choice of the name: " ... a title that causes more questions than the film has answers". And later, that it "makes you think of a film's beginning, but, this is the film". While the meaning of the title, 1933, is enigmatic and has no real and ostensible relationship to the film's street scene and white streaked section, in its systematic use as subtitle, it becomes an image incorporated into the film. It is not the title of a longer work, but an integral part of the work.

And while the title remains unexplained, so does the brief loop action of the street in fast motion, slowing down for a moment and then resuming its speed. It is merely a fragment of incomplete action, moving in and out of and around the frame. Each time something else is perceived. Not only is the street footage seen over and over, but it is seen in unreal time. And its illusory three-dimensionality is sharply contrasted with the flatness of the white section. Even more markedly than in SAILBOAT, all of these factors become, to use filmmaker Ken Jacobs's term, "illusion-defeating devices", which call attention to the strip of film as film. And the white dominated sections incorporated into the film assert themselves as valid images, equal to the street scenes.

Wieland's DRIPPING WATER (1969) was conceived by her and directed with her husband, artist and filmmaker Michael Snow. The idea came from a tape made by Snow of dripping water and street sounds, and this tape accompanies the film image. A section of the dish into which the water is seen dripping is off screen, and is apparently the source of the water's escape, for the water level in the dish remains the same throughout the film. The off-screen activity and the fixed camera, never moving to reveal the source of the water nor its escape, nor the source of street noises heard on the sound track, serve to emphasize the film frame. One becomes acutely aware of these presences somewhere beyond the perimeters of the frame. The irregularity of the dripping causes curious patterns to form which, at certain rhythms, look like oscillating grains of film emulsion, reminding one again of the film material itself. The sound of the water is at times synchronous and other times asynchronous with the visual drip, and this vacillation draws the viewer's attention more closely to the image, heightening the complexity of the experience.

In HAND TINTING (1967-8) poor young white and black women in an "education centre" dance, swim, and observe each other's recreation. For this work, Wieland used black-and-white outtakes from a Job Corps Project on which she worked as a camerawoman in 1965-6, and as described earlier, hand tinted the footage with fabric dyes. Various shots are repeated in different tints. Yellows, reds, blues, violets and greens dominate. As in 1933, no action is completed and every action is fragmented. Often movements seem frustrated because of the repetitions and the occasional alterations in camera speed. The abstractions created by the medium shots and close-ups, by the repeated shots, and by the tinting, often streaked and uneven as if tie-dyed, disorient the viewer. Moreover, the film's silence underscores the strange and sad setting. While creating a series of single and group portraits of the young women, Wieland at the same time allows the permutations to protrude upon the images. The short repetitions, the tints and their irregularities, the added tinted sections between shots and scenes with their occasional perforations, the film grain which at times becomes pronounced, and the fleeting segments of other unrelated footage—the very things which break through the illusions, paradoxically strengthen the work both as portrait and as film object.

CATFOOD and RAT LIFE AND DIET IN NORTH AMERICA, both made in 1968, have as their titles suggest, animals as subjects. Less concerned with film's dual potential for producing tactile illusions and at the same time breaking through these illusions and pointing to the materials of film, as in the works discussed above, these films concentrate on the images, highlighted through colour and texture. In CATFOOD, a large, sensuous and relaxed cat approaches one fish at a time and begins to eat, usually starting at the fish's tail. Soft fur and whiskers are contrasted with firm and scaled silver blue and silver green bodies. There is a curious impression of displacement created by the cat eating the dead fish on a white tablecloth, accompanied by the sounds of the sea. As the filmmaker herself describes it, it is as if the cat were in a box, "enclosed with the sound of the sea". The sound, because it is present throughout the film, and although it is spatially displaced, enforces the feeling of continuity in time. And the use of close-ups and medium shots on the cat and his eating habits concentrates it even further.

In notes for RAT LIFE AND DIET IN NORTH AMERICA, Wieland writes: "I shot the gerbils for six months, putting different things in their cages: food, flowers, cherries, grass, etc.... When I put them in the sink in an inch of water I began to see what the film was about... a story of revolution and escape." It is a beast fable with gerbils as the oppressed and the cats as the oppressors. Once again titles are used, but not as in SAILBOAT and 1933; here sometimes they are flashed on the screen over action, at other times they serve to introduce subsequent episodes. The allegory relates the escape of the gerbils from an American political prison in 1968 to freedom in Canada, and how they take up organic gardening in the absence of DDT, occupy a millionaire's table, and enjoy a cherry festival and flower ceremony. However, it ends on a less than humorous note: an American invasion. The film is very meticulously shot and controlled, and even more than in CATFOOD, the colour and delicacy of Wieland's approach to the animals and their surroundings create sensuously textured images and relationships.

With RAT LIFE AND DIET IN NORTH AMERICA as the first, LA RAISON AVANT LA PASSION (1967-8) becomes the second part of what Wieland characterizes as a political trilogy, to be completed by a work still in the planning stages, "True Patriot Love" [which became THE FAR SHORE]. LA RAISON AVANT LA PASSION is her longest film to date, and takes the form of a prelude and three parts. In the prelude, the Canadian theme is unfurled in the shape of the Canadian flag and the singing of "O Canada". Part I begins with Pierre Trudeau's statement in French and English: "La raison avant la passion; c'est la thème du tous mes ecrits." "Reason over passion; that is the theme of all my writing." The first and third parts consist of a journey across Canada; in the centre section, a French lesson is followed by a portrait of the prime minister. As Wieland has stated in notes: "The Trudeau portrait is sandwiched into my film where Ontario should be."

The film opens on shots of waves at Cape Breton on the Atlantic and ends at Vancouver on the Pacific with a postcard shot of a steamer, accompanied by "O Canada". It avoids cities for the most part and concentrates on the expanses of fields, lakes, streams, and mountains. There is almost constant movement during the first and third parts; when there is no movement of the camera, we see a figure crossing the screen, or waves in water or wind through flowers and trees. Across and into the illusionistically deep space of the screen, the film proceeds, revealing the beauty of the land through car and train windows, shot at different times of day, on various stocks and at varying exposures. These streams of moving abstractions remain always concrete, bound by the textures of the changing water, sky, and landscapes. And the illusions of depth are constantly qualified by the flat computerized permutations of the English phrase "reason over passion", which flash on the screen and over the images in 537 different forms.

Wieland commented in an interview on the heard but unseen language lesson which precedes the Trudeau portrait: "The French lesson is a direct reference to Trudeau's idea of bilingualism. We must all speak French so that the French Canadian will feel at home in his own country. I found the teaching record in a stack of our old records. Luckily the man on the disc pretending to be a school child is named Pierre. And he is supposedly only eight years old." At the same time the lesson satirizes the simplistic and inadequate level at which the cultural need for bilingualism has been fulfilled. The portrait of Trudeau stands in the heart of the film. Is it an homage or a criticism? Or is it simply meant to be ambiguous? It was shot when Trudeau was on his way to the prime ministry, at a time when he was Canada's hope. As American film critic Manny Farber describes it in *Artforum* (February 1970): "LA RAISON AVANT LA PASSION is a clutter of love for Canada, done in the nick of time before it changes completely into a scrubby Buffalo suburb."

As a Canadian, Wieland feels strongly about the politics of technology and the presence of U.S. technological enterprises in Canada which are gradually spreading across the country, in economic and spiritual domination. While this concern is evident in RAT LIFE AND DIET IN NORTH AMERICA and implicit in LA RAISON AVANT LA PASSION, her next long work, True Patriot Love", subtitled "A Canadian Love, Technology, Leadership and Art Story", will be her most direct film statement on the subject. A romantic narrative, it will be formal in conception. Working on the script has occupied Wieland for the past two years and it should be four or five years before the projected two-and-a-half-hour work is ready. "True Patriot Love" will be a bilingual allegory. Subtitles will be used in a form more complex than in any of her previous films. Set in Canada in 1919, the film will include both real and fantasy technology. French and English cultural differences and difficulties will be stressed.

The dialogue between film and other media will be continued in "True Patriot Love". One can really predict of that dialogue only that it will proceed in unique ways.

The Life & Times of Michael Snow

Interview by Joe Medjuck

In October 1971, Take One associate editor Joe Medjuck conducted the following interview with Canadian filmmaker Michael Snow, in Toronto. Slight revisions and additions were made in December 1971. The interview began with a discussion of a conference of Canadian artists, from which Snow had just returned.

Michael Snow: [It was] a political thing rather than an art-political thing. Just the fact that a lot of fine artists can get together, and have some kind of organization that might have some kind of effect on the situation.

Joe Medjuck: I guess that especially for a group of artists it must be very hard to get organized. If you see yourself as an individual it may seem like some kind of sacrifice to have to work as part of a group.

MS: Right, but I think it's necessary. If you feel it's a crisis... it's not like the Battle of Britain, the bombs aren't falling; it's more insidious than that. So you do what you can, and it seems to me that the organizing of artists is something that can be done. We did some mild things: telegrams to Trudeau and Nixon about the Amchitka thing, and votes about the proportion of art teachers who should be Canadian. Things like that. One of the things we talked about was *artscanada*, and I surprised a lot of people by framing the motion that we suggest that *artscanada* should be on Canadian art and, to protect myself, the activities of Canadian artists elsewhere. And that it be as much written by Canadians as possible.

JM: Does it try to be international now?

MS: Yeah, for them to keep going Ann Brodsky has tried successfully to sell it elsewhere, and she's tried to cover more than Canadian art. I think it was reasonable for us to say that there are other magazines that cover what goes on elsewhere, and you can buy them here.

JM: Do you feel a part of any tradition? A New York tradition?

MS: No. I went to New York because I wanted to get out of me what I hoped was there. I think you're exposed there to a level of effort that makes you find out what's possible for yourself. The thing that made it possible for Joyce (filmmaker-artist Joyce Wieland, Snow's wife) and I to do what we wanted to do has a lot to do with Jonas Mekas. He was able to make a place where you could show your films to other interested people. It was fantastic, and Jonas maintained this thing. We'd made films here, but never with the thought anyone could possibly be interested. In New York it was a small group, held together mostly by

Reprinted from *Take One*, vol. 3, no. 3 (January-February 1971).

Jonas. And that group disseminated a whole new thing about the kind of effort you could make: that it was possible to make a film independent of the movie business.

JM: Do you still live in New York, and do you still feel a part of that scene, or have you left that?

MS: Oh, no. We still have a studio in New York. I couldn't leave it completely right now. Both of us are really torn apart about all that. In a lot of ways it's so bad, life in New York, but yet in the last year or two in New York there's been a serious interest in what I've been doing—which I've never really had before. So, simultaneously with wanting to leave, I'm now beginning to have an effect—in terms of influencing other people and in terms of recognition of what I've been doing.

JM: When you have to fill in forms that ask for your occupation, what do you put down?

MS: I say "artist".

JM: What does that include for you?

MS: Well, I'm interested in sound, and I've been a musician and I do things that are just sound. And I have been a painter—things that go on walls. I still do photograph pieces and films. Sculpture too. I think saying "artist" doesn't mean the material you use, but that you do things of a certain kind.

JM: Do you now spend more time with films than with other things?

MS: Well, I'm specifically interested in film really. For the last few years I've been more interested in film than anything else. But I've made films for years and a lot of the things that were previously separated in my work have come together in the films. Like the sound thing was a separate thing for a long time, but in film there's a way I can use it with the image thing.

JM: What kind of sound things did you do?

MS: Well, I worked professionally as a jazz musician for about two years—'59 and '60, I think—playing all over Toronto, on TV, and at the Park Plaza, The Colonial, George's, etc.

JM: Do you think that you'll continue with films, or do you see it as just one aspect of your work?

MS: No, I think that that's where it's going to be.

JM: Does that mean you've been doing less work in the plastic arts recently?

MS: Yes. I haven't been doing any work of that kind.

JM: How did you first decide that you wanted to be involved with art?

MS: In my last year of high school I was awarded a prize; it was a book called something like *The Artist's Handbook*—it was about how to prepare paints and stuff like that. Somebody apparently decided that I was talented as an artist, but I could never figure out why. I never did anything at all in high school. Anyway, I got this book and I decided that maybe I should go to art college.

JM: Where did you go to art college?

MS: I went to The Ontario College of Art. I'd just started playing music before I went there, in high school, so while I was at art college I did more of that. I took a compromise course called "Design", because I didn't know whether I was going to turn out to be a commercial artist or what the fuck. So I started to paint while I was there but I didn't want to go into a drawing and painting course, because I had this idea that when you got out you had to have an occupation of some kind. Not a career, but a business. When I got out I had a job in some horrible advertising art thing, and I kept on painting and playing music.

JM: Do you think anyone taught you anything while you were at art college?

MS: Mostly it was a guy named John Martin (he's dead now)—he showed me books of reproductions, and discussed the stuff I was doing outside of school. He wanted to see the paintings, and I showed them to him, and he said some beautiful things. He'd say "Why don't you check out Paul Klee?" and I got very interested in him. And he'd tell me about different things I should look at, so he was very helpful.

JM: Were you still at the advertising agency when you made A TO Z?

MS: No. I went to Europe for a year, and I supported myself by playing music. I drew and painted a lot while I was there. Then I came back, and I had an exhibition at Hart House (University of Toronto).

JM: How did that come about?

MS: I don't know. It was with Graham Coughtry.

JM: Had you met him at art school?

MS: Yeah, he was in art school with me. And George Dunning, the man who directed YELLOW SUBMARINE, saw the show and he liked it a lot—and he thought, for some reason, that there was something to do with film. Anyway, he phoned me up and asked if I'd like to have a job working in film, which I'd never thought about before. He had this company, Graphic Films, which had a lot of people working at it. Graham was there, Warren Collins, Richard Williams, Sid Fury, Jim McKay, an animator who's been at the film board too. So I took the job, and I met Joyce there. That was my first contact with film. They did some live stuff there—that's what Sid Fury was doing—but mostly they did animation, and that's what I was doing. For a while I was director of the Animation Department—just before the place folded.

JM: What happened between '59 and '63?

MS: I worked for a year and a half at Graphics, but I was still playing and painting at the same time. And when that company folded, Joyce and I went to Cuba for a few months. I don't remember exactly why. That was when the fighting was on, actually. We left a couple of weeks before Castro arrived in Havana, so we saw what the Batista scene was like. Then I got really into working in music, but I was still painting and having shows and things. That was really a nice life. It was really beautiful—working at music, getting drunk, all that stuff. And I still had time for my painting. Have you ever seen TORONTO JAZZ?

JM: Don Owen's film? Yeah, sure. Are you in that? I don't remember.

MS: Well, I had a beard then. I'm in Alf Jones' quartet; we're at The House of Hamburg. In fact we play a tune of mine in it.

JM: Is that what you were doing until you went to New York?

MS: Yeah, we went to New York in '63.

JM: How did you meet Jonas Mekas and decide to continue making films?

MS: I didn't meet him for a long time. I was just digging what was going on around there, following everything, going to see dance things and everything else—especially music things. For a couple of years I had a studio that a lot of "free jazz" musicians—Cecil Taylor, Albert Ayler, Archie Shepp and all those guys—were playing at, because they had no other place to play. And then I made NEW YORK EYE AND EAR CONTROL, using a group which I chose.

JM: Was the music composed especially for the film?

MS: It was played especially for the film, yeah. I assembled the band, and we made the tape.

JM: Had they seen the visuals when they recorded the music?

MS: No. All I asked of them was whatever length it was of ensemble playing. I said, "No solos please."

JM: How about that very brief—

MS: That's Don Cherry, a trumpet solo. That just came from a sort of scrap piece of tape, from when everybody was playing around. And I hadn't planned that originally. I was going to have that part of the film completely silent, but that piece seemed an interesting way—

JM: It fits in, and is really very powerful there. What sort of work were you doing in '63?

MS: I was painting. It was in my studio that all these sessions happened. I did a lot of sculptures too. I'd started the walking woman series in '61, and I was really into that then. And I was making that film too, and that was like a part of the walking woman works.

JM: What are the implications of the title, NEW YORK EYE AND EAR CONTROL?

MS: I tried to do something in which the sound and the image had an equal power. You can take any piece of film and play any kind of music with it, and no matter how great the music is, it will become subservient—it will be used the way Bach is used in some French movies. It's still great music, but it becomes some other thing because it helps to set moods and you don't hear the music any more; and I was interested in doing a thing where you could see and hear at the same time. So I made a counterpoint with the images—which were measured and classical—as opposed to this very spontaneous, very emotional sound.

JM: Do you see this film as an adjunct to the walking woman works?

MS: That's a long story. Let me try to track it down. I'd been thinking of making other films since I'd made A TO Z but the occasion hadn't come up and the logistics were difficult; we didn't have a camera, and things like that. When I'd made A TO Z I was at Graphics, and I used their equipment and Warren Collins helped shoot it. So it was sort of easy. I had been doing photograph pieces, documentation art-pieces. I did one here in '62 and from doing that I got an idea for a film that I wanted to do. When I first went to New York to see what we might do there in the summer of '62, I met this guy and somehow told him about the film. Ben Park was his name, and he was a partner with Hugh Downs in some TV thing. Anyway, he was really taken, either with me or the idea, and he put up the money to start the film. So we shot a lot of film—at least six hours—and it seemed really interesting, but all of a sudden he just lost interest in it. He'd just realized what he'd done, I guess. He still has the film. I really wanted to do that, but I went on from that and made EYE AND EAR CONTROL.

JM: Did anything spectacular happen with NEW YORK EYE AND EAR CONTROL to make you decide you wanted to continue with films?

MS: Both of the occasions when it was first shown resulted in riots. (*Laughter*) One performance was in New York Cinémathèque and the other was in Toronto. It was partially financed by Ten Centuries Concerts, and they really hated it. They just couldn't believe how awful it was. It was shown, and there were about 300 people there, and then somebody wrote a review with a headline saying: "300 Flee Far Out Film". I was always sort of mad that there weren't 400 there to complete his alliteration. (*Laughter*) At the end of the screening there were still a few friends there. My mother didn't come, or she would have stayed too, I think. And then, at the Cinémathèque, there were people throwing things at the screen. I showed it, and Andy Warhol showed something that he'd just finished, and a lot of his gang were there and they didn't like my film much—except that Andy liked it and Gerry Malanga liked it. Which shows something or other.

JM: How did you like the other films being shown at the Cinémathèque at that time? How did the audience respond to other people's films?

MS: Reactions were more violent then. There were all kinds of levels of things going on. There were people who could really dig it in the midst of the din. At the same time, there were people very violently opposed to things. People would try to rip the film out of the projector even as late as when the Cinémathèque was up on Forty-first Street. When Bob Cowan was projectionist, one time a guy ran up and into the projection room and tried to rip a film out of the projector. I forget which film it was—I think it was one of George Landow's. I saw Jack Smith's FLAMING CREATURES, which I think is a great film, and the time I saw it there were people making just so much fucking noise it was hard to really groove with it, but you could still recognize that it was a great film. There's not much of that any more, which is both bad and good I guess. I don't know what it means.

JM: I find EYE AND EAR CONTROL a very emotional film. It begins with the walking woman figure lying on the shore, and then that fantastic, bluesy Don Cherry solo comes in. It seems to me there are very definite changes of emotion in the film. Do you see it that way?

MS: Well, emotions aren't unimportant, but they're not the stuff I work with. I put the things together, and the emotions are a by-product of having done a certain thing. But I don't try to make you happy or sad or anything like that. In relation to that I'd like to add this: the meaning is not on the screen.

JM: Do the images have emotional connotations for you?

MS: Yes, but it's a by-product of experiencing that particular image plus sound, or whatever. Like, that film was meant to deal with opposites, or supposed opposites. Fast-slow, city-country, etc. It's in black-and-white, and it ends with a black man and a white woman. They're the only two people you ever see together. It's a gradual progression of life-likeness in the representational sense, as far as the image goes.

JM: How do you feel about someone missing what you see as a definite structure? I mean, obviously I see the film differently than you do, for example.

MS: I think that's perfectly valid. When you're making something you have to have something in your hands, so to speak. That's the way I work. I work with material and it interests me to arrange things in a certain way. That sounds clearer than it is. But I don't believe that I can calculate an effect. You can use my films to laugh or cry, and that's your prerogative, but I don't aim to do that. I think that's what I object to in most other films, and why I don't go to the movies. I don't like that sort of artificial laugh or cry. It doesn't interest me; I'd rather have it actually happen.

JM: Aren't you interested in any films?

MS: Well, I like Ken Jacobs' films, George Landow's films, Hollis Frampton, Joyce Wieland, Paul Sharits, Ernie Gehr....

JM: Do you think you're influenced very much by anyone—including Joyce?

MS: No.

JM: Have you ever seen anything by Robert Bresson?

MS: Yes, A MAN ESCAPED. It's very good.

JM: Your films remind me of Bresson to some extent.

MS: Yeah... but I'd like to have even more distance than that. With LA REGION CENTRALE I really wanted to set up a phenomenon that exists in front of you, so that it's your choice, in a way, to become part of it or not.

JM: Are you very interested in narrative films?

MS: I've got some notes for things that could be called narrative films. I'd like to make a dialogue film. There I was thinking of the emphasis being on the sound. But I guess I don't think of that one being narrative either.

JM: Do you consider SHORT SHAVE a minor piece?

MS: Yeah, that's my worst film.

JM: What does "worst" mean?

MS: Well, I think it's pleasant, but well... you know that thing at the end where I sort of hold things up in front of me, that's part of a stage piece. That's sort of appended. I think it's relevant. But I don't think you can see that film very often. The other films, you can see them again and again, even when you know where they're going. They may even be better after the first time. But I don't think you can do that with SHORT SHAVE.

JM: NEW YORK EYE AND EAR CONTROL seems to me to be an extension of what you were doing in the plastic arts at the time. Do you see any of your films that way?

MS: I don't know. I always try to work within the possibilities of whatever medium I happen to be working in. That's why I have a certain attitude about what I think my films ought to be like. I don't know how to put this. There are certain possibilities in a medium that make it a distinct thing as opposed to some other thing. And I've thought about what I think you can get out of films as a medium. And I haven't thought about other films so much as I've thought about, you know, they have this strip of stuff and it goes through a machine. But there are all sorts of relations. The walking woman thing was a whole sort of variation which is related to jazz. The theme and variation thing. And while I was doing them I was thinking that maybe a lot of the paintings I did should be seen in time—that there should be a serial display of the variations. That was one of the things that preceded making WAVELENGTH. This idea of having the variations follow each other in time is like jazz, or any music. "The Goldberg Variations" especially.

JM: Do you see WAVELENGTH as an important point in your career?

MS: Yes, and it was important before it got noticed; it was like a crisis of all the things that I'd been doing. A lot of things came together.

JM: How about after it was noticed?

MS: Well, how do you talk about that? I thought it was great, and I thought EYE AND EAR CONTROL was great too. And it didn't really get noticed. I didn't think WAVELENGTH would be either. You know, I'd do it, it would be shown a couple of times, and that would be the end of it. Actually, here's where Jonas comes in. I wouldn't have sent it to the Belgium film thing (4th International Experimental Film Festival, Knokke-Le-Zoute, Belgium, 1967) if it wasn't for Jonas. He saw it, really liked it, and said it would be a good idea if I sent it. Then it got the first prize, people began to notice it, and some attention was put on that particular work, which gave me some encouragement.

JM: How would you describe your films to someone who's never seen them?

MS: (*Laughter*) Gee, I don't know.

JM: How would you describe WAVELENGTH?

MS: I'd probably say that it's a long zoom. Which is what most people do, and that's great because it's meaningless.

JM: Is that how you conceived of it?

MS: I think that that idea happened along with the idea of variations in time. But a lot of other things too. In '66, I guess, I had acid for the first time and that was related to it.

JM: Do you think that dope in any way affects the product—what comes out of you?

MS: Yeah, I think so.

JM: Why did you decide on a zoom?

MS: I don't remember exactly.

JM: That was sort of a loaded question. What interests me about the zoom is that it's one thing the camera does that we can't do with our eyes. And one of the things I find in the film is the way the slow zoom questions the whole meaning of the zoom. I mean, you keep coming closer to the wall, but the sides don't disappear. You do lose some of the sides, but not much. You're really changing people's perspective rather than their point of view.

MS: I wrote a thing, originally for the New York Filmmakers' Cooperative catalogue, but it's appeared other places—this was before the film had received any acclaim—and I said that I had wanted to make a definitive film. And it's true. All that year I'd been thinking about an essential film. Like it's coloured light on a flat surface. And the material of it is light and time. And the depiction of space.

JM: How do you conceive of the dramatic events in your film? It's funny to call them that, but because there are so few they take on even more dramatic significance. I mean in the middle of WAVELENGTH there appears to be a death.

MS: That's the basic idea, but the original idea was even cooler. I wanted to have a body on the floor and have the camera pass over it. It's like the bookshelf moving in, which is really not so dramatic, but there's metaphoric connections between those boxes and looking out the windows and they're empty. And I wanted something that had some weight to be moved through the space. When you see the room for a long time, you lose the sense of how big it is, but when somebody traverses it, you get an idea again of how long it is. So the thing—the room, the space—gets flatter and flatter, which is its real reality, since it's coloured light on a flat surface—and then all of a sudden the surface is broken by this illusion of people, or whatever it is, that's moving in there. So that's what I was working with: the different kinds of realities involved.

JM: So the drama is secondary?

MS: It's secondary in that it was trying to position these things in time, and to work with the space. Then I thought about the kinds of connections between the events, and I wanted to have a range of connections. And this one thing, the phone call about the body, is a distinct kind of a narrative intimation compared with the other things. Besides, other things in the film, like the colour things, are also events and have drama.

JM: Did you know when you first conceived the film that you would end on the shot of the water?

MS: No, it went through a lot of things, and I've got all kinds of notes. For a while I thought I might end on a still photo of the opening shot. That was a terrible idea. We went through a lot of things the zoom might move towards. One of them was a life of Duke Ellington.

JM: Were you aware of how the final superimposition would look?

MS: No, and that's one of the things I've worried about when I've seen it. I'm not sure it was a good idea.

JM: I really like it. I've always been surprised that more people haven't picked up on the idea: a superimposition of the larger image over the smaller which gives a depth thing, but I guess that destroys your idea of the flat surface.

MS: Well, it leads you to the flat with a kind of mirage. Sometimes I've seen it and I think I should have just continued the zoom. I like the supering too, though. It happens other times in the film, where the zoom catches up and then the two images are together. But it worried me that I might be destroying the fact that you were still in the same space. But I guess it doesn't.

JM: Is there much or any editing in WAVELENGTH, or is it all done in the camera?

MS: It took a little while, but I guess that's not much of what's usually called editing. I shifted things a little bit. In BACK AND FORTH (⟷) I edited. Or maybe that's not the right word. I worked on it after the shooting for four or five months. And it doesn't look like an edited film. Sometimes the people cut on or off or the pan doesn't go all the way. And I'd include some things in some versions that I'd shorten on others.

JM: Do you have a soundtrack in mind before you shoot your films?

MS: Well, with WAVELENGTH it was planned before I shot the film, because I decided that I wanted to have an ear equivalent to what a zoom was. Which I guess would have been a crescendo. But a glissando seemed more discernible. And I didn't know how to do that, and I could have used any way to get a glissando, but I asked around and talked to a couple of people—Max Neuhaus, who's a composer—and I'd ask casually, "How would you make a forty-minute glissando?" And he told me to call up Ted Wolfe, who's an engineer. I thought maybe I could do it with a piano, by sounding all the notes and running them all together. I just wanted to start at the bottom and go to the top.

JM: So the soundtracks of the films don't require special electronic instruments?

MS: WAVELENGTH did, because we used a sine wave generator. Ted Wolfe made a little motor that turned the thing up from sixty cycles to—I don't know what it was—12,000 cycles or something like that, over a period of forty minutes. I hadn't thought of using something electronic. Any way of doing it would have been O.K., but it turned out that it was electronic.

JM: Was it you who arranged to have the music from EYE AND EAR CONTROL released as a record?

MS: Yeah, through ESP records. I wanted to use the walking woman insignia for some company that manufactured things, so I'd be able to see it on trucks and billboards and things like that. For a while I thought we might get to use the walking woman for the record company. Before Bernard Stollman went ahead with ESP he was considering making it "Walking Woman Works Records".

JM: How would you describe STANDARD TIME?

MS: I don't know. Thinking about WAVELENGTH made me think about using other kinds of basic film vocabulary things. And that was like a sketch that showed a lot of possibilities. It's my home movie, really.

JM: Do you mind people calling your films structural or conceptual films?

MS: They're conceptual in that they're planned. Some people—take Jonas, he shoots a whole lot of stuff, then he edits it. It's not conceptual, it's a whole other thing. I plan them as carefully as I can, although it doesn't always come out that way.

JM: Do you allow chance to play any part in your films?

MS: Quite a lot. I make a kind of container that makes fortuitous things belong.

JM: Did you have any reason for picking the particular dramatic events that take place in BACK AND FORTH (⟷)?

MS: Yeah, but it was a different kind of reason than with WAVELENGTH. It was connected in some ways, in that I wanted to inhabit the place in various ways.

JM: What is the place, by the way?

MS: It's a classroom at Fairleigh Dickinson University, which is in New Jersey. I was there for, I don't know what it was, an artists' seminar, I guess. I was there for three weeks, or a month, in the summer of '68. Emmet Williams, the poet, Max Neuhaus, Alan Kaprow were there. They're in the film. Jud Yalkut was there for a while.

JM: Did you have a special reason for titling BACK AND FORTH (⟷) with an arrow?

MS: Only that it's a visual rather than a verbal thing.

JM: Both (⟷) and LA REGION CENTRALE have a change in camera movements near the end.

MS: I think it comes about two-thirds of the way through in (⟷) whereas in THE CENTRAL REGION it is near the end. In (⟷) it goes to its fastest speed back and forth, and then cuts to up and down. Then it slows down and finally there's a kind of coda which is all the different stuff that's happened superimposed over each other. It's sort of like your memory. You don't think of things in their order, really. When you come out of that film you don't really remember what order things happened in. You remember this scene, or that scene, and the feeling of it.

JM: One of the things that gets me in WAVELENGTH and in LA REGION CENTRALE is that, although the photographed space is quite small, because of the camera movement I can't take it all in at any given moment, and I find myself looking really closely—at the edges in WAVELENGTH because they're always disappearing. And even though REGION is three hours long, at the end I still have the feeling that I haven't seen all there is to see of the area you're showing.

MS: That's really nice, because that's something that's important in them to me—that there really is a lot to see. It may seem like it's a simple subject, but there really is a lot.

JM: In (⟷) it seemed to me that the dramatic actions you present are rather ominous. Especially the policeman at the end.

MS: The film is really relationships—reciprocity. There's a teacher and students, lovers—the whole thing is action and reaction. Two people toss a ball. And somehow or other the cop enters into that.

JM: Are you very aware of the rhythm and structure of your films?

MS: Sure. (⟷) is easy to talk about that way because it's about the speed of panning. It starts at that medium speed where strobing happens, and it slows down to a medium speed where you can more clearly identify and believe in the things you see. I think the slowest point is where the teacher draws the symbol, and they're all facing the green board. Then it gradually picks up speed again, until it reaches the ultimate speed possible.

JM: How did you do that? Manually?

MS: Yes, but there's a little trickery. I change the shooting speed.

JM: Do you change the shooting speed in REGION?

MS: Not at all, it's all twenty-four.

JM: How did you get that sunset? Is that how it really looks there?

MS: Oh yeah. That's all real-time.

JM: It seems to me that one of the implications of a lot of contemporary art—maybe including yours—one of the constant "messages" to the audience is that they could be doing this too. Do you see much of a differentiation between the artist and the audience?

MS: Well, I'm specifically spending all my time working on this thing, and I presume that I know more than other people who aren't.

JM: It seems to me that one of the implications of, say, Andy Warhol's work is that there are no artists. Or, rather, we're all artists. We have no art, we do everything as well as we can, and all that shit.

MS: I would never draw that implication from Andy's films, because all the people in them are actor-personalities, and they've been chosen, and they've been placed. There may be a certain passivity compared to the way I work, which is theoretically more controlled. Perhaps it isn't in practice—whether that means anything or not. But it's like any other thing, really. I'm not very interested in hockey and if I watch a hockey game I won't see as much as someone who does know about it, especially a player. I've spent my life being involved with art, and I'm not sure what conclusions you can draw from that except that I think I know something about art. (*laughter*) There may be an argument that everybody's an artist, but some people don't seem to use that capacity if they are.

JM: Are you interested in having your films seen by as many people as possible?

MS: Yes. I don't make the films with a particular audience in mind, or aim it at all people. But I'm human too, and it might interest some people, it could be that something could become very popular, but it doesn't have anything to do with anything. They're not made for two or three people. It pleased me that WAVELENGTH got some attention. It was satisfying attention, because it had to do with what I'd done and what I knew I had done. It pleases me and it wouldn't hurt me at all if a lot more people liked the films. And I guess it would hurt me if a lot less people liked the films. But it wouldn't affect what I did. Like, it's been really not very easy. It's hard work being an artist. And it's a very interesting thing trying to do something that's your own. It's a struggle. But it's worthwhile I guess.

JM: How do you feel about the audience response? I mean, what if the audience obviously hates your film?

MS: I don't really like it too much when that happens. Because usually I enjoy watching them myself, and that disturbs me.

JM: How do you feel about the audience being stoned watching your films?

MS: Nice.

JM: Have any really violent things happened during screenings of your films?

MS: There have been quite a few things happen. One of them I didn't see was in Amsterdam. WAVELENGTH was shown, and there was a huge audience and somebody tried to rip down the screen.

JM: Well, we're laughing about that now, but does it bother you when it happens?

MS: No, it doesn't really bother me, but obviously you can't really groove on a film when people are trying to pull the screen down. (*Laughter*)

JM: Is DRIPPING WATER the only film you've collaborated on with Joyce?

MS: Yes. We help each other, but there are no real, actual collaborations. That one came from a tape that I'd made.

JM: For ONE SECOND IN MONTREAL you re-photographed stills.

MS: Yeah. They're stills that were printed offset lithography or something.

JM: You've made a film that I haven't seen...

MS: SIDE SEAT PAINTINGS SLIDES SOUND FILM

JM: Yeah, and this time I really haven't seen it, so how would you describe it?

MS: It came out of doing my book, *A Survey*, for the Ontario Art Gallery show, in February 1970. And also the whole retrospective thing that made me look back at my work for the first time. I was interested in the idea of using the records of old work as the material for new works. The book uses still photos. The film uses slides. Not very many. And it's like a filming from a very bad seat of the slides being shown on a screen. It's a side seat.

JM: What's the soundtrack?

MS: The names, sizes, mediums, and dates of the works on the slides. You can't see the paintings very well. I mean, you can tell they're slides of paintings, but it's all to do with... it slows down.

JM: How did you get the idea for LA REGION CENTRALE?

MS: I'd been thinking about the idea for a long time. I'd been thinking about types of subjects. The traditional painting division of subjects seems to me to be still applicable—portraiture, landscape, still life, etc. There are good reasons why those divisions are still used. It's like animal, vegetable and mineral—those things do exist. And I thought about how you could make a landscape film.

JM: This is dangerous to say, since I haven't seen your next film yet, but it seems to me to be a culmination of your past films—particularly those since WAVELENGTH.

MS: Yeah, I think it wraps up the whole thing about panning.

JM: Does that mean you aren't going to make any more films about camera movements?

MS: I've got a couple of ideas, but this one was so torturous to make.

JM: The conception involved a fairly expensive machine, which you invented, I guess. How did you operate it?

MS: It was operated from a distance. There could be different ways. You could prepare the tapes ahead of time, and the tapes could operate the machine, but there's also a set of controls—horizontal, vertical, rotation, and speed for each one.

JM: How long did it take to shoot the film?

MS: We were up there five days, but it was supposed to be just four. We were left there by a helicopter. It's about 100 miles north of Sept-Iles in Quebec, which is about the same latitude as James Bay.

JM: How did you pick the spot?

MS: I spent a lot of time looking for a place with a car or truck. I wanted complete wilderness with nothing man-made, and we never could find anyplace. There was always something wrong. Joyce and I took a whole bunch of trips, all over, with a car. So finally I decided to narrow it down with aerial photographs, and we found an area that seemed pretty interesting. So I rented a helicopter and looked at the place. That was really thrilling.

JM: You had to reassemble the machine up there, I guess.

MS: Yeah, it was really weird. We were left on a mountain top, and the helicopter went away. It was really fantastic. We had all this sophisticated machinery up there in this complete wilderness. We had a tent, and it was cold. Joyce was hoping to shoot something of the machine working, but unfortunately she never did. It was really nice just to see the thing moving around. Like if anybody'd flown by...

JM: In the film you can see the shadow of the machine. It's really nice.

MS: It's nice that it happens where it does, too; it happens near the beginning of the film, where perhaps you need a clue to exactly what it is that's going on. And it happens at the end, too.

JM: Did it take long to design the machine? Did you do that yourself?

MS: No, I had a clear idea of what I wanted the machine to do, but I didn't know how to do it. Graham Ferguson, who made NORTH OF

SUPERIOR, had worked with Pierre Abbeloos and suggested him to me. So I went to Montreal and Pierre and I talked about it. He came up with a set of axles that combined to make it possible to make all the possible movements without photographing the base. He's really brilliant.

JM: The camera can move in four directions at once with it, I guess.

MS: It can move horizontally and it can move vertically, while the camera itself can move centred on the lens. So it's like a bodyless eye—an eye floating in space.

JM: Usually, with films, we describe what we see as a camera movement—we say the camera moved left, we don't say the scene moved right. But there's one moment in your film—it's in the second section, I think—where I was convinced that the camera wasn't moving but that the earth was spinning.

MS: That's nice. That should happen, because that's the other way of reading the image. There is a reversal when you project the film. I mean that's one thing you can do with a camera that has hardly been touched upon—the thing has no up or down. And the whole film is meant to work on your sense of gravity.

JM: How did you go about arranging financing for the film?

MS: I don't know how I heard about the CFDC (Canadian Film Development Corporation) but I wrote the whole thing out and applied for a grant.

JM: Did you get a grant from them, or an investment?

MS: It was a grant. The CFDC gave me half of what I asked for, so I had to try some other way of getting the rest of the money. I spent a long time looking, and then went to Famous Players. Theirs is an investment. They want to get their money back.

JM: Do you think they're going to?

MS: Gee, I don't know. But they don't own the film. It's my film, and they get a percentage of the profits. The money was put up for lab costs. I didn't make a cent out of it. Oh yes, I did. I got 10 per cent—$1,500 for my work, or whatever.

JM: So how much money did the film actually cost?

MS: Twenty-seven thousand dollars. They were all pretty good about it. They made the money available at the lab, and pretty well left me alone. I guess I have a rather peculiar status, sort of like McLaren at the film board—a kook who they sponsor. I don't think they expect to make any money from the film.

JM: Have you started work on anything since LA REGION CENTRALE?

MS: No. I have a lot of ideas, but I haven't started anything. I did a kind of video installation piece at the National Gallery in Ottawa. It was pretty successful. It's an adaptation of the LA REGION CENTRALE machine as a moving sculpture. The machine, with a video camera, is set in various motions. The path of the camera eye is shown on four monitors, and the audience is in the images.

JM: Do you think you'll have problems getting LA REGION CENTRALE shown?

MS: I'd like to get it into a theatre, but I can't convince anybody on the basis of any kind of commercial record at all. And yet, it would need some kind of promotion that I'm not prepared to do. And the fact that it's three hours long will be a difficulty. I mean it isn't three hours long because I wanted to make it a three-hour-long film. It just takes that long to have it happen.

JM: What is the relationship of the soundtrack to the camera movements in the film? There seemed to be a corresponding sound for every movement.

MS: There is. We made tapes to operate certain sections of the thing, but I couldn't use the original sound that was made to trigger the machine because some of it was too high for optical soundtracks. I'd known that, but I thought I'd be able to shift it all down. But that wasn't possible, so I had to reconstruct it. Originally, the sound was intended to dictate the movements. Actually, though, I was thinking about Bach—the "St. Matthew Passion" and that sort of thing.

JM: But you would never use that on the soundtrack.

MS: Oh, God no. But I was thinking about that kind of weight. I guess that would be my ultimate ambition, to do something that was as good as something by Bach.

Postscript (1976)

Since the above interview was published, Michael Snow has finished two more films: RAMEAU'S NEPHEW BY DIDEROT (THANX TO DENNIS YOUNG) BY WILMA SCHOEN (1973-4) and BREAKFAST (1972-6). RAMEAU'S NEPHEW is Snow's first "true talking picture". It is 285 minutes long and is divided into twenty or so sections which are related to each other by theme rather than by narrative, the most obvious theme—one which nearly every scene explores—being the relationship of the film's soundtrack to its image track.

RAMEAU'S NEPHEW also deals with the meanings of words as well as their sounds, and the film is full of puns, quotes, and various kinds of word play. Though the sequences could be shown separately (indeed, the Canadian Filmmakers' Distribution Centre catalogue gives rental prices for each of the film's six reels) many of the themes of RAMEAU'S NEPHEW (e.g., its concern with memory and the various uses of the wordsound "forfourfore") only become apparent when the film is seen as a whole.

Michael Snow has described RAMEAU'S NEPHEW as a musical comedy.

BREAKFAST was shot in 1972 but the soundtrack was not added until 1976. It is ten minutes long and the visuals consist of one slow tracking shot across a table laden with breakfast foods (most of them packaged). The camera pushes the breakfast across the table, smashing it slowly onto a wall against which the table has been placed. (In actuality, a piece of plexiglass was placed in front of the camera.) At the end of the film the camera tracks quickly back and then forward again to make it apparent what has transpired. The effect of the initial track is especially startling before one understands what is happening; all one sees on the screen is the breakfast materials moving and metamorphosing in shape.

The soundtrack to BREAKFAST consists of the noises of dishes being cleaned up while a radio tuned to a "morning show" is played.

In 1974 Snow completed an installation involving film called TWO SIDES TO EVERY STORY. It is comprised of two films taken at the same time by cameras facing each other and is screened with two projectors onto a hanging screen. (8 min. Colour. Sound.)

It should perhaps be added that after the above interview was published, Michael Snow wrote a letter to *Take One*, which read in part:

> It's true that it's funny to talk about when you're talking about it and feeling funny, but there seem to be so many mentions of riots and other acts-of-man—starting with the "300 Flee Far Out Film" cover (which is funny too)—in my interview and elsewhere in the last issue of *Take One* that I felt sad about the possibilities of the expectations of newcomers to my films being formed by descriptions of such events.
>
> My films are made for attention, contemplation, meditation, and if they are met in those sorts of ways some very rewarding and subtle sensory, sensual and psychic states can be experienced, so please don't riot until intermission. (They're often met appreciatively.)... I'm a respecter and observer, as well as a shaper, of the unities of occasions (which is why I made very very few changes in the transcript of our discussion). This is another occasion.

Michael Snow's "Wavelength"

Bruce Elder

One of the most encouraging features of a certain mainstream of contemporary advanced art has been the interest it has taken in important epistemological questions. The signs of this are widespread but nowhere are they more striking than in the exploration of illusionism which characterizes much of contemporary artistic production—an exploration which, inasmuch as it surveys both the nature of the material relations constructed in the work of art and the effect of those relations upon the perceptual processes of the viewer, raises a whole gamut of questions concerning the nature, conditions and validity of experience.[1]

Among those artists concerned with epistemological questions, many have found in the cinema an art form uniquely qualified to present their ideas. The reasons for asserting that the cinema occupies such an epistemologically privileged position have been various. For some of these artists, the claim rests upon the fact that the flow of images in a film can directly represent the ever-changing contents of consciousness.[2] Others have claimed that the cinema offers a structure or set of structures isomorphic to certain structures (usually temporal) of consciousness. In consequence, in the work of this second group the other great concern of the mainstream of contemporary advanced art, the self-reflexive concern with the forms and structures of art objects, converges with the inquiry into the structures of consciousness.

This latter school finds an exemplary figure in the person of Michael Snow. It is well known that much of Snow's work consists in part of an exploration of the forms and structures of art objects and of their effects upon the perceptual processes; here it suffices to submit as evidence that several of his works consist of an examination of the effects of certain operations of recent cinema. Examples of this are (   ), which surveys the effects of various tempi and frames[3] of the operative action of panning and tilting; ONE SECOND IN MONTREAL, which, by projecting a number of still images for varying lengths of time, illustrates the way in which temporality is inscribed in the cinematographic image[4]; LA REGION CENTRALE which is in part a meditation upon the relations between the frame, the image and the photographic subject dealing with the way in which the frame's function of isolating a portion of space acts also to imply a spatio-temporal continuum outside its bounds;[5] and of course WAVELENGTH, which demonstrates the effects on the perceptual mechanisms of the viewer of a continued zoom across a loft.

But to claim, as several commentators have, that such descriptions as these exhaustively define the areas of concern of Snow's work would be

Reprinted from *Descant*, no. 8-9 (Spring-Summer 1974).

to commit a grave error. One fault of such descriptions is that they fail to mention the spiritual dimension of Snow's work. Evidence that such concerns have preoccupied Snow throughout his career could be found in almost any of Snow's works as a filmmaker, as in much of his art-work *in toto*. Restricting ourselves to educing evidence from the works cited above, we would refer to the fact that (⟵⟶) is structured around a series of opposites which are unified by the velocity of the panning movement and so offers us, as Snow himself has pointed out,[6] an analogue to religious transcendence; that LA REGION CENTRALE, in its positing within the cascading tumult of images a central point of absolute stillness, offers an analogue to the zero point of nirvanic consciousness which lies behind the flow of images in consciousness; and that WAVELENGTH explores the possibility of transcendence.

To point out merely this, however, is still to miss the most damning refutation of the view that Snow is an artist/filmmaker whose concerns are exclusively formal and to ignore a central feature of his work—a feature which, I contend, justifies the claim that Snow is a filmmaker of major importance.

The feature of Snow's work to which I refer is, of course, Snow's use of art to explore epistemological problems. The fact that this feature, though both prominently foregrounded and recurrent in his work, has been little mentioned[7] in the now somewhat extensive literature on Snow's work indicates that there is a need to explore this idea at some length. Epistemological problems have occupied a central place in Snow's work ever since the beginning of his career; for example the famous "Walking Woman" is really in theme and structure a "declension of ideas" on the modes of illusionism. But it is with the film WAVELENGTH—a film which even according to Snow's own admission[8] represented both a summation of his previous art-work and a projection toward his future film work—that the total range of his epistemological preoccupations was pressed into the service of a single unified work rather than explored piecemeal. For this reason, we shall undertake an analysis of WAVELENGTH as a demonstration of the way in which epistemological and formal inquiry converge in his work.

First a rather brief description of the film. Snow's own description of the film, prepared for the 1967 International Festival at Knokke-le-Zoute, reads in part as follows:

> The film is a continuous zoom which takes forty-five minutes to go from its widest field to its smallest and final field. It was shot with a fixed camera at one end of an eight-foot loft, shooting the other end, a row of windows and the street. Thus the setting and the action which takes place are cosmically equivalent. The room (and the zoom) are interrupted by four human events, including a death. The sound, music and speech, occurred simultaneously with an electronic sound, a sine-wave which goes from its lowest (fifty cycles per second) note to highest (19,200 c.p.s.) in forth minutes.

One would want to add to this description only five things. First, the event to which Snow unambiguously refers as a death in this text is not presented so unambiguously in the film; in the film, a man staggers into the room and falls on the floor apparently drunk or dead; later, when a woman places a telephone call, in referring to the body lying on the floor she insists that it is that of a dead man. Second, there is a striking dissimilarity among the four "human events" in that each successive event occurs in a flatter space than the previous event and marks an increase in mobility and dramatic effect over the previous one. Third, as a result of changes in the film stock exposure and time of day, the space inside the loft and that outside the loft vary in visibility: at times only the loft is visible, the windows being blocked up by light or darkness; at other times the loft is itself next to invisible while the streets, store offices and light outside are clearly visible, and at still other times, the loft and the outside are both clearly visible. Fourth, the film concludes with the zoom centering upon a photographic image of a wave. And fifth, the zoom is not smooth and continuous but is disrupted by events of four sorts: a) a stammering or faltering in the progression of the zoom; b) colour flashes of an extraordinary intensity; c) changes in grain created by the use of filters, negative printing and a variety of film stocks; and d) the superimposition over the progression of the zoom of images with wider field, echoing images from a previous point in the film.

A central aspect of the film is the exploration of various modes of cinematic experience. This exploration is initiated right at the beginning of the film by the use of two very different cinematic styles. The film opens with the first of the "human events"—two men, supervised by a woman, move a large bookcase into the room. Several devices are used to give this portion of the film a highly mimetic character. The use of the shortest focal length of the zoom lens, the placing of the camera at an oblique angle to the wall, and the recession of people and objects through the field all help to create the illusion of deep space. At the same time, synchronous sound and naturalistic colour and lighting contribute further to the "realistic texture" of the image. Shortly after this "human event" is completed, however, the mimetic character of the image is quickly destroyed. A number of strategies are used to accomplish this. In the first place, narrative transitivity is destroyed: this first event does not initiate a series of subsequent dramatically related events. And secondly, the zoom begins to stammer and falter its way forward, while light and colour changes of an extraordinary intensity occur.

As would be expected, one reacts to these two portions of the opening section of the film in very different ways. At first, the audience responds to the film much as it would to any traditional illusionistic dramatic film. This response, however, is soon undercut: in the second portion the use of colour and light changes, the duration of the extension of the zoom and the absence of dramatic action (at least dramatic action as we usually conceive it) cause the audience to redirect its attention to the material nature of the film.

The differences in nature of these two kinds of responses need to be further elaborated, for an understanding of these differences is necessary to a comprehension of Snow's thoughts on illusionism. When viewing the first portion of the film, as when viewing any well-plotted film, one's attention tends to focus upon the elaboration of the "intrigue". One's energies tend to be expended upon arriving at an understanding of "what is happening", i.e. in giving a reading of the text of the film-deciphering the meaning of objects and action which the film presents. Because one's energies are expended upon such conceptualizing activities, and because in a plotted film the objects on the screen undergo frequent displacement, one's relationship to the objects presented in the film is of a specific nature: one tends to apprehend these objects "in the mode of distraction", to think about the objects rather than to open oneself to experiencing them sensually.

As the plot thins and disappears, and as the objects presented, rather than undergoing frequent displacement begin to remain on the screen for a considerable period of time, the nature of one's response changes. One's mode of apprehending the objects becomes less conceptual and more perceptual. One's energies begin to be directed less on determining the signifying function of the various objects in the film and more on actually scrutinizing their appearance and appreciating their sensual properties. (Consider, for example, the care one takes in examining the yellow chair.[9])

It will be recognized upon reflection that the second type of response is characteristic of one's response to the traditional static visual arts. At one level then, the difference in the modes of response to the two cinematic styles alerts the viewer to the crucial difference between his mode of response to a work of one of the static visual arts and to a moving picture and so demonstrates the effect of the introduction of movement into the image.[10] But more profoundly it marks a reflection upon and a vigorous refutation of the notion that the experience of presence can be used as an index of "disillusionment". Traditionally the experience of "presence" in a drama has been considered a way of combating the illusionism inherent in the conventional drama. In showing that by concentrating one's attention on the individual objects one can evoke a sense of presence, Snow is demonstrating that the experience of presence does not depend upon the degree to which the "actualness" of the objects asserts itself over the illusion fostered by the material and formal conditions of the work. It depends rather on the degree to which the material and formal conditions of the work focus and concentrate one's perceptual energies. Snow thus refutes the traditional theories of presence.

The conjunction of these two cinematic styles also demonstrates certain facts about our apprehension of the "passage of time" while viewing a film. When viewing the dramatic portion, as when viewing any plotted film, we are frequently almost unaware of the "passage of time". It seems as though the attention which we devote to "giving a reading" of the action diminishes the extent to which we are aware of the flow of time. During this portion our apprehension of time (when we are aware of time at all) is controlled by the intensity and tempo of the dramatic action rather than by the actual running time of that action. During the other portion, however (wherein nothing happens except the extension of the zoom), we are, precisely because nothing happens, very much aware of the actual running time of the piece. Thus the conjunction of these two cinematic styles establishes the difference between actual running time and apprehended time.

The establishment and subsequent replacement of the dramatic mode carries yet another meaning. When viewing the opening portion of the film (representing the first of the "human events"), one tends to anticipate succeeding human actions. This event, then, establishes the expectation that it will be the initial member in a series of interrelated human actions. This expectation is however frustrated when for a considerable period of time no further "human events" occur. One eventually realizes that it is the extension of the zoom that constitutes the major action of the film, and begins to anticipate not the human action to follow but rather the next movement of the zoom.

This feature of the work thus demonstrates that the experience of film-as-drama is anticipatory in character, i.e., that the experience of viewing a film structured upon the dramatic form is characterized by a sense of anticipation and expectation of forthcoming action. It also identifies the structural feature of a drama which conditions this experience—namely, that the events in a drama function not as independent entities but as relational units whose very nature is determined by the way they lead to subsequent events in the drama. Thus the trajectory described by the continual progression of the zoom stands as a grand metaphor for the viewer's experience of a drama and for the dramatic form itself. The motivating force for this metaphor lies in the isomorphism in temporal structures inherent in the progression of the zoom, the experience of a drama and the dramatic form itself, an isomorphism which rests in the way in which all these structures project forward in time.[11] This isomorphism establishes the possibility of using the continual progression of the zoom as a structural principle for a work which, although lacking any dramatic action, will nevertheless possess the structural tensions of a drama. It also makes it possible to use the quintessential features of the operation of the zoom to comment upon and to elucidate the essential features of the viewer's response to drama and of the dramatic form itself.

We have seen, then, how the structure of the film evokes a sense of anticipation. One important effect of this anticipation is that it tends to annihilate one's sense of the present. At the same time, however, one is also under the influence of a force working against this annihilation—a kind of perceptual tug which pulls one back from the anticipation of what is to follow to the apprehension of the image in (to corrupt an expression from Whitehead) the mode of presentational immediacy. This tension of course alerts one to a duality in the temporal characteristics of any filmic image which has been subsumed into a drama. Because of its photographic character, a filmic image demands to be experienced in the mode of presentational immediacy: at the same time, when it is subsumed into a drama, it evokes an anticipation of actions or events. It is as though the image demands to be experienced both as something existing in the present and as something pointing away from the present and toward the future—both as an entity in itself and as a relational unit.[12]

Soon the mesmerizing power of the soundtrack,[13] the film's minimal form and extended duration take effect on the viewer; one finds that at times one's attention is directed not towards the film but towards his/her own mental processes. In this state of self-reflection one becomes aware of another important fact—that the temporal character which we have described as belonging to the experience of drama in fact belongs to all experience. All experience, we realize, is anticipatory in nature and projects itself forward towards an horizon.

We discover, then, that the isomorphism which we have described as existing between the basic structural features of the over-all shape of the film, the experience of the drama and the dramatic form itself can be extended to include the basic temporal structures of experience in general. The addition of this new term opens a new and profound dimension of meaning in the film. Because temporality is basic both to drama and to experience and because there exists an isomorphism between the temporal structures of drama and experience, it becomes possible to use the structural features of drama to comment on and elucidate the essential structures of experience. And this provides the basis for a new kind of epistemological cinema; the old epistemological cinema[14] utilized the illusion-conjuring potential of film to explore the influence of material objects on the perceptual processes of the viewer, and so to conduct an inquiry into the nature, conditions and validity of experience. With WAVELENGTH, a new epistemological cinema emerges, one which utilizes the structure of the film to comment upon the structure of experience.

The fact that the film is built upon the continual extension of the zoom has other implications. One effect of building the film on a single operation is to create the impression that the film is constituted by a single shot. This serves to suggest a unity or continuum between the different types of events occurring in the film; thus, the continuum established alludes to the transcendental unity of consciousness which underline all ideas in consciousness and serves to unify them into a single flow.[15] In this way, then, building the film upon a single operation articulates an analogy to the unity underlying experience while the fact that this operation is one of projection forward articulates an analogy to the way in which, within this continuum of experience, one event leads to another. Snow himself directed attention to this aspect of the work, for in an interview in *Take One* (vol. 3, no. 3) he says, "Then I thought about the kinds of connections between events, and I wanted to have a range of connections."

The fact that the film appears to be recorded in a single shot also serves to suggest that the film was recorded in real, continuous time. And analogously, by confining the major action of the film to events occurring within the space of the loft[16] and by emphasizing that the action is recorded in a single space. Snow thus creates the illusion that the film's space-time is single, fixed and continuous.

We have commented already on the fact that this film is, in part, a meditation on the drama in film. The use of this space-time develops further this line of thought. One important basis of drama, as Bazin repeatedly pointed out, is the continuum of space-time in which the different elements in the action are held together in a dramatic tension. The use of what appears to be a single shot then serves both to establish the continuum and to draw attention to the fact that this continuum is a condition of drama.

The effect on the temporal structure of the film of building it on this single operation is even more important and embodies an insight that appears all the more remarkable when the film is considered in the context of the tradition in which it exists, the tradition of innovational filmmaking. One important feature of innovational filmmaking in all its phases has been the use of disjunctive strategies ranging from the deconstruction of narrative transitivity to the use of an assertive editing style or to the gestural use of camera movement. The motivating impulse for this disjunctive style has been the desire, common to innovational artists of the past half-century ranging from the surrealists and Gertrude Stein to Maya Deren[17] and Stan Brakhage, to create a sense of immediacy, of perpetual present in the art-work. The effect of this, of course, was to destroy the sense of the future, to annihilate the feeling of anticipation and expectation which, we have seen, evokes the tension of a drama. With remarkable insight, Snow eschewed the use of these disjunctive strategies, and re-establishes the continuum of time which subtends the action of a drama and reaffirms the sense of the flow of time which conditions the tension evoked by that action.[18]

In a similar way, the traditional concerns which shaped the evolution of the style of innovational filmmaking had led to the widespread use of such strategies as the flattening of space, painting on film, and an associationist editing style which recreated on film a subjective space, the space of vision and imagination. In reaction to this, the fixed unblinking stare of the camera in WAVELENGTH re-establishes the real continuous space that subtends the action of the drama and makes the viewer very aware of that continuity.

This idea that the film is constituted by a single shot and so is recorded in real space and time is, however, contradicted by a certain feature of this work. During this portion of the film there occur, as was noted above, a number of light changes which indicate passage from day to night and back to day again. The contradiction between these light changes, which indicate that the film time has been synthesized from a number of different takes, and the general shape of the film, which being based upon a continual zoom suggests that the film is recorded in real time, both exposes the differences between film time, real time and narrative time and reveals the synthetic and constructed character of film time.

Suddenly one's attention is diverted from the continual extension of the zoom. There occurs the second of the "human events": two women, one of whom we saw previously supervising the moving into the room of the bookcase, walk into the room and listen to a radio broadcast (supposedly) of the Beatles' recording "Strawberry Fields Forever".[19] In part, this portion of the film reiterates the contrast between the two cinematic styles discussed above. There is, however, a marked contrast in the manner of presentation of this "human event" and that of the first, for as a result of the extended use of a filter, the coloration of the image representing the later event is, for a considerable period of time, non-naturalistic. This contrast between the naturalism of the representation of the first event and the non-naturalism of the second demonstrates the importance of mimeticism for sustaining the dramatic illusion. The same fact concerning sound is demonstrated through the contrast in the manner in which the exits of the two women are presented, for in one case the act is accompanied by sync sound, in the other case not.

Just as suddenly as the "human event" began, it comes to an end and some of the most striking visual effects of the entire film occur. For a moment the image disappears entirely and the frame becomes a solid colour field. This portion of the film marks Snow's most intense reflection upon light as a material of film. This meditation bears on several topics and is articulated in several ways. In the first place, the disappearance of the image and the resultant transformation of the frame into a solid colour field creates an environmental condition which shifts the viewer's attention away from the illusionary depth which appears to lie behind the screen and towards the space in front of the screen. As a result of this shift of attention, the viewer becomes intensely aware both of the light reflected into the space from the cinema screen and the light transmitted through that space in the form of the projection beam.

The pure colour fields of this portion of the film are replaced by startlingly coloured negative images of the loft whose visual field is the same as that of the image which preceded the pure colour fields. This image is followed by several others, all in non-naturalistic colours of like intensity. As these images succeed each other on the screen, the zoom continues its extension forward.

This portion of the film is significant in many ways. In the first place, the non-naturalistic negative coloration of the images causes an apparent flattening of space. This, of course, directs the viewer's attention to one of the essential facts concerning the material of film, namely that the filmic image consists of an arrangement of forms on a two-dimensional surface. Secondly, the startling colour of the image again reminds the viewer (especially since it follows on that portion of the film just described) of the projection beam.

When one realizes that Snow is contriving a number of devices to draw attention to the projection beam, one comes to realize that the over-all structure based upon the continual extension of the zoom figures a brilliant spatial analogy to the projection beam and the screen.[20] The lengthening of the zoom has a two-fold effect on the image: it causes a continual flattening of the image and it causes a progressive restriction of the visual field of the image. Thus in the course of the film there is described a sideways-lying pyramidal figure—a figure similar to that formed by the projection beam—adjacent to a flat surface. The fact that the over-all shape of the film and the shape of the projection beam share a common spatial character justifies the extension of the four-termed homology of the structures of the film, the viewer's response to a drama, the dramatic form itself and experience in general to include a fifth term: the structural features of the projection beam.

As the zoom continues its slow progression across the room and the visual field continues to be reduced, one becomes conscious that on the central panel of wall facing the camera there are a number of rectangular objects. Soon after becoming conscious of the presence of these objects one comes to sense that the camera's movement is destined to end by centering on one of these objects.[21]

This feature of the work demonstrates further aspects of the homology of the over-all structure of the film and the structure of the viewer's response to film-as-drama. One's initial response to the film is of course that of uncertain anticipation: one waits for some action to follow the first though one is uncertain what to expect. As it becomes clear that the over-all shape of the film is based upon the continual progression forward of the zoom, one's response changes in character: one still expects action but now one has an expectation about the general nature of that action: it will, one expects, be a further extension of the zoom. Up to this point, however, a considerable uncertainty characterizes one's anticipation, for as yet one is still in doubt about the eventual outcome of the zoom's progression forward. But as the rectangular objects on the central panel of the wall facing the camera come to occupy a larger and larger portion of the screen, this uncertainty is reduced, as one comes to expect that the film will end with the camera centering on one of the objects. As the zoom's progression continues further, uncertainty is eliminated as it becomes clear that the progression is leading toward the image of the sea waves. At this point, one is so certain about the eventual outcome of the film that the camera's movements seem destined. In short, the overall trajectory of the movement of the viewer's response to the film is from uncertain anticipation to certain expectation.[22] In overall structure, based as it is upon the continuous extension of the zoom figures, a brilliant spatial metaphor to the general trend of this movement is developed. One effect of the extension of the zoom is the continual restriction of the visual field of the image; this of course parallels the growing certainty one feels about the future development of the film. One could therefore say that the long open space of the loft as seen at the beginning of the film stands for the open possibilities which cause the initial response of uncertain anticipation, and that the restriction of the space brought on by the continual extension of the zoom stands for the diminishing of the field of possibilities which causes the viewer's response to change from uncertainty to certainty.

The structural feature of the restriction of space brought on by the progression of the zoom stands also as an analogue to certain structural features of drama and so serves to demonstrate further aspects of the isomorphism of the structure of the film and the structure of drama that was noted earlier. The long open space seen at the beginning of the film stands as an analogue for the wide range of possible action which characterizes the beginning of a drama, while the continual restriction of space parallels and emblemizes the progressive restriction of the range of possible further actions which occurs during the course of a drama. The presence of the rectangular objects on the wall facing the camera and their subsequent elimination develops a similar idea, for their multiplicity stands for the range of possible outcomes of the drama[23] while the elimination of some of the rectangular objects by the forward progression of the zoom stands for the elimination of some of the possible outcomes which occur in the course of the drama.

The presence of these rectangular objects and subsequent elimination from the field of view of all but one of them also serves to develop further that analogy between the over-all shape of the film and the structure of experience which we noted earlier. Just as the zoom projects forward towards the rectangular objects on the wall, so also much of our experience is "intensionally oriented", i.e. projects forward to an horizon of anticipated outcomes. And just as the visual field of the image narrows and as a result all but one of the images on the wall facing the camera are eliminated, so too in the course of an experience the range of possible outcomes is progressively reduced until one outcome becomes inevitable.

As a result of sensing that the zoom has a destination, one comes to feel during the course of the film that the space of the loft is held in the sway of inevitably unfolding forces. At the same time, however, a series of events occur the effect of which is the polar opposite of this, for they act to subject the room to the influence of a number of arbitrary happenings.[24] These events are of three sorts. One class of events includes random alterations of the colour characteristics of the image caused by the changes in film stock and the use of filters. The second class includes sudden and arbitrary changes in light caused by shooting the film at various times of day and night. The third class includes the events which occur outside the loft seen through the windows[25] on the wall facing the camera—the passing of trucks, the whirling of the lights of automobiles passing in the night, etc.[26] The opposition between the arbitrariness of these events and the inevitability of the actions which constitute the drama of the zoom's forward progression creates a contrast of response the effect of which is to highlight the structural tensions at work in a drama and the manner in which these structural tensions serve to hold the events in the drama in a nexus of apparent inexorable inevitability.

Suddenly the resolute tranquility of the progression of the zoom across the room is disturbed by the sound of breaking glass and a man climbing stairs off-screen and what seems to be stumbling or scuffling. Finally, a man[27] staggers into the room and falls on the floor, apparently drunk or dead.[28]

There immediately follows a passage of filter effects, colour changes and superimpositions of considerable duration. Then, as suddenly as the previous one began, the fourth in the series of "human events" is introduced. A woman enters the room and places a call to a man named Richard. She reports that there is a dead man on the floor, reiterates that he is dead and not drunk, arranges to meet Richard downstairs, and leaves.

The interrelationship between these two events, the latter of which presents a dramatic development upon the former but is separated from it by an interpolated passage,[29] is remarkably well-conceived.[30] In part the significance of this portion of the film lies in the way it demonstrates further aspects of the temporal structures of film and drama, and of our experience of temporality in film and drama. For when, during the second of these events, the woman makes a reference to the corpse lying on the floor, our thoughts are immediately cast back to the time and space at which we saw the man staggering into the room and falling on the floor. The temporal and spatial separation of the two events by the interpolated passage and by the change from day to night intensifies and heightens the effect of the passage of thought between the reference and event referred to.[31] Secondly, the relation between these two events serves to demonstrate the way in which the subsequent development of a narrative can act to clarify prior events and to reduce any ambiguity concerning them. At the end of the earlier of these two "human events" we are left in a state of doubt as to whether the man we have seen collapse on the floor is drunk or dead. The woman's insistence in the subsequent event that the man is not drunk but dead serves as clarification thereby reducing the vexing ambiguity associated with the event. The pattern of reduction of ambiguity is of course isomorphic with that pattern of the reduction of the visual field which we noted earlier was an important structural feature of the work.

These aspects of the relation between the two events serve to develop further the demonstration of the isomorphism of the structure of the film-as-drama and the structure of experience in general. For just as in a drama, later events have a connection with earlier events and reduce their ambiguity, so too in experience in general we look back to earlier events to clarify our understanding of them. In all these cases a reservoir of past information acts on the present.

There is a further aspect of these events which bears remarking upon. The film is in a certain important regard symmetrically structured, for both at the beginning and near the end of the film a "human event" takes place. Nevertheless, an important asymmetry attaches to the spatial character of each of the two events. At the beginning of the film, the zoom is set at its widest field and an illusion of deep space is created. In consequence, the events are presented in a very "realistic" manner. In the later events the zoom is quite far extended which flattens the space of the image and presents the event in an unrealistic manner. This asymmetry between the two sets of events and the contradiction between the spatial demands of dramatic action and the quality of space used to present the latter dramatic action (a contradiction heightened by the intensity of dramatic effect of these episodes) demonstrate that the impression of deep space is necessary to sustain the illusion of dramatic action.

The fact that the nature of the relation between these two events forces one to recollect a past event also extends one's thinking about the temporal structures of drama and experience. We have already seen that certain features of the work cause us to anticipate events while others cause us to experience events in the mode of presentational immediacy. Now we see that yet other features cause us to recollect events.

In part this serves to demonstrate further aspects of the homology of structures between the structures of this film and of drama and experience, for it is clear that in drama as in experience present events are qualified by past events and events to come. Perhaps more important, however, is the fact that as a result of these devices, events in the film are experienced in three ways: they are anticipated, they are perceived and they are remembered. In contrasting these three kinds of experience, Snow demonstrates with remarkable cogency the way in which the temporal character of the intensional objects of experience affect the nature of that experience. We can view the inexorable forward movement of the zoom, which continually brings the more distant nearer, as articulating an allusion to "the passage" (to speak loosely) of time, which continually brings the future into the present, and to the process of passage from one kind of experience to another. Thus another aspect of this rich work is that it constitutes a phenomenological inquiry into temporality which resembles Sartre's in its concern with the "process by temporality" and with the way in which the temporal character of the intensional objects of experience affects the nature of experience.

Shortly after the "human event" ends, and before the tension generated by it has dissipated, an extraordinary event occurs: suddenly a ghost image, in negative superimposition, of the woman making the phone call appears and is repeated several times. This event serves to develop several ideas. For one thing, it reiterates the way in which later events in a drama connect with prior events, for just as the woman's reference to a corpse lying on the floor refers back to the episode of the man's entering the room and falling on the floor, the phantom images of the woman making the call are used to allude to events in the past.

But more importantly the relationship between the actual "human event" and this more abstract echo of the event also serves to extend the discourse on the kinds of connections between events—a topic which, as was previously noted, is of great interest to Snow. The image in negative superimposition carries almost the same dramatic and emotional burden as the actual acted version. This establishes a further kind of continuum between these seemingly diverse sorts of events, for the one event is an equivalent of the other. This sense of the two objects being joined in a continuum is further strengthened by the fact that the actual event and its echo are related in a kind of dramatic causal nexus, since the dramatic intensity of the actual human event seems to cause the film to bring forth the negative superimposition.

In the last few minutes of the film, the meditation on illusionism conducted throughout the film is recapped and in some ways even further extended. During this portion of the film, the zoom continues its inexorable march across the final few feet of the empty loft. One effect of the extension of the zoom in this portion of the film is to eliminate the floor and ceiling from the image, leaving only a portion of the wall opposite the camera open to view. As a result, the illusory space in front of the wall articulated by the converging lines of the floor and ceiling is removed from view and one is presented with an image of flat field. Thus in the course of the film even the representational image changes from an image creating the illusion of deep space to one that appears flat.[32] The movement of the zoom could be seen as a track towards the true nature of film.

During these final five minutes of the film another process occurs, namely the emergence to clarity of the photographic images tacked on the wall opposite the camera. When the images become clear we see there are three of them. One, centered on the wall below the other two images, is a shot of waves. Above this and to the right is a front and back composite photograph of a nude girl. To the left, there are two white on black silhouettes of the "Walking Woman"; one of these, a larger figure than the other, is tacked onto the smaller figure and separated from it by a white border.

We have commented above on the fact that this array of images sets up a field of possibilities for the outcome of the film and in so doing articulates an allusion to fundamental structural features of our experience of the film-as-drama, of drama itself, and of experience in general. It also demonstrates further aspects of cinematic illusionism. Particularly significant in this regard are the silhouette figures of the "Walking Woman". By setting the larger figure on top of the smaller, Snow shows how a divergence of object size on a single flat plane can create the illusion of depth. This manner of creating the illusion of depth is of course characteristic of representational images in film. Also of significance is the white border separating the two figures, for it is the border which exposes the means by which the illusion is created.[33]

The film concludes with the zoom centering on the image of sea waves. The selection of this image is significant for several reasons. First, of all the images on the wall this image is the most illusionistic. Thus, as the image comes to fill the frame, the illusion of deep space, destroyed in the course of the film by the flattening of the image attendant upon the extension of the zoom to its furthest ranges, is re-established. In a sense, therefore, the film possesses a cyclical structure, for it begins and ends with a naturalistic image. At the end of the film, however, the viewer is aware as he was not at the beginning of the illusory character of the deep space. Secondly, the oceanic character of the image serves to articulate a further reference to the unity of the continuum, an idea in which Snow was, as we have seen, greatly interested when he made this film. One might even feel compelled to suggest an analogy between the ocean and the continual flow of events and between the waves and the events within this continuous flow. And third, no better image could have been found to define a space which appears to stretch beyond that which could be enclosed by the loft. This feature of the image, as we noted earlier, is used to articulate thoughts on the nature of consciousness and on the possibility of transcendence.

One final topic demands comment and that is the nature of Snow's relationship to the traditions of innovational filmmaking which existed at the time he began making films. Until now we have spoken as if this relation were simply one of rejection. This has of course been an over-simplification; it is no more true of Snow than of any other innovational artist that he simply rejected the traditions which preceded him. The relation is much more complex; in part it is one of rejection and in part one of assimilation, extension and transformation. I should like to show now how certain features of Snow's work are founded on a transformation of features of the traditions of innovational filmmaking which preceded him. In particular, I should like to discuss Snow's relationship to a certain aspect of Brakhage's work, since Brakhage epitomizes that tradition.

Brakhage's work is justly celebrated as an exploration of camera movement. By positing a somewhat extraordinary convergence between vision and expression, Brakhage used camera movements in such a way that they possessed both gestural and mimetic significance, since they were to be taken both as records of behavioural acts in which could be read the subjective state of the filmmaker at the time of making the work and as imitative of the mechanism of vision. In a movement towards reification[34] which has characterized many recent developments in art, Snow voids camera movements of any behaviourist or mimetic import[35] and uses movement instead as a formal principle for the organization of the film. And as a further extension of this process, Snow makes one simple operation the principle of formal organization of the entire work.[36]

The result of this voiding of the camera movement of expressionist and mimetic import and of using the transformed camera movement as a principle of formal organization of the work is that the conceptual import of the work is conveyed in an unusual manner. Here the content of the work is not something different from that expressed through the structure of the work; the structure of the work becomes the content.

This has important consequences for the manner in which one reads the meaning of the work. For no longer do the events in the film constitute a sign system which must be interpreted in order to decipher the meaning of the film. Rather the work becomes an object to be experienced, and it is through a consideration of the experiences evoked by the work that its "meaning" will be discovered. Such works as this, then, invite reflections upon and considerations of the mind in the processes of experiencing. On this ground, artistic production converges with epistemological inquiry.

Afterword on WAVELENGTH (1976)

Though on the whole I still subscribe to the aesthetic position which underlies this paper, the polemical impulse which led to its writing resulted in a study of the film which has many serious flaws. The most important of these, I feel, is that it fails to focus on the fact that the structure of the film operates to evoke an anticipatory sense, which then, by a range of strategies that can only be characterized as staggering (in view of the radically minimal character of the work), is frustrated. Thus, the article is not centred upon the aesthetic, i.e. tensional, basis of the film. A second serious flaw is that the article fails to stress the importance of the role which chance occurrences play in the film. A very important tension system in the film is that which operates between the radically determined over-all structure of the film and the chance occurrences which occur within this over-all structure.

All-in-all, in order to combat the prevailing approach to the independent cinema—an approach which characterized the independent cinema as engaged in a struggle for sensual liberation—I tended to overstress the extent to which the structure of the film can be seen as a determined system of very rigorous inquiry, and underplayed precisely those phenomenological tasks which are the real aesthetic imperatives of sound criticism.

The thought of revising the paper taking this shortcoming into account occurred to me, but I rejected the task when I realized that the polemical demands of today, though of vastly different character, would be just as great. The fact that today, in what is taken as serious criticism, WAVELENGTH can be discussed as a film which parallels the work of the Dziga-Vertov film group in undertaking a kind of cinematic deconstruction, I find so utterly discouraging that I can no longer believe that reasoned and informed critical discourse in the realm of the independent cinema serves any useful purpose whatsoever.

The New Canadian Cinema

Images from the Age of Paradox

Gene Youngblood

Men must have been in critical life-sustaining crises to have invented words. When we have something vital to say we can usually develop the means of communication. Today with our great vocabulary inheritance we squander meanings on unworthy causes and communicate little that needs to be said. —*R. Buckminster Fuller*

It seems to me that in the 1970s when you talk about film you're talking about media, and when you're talking about media you're talking about the messages, the cultural gestures, of society. Humanity is involved in a vast cultural revolution that is directly linked with the messages of the intermedia network, which now functions as nothing less than the nervous system of mankind. It's important that we begin thinking about movies in comprehensive ways. So before discussing the specific films that are the subject of this essay, I want to establish a context that will place them in proper perspective.

Reprinted from *artscanada*, April 1970.

The young of today with their transcultural video consciousness, free of the conditioning and nostalgia of past environments, have intuited something fundamentally inadequate in prevailing notions of reality. We're groping for new models of human behaviour to accommodate our perceptions. We have something vital to say. But the message has had no suitable medium. Our intuitions have remained inarticulate. We see the need for new concepts regarding the nature of human existence; but concepts are expanded or constricted in direct relation to the relevancy of prevailing languages: we've been in bondage to our metaphysical heritage.

Buckminster Fuller has said that words are "memorials of metaphysical victories of the mutual understandings of humanity". Clearly, the generation gap is a communication gap. We've lost our mutual understandings because the generations quite literally perceive two different worlds. Young people feel that the masters of the media squander meanings on unworthy causes and communicate little that needs to be said.

Indeed, the accelerations of radical evolution have caught us by surprise: the messages of society as expressed in the global intermedia network have become almost totally irrelevant to the needs and actualities of the organism. The situation is equivalent to one's own nervous system transmitting erroneous information about the metabolic and homeostatic condition of one's body. Fortunately, however, technology is decentralizing and individualizing the communication channels of humanity. And we find that personalized communication means the end of "official" communication structures such as the genre of drama, resulting in more poetic interpretations of previously standardized forms such as movies.

When the proliferation of technology reaches a certain level of saturation in the environment we cease to be separate from it. Communications technologies shape and record the objective and subjective realities of Everyman. The intermedia network becomes metabolically and homeostatically interfaced with each human being. To unplug and one of the advanced nations from the global telephone network, for example, would be a more extreme deterrent than any bomb; and world television linkages soon will become equally as vital.

In the past we've had two mass personalities, our media personality and our "natural" personality. Pioneering radio and television announcers adopted a mode of speech and behaviour essentially unnatural, a formal way of talking and acting through the media. In one sense, the media function as behaviour-altering agents for special occasions called "shows", much the same as alcohol is a behavior-altering agent for special occasions called "cocktail parties". But the recent phenomena of "underground" FM radio and "two-way" or "conversation" radio and television is evidence we're feeling more comfortable with our extensions. Soon we'll converse as intimately over television and radio as we do now over telephones.

The increasing number of twenty-four-hour all-news radio stations is a symptom of humanity's growing awareness of the monitor function of the media, even though today's profit-motive news might well be described as "tactical misinformation". The notion of putting on a "show", while still prevalent in namesake at least, is losing its meaning. Inevitably, show business is becoming communication business, which in turn is becoming education business. And thus begins the revolution.

The mass-audience, mass-consumption era is beginning to disintegrate like Hesse's alter-ego Harry Haller in *Steppenwolf*, who regretted his dual nature until he realized that he not only had two selves but quite literally dozens. The environmental saturation of inexpensive 8mm and 16mm filmmaking technology qualitatively transforms the nature of movies in a given culture. Symbiotically interfaced with this extension of his nervous system at twenty-four frames per second, the filmmaker is economically and aesthetically liberated from all social pressures; and a new personal cinematic statement results.

The majority of college students may stand in line to see EASY RIDER or ALICE'S RESTAURANT, because they have little choice. But it's significant that when they make their own movies, the output is qualitatively different from the input: they just don't make the kind of movies they've been raised on. Thus it's clear that in the new cinema the young have found a means of communicating their inarticulate awareness of a critical life-sustaining crisis—a crisis in the life of the mind. They've achieved a metaphysical victory of mutual understanding of a strange new reality looming on the horizon of civilization.

Slavko Vorkapich: "Most of the films made so far are examples not of creative use of motion picture devices and techniques, but of their use as recording instruments only. There are extremely few motion pictures that may be cited as instances of creative use of the medium, and from these only fragments and short passages may be compared to the best achievements in the other arts."[1]

It has taken seventy years for man to come to terms with the cinematic medium, to liberate it from the umbilical to theatre and literature. We had to wait until our consciousness caught up with our technology. If we've tolerated a certain absence of discipline, it's been in favour of a freedom through which new language hopefully would be developed. With a fusion of aesthetic sensibilities and technological innovation that language finally has been achieved. The new cinema has emerged as the aesthetic language best suited to the environment in which we live.

Emerging with it is a major paradigm: a conception of the nature of cinema so encompassing and persuasive that it promises to dominate all movie-making much the same as the theory of general relativity dominates all physics today. I call it *synaesthetic cinema*. In relation to traditional cinema it's like the science of bionics in relation to previous notions of biology and chemistry: that is, it models itself after the patterns of nature rather than attempting to "explain" or make nature conform in terms of its own structure. The new filmmaker, like the new scientist, does not "wrest order out of chaos". Both realize that supreme order lies in nature and traditionally we've only made chaos out of it. The new filmmaker and the new scientist recognize that chaos *is* order on another level, and they set about to find the rules of structuring by which nature has achieved it. That's why the scientist has abandoned absolutes and the filmmaker has abandoned montage.

In a 1934 essay, Erwin Panofsky wrote: "To pre-stylize reality prior to tackling it amounts to dodging the problem. The problem is to shoot and manipulate un-stylized reality in such a way that the result has style." Panofsky was concerned with the two properties unique to cinema: (a) its ability to capture and preserve a picture of time, and (b) its ability to post-stylize the natural reality that has been captured. To understand these concepts we must examine the three general purposes to which filmmaking historically has been applied: fiction, documentary, cinéma vérité.

Cinematic fiction should be understood as pre-stylized or manufactured reality that did not exist prior to the making of the film, i.e., the costuming of actors to represent cowboys, gangsters, etc., and the construction of sets as false environments.

A documentary also deals with pre-stylized reality. The documentary filmmaker shifts and reorganizes unstylized material into a narrative form that explains that reality to the viewer. Thus a documentary is not an explanation of reality, but the reality of an explanation.

Cinéma vérité, or direct cinema, is based on recording actual unstylized reality as it exists at a particular moment before the camera. The filmmaker is never to intrude by directing the action, or in any way to alter the events taking place (that is, beyond the unavoidable alterations caused by his very presence). The filmmaker's refusal to intervene directly in the reality before his camera, and the resultant loosely-organized structure, bring this type of cinema closer to the truth of the way events move in actual reality.

Synaesthetic cinema is all and none of these. It's not fiction because, with few exceptions, it's based wholly on unstylized reality. It's not documentary because the reality is not organized into an explanation of itself. And it's not cinéma vérité because the filmmaker shoots and manipulates his unstylized reality in such a way that the result has style. This process, best described as "synaesthetic post-stylization", results in an experience that is not "realistic", but neither is it "fiction" as generally understood, because none of the elements are stylized prior to filming.

At the beginning of ALPHAVILLE, Godard states: "There are times when reality becomes too complex for communication. But legend gives it a form by which it pervades the whole world." This is the legitimate role of fiction: to establish a framework that provides insights into otherwise inaccessible regions of the living present. But most insights inherent in fiction as the simulation of objective reality have been absorbed by the collective consciousness. We've learned from cybernetics that the structure of a system is an index of the performance that may be expected from that system. The simulation of reality has delivered its maximum performance. It no longer benefits us as it has in the past, primarily because television renders cinema obsolete as communicator of objective reality. There is no longer a need to represent the human condition through art: we see it daily on television.

Obviously filmmakers will continue to pre-stylize reality; in one sense the essence of art is the rearrangement of the environment for greater advantage to humanity. Yet this pre-stylization will not be so clearly separated from "reality" as it has in the past. Because of technology we've reached the point at which it's possible to manipulate reality itself in order to create new legends. Fiction, legend, parable, myth, traditionally have been employed to make comprehensible the paradoxes of that field of non-focussed multiplicity that is life. Synaesthetic cinema, whose very structure is paradox, makes paradox a language in itself, discovering the order (legend) hidden within. It is quite likely that insights most relevant to contemporary experience will be achieved primarily through this language.

In addition to the intuitively spontaneous inclination towards the cinema on the part of the young in general, we find that many professional artists who have worked exclusively in other media are now turning to the movies as a means of extending their formal preoccupations. Artists like Kenneth Noland, Frank Stella or Larry Poons achieved significance as painters in the last decade primarily because they kept the game going; one was impressed merely that they discovered new possibilities for a two-dimensional surface on stretchers. Obviously, men will continue to paint pictures; but for artists involved in certain formal problems the possibilities are so narrow today that soon there'll be nowhere else to go but to the movies. Thus the intuitive grass roots cinematic language unconsciously developed by the young non-artist is refined and made more eloquent through the aesthetic discipline of the professional artist.

Apart from Michael Snow... the most prominent examples of this trend toward the cinema on the part of Canadian artists may be found in John Chambers and Greg Curnoe of London, Ontario, and Gary Lee-Nova of Vancouver. Chambers, in my estimation one of the most important painters at work today, manages to invest his films with that special quality of "cosmic fantasy" that characterizes his paintings. Indeed his first film, MOSAIC (1966), was typically transitional in that Chambers was attempting to do in film almost precisely what he had done in painting.

MOSAIC is characterized by the same low horizons, expansive skies, and blank-space perspectives that inform the paintings. It was masterfully controlled for a first film, especially in its astonishing qualities of light. The light in MOSAIC is beautifully sculpted, defining the architectural trajectories of the graphic composition with a clear pellucid grace. Like certain images in Antonioni's early work (IL GRIDO, ECLIPSE), Chambers' compositions are characterized by long shadows raking across clipped bowling green lawns, stark juxtapositions of isolated verticals in an over-all horizontal vastness.

The film's mosaic of life and death, regeneration and entropy, is flawlessly evoked in ethereal, timeless, oceanic image-event sequences: a dead racoon, a new baby, an old man walking with a cane, a lithe young man running past him, a beautiful woman in a diaphanous white gown, arms outstretched against the sky, tossing rose petals to the wind, or suckling her child while bathed in pristine afternoon light in the windblown expanses of a park. MOSAIC is a metaphysical rondo that expresses what Chambers has described as "the inherent gentleness in the inter-communion of oneself with things".[2]

The influence of his paintings was almost negligible in Chambers' second film, R34 (1967), a rhythmic collage of the life and work of collage-maker, painter Greg Curnoe. R34 is, in effect, an interpretive documentary-commentary on the "reading paintings", box constructions, collages and other objects in Curnoe's studio—and their relation to the artist's personal life and cosmology. The film is a tight, brisk staccato of compact metaphors sprayed across the frame with burp-gun insistence, yet is choreographed so nimbly that the barrage is repeatedly spaced with wedges of oblique insight. For example, a blast of particoloured single frames that are pulverizing a collage might be punctuated with a long tender gaze at Curnoe's wife brushing her flaxen hair, or of the artist sitting contemplatively inside one of his objects with his child upon his lap. Volumes, scales, durations and textures become a combined gesture of intellectual montage that circumscribes the parameters of one human being's presence.

Inevitably, it was the notion of presence, of a sense of place, that Chambers undertook to explore in his next film, CIRCLE (1968-69). The subject of this film is light—light as contained within a closed space, and light as arbiter of physical and perceptual change within that space. As in Michael Snow's WAVELENGTH, with which it has much in common, the underlying device of CIRCLE is disarmingly simple: Chambers set up his camera in the same spot at ten a.m. each morning and exposed four seconds of film of his backyard each day for one year. Since the aperture and camera position were never altered, the only "action" in the film is inherently natural: the daily changes in light and colour become the protagonists of the film without any intervention on the part of the filmmaker.

CIRCLE is a natural film for Chambers to have made. Not only is its preoccupation with light a logical extension of the paintings (he has described his silver paintings as "light layouts"); it is equally a statement on the nature of photography, because here he allows the intervals between frames to function as his "painting". For this reason CIRCLE is only coincidentally a film that also belongs to a more general trend in structural cinema, characterized by the work of Snow, Joyce Wieland, George Landow, Bruce Baillie, and others. Although this particular school of filmmaking commonly is described as "minimal", to me its implications are more metaphysical than literal, more romantic than reductivist. CIRCLE, like WAVELENGTH, is a romantic film.

The environmental ambience of CIRCLE can be seen as one extended haiku, or 365 four-second haikus, but in any event I find the haiku analogy appropriate. A great metaphysical reality is conveyed with minimal language. The film is, in effect, one image in continual metamorphosis. The effect is overwhelming: the qualities of light impinge so radically upon the physicality of the scene that each shot seems to be of an entirely different location. Snow, leaves on the ground, shadows, clouds, sunlight, objects (toys, lawn chairs, etc.), clothes on the line, windblown trees, rain—separately and together they transform our perception of a place that is also an event, that is also a process. Romance occurs in the intervals between events. "Everything and anything that one sees," wrote Chambers, "is in its actual presence also more than we can, in any one way, understand it to be."[3]

Greg Curnoe presently is involved in intermedia inter-disciplinary records of real-time unstylized pattern-events. Art for Curnoe exists in the faithful cataloguing of the facts of experience—including a record of the process of that cataloguing. His current range of working media includes films, typed and stamped words, paintings, collages, box constructions, painted sculptures, audio tapes, video tapes, still photographs and computer printouts—all applied to the documentation or description of one subject. It is impossible and unfair, therefore, to discuss the films separately from this context. Indeed, the films (I saw only two) are negligible as "art", and assume relevance only in the home-movie context of their integration into Curnoe's multi-media documentation of regionalism as manifested in pattern-events and objects.

Thus he describes CONNEXIONS (1969-70) as a "biographical documentary", composed of three-minute reels of footage shot in and around London, Ontario. We hear Curnoe's voice (ostensibly reading from some sort of printed matter) describing the various houses, streets, events and personages that comprise the local milieu. CONNEXIONS thus becomes a diary-narrative-biographical-auto-biographical home movie of regionalism-provincialism. It is funny, naive, crude, unique. ("... Here's Sintzel's Cleaners. Johnny Sintzel married my cousin.... Here's the house where Jack Chambers was arrested trying to sneak into his girlfriend's window... it was the wrong window.... Here's the jail where they took him... ")

In Vancouver, Gary Lee-Nova showed me approximately forty-five minutes of unedited footage that constitutes all of his film work over the last two years. He's interested in film as process-documentation of art, *as* art. He's interested also in what he calls "sculpture as theater", which is suggested in a brilliant segment from his work-in-progress: a grotesque man with a box for a head and box feet clambers surrealistically around in a strange room with oversized perspectives and an outlandish TV set that shows a parade of other boxes just like him. The effect was indeed both sculptural and theatrical, as well as cinematic in Lee-Nova's sensitive lighting and camera work. Elsewhere in this workprint there's a humorous yet curiously metaphysical documentation of the making of a rainbow-coloured monolithic painted sculpture: a man breaks out of a huge box, paints a stripe on the sculpture, jumps back in the box, seals himself in, jumps out again, paints another stripe, returns to the box, etc. It seems to me that Lee-Nova is on the verge of a fairly important interface between film and the other plastic arts.

Of course STEEL MUSHROOMS (1967), made jointly by Lee-Nova and Dallas Selman, already is somewhat of a classic in the new Canadian cinema. A hyper-collage film in the style of Bruce Conner, it manages to pack a lifetime of steely urban paranoia into seven frantic minutes that also convey a sense of the beauty of the urban landscape. There's a powerful sense of dynamic thrust and driving kinaesthesia that culminates with a cartoony atomic mushroom cloud that folds in upon, and extinguishes, itself.

The highlight of my introduction to the new Canadian cinema came with my discovery of... David Rimmer, a really major talent. I can say with some authority that Rimmer is making movies of much greater merit than many filmmakers who have reputations only because they happen to work in cultural centres like New York, Toronto or San Francisco. SQUARE INCH FIELD (1968) and MIGRATION (1969) are poems in the finest tradition of synaesthetic cinema. They represent post-stylization of unstylized reality at its most refined level of intuitive language, striking deep in the inarticulate consciousness. Rimmer exerts a masterful command over a syncretistic field of complex image-events, suffusing the whole in synaesthetic alloy.

In thirteen closely-packed minutes SQUARE INCH FIELD surveys the micro-macro universe as contained in the mind of man. In that square inch field between the eyes known in Kundalini Yoga as the *Ajna Chakra*, Rimmer projects a vision of the great mandala of humanity's all-time experience in spacetime. A collection of archetypal faces accelerates to twenty-four per second and we're thrust into a cosmos of the elements, earth, air, fire, water, metamorphosing with icons, molecular structures, constellations, spider webs, snow crystals, and a time-lapse sunset over English Bay. All of this is viewed through a kind of telescoped iris aperture—peering outward from the mind's eye. The final image is the smiling face of an innocent child. This description does not begin to communicate the powerful aesthetic integrity with which Rimmer has compounded and orchestrated his universe of harmonic opposites: a revelation of cosmic unity.

Whereas SQUARE INCH FIELD was composed largely in the camera, Rimmer's next film, MIGRATION, made full use of rear-projection rephotography, stop-framing, multiple-framing, and slow motion. The migration of the title is interpreted as the flight of a ghost bird through aeons of spacetime, through the micro-macro universe, through a myriad of complex realities. A seagull is seen flying gracefully in slow motion against a grainy green sky; suddenly the frame stops, warps and burns, as though caught in the gate of the projector. Now begins an alternation of fast and slow sequences in which the bird flies through time-lapse clouds and fog and, in a stroboscopic crescendo, hurtles into the sun's corona. Successive movements of the film develop rhythmic, organic counterpoints in which cosmic transformations send jellyfish into the sky and ocean waves into the sun. It concludes with stop-frame slow-motion of the bird, transformed once again into flesh.

Rimmer also showed three short workprints, DANCE FILM, CELLOPHANE WRAPPER, and SURFACING ON THE THAMES, all dated 1970, all approximately five minutes long. SURFACING is a brilliant film which, in its way, belongs in the same class as Snow's WAVELENGTH. I've never seen anything like it. Rimmer rear-projected a ten-second sequence of old World War II footage showing two ships passing on the Thames. He rear-projected each frame, filmed it for several seconds, then lap-dissolved to the next frame, filmed it for several seconds, etc. The result is a mind-blowing film of invisible motion. The ships pass one another like the hands of a clock, without apparent motion.

SURFACING ON THE THAMES is the ultimate metaphysical movie, the ultimate post-minimal movie, one of the really great constructivist films since WAVELENGTH. It confronts empirically the illusions of space and time in the cinema and, in my estimation, is at least as important as WAVELENGTH as a statement on the illusionistic nature of cinematic motion. If SURFACING had been made in New York, Rimmer would be famous today. As it is he'll have to wait a bit; but this young artist is destined for recognition.

Keith Rodan is another talented filmmaker on the Vancouver scene. His CINETUDE #2 and CINETUDE #3 are brilliant studies in concrete motion graphics in the tradition of Len Lye, Jordan Belson (the films up to and including ALLURES), Harry Smith, Paul Sharits and Barry Spinello. Like Vasarely op mandalas, Rodan's graphics pop and scintillate with a slick Ultramoderne dynamism that strikes a neat balance between Bauhaus and 2001. Polka dots, serial modular grids, tetrahedronal configurations and pastel-tinted moiré patterns interact with mathematical precision that always teeters on the edge of be-bop frenzy. Rodan pastes Zip Tone acetate directly on film and combines his patterns in optical printing and various other animation techniques. It's a difficult kind of film to make, and Rodan is among the few today who are able to bring it off with the kind of kinaesthetic balletic grace that makes you sorry when the film is over. It was apparent from what I saw of his work that Rodan is well on his way to developing a viable vocabulary of concrete graphics in motion.

In London, Ontario, the young mathematician Keewatin Dewdney has produced two excellent movies, MALTESE CROSS MOVEMENT (1968) and SCISSORS (1967). Dewdney is archetypal of the new consciousness, a blend of science and psylocibin. MALTESE was made following a DMT drug experience. It's composed of a rapid panoply of live-action scenes intercut with Dewdney's arcane collages, mystical assemblages. In the film's first section, words or fragments of words are heard in conjunction with photographs of corrsesponding objects: idea and experience are not yet integrated; experiences must be *named* in order to have meaning. A little girl repeatedly asks: "Are you ready?" (for the drug experience). The remainder of the film represents post-drug ego-death: the hyper-collage proceeds nonverbally toward its staccato crescendo.

In SCISSORS Dewdney demonstrated considerable talent with the pixillation technique of animation: a pair of scissors live out a life-cycle drama of fighting, making love, giving birth to a covey of little scissors. Both MALTESE and SCISSORS owe something to the iconographic collage work of Stan Van Der Beek's early films; but in my estimation they're slightly more original than many of Van Der Beek's hastily-assembled gestures.

Under the guidance of Intermedia director Werner Aellen, the tutelage of Simon Fraser University's Stan Fox [now at York University], the Vancouver scene is prospering as regards the independent filmmaker. A series of generous grants from Canada Council and the Canadian Film Development Corporation is allowing the Vancouver, Montreal, and Toronto filmmakers co-operatives to join together with a community fund of some 100 films in a bilingual catalogue. The promise of an effective distribution network, coupled with the new videotape cassette image-publishing industry, indicates a revolutionary and quite unexpected future for the personal filmmaker.

Although commercial restrictions are inevitable in the early stages of videotape cassette image-publishing, we soon will find that the personal filmmaker is equivalent to the major studio. Sooner than we think, it will be possible to collect hundreds of cartridges of one's own synaesthetic cinema—images of one's actual life preserved out of time—for documentation, post-stylization and study. For the first time in history every human being now has the ability to capture, preserve, and interpret those aspects of the living present that are meaningful to him. The key word is *interpret*. In a very real sense we can now show both our experiences and our emotions to one another, rather than attempting to explain them in verbally abstracted language. We can now see through each other's eyes, moving toward expanded vision and inevitably expanded consciousness. Wallace Stevens: "It is the explanations of things that we make to ourselves that disclose our character; the subjects of one's poem are the symbols of one's self or one of one's selves."

Review of "The Hart of London"

Seth Feldman

Through the crushing banality of local television news images, we learn that a deer has wandered into downtown London, Ontario, during the winter of 1954. After jumping the fences separating the city's backyards, the deer is captured by local police. It is bound and placed in a cage made of storm fencing. A policeman pats it on the head. Then a man dressed as a hunter balances his rifle through the wires of the fence. We don't actually see him pull the trigger.

These are the events described by the title of Jack Chambers's film, THE HART OF LONDON. Like most Canadian films—from National Film Board documentaries through the features produced by the infant French and English film industries and the work of the Canadian avant-garde—Chambers's film centres around the exploration of a particular Canadian place. Yet THE HART OF LONDON, made by one of the most sophisticated theorists of realism in this documentary-oriented nation, goes further than most other Canadian films. Like a drummer, Chambers beats upon the core images with a rhythmic persistency until they yield a rich interweaving of personal consciousness, news, and history.

THE HART OF LONDON grows, more than anything else, out of Chambers's own evolution as an artist. He is, by profession, a painter. Unlike most Canadian artists, however, Chambers was not trained in the modernist schools of Toronto, New York, London, or Paris. He chose, instead, to undertake the rigorous classical training of the Spanish Royal Academy of Art, wishing, from the outset of his career, to acquire the precision of a Renaissance master in capturing the world around him.

After graduating from the Royal Academy, Chambers remained in a small village in Castile where he underwent what he called "a series of births", experiences that grew out of a synaesthetic perception of the Castilian landscape and a simultaneous realization that the landscape would be eternally impenetrable to him. It was this latter realization that caused Chambers to decide, in 1961, to return to his birthplace: London, Ontario.

During his late Spanish and early London period, Chambers harnessed the disciplined technique of the Royal Academy to an attempt to render some of the states of mind induced by his "series of births". The first attempts were highly expressionistic fantasy images. Slowly, though, throughout the sixties, Chambers's work began to demonstrate a realization that the impressions, the "wow moments" he wanted to create, would not be found in a compromise between mental and corporeal images. His work evolved, instead, toward the exact reproduction of

Reprinted from *Film Quarterly*, University of California Press, vol. 29, no. 4 (Summer 1976).

mechanically perceived reality on canvas. Using photographs of his family, his friends, and his geographic environs as models, Chambers created compositions that modified the photos in terms of saturation, colour, and details of subject matter. This modification became less and less pronounced and, by 1969, it disappeared altogether.

It was in October 1969 that Chambers published his manifesto "Perceptual Realism" in *artscanada*. The piece announced his intention to directly imitate the experience of perception by creating exact renderings of photographs. At the same time, however, the paintings were meant to be seen as paintings. Chambers did not and does not work to achieve a super-realist sense of *trompe l'oeil*. Instead, his intention is to invite the viewer to attempt to understand the artist's experience of the chosen subject. He has, since 1969, worked to separate style and ego, to make his presence felt not by imposing upon reality but by coming to terms with it.

Chambers released THE HART OF LONDON in 1970. On its most basic level, the film is an eighty-minute discourse on the evolution of Chambers's modes of perception, the growth of his realization that he could render the multi-sensuous impressions he desired only through precisely reproduced images of the world around him. Like Brakhage's SCENES FROM UNDER CHILDHOOD, the film is about an opening of eyes. But it is not a general statement about the nature of perception. It is, in a typically Canadian fashion, a chronicle that documents the reconcilliation of one man and one place over time.

THE HART OF LONDON begins with an exposition of the core incident described above. Beginning with the second image of this sequence, however, the reality of the news story comes to us not with the dubious clarity of a television news item, but rather with the flickering perception of a twenty-year memory. Printing multiple exposures of positive and negative images and overexposing single images, Chambers creates a winter within the winter of 1954. The frequent whiteouts, the failures of perception, also evoke an awakening consciousness which cannot yet fully experience and thus retain an image. The content of the news story, the automatic and pointless destruction of a graceful and innocent animal, would seem a metaphor for Chambers's conception of his own situation in the Canada of the early fifties before his departure for Spain.

While continuing the cinematic winter of over- and multiple exposures. Chambers adds to the deer incident shots of hunters piling up the frozen bodies of masses of dead deer in a setting unrelated to that of the news story. There then follows the longest sequence of the film, the compilation and reorganization of found images into a visual history of London. We see a barrage of single-frame images of maps, drawings, portraits, and photographs from London's precinematic past arranged in an approximately chronological order. We then see the relics of London's cinematic history, bits of archival footage dating from the late twenties or early thirties.

The contents of these shots show a personal memory rather than a textbook history. Rather than news events, we see what appear to be establishing shots for news stories: street scenes, factories, old-fashioned fashions surrounding local landmarks. Humans can be identified only as "group of wealthy looking men in front of doors to large building", "coeds of the forties on University bridge" and "worker at bench holding something". All the shots used recur again and again in the sequence. by themselves, superimposed on other shots, in negative, superimposed on their own negatives, reversed and overexposed to the point of illegibility—techniques, it would appear, that arc direct visual metaphors for states of memory.

The shots that recur the most in this sequence are those having to do with the mass slaying of deer with which the sequence began. By repeating these shots in the history sequence, Chambers successfully generalizes the deer incident, making it a metaphor for the place he is describing. Just as the hapless single deer jumped over backyard fences in his doomed efforts to escape London, the dead masses of deer are an involuntary part of the city's frozen landscape. The double meaning of the title, engendered by an invitation to pun on the word "hart", becomes clear.

The first two sequences of the film are unified not only by the techniques of cinematic winter but also by their mutual soundtrack—the slow, repetitive sound of waves breaking against a shore. The net effect of the images/sound montage during these first two sequences is that of time passing, of waves of memory drawing up and washing away the past, just as waves of light create and wash out images. Toward the end of the history sequence, however, the sound of waves is abruptly replaced. The sounds of the backwashes of waves heard in the first two sequences are the audio negative of the first sounds in the film.

The change in the soundtrack accentuates an equally abrupt reversal in the nature of the images. We go from the stock shots of London to shots, probably taken by the filmmaker, on the general theme of the coming of a literal and figurative spring. The cinematic winter of optical techniques gives way to clear black-and-white photographed imagery of the budding of plants, the plowing of a field, spring floods, children out for a walk. It is a step forward in an opening of the eyes, a giving back of images to the world that has produced the memories seen previously. In autobiographical terms, the film at this point leaves London, just as Chambers left it for Spain. The film temporarily abandons the experiencing of a single place in favour of the exploration of experience itself.

The "series of births" that Chambers experienced in Spain is re-created not only with shots of a human birth but also with shots of birth intercut with those of death. We see muscles spewing forth life and life becoming meat. There are shots of babies and a baby's genitals. The sequence begins subtly with close-up tracking shots of shears going through a hedge. It never really ends, but rather is subliminated into sequences made up of different kinds of images.

The "series of births" sequence is awkward. The human nativity and the stuff of death that one sees upon the screen cannot be favourably compared to Brakhage, or even to Brakhage's more skilled imitators. The cutting of the sequence is undeniably hackneyed. It is a montage exercise that was undoubtedly old when Dovzhenko used it in EARTH and all but exhausted when Vertov was through with it in MAN WITH A MOVIE CAMERA.

Chambers may well mean the sequence to be awkward as a reflection of his difficulty in attempting to assimilate his Spanish experiences. If so, then this admission of difficulty also contains a hint of Chambers' eventual solution to his perceptual dilemma. For while the cutting of the sequence is weak and most of the images uninteresting, one shot of the sequence stands out as the most poignant image of the film. The shot is a straightforward "wow moment" of perceptual realism in which we see a sheep bleeding to death on a large stone slaughterhouse table. We have previously seen part of this same shot in black and white. But now, for the first time, THE HART OF LONDON is in full colour. The sheep raises its head imploringly toward the camera, then lowers it back to the table. The camera is stationary and, as the sheep bleeds to death, the film runs through the camera, until both are bled white. All this is to the sound of backwards waves.

The film returns to London, Ontario. The first images of home are the midwinter burning of Christmas trees in a large bonfire surrounded by onlookers and a water truck marked "London Fire Dept." The shots are tinted red, as if by the blood of the previous sequence. They are followed by an intercutting of rather innocuous colour home-movie shots with colour shots of images from the previous sequence. The "series of births" sequence comes out red from the blood and the muscles photographed. The shots taken in London include or imply water. London water, then, in conjunction with the soundtrack, attempts to put out the red fire of Spanish images.

It does not entirely succeed. For while the Spanish images disappear, along with a temporary disappearance of colour in the film, the water shots also disappear. They give way to a series of fifteen minor news and human interest stories—the descendants of the previously viewed archival footage—that frequently present grotesque images of the waters of London. We see a swimmer taking a midwinter dip in the river—only to be escorted, along with his friends, to a London Police paddy wagon. We watch the pulling down of some water towers. We are taken to a mental patient's field day, at which one athletic event involves the soaking of participants. We are introduced to a man who keeps his sunflowers dry with a garden full of umbrellas.

The fifteen items are also the beginning of a summary of all that has come before. The second item, for instance, in showing the survivors of an earthquake being dug out of rubble, keeps alive the thought of death amid the much more innocuous material that surrounds it. The twelfth item shows old people looking at some of the old photos we looked at briefly earlier in the film. The fourteenth item is a local news report of a farmer who shot a timber wolf during the winter. The farmer and his wife play with the dead animal and then he poses beside it for the camera.

The last item of the series seems almost a parable, a summation of the film. An elderly lady pours water into the feeder on the side of a parakeet cage. We discover that the cage is only one of many assembled in a living room. A well dressed middle-aged gentleman and a policeman take several cages each and exit. They are seen entering another house in which a working-class couple is trying rather desperately to get their brain-damaged child to lift his head and look into the camera. The aristocratic man presents the child with a caged parakeet. Close-ups of the child's terribly distorted face are intercut with close-ups of the parakeet. And then there is an abrupt change in the soundtrack. We hear the sounds of screeching birds. But the sound comes not over a close-up of the parakeet but rather over the last close-up of the child, a shot in which he is frantically moving his lips.

There are approximately five minutes left to the film at this point and it takes about two minutes to discern the exact nature of the soundtrack. The sound of birds continues over more local news items, including shots of people sleeping on a local beach, London's own UFO, and the dismantling of the old city gates. The bird sounds merge into those of passing traffic and children's voices. As we see a home movie of Chambers pushing his lawnmower, we begin to hear adult voices talking to the children. A man and a woman are warning them to be careful, not to get too close. There is a cut to far away, from a travelogue perhaps, in which a European and an Arab stand in caves on a mountainside.

Then, as climax, we have what Peter Kubelka calls "synch event". We discover that the soundtrack to which we have been listening is a recording of a day at a local children's zoo. Chambers is with his wife Olga and their children, John and Diego. The children are feeding the deer.

The film contains an epilogue. It is a simple epilogue, consisting of four semicircular camera movements shot along the banks of the Thames. (Indeed, London has a Thames River, and an Oxford Street and a Covent Garden Market. When you take a picture of London, Ontario, you get a reflection of a reflection.) The camera moves toward the right along the bank, tilts up into the sky and then returns approximately the same distance. The soundtrack continues to the end of the first three sweeps at which point it ends on Olga's saying "You've got to be careful." The camera sweeps once more in silence, this time at sunset, around a very dark screen.

338 *Experimental Filmmaking*

Bibliography

Chambers, John. *John Chambers Interviewed by Ross Woodman*. Toronto: Coach House Press, 1967.

——— . "Perceptual Realism". *artscanada* 26, no. 5 (October 1969) pp. 7-13.

Magidson, Debby. "The Art of Jack Chambers". *Art Magazine* 6, no. 19 (Fall 1974) pp. 19-21.

Shadbolt, Doris. "On the Evolution of John Chambers' Perceptual Realism". *artscanada* 27, no. 5 (October-November 1970) pp. 57-62.

Woodman, Ross. "Canada's Finest Painter". *The Business Quarterly* 27, no. 4 (Winter 1972) pp. 72-6.

——— . "The Realism of John Chambers". *Art International* 14, no. 9 (November 20, 1970) pp. 37-41.

David Rimmer: A Critical Collage

compiled by Joyce Nelson

"While the emphasis of the Quebec cinema has been in the feature film, the Vancouver filmmakers have developed a concise, imaginative, evocative and intense work, the highly personal, individual concentration permitted only in the short film. And headed by such filmmakers as Dave Rimmer, Keith Rodan, Al Razutis, Gordon Fidler, Peter Bryant and many others, the evolution of a west coast cinema has reached such a level of accomplishment that recognition is long over-due. Even more so in the immediate present, for the active filmmakers have had an opportunity to develop their first works and refine ideas and penetrate into new perspectives, with each new film. Such is the case with Dave Rimmer...." (Kirk Tougas, *Take One*, vol. 2, no. 11.)

"Rimmer, who came to film via economics, math and graduate English (UBC and Simon Fraser) didn't start making films seriously till about a year and a half ago [1967]. SQUARE INCH FIELD (1968, 13 minutes, colour), which was only his second in 16mm, has been called the best film ever to come out of Vancouver. Composed of thousands of very brief images edited almost entirely in the camera, it is a thirteen-minute celebration of human life, of the multiplicity of Creation, and of the interconnectedness of all things. The film opens with shots of faces—all races, ages, expressions—accelerating up to twenty-four different faces per second. We then enter the square inch field—the mind of a man, which contains and is contained by the universe—through the windows of the eyes. And here we are confronted with life in all its aspects. In quick succession the images flash by, and are compounded: images of earth, air, fire and water, of birth and death, creation and destruction, the land and the city, the micro- and the macrocosm. And through it all the eye-globe-circle image reappears, uniting man and the universe in a band of being. It appears variously as a mandala, a galazy, or a spiderweb, but its chief representation is the iris, the circle of vision through which things are seen, alternated, and related. As the film progresses, the images tend to become more anguished: war, burning, violence, a deathmask. Then, sunset, a gull taking off from the waves, clouds; images of various religions; the universe is a flower, and now we are pulling back from the eyes to see faces again, first a blur but then separately discernable, slowing and finally coming to rest on the happy, lively face of a child—a moving statement of faith." (Tony Reif, *Take One*, vol. 2, no. 2.)

"... SQUARE INCH FIELD is a rapid-fire montage, a dynamic juxtaposition of the world's vital and destructive forces. The title originated in a Chinese book called *Secret of the Golden Flower* in which the Square Inch Field refers to the Third Eye. The filmmaker's own excellent eye is revealed in his beautifully composed nature shots and his forceful images of human life.... By quick cutting and fast zooms he telescopes an enormous amount of visual material together into a kaleidoscopic survey of our world." (Kristina Nordstrom, *Village Voice*, April 6, 1972.)

"MIGRATION (1969, 11 minutes, colour) appears to be a vision of motion described from the point of view of a bird flying through space. It opens with the black silhouette of a seagull flying in slow motion against a white background. Suddenly, the film stops, burns, and bubbles appear on the surface. This is followed by a more abstract, white silhouette of the bird, again in flight. Rapid dolly shots past trees and fast pans over the earth's surface vegetation symbolize the bird's speed. One particularly impressive shot records glimpses of the sun flashing behind a dark web of foreground trees; these glittering lights being visually analogous to the rapid wing motion of a bird in flight. At one point the bird's journey is interrupted; he falls from the sky as a bloody mass of flesh. Other carcasses of dead animals are cut in to remind us of the immobility of death immanent in life itself. The film essentially celebrates the movement of natural forms: birds, seals, a jellyfish, the waves, clouds, trees; it is a poem of motion.... Even the opening title and closing credit lines were made to vibrate by scratching the words by hand onto each individual frame." (Kristina Nordstrom, *Village Voice*, April 6, 1972.)

"... It's less a film of associations than of startling visual effects and rhythms.... The continuing migration is expressed in two ways: shots of the bird matted in white 'through' various scenes; and by a unique method of editing which seeks to emulate the rhythms of flight, and gives the film at times a powerful organic rhythm, a heartbeat of its own." (Tony Reif, *Take One*, vol. 2, no. 2.)

"Perhaps Rimmer's best quality is his immensely appreciative irreverence for the filmed image and for his own ways of reshaping it. Thus, SURFACING ON THE THAMES (1970, 5 minutes, colour), the loveliest Rimmer film (and the cleverest Rimmer title) shows a river boat slowly steaming past the Houses of Parliament—so slowly that it almost seems not to be moving, and surrounded by such a grainy luminous mistiness that one critic is supposed to have thought he was looking at a Turner painting rather than at film footage. Gradually the surface of the film begins to wrinkle slightly, to spot, to show minor blemishes—in a sense, to assert *itself* above and before the rich density it contains. The gesture is tentative and discreet, but it is also unsettling and liberating in ways that seem central to the gentle invocations of dissolution that are a basic feature of David Rimmer's world." (Roger Greenspun, *New York Times*, October 8, 1972.)

"The basis of the film is the shot of two ships passing each other as they move in opposite directions along the river Thames. By projecting it and rephotographing it frame by frame, Rimmer slowed down the film's speed so that the movement of these two boats becomes barely perceptible. He concentrates the viewer's attention on the grainy texture of the film stock itself, the lens through which it was projected, and the movement of hairs and specks of dirt in the gate. The shot was originally black-and-white, but he created its golden tonality by printing it on colour stock. The graininess, too, was increased through laboratory techniques." (Kristina Nordstrom, *Village Voice*, April 6, 1972.)

"SURFACING ON THE THAMES... denies normal time to emphasize a continuing motion. By expansion (the reverse of LANDSCAPE) Rimmer captures the illusion of the film medium, the twenty-four-frames-per-second fiction of motion; the breathing between each frame. Moreover, this film penetrates into the emulsion itself with its vivid and ever-changing abrasions and scratches, and, through its denial of its 24 fps reality, expounds on its own celluloid life." (Kirk Tougas, *Take One*, vol. 2. no. 11.)

"LANDSCAPE (1970, 11 minutes, colour) is single-framed during eighteen hours, dawn to dusk, from an unchanging camera position. Its drastic compression of time permits participation in a vision of the sculpture of landwater coming alive with otherwise imperceptible motion and colour fluxes. However, what is perhaps more important to this work is a positive force deriving from a negation. For the film asks for a response: the contemplative attitude associated with nature, the aura of peace and the realm of tranquility inhabited by any person fortunate enough to restfully settle down on a deserted seashore. The film asks for relaxation, for thought, for dreams, for drifting, for humanity. Without pretensions, without theories or logic, it is a film, a technological medium, used to reach an audience which seems more frequently to insist upon the involvement and entertainment of technology, rather than the simple charms of a landscape. It is a film that requests the renouncing of concrete, the negation of fumes and electronic pulses for at least a few minutes, and, without being pompous, is a warm reminder to live." (Kirk Tougas, *Take One*, vol. 2, no. 11.)

"BLUE MOVIE (1970, 5 minutes, colour) is a more abstract study of natural motion in which blue and white forms continually displace each other. It opens with a solid frame of bright blue. Suddenly clouds appear and move rapidly over the surface until the frame is totally white. Immediately, another mobile pattern is introduced, that of ocean waves which sweep white froth over the intense blue ground. The abstract effect is increased by looping some of the shots to repeat the same wave patterns again and again. Sometimes the colours are arbitrarily reversed. In the final segment the ocean appears more serene; the colours do not compete as violently as they had in the two earlier sequences, but vibrate quietly on the surface.... Rimmer's BLUE MOVIE recalls Franz Marc's "Fighting Forms", a powerful exercise in dynamic movement." (Kristina Nordstrom, *Village Voice*, April 6, 1972.)

"THE DANCE (1970, 4 minutes, black-and-white) begins with the shot of a theatre curtain being drawn open to reveal a packed audience. Then comes a dancehall scene with a jazz band playing in the background and a couple whirling around the dance floor. The picture is looped so that the dancers repeat their steps over and over again, while the music is allowed to develop into a finished jazz piece. The dancers end with a flourish (a smaller loop with the dancers twirling in one spot) and receive a huge bouquet of flowers. The film closes with the first shot of the film run backwards, drawing the curtains together again." (Kristina Nordstrom, *Village Voice*, April 6, 1972.)

"If you think about those dancers, who danced before a camera maybe a half a century ago, and who are now imprisoned in a repetition of those same few lively steps, it is tempting—and I think dangerously tempting—to see in the mere concept of the loops a kind of instant profundity. That Rimmer is aware of the profundity—and of the temptation—seems likely from what he does in VARIATIONS ON A CELLOPHANE WRAPPER." (Roger Greenspun, *New York Times*, October 8, 1972.)

"... Although Dave indicated to me that SURFACING ON THE THAMES was his preferred film, I feel the ultimate progression of his four recent works is more completely contained in the last: VARIATIONS ON A CELLOPHANE WRAPPER (1970, 8 minutes, colour). Firstly, whereas LANDSCAPE, THE DANCE and SURFACING are intricate units which modulate only within very restricted limits, this... work follows a *process*, embracing the intuitive concepts of the previous three films but juxtaposing their ideas, feeling for relationships. It is an odyssey into subject, motion, colour, image, and medium. The breakdown of these intrinsically becomes a constructive power within a changed dimension, the division-manipulation of elements evolves an accentuated whole. Commencing with an image-loop of a young woman shaking a large sheet of cellophane, Rimmer explores and rearranges the inherent reality of image, motion and sound present in a piece of film. The film rips at visual and sound relationships, elicits positive and negative image and defines the tensions and motion between them, breaks down colour and reveals visual emotive intensity in staccato bursts, sculpts darkness and light, and the contrast of spaces. Ultimately, as the image in motion links with the breaking of waves on a shore, the image of cinema arrives at a redefinition in two dimensions, linearity." (Kirk Tougas, *Take One*, vol. 2, no. 11.)

"VARIATIONS begins with a shot of a woman worker unrolling a large heavy sheet of cellophane before the camera in a most mechanical movement. In the course of the opening eight-second sequence the sheet unfurls to its full length in a brisk succession of undulating waves. The fine gradations of grey tone in the original shot progressively dissolve into high contrast, over-exposed, solid black and white areas. The very next sequence is shown in negative images. Eventually the representational forms are reduced into simple black and white patterns. As the tempo of the film increases the patterns themselves give way to nervous flickering dots and dashes and colour is introduced. Throughout each of the successively attenuated variations the dominant rhythms of the fluttering wave of the unfolding sheet remain present. It is almost as if the rhythm has become part of us, is in us. While the visual images virtually disintegrate into a staccato blur before our eyes, it is this dominant rhythmic undercurrent which gives the film its palpable, very real, cohesion.

"The principle action of the film is a progressive reduction.... The straightforward, descriptive shot of the woman worker performing her act of labour becomes an abstract gesture defined by rapidly alternating broad areas of black and white. This gesture is further abstracted into pure rhythmic flashes of primary colours. The progression from an illusion of background-foreground to a series of simple, alternating black and white patterns and finally to scintillating fields of pure colour washes is punctuated by an apparently random assortment of spots of contrasting colour.... VARIATIONS' abstractness works on other, deeper levels as well. Film, unlike painting, has a definite, highly structured temporal aspect to it. Rimmer utilizes this essential element of the medium to underscore the tendency within recent avant-garde art away from a concern with the content of a work of art to a concern with the process involved in its making." (Walter Klepac, *Mind & Matter*.)

"In SEASHORE (1971, 12 minutes, colour) Rimmer also repeats actions to set up a series of rhythmical patterns. The basic image derives from a shot from an old movie depicting women in long dresses standing along the edge of the ocean. Within this several-seconds loop he cut shorter ones, so that the film actually contains loops within loops. For example, the activity of a central group of three women is cut so that the figures repeat certain motions over and over again; one woman keeps kicking out her foot, the person in front of her continues touching her hand to her leg, while at the edge of the frame another woman keeps tidying her hair. Rimmer also chose to use the forms of surface imperfections, the scratches and dirt patterns, as bases for his loops. Other ways of stylizing the images include freezing the frame in which a distinct pattern of dirt appears, contrasting positive and negative images, and reversing the entire scene. At one point the original scene is confronted with its mirror image to create a bilaterally symmetrical pattern.

"Rimmer used other techniques in REAL ITALIAN PIZZA (1971, 12 minutes, colour), a film diary of the façade of a New York pizza parlor recorded from September 1970 to May 1971. On the soundtrack we hear street noises and popular music. In this film Rimmer combines the cinéma vérité approach of capturing actual people in segments of real life with stylized abstractions of those people.... As figures saunter past, enter or leave the restaurant the film suddenly jumps ahead in time to find them in a new posture. Their movements have become fragmented, set off, isolated as if their bodies had been lit by strobe lights. In these scenes, Rimmer condenses time, eliminating all inessential activity in order to emphasize certain special moments. In other sequences Rimmer expands time by capturing figures in slow motion. The shot of one young man dancing gracefully along the sidewalk is particularly memorable. The filmmaker has capsuled into this twelve-minute film several months of New York life. People walk by, carrying packages; they dance and fight (in the dancing and fighting sequences he looped some of the individual movements for a rhythmical effect); a firetruck stops; we even witness an arrest. In one humorous sequence two men shovel snow off the sidewalk, the filmmaker speeding up the action as it nears completion. One of the men suddenly twirls his shovel in a delightfully human way. This interest in anecdote combine with the film's formal structure reminds me of the paintings of Edward Hopper." (Kristina Nordstrom, *Village Voice*, April 6, 1972.)

"By and large, the structure of David Rimmer's lucid and remarkably self-contained films resemble nothing so much as a set of musical variations. After his first two films, SQUARE INCH FIELD and MIGRATION, both of which abound in a dense profusion of diverse but thematically interrelated visual images, Rimmer restricts himself to creating variations on a single motif. The source of these variations is derived from the formal properties of the film medium itself and from the basic techniques of film processing—splicing, repetition, reversing the original sequences, over- and under-exposing, introducing colour filters, and even altering the actual surface of the film strip itself. All are used to expand and transform the brief segment of film (i.e. the motif) into a unique visual experience.

"The films after MIGRATION achieve a power of abstraction which is close to astonishing. Such is the clarity of Rimmer's over-all conception and the aptness of his invention that these films totally engage and convince the viewer, both seasoned film enthusiast and man in the street. Another reason Rimmer's abstract mode has such a strong effect even on a relatively unsophisticated viewer is that he starts out with an image which anyone can recognize and identify. This gives us an immediate sense of orientation so that we are led by degrees and entirely through our senses to experience the ensuing variations and subtle transformations in completely cinematic terms. For soon after the film begins, Rimmer's brilliantly inventive variations obliterate the literal image of the given motif and force us, usually unwittingly, to take in the rest of the film in an entirely new and different way; Rimmer has, in effect, made the medium of the film into a mode of direct sensuous perception and experience, in itself and very much on its own unique terms.

"By acknowledging and then mastering the essential characteristics of the medium, Rimmer has created a number of extraordinary films which expand our visual-perceptual vocabulary and enable us, on reflection, to gain a clearer, more direct understanding of the very processes of human perception. In his best work, Rimmer, like the more important artists of the current avant-garde, transcends the traditional thematic, narrative, or even 'psychoanalytic' functions of a content-oriented art and opens up to us the phenomenological, perceptual and physiological aspects of art." (Walter Klepac, *Mind & Matter*.)

Rimmer's other films are HEADEND (1970, 2 minutes, colour), TREEFALL (1971, 5 minutes, colour), FRACTURE (1973), WAITING FOR THE QUEEN (1973). CANADIAN PACIFIC PART I (1974), and CANADIAN PACIFIC PART II (1975).

V

"THE POSSIBILITIES ARE TRULY GREAT"

CONTINUED

A Place Like Home

Robert Fothergill

How variously and how well have English Canadian movies shown us the country we live in? Imagine a foreigner who had derived his impressions of life in Canada from an immersion course in our movies: what sense would he have of the look and sound of Canadian places—cities and small towns, farm-land and wilderness? How much would he know of the ambience of the different regions—the Maritimes, Montreal, Ontario, the prairies, and the west coast? What impression would he have gained of the feel of life—various social contexts and pockets of culture—their emotional climate and everyday texture? How truly could he say that he felt as if he had lived here? Of course, there is no definitive reality to the Canadian milieu, nor do we require of movies that they should be trying to capture such a thing. But most movies do indeed convey, inadvertently or by design, some fragmentary image of a milieu within which their stories are set. This essay proposes to scrutinize some of those fragments.

Most Canadian films are situated more or less specifically in a Canadian location. Sometimes, admittedly, the location has no identifiable features, and could be some vague tract of land anywhere in North America—as in EVER AFTER ALL by Barrie Angus McLean. But, as a rule, the action takes place in a locale which the inhabitants at least, if not the audience at large, can recognize. Sometimes this locale is specifically identified, in conversation, by road-signs, etc., or is so universally recognizable as not to need naming. (Vancouver and Montreal are unmistakable in any movie.) In other cases, the setting of the story is quite particular—an Ontario small town, for instance—but its actual identity is masked, so that only those people familiar with the area can detect in the background the sights of St. Thomas or Elora, Paris or Peterborough. The purpose for such masking is apparently to generalize the story to some extent, and to achieve a measure of elusiveness, so that no one can dismiss the story as utterly implausible or a slander. In still other films an effort is made to disguise, for example, Toronto as any North American city. Licence plates are concealed, police uniforms are subtly generalized, streetcars are kept out of sight, and so on. In BLACK CHRISTMAS, a small U.S. flag can be seen on the corner of a police officer's desk shyly hinting to American patrons that this is a film they can recommend to their friends as 100 per cent apple-pie entertainment.

But questions about milieu in movies go deeper than whether we can read the licence plates on cars and the name of the city transportation commission on the sides of buses. Concealment of the locale is not necessarily a crime; certain kinds of fiction positively require a vague location, free of specific associations. Conversely, plunking the action down in Toronto for all to see doesn't automatically guarantee that the film will be rich with concrete social observation, or that the fiction will be woven into the fabric of a particularly rendered human milieu. And here, of course, we are introducing another kind of interrogation. It's not enough to ask what role the physical locale plays in a given film, how faithfully the plot respects and incorporates the geography of streets and fields, the interiors of "beverage rooms" (grotesque name!) and farmhouses. More important are the questions about the relations which are established between the lives of the fictional characters and what we may glibly call "the real world". On one level, these continue to be questions about how the shooting of the film employs locations—which may or may not include people going about their regular lives. On another level, however, we come to enquire about the screenplay, the author's conception of a dramatic action involving several people over a space of time. Does this conception encapsulate the characters in an essentially private world, or does it, in some way or another, locate them in the web of social inter-connections that ultimately entangles the entire population of the earth? To the incorrigibly classifying mind it appears that when its milieu is not definitely Somewhere, a film will have its setting Elsewhere, Anywhere, or Nowhere.

It is one of the increasingly obvious presumptions of this article that Canadian filmmaking has been artistically most successful when it has sailed close to the winds of realism. Where milieu is concerned, this entails a conscientious exercise of the sociological imagination, to plant the fiction in those social facts that largely condition it. But there are also some commendable films espousing a deliberately different mode, to which different criteria should be applied. Such films may be said to be located Elsewhere—a specially created and particular Unreal place. In his futuristic extravaganzas, for example, David Cronenberg is concerned to establish environmental contexts which are deliberately unfamiliar. In STEREO and CRIMES OF THE FUTURE his characters wander through stark, depopulated institutional edifices of steel and concrete and plate glass. We are inside quarantined communities, insulated from whatever may be supposed to remain of society at large. Inherent in the conception of these films is the creation of a counter-milieu—one in which the conditions of human intercourse will have been radically transformed. To put Paul Almond's film JOURNEY next to those of Cronenberg may seem incongruous, but Almond too creates an Elsewhere, a self-contained community in which life is lived on different terms from what we take to be the norm. Unlike Cronenberg's, however, Almond's artificial community eschews all artifice. The inhabitants of

"Undersky" have created for themselves a pre-industrial subsistence commune. On a few acres reclaimed from the wilderness, on the banks of the Saguenay river, they farm with hand-made implements, live in hand-hewn log cabins, and play on (presumably) hand-hewn guitars. Only their glasses are unaccounted for. The lovely thoroughness of the set-construction combines with the changeable beauty of the location to make this milieu the most satisfying element in the movie. Deliberately, as an element of the film's mystique, Almond seeds ambiguous suggestions that the protagonist, Geneviève Bujold, may be visiting the commune in a dream or in some sort of time-warp, there to encounter potential deliverance from the prison of her urbanized, neurotic psyche. After a number of therapeutically elemental shocks, including the birth and slaughter of animals, and a primal fuck administered by the community head-man, Boulder, she floats back to a world that distant lights and harbour sounds suggest may be our own. Film audiences, who are not backwoods buffs on the whole, find this return to the real of technology rather a relief.

"Elsewhere" in these films by Cronenberg and Almond is elaborately stylized, set over against the world of supermarkets and bus depots, and standing in relation to that world as an anti-type. In a different way, the actions of Morley Markson's ZERO THE FOOL and MONKEYS IN THE ATTIC are removed from everyday reality by a process of insulation. They are neither out of this world nor in it. The setting for ZERO is a cabin in the woods in winter; for MONKEYS, the interior of a house. The clusters of characters—a trio and a quartet, respectively, with one additional arrival in each case—are presumed to have come from an everyday world that surrounds their isolation. They buy their food in stores and their gas at gas stations. But for the purposes of the dramatic action, this larger milieu has no existence. Entering the pressure-cooker that Markson has created, they are shorn of occupation, personal history, role in society. They are participants in a collective hysteria generated by the filmmaker. In ZERO the persons are interacting as themselves; in MONKEYS they are actors animating a script by playwright John Palmer. In MONKEYS, especially, the setting contributes powerfully to the emotional tone of the film. From ground floor to attic (where the "monkeys" prance and cavort) the house is an active element in the chemistry, which the camera-work intensifies by peering crazily up and down stairwells, in and out of rooms. But, for all that the opening shot shows us the Toronto skyline, this surreal theatre is situated Nowhere.

On first thought, Jack Darcus's PROXY HAWKS appears to be another Nowhere film. This very private drama of the battle between a man and a woman for control over the space between them takes place in a cabin in the woods. It is near a golf course and a river, and other people are occasionally to be seen passing like phantoms. Dramatically more prominent than any other people, however, are the many ravening birds, including a wounded eagle, that the couple keep caged, for no very obvious reason. Alternately threatening and helpless, these birds (the "proxies" of the title) become symbolically identified with the images that the couple have of each other. But while this psychic drama occurs in isolation from the world, it is not insulated from it. The woman's crisis of revulsion against ravening maleness is precipitated by the account she finds in an illustrated magazine of the My Lai atrocities. This reference has the double effect of generalizing the thematic scope of the film's central conflict, and at the same time of particularising its historical situation. Many other signs in PROXY HAWKS combine to evoke a pretty specific cultural locus for the drama. The style of dress of the two characters, their hair, their physical posture even, and what we see of their life-style, all proclaim unequivocally the radical counter-culture, back-to-nature ethos of the late sixties. And in fact the physical location of the story, while not stated, is unquestionably precise also. This cabin in the woods, which might be in Maine or Oregon, is actually close to the Fraser River, at the south end of Vancouver. It wasn't built on a studio lot to look as general as possible: it was Jack Darcus's own home at the time, and it just happens to look a lot like other cabins in the woods.

Well, you might say, but the house in MONKEYS is actually Morley Markson's own home in Toronto. True enough, but whereas Markson populates his home with a quartet of theatrical personages and a pizza delivery boy, for a night of Absurdity, Darcus himself takes the leading role in a drama that seeks to give expression in natural imagery to the tendency to polarizattion of male and female in actual everyday life. The mode of Darcus's fiction calls for a naturalistic locale, to confirm its connection to reality. Palmer and Markson, on the contrary, in staging a fantastical play of "exploding dreams" (as the extended title calls it), require an imaginatively closed space.

With a few exceptions, Canadian dramatic fictions, as written and as photographed, occur Somewhere—in and against a larger social setting. The variety of locations is respectable, even though a good many interesting and distinct locales have yet to make an appearance. Contrary to what one might expect, relatively few films are situated in the mighty wilderness. Nor, for the most part and speaking only of films in English, do they take place amid the winter's snow. Perhaps for no better reason than convenience, the season is usually summer or fall, and the place fairly civilized, i.e., not too far from a processing laboratory. Montreal, Toronto and Vancouver have got into the picture often enough to satisfy and local chamber of commerce, but the cities of the Maritime provinces and of the prairies have put in hardly a single appearance. Indeed, THE ROWDYMAN, with its jaunty, down-home, in-and-out-the-houses look at Cornerbrook, Newfoundland, must be the only feature film to be located east of the province of Quebec. It's true that Maritime locales have had their moments of glory in NFB travelogues—those rather ingratiating little pieces which ask cutely: "Did you know that there's a place in X (fill in name of province) where you can still find people doing Y (fill in name of improbable activity like tossing the caber or cheese-rolling)?" But if any dramatic screenplays have been situated in that old and weather-beaten part of the cultural mosaic, they haven't yet found their way into production.[1]

THE ROWDYMAN does Cornerbrook proud, and no wonder the inhabitants loved it. Author and actor Gordon Pinsent isn't setting out to compose a sociological document, but rather to evoke a spirit-of-place to chime with popular mythology. Yet this fiction seems, to one who has never been there, to bottle the spirit of that community with at least as much fidelity as a sober documentary could do. Beginning with the look of the place—the pale and chilly light of a harbour on the St. Lawrence Gulf, the hilly streets climbing away into the surrounding heath—the film goes on to summon up the flavour of life there, the tone and tempo of its daily music. Granted that Will Cole may be something of a fantasy, an anthropologist's reconstruction of Newfoundland Man, nevertheless he is located in a community of work and play which has substance and detail. We know the inside of his house, of the pulp-mill where he works, of the pub and the police-station. We see him with his work-mates on their lunch break; at some kind of a town fair; and inside the jolliest brothel you could ever dream of. Such is the realism of a short café sequence that one of the background characters actually bears a haunting resemblance to Michael Spencer, executive director of the CFDC.

Swing for a moment *a mari usque ad mare*, and compare THE ROWDYMAN to George McCowan's film THE INBREAKER, set in a fishing port on the north end of Vancouver Island. The physical land and sea-scapes of Alert Bay are presented with postcard vividness; small boats jiggle and joggle at their moorings under skies of cloudless blue. And, to give the film its due, the long scenes of herring fishing out on the ocean are done with commendable attention to the arduous processes involved. But the life of the fishing community on shore, with its bitter hostility between Indian and white, is conveyed in a most perfunctory fashion. We get a glimpse of the offices of the fish-packing depot, a couple of scenes in a beverage room, where most of the patrons have the look of extras acting natural—and not much more. Rather than growing out of its location, the story was parachuted into it. Alert Bay was selected, one imagines, by a "location-finder", mainly for its scenic suitability.

What is to be said, in this connection, of PAPERBACK HERO? The setting is Delisle, Sask., no bones about it. (Rick Dillon's red Thunderbird is now enshrined in a local showroom.) Don Wilder's photography shows off to advantage the beauties of the surrounding landscape, and captures the sprawling, wide-open, dusty look of the prairie town.[2] The local hangouts are authentically rendered, along with the drygoods store, the police station and the hockey arena, where the on-ice sequences are most excitingly done. We know we are in a real place, right enough. But beyond this depiction of the physical milieu of Rick Dillon's decline and fall, has the social milieu been convincingly established? This is particularly important because the character of Rick Dillon is not a detached conception, but involves his relation to the community. To some extent, we are to understand that he is a creation of that community, inconceivable in isolation from its ethos. He embodies an aspect of its collective self-image, and performs, like any idol, in obedience to the demands of the fickle. In a sense, then, Dillon and Delisle, figure and ground, must both be got right if either one is to be convincing. And Keir Dullea's performance, though displaying an energetic bravado in places, is not attuned to the ambience of a hockey town in Saskatchewan. Too many elements of character and social situation are overdrawn, caricatured, distorted. The hockey heroes of the west may be loud, uncouth, boisterous jocks, but glassy-eyed psychopaths they surely are not. There is a violent craziness latent in Dullea's Rick Dillon, a total lack of easiness with himself. His hollowness is too hollow, his brutality too brutish. He didn't grow up laying minor hockey in the bush leagues, and the people of Delisle wouldn't have loved him. The conception of "Marshall" Dillon, the gun-toting, erstwhile darling of Delisle, is an imported one. An indication of its falsity may be detected in the movie's theme song, Gordon Lightfoot's "If You Could Read My Mind". Appropriate neither as an expression of the protagonist's sensibility nor as an authorial comment, the song serves only to smudge and sentimentalize the tone of the film, in the same way that Leonard Cohen's songs are pasted onto MCCABE AND MRS. MILLER.

Two ways to go for a contrast to PAPERBACK HERO: east to Toronto, west into Alberta. Either way, the comparison favours Pearson's film. FACE-OFF takes us to the glamorous, blazers-and-trench-coats world of Hockey "down east", where Billy Duke, getting the break that poor Dillon never had, has been drafted to the Maple Leafs. Beware of any Toronto movie in which the romantic leads run hand in hand along Yorkville in the rain! If Pearson's protagonist is the creature of a TV series, the hockey players in FACE-OFF have leapt clean out of the commercials, poised to endorse a hair-conditioner or a garbage bag at the drop of a cheque. The world in which they move, in which Duke has to choose between his loyalties to The Team and to a pretty singing lady, is vintage, well-lit glossy (photography: Don Wilder again). In literal terms, of course, it's all as authentic as can be. There they are on the ice at the gardens, and now they're in the Hot Stove Room, and Gee, there's the real Eddie Shack! But the social ethos created by the script is crossbred soap-opera and sports-page. It exhibits no feel at all for the daily texture of life among professional athletes—or among pop celebrities, for that matter; a wholly plastic film.

SLIPSTREAM turns in the other direction, towards the rolling foothills of southern Alberta and a life of calculated withdrawal. There are splendid landscapes, and a skyful of twinkling stars that cost a small fortune at the optical printer's, but the screenplay doesn't effectively situate itself in a particularized Canadian locale. To be fair, the film doesn't actually conceal its whereabouts, and on the licence-plate test it makes a respectable score. But the nearest urban centre to Mallard's electronic hideaway is never called Lethbridge, but always "the city", allowing viewers to think of it as Salt Lake or Oklahoma, as seems good to them. The dramatic action involving Mallard, a bunch of kids from "the city" (one of whom stays with him), and the manager of the radio station, is pretty well self-contained, and exists independently of any surrounding milieu. Although shot in a rural *location*, Acomba's movie from Bill Fruet's script, has nothing to show about the indigenous quality of that region of Alberta. Not much more satisfactory, from this point of view, is Harvey Hart's production of GOLDENROD, maladapted from the novel by Herbert Harker. The story of the fall and rise of a champion bronco-buster has all the right ingredients for bringing out the local flaour, but the made-for-U.S.-TV movie wastes them unforgivably. The imported stars talk with hillbilly accents; Harry Makin's photography contrives to make the distant Rockies look like painted backdrops; and, with a touch of supreme indifference, the script sends its Alberta dirt-farmers to Estevan for their Saturday-night boozing. What the hell? Who's going to know that Estevan is several hundred miles away, on the far side of Saskatchewan? Answer: readers of *Who Has Seen the Wind*. At the time of writing, Allan King's production of W.O. Mitchell's story is the one to be on as a prize-winner in the prairie location contest.

Among a number of movies set in a rural milieu, two stand out (in contrasting ways) for the effort displayed in both screenplay and shooting to convey the spirit and feel of their particular locales. In BEST DAMN FIDDLER FROM CALABOGIE TO KALADAR (set, as the title proclaims, in the depressed rural area of eastern Ontario), and in ISABEL (set in a village on the Gaspé coast), a girl is struggling against entrapment by the place of her birth. Both directors, Pearson and Almond, take pains to show the physical and social environments which oppress their characters. Rosie (Margot Kidder), eldest daughter of the "Fiddler", still lives in his impoverished, ramshackle, child-littered farmhouse. The black-and-white photography conveys vividly both the squalid and the picturesque aspects of this backwoods habitation, and of the surrounding social milieu, which is evoked in rowdy scenes at a Saturday night dance and at a wedding. But in the fate of her mother (Kate Reid), Rosie can see all too clearly what would follow from marriage to the man who seduces her so merrily in the back of his panel-truck. The men of this community, her father especially, embody a kind of irresponsible vitality, and family life has a primitive closeness and warmth; but it is also a kind of death, particularly for a woman, who will become nothing but a permanently pregnant drudge.

Isabel (Geneviève Bujold) has made an escape already, but her mother's funeral draws her back towards a trap which, as Almond conceives it, is more psychic than social—a farm and a helplessly bereaved uncle called for her care. With a poetry of visual images that has been justly praised, Dufaux's cinematography evokes the sight and sound, and almost the smell, of winter releasing itself into spring around the old farmhouse. But, as Isabel experiences it, the spirit of the rural Gaspé that clutches at her spirit has something of the demonic. The past threatens her with more than merely the drag of stagnation and servitude, as it did Rosie; rather, it haunts her with the ghosts of the unappeased dead. Beyond the physical brutishness of the rural milieu, incarnate in the village louts who try to rape her, Almond depicts the farm as a nightmare from which Isabel is struggling to awake.

These two films proceed from radically different imaginations. Pearson's latent Romanticism is detectable in the characterization of the indomitable Fiddler (Chris Wiggins), and in the choice of lyrical snatches of Berlioz to sweeten the movie's interludes; but it looks like the severest naturalism beside Almond's gothic intensities. Pearson lets us see and feel the oppressive stagnation threatening Rosie in the tangible details of everyday life; Almond spooks us with the ghostly figures and looming irrationalities that terrorize his Isabel. In both movies, however, we have strong examples of milieu-as-theme. Reflecting one of the central dichotomies of the fictive imagination, they invoke the opposition of country and city as social and spiritual climates. Sometimes this dichotomy can appear as a simple contrast of better and worse: warm, natural, wholesome country versus cold, corrupt, alienated city; or liberating, energetic city versus stifling, stagnant country. But in any complex work the ambivalence of both terms is at least suggested, if not thoroughly explored. (Rosie, for example, makes her "escape" to a job as a switchboard operator for Bell Telephone.) Furthermore, the quality of each mode of existence is seen to depend to some extent on the temperament of the person confronting it. Life, as they say, is what you make it.

"Life in the country" and "Life in the city", while they have certain intrinsic realities, are also, in an important way, ideological notions that people in either one of the two situations have about the other. Both pathos and ironic comedy reside in the encounter between a person armed with such notions and the realities by which they are challenged. There was a time, long ago it seems, when the attempts of a bewildered rustic to cope with the jazzy, bustling city was surefire comedy. But the buoyantly patronizing laughter has died away, and the plight of naive newcomers like Shebib's Pete and Joey, in GOIN' DOWN THE ROAD, is seldom the occasion for amusement. On the whole, the comic version of the encounter appears to be the one between a city person and country conditions. In Shebib's second feature film, RIP-OFF, four suburban youths excite themselves with ideas of establishing a rural commune in the Ontario north woods. The dominant joke of the movie is their rapid disenchantment with that grand old Canadian notion, roughing it in the bush. After a couple of days of roughing it with a derelict cabin, inedible whole-earth food, a radio beyond the reach of any stations, and the onset of total boredom, they trundle back to the comforts of home. "The country" had been a romantic idea to them, a notion of some sort of liberating transformation of the self. They had been duped by a line of counter-culture advertising: New Formula "Nature", easier than ever to apply; after just three days, you will feel like a new person. In similar fashion, the hippie-hero of David Beck's FOLLOWING THROUGH betakes himself to the country for a groovy summer of work on a farm. In his case, the comedy extends beyond his defeat by the physical conditions, to his psychological rout at the hands of the local community. In some ways, the film resembles a farcically invented JOURNEY. In JOURNEY, as described earlier, the leading character finds herself in a radically anti-urban milieu, surrounded by fundamentalist adherents to the Primitivist faith. The thousand natural shocks to which she is exposed constitute a healing trauma for her, while her unsettling vibes threaten to disrupt the commune's hard-won harmony. In contrast to these philosophic solemnities, Beck's film mocks the discomfiture of a Nature fan hitting the shit.

The country-city polarity makes another appearance in Robin Spry's PROLOGUE, as an element in a larger treatment of opposing paths to personal commitment and choice of life-style. Suffice it to say at this point that Spry divides his questing sensibility into two characters, and sends one of them off to try the life of a drop-out commune. The milieu thus explored is not so much agricultural as counter-cultural. Living close to nature and baking their own bread expresses the commune's dedication to a different mode of social and personal interaction. Like the character, the film visits the commune as a fairly casual quest, and registers little of the daily actualities of farm work. The life of the commune, and the rural milieu, stand more for the repudiation of involvement in mass society and its political problem than for the positive espousal of a rural ideal. A long dinner-table debate on this theme compromises the film's most elaborate presentation of the milieu—in theoretical rather than in dramatic terms.

One other movie that calls out for mention in this context, though not strictly speaking a dramatic feature, is THE CLINTON SPECIAL—Michael Ondaatje's film version of Paul Thompson's production of the Theatre Passe Muraille's theatrical portrait of an Ontario farm community. Originally entitled THE FARM SHOW, the stage production was a kind of documentary pantomime. A group of Toronto actors went to live and work for a summer on farms in the neighbourhood of Clinton, Ontario. (Some of their experiences, as rendered in the stage-show, reflected exactly the comedy situations of soft-handed city people being felled by the rigours of farm labour.) While there, they gathered detailed impressions of the life around them—of individual characters and daily activities and social events—which they then worked up into an evening's theatre. This mixture of wicked impersonations, tumultuous mimes, and poignant stories of personal disappointment and loss was first presented to a Clinton audience which apparently howled in dismayed delight at the mirror thus held up to them. In making a movie version of this lovely theatrical concoction, Ondaatje takes the cast back to Clinton and reconstructs the evolution of the show. What we see, therefore, is not only a mimic representation of a social milieu, rich in expressive detail, but also the milieu itself—the physical place and some of the very people whom the actors impersonated. Culminating in a live performance of THE FARM SHOW in a local cattle-auction arena, the film captures an actual face-to-face encounter of country-life, city-life. The actors, having exposed their urban vulnerability to the farm community, now in turn show the community its own *comédie humaine*, for laughter and for genuine tears.

The comic encounter between urban and rustic rises to more extravagant levels in LA VRAIE NATURE DE BERNADETTE, directed by Gilles Carle. To begin with, the joke is on the city lady who imports to a Quebec farm community a bunch of fanciful notions about the innocent simplicity of pastoral life. We recognize the format: love and macrobiotic food meets the unturned sod. The bounteous idealism of this aspiring earth-mother even extends to relieving the sexual (and other) needs of senior citizens, who take every advantage of her that she offers. Carle's rustic milieu, like the various milieux established in his other films, is a community of more or less comic grotesques, caricatures observed by the satiric eye. The society he has created for Bernadette's zealous invasion is lavishly detailed and constantly hilarious. Midway through the film, however, the satiric forms lengthen. The community, which Bernadette has attempted to transfigure through the power of love, betrays her generous faith. Simultaneously venerated as a wonder-worker and abused as a credulous fool, she comes to incarnate a disenchanted utopianism. In a satiric parable for Quebec, she learns that her society is less susceptible to redemption from its own nature than she had naively hoped.

Between the city and the country, as a place to stand and as a location for movies, there is the small town. Eli Mandel has remarked that in Canadian literature the small town is frequently evoked nostalgically as a place in the past, a context of irrecoverable childhood.[3] Even though that small-town childhood may have been stifling and painful, language tends to bathe the quiet old streets and well-kept houses, the dusty lanes and tree-fringed river (more of a creek, actually) in a sentimentalizing glow. The "language of movies", however, displays a contrary tendency. Take a camera to one of those little towns, and unless you are extremely careful it will record the junky clutter of assorted storefronts, the faded, ramshackle hotel, the A&W drive-in, piles of rusty Things around the train station, and a general air of seediness. This emphasis, equally one-sided, is not to be mistaken for the mere truth, but it contributes to a cinematic tone which counterbalances the *temps perdu* flavour described by Mandel.

Falling somewhere between the raw and the remote in its treatment of the small town is Martin Lavut's CBC feature document, ORILLIA, OUR TOWN. In this work Lavut achieves the curious and rather despicable feat of inducing a good number of the inhabitants of Orillia to pose as specimens of comic quaintness. Exploiting their submissive awe of the CBC, he assembles them in ludicrous, old-fashioned, photographer's-studio poses, and encourages them to tell about themselves with trusting candour. Where THE FARM SHOW offered a partly humorous imitation of a community and its members, ORILLIA tricks its participants into composing a kind of freak-show; they themselves unwittingly create the comic spectacle. Little do they know that audiences of city sophisticates will giggle condescendingly at their lovable innocence. Mandel says the small town is a region of the mind called childhood. Lavut arranges for a small town to reveal itself as still populated by slightly simple-minded children, saying the darn'dest things. For the first third of the film, the effect certainly is very funny, but the viewer gradually recognizes that the members of any community could be made to appear quaint and guileless by the application of this technique. One is not watching a composite portrait of Orillia, but a particularly insidious version of "Candid Camera", in which the victims know they are on film, but do not realize how their earnestly sincere performances are going to be exploited.

In addition to PAPERBACK HERO and ROWDYMAN, already noticed, several other fictional screenplays have been situated in a small Canadian town, to various thematic purpose and with differing effect. A pair of low-budget features, THE HARD PART BEGINS and 125 ROOMS OF COMFORT, are both located in southern Ontario, and both, in their admittedly contrasting modes, revolve around the return to his home town of a professional entertainer. But whereas the hard part of Jim King begins in the quite elaborately sketched town of "West Eden" (shot in Ayr, Paris, and Brantford), Billie Joyce's discomfort is mostly confined to the rooms of the Grand Hotel in the town of St. Thomas. The hotel of Loubert's film tends towards allegorical generalization—its impending takeover by an ambitious American is a focal element of the plot —whereas the small town established by John Hunter and Paul Lynch is principally a typical place in the actual world where a certain country-and-western singer encounters more personal complications than he could wish for. In 125 ROOMS the photography shows us the hotel from peculiar angles which conspire to make it into a bizarre locale, a Kafkaesque environment whose inhabitants are mostly rather strange. Projecting the schizoid psyche of the protagonist onto his milieu, the film seeks to imbue the physical setting, and many of the dramatic situations, with a quality of waking nightmare. Occasionally we catch glimpses of an everyday world outside, but our main introduction to the surrounding town is by way of an elaborate title-montage in which the streets and storefronts shimmer in a kind of kaleidoscopic miasma. HARD PART, on the contrary, takes a matter-of-fact approach to the tawdry actualities of bar and restaurant, hotel room and service station. As a social milieu the small town is neither romanticized nor caricatured, though a tendency in the latter direction reveals itself in some of the minor characterization. As "King and Country" play their sets, the camera scrutinizes the local faces that compose a dwindling audience. Jim's fate depends upon these people. His future as an entertainer is bound up with cultural and social evolution of "West Eden". As the clientele drifts away from the old hotel beverage room to the rock bands at the new motel outside town, "King and Country" must change their act or go into oblivion.

THE HARD PART BEGINS earns respect also for its observation of the signatures of social and economic class. When a movie fiction is situated in a purely rural setting, the question of class-milieu remains relatively marginal. True, there are class stratifications in rural society, as marked as those in the urban environment. BEST DAMN FIDDLER, for example, dramatizes the situation of a "busher", a shiftless kind of pioneer-manqué, eking a subsistence for eight or ten children out of a few acres of bush. The screenplay takes note of his economic plight, his discomfort in the bourgeois bastion of a hospital, and his repudiation of brisk, officious welfarism. But it seems that the boundaries between economic classes, as marked by ocuupation, dwelling, neighbourhood, tastes in recreation, social attitudes, opportunities, etc., became more pronounced in towns and cities. They exist unmistakably, to be observed by the screenplay-writer and director who will pay attention to them, as conditions which bear upon individual experience. Of course a fiction may be concocted in almost total disregard for the realities, visible and invisible, of socio-economic class; the characters may collect apparently unearned incomes, and live in well-upholstered movie-starlet ghettoes whose inhabitants do nothing much except have love affairs. Some films exhibit no awareness of class because it is foreign to their particular mode of fiction; others because the authors never gave it much consideration. In the establishment of milieu, the writing and the direction of THE HARD PART BEGINS are decently alert to the social stratum in which the fiction moves. For instance—not to make extravagant claims—Jim King's ex-wife is now married to a truck-driver who delivers her request to Jim that he come to see her; the home which he visits expresses pointedly that life-style, between poverty and gentility, of a working man who can afford, in a small town, to carry the payments on a cheap new house. The large kitchen, with its appliances and fitted cabinets, has nonetheless a graceless air, verging on the tawdry. Children scrabble underfoot as the distraught wife at the sink bewails her sad existence. The son of her marriage to Jim—a marriage which she traded for her present "security"—is in a reformatory. While this is not a sociological case-study, the character initially conceived of as "Jim's ex-wife" has been installed in a particularly envisaged socio-economic situation.

Written and directed by Bill Fruet, WEDDING IN WHITE is another film situated in the working-class stratum of a small town, in this case somewhere on the prairies. However, this film has a temporal as well as a spatial milieu, being set in the year 1943. Unlike a film set in the unspecified present, and hence needing no deliberate creation of a place-in-time, the "remember-when" movie faces special problems with milieu, problems which are different again from the genuinely historical movie, the costume-drama. "The past is a foreign country," says the opening line of *The Go-Between*; "they do things differently there." But remember—when films evoke, not the foreign past, but the day-before-yesterday, a time within the memory of most of the audience. Familiar yet bizarre, it is like seeing oneself in the crazy mirrors at a fairground —especially when the different length of dresses and jackets gives the figures a stunted or elongated look. Films in this vein can maximize this particular kind of endistancing effect, playing it for laughable weirdness or for nostalgia, or they can keep it to a minimum. In the former case, with its abundance of funny clothes, quaint idioms and vintage Coke bottles, the style of acting tends towards caricature. Instead of projecting imaginatively into people who experienced themselves as no more dotty and freakish in their dress and behaviour than we do in ours, the actors give campy imitations of external mannerisms. The resulting impression is that people "in those days", like the inhabitants of ORILLIA even now, were unself-consciously ludicrous to a degree that would be impossible nowadays. It is only a short step to believing that people in the early nineteen-hundreds scuttled about with a peculiar jerky rapidity, or that Shakespeare's contemporaries fpoke ftrangely and fuggeftively in a foft whifper.

WEDDING IN WHITE goes to more trouble to establish its time than its place, but only seldom falls into the camp routine. The character of Dolly, Jeannie's tarty friend, is mostly played as a set of exaggerated quirks, and a café scene, in which the two girls meet a pair of droopy guys in zoot-suits, tilts into clowning. On the whole, however, the screenplay evokes its distinct time-place in the archaic narrow-mindedness and primitive level of personal development in which the characters are stuck. Physical location is not specific, and the filming sketches it with only a few strokes. In fact the film wasn't shot in a prairie town, but in Toronto, and the exterior locations are so tightly framed that we never see more than a back-alley, a couple of house-fronts, a dark roadway, and the inside of an old Kresge's store. The resulting effect of claustrophobia and isolation is rather artificially expressionistic, conveying the unnatural impression that nobody in this little purgatory ever sees the sky or trees or any length of street. But within the home of the Dougal family, a sensation of physical confinement effectively matches the emotional pressures of the human milieu. This human milieu, sharply circumscribed and not stretching away into a "real world", comprises the friends, neighbours of the central family, and especially the legion-hall cronies of Jim Dougal, played by Donald Pleasence. Poor abused Jeannie cowers among drunken, stupid, brutal males, and oppressed females who all-too-readily turn on each other. Add to time and place the cultural inheritance of émigré Scots Calvinism, the social pretention to "respectability", economic depression, and a militaristic brand of male chauvinism, and you have a pretty ghastly dungeon of the spirit.

The action of Murray Markowitz's third feature, RECOMMENDATION FOR MERCY, occurs in another small town whose social climate victimizes a helpless young protagonist, and in a temporal milieu set in the recent past. But this dramatization of the 1959 trial of Stephen Truscott[4] reduces to a minimum the endistancing awareness of way-back-then. For one thing, the visible signs of the times are much less prominent in a country town in summer than they would be in a city. And Markowitz has for the most part decided against the inclusion of golden-oldie pop-songs and distinctively dated speech-idioms. His major lapse of judgment in this respect releases a flood of schmalzy romance music over a scene of adolescent passion. Theoretically defensible as expressive of the teenagers' own phase of romantic sensibility, the music in fact makes a travesty of the situation. But in general the film avoids the pitfalls inherent in attempts to date the action. That the crop of listless adolescents surrounding "John Robinson" didn't ripen this year is detectable mainly in the *absence* of certain signs rather than by their presence. No long-hair, no transistorized rock, no veneer of sophistication—perhaps to contemporary teenagers or schoolteachers these kids in the movie may look more obviously foreign, but they don't in general strike an audience as objects of amusement. They are part of a convincingly established social milieu in which callousness and prejudice prevail over justice. The whole community is implicated in the process that selects a fourteen-year-old boy as the rapist-murderer of the daughter of the town's leading employer, subjects him to a travesty of judicial procedures, and condemns him to hang. Like an election or a strike, a trial can lend itself very effectively to the dramatization of complex social currents catching up the lives of individuals. Though he focusses as well on the accused boy's private torment, Markowitz endeavours to bring the town itself into the picture, as a physical and social conglomerate. Unlike WEDDING IN WHITE, the film amply displays the physical settings in and around the town, and, with a large cast of actors, presents a cross-section of its population. While not uniformly successful, this attempt raises an otherwise rather journalistic kind of sensational human-interest into a social investigation.

Unfortunately for the English-Canadian patriot, the Québécois again take the gold medal when it comes to the dramatic realization on film of a small-town milieu. This is not the place for detailed appreciation of —yes, you've guessed it—MON ONCLE ANTOINE; suffice it for the moment to notice the rich human and sociological texture of Perron and Jutra's day-in-the-life of a small village in the asbestos-mining area of

Quebec. So many personalities, so many currents of social interaction converge on Antoine's general store that Christmas Eve of a generation ago! One would like to see an English-Canadian rival to this kind of work, but the prospect doesn't seem imminent. Is this a matter of individual talent, simply? Or is French-Canadian society intrinsically more variegated and distinctive than English—in the way that an ethnic neighbourhood has more "character" than a suburb? Or, again, does the experience of living in present-day Quebec cultivate a livelier kind of social-critical awareness? Certainly the process of decolonizing the Canadian imagination may accompany and promote a sharper depiction of society in the cinema. Québécois filmmakers are not hoping to sell to the U.S., or even the English-Canadian, market, nor (by and large) to that of France. Hence they are not caught in the half-conscious habit of diluting the cultural consciousness that is the case among the Anglophones. Filmmakers in Montreal are actually interested in one another's work from the point of view of what it has to say and what its social and political implications might be.

Coming around at long last to consider the cinematic treatment of contemporary urban milieux, it is appropriate to notice first a couple of films, set in the English-speaking side of Montreal, in the period immediately following World War II. Released in 1974, set in 1947, THE APPRENTICESHIP OF DUDDY KRAVITZ and WHY ROCK THE BOAT? (which could well be entitled "The Apprenticeship of Harry Barnes") both deal with the achievement of "manhood", as they say, by their protagonists. A lot of money and invention and talent went into creating the working-class Jewish milieu of St. Urbain whence Duddy makes his unscrupulous exodus. Yessiree, Bob! Rather less of each went into setting up the arena of Montreal daily journalism where Harry the novice reporter endures editorial oppression and sexual privation. Actually it's hardly fair to compare the two movies. Not only did the producers of DUDDY KRAVITZ command much greater resources, but Richler's comic panorama embraces a pungently-flavoured ethnic sub-culture, whereas Weingraub and Howe are working with the relatively bland and featureless milieu of bourgeois Waspery. "Eddy's Cigar and Soda" and the bar of the Windsor Hotel epitomize the contrast. Time and again, DUDDY KRAVITZ exploits to the full the opportunities furnished by the screenplay to render satirically the style and ethos of the Jewish community. WHY ROCK THE BOAT? tends to minimize the difficulty and expense of creating a period look by avoiding wherever possible those exterior shots that call for old cars and vintage billboards. It concentrates instead on establishing a dated style of social behaviour, notably in the area of sexual mores. Thus the film furnishes an example of temporal milieu as theme, the hero's archaic notions about love and lust being the chief ingredient of its historical endistancing. DUDDY KRAVITZ, on the contrary, luxuriates in the dated look of places and things, but there is nothing naively quaint about individual behaviour. Duddy himself exhibits a breathtaking innocence in the midst of his guile, but we are not being invited to laugh indulgently at the simple-mindedness of "those days"

Beautiful Westmount has been the setting for several glossy and pretentious fictions situated in Montreal. But the film which declares in its very title the central role of milieu in its imaginative design is MONTREAL MAIN (Frank Vitale, 1973). More than just a strip of bars, all-night hangouts, and amusement arcades, lower St. Laurent, "The Main", is not exactly a community. It is an ambience, a spirit in the air that seeks out its destined habitués and draws them with its scent. Vitale sets up the spirit of the Main as one of the dramatic antagonists in his story of the love conceived by a gruffly reserved photographer (Frank himself) for a thirteen-year-old boy. In a human milieu where the shrill, narcissistic voices of a homosexual coterie compete to wither innocence, this shy passion is also under attack from the boy's pseudo-hip parents. A particular strength of Vitale's film is the creation out of physical settings, photographic style, and dramatic performances, of a psychological climate inimical to the central relationship. The gay world, of which Frank is a kind of non-playing member, appears as a menagerie of exotic, slightly hysterical creatures who will pounce on "Frank's new friend" and mesmerize him with their routines. An altogether stunning double-bill would put MONTREAL MAIN before IL ETAIT UNE FOIS DANS L'EST, directed by André Brassard from a screenplay by Michel Tremblay. The Brassard-Tremblay film takes the same locale as Vitale—the Main—and creates out of it a veritable hell, populated by hysterical predators, lost souls tearing at each other in their desperation.

Toronto doesn't lend itself to the imagination like Montreal as a place of drama and intrigue, of theatricality and passion. There is something implacably "real" about Ontario's capital that resists romanticization. For all its cleanliness and safety and bank-towers and Ontario Place and a reform-minded council and the Maple Leafs and ethnic diversity and the tallest free-standing thing in the world—it has no magic. "There must be more to life than this," you feel; yet an attempt to say what you mean sounds like crying for the moon—which, indeed, it is. Movies convincingly imagined for Toronto tend, accordingly, to have a sociological bent, and to derive their virtue from a seriousness about the actual. They don't stray far into romance or melodrama—unless they want to risk derision. NOBODY WAVED GOODBYE has the Toronto touch; Clarke Mackey's THE ONLY THING YOU KNOW has it. But Don Shebib is Toronto's director-laureate, and his GOIN' DOWN THE ROAD is the film which most pervasively and integrally establishes Toronto as a milieu.

In a sense Toronto itself is really the subject of GOIN' DOWN THE ROAD—or rather, the object. Peter and Joey, the migrant Nova Scotians, are the subjects, and Toronto is what they find. The audience discovers Toronto along with them, and from their perspective. At first it presents itself as an exhilarating concentration of buildings seen from the

Expressway—a big city; but within hours it has become a place to spend a night at the Sally Ann hostel. When they start to look for work, Pete's fantasy takes him to an office-tower looking for an executive position in advertising; Toronto's reality offers them jobs in a soft-drink plant. Saturday-night entertainment takes them down Yonge Street, to the aimless milling-about in the exhaust fumes that passes for Having a Good Time. From here, an amazingly short drive shows them the impregnable chateaux of Rosedale, (a Toronto principality where, at election time, the voters' lists on the telegraph poles include a number of persons with the occupation: butler). When the soft-drink job fails at the end of the summer, Toronto offers them a whirl at car-washing, leaflet distribution, and (for Pete) setting up the pins at a pre-automated bowling alley. Toronto ferries them over to Centre Island, where Joey chats up a waitress in the breezy afternoon sun. But, come fall, Toronto also takes back Joey's high-rise apartment and his no-down-payment furniture, and sends him with his pregnant bride to share a room-and-a-half in Cabbagetown with Pete.

It would become repetitious to scan the whole collection of urban-located movies, from Vancouver as well as Toronto, noting the relative effectiveness and range of their dramatic milieux. Few among them, let it be said, can stand comparison on this score with the healthy, though by no means definitive standard established by Don Shebib, in conjunction with scriptwriter Bill Fruet. The evocation of an actual place, experienced by particular sensibilities from a particular disadvantage point, is admirably done in GOIN' DOWN THE ROAD. The achievement amounts to more than the choice and juxtaposition of many expressive locations —locations which testify to the economic and social structure of the world the characters inhabit; more than the "vérité" style of Leiterman's photography and the inclusion of such telling details as the police-officer descending the stairs in the Cabbagetown rooming-house—a presence worth a thousand words on the subject of slum-lodgings. It amounts, finally, to an attitude towards the telling of a story, an angle of concern. GOIN' DOWN TIHE ROAD proves that such an attitude need not preclude humorous and moving dramatic entertainment; the film's popularity in Canada suggests that critical social awareness in the creation of milieu, while it may not guarantee a movie's success, at least can do it no harm.

Statement from the Council of Canadian Filmmakers

Sandra Gathercole

The Canadian feature film industry is swamped by problems, and has been since it began in earnest seven to eight years ago.

Depending on whom you talk to, *the* problem is lack of scripts; lack of producers; lack of money; lack of popular appeal with audiences; lack of distribution; lack of investors; lack of return of investment; lack of a star system; self-indulgent directors; too much or too little commercialism.

And they're all right. These are very real problems. But the root problem for Canada, in attempting to build a feature film industry, is the same problem which every film producing country has faced: Hollywood's monolithic economic control of the world film market.

That control has been real and dominant enough to require every film producing country outside the United States to institute some form of control in its own marketplace in order to offset, or counterbalance, the dominance of U.S. films. One hundred and four countries discriminate against Hollywood films—usually in the form of quota restrictions on exhibition and a tax or levy on American box office revenues. Canada is not among the 104 countries, but remains the only film producing country without any form of protection for its own films, in their own market. Compared to this problem, the others pale into growing pains.

The reason Hollywood's control is ruinous to the development of a film industry in Canada, as in other countries, is simple enough. It's economics. Adolph Zukor, the Hollywood mogul of moguls, earned the title by a shrewd appreciation of the basis of the film industry. In his words: "Who controls the box office, controls the industry."

Truer words were never said. Because film production costs vast amounts of money, it cannot be viable unless it is directly connected to, and supported by, the similarly vast amounts of money generated at the box office.

From the first days of film production, the Americans understood this, and Hollywood studios quickly developed distribution and exhibition arms to ensure their access to—and control of—the pay wicket. These distribution arms were extended around the globe, with full support of the U.S. State Department which was not slow to understand the immense propaganda power of having American images universally projected on the silver screen. Antitrust rulings in 1948 somewhat mitigated this vertically integrated system within the U.S., but permitted such monopoly practices to be carried on abroad. In Canada, for

Reprinted from *Criteria*, February 1976.

instance, the largest theatre chain—Famous Players—is owned by the same parent corporation—Gulf and Western—as one of the major U.S. producers and distributors—Paramount Pictures.

Canada is, in fact, a prime example of how the Hollywood monopoly works beyond American borders. Film exhibition throughout Canada is controlled by two major theatre chains, Famous Players and Odeon. Together these two chains own or control 427 theatre screens, which include virtually all of the prime urban locations. In Ontario, in 1972, they controlled 92.1 per cent of the regular theatre screens in urban centres with a population between 35,000 and 100,000, and 75.4 per cent in urban centres with a population over 100,000, and had an average of 78.3 per cent of the total Ontario market.

Famous and Odeon operate in a closed circuit "family compact" with the seven major Hollywood producer-distributors (Universal, Paramount, United Artists, 20th Century Fox, Columbia, Warner Brothers). Operating a functional monopoly, they divide the Canadian market tidily between them. Screen time is guaranteed to the Hollywood product by the chains. In return, they are guaranteed the "blockbuster" films like JAWS along with the less popular successful films which are "tied-on" to the big name products.

Here's how it works, according to George Destounis, president of Famous Players, speaking in an interview for the CBC Culture Series telecast March 17, 1976:

> It's been an historical fact that... major distributors aligned themselves with either one circuit or the other. People like Paramount, Warners and United Artists will play 100 per cent Famous and people like Columbia, and two-thirds Universal and one third Fox would play Odeon.... It was agreed, I understand, (in the) early forties how the breakdown (worked) when Odeon was first formed.

In other words, there is a quota—guaranteed screen time—for Hollywood films in the majority of theatres in Canada. It works well. The system is efficient, effective and profitable—for the foreign corporations.

How profitable? The total Canadian box office is approximately $220 million annually. Of the total earned at the box office, roughly one-third goes to the distributors as rental fees, and two-thirds remains with the exhibitors. Between 1970 and 1974, the revenues taken out of Canada by the seven major distributors increased 98.9 per cent to $54.4 million in 1974. (Source: Motion Picture Export Association of America, as published in *Variety*.) The 1975 figure was $63 million.

Famous Players revenues have increased more than 100 per cent in the same period. According to *Canadian Cablesystems Interim Report to Shareholders* for the First ¾ of the Fiscal Year 1975 (Canadian Cablesystems is a shareholder in Famous Players), Famous Players Ltd.

revenues for the first three-quarters of 1975 were $76.6 million, up 22 per cent from $62.9 million for the same period in 1974. The same source states Famous Players profits, after tax, for the first three-quarters of the fiscal year 1975 to be $5.9 million. This is an increase of 90 per cent from $3.1 million for the same period in 1974.

One result of these leaping profit figures has been a corresponding leap in Canada's relative worth to Hollywood. Six years ago Canada was the sixth largest foreign market for Hollywood films: today Canada is Number One. The fact that we have become Hollywood's biggest foreign customer is not justified by the size of our population, but rather by the fact that we are the only country which still permits unimpeded entry of American films, and unimpeded export of their revenues.

How does all this relate to Canadian feature film production? Not very well. During the same four years in which foreign profits from the Canadian box office doubled, Canadian feature film production was on a reverse curve. In English Canada, production of big budget Canadian feature films collapsed abruptly:

Year	Major English Feature Films Produced
1972	13
1973	6
1974	4
1975	0

(As of mid-summer—a number of features went into production in the latter part of the year due to the "voluntary agreements" referred to below.)

Juxtaposition of the growth rate for film production and film distribution-exhibition in Canada in the last four years confirms the central reality of the Canadian film industry: film production is disconnected from its own market in Canada, and does not benefit from the enormous profits generated by that market.

If Canada had never entered into feature film production, but had remained a producer of shorts and documentaries as we were for many years; or had Canada entered feature film production without involving millions of public funds through the investment program of the Canadian Film Development Corporation; or had the Canadian Film Development Corporation been given a mandate to bypass the existing commercial system by fully funding feature film production—then the fact that Canadian films had no entry to their profitable market would merely have been a sad cultural loss. But given that the CFDC was instead set up on the premise that Canadian films would be a commercial venture—that the twenty odd million of public funds invested would be matched by private investment, and that the films thus produced would have commercial distribution and pay back their investors—the situation amounts to a national disgrace.

From its inception, the CFDC chose to ignore the problem of distribution for the films it was investing in. In the beginning that approach seemed to work because it was buoyed up by a tax loophole which allowed investors sizable tax write-offs. When that bubble burst in 1972, the fact that Canadian films were not being properly distributed and were not returning to their investors, became a critical issue. Left with no incentive to invest in Canadian films, private investors evaporated and left the CFDC about as functional as a one-armed pair of scissors. Film production began its downward spiral, unemployment in the film industry rose to frightening proportions, and the filmmakers who had had their expectations raised by the initial boom of the CFDC tax write-off investment became politicized.

By the spring of 1973 the major film production unions and organizations in English Canada formed a national association—the Council of Canadian Filmmakers—to try to deal with the mounting problems, and the apparently mounting government indifference to those problems. There was consensus on the grim realization that the young industry had to have two things, without which it was more likely to go down the drain than down the road. It had to have access to Canadian theatres for Canadian films; and it had to have a reasonable return on box office earnings. The same measures employed in every other film producing country—quota and levy—were advanced as the essential means of righting the listing industry.

A quota would ensure that Canadian films were shown in Canadian theatres not just in major cities, but across the country and the people who had invested in them—the Canadian taxpayers—would at least have the choice of whether or not to see their investment. A levy would compensate for the low ratio of return which afflicts those few Canadian films that are shown (PAPERBACK HERO returned on an eleven to one ratio and DUDDY KRAVITZ five to one, as opposed to two-and-a-half or three to one ratio of return on investment which is normal for American films). By ensuring a return "off the top" on film earnings, a levy also dramatically increases a film's chance of paying back its investment and thus attracting new private investment for future production. There are a variety of forms of box office levy used in European countries and without them the films of Ingmar Bergman, Satyajit Ray and Fellini, among others, would not be made.

Both quota and levy appear to be arbitrary measures designed to give advantage to the films of their own country. They are, in fact, measures to counterweight the unofficial "quota" biased economics of the entrenched and overpowering Hollywood system, and to put indigenous films on an equal footing with imported films. If (as a federal MP once asked in the House) American films have a quota in Canadian theatres why shouldn't Canadian films also have a quota, and if foreign corporations are going to cream hundreds of millions off the Canadian box office why shouldn't they be made to pay a "cost of doing business" allowance for the privilege, which would serve to support Canadian production on a level at which it might more fairly compete with its foreign counterpart?

The Council of Canadian Filmmakers and other industry groups have in the last four years written briefs, attended meetings, sat on committees, talked to the media, researched and drafted proposals to government endlessly. Government response has been a perverse blend of apathy, buck-passing and suspicion, interspersed with bursts of half-measure solutions.

The fact that quota and levy legislation falls under the jurisdiction of the provinces, due to vagaries of the BNA Act, confused the issue. So did various committees of government assigned to develop a film policy. None of these bodies ever developed a functional film policy but they did serve to delay action on the basis that nothing could be done until they reported. (Despite the fact that these committees seem impotent to produce the long-awaited film policy, they do seem to reproduce themselves in ever new guises with rabbit-like efficiency.)

Then, four years after the federal government announced its intention to develop a film policy, and three years after the film industry began inundating government with detailed explanations of what was required in the industry, something did happen in mid-1975. The first movement came from the Ontario government. In July, enabling legislation was passed by the Ontario Legislature which would permit the introduction of a quota for Canadian films in Ontario theatres.

The following month, then Secretary of State Hugh Faulkner announced an accommodation reached with the two major exhibition chains, whereby the two chains would "voluntarily" show Canadian films for four weeks a year, and would "voluntarily" contribute a total of $1.7 million to Canadian film production. He also announced an increase in the capital cost allowance from 60 per cent to 100 per cent for film investment.

Both moves sounded better than they were. The enabling legislation in Ontario was just that: it enabled Ontario to impose a quota but did not commit it to actually implement one. To date no further action has taken place on quota although Ontario is actively meeting and discussing the levy concept.

Mr. Faulkner's "voluntary agreement", which has succeeded in getting several films into production in the last few months, still contains some lethal flaws. First, it is voluntary, rather than legislated, and so works on sufferance from the chains while defusing pressure that had been mounting for a legislated version—a toothless tiger which served to buy off the threat of the real thing. Second, the definition of a "Canadian" film announced by Mr. Faulkner barely distinguished it from an American film. This definition, combined with the fact that the chains have complete control over which films are invested in and, in fact, send the scripts to New York for selection, invites the worst kind of branch plant situation. Essentially American films can masquerade as Canadian and receive unto themselves benefits of investment and tax write-offs which were designed to compensate for their control, rather than augment it.

However meagre these compromise solutions, they are, at least, historically true to form. Our past is riddled with examples of outrageous submission to Hollywood on the part of the Canadian government. Pierre Berton recounts in *Hollywood's Canada* the most notable government boondoggle—the Canadian Co-operation Project. The last time the Canadian government considered a feature film industry for Canada was in the days of C.D. Howe. Presumably mustering courage to tackle the proposal, Mr. Howe walked into the office of the then president of Famous Players and suggested that the company was taking a lot of money out of the country each year and it might be a good idea if it were to invest a portion of its earnings in developing a Canadian film industry. Whatever transpired in the interim, by the time Mr. Howe walked out of the office he had settled instead for a scheme whereby Hollywood would mention Canada in its movies occasionally and presumably thereby increase tourism and thus revenue. This ill-fated project accounts for the inappropriate and occasional reference made to Canada (usually as the place where the outlaw escaped to or the heroine's sister died) in the late shows.

Mr. Faulkner's voluntary agreement of this year, also a proposal originating in New York as an alternative to more ambitious alterations in the system, seems destined to be a repeat of the Neville Chamberlain-style "peace" with Hollywood which our governments have used to get us where we are today with the film industry. Obviously there is not going to be a Canadian film industry—though there may well be a film industry in Canada—until governments, provincial and federal, come to terms with the very obvious fact that we cannot have a Canadian culture which is controlled by Americans.

Canadian theatres were set up to show American films and primacy —or access, promotion and financial return—in those theatres still belongs to American films. Canadian films are, as a result, foreign in their own market. Despite this, some are succeeding in winning large audiences and making large profits, though few if any are returning much of their profits to their producers. Lest we still harbour doubts that the *real* cause of the problem is that the films are no good, it is interesting to note that the three top money-earners for Canada's largest distributor, Astral, in 1975 were Canadian films: DUDDY KRAVITZ, RECOMMENDATION FOR MERCY and LIES MY FATHER TOLD ME. DUDDY KRAVITZ, by earning over $2 million at the Canadian box office, placed as one of the top twenty-five money-earners in Canada in 1975. But these films are succeeding despite the system, not because of it.

Government timidity and half measures, which have perpetuated our branch plant position in distribution and exhibition, now seem to be extending it into production. But surely the CFDC was not set up and funded with $20 million in order to facilitate a branch plant for Hollywood. Surely before we worry about foreign markets we have to deal with the problem of a right of way to our own market. Surely the mandarins can confront the majors, instead of endlessly tip-toeing around them.

Introduction

Peter Harcourt

The Canadian feature film industry remains an immensely undervalued achievement, especially in English Canada. There are several reasons for this.

First of all, we see so few Canadian films. Glancing through the list of films in this volume (*Film Canadiana 1975-1976*). I am amazed at how few films I have even heard of, let alone seen. Yet I live in Toronto —supposedly a film centre—and I am certainly dedicated to the concept of an indigenous film culture, whether in the theatres or on television. But so few of the films made here really get talked about. Certainly, few French-language films are mentioned in Ontario; and I imagine that few English language films get talked about in Quebec. Quebec filmmakers can find more distribution outlets for their work throughout the many countries of Europe than they can within English Canada; while even what we might describe as "schlock" English-language films like SUDDEN FURY or THE PARASITE MURDERS (now called SHIVERS) can regain their costs more efficiently in Japan than in Canada. So somebody is seeing our films, but not many Canadians. Why is this?

One might begin with the cliché that an artist is often initially more appreciated outside his own country than he is at home. Except that when talking about filmmakers from *any* country, we are only tangentially talking about artists. We are talking about a variety of people attempting to earn their living within a highly technologized, international industry—an industry basically controlled by American capital. With the rare exception of a Jean-Pierre Lefebvre or a Denys Arcand, most filmmakers are aiming at world-wide distribution. But why must this distribution by-pass Canada?

Reprinted from *Film Canadiana 1975-1976* (Ottawa: Canadian Film Institute).

If I had all the answers to that question, I should be working in the Secretary of State's office (which perhaps I should be in any case!); but what I would like to do here is simply play with the question to see where it leads us. Let me begin with an anecdote.

In April of this year (1976), I had the privilege of sitting in on a conference of television writers organized by the Toronto office of CBC drama. As part of this conference, two prestigious BBC writers had also been invited, to show examples of their work and talk about both the challenges and restrictions of writing for television. A number of Canadian writers were present, plus one or two cultural commentators like myself to lend, I suppose, some kind of critical perspective. I am certainly pleased I was there; for the tone of the conference taught me a great deal about the problems of the film—or television—writer working in Canada.

As the conference was not open to the public, perhaps within the context of this article everyone should remain nameless—or at least almost everyone. In any case, what I am trying to do here is less to "sum up" the results of the conference than to present my own personal interpretation of it, my way of "reading" the event in the light of current problems. Two BBC-TV dramas were screened which had been written by our two invited guests. Both plays were greatly appreciated. They were, indeed, in their different ways, both highly distinguished. They generated a great deal of excitement but also a kind of uneasiness. "Why can't we be doing things like that at the CBC?" seemed to be the question that underlay everything else that was said. There was an atmosphere of sadness (I think I might call it) if not of desperation that pervaded the room.

But there was another TV drama screened as part of the conference—a CBC-TV drama, the show I must name. It was the last of the journalistic-drama series that were screened during the last few weeks of this season of CBC's "Performance" series—fictionalized accounts of events that had actually happened, as indeed, one of the BBC-TV dramas had been. The show screened was WHAT WE HAVE HERE IS A PEOPLE PROBLEM, written by Michael Mercer (an anglophone from the west coast) and directed by Francis Mankiewicz (a francophone from Quebec). It was *a real Canadian drama*—indeed, I would go so far as to say *a real Canadian film*.

I mention it here simply to state that no one at the conference, especially the Canadians, seemed to care much about it. It is not that they didn't *like* it exactly: there was just the general assumption that it was *less* in some way, inferior to its BBC competitors. No one really wanted to talk about it. Certainly, no one seemed *proud* of it. These Canadian writers seemed more interested in what the BBC was doing —interested and envious.

I *am* pleased I was at that conference because at this stage I hit the roof! The British shows were densely psychologized—"dramatized" in the conventional sense of the word. There was lots of action and most of all (bouyed up by the strong theatrical tradition that has always informed even the *worst* of British television and cinema), a strong sense of character. Solid British television drama which, I assured the group (especially the British writers!), I admired as much as anyone. But it is so *easy* to do that kind of thing in England, I explained. Of course, budgets and fresh ideas always have to be fought for; but there are so many established traditions and such a densely populated society of viewers to support that struggle. Furthermore, there isn't the threat of unrestricted competition from American cable input. The British shows, distinuished though they were, were produced within what is a highly protected, self-sustaining culture. The Canadian show, on the other hand, grew out of a very different and more precarious cultural situation.

What I was arguing then as I am trying to argue now is that within the different cultures that had produced the different shows, the Canadian show took more risks, was far more individual, in my view was even more distinguished and original than the British shows really were. This is not to diminish the quality of the British shows; it is simply to establish a context in which they could be seen. Similarly, if we really want to understand the problems of Canadian film culture—whether for the theatres or for television—we would have to establish a context in which the Canadian shows could be seen.

The British shows, especially the "documentary" one, were working firmly within the tradition of what we might call psychological realistic drama. The Canadian show, I suggested, was working in a different mode. "What mode is that?" Someone asked me—not an easy question to reply to off the cuff. But I will try to reply to it now.

It is a mode, I want to suggest, that touches upon fable, that *implies* more than it says, that is rich in connotation, in visual impressions and in atmosphere; but it is a mode that does not spell out with great psychological authority a specific social problem. While the show actually dealt with a particular social problem—the attempt of some developers to evict an old man—it didn't make explicit just who had won by the end. While there *is* a personal victory—the old man is not evicted—perhaps there is also, ultimately, a political defeat. The developers go on developing. They simply take another route—possibly (one might imagine) evicting someone else!

Maybe the film is too subtle for television. Maybe it is even too subtle for Canadians. But I do not believe this. For those of us privileged enough to have seen Francis Mankiewicz's LE TEMPS D'UNE CHASSE a couple of years ago (I believe it lasted about ten days in Toronto), we might even have been able to recognize some of the same qualities: a sensitive feeling for landscape which is both beautiful and menacing; plus a view of the male adult world which gradually discloses the violence which is part of that world.

What I am trying to suggest here is that there are conventions at work in these two films directed by Francis Mankiewicz—one made for the theatres and the other for television—that are distinctly Canadian, which in this case even transcend the basic cultural division that exists between French and English Canada. These conventions are different from the conventions that we associate either with "entertaining" American movies or with "prestigious" BBC television drama. They are less "exciting", possibly (in the conventional sense) less "dramatic". But perhaps "excitement" and "drama" as we have been trained to understand the terms belong more naturally to societies more densely populated than our own, societies that are more sure of themselves. Perhaps we should be trusting more our own, indigenous modes.

Another cliché often put forward about Canadian cinema is that the scripts are so bad. Apparently, we lack writers. What this means, in my view, is that we lack writers who can operate comfortably, within our own country, either in the American or the British vein. But it may also mean that we do lack writers who are committed to writing for the cinema and television.

If this is so, this is disastrous. If our writers think of themselves primarily as novelists or playwrights but are prepared to work for television "for the money", then we can never build up a complex of writers who are *actually excited* about the medium they are working in and by the collective nature of that kind of collaboration. And if our television networks (is there really more than one?) and our precarious film production companies cannot help create that kind of *atelier* atmosphere, then it is doubtful if we will ever achieve much momentum or much sense of continuity in whatever we manage to do.

Personally, I don't get the feeling that the scripts are that bad for Canadian movies. They are simply different. They are often more tentative, less sensational, less able to create a density of characterization than either the American or the British models. But this is their integrity—an integrity that reflects our own social uncertainties—both our uncertainty of action as a nation (look at the uncertainty of action within the Secretary of State's office!) and our own present lack of security in dealing with the ethnic and cultural problems which, throughout our vast nation, are trying to define themselves.

In her seminal sketch for a thematic approach to Canadian literature, *Survival*, Margaret Atwood quotes a challenging comment from Germaine Warkentin:

> Searchers for a Canadian identity have failed to realize that you can only have an identification with something you can see or recognize. You need, if nothing else, an image in a mirror. No other country cares enough about us to give us back an image of ourselves that we can even resent. And apparently we can't do it for ourselves, because so far our attempts to do so have resembled those of the three blind men trying to describe the elephant. Some

of the descriptions have been worth something, but what they add up to is fragmented, indecipherable. With what are we to identify ourselves?[1]

My basic argument is that (a) if we could be persuaded to watch our own television programmes; (b) if through our predominently foreign-owned distribution and exhibition system, we were allowed to see more of our own movies as well as a far greater number of films from other foreign cultures; and that (c) if we could stop constantly comparing our own product with the British or American models, we might be surprised to find that, in its tentative way, that mirror is beginning to form itself, that there is something there on our screens to be deciphered. Even in their weaknesses (if we want to call them that), our Canadian films are striving to tell us something—something about ourselves that is important to ourselves if we want to develop culturally as a nation.

"The answers you get from literature depend on the questions you pose," as Margaret Atwood has said. So it is with the movies. If what we want is distraction—"just entertainment", as people keep saying—then perhaps the Americans can go on doing this for us, with their far greater resources, years of experience, and (judging from the Canadian attempts to imitate the American style in films like BLACK CHRISTMAS and SHIVERS) better taste. The Americans can go on doing this for us and go on diminishing us as a nation—offering us a mirror in which we see reflections which, while they might seem similar in many ways, are not really our own. And if what we want is cultural uplift, the reflected sense of ourselves as cultivated people possessing erudition and refined taste, then we can let BBC-TV do this for us (although, even here, we can probably pick up more of it through the American PBS channels than we can through the CBC). But if what we *really* want is an intensified sense of ourselves as a nation—both light-hearted and serious, bilingual, multi-cultural, or whatever—then we have to fight for the right to gain exposure for our own film product, both in English and in French.

All knowledge is the result of experience. Comprehension (the ability to decipher) is the result of repeated exposure. It is like learning a language. When we are first exposed to a foreign language, we are immediately made conscious of all the idiomatic and syntactic conventions that are different from our own. The linguistic conventions are "foregrounded", as the theoreticians say—so much so that our first attempts to read a novel in a foreign language tend to make us more aware of all these unfamiliar grammatical conventions that we are of the meaning. We cannot simply *experience* the meaning with the same directness that we can experience the meaning of a novel in our own language, reading through the conventions *as if they were invisible* to the meaning they contain.

So it is with the movies. Except that the movies, for the majority of

Canadians, our own cinema is like a foreign language. The cinema we experience directly, as if without effort, is the American cinema; and that is simply the result of the repeated saturation we have had in the American product.

Don't misunderstand me: I am not *against* the American product. I am as thrilled as anyone by THE GODFATHER, NASHVILLE, or TAXI DRIVER; and I admire infinitely the skill and sensitivity with which such expensively comprehensive statements on American society can be made. But what I do resist strongly is the often unvoiced suggestion that, for instance, the mighty NASHVILLE might provide a standard against which we should judge the delicate and distinguished THE HARD PART BEGINS.

If we see ourselves as an emerging culture, as an over-developed Third-World country (as I have grown fond of saying), we have to be wary of importing critical standards from more established cultures, important though at times this exercise may be. It is really only the international money market that has encouraged us to believe that there are international standards in art. While we are all pleased if a Canadian film is well received at that international cinematic supermarket held each year at Cannes, I think it would be culturally disastrous for any nation to try to make films especially *for* that market. In fact, within the English-Canadian situation, the fine tribute paid there last year (1974) to Michel Brault for LES ORDRES has not helped the commercial life of that film in this country at all!

In her suggestive article on "The Documentary Poem: A Canadian Genre", Dorothy Livesay has written:

> ...our narratives reflect our environment profoundly; they are subtly used to cast light on the landscape, the topography, the flora and fauna as well as on the social structure of the country.

And after this, she goes on to suggest that, within this kind of genre,

> What is remarkable throughout is the interplay of the characters with the natural world they set out to dominate.[2]

If we look at just a handful of the films made this year, we can see how these comments might be related, in different ways, to THE FAR SHORE, LIES MY FATHER TOLD ME, SECOND WIND and (of course) WINGS IN THE WILDERNESS; and if we take the relationship of characters to landscape, or more generally to the social world that we, as Canadians, have to live in, then these films join a host of others that have been made over the last ten years—films such as NOBODY WAVED GOODBYE; LE CHAT DANS LE SAC, *all* the films of Don Shebib, including his CBC documentary on war veterans, GOOD TIMES, BAD TIMES; MON ONCLE ANTOINE; KAMOURASKA; THE HARD PART BEGINS; LE GRAND ROCK; LE TEMPS D'UNE CHASSE; LA VIE

REVEE; LES ORDRES; and really countless others—including SWEET MOVIE!

When we begin to respond to Canadian films thematically in this way, then (possibly) critical distinctions can be made between them. But initially, we have to see what they are *in themselves*. We have to recognize that they are trying to tell us something about ourselves and the world we live in—not the world we are surrounded by but the world we actually live in; and when we begin to think this way, we are beginning to think helpfully about the Canadian cinema. We are beginning to recognize that there is, in fact, a Canadian cinema that is *inferior to nothing*.

Certainly, its conventions are different as are the economic and cultural conditions in which it is produced. If we begin to think this way, then even the tastelessly clever excesses of SHIVERS might begin to make sense. They make sense as an expression of an attitude that is desperate to draw attention to itself (and, of course, to recover its costs), no matter what lengths it has to go to achieve this kind of attention. In my view, SHIVERS reflects the desperation of total cultural cynicism—a cynicism that believes an indigenous Canadian product is neither possible nor worthwhile.

Ultimately, I believe that if there is to be a *recognized* Canadian cinema, there will have to be some form of continued government subsidy. But the subsidy as it has existed so far, through the CFDC, the Canada Council, and the local arts councils, has been partial and inadequate. It has only concerned itself with aiding production, while ignoring the problems of distribution and exhibition and all the publicity that must accompany the production of a film. Any Hollywood tycoon worth his salt knows that it can cost almost as much to sell a film as to make it; but since in this country, the American product arrives pre-sold—the "stars" already familiar, the reviews already printed in the American press—no one in Canada has taken this part of our industry very seriously. Furthermore, there has been little done to encourage the screening throughout Canada of the non-American product—films from Europe and Asia—films that could help give Canadians the sense that there are other cinematic conventions than the American ones that the films can draw upon.

For we *do* have a Canadian cinema; and each year, we produce several films of quality. But whether or not the Canadian government is ever going to have the courage to interfere sufficiently with established commercial interests in this country to encourage these films to be seen is still a matter that hangs in the balance.

And that, of course, involves a whole new range of questions.

Notes

Preface

[1] Kh. Abdul-Kasimov, et. al, *Istoriia Sovetskovo Kino* (Moscow, 1969).
[2] Istvan Nemeskurty, *Word and Image: History of the Hungarian Cinema* (Budapest, 1968).
[3] Jorge Ayala Blanco, *Adventure del Cine Mexicano* (Mexico City, 1968).
[4] Pierre Leprohon, *The Italian Cinema* (New York, 1972).
[5] The best collection of work in this area is in *Artforum*, vol. 11, no. 5 (January 1973).
[6] Noel Burch, "Towards a Theory of Japanese Film", *October*, vol. 1, no. 1 (Spring 1976).
[7] Andrew Sarris, "Notes on the Auteur Theory in 1962", *Film Culture Reader* (New York, 1970), p. 130.
[8] In conversation, December 1976.
[9] E.M. Forster, *A Passage to India* (New York, 1924), p. 322.

I. "The Possibilities Are Truly Great"

American Domination of the Motion Picture Industry: Canada as a Test Case

[1] William Marston Seabury, *The Public and the Motion Picture Industry* (New York: The MacMillan Company, 1926), p. 240.
[2] Ibid., pp. 240-1.
[3] Rachel Low, *The History of the British Film, 1918-1929* (London: George Allen and Unwin Ltd.), p. 79.
[4] Seabury, *Public and Motion Picture Industry*, p. 252.
[5] *Film Daily Yearbook 1922*, p. 271.
[6] National Council of Public Morals, *The Cinema: Its Present Position and Future Possibilities* (London: Williams and Norgate, 1917), p. xxi.
[7] Arthur Weigall, "The Influence of the Kinematograph upon National Life" in *The Nineteenth Century*, April 1921, p. 668.
[8] Ibid., pp. 670-2.
[9] *New York Herald Tribune*, January 29, 1927, p. 5.
[10] Seabury, *Public and Motion Picture Industry*, p. ix.
[11] Ibid., p. 187.
[12] Ibid., p. 178.
[13] J.S. Woodsworth, *My Neighbour* (Toronto: University of Toronto Press, reprint edition, 1972) pp. 92-3.
[14] H.F. Angus, ed., *Canada and Her Great Neighbour* (Toronto: The Ryerson Press, 1938), p. 126.
[15] Ibid., p. 127
[16] Ibid., p. 129.

II. The National Film Board of Canada

Grierson's First Years at the NFB

[1] H. Reginald Hardy, *Mackenzie King of Canada* (London: Oxford University Press, 1949), p. 128.

[2] Mrs. Gudrun Parker in a conversation held August 1962, and many other sources.

[3] Grierson, "Documentary: A World Perspective" in *Grierson on Documentary*, ed. Forsyth Hardy (Berkeley: University of California Press, 1966), pp. 365-71.

[4] Hardy, *Mackenzie King of Canada*, p. 88.

[5] Ibid., p. 252.

[6] Grierson, interview, September 1966. He had been introduced to Haushofer's theories by a young Scottish teacher while still in secondary school; he knew about Geopolitik before Hitler did, he said.

[7] Hardy, *Mackenzie King of Canada*, pp. 253-4.

[8] Ibid., p. 311.

[9] Ibid., p. 309.

[10] Grierson, *Grierson on Documentary*, p. 29.

[11] Ibid., p. 26.

[12] "New Documentary Films" in *Documentary News Letter* I (May 1940), p. 7.

[13] "Films Across Canada" in *Documentary News Letter* I (January 1940), pp. 9-11.

[14] National Film Board Information Section, "The National Film Board: A Survey", mimeographed (Ottawa: National Film Board, June 1945).

[15] Grierson, "Postwar Patterns" in *Hollywood Quarterly* I (January 1946), pp. 159-65.

[16] James Beveridge, interview, September 1962.

[17] Stuart Legg, interview, September 1966.

[18] Julian Roffman, interview, August 1962.

[19] "Who's Who in Filmmaking: John Grierson" in *Sightlines* I (November-December 1967), pp. 4-5.

[20] Marjorie McKay, interview, August 1962.

[21] Ibid.

[22] Grierson, "The Documentary Idea, 1942" in *Documentary News Letter* III (June 1942), pp. 83-6; reprinted in *Grierson on Documentary*, pp. 248-58.

[23] Gordon Weisenborn, interview, September 1963.

[24] Beveridge interview.

[25] "Australia" in *Film News* XX, no. 4 (1963), pp. 6-7.

[26] Roffman interview.

[27] Norman McLaren, interview, August 1962; and Alan Phillips, "The Inspired Doodles of Norman McLaren" in *Maclean's*, c. 1952.

[28] National Film Board Information and Promotion Division, "The National Film Board of Canada", mimeographed (Ottawa: National Film Board, September 1953).

[29] Paul Rotha, Sinclair Road, and Richard Griffith, *Documentary Film* (London: Faber and Faber, 1952), p. 327.
[30] McKay interview.
[31] Roffman interview.
[32] Ibid.
[33] Grierson, "The Documentary Idea, 1942".
[34] Tom Daly, interview, August 1962.
[35] Michael Spencer, interview, August 1962.
[36] Raymond Spottiswoode, "Developments at the National Film Board of Canada, 1939-44" in *Journal of the Society of Motion Picture Engineers* XLIV (May 1945), pp. 391-400.
[37] NFB, "The National Film Board of Canada".
[38] Grierson in a letter to Basil Wright, October 1940.
[39] Donald Fraser, interview, August 1962.
[40] McKay interview.
[41] Grierson to Wright.
[42] Grierson, "The Eyes of Canada", mimeographed (January 1940).
[43] Stuart Legg in a letter to Basil Wright, December 1940.
[44] Margaret Grierson in a letter to Basil Wright, February 1941.
[45] "News from Canada" in *Documentary News Letter* II (April 1941), p. 76.
[46] McKay interview.
[47] NFB, "The National Film Board of Canada".
[48] Grierson, "A Film Policy for Canada" in *Canadian Affairs* I (June 15, 1944), pp. 3-15.
[49] Rotha, Road, Griffith, *Documentary Film*, p. 331.
[50] Grierson, "A Film Policy for Canada".

Before the Guerillières: Women's Films at the NFB During World War II

[1] Susan Trow and Olga Denisko, eds., *Four Days in May* (NFB, 1975).

The Innocent Eye: An Aspect of the Work of the National Film Board of Canada

[1] (1976) At the time of writing, I was scarcely aware of the role played within this unit by Terence Macartney-Filgate. In the early days of cinéma-vérité, his camera work quickly gained for him an international reputation; and judging from the films he made with Unit B—films such as THE DAYS BEFORE CHRISTMAS (1958), BLOOD AND FIRE (1958), and THE BACK BREAKING LEAF (1959)—Filgate was very much concerned with using the camera as a tool for social investigation. He expressed this concern again when he returned to the board to make UP AGAINST THE SYSTEM for George Stoney in 1969.

On the Candid-Eye Movement

[1] Frequently, melodramatic narratives were used in the works of these schools in order to sketch in outline the architectonic of the dramatic form. Thus, the outline of the formal structure of the narrative, to be completed by the

integration of the real, is presented almost schematically.

[2] On a theoretical level, this tendency was defended by André Bazin in his article, "Montage Interdit". This article presents an argument to the effect that integration of reality and the drama is an essential feature to truly cinematic works.

[3] The first fully developed "direct cinema" works in Canada date from 1958 (BLOOD AND FIRE, THE BACK-BREAKING LEAF)—anticipating the Drew/Leacock PRIMARY by almost two full years—and the roots of the style in Canada can be traced back to at least 1952.

[4] On this topic, see Mamber's incisive study of American-type cinéma-vérité, *Cinéma-Vérité in America*.

[5] Ibid.

[6] Perhaps explaining this idea in another manner would help to clarify it. By basing the films on a contest-type situation, one is guaranteed that there will be a central problematic posed by the film which can be expressed in the form "Will A win over B" and that this question will be answered by following the external course of development of the event. This entails that the course of the unfolding of the physical event is homologous with the form for the drama and thus that a document of the unfolding of the event will possess at least a degree of dramatic intrigue.

[7] As an interesting aside to this point, one might note how in these films the conception of a man's real nature is ideologically bound. In every case, man is shown to have the ability to survive under stress, to carry on his struggle despite defeat. As Mamber points out, this is a very American conception of human nature. Mamber compares the depiction of the central protagonist in the Drew films to Hawks's conception of hero. (Though the idea of hero is opposite, I should think the best parallel would be found in the works of Hemingway.) Mamber fails to note, however, how often this depiction of the American is permeated with that strong tone of condescension, even contempt, which is so typical of the eastern American attitude toward the ideals of Middle America. Leacock is most guilty in this regard: HAPPY MOTHER'S DAY is thoroughly infected with an attitude of contempt only partially redeemed by his so obvious humane sympathy for Mrs. Fisher. Furthermore, Mamber fails to note how the ambitious, striving American-hero character is consistently depicted in these works as a mask, disguising the underlying essence. The importance of the crisis-type of situation is precisely that it provides the stress to crack open this mask and reveal the real nature of the human character.

[8] The fact that this conception of the character's real nature is ideologically determined does nothing to refute the claim that the work derives its structure from reality, for the character's revelation of himself at the moments after the crisis surely admits of something that is undeniably real. What is ideologically determined is the conception that what is revealed in the aftermath of the crisis situation is more basic to the human constitution than what is revealed in the character's choices of his goals. This conception of the unity of truth and beauty, of the affinity between natural and artistic forms (indicated by the use of natural activities to provide the structure by which aesthetic tensions are resolved) and of the organic character of a work of art indicates the allegiance of this kind of cinema (and more generally of the stream of modernism with which it is associated) to the aesthetics of Romanticism.

[9] It should go without saying that the ideological implications of this shift in direction in the film are quite profound and disturbing.

[10] The examples I have chosen are not isolated cases of the refusal to use dramatic forms for the documentation of situations which have an inherent dramatic potential; indeed, the entire history of the Candid-Eye movement is a succession of crisis-type situations refused, of conflicts not taken into account. Two further examples one could point to are BLOOD AND FIRE which could have been developed as a drama of the struggle to save souls, and I WAS A 90-POUND WEAKLING which could have been a dramatic presentation of individuals striving to overcome their physical limitations.

[11] This influence has been attested to by the Candid-Eye filmmakers themselves, for example, Terence Macartney-Filgate in an interview with Sarah Jennings (see "An Interview with Terence Macartney-Filgate" in this book).

[12] This approach places the work of Cartier-Bresson within the streams of modernism which eschewed the use of dramatic forms because they tended to privilege certain moments over others. The logical extension of this trend was to repudiate even Cartier-Bresson's "decisive moment" (which will be discussed shortly) and to capture the moments before or after it. This was the step taken by Robert Frank in his important ground-breaking book, *The Americans*.

[13] The idea that photography developed when a series of technical innovations made it possible is simply historically false; all the technical components necessary for the development of photography were in existence at least two hundred years prior to its invention.

[14] This chronological method of presentation of course oversimplifies and distorts the actual history, for there were at all times literalist as well as pictorialist tendencies co-existing; in fact, at times literalist and pictorialist features co-exist in the work of a single photographer. This chronology does, nonetheless, outline some essential tendencies in the history of photography. (A cogent presentation of the conflict between these two modes of photography is Walker Evan's article in *Hound and Horn* no. 37.)

[15] Here I use the term "modernism" not to refer to those tendencies described by Clement Green as defining modernist painting, but to refer to that stream of art flowing from impression.

[16] Hence the resemblence between the object matter of much of literalist photography (and of the affinities of photography discussed by Kracauer in his *Theory of Film*) and the object matter of much of impressionist painting.

[17] Susan Sontag has described the way in which Surrealism lay close to the heart of the photographic enterprise itself, and showed how those photographs which eschew the decorative convention introduced by Surrealism into the other arts and cling more nearly to the reproductive process are the most likely to be surreal. An overwhelmingly powerful demonstration of this in films is, of course, Luis Bunuel's LAS HURDES. (See Susan Sontag, "Shooting America", *The New York Review of Books*, April 18, 1974.)

[18] An alternate approach of the early photojournalist was to deal with the noteworthy, even the spectacular. But here again, the real was allowed to enter the work of art only by virtue of its dramatic qualities.

[19] It was not until Robert Frank's publication of *The Americans* that this approach was rejected. Frank refused to select those climactic moments which constituted the object matter of Cartier-Bresson's photographs and instead selected

moments precisely on the basis of their ordinariness—of their being typical of the run of events.

[20] So extreme is Cartier-Bresson's stance on this matter that he photographs only with a 50mm lens—a lense the angle of acceptance of which most nearly approximates the angle of acceptance of human vision, and he refuses to crop or otherwise manipulate the print in printing.

[21] This principle underlying Cartier-Bresson's practice is allied very closely with that principle of non-interference in the pro-filmic event so dear to all practicioners of "direct cinema" in North America. No doubt this accounts in part for the affinity which the Candid-Eye filmmakers felt for his work.

[22] This tendency in the practice of photography of this period also finds expression in the theories of photography which evolved contemporaneously. Aestheticians of the time often made claims for the virtues of photograph quality self-effacement. It is noteworthy that these claims for objectivity, for the detached, unmanipulative characteristics of photography, arose only in the mid-fifties.

[23] This sort of structure was first used in cinema in the works of Robert Flaherty. It is noteworthy that Flaherty felt compelled to resolve such a structure with a dramatic finale, while the Candid-Eye filmmakers felt no such compulsion.

[24] "On National Culture", *The Wretched of the Earth* (New York: Grove Press, 1968).

What Challenge? What Change?

[1] See "Memo to Michelle about Decentralizing the Means of Production",

Saint-Jérôme: The Experience of a Filmmaker As Social Animator

[1] The Saint-Jérôme Chamber of Commerce, since that time, has asked that the film be restricted to specialized audiences, only to find the principal community organizations in Saint-Jérôme rising up in defence of the film.

III. Feature Filmmaking

The Years of Hope

[1] This article is a reworking of *Movies & Mythologies*, prepared for CBC's "Ideas". A book based on the material was published in 1977. All quotations are courtesy of CBC sound archives.

[2] See "The Innocent Eye", page 67.

[3] Ibid.

Men of Vision: Some Comments on the Work of Don Shebib

[1] For instance, see the section on Don Shebib in *Inner Views: Ten Canadian Film-Makers*, by John Hofsess (Toronto: McGraw-Hill Ryerson, 1975), pp. 67-79.

[2] In *Marshall Delaney at the Movies*, by Robert Fulford (Toronto: Peter Martin Associates, 1974).

[3] Ibid, pp. 70-71.

[4] "The End of the Road", by John Hofsess, in *Weekend Magazine* (Toronto) 28 February, 1976, pp. 16 ff.

[5] See "Introduction", pp. 372-376.

An Account By a Privileged Hostage of "Les Ordres": Brault Has Missed His Shot

[1] Around 1973-4, a rallying slogan for the Parti Québécois was "J'ai le goût du Québec".

IV. Experimental Filmmaking

Michael Snow's "Wavelength"

[1] This concern with the problems of illusionism is, of course, also partly grounded in the belief in the importance of re-sensitizing which has characterized much of modern psychological thought. To a large extent, speculation on this problem can also be seen as the inevitable consequence of the attempt to insert subjectivist and expressionistic ideas into an aesthetic tradition which had been founded upon the concept of mimesis.

[2] This view has been most powerfully argued by Stan Brakhage.

[3] E.g., the fixed point of view of the camera, the limits of its field of view and the limits of the camera's movements. The polarity between a fixed space and a fixed tripod on the one hand and the free movement of the camera (panning, tilting, and zooming) within these fixed limits on the other hand is a common feature of the structuralist film, as Sitney points out in his important article on "Structural Film" (*Film Culture* no. 47, Summer 1969). The antecedent for this technical characteristic is found in the work of Warhol (e.g., PARTY SEQUENCE: POOR LITTLE RICH GIRL, and the Marie Menken episode of THE CHELSEA GIRLS).

[4] This film gives the lie to Youngblood's claim (*Expanded Cinema*, p. 122) made in connection with WAVELENGTH that "by introducing the element of motion, specifically invisible motion [but the motion referred, the extension of the zoom, is perceivable] like the hands of a clock [why like the hands of a clock? Why not like the growth of a flower or to use Youngblood's ungrammatical construction, like a flower? Is he perhaps trying to sneak in the idea of temporality?], the filmmaker adds the temporal element [adds the temporal element?! Any film exists in time!] to a composition that in all other respects appears static. [What are these other respects? What are the characteristics other than the lack of motion by virtue of which an image is static?]. Motion is the only phenomenon that allows the perception of time." Snow demonstrates the falsity of this last claim by pointing out that the awareness of subjective time is part of the experience of a film.

[5] This concern with framing is a concern which Snow has expressed repeatedly during his career. Consider as outstanding examples: "8 x 10", "Portrait of 1967", "Sight 1967", the photographic images of the tray of ice and, most closely relating to LA REGION CENTRALE, the Canadian landscape seen through a windshield and rear-view mirror. Interestingly, this concern represents a deviation of Michael Snow from the "modernism" of the sixties with which he is often identified. Snow continually justifies his opposition to the strategy of rejecting actual physical containment in favour of the use of closed forms by pointing almost obsessively the way in which the frame transforms that which is framed into a distinct self-reflexive entity.

[6] Convering on LA REGION CENTRALE: Michael Snow in Conversation with Charlotte Townsend", *artscanada*, no. 28, pp. 46-7 (February 1971).

[7] A most important exception is, of course, Annette Michelson (see "Towards Snow", *Artforum*, no. 9, pp. 30-7 (June 1971).

[8] *Film Culture*, no. 46 (Autumn 1967).

[9] This intensification of interest in the plastic character of images in the film by the devaluation of the narrative is a prevalent though little noted feature of the modern cinema; it largely accounts for the strength of the effect of the imagery in the films of Antonioni and more especially Bresson.

[10] As might be expected in the case of a photographer/painter turned filmmaker, this matter has been a recurrent concern in Snow's films. ONE SECOND IN MONTREAL, for example, demonstrates that by transposing photographs into a film, one alters the nature of the viewer's response to them.

[11] That this film deals with the structural homology of drama and experience was first pointed out by Annette Michelson in her characteristically brilliant article on Michael Snow in *Artforum* (previously cited), to which I am greatly indebted.

[12] The fact that the dramatic film image exists in a field charged between the poles of the present and the future is a fact Snow brilliantly demonstrates in ONE SECOND IN MONTREAL.

[13] A note on the soundtrack is in order. The soundtrack, as was noted earlier, consists of a nearly continuous extended *glissando* interrupted only by real, synchronous sound during the human events. The soundtrack thus parallels the visuals, for like the visuals it is for the most part structured upon a single extended operation. Moreover, like the forward progression of the zoom, the increase in the frequency of the sound on the track parallels the increase in tension which occurs during the course of a drama. In my opinion, however, the track is much less successful than the visual film, for the sound, having no discernible "destination", fails to create the structural tensions which are attendant upon the anticipation of a range of possible outcomes.

[14] Typified surprisingly enough by another film of this remarkable filmmaker, NEW YORK EYE AND EAR CONTROL.

[15] This idea was extended and developed in LA REGION CENTRALE.

[16] I am here speaking somewhat loosely. There is, of course, a play of spaces in film—between the illusory three-dimensional space of the loft and the real two-dimensional surface of the screen, between the space inside the loft and the space outside the loft, and between the surface of the screen and the space of the viewing room in front of it.

[17] Maya Deren's important contrast between vertical and horizontal structures is, for all the abuse it received, one of the most cogent theoretical formulations of the problematic defined by this desire (see Sitney, ed., *Film Culture Reader*, pp. 173 ff.).

[18] This feature of the work gives the lie to yet another claim advanced by Gene Youngblood (*Expanded Cinema*, p. 125), namely, that the work is nonlinear. What could be more linear than the use of this continual forward extension of the zoom to articulate a sense of the continual stream of time? His characterization of the work could, in fact, be applied much more accurately to works of that very tradition against which Snow, as we have noted here, reacted—the tradition which culminates with the early work of Peter Kubelka (e.g., MOSAIC IN CONFIDENCE—the very title is suggestive!), the incredibly assertive

Notes   385

and disjunctive style of Stan Brakhage or the rapid single-frame animation of Robert Breer whose films truly do establish a nonlinear *gestalt*.

[19] A song which, appropriately enough, deals with the idea of illusion and reality.

[20] An important compositional feature of this work which merits comment is the use of strategies within the over-all structure of the work to put the viewer in mind of those features for which the over-all structures of the film stand as a grand metaphor. A further example of this is the introduction of dramatic moments into the film which cause the viewer to question the role of drama in the film.

[21] The time of this realization will, of course, vary from person to person.

[22] The tension conditioned by an expectation of a conclusion about which one is certain is also one of Robert Nelson's. In BLEU SHUT he develops a strategy to evoke that tension which, in its regorous purity, is reminiscent of WAVELENGTH: at the beginning of the film someone announces that the film will last thirty minutes and throughout the film there is a clock on the screen which enables the viewer to gauge how much longer the film will run (or more accurately which persuades the viewer that he/she can gauge this, since the film is in fact thirty-eight minutes long). The similarity of this film to WAVELENGTH is even more marked, for like WAVELENGTH this film demonstrates that the temporal structures of a film ground our experience of expectation.

[23] Remarkably, when the viewer becomes conscious that the camera movement will end by centering on one of these objects, he feels the same sort of tension as that brought on by the anticipation of the range of possible outcomes of a drama. This points up the fact that this film, though for the most part lacking in the kind of action traditional in the drama, possesses nonetheless the structural tensions of that form.

[24] The character and influence of these events were first pointed out by Sitney ("Structural Film", *Film Culture*, no. 47, Summer 1969, p. 4.).

[25] There is a further randomness associated with these events occurring in the space outside the loft. As a result of the changes in film stock, filters and printing processes the windows of the loft appear sometimes as blocked up with light or darkness, sometimes as transparent, rendering the events outside the loft sometimes observable, sometimes not. There seems to be no discernible pattern to these changes.

[26] The confining of the action to a single space, the play between the space inside the loft and that outside the loft, and the movement of the zoom towards that space outside the loft have yet another significance: they define the problem of establishing that consciousness has access to things outside the circle of ideas, and they reincarnate the drama of the quest for transcendence. (Snow himself has directed attention to this aspect of his work by saying, in his statement prepared for the Knokke-le-Zoute Festival, that the work is a "summation of my religious inklings". He has also related the work to his first experiment with lysergic acid.) The film concludes with an image which appears to be that of a space beyond that of the loft but is in fact enclosed within the loft, and this of course reiterates the idealist position. This aspect of the work is interesting, for it separates Snow from the analytic and objectifying tradition which has been the context of the bulk of innovational art-work of the last few years—a tradition with which Snow is often identified. The aspirations of those belonging to this tradition have been consistently and thoroughly secular and materialist in

character. Snow's work clearly belongs to the tradition of Romantic idealism which for decades has sustained experiment in the cinema.

[27] He is Hollis Frampton, a friend of Michael Snow's and a distinguished structuralist filmmaker in his own right.

[28] An interesting aspect of these episodes is connected with the treatment of the man lying on the floor. As the man tumbles onto the floor, he falls almost out of view of the camera. A slight progression of the zoom then totally removes the man from view and gives the impression of the camera passing over him. The effect is to render the man almost insignificant in comparison with the general flow of events. Thus this treatment of the man stands, I believe, as an analogy to the way in which events and objects within the context of a dramatic film tend to be "carried away" by the momentum of the unfolding story—to cease to be events which stand as entities in themselves and to become "relational units", units whose nature and importance are determined by their relationship to past events and events to come and which are entirely subsumed into the dramatic structure.

[29] This feeling of temporal separation is enhanced by the apparent change from day to night between the two events. Thus the conjunction of these passages also articulates a play between real time and film time.

[30] We have already noted that the film deals with various kinds of connections between things. Here another kind of connection is demonstrated, namely the connection of events in a dramatic sequence. In this connection, the relationship between the four "human events" should be commented upon. Each successively occurring "human event" in the film marks an increase in mobility and in dramatic intensity culminating, in fact, in the fourth episode, with a moment of dramatic action, rare in the experimental film. In this regard, the relationship of the four "human events" is structurally similar to the relationship of the events in a drama, each of which increases the dramatic tension.

[31] One suspects that this separation of events serves other functions as well. Inasmuch as this film is in part a study of the mode of cinematic illusionism, one can perhaps see the separation as making a reference to the separateness of the frames upon which all illusionism in film is ultimately based. And inasmuch as this film is, in part, a study of dramatic structures in film, this separateness can perhaps be seen as making a reference to the fragmentation of scenes upon which the articulation of the drama in film has, since the days of Griffith, been based. In addition, the interpolation of the passage of superimpositions into this passage, by breaking up the dynamics of the unfolding story, demonstrates the way in which the eschewing of a story forces the viewer to contemplate the graphic character of the images, and to consider the objects represented not relationally but for what they are in themselves. Thus the contrast between the two filmic styles in this portion of the film demonstrates different modes of cinematic experience.

[32] This of course recreates in the over-all structure of the film, the play between images creating the illusion of deep space and images which appear flat. This play occurred early in the film in the contrast between naturalistic images on the one hand and the images in photographic negative or the pure colour fields on the other.

[33] It has already been remarked that this concern with framing has been a recurrent feature of Snow's work.

[34] This movement towards reification is also exemplified in the attempt to create a work which for the most part lacks the human action typical of the drama but which possesses the structural tensions inherent in that form.

[35] The strategies which Snow uses to void these movements are remarkable. Snow has throughout his *oeuvre* chosen movements which have no counterpart in ordinary human vision. Nothing in human vision approximates the mechanism of the zoom in WAVELENGTH, the panning and tilting or the whirling camera in LA REGION CENTRALE. In order to void these movements of any expressionistic import, Snow has so reduced and protracted the camera movements that a single type of operation becomes the structural principle for an entire work.

[36] The resultant monomorphic structure is in marked contrast to the polymorphic structure which had become traditional in innovational filmmaking. This feature of Snow's work, too, demonstrates that Gene Youngblood's use of the term "constructivist" as an appellation for Snow's kind of cinema is a frightful misappropriation. For, although the issue is made somewhat complex by the fact that the minimalist style in art has forced a reconsideration of aspects of the constructivist experiment in the arts, and although Snow's cinema shares certain features with minimalism, Snow's work is a great distance from the constructivist experiments in both constructivist theatre and cinema which, being founded on the concept of a montage of discrete particles, was polymorphic in character. Furthermore, the spiritual concerns of Snow's work are at a great remove from the thoroughly secular and objectifying concerns of the constructivist tradition.

The New Canadian Cinema: Images from the Age of Paradox

[1] Slavko Vorkapich, "Toward True Cinema" in *Film: A Montage of Theories*, edited by Richard Dyer MacCann. (New York: E.P. Dutton & Co., Inc., 1966), p. 172.

[2] John Chambers, "Perceptual Realism", *artscanada* (October 1969), p. 13.

[3] Ibid.

V. "The Possibilities Are Truly Great" Continued

A Place Like Home

[1] Honourable mention should be made of a TV-film like SPRING HILL. Ron Kelly's powerful dramatization of survivial in a mine disaster.

[2] Unfortunately, 16mm, the format in which many audiences get to see Canadian films, sadly reduces the breadth of a prairie sky, and many another noble prospect.

[3] In a talk in the Victoria College Alumni Lecture Series at the University of Toronto, October 1974.

[4] "All resemblances to actual persons, etc., etc.... coincidental."

Introduction

[1] Margaret Atwood, *Survival* (Toronto: Anansi, 1972), p.9.

[2] Eli Mandel, ed., *Contexts of Canadian Criticism* (Chicago: University of Chicago Press, 1971), pp. 269 & 274.

A Selected Bibliography

I. "The Possibilities Are Truly Great" (Pre-NFB)

Backhouse, Charles F. *Canadian Government Motion Picture Bureau: 1917-1941*. Ottawa: Canadian Film Institute, 1974.

Berton, Pierre. *Hollywood's Canada*. Toronto: McClelland & Stewart, 1975.

Côté, Guy L. *Hommage à M.L. Ernest Ouimet*. Montréal: La Cinémathèque canadienne, 1966.

Cowan, James A. "The Battle for Canadian Film Control". *Maclean's*, October 1, 1930.

——. "Is There a Chance for Empire Films?" *Macleans*, October 15, 1930.

Cox, Kirwan, "The Majors and the Mandarins: Through the Years". *Cinema Canada*, no. 22 (October 1975).

Duvan, Allan. "Canada Has a Movie Future". *Maclean's*, February 1, 1920.

Evans, Gary. "First Films in Canada". *Cinema Canada*, no. 26 (March 1976).

Ibrányi-Kiss, Á. "DREAMLAND: Kirwan Cox and Donald Brittain". *Cinema Canada*, no. 16 (October-November 1974).

Mitchell, M. "Ernest Shipman". *Motion*, no. 1 (1972).

——. "Oh Canada: 1919-1930". *Motion*, March-April, 1973.

——. "Quickies à la Canadienne". *Motion*, vol. 5, no. 5 (October 1976).

——. "The Silhouette Films of Bryant Fryer". *Motion*, vol. 5, no. 3 (1976).

Morris, Peter, "Canada's First Movie Mogul". *Take One*, vol. 1, no. 1.

——. *Canadian Feature Films: 1913-1969. Part I: 1913-1940*. Ottawa: Canadian Film Institute, 1970.

——. "The First Films in Canada: The True Story (Part I)". *Cinema Canada*, no. 29 (June-July 1976).

——. "The First Films in Canada: The True Story (Part II)". *Cinema Canada*, no. 30 (August 1976).

Nowry, Lawrence. "Early Scenario of Ernest Ouimet, Grand-père of Film". *Montrealer*, no. 40 (August 1966).

Ryval, Michael. "Those Were the Days: Interview with Roy Tash, C.S.C." *Motion*, vol. 5, no. 3 (1976).

Turner, D. John. "Ernest Ouimet: Exhibitor". *Cinema Canada*, no. 22 (October 1975).

——. "Ernest Ouimet: Filmmaker and Distributor". *Cinema Canada*, no. 24 (December-January 1976).

II. The National Film Board of Canada

Andrew, Geoffrey. "John Grierson: 1898-1972". *Canadian Forum* (April 1972).

"Animation". *Pot Pourri*, April 1972.

Barlow, Roger. "Documentary in Canada". *Documentary Newsletter*, February 1942.

Barsam, Richard. *Non-Fiction Film*. New York: E.P. Dutton, 1973.

Bennet, Deborah J. "George C. Stoney: An Interview". *Journal of the University Film Association*, vol. 25, no. 4 (1973).

Block, R. "Canada's War Baby Comes of Age". *National Home Monthly*, October 1943.

Blumer, Ron. "John Grierson: I Derive My Authority from Moses". *Take One*, vol. 2, no. 9 (January-February 1970).

_____. "NFB: Is This the End?" *Take One*, vol. 2, no. 3 (January-February 1969).

Boissonnault, Robert. "Les Cinéastes québécois et l"Office national du film". *Cinéma-Québec*, vol. 2, nos. 2-4.

Bonneville, Léo. "Crise à l'ONF". *Séquences*, no. 60 (fevrier 1960).

Buchanan, D.W. "Canada on the World's Screen". *Canadian Geographic Journal*, March 1944.

Buchanan, Donald. "A Canadian Experiment". *Documentary Newsletter*, June 1942.

Callenbach, Ernest. "Grierson". *Film Quarterly*, Winter 1973-4.

Cinema Canada, no. 15 (August-September 1974). Special issue on NFB.

Collins, Maynard. *Norman McLaren*. Ottawa: Canadian Film Institute, 1976.

Cutler, May E. "The Unique Genius of Norman McLaren". *Canadian Art*, no. 97 (May-June, 1965).

Elliot, Lawrence. "Norman McLaren: Gentle Genius of the Screen". *Reader's Digest*, August 1971.

"En tant que femmes". *Access*, Summer 1973.

"The Fight for the NFB". *Canadian Dimension*, April-May 1970.

"Film Board of Canada". *Documentary Newsletter*, January 1943.

Gauthier, Guy. "L'Office national du film canadien". *Image et Son,* mai 1964.

Glover, Guy. "Nine Film Animators Speak". *artscanada*, April 1970.

Gobeil, Charlotte, ed. *Terence Macartney-Filgate: The Candid Eye*. Ottawa: Canadian Film Institute, 1966.

Grant, Connie. "A Mirror for Canadians: André Lamy, NFB". *Motion*, vol. 5, no. 2.

Greenwood, K.M. "Role of Documentary Films in Canada". *Public Affairs*, no. 10 (1946).

Grierson, John. "O Canada! We Stand on Guard for Thee". *Documentary Film News*, March 1948.

Hardy, Forsyth, ed. *Grierson on Documentary*. London: Collins, 1946; New York: Praeger, 1971.

Hill, Derek. "The Documentary Movement". *Sight and Sound*, Spring 1976.

James, C. Rodney. *Film as a National Art*. New York: Arno Press, 1977.

James, Rodney. "The Film Board Idea". *Journal of the University Film Association*, vol. 23, no. 1 (1971).

——. "John Grierson: England, Canada, the World". *Journal of the University Film Association*, vol. 24, no. 3 (1972).

——. *The National Film Board of Canada and Its Task of Communication*. Washington: U.S. Dept. of Health, Education and Welfare, 1968.

Jordan, William E. "Norman McLaren: His Career and Techniques". *Quarterly of Film, Radio and Television*, vol. 8, no. 1 (1954).

Jutra, Claude. "En courant derrière Rouch". *Cahiers du cinéma*, novembre 1960, janvier 1961, fevrier 1961.

Larsson, Rose-Marie. "Silencing the Workers: Censorship in the NFB–ON EST AU COTON". *Transformation*, Summer 1972.

Lefebvre, Jean-Pierre. "Colin Low: Poète de la survivance". *Objectif*, 1968.

Levine, Holly. "The NFB Remembers". *Motion*, vol. 5, no. 3 (1976).

Lovell, Alan, and Hillier, Jim. *Studies in Documentary*. London: Secker & Warburg, 1972.

Lysyshyn, James. *A Brief History: The National Film Board of Canada*. Montreal: NFB, 1968.

McCann, Richard Dyer. "The National Film Board of Canada". In *The People's Films*. New York: Hastings House, 1973.

McInnes, G.C. "Canada Carries On". *Maclean's*, March 15, 1941.

McKay, Marjorie. "Proposals for the Future". *Interlock*, nos. 4-5 (1976).

McLaren, Norman. "Animated Films". *Documentary Film News*, May 1948.

McLean, Grant. "Canada Goes To China". *Documentary Film News*, June 1948.

"Media in the Arctic". *Pot Pourri*, Spring 1976.

Michener, W. "Through a Multi-screen Darkly". *Maclean's*, September 17, 1966.

Morris, Peter, ed. *The National Film Board of Canada: The War Years*. Ottawa: Canadian Film Institute, 1965; reprinted 1971.

Movie, no. 8 (April 1963).

"NFB Film Workshops". *Pot Pourri*, Spring 1976.

Paquet, André, ed. *How to Make or Not to Make a Canadian Film*. Montreal: La Cinémathèque canadienne, 1967.

Ropchan, P. "The Career of Norman McLaren". *Cinema Canada*, no. 9 (August-September, 1973).

Rosenthal, Alan. *New Documentary in Action*. Berkeley: University of California Press.

Rubenstein, Lenny. "SAD SONG OF YELLOW SKIN". *Cinéaste*, vol. 4, no. 4 (Spring 1971).

Summers, Bob. "Challenge for Change". *Cinéaste*, Spring 1970.

Sussex, Elizabeth. "The Golden Years of Grierson". *Sight and Sound*, Summer 1972.

_____. "Grierson on Documentary: The Last Interview". *Film Quarterly*, Fall 1972.

Stoney, George C. "Film, Videotape and Social Change". *Journal of the University Film Association*, vol. 23, no. 4 (1971).

Tadros, Connie. "The Testing Ground: Atlantic NFB". *Cinema Canada*, no. 32 (November 1976).

Warkentin, Germaine. "Norman McLaren". *Tamarack Review*, no. 5 (Autumn 1957).

Wilson, C.P. "History in Motion Pictures". *Canadian Historical Review*, March 1942.

"Women Making Films". *Pot Pourri*, June 1974.

"Working with Film: Experiences with a Group of Films about Working Mothers". *Access*, no. 14 (Spring 1975).

III. Feature Filmmaking

"The Actor". *Motion*, July-August 1974. Special issue.

Ammon, Jack. "Scanlon's Overview". *Cinema Canada*, no. 24 (December-January 1975-6).

Armatage, Kay, and Beath, Linda. "Canadian Women's Cinema". *Women and Film Festival Notes*, 1973.

Association of Quebec Cinéastes. "Cinema: Another Face of Colonized Quebec". *Cinéaste*, Summer 1972.

Bawden, Liz-Anne, ed. "Section on Canadian Film". *Oxford Companion to Film*. New York: Oxford University Press, 1976.

Beattie, Eleanor. *The Handbook of Canadian Film*. Toronto: Peter Martin Associates and Take One, 1977. 2nd ed.

Berson, Alain. *Pierre Perrault*. Montréal: Conseil québécois pour la diffusion du cinéma, 1970.

Beveridge, James. "The Living Story: Crown and Canada". *Sight and Sound*, April-June 1952.

"Bill Fruet's WEDDING IN WHITE". *Cinema Canada*, no. 3 (August 1972).

Bonneville, Léo. "Dieu n'est pas mort dans le cinéma canadien". *Séquences*, no. 51 (fevrier 1968).

──── . "Qu'est-ce que le cinéma canadien?" *Séquences*, no. 53 (avril 1968).

Chabot, Jean. *Claude Jutra*. Montréal: Conseil québécois pour la diffusion du cinéma, 1970.

──── . "Jean-Pierre Lefebvre". *Second Wave*. Edited by Ian Cameron. London: Studio Vista, 1970.

"Chalmers Adams: A Producer's View". *Criteria*, February 1976.

Charent, Brian; Harcourt, Peter; and Blacknell, Margo. "THE FAR SHORE: Interview with Wieland". *Motion*, vol. 5, no. 2 (1976).

Chesley, Stephen. "BINGO: Lord". *Cinema Canada*, no. 18 (March-April 1975).

──── . "William Weintraub, Producer". *Cinema Canada*, no. 15 (August-September 1974).

Chesley, Stephen, and Ibrányi-Kiss, Á. "Bloomfield". *Cinema Canada*, no. 17 (December-January 1974-5).

──── . "Pilon". *Cinema Canada*, no. 17 (December-January 1974-5).

Clancy, Brian. "An Interview with Michel Tremblay". *Cinema Canada*, no. 19 (May-June 1975).

Clarke, Cheryl. "Peter Pearson". *Motion*, vol. 5, no. 4 (1976).

Cook, Bruce. "The Canadian Dilemma: A Problem of Identity". *Journal of the University Film Association*, November 1975.

Côté, Guy. "Anybody Making Shorts These Days?" *artscanada*, April 1970.

Cox, Kirwan. "Association coopérative des productions audio-visuelles". *Cinema Canada*, no. 6 (February-March 1973).

──── . "KAMOURASKA: Claude Jutra". *Cinema Canada*, no. 7 (April-May 1973).

──── . "Rocca's Big Fight". *Cinema Canada*, no. 25 (February 1976).

Comolli, Jean-Louis. "Situation du nouveau cinéma: Canada". *Cahiers du cinéma*, octobre 1967.

Crowdus, Gary. "The Montreal New Cinéma Conference". *Cinéaste*, vol. 6, no. 3 (1975).

Csaba Köller, George. "About Rape and Recent Releases". *Cinema Canada*, no. 16 (October-November 1974).

──── . "Carle's Heavenly Bodies". *Cinema Canada*, no. 13 (April-May 1974).

──── . "Interview with Claude Jutra". *Cinema Canada*, no. 23 (November 1975).

──── . "Jacques Godbout". *Cinema Canada*, no. 7 (April-May 1973).

──── . "Leiterman in China". *Cinema Canada*, no. 12 (February-March 1974).

──── . "Paul Almond's JOURNEY: Dream and Reality". *Cinema Canada*, no. 4 (October-November 1972).

_____. "THE ROWDYMAN: Interview with Peter Carter". *Cinema Canada*, no. 2 (May-June 1972).

_____. "To Chase the Elusive: George Kaczender". *Cinema Canada*, nos. 10-11 (October 1973, January 1974).

_____. "The True Nature of Micheline Lanctot". *Cinema Canada*, nos. 10-11 (October 1973, January 1974).

_____. "Vancouver Independent Filmmaking: Peter Bryant". *Cinema Canada*, no. 7 (April-May 1973).

Csaba Köller, George, ed. "Richard Leiterman". *Cinema Canada*, no. 1 (March 1972).

Dancyger, Ken. "The Point of Returns: Ed Hunt". *Cinema Canada*, no. 33 (December-January 1976-7).

Daudelin, Robert. *Gilles Groulx*. Montreal: Conseil québécois pour la diffusion du cinéma, 1969.

_____. "Gilles Groulx". In *Second Wave*. Edited by Ian Cameron. London: Studio Vista, 1970.

_____. "1945-1955: Le Préhistoire". *Objectif,* mai 1967.

_____. *Vingt ans de cinéma au Canada français*. Québec: Ministre des affaires culturelles, 1967.

Daudelin, Robert, et Frappier, Roger. *Gilles Carle*. Montréal: Conseil québécois pour la diffusion du cinéma, 1970.

Delaney, Marshall. "Canada's Trauma Produces a Major Work of Art". *Saturday Night*, June 1975.

_____. "Canadian Sex and the Multinational Menace". *Saturday Night*, October 1976.

Delisle, Martin. "Rencontre avec Gilles Carle". *Motion*, vol 5, no. 4 (1976).

Denton, Clive. "Furie, Then and Now". *Cinema Canada*, no. 26 (March 1976).

"Distribution". *Motion*, vol. 5, no. 5 (October 1976). Special issue.

Drabinsky, Garth. *Motion Pictures and the Arts in Canada*. Toronto: McGraw-Hill Ryerson, 1976.

Dumas, Carmel. "An Artisan in Show Biz: Claude Fournier". *Cinema Canada*, no. 32 (November 1976).

Edell, Frederick. "Films: Claude Jutra". *Canadian Dimension,* March 1976.

Edsforth, Janet. *Paul Almond: The Flame Within*. Ottawa: Canadian Film Institute, 1972.

Edwards, Natalie. "Talking with Leonard Yakir". *Cinema Canada*, no. 21 (September 1975).

Edwards, Natalie, and Irwin, Mark. "Reg Morris, C.S.C.: Past, Present, and Future". *Cinema Canada*, no. 25 (February 1967).

Evanchuck, P.M. "Breathing Heavy: Or is Don Getting Second Wind?" *Motion*, January 1976.

———. "Conversation with Arla Saare". *Motion*, March-April 1973.

———. "The Idea of Life and Death: Francis Mankiewicz". *Motion*, May-June 1973.

———. "Interview with Don Shebib". *Motion*, March-April 1973.

———. "Kelly Duncan, C.S.C." *Motion*, November-December 1973.

———. "Regina You Say: John Vernon". *Motion*, May-June 1973.

———. "Second Fiddle: Peter Pearson". *Motion*, January 1976.

———. "Three Years Ago: Doris Petrie". *Motion*, January-February 1973.

———. "Tracing a Visual Career: Jackson Samuels, C.S.C." *Motion*, January-February 1973.

———. "Werner Aellen: Four More Pictures". *Motion*, November-December 1973.

———. "WOLFPEN PRINCIPLE: Jack Darcus". *Motion*, November-December 1973.

Forrester, James. "La Tête de Gilles Carle". *Motion*, vol. 5, no. 4 (1976).

Fothergill, Robert. "Paperback Heroism: Three Canadian Films". *Canadian Forum*, February 1974.

Fox, Joseph. *The Canadian Film Industry: Past, Present, and Future.* Ottawa: Carleton University, 1971.

"Friendly Neighbourhood Cinéastes". *Maclean's*, January 1972.

"The Film Critic". *Pot Pourri*, November 1974. Special issue.

Fulford, Robert. *Marshall Delaney at the Movies.* Toronto: Peter Martin Associates and Take One, 1975.

Gathercole, Sandra. "Just Between Friends: Don Shebib". *Cinema Canada*, nos. 10-11 (October 1973, January 1974).

Gelinas, Marc. "Quelques acres d'histoire". *Le Maclean*, mars 1972.

———. "Une problème de pays". *Le Maclean*, août 1971.

Gobeil, Charlotte, ed. *The Film and Ron Kelly.* Ottawa: Canadian Film Institute, 1965.

———. *Terence Macartney-Filgate: The Candid-Eye.* Ottawa: Canadian Film Institute, 1966.

Godbout, J. "Pour un cinéma québécois". *Cinéma-Québec*, janvier-fevrier 1972.

———. "Le Temps de la poésie du cinéma". *Canadian Literature* no. 46 (Autumn 1970).

Hamelin, Lucien, et Houle, Michel. *Fernand Dansereau.* Montréal: Conseil québécois pour la diffusion du cinéma, 1972.

Handling, Piers. *Canadian Feature Films: 1964-1969.* Ottawa: Canadian Film Institute, 1976.

———. *Don Shebib.* Ottawa: Canadian Film Institute, forthcoming.

———. "A New Canadian Wave". *Canadian Review*, February 1976.

———. "Visits to the Canadian Countryside". *Cinema Canada*, no. 22 (October 1975).

Hansauter, Alexander. "Film in Quebec: What Now?" *Motion*, 1974.

Harcourt, Peter. *Movies & Mythologies*. Toronto: CBC, 1977.

Harris, John K. "Screening the Canucks in Mid-town Manhattan". *Saturday Night*, April 1976.

Hartt, Laurinda. "Interview with Donald Pleasence". *Cinema Canada*, no. 8 (June-July 1973).

———. "THE RAINBOW BOYS: Interview with Gerald Potterton", *Cinema Canada*, no. 8 (June-July 1973).

Haynes, Peter. "WHY SHOOT THE TEACHER: Interview with Silvio Narizzano". *Cinema Canada*, no. 33 (December-January 1976-7).

Hofsess, John. "The Emergence of Claude Jutra". *Maclean's*, August 1973.

———. "The End of the Road". *Weekend*, February 28, 1976.

———. *Inner Views: Ten Canadian Film Makers*. Toronto: McGraw-Hill Ryerson, 1975.

———. "Looking for Bergman". *Maclean's*, January 1972.

Hofsess, John, and Fothergill, Robert. "The Rich Get Richer: A Dialogue on DUDDY KRAVITZ". *Canadian Forum*, October 1974.

Horsman, Joan. "The Politics of Film". *Arts Bulletin*, October-November 1976.

Ibrányi-Kiss, Á. "Carol Betts on Camera". *Cinema Canada*, no. 16 (October-November 1974).

———. "Fantasy, Film and Feminism, Or an Affirmation of Male Paranoia". *Cinema Canada*, no. 19 (May-June 1975).

———. "How to Have Your Cake and Eat It Too . . . à la Denys Arcand". *Cinema Canada*, no. 13 (April-May 1974).

———. "Roger Frappier". *Cinema Canada*, no. 9 (August-September 1973).

Ibrányi-Kiss, Á., ed. "Harvey Hart's Back in Town". *Cinema Canada*, nos. 10-11 (October 1973, January 1974).

Ibrányi-Kiss, Á., and Csaba Köller, George. "Francis Mankiewicz". *Cinema Canada*, no. 7 (April-May 1973).

———. KAMOURASKA: Geneviève Bujold". *Cinema Canada*, no. 7 (April-May 1973).

———. "KAMOURASKA: Michel Brault". *Cinema Canada*, no. 7 (April-May 1973).

"Interview with Murray Markowitz". *Cinema Canada*, no. 6 (February-March 1974).

"Interview: Norman C. Allin, C.S.C." *Cinema Canada*, no. 1 (March 1972).

Jacobs, Lewis. *The Documentary Tradition*. New York: Hopkinson and Blake, 1971. (Material on Allan King.)

"Jan Kadar". *Motion*, vol. 5, no. 4 (1976).

Jeancolas, J.P. "Gilles Carle, LES MALES, BERNADETTE". *Jeune Cinéma*, no. 70 (avril-mai 1973).

Katz, John. "Kotcheff: An Interview". *Cinema Canada*, no. 20 (July-August 1975).

Kirshenbaum, Harris. "Alberta in Todd-AO: David Acomba". *Cinema Canada*, nos. 10-11 (October 1973, January 1974).

———. "Roy Tash, C.S.C." *Cinema Canada*, no. 16 (October-November 1974).

Knelman, Martin. "Claude Jutra in Exile". *Saturday Night*, March 1977.

Laforest, Thérèse. "L'Hiver dans le cinéma canadien". *Séquences*, no. 51 (décembre 1967).

Lamothe, Arthur. "Cinéma et culture". *Liberté*, no. 8 (mai-juin 1966).

LaRochelle, Réal. *Denys Arcand*. Montréal: Conseil québécois pour la diffusion du cinéma, 1971.

———. *Jean-Claude Labrecque*. Montréal: Conseil québécois pour la diffusion du cinéma, 1971.

LaRochelle, Réal, and Maggi, Gilbert. "Political Situation of Quebec Cinema". *Cinéaste*, vol. 5, no. 3 (Summer 1972).

La France, André, et Marsolais, Gilles. *Cinéma d'ici*. Montréal: Les Editions Lemeac, 1975.

Lefebvre, Jean-Pierre. "La Crise du langage et le cinéma canadien". *Objectif* avril-mai 1965.

———. "Les Paradis perdus du cinéma canadien". *Objectif*, nos. 1 (novembre-décembre 1966), 2 (mai 1967), 3 (août-septembre 1967).

Lever, Yves. *Cinéma et société québécoise*. Montréal: Editions du Jour.

———. "Une Histoire à suivre: octobre '70 dans le cinéma québécois". *Cinéma-Québec*, vol. 4, no. 5 (1975).

Magidson, Debbie, and Wright, Judy. "Why THE ROWDYMAN Never Reached Medicine Hat: Film Distribution in Canada". *This Magazine*, June 1974.

Marsolais, Gilles. *Le Cinéma canadien*. Montréal: Editions du Jour, 1968.

———. *Michel Brault*. Montréal: Conseil québécois pour la diffusion du cinéma, 1972.

Martin, Ivan. "Profile Shot: Ken Heeley-Ray". *Canadian Film Editor*, July-August 1975.

Matheson, Gwen. "Two French-Canadian Films (Pierre Perrault)". *Canadian Forum*, December 1972.

McLarty, James. "Arthur Hiller, Director". *Motion*, March-April 1973.

———. "Gilles Carle". *Motion*, November-December 1973.

———. "The World According to John Herbert". *Motion*, March-April, 1973.

McPhedran, Phillip. "Personality Focus: Harry Makin, C.S.C." *Cinema Canada*, no. 1 (March 1972).

McPherson, Hugo. "Write Me a Film: A Symposium by Canadian Film Makers". *Canadian Literature*, Autumn 1970.

Miller, Mark. "The Quebec Crisis: Once More with Feeling". *Cinema Canada*, no. 20 (July-August 1975).

―――. "Will the Real Johnny Canuck Please Stand Up". *Cinema Canada*, no. 18 (March-April 1975).

Morisset, Micheline. "The Man André Forcier". *Cinema Canada*, no. 19 (May-June 1975).

Morris, Peter, ed. *Canadian Feature Films: 1941-1963*. Ottawa: Canadian Film Institute, 1974.

Moses, Michelle, ed. "Fellini's Not Bad, Bergman's Okay, But How About Me; Peter Pearson". *Cinema Canada*, nos. 10-11 (October 1973, January 1974).

Noguez, Dominique. "Un Cinéma de l'errance". *Vie des arts*, no. 55 (été 1969).

―――. *Essais sur le cinéma québécois*. Montréal: Editions du Jour, 1970.

―――. "La Jeunesse dans le cinéma québécois". *Vie des arts*, no. 54 (printemps 1969).

Ott, Gunter. "Ontario Gothic". *Cinema Canada*, no. 24 (December-January 1975-6).

Owen, Don. "Adrift in a Sea of Mud". *Take One*, vol. 1, no. 6.

Paquet, André. "Qu'est-ce que le cinéma canadien". *artscanada*, April 1970.

Paquet, André, ed. *How to Make or Not to Make a Canadian Film*. Montréal: La Cinémathèque canadienne, 1967.

Patry, Yvan. *Arthur Lamothe*. Montréal: Conseil québécois pour la diffusion du cinema, 1971.

―――. "Cinema as It Relates to the Forces of Our Society". *Cinéaste*, vol. 5, no. 3 (Summer 1972).

―――. *Jacques Godbout*. Montréal: Conseil québécois pour la diffusion du cinéma, 1972.

Patry, Yvan, et Bérubé, Renald, eds. *Le Cinéma québécois: tendences et prolongements*. Montréal: Editions Ste-Marie, 1968.

Patterson, Grant. "It's a Long Way to Paradise: Tom Shandell". *Motion*, May-June 1973.

Pearson, Peter. "Filmmaking as a Political Primer". *Cinema Canada*, no. 25 (February 1976).

Pratley, Gerald. "Films in Canada". *Queen's Quarterly*, Winter 1955.

Predal, René. *Jeune cinéma canadien*. Lyon: SERDOC, 1967.

"Quatre questions sur le cinéma canadien". *Objectif*, octobre 1961.

"Les Québécois: Jean-Pierre Lefebvre". *Cinema Canada*, no. 3 (July-August 1972).

Raboy, Marc. "Political Cinema in Quebec". *This Magazine*, January-February 1975.

Rasselet, Christian. *Jean-Pierre Lefebvre*. Montreal: Conseil québécois pour la diffusion du cinéma, 1972.

Reid, Alison. *Richard Leiterman*. Ottawa: Canadian Film Institute, forthcoming.

Reid, Alison, ed. *Allan King: An Interview with Bruce Martin and a Filmography*. Ottawa: Canadian Film Institute, 1970; revised 1971.

──. *Canadian Women Film Makers: An Interim Filmography*. Ottawa: Canadian Film Institute, 1972.

Richler, Mordecai. "Writing for the Movies". *Take One*, vol. 1, no. 12 (November 1968).

Rolfe, Lee. "WHO HAS SEEN THE WIND: Visiting Arcola". *Cinema Canada*, no. 33 (December-January 1976-7).

Rosenthal, Alan. *The New Documentary in Action*. Berkeley: University of California Press, 1971. (Chapters on Richard Leiterman and Arla Saare.)

Ryan, Elaine. "Profile Shot: Interview with Gerry Arbeid, Producer". *Canadian Film Editor*, October 1974.

Saint-Jacques, A. "Art et morale au cinéma". *Revue de l'Université Laval*, automne 1966.

Shek, Ben, "En Français: Cinema from Quebec". *Performing Arts in Canada*, Winter 1972; Spring 1973; Summer 1973.

──. "Quebec Films: Sharp Image of a Separate Society". *Performing Arts*, no. 11 (Fall 1974).

Silverman, D. "Writers Are Also Part of the Film Industry—Or Are They?" *Performing Arts*, no. 12 (Spring 1975).

"Six Interviews with Canadian Writers". *Pot Pourri*, Summer 1976.

Slade, Mark. *Language of Change*. Toronto: Holt, Rinehart & Winston, 1970.

Spencer, Michael. "In Defence of the CFDC". *Saturday Night*, December 1975.

Stewart, Craig. "A Canadian Film Editor and Me: Interview with Stan Cole". *Canadian Film Editor*, November 1974.

Street, B. Jeffrey. "Budge Crawley". *Motion*, vol. 5, no. 2 (1976).

Tadros, Connie. "Le Cinéma québécois". *Cinema Canada*, no. 5 (December-January 1972-3).

Tadros, Jean-Pierre. *Le Cinéma au Québec: bilan d'une industrie*. Montréal: Cinéma-Quebec, 1975.

──. "A Conversation with Hugh Falkner". *Cinema Canada*, no. 28 (May 1976).

"Ten Questions to Five Canadian Filmmakers". *Cahiers du Cinema in English*, no. 4 (1961).

Thorvaldson, Patricia. "Interview with Bill Reid". *Pot Pourri*, April 1974.

Tremblay, Gisèle. "Le Couple dans le cinéma canadien". *Séquences*, no. 50 (octobre 1967).

Turner, D. John. "Le Cinéma Québécois: Canada's French Language Feature Film Industry". *Journal of the University Film Association*, vol. 27, no. 3 (1975).

Varda, Agnes. "Notes sur Toronto". *Image et Son*, no. 283 (avril 1974).

Wark, Brian J. *The Canadian Film Industry*. The Banff Centre Press, 1974.

Wronski, Peter. "Interview with Claude Jutra". *Cinema Canada*, no. 23 (November 1975).

IV. Experimental Filmmaking

Armatage, Kay. "Interview with Joyce Wieland". *Take One*, vol. 3, no. 2 (November-December 1970).

Chandler, John Noel. "Reflections on/of Michael Snow". *artscanada*, Spring 1974.

Cowan, Bob. "New York Letter: LA REGION CENTRALE". *Take One*, vol. 3, no. 3 (January-February 1971).

Csaba Köller, George. "Interview with Michael Snow". *Cinema Canada*, no. 4 (October-November 1972).

———. "Vancouver Independent Filmmaking". *Cinema Canada*, no. 7 (April-May 1973).

Edwards, Natalie. "It's Film All Right, But Is It Art?" *Cinema Canada*, no. 26 (March 1976).

———. "Moving Art". *Cinema Canada*, no. 13 (April-May 1974).

———. "Ondaatje and Snow: Two Artist/Filmmakers". *Art Magazine*, vol. 6, no. 19 (Fall 1974).

Fleisher, Pat. "John Gould: Artist/Filmmaker". *Art Magazine*, vol. 5, no. 17 (Spring 1974).

Hale, Barrie. "The Vanguard of Vision: Notes on Snow and Wieland". *Saturday Night*, June 1974.

Ibrányi-Kiss, Á. "Snow's Sin(ema) Soufflé". *Cinema Canada*, no. 19 (May-June 1975).

Lord, Barry. "Let There be Darkness". *artscanada*, December 1968.

Magidson, Debbie. "The Art of Jack Chambers". *Art Magazine*, Fall 1974.

———. "Joyce Wieland's Vision". *Canadian Forum*, September 1975.

Marcorelles, Louis. "Snow Storms Italy". *Cinema Canada*, no. 6 (February-March 1973).

Michelson, Annette. "Towards Snow". *Art Forum*, June 1971.

"Mike Snow: An Interview". *Criteria*, March 1975.

Rosenbaum, Jonathan. "RAMEAU'S NEPHEW". *Sight and Sound*, Winter 1975-6.

Ryan, Terry. "Six Filmmakers in Search of an Alternative". *artscanada*, April 1970.

Sitney, P. Adams. "There Is Only One Joyce". *artscanada*, April 1970.

———. *Visionary Film*. New York: Oxford University Press, 1974. (Chapters on Wieland and Snow.)

400 *Bibliography*

Woodman, Ross. "The Realism of John Chambers". *Art International*, November 20, 1970.

Wordsworth, Anne. "Interview with Joyce Wieland". *Descant*, Spring-Summer 1974.

Youngblood, Gene. "Icon and Idea in the World of Michael Snow". *artscanada*, February 1970.

Index

A

Abbeloos, Pierre 305
L'ACADIE, L'ACADIE 24, 149-51
Acomba, David 249, 353
ACTION STATIONS! 43
ACT OF THE HEART 247
Adamson, Margaret Ann (now Lady Elton) 62
THE ADVENTURES OF PRINCE AHMED 59
Aellen, Werner 268, 332
AFFAIR OF THE SKIN 154
Agostini, Lucio 28
AIR CADETS 63
Alexeieff, Alexander 43, 102
ALEXIS TREMBLAY 63
ALICE'S RESTAURANT 325
Allan, Ted 262
ALLEGRO 95
ALLURES 331
Almond, Paul 247, 253, 348, 353-54
ALOUETTE 95
Alpert, Harry 43
ALPHAVILLE 326
Anderson, Lindsay 78, 145, 153
AND NO BIRDS SING 236
AND SO THEY LIVE 43
Anka, Paul 71, 75-76, 81
ANOTHER DAY 48
Ansty 52
Antonioni, Michelangelo 154, 216, 328, 383
THE APPRENTICESHIP OF DUDDY KRAVITZ 250, 258-62, 274, 361, 367, 369
Arcand, Denys 217-34, 370
Arling, Charles 19
A SAINT HENRI, LE 5 SEPTEMBRE (SEPTEMBER 5 AT SAINT-HENRI) 76, 128-31, 162
Ashworth, Clarke 22
Astruc, Alexandre 144
ATLANTIC CROSSROADS 53
ATLANTIC PATROL 52
A TOUT PRENDRE 76, 153-56, 160, 240-41
A TO Z 294
Atwood, Margaret 245, 373-74
Auden, W.H. 97, 162
AUGUST AND JULY 240
Auzepy, Patrick 251, 253
Ayler, Albert 292

B

BACK AND FORTH (⟷) 299-301, 308-09
THE BACK-BREAKING LEAF 80, 85, 89, 140, 379
BACK TO GOD'S COUNTRY 16, 18, 20
Badgley, Frank C. 22, 27, 40, 43-44
Baillie, Bruce 329
THE BALCONY 154

BALKAN POWDER KEG 54, 56, 57
THE BALLAD OF CROWFOOT 117
Ballantyne, Tanya 114, 121
BALLET ADAGIO 95, 101-2,
BAREE, SON OF KAZAN 17
Barlon, Roger 43
Barnum, P.T. 14
Baroja, Pio 258
BATTLE FOR OIL 53
BATTLE IS THEIR BIRTHRIGHT 55
BATTLE OF BRAINS 53
BATTLE OF BRITAIN 28
BATTLE OF EUROPE 53
BATTLE OF THE HARVESTS 53
Bauhaus 331
Bazin, André 379
Beauchemin, Serge 232
Beck, David 238, 355
Bedelia, Bonnie 214
Beesley, Ross 26
BEGONE DULL CARE 95, 99-100
Bellow, Saul 258
THE BELOVED FISH 28
Belson, Jordan 331
Benedict, Lawrence 280
Benoit, Denyse 60
Bergman, Ingmar 216, 367
Berton, Pierre 74, 140, 166, 369
Bertram, Beth 62
BEST DAMN FIDDLER FROM CALABOGIE TO KALADAR 353, 358
BETHUNE 104, 107-08
Bethune, Norman 262
BETWEEN FRIENDS 212-16, 249
Beveridge, James 41, 44, 49, 80
Biggs, Julie 157, 173
BILLY CRANE MOVES AWAY 122
BIRDS OF CANADA 48
Birman, Len 263
Bjerring, Gudrun Parker 51, 61
Bjoernson, Margaret Anne 51
Blackburn, Maurice 102
THE BLACK CAT 276
BLACK CHRISTMAS 274, 347, 374
Blaisdell, Margot 25
Blassco, Joe 277
BLEU SHUT 384-85
BLINKITY-BLANK 95
BLOOD AND FIRE 79, 82, 85, 140, 379-80
BLUE MOVIE 341
BLUE WATER 14
LA BONNE 153
Bonnière, René 144
BOOK BARGAIN 97
Boulton, Laura 61
Bourassa, Robert 228, 267
Bradley, Paul 237, 239
BRAHM'S HUNGARIAN DANCE 95
Braidwood, Tom 270
Brakhage, Stan 314, 321, 334, 336, 383-84
Brassard, André 362
Brault, Michel 76, 78-79, 144-145, 147, 150, 153, 219, 264-268, 375

Brayne, William 179
BREAKFAST 306-307
BREAK-THROUGH 53
BREATHING TOGETHER 246
BREATHLESS 162, 165
Breer, Robert 384
Bresson, Robert 152, 296, 383
BRIDE OF FRANKENSTEIN 276
Brittain, Donald 103-112, 166
Britten 97
Brodsky, Ann 290
Browning, Ted 276
Brown, Lawrence 271-272
Bryant, Peter 270, 338
Buchanan, Donald F. 50
LES BUCHERONS DE LA MANOUANE 76
Bujold, Geneviève 247, 349, 353
Bunuel, Luis 258, 381
Burroughs, Jackie 167, 173
Byram, Ronald 19
BY THEIR OWN STRENGTH 49

C

Cahan, Abraham 258
Callaghan, Morley 42, 51
CAMERA MAKES WHOOPEE 96
CAMERON OF THE ROYAL MOUNTED 15
Campbell, J.C. 25
CANADA AT WAR 13, 107
CANADIAN LANDSCAPE 49
CANADIAN PACIFIC, PART I 344
CANADIAN PACIFIC, PART II 344
CANNIBAL GIRLS 105, 278
CANON 100-101
Carle, Gilles 141-142, 199-207, 232, 239, 245, 356
CARNIVAL ON SKATES 25
CARRIE 276
Carrière, Marcel 71, 76
CARRY ON SERGEANT! 22
Carter, Peter 238
Cartier-Bresson, Henri 80, 90-92, 145, 380-81
Carver, H.P. 18
Cary, Joyce 210
THE CASE OF CHARLIE GORDON 50-51
Cassavetes, John 77, 162, 252
CATFOOD 287-288
Cavalcanti, 97
Cavanaugh, W.H. 29
CELLOPHANE WRAPPER 331
A CHAIRY TALE 95-96, 102
Chambers, Jack 333-338
Chambers, John 327-329
Chambers, Marilyn 274, 277
Chambers, Olga 337
Chaplin, Charlie 3, 96
LE CHAT DANS LE SAC 76, 141-142, 146, 163, 373
THE CHELSEA GIRLS 383
Cherry, Don 292, 295

Cherry, Lawrence 49-50, 61
CHESTER ANGUS RAMSGOOD 238
Chesterton 55
Chevalier 22
Chicoine, Michele 167, 173
UN CHIEN ANDALOU 260
Chilcott, Barbara 263
THE CHILDREN OF FOGO ISLAND 122
CHRONIQUE D'UN ETE 153
CHURCHILL'S ISLAND 53
CINETUDE #2 331
CINETUDE #3 331
CIRCLE 328-329
CITIZEN HAROLD 121
THE CITY 43
CITY OF GOLD 70, 72, 74-75, 140-141
Clandfield, David 198
Clarke, Shirley 154
Clawson, Del 19
THE CLINTON SPECIAL 355
Clish, Stanley 107
CLOSELY WATCHED TRAINS 271
Cohen, Leonard 104, 161, 166, 170, 174, 352
Cohl, Emile 102
Colbert 22
Collins, Warren 291, 294
LES COLOMBES 245
COLOUR BOX 95
COLOUR COCKTAIL 96
Colvin, Bill 19
THE CONNECTION 154
Conner, Bruce 330
CONNEXIONS 329
Connolly, Cyril 83
LES CORPS CELESTES 205-206
CORRAL 74, 140
Corso, Sam 22
Costa Gavras 228, 265
Côté, Guy 72
Coté, Phileas 51
Coughtry, Graham 174, 291
A COUNTRY HARVEST (COUNTRY THRESHING) 79
Cowan, Bob 295
COWBOY AND INDIAN 162, 174-175
Crawley, F. Radford "Budge" 44, 48-49
Crawley, Judith 61
CRIMES OF THE FUTURE 278, 348
Crist, Judith 164, 172, 193
Crone, Bob 254
Cronenberg, David 274-278, 348-349
Crosby, Bing 20
Cross, A.E. 18
Cross, James 266
Crowther, Bosley 104, 164
LA CRUE 60
CRYSTAL BALLET 26
Cukor, George 22
Curnick 238
Curnoe, Greg 327-329
Curwood, James Oliver 17, 19
Cushing, Peter 274

D

Daly, Tom 44, 51, 71, 73, 76, 80, 104, 106, 140, 161-163
THE DANCE 341
DANCE FILM 331
A DANGEROUS AGE 77
Dansereau, Fernand 115-116, 128-131
Dansereau, Jean 219
Dansereau, Mireille 60, 240, 250-258
Darcus, Jack 240, 248, 250, 268-273, 349-350
A DAUGHTER OF THE GODS 19
DAVID AND LISA 154, 156
Davidson, J.D. 42
Davidson, Joyce 157
DAWN 13

THE DAYS BEFORE CHRISTMAS 78, 145, 379
DAYS OF WHISKY GAP 74
Dean, James 158
DEATH WEEKEND 274
de Beauvoir, Simone 67
De Broca 238
DEFENCE OF MADRID 97
de Lom, Caesar 27
Deren, Maya 314, 384
DESIGN FOR SWIMMING 27, 28
Destounis, George 365
DEUX FEMMES EN OR 274
DEUX OU TROIS CHOSES QUE JE SAIS D'ELLE 201
Dewdney, Keewatin 332
Disney, Walt 59, 100
DOLLAR DANCE 42,
DON'T LET THE ANGELS FALL 237
Dostin, Alain 232
DOTS 95
Dovzhenko 336
Downs, Hugh 294
DRACULA 276
Drapeau, Jean 228
Drew, Robert 90, 94, 379-80
Dreyer, Carl 276
Dreyfuss, Richard 259, 261
DRIFTERS 45
DRIPPING WATER 285-286, 303
DR. JEKYLL AND MR. HYDE 276
DRYLANDERS 76, 160, 247
Dufaux, Georges 79, 354
Duke, Daryl 272
Dullea, Keir 352
Duncan, Alma 62
Dunning, George 103, 291
Dunning, John 275
Dunn, Willie 117
Duplessis, Maurice 195, 217, 266
Duprey, Don 115
Duras, Marguerite 59

E

EARTH 336
EASY RIDER 193, 325
ECLIPSE 328
ECSTASY 20
EDDIE SACKS 88
Edwards, Billy and Antoinette 179-194
Ellington, Duke 299
Elliot, Denholm 260
Englehart, Gloria 25
THE ERNIE GAME 167, 169-173, 177, 238
ESKIMO ARTS AND CRAFTS 61
Euler, W.D. 46
EVANGELINE 29
Evans, Walker 90-92
EVER AFTER ALL 239, 345
THE EXORCIST 276

F

FACE-OFF 239, 274, 352
THE FALL OF THE ROMANOV DYNASTY 59
Fanon, Frantz 93
A FAN'S NOTES 238
FANTASIA 100
Farber, Manny 289
THE FARM SHOW 355-57
THE FAR SHORE 60, 250, 279-282, 375
Faulkner, Hugh 368-69
LA FÉE AUX CHOUX 59
Feld, Irving 75
Fellini 367
UNE FEMME EST UNE FEMME 165
Ferguson, Graham 304
Ferno, John 43, 51
FERRY PILOT 52
FEUERTAUFE 53

FIDDLE-DE-DEE 95, 99
FIDDLER ON THE ROOF 263
Fidler, Gordon 338
FIELDS OF SACRIFICE 104, 111
THE FIGHTING DUTCH 53
FIGHTING NORWAY 53
Finesmith, Jared 125
THE FINISHING TOUCH 239
FIRST OFFENSE 163
Fischinger, Oscar 95, 102
FISHERMAN'S MEETING 122
FISHERS OF GRANDE ANSE 48
FISHING MY FATHER FISHING 178
FIVE FOR FOUR 42
FIVE MEN OF AUSTRALIA 53
Flaherty, Robert 43, 48, 78, 112, 145, 155, 164, 380
FLAMING CREATURES 295
Fogg, Howard 24
FOGO 116
FOLLOWING THROUGH 238, 355
FOOD, SECRET OF THE PEACE 53
FOOD, WEAPON OF CONQUEST 53
Ford, John 216
Forest, Léonard 123, 127
FORTRESS JAPAN 53, 57
FORWARD COMMANDOS 53
FORWARD WITH CANADA 23
Fournier, Claude 76, 170
THE FOUR SEASONS 49
Fox, Joan 171
Fox, Stan 332
Fox, William 17
FOXY LADY 238
FRACTURE 344
FRAME BY FRAME 102
Frampton, Hollis 296, 385
Franju, Georges 72, 209
Frankenheimer, John 154
FRANKENSTEIN 276
Frank Robert 381
Francks, Don 162
Fraser, Donald 44, 51
FREAKS 276
FREIGHTERS UNDER FIRE 52
FROM THE DRAIN 278
Fruet, Bill 239, 353, 358, 363
Fulford, Robert 164, 172, 212-213, 278
Fuller, R. Buckminster 323-324
Furie, Sidney 77, 291
A FURTHER GLIMPSE OF JOEY 170

G

Gagne, Danielle 251, 254-255
GALLERY: A VIEW OF TIME 173, 177
Gascon, Gilles 80
THE GATES OF ITALY 53, 57
GATEWAY TO ASIA 52
Gault, Judith 173
Gauthier, Guy 151
Gehr, Ernie 296
THE GENERAL LINE 67
GEOPOLITIX, HITLER'S PLAN FOR CONQUEST 53
Gill, Brenden 164
Gill, François 254
Gilmour, Clyde 171
GINA 218
GINGER COFFEY 237
GLOBAL AIR ROUTES 52
Glover, Guy 44
Godard, 142, 146, 154, 162, 165, 201, 229, 326,
Godbout, Claude 146, 251
THE GODFATHER 193
GOD'S COUNTRY AND THE WOMAN 17, 18
GODZILLA 274
GOIN' DOWN THE ROAD 211-212, 214-215, 237, 239, 354, 362-363

402 Index

GOLDEN GLOVES 146
GOLDENROD 250, 353
THE GOLDEN SNARE 21
Gold, Jack 190
Gold, Mike 259
Golightly, J.P.R. 42
GONE WITH THE WIND 275
GOODBYE COLUMBUS 259, 260
GOOD TIMES, BAD TIMES 209, 375
Gosselin, Bernard 149, 219
Gould, Glenn 79
LE GOUT DE LA FARINE 152
LE GRAND ROCK 375
Grass, Gunter 258
GREAT COUPS OF HISTORY 240, 248, 268-269, 271
Greaves, Phil 80
GREENHOUSE BLUES 178
Greenspun, Roger 340-341
GREY OWL AND THE BEAVER 48
GREY OWL'S LITTLE BROTHER 25
Grierson, John 34-47, 48-52, 60-64, 94, 96-98, 112-113, 120, 127, 132-136, 139, 143, 161
GRIEVANCE 113
Griffith, D.W. 29, 159, 386
Grosz, George 258
Groulx, Gilles 76, 141-142, 145-147, 163, 219, 224
GROUP PORTRAIT 178
GUARDS OF THE NORTH 52
Guilbeault, Luce 218
GUNS OF THE TREES 154
Guy, Alice 59

H

HABITANT 63
Haldane, Don 247
HALLELUJAH THE HILLS 154
HAND TINTING 285, 287
HAPPY MOTHER'S DAY 380
THE HARD PART BEGINS 250, 357-58, 375
Hardy, Forsyth 38, 62
Hardy, Hagood 215
Harker, Herbert 250, 353
Hartford, David M. 19, 21
Hart, Harvey 250, 353
THE HART OF LONDON 333-338
Hart, Roger 123, 126
Hawes, Stanley 42-43, 51, 66
HEADEND 344
THE HEARTBREAK KID 259
HELLO, DAD! 18
HELL UNLIMITED 97
HEN HOP 42, 95
Henning, Doug 278
Hepburn, Mitchell 13
HERITAGE 50
HEROES OF THE ATLANTIC 52
Héroux, Denys 245
HIGH OVER THE BORDERS 42-43, 52
HIGH STEEL 165-166, 177
HISTORY OF POWER IN CANADA 49
Hofsess, John 216
Holland Brothers 29
Holmes, David and Anna Marie 101
UN HOMME ET UNE FEMME 144
Hopper, Edward 343
HOTEL DES INVALIDES 209
HOUSING PROBLEMS 133
Howe, C.D. 369
Hudson, Terry 269
LAS HURDES 381
Hynes, Jack 28

I

Ibert, Jacques 98

Ibsen, Enrik 258
IL ETAIT UNE FOIS DANS L'EST 362
IL GRIDO 328
THE INBREAKER 351
THE INCREDIBLE SHRINKING MAN 276
Inge, William 159
INSIDE FIGHTING CANADA 63
INSIDE FIGHTING CHINA 53
INSIDE FIGHTING RUSSIA 53
INSIDE FRANCE 53, 55
IN THE WAKE OF THE ARMIES 53
INVASION OF EUROPE 53
L'INVITATION 274
ISABEL 247, 353
L'ISLE D'ORLEANS 48
IVENS, JORIS 43, 51
I WAS A 90-POUND WEAKLING 72, 75, 140, 380

J

Jackson, Stanley 72, 106
Jacobs, Ken 286, 296
Jacoby, Irving 42-43
Jacquemin, Alfred 26, 27
JALNA 50
JANE FONDA 88-89, 93
JAWS 276
Jennings, Humphrey 72
JESUS CHRIST SUPERSTAR 269
JIM DECKER BUILDS A LONGLINER 122
Johannsen, Peggy 26
JOHN BULL'S OWN ISLAND 53, 56
JOHN HUSTON 179
Jones, Alf 292
Jones, Dallas 51
Jones, Peter 107
JOURNEY 247, 249, 348, 355
JUDITH OF BETHULIA 29
Junker, Howard 160
Jutra, Claude 76, 102, 142, 153-155, 160, 194-199, 241-242, 360

K

Kaczender, George 237
Kadar, Jan 262-264
KAMOURASKA 375
Kanner, Alexis 171, 173
Kaplan, Sol 263
Kaprow, Alan 300
Karen, Kenny 263
Karloff, Boris 276
Kastner, Peter 156-158, 167, 173, 246
Kaufman, Boris 43
Kazan, Elia 43, 159
Kellerman, Annette 19
Kelly, Ronald 170, 387
Kennedy, Tim 126
Kent, Larry 269
Kidd, Bruce 76, 158, 161-162
Kidder, Margot 353
King, Allan 82, 103, 179-194, 353
King, Charmion 157
KING KONG 274, 276
King, Mackenzie 13, 36-38
KING OF HEARTS 238
KING OF THE HILL 111-112
Klee, Paul 133
Klepac, Walter 342, 344
Knelman, Martin 168
Koenig, Wolf 71-75, 78, 80, 89, 106, 140, 145, 161
Kotcheff, Ted 260-261
Kracauer, 30, 381
Kramer, Stanley 154
Kroiter, Roman 71-76, 78-80, 89, 106, 108, 145, 161, 163
Kubelka, Peter 337, 384
Kuleshov 54

L

LABOUR FRONT 53
Labrecque, Jean-Claude 80, 170, 245
LABYRINTH 139, 141
La Chapel, France 232
LADIES AND GENTLEMEN, MR. LEONARD COHEN 166
Lafleur, Father 48-49
Laidlaw, Ralph 19
Lamarr, Hedy 20
Lambart, Evelyn 62, 99
Lamy, Pierre 207, 232
Lanctot, Micheline 259
LANDMARKS OF THE PRAIRIES 50
Landow, George 295, 296, 329
LANDSCAPE 340-341
Lang, Fritz 258
Laporte, Pierre 266
Lapp, Horace 24
Larente, Arthur 29
Lasey, Fred 43
THE LAST DETAIL 259
Lavut, Martin 357
Layton, Irving 161
Lazare, Carole 263
Leacock, Richard 81, 89, 93, 103, 144, 151, 154, 180, 379-80
Lee, Christopher 274
Lee-Nova, Gary 327, 329-330
Lefebvre, Jean-Pierre 269, 370
Legg, Stuart 38-40, 42, 50-54, 63
Leiterman, Richard 179, 182-185, 281, 363
Lelouch, Claude 144
Lenauer, John 43
LETTER FROM ALDERSHOT 52
LETTER FROM OVERSEAS 52
Lévesque, René 149, 267
LIES MY FATHER TOLD ME 262-264, 274, 369, 375
Lightfoot, Gordon 352
Lightstone, Marilyn 263
Lilly, Daphne (Anstey) 62
LINES VERTICAL 102
Link, Andre 275
Lipsett, Arthur 75
Livesay, Dorothy 375
THE LIVING MACHINE 67, 70-73, 141
Livingston, Ken 269
Lobianco, Tony 250
Loew, Marcus 17
Lombardo, Guy 209
Lomez, Celine 280
LONELY BOY 70-72, 75, 81, 93, 106, 141, 156
LOOK TO THE NORTH 52
Lord 245
Loubert, Patrick 250
LOVE ON THE WING 95, 98, 101
Low, Colin 71-75, 112-113, 122, 127, 140, 161
Lubitsch 22
Lugosi, Bela 276
LA LUTTE 76, 162
Lye, Len 95, 97, 102, 331
Lynas, Jeffrey 263
Lynch, Paul 250

M

McAllistair, Stewart 95-96
McCABE AND MRS. MILLER 352
McCann, Sean 280-281
Macartney-Filgate, Terence 140, 145, 379-80
McCowan, George 239, 351
McCracken, Melinda 172, 173
MacDonald, Sally 61
McGrath, Doug 237, 239
McInnes, Graham 49, 51
McIntyre, Jean 40

McKay, Jim 291
McKay, Marge 61
Mackenzie, William Lyon 36
Mackey, Clarke 237, 362
McLaren, Norman 42, 44, 62, 75, 94-103, 143, 153, 305
McLean, Barrie Angus 347
MacLean, Rory 96
McLean, Ross 40, 43-44, 239
McLuhan, Marshall 84, 132, 172
McMahon, Alex 166
MacPherson, Hugo 224
Maddow, Ben 154
MADELEINE DE VERCHERES 29
MADELEINE IS 60, 240, 271
Magidson, Debbie 338
MAIL EARLY 42
Mailer, Norman 259
Makavejev, Dusan 252
Makin, Harry 353
Malamud, Bernard 259
Malanga, Gerry 295
LES MALES 203-204, 206, 241
Mallard, Mike 250, 353
MALTESE CROSS MOVEMENT 332
Mamber 87, 90, 379-80
Mamoulian 22
A MAN AND HIS JOB 51
Mandel, Eli 356-57
A MAN ESCAPED 296
Mankiewicz, Francis 241, 371-73
MAN WITH A MOVIE CAMERA 336
Marc, Franz 341
MARCHING THE COLOURS 44
MARIA CHAPDELAINE 50
Marker, Chris 72
Markle, Robert 175
Markowitz, Murray 240, 360
Markson, Morley 246, 349-350
A MARRIED COUPLE 179-194
Marshall, W.R. 18
Marsh, Jane 63-66
Martin, Bob 26, 27
Martin, John 291
Marx Brothers 178
THE MASK OF NIPPON 53, 57, 66
Matuszewski, Bdeslas 30
LA MAUDITE GALETTE 217-218, 225-227
Maurois, André 9
Maysles, Al 81, 103, 144, 154, 180
Mekas, Adolfas 154
Mekas, Jonas 154, 290, 292
MEMO FROM FOGO 123
MEMORANDUM 104, 107-110
Menken, Marie 383
Mercer, Michael 371
Mercier, Margaret 102
LE MERLE 95
Methe, Jacques 232
Michelson, Annette 384
Michener, Wendy 172
MIGRATION 330-331, 339, 344
Milliken, Carl
Mitchell, Mike 117
Mitchell, W.O. 353
MOMMA DON'T ALLOW 78
MONIQUE LEYRAC IN CONCERT 167
MONKEYS IN THE ATTIC 349-350
MON ONCLE ANTOINE 194-199, 242, 360, 375
Montagu, Ivor 97
MONTREAL MAIN 250, 362
MONTREAL UN JOUR D'ETE 217
Moore, Brian 237
Moore, Frank 276, 280
Morin, Nicole 137
Morriss, Frank 164
LA MORT D'UN BUCHERON 204-207, 241
Morton, William 24
MOSAIC 102, 327-328, 384
Moseley, Peter 179

Munch 258
Munro, Grant 100-101
MUSIC FROM THE STARS 24
Myers 154
MY PLEASURE IS MY BUSINESS 274

N-O

NASHVILLE 375
NEIGHBOURS 95-96, 101-102
Nelson, Robert 384
NEPTUNE'S DAUGHTER 19
Neuhaus, Max 299, 300
NEVER A BACKWARD STEP 104
NEW HORIZONS 49
Newman, Sydney 120, 225
NEW YORK EYE AND EAR CONTROL 294-297, 300, 384
NIGHT AT THE CIRCUS 178
NIGHTMAIL 85
NIGHT ON BALD MOUNTAIN 43
1933 285-286, 288
Nixon, Richard M. 290
NOBODY WAVED GOODBYE 76-77, 141-142, 156-160, 160, 163-165, 167, 169, 246, 362, 375
LA NOCE N'EST PAS FINIE 123, 127
Noland, Kenneth 327
NOMADS OF THE NORTH 21
Nordstrom, Kristina 339-341, 343
Norrish, B.E. 23-24, 27, 28
NORTH OF SUPERIOR 304-305
NOTES FOR A FILM ABOUT DONNA AND GAIL 167-169, 175, 177
NOT FAR FROM HOME 178
NOW IS THE TIME 95
NOW—THE PEACE 53, 56
NUIT ET BROUILLARD 209
Oakman, Wheeler 19
THE OBEDIENT FLAME 98
Odets, Clifford 259
Oliver, Bill 25, 48
THE OMEN 276
Ondaatje, Michael 355-56
125 ROOMS OF COMFORT 250, 357
ONE POTATO, TWO POTATO 158
ONE SECOND IN MONTREAL 303, 308, 383-84
ON EST AU COTON 217, 220-227, 232
THE ONLY THING YOU KNOW 247, 362
ON THE BOWERY 179
Ophuls, Max 161
LES ORDRES 264-268, 375-76
ORILLIA OUR TOWN 357, 359
OTTAWA ON THE RIVER 49
OU ETES-VOUS DONC? 147
Owen, Donald 76, 141-142, 156-160, 160-178, 238, 246, 292
Owen, Suzanne 175, 177

P-Q

PAINTERS OF QUEBEC 49
Palmer, John 349-350
Panofsky, Erwin 30, 326
PAPERBACK HERO 249, 274, 351-352, 357, 367
Paquette, Vincent 51
PARCS ATLANTIQUES 217
Park, Ben 294
Parks, Michael 214, 249
PARTNERS 178, 250
PARTY SEQUENCE: POOR LITTLE RICH GIRL 383
PAS DE DEUX 95-96, 101-102
Patton, G.E. 4
PAUL TOMKOWICZ, STREET RAILWAY SWITCHMAN 74
UN PAYS SANS BON SENS 149-151

Pearson, Peter 249, 352-354
Pedlar, Madeleine 24
Pelletier, (Hon.) Gérard 265
Pennebaker, Donald 89, 93, 144, 180
PEOPLES OF CANADA 45
Perrault, Pierre 144-152
Perron, Clement 242, 246, 360
Perry, Frank 154
Perry, Margaret 61
Peterson, Oscar 100
Petrie, Susan 240
Pickford, Mary 3, 157
PILOT X-15 81
PINCERS ON AXIS EUROPE 53
Pinney, Chris 125
Pinsent, Gordon 351
Playter, Wellington 19
Pleasence, Donald 239, 360
Poirier, Anne-Claire 60
Polanski, Roman 276
Pontecorvo 228
Poons, Larry 327
PORTAGE 48
POTEMKIN 67
Potterton, Gerald 238
POUR LA SUITE DU MONDE 76, 144, 147-148, 153
Pratley, Gerald 171
Pratt, John 28
Preminger, Otto 104
Price, (Hon.) Wm. H. 3
PRIMARY 81, 88, 379
Pritchard, Ann 281
PROLOGUE 246, 355
Proulx, Reverend Maurice 48-49
PROXY HAWKS 248, 268, 270-272, 349-350
LA P'TITE BOURGOGNE 115-116
Pudovkin, 54
Q-BEC MY LOVE 269
Quaid, Randy 259
QUEBEC: DUPLESSIS ET APRES 217, 226, 232
QUEBEC, PATH OF CONQUEST 52
QUELQUES ARPENTS DE NEIGE 245

R

RABID 274-278
THE RAINBOW BOYS 238
LA RAISON AVANT LA PASSION 285, 288-289
RAMEAU'S NEPHEW BY DIDEROT (THANX TO DENNIS YOUNG) BY WILMA SCHOEN 306-307
Ramsaye, Terry 22
Randall, Harry 43
LES RAQUETTEURS 76, 145
Rathburn, Eldon 72, 74-75, 140
RAT LIFE AND DIET IN NORTH AMERICA 280
Rawson, Harold 43
Ray, Satyajit 367
Rayner, Gordon 175
Razutis, Al 270, 338
Read, Nicholas 41, 43, 51
THE REAL BIG SOCIETY 172
REAL ITALIAN PIZZA 343
RECOMMENDATION FOR MERCY 274, 360, 369
RED 202, 204, 206-207
REGARDS SUR LA FOLIE 153
LA REGION CENTRALE 296, 300-301, 303, 305, 306, 308-309, 383-84, 386
LE REGNE DU JOUR 147-148
Reid, Kate 238, 353
Reif, Tony 339-340
Reiniger, Lotte 59
Reitman, Ivan 238, 275, 278
Reitze, Elvira 172
REJEANNE PADOVANI 218, 226-228, 230, 232-233

Index

Renoir, Jean 180
Resnais, Alain 147, 209
RHAPSODY IN TWO LANGUAGES 23
Rhodes, Donnelly 250
RHYTHMETIC 101
Richler, Mordecai 174, 361
RICHLER OF ST. URBAIN 173-174
Riefenstahl, Leni 112
Rill, Eli 249
Rimmer, David 270, 330-331, 338-344
RIP-OFF 212, 238, 240, 354
ROAD TO THE REICH 53
THE ROAD TO TOKYO 53
Robbins, Leroy 43
Roberge, Guy 153
Rodan, Keith 331-332, 338
Roffman, Julian 43
Rogers, Norman 40
Rogosin, Lionel 179
ROMANCE OF TRANSPORTATION IN CANADA 74
ROSEDALE LADY 169, 176, 178
Rose, Les 103
Rosenthal, Joe 29
Roth, Philip 259
Rouch, Jean 153-154
LA ROUTE DE L'OUEST 217
THE ROWDYMAN 238, 350-351, 357
ROYAL BANNERS OVER OTTAWA 27
THE ROYAL TOUR 40
UN ROYAUME VOUS ATTEND 152
R34 328
Rugoff, Dan 164
RUMBA 95
Runge Janis 126
RUNNER 76, 158, 161-162, 165
RUNNING AWAY BACKWARDS 179
Ruspoli, Mario 153
RUSSIA'S FOREIGN POLICY 53
Ruvinsky, Morrie 239, 269

S

Saare, Arla 182, 189
SAILBOAT 285-286, 288
Salinger, J.D. 259
SAMUEL DE CHAMPLAIN 217, 219
Sanders, Denis 154
Sandwell, B.K. 23, 25
Sartre, Jean-Paul 319
Satie, Erik 211
Sauriol, Brigitte 60
THE SAVAGE EYE 154
Scellen, Janet 40
SCENES FROM UNDER CHILDHOOD 334
Schenk, Joseph 17
Schooler, Zvee 260
Schulberg, Budd 259
SCISSORS 332
Scott, J.B. 50
Seabury, William Marston 9
SEASHORE 342
SECOND WIND 208, 212, 215, 250, 375
Selman, Dallas 330
Seltzer, Leo 43
SETTING FIRES FOR SCIENCE 107
SEVEN TILL FIVE 96
Shadbolt, Doris 338
SHADOW OF THE HAWK 274
SHADOWS 77, 153, 162
Shurits, Paul 296, 331
Shebib, Don 208-217, 354, 362-363, 375
SHE CLIMBS TO CONQUER 25
Shepp, Archie 292
Shiffman, Milton 43
Shipman, Barry 17

Shipman, Ernest 14-21
Shipman, Nell 14, 17, 19, 21, 60
SHIVERS 274-278, 370, 374, 376
SHOOT THE PIANIST 155
THE SHOP ON MAIN STREET 263
SHORT SHAVE 296
Shub, Esther 59
SHYNESS 72
SIDE SEAT PAINTING SLIDES SOUND FILM 303
SIEG IN WESTEN 53
Silver, Joe 260
Sitney 383, 385
SITZMARKS THE SPOT 28
SKID ROW 179-180
Slade, Mark 171
SLIPSTREAM 249-250, 352-353
LES SMATTES 245
Smith, Harry 331
Smith, Jack 295
SNOW IN VENICE 173-174
Snow, Michael 162, 173-175, 286, 290-307, 308-323, 327-329, 331, 383-87
Snyder, Norman 176
SOD-BUSTER 4
SOIL FOR TOMORROW 50
THE SONGS OF CHRIS COBB 122
Sontag, Susan 381
Sparling, Gordon 22-28
Spencer, Bernard Cole 169
Spencer, Michael 44, 51, 253, 351
SPHERES 99
Spice Cherry, Evelyn 40, 43, 49-50, 61, 97
Spinello, Barry 331
Spottiswoode, Raymond 40, 42-45, 51
Spotton, John 80, 163
SPRING HILL 387
Spring, Sylvia 60, 240, 271
Spry, Robin 246, 355
SQUARE INCH FIELD 330-331, 338-339, 343
STANDARD TIME 300
Starblanket, Noel 117
STATE OF SEIGE 228, 265
STEEL MUSHROOMS 330
Steiglitz, Alfred 90-92
Stein, Gertrude 314
Stella, Frank 327
Ste. Marie, Buffy 117
Stendhal 239
STEREO 278, 348
Stevens, George Jr. 81
Stevens, Wallace 332
Stollman, Bernard 300
Stoney, George 112-113, 115, 117
Strand, Paul 90-92
Strange, Marc 247
STRATEGY OF METALS 53
Strick, Joseph 154
STRIKE 113
STUDY OF SPRING FLOWERS 48
SUDDEN FURY 370
Sullivan, E.P. 29
SURFACING ON THE THAMES 331, 340-341
SUSAN STARR 88
Sutherland, Donald 247
Sutherland, Harry 125
SWEET MOVIE 376
SYNCHROMY 102

T

Taafe, Gerald 167
Tash, Roy 23, 27
TAUREAU 246
TAXI DRIVER 375
Taylor, Cecil 292
Taylor, James 126
Taylor, N.A. 156
LE TEMPS D'UNE CHASSE 241, 372, 375

THE TENANT 276
TENTH VICTIM 78
LA TETE DE NORMANDE ST. ONGE 199, 205-207
Thatcher, Leslie P. 48
THE THING 276
THE THINGS I CANNOT CHANGE 114-115, 121
13 PLATOON 43
THIS IS BLITZ 53
Thompson, John 236
Thompson, Paul 355
Thomson, Corey 25
THE THOUSAND DAYS 24
THURSDAY'S CHILDREN 78, 145
Till, Eric 238
TOMORROW'S WORLD 53
TORONTO JAZZ 162-163, 174, 292
Tougas, Kirk 270, 338, 340-342
TOUT LE TEMPS, TOUT LE TEMPS, TOUT LE TEMPS 115-116
Townsend, Charlotte 383
THE TRAIN 179
TRANSFER 278
TREEFALL 344
Tremblay, Michel 362
THE TRIAL 101
Trudeau, Pierre 267, 288-289, 290
Truffaut, François 154
Truscott, Stephen 360
24 HOURS AND AFTER 224
TWO SIDES TO EVERY STORY 307

U

Ulrich, Barbara 146
UNIVERSE 70, 72, 73, 141
UNRRA 53
UP AGAINST THE SYSTEM 119, 379

V

Valenta, Vladimir 271-272
VALERIE 274
VAMPYR 276
Van Der Beek, Stan 332
Van Every-Taylor, Elizabeth 126
Van Tuyle, Bert 19
VARIATIONS ON A CELLOPHANE WRAPPER 341-342
Vas, Robert 72
Vasarely 331
Vernon, John 157
Vertov 323, 336
VERY NICE, VERY NICE 75
V FOR VICTORY 42
LA VIE HEUREUSE DE LEOPOLD Z 141, 199-200
LA VIE REVEE 240-250-258, 375-76
Vigneault, Gilles 177
VILLE-MARIE 217, 219
Vineberg, Dusty 168
VIRGIN SPRING 241
Vitale, Frank 362
VIVRE SA VIE 142, 165
LE VIOL D'UNE JEUNE FILLE DOUCE 201-202, 204, 206-207, 241
VOICE OF ACTION 52
LES VOITURES D'EAU 147-149
VOLLEYBALL 217, 219
Vorkapich, Slavko 325
LA VRAIE NATURE DE BERNADETTE 203-204, 206-207, 245, 356

W

WAITING FOR CAROLINE 170
WAITING FOR THE QUEEN 344
Walker, Joe 19
Wanger 22
Wangler, Chris 183-184

WAPI, THE WALRUS 18
WAR BIRDS 52
WARCLOUDS IN THE PACIFIC 52
Warden, Jack 259
THE WAR FOR MEN'S MINDS 53, 57, 66
Wargon, Allan 106
Warhol, Andy 295, 302, 383
WAR HUNT 154
Warkentin, Germaine 373-74
THE WARNING 40
Warren, Vincent 102
WARRENDALE 179, 181, 183
Watson, Patrick 167
WAVELENGTH 173, 297-304, 308-323, 383, 385-86
WEDDING IN WHITE 239, 358-60
Weigall, Arthur 8
Weinberg, Herman 195
Weingartner 239
Weintraub, William 238
Weisenborn, Gordon 43
Welles, Orson 101
WEST WIND 49
WE'VE COME A LONG WAY TOGETHER 209
WHAT WE HAVE HERE IS A PEOPLE PROBLEM 371
WHEN ASIA SPEAKS 54
WHO WILL TEACH OUR CHILDREN? 113
WHY ROCK THE BOAT? 238, 361
Wieland, Joyce 60, 279-282, 285-289, 290, 296, 303, 304, 329
Wiggins, Chris 354
Wilcox, Herbert 13
Wilder, Don 351-352
Williams, Emmet 300
Williams, Richard 291
Wilson 238
WINGS IN THE WILDERNESS 375
WINGS OF A CONTINENT 52
WINGS OF YOUTH 42-43, 53
WINGS ON HER SHOULDERS 65
WINTER BUILDING, IT CAN BE DONE 107
Wiseman, Fred 103
Wiseman, Joseph 261
Wittig, Monique 58
WOLF PEN PRINCIPLE 250, 268, 271-272
Wollstonecraft, Mary 63
WOMEN ARE WARRIORS 53, 63-66
WOMEN AT WAR 64-65
WOMEN IN THE WAR 43
Woodman, Ross 338
Woodsworth, J.S. 10
Woolf, Virginia 67
WORK FOR WOMEN 63, 65
Wright, Basil 42
Wright, James 51
Wright, Richard 43

Y

Yadin, Yossi 263
Yalkut, Jud 300
YELLOW SUBMARINE 291
YOU ARE ON INDIAN LAND 117
YOU DON'T BACK DOWN 166, 168
Youngblood, Gene 383-384, 387
YOUTH IS TOMORROW 50

Z

Z 228
Zavattini 132, 135
ZERO HOUR 53
ZERO THE FOOL 349
Zinkan, Beth 61
Zolf, Larry 115
Zukor, Adolph 7, 17, 364